P9-DED-139

NEW!

8th edition

BABY

BARGAINS

S E C R E T S

to saving 20% to 50% on
baby furniture, equipment,
clothes, toys, maternity wear
and much, much more!

Denise & Alan Fields
authors of the best-sellers
Bridal Bargains, Baby 411

Copyright Page and Carbon-Neutral Credits

Saxophone, lead guitar and breast-feeding by Denise Fields
Drums, rhythm guitar and father stuff by Alan Fields
Congas on "Grandparents" by
Max & Helen Coopwood, Howard & Patti Fields
Cover/interior design and keyboard solo by Epicenter Creative
Screaming guitar solos on "(Let's Go) Perego" by Charles & Arthur Troy
Additional guitar work on "Diaper Changing Blues" by Todd Snider
Backing vocals on "(She's Got A) LATCH Car Seat" by Ric Ocasek
Band photography by Moses Street

*This book was written to the music of Barenaked Ladies,
which probably explains a lot.*

To order this book, call 1-800-888-0385. Or send $17.95 plus $3 shipping to Windsor Peak Press, 436 Pine Street, Boulder, CO 80302. Questions or comments? Please call the authors at (303) 442-8792. Or fax them a note at (303) 442-3744. Or write to them at the above address in Boulder, Colorado. E-mail the authors at authors@babybargains.com.

Learn more about this book online at www.BabyBargains.com

Distributed to the book trade by National Book Network, 800-462-6420.

Library Cataloging in Publication Data

Fields, Denise
Fields, Alan
    Baby Bargains: Secrets to saving 20% to 50% on baby furniture, equipment, clothes, toys maternity wear and much, much more/ Denise & Alan Fields
    608 pages.
    Includes index.
    ISBN 978-1-889392-33-2
    1. Child Care—Handbooks, manuals, etc. 2. Infants' supplies—Purchasing—United States, Canada, Directories. 3. Children's paraphernalia—Purchasing—Handbooks, manuals. 4. Product Safety—Handbooks, manuals. 5. Consumer education.
    649'.122'0296—dc20. 2009.

We miss you Dee Dee.

Version 8.0

CONTENTS

Chapter 1

"IT'S GOING TO CHANGE YOUR LIFE"

Chapter 2

NURSERY NECESSITIES: CRIBS, DRESSERS & MORE

Chapter 3

BABY BEDDING & DECOR

Chapter 4

THE REALITY LAYETTE: LITTLE CLOTHES FOR LITTLE PRICES

Chapter 5

Chapter 6

Chapter 7

AROUND THE HOUSE: MONITORS, DIAPER PAILS, SAFETY & MORE

Chapter 8

CAR SEATS

Chapter 9

STROLLERS, DIAPER BAGS, CARRIERS AND OTHER TO GO GEAR

Chapter 10

CHILD CARE: OPTIONS, COSTS & MORE

Chapter 11

CONCLUSION: WHAT DOES IT ALL MEAN?

ICONS

 Getting Started

 Money-Saving Secrets

 Sources

 Best Buys

 Parents In Cyberspace

 The Name Game

 What Are You Buying?

 Do it By Mail

 Safe & Sound

 Email from the Real World

 Smart Shopper

 More Money Buys You . . .

 Wastes of Money

 Bottom Line

CHAPTER 1

"It's Going to Change Your Life!"

Inside this chapter

T hat had to be the silliest comment we heard while we were pregnant with our first baby. Believe it or not, we even heard this refrain more often than "Are you having a boy or a girl?" and "I'm sorry. Your insurance doesn't cover that." For the friends and relatives of first-time parents out there, we'd like to point out that this is a pretty silly thing to say. Of course, we knew that a baby was going to change our lives. What we didn't realize was how much a baby was going to change our pocketbook.

Oh sure, we knew that we'd have to buy triple our weight in diapers and be subjected to dangerously high levels of the Wiggles. What we didn't expect was the endless pitches for cribs, gear, toys, clothing and other items parents are required to purchase by FEDERAL BABY LAW.

We quickly learned that having a baby is like popping on the Juvenile Amusement Park Ride from Consumer Hell. Once that egg is fertilized, you're whisked off to the Pirates of the Crib ride. Then it's on to marvel at the little elves in StrollerLand, imploring you to buy brands with names you can't pronounce. Finally, you take a trip to Magic Car Seat Mountain, where the confusion is so real, it's scary.

Consider us your tour guides—the Yogi Bear to your Boo Boo Bear, the Fred to your Ethel, the . . . well, you get the idea. Before we enter BabyLand, let's take a look at the Four Truths That No One Tells You About Buying Stuff For Baby.

The Four Truths That No One Tells You About Buying Stuff for Baby

1 **BABIES DON'T CARE IF THEY'RE WEARING DESIGNER CLOTHES OR SLEEPING ON DESIGNER SHEETS.** Let's be realistic. Babies just

want to be comfortable. They can't even distinguish between the liberals and conservatives on "Meet the Press," so how would they ever be able to tell the difference between Baby Gucci crib bedding and another less famous brand that's just as comfortable, but 70% less expensive? Our focus is on making your baby happy—at a price that won't break the bank.

2 **YOUR BABY'S SAFETY IS MUCH MORE IMPORTANT THAN YOUR CONVENIENCE.** Here are the scary facts: 66,400 children under age five were injured (requiring emergency room visits) by nursery products. During a recent three-year period (2002-2004), those same baby products caused 80 deaths per year. (source: 2008 Consumer Product Safety Commission report based on 2006 data).

Each chapter of this book has a section called "Safe & Sound" to arm you with in-depth advice on keeping your baby out of trouble. We'll tell you which products we think are dangerous and how to safely use other potentially hazardous products.

3 **MURPHY'S LAW OF BABY TOYS SAYS YOUR BABY'S HAPPINESS WITH A TOY IS INVERSELY RELATED TO THE TOY'S PRICE.** Buy a $200 shiny new wagon with anti-lock brakes, and odds are baby just wants to play with the box it came in. In recognition of this reality, we've included "wastes of money" in each chapter that will steer you away from frivolous items.

4 **IT'S GOING TO COST MORE THAN YOU THINK**. Whatever amount of money you budget for your baby, get ready to spend more. Here's a breakdown of the average costs of bringing a baby into the world today:

The Average Cost of Having a Baby

(based on industry estimates for a child from birth to age one)

Crib, mattress, dresser, rocker	$1500
Bedding / Decor	$325
Baby Clothes	$600
Disposable Diapers	$860
Maternity/Nursing Clothes	$1130
Nursery items, high chair, toys	$475
Baby Food / Formula	$950
Stroller, Car Seats, Carrier	$600
Miscellaneous	$600
TOTAL	**$7,040**

The above figures are based on buying name brand products at regular retail prices. We surveyed over 1000 parents to arrive at these estimates.

Bedding/Decor includes not only bedding items but also lamps, wallpaper, and so on for your baby's nursery. Baby Food/Formula assumes mom breastfeeds for the first six months and then feeds baby jarred baby food ($425) and formula ($525) until age one. If you plan to bottle-feed instead of breastfeed, add another $525 on to that figure. (Of course, the goal is to breastfeed your baby as long as possible—one year is a good target.)

Sure, you do get an automatic tax write-off for that bundle of joy, but that only amounts to about $3500 this year (plus you also get up to an additional $3000 child care tax credit, depending on your income). But those tax goodies won't nearly offset the actual cost of raising a child. And as you probably realize, our cost chart is missing some expensive "extras" . . . like medical bills, childcare, saving for college and more. Here's an overview of what can add to the tab.

Scary Number: The Cost of Raising Baby to Age 18

$204,060. That's what the federal government says it costs to raise a child born in 2007 (the latest year stats are available) to age 18. Those costs include food, transportation, housing, clothes and child care.

But let's talk about child care. Critics point out the federal government grossly underestimates this cost (the feds say parents spend $1220 to $3020 on child care each year for the first two years). But the government averages in parents who pay nothing (grandma watches baby) with those who pay for child care.

So what does child care really cost? According to the National Association of Child Care Resource and Referral Agencies, the average annual bill for center care is $4,388 to $14,674. Want to hire a nanny? That can run $30,000 per year in big cities, plus another $6,000 in taxes.

College is another expense the government leaves out of their figures. Financial planners say new parents should save a minimum of $1000 per child per month. So that's another $24,000 for the first two years alone.

The take-home message: raising a baby ain't cheap. It's important to start saving your pennies now, so you can start saving for those important items (college, etc.) down the road.

Reality Check: Does it Really Cost that Much to Have a Baby?

Now that we've thoroughly scared you enough to inquire whether the stork accepts returns, we should point out that children do NOT have to cost that much. Even if we focus just on the first year, you don't have to spend $7040 on baby gear. And that's what this book is all about: how to save money and still buy the best. Follow all the tips in this book, and we estimate the first year will cost you $4149. Yes, that's a savings of $2891!

Now, at this point, you might be saying "That's impossible! I suppose you'll recommend buying all the cheap stuff, from polyester clothes to no-name cribs." On the contrary, we'll show you how to get *quality* name brands and safe products at discount prices. Most importantly, you will learn how not to WASTE your money on dubious gear. And much more. Yes, we've got the maximum number of bargains allowed by federal law.

A word on bargain shopping: when interviewing hundreds of parents for this book, we realized bargain seekers fall into two frugal camps. There's the "do-it-yourself" crowd and the "quality at a discount" group. As the name implies, "do-it-yourselfers" are resourceful folks who like to take second-hand products and refurbish them. Others use creative tricks to make homemade versions of baby care items like baby wipes and diaper rash cream.

While that's all well and good, we fall more into the second camp of bargain hunters, the "quality at a discount" group. We love discovering a hidden factory outlet online that sells goods at 50% off. Or finding a designer stroller on Craigslist at 75% off its original retail. We also realize savvy parents save money by not *wasting* it on inferior goods or useless items.

While we hope that *Baby Bargains* pleases both groups of bargain hunters, the main focus of this book is not on do-it-yourself projects. Books like the *Tightwad Gazette* (check your local library for a copy) do a much better job on this subject. Our main emphasis will be on discount web sites, catalogs, outlet stores, brand reviews and identifying best buys for the dollar.

What? There's No Advertising in This Book?

Yes, it's true. This book contains zero percent advertising. We have never taken any money to recommend a product or company and never will. We make our sole living off the sales of this and other books. Our publisher, Windsor Peak Press, also derives its sole income from the sale of this book and our other publications. **_No company recommended in this book paid any consideration or was charged any fee to be mentioned._** (In fact, some companies probably would offer us money to leave them *out* of the book, given our comments about their products or services).

As consumer advocates, we believe this "no ads" policy helps to ensure objectivity. The opinions in the book are just that—ours and those of the parents we interviewed.

We also are parents of two kids. We figure if we actually are recommending these products to you, we should have some real world experience with them. (That said, we should disclose that our sons have filed union grievances with our company over testing of certain jarred baby foods and that litigation is ongoing.)

Of course, given the sheer volume of baby stuff, there's no way we can test everything personally. To solve that dilemma, we rely on reader feedback to help us figure out which are the best products to recommend. We receive over 100 emails a day from parents; this helps us spot overall trends on which brands/products parents love. And which ones they want to destroy with a rocket launcher.

Parents post reviews of products to our web site, message boards and blog. Of course, one bad review from one parent doesn't mean we won't recommend a product—we combine multiple review sources to come up with an overall picture as to which products and brands are best.

What about prices of baby products? Trying to stay on top of this is similar to nailing Jell-O to a wall. Yet, we still try. As much as we can confirm, the prices quoted in this book were accurate as of the date of publication. Of course, prices and product features can change at any time. Inflation and other factors may affect the actual prices you discover in shopping for your baby. While the publisher makes every effort to ensure their accuracy, errors and omissions may exist. That's why we update this book with every new printing—make sure you are using the most recent version (go to BabyBargains.com and click on Which Version?).

Our door is always open—we want to hear your opinions. Email us at authors@BabyBargains.com or call us at (303) 442-8792 to ask a question, report a mistake, or just give us your thoughts.

So, Who Are You Guys Anyway?

Why do a book on saving money on baby products? Don't new parents throw caution to the wind when buying for their baby, spending whatever it takes to ensure their baby's safety and comfort? Ha! When our first son was born, we quickly realized how darn expensive this guy was. Sure, as a new parent, you know you've got to buy a car seat, crib, clothes and diapers . . . but have you walked into one of those baby "superstores" lately? It's a blizzard of baby stuff, with a bewildering array of "must have" gear, gadgets and gizmos, all claiming to be the best thing for parents since sliced bread.

Becoming a parent in this day and age is both a blessing and curse. The good news: parents today have many more choices for baby products than past generations. The *bad* news: parents today have many more choices for baby products than past generations.

Our mission: make sense of this stuff, with an eye on cutting costs. As consumer advocates, we've been down this road before. We researched bargains and uncovered scams in the wedding business when we wrote *Bridal Bargains*. Then we penned an exposé on new homebuilders in *Your New House*.

Yet, we found the baby business to be perilous in different

The 7 Commandments of Baby Bargains

Yes, we've come down the mountain to share with you our SEVEN commandments of *Baby Bargains*—the keys to saving every parent should know. Let's review:

1 **SAFETY IS JOB ONE.** As a parent, your baby's safety is paramount. We never compromise safety for a bargain— that's why hand-me-down cribs or used car seats are not a good idea. Good news: you can subscribe to our free blog to get an email or instant message when a baby product is recalled. Go to BabyBargains.com/blog and enter your email address in the box at the right.

2 **FOCUS ON THE BASICS.** Big box baby stores are so over- whelming, with a blizzard of baby products. Key on the basics: setting up a safe place for baby to sleep (the nursery) and safe transport (car seats). Many items like high chairs, toys, and so on are not needed immediately.

3 **WEED OUT THE FLUFF.** Our advice: take an experienced mom with you when you register. A mom with one or two kids can help you separate out needed items from the fluff!

4 **TWO WORDS: FREE MONEY.** As a parent, you NEVER pass up free money! From tax deductions to tax credits, being a ways—instead of outright fraud or scam artists, we've instead discovered some highly questionable products that don't live up to their hype—and others that are outright dangerous. We were surprised to learn how most juvenile items face little (or no) government scrutiny, leaving parents to sort out true usefulness and safety from sales hype.

So, we've gone on a quest to find the best baby products, at prices that won't send you to the poor house. Sure, we've sampled many of these items first hand. But this book is much more than our experiences—we interviewed over 10,000 new parents to learn their experiences with products. Our message boards have over 20,000 members, buzzing with all sorts of product feedback and advice. We also attend juvenile product trade shows to quiz manufacturers and retailers on what's hot and what's not. The insights from retailers are especially helpful, since these folks are on the front lines, seeing which items unhappy parents return.

parent means freebies. And don't overlook your employer: take advantage of benefits like dependent care accounts—using PRE-TAX dollars to pay for child care will save you HUNDREDS if not THOUSANDS of dollars.

5 MORE FREEBIES. Many companies throw swag at new parents, hoping they will become future customers. We keep an updated freebie list on our web site—get free diapers, bottles, supplies and more. Go to BabyBargains.com/freebies for the latest update!

6 SHOP AT STORES THAT DO NOT HAVE "BABY" IN THEIR NAME. Costco for diapers? Pet web sites for safety gates? Regular furniture stores for rockers and dressers? IKEA for high chairs? Yes! Yes! Yes! You can save 30% or more by not buying items at baby stores.

7 ONLINE SHOPPING SAVVY. Let's face it: as a new mom and dad, you probably won't have much time to hit the mall. The web is a savior—but how do you master the deals? One smart tip: ALWAYS use coupon codes for discounts or FREE shipping before you order. We keep a list (updated daily!) of the best coupon codes on our Bargain Alert Forum on our free message boards (BabyBargains.com).

What you need, when

Yes, buying for baby can seem overwhelming, but there is a silver lining: you don't need ALL this stuff immediately when baby is born. Let's look at what items you need quickly and what you can wait on. This chart indicates usage of certain items for the first 12 months of baby's life:

ITEM	MONTHS OF USE				
	BIRTH	3	6	9	12+
Nursery Necessities					
Cradle/bassinet	▓▓▓▓				
Crib/Mattress	▓▓▓▓	▓▓▓▓	▓▓▓▓	▓▓▓▓	▓▓▓▓
Dresser	▓▓▓▓	▓▓▓▓	▓▓▓▓	▓▓▓▓	▓▓▓▓
Glider Rocker	▓▓▓▓	▓▓▓▓	▓▓▓▓	▓▓▓▓	▓▓▓▓
Bedding: Cradle	▓▓▓▓				
Bedding: Crib	▓▓▓▓	▓▓▓▓	▓▓▓▓	▓▓▓▓	▓▓▓▓
Clothing					
Caps/Hats	▓▓▓▓	▓▓▓▓	▓▓▓▓	▓▓▓▓	▓▓▓▓
Blanket Sleepers	▓▓▓▓	▓▓▓▓	▓▓▓▓	▓▓▓▓	▓▓▓▓
Layette Gowns	▓▓▓▓				
Booties	▓▓▓▓	▓▓			
All other layette	▓▓▓▓	▓▓▓▓	▓▓▓▓	▓▓▓▓	▓▓▓▓
Around the House					
Baby Monitor	▓▓▓▓	▓▓▓▓	▓▓▓▓	▓▓▓▓	▓▓▓▓
Baby Food (solid)			▓▓▓▓	▓▓▓▓	▓▓▓▓
High Chairs			▓▓▓▓	▓▓▓▓	▓▓▓▓
Places to Go					
Infant Car Seat	▓▓▓▓	▓▓▓▓			
Convertible Car Seat*			▓▓▓▓	▓▓▓▓	▓▓▓▓
Full-size Stroller/Stroller Frame	▓▓▓▓	▓▓▓▓	▓▓▓▓	▓▓▓▓	▓▓▓▓
Umbrella Stroller			▓▓▓▓	▓▓▓▓	▓▓▓▓
Front Carrier	▓▓▓▓	▓▓▓▓			
Backpack Carrier			▓▓▓▓	▓▓▓▓	▓▓▓▓
Safety items		▓▓▓▓	▓▓▓▓	▓▓▓▓	▓▓▓▓

You can use a convertible car seat starting immediately with that first ride home from the hospital. However, it is our recommendation that you use an infant car seat for the first six months or so, then, when baby grows out of it, buy the convertible car seat.

Our focus is on safety and durability: which items stand up to real world conditions and which don't. Interestingly, we found many products for baby are sold strictly on price . . . and sometimes a great "bargain" broke, fell apart or shrunk after a few uses. Hence, you'll note some of our top recommendations aren't always the lowest in price. To be sensitive to those on really tight budgets, we try to identify "good, better and best" bets in different price ranges.

We get questions: Top 5 Questions & Answers

From the home office here in Boulder, CO, here are the top five questions we get asked here at *Baby Bargains*:

1 **How do I know if I have the current edition?** We strive to keep *Baby Bargains* as up-to-date as possible. As such, we update it periodically with new editions. But if you just borrowed this book from a friend, how do you know how old it is? First, look at the copyright page. There at the bottom you will see a version number (such as 8.0). The first number (the 8 in this case) means you have the 8th edition. The second number indicates the printing—every time we reprint the book, we make minor corrections, additions and changes. Version 8.0 is the initial printing of the 8th edition, version 8.1 is the first reprint of the 8th edition and so on.

So, how can you tell if your book is current or woefully out-of-date? Go to our web page at BabyBargains.com and click on "Which version?"—this shows the most current version. (One clue: look at the book's cover. We note the edition number on each cover. And we change the color of the cover with each edition.) We update this book every two years (roughly). About 30% to 40% of the content will change with each edition. Bottom line: if you pick up a copy of this book that is one or two editions old, you will notice a significant number of changes.

2 **What if I see a new product in stores? How can I find info on that?** First, make sure you have the latest edition of *Baby Bargains* (see previous question). If you can't find that product in our latest book, go to our web page at BabyBargains.com. There you will find a treasure trove of information. First, check out our blog, which tracks the latest news on baby gear. Second, search our message boards section to see if other readers have tried out the product and reported to us on their experiences. Finally, click on Reviews to read parent-penned reviews of baby products. Of course, you can email us with a question as well (see the How to Contact Us page at the back of this book). Be sure to sign up for our free e-newsletter to get the latest news on our book, web page, product recalls and more. All this can be done from BabyBargains.com. (A note on our privacy policy: we NEVER sell reader email addresses or other personal info).

Even though we have a treasure trove of FREE stuff on our web page, please note that we do not post the entire text of *Baby Bargains* online (hey, we have to make a living somehow). If a friend gives you a ten year-old edition of this book, you can't go online and just download all the changes/updates for free. We appreciate your purchase of the most recent edition of this book.

3 **I AM LOOKING FOR A SPECIFIC PRODUCT BUT I DON'T KNOW WHERE TO START! HELP!** Yep, this book is 600+ pages long and we realize it can be a bit intimidating. But you have a friend in the index—flip to the back of the book to look up just about anything. You can look up items by category, brand name and more.

If that doesn't work, try the table of contents. We sort the book into major topic areas (strollers, car seats, etc). FYI: Some companies have sub-brands—we list these aliases alphabetically and refer you to the main company review (for example, Cocoon cribs are made by Baby's Dream; we discuss Cocoon in the Baby's Dream review.)

Don't forget the handy Telephone/Web Site Directory in the back of the book as well. You can pop to any company's web page to find more details about a product we review in *Baby Bargains*.

4 **WHY DO YOU SOMETIMES RECOMMEND A MORE EXPENSIVE PRODUCT THAN A CHEAPER OPTION?** Yes, this is a book about bargains, but sometimes we will pick a slightly more expensive item in a category if we believe it is superior in quality or safety. In some cases, it makes sense to invest in better-quality products that will last through more than one child. And don't forget about the hassle of replacing a cheap product that breaks in six months.

To be sure, however, we recognize that many folks are on tight budgets. To help, we offer "Good, Better, Best" product suggestions that are typically sorted by price (good is most affordable, best is usually more expensive). Don't torture yourself if you can't afford the "best" in every category; a "good" product will be just as, well, good.

Another note: remember that our brand reviews cover many options in a category, not just the cheapest. Don't be dismayed if we give an expensive brand an "A" rating—such ratings are often based on quality, construction, innovation and more. Yes, we will try to identify the best values in a category as well. But we realize that some folks want to spend more on certain items (car seats, for example)—hence we try to identify the best of the best, not just the cheapest.

Why does our advice sometimes conflict with other publications like *Consumer Reports*? Simple reason: we have different research methods. Most *Consumer Reports* reviews are based on lab tests; we rely on more on parent feedback, culled from hundreds (and sometimes thousands) of reviews, interviews and emails. That's our secret sauce.

More often than not, our picks and *Consumer Reports* usually match; when we don't agree, we try to point out the differences, both in our book and blog. Of course, we review and rate many more products than *Consumer Reports*, as our focus is just baby gear. We know you want in-depth info to make the best decisions . . . that's why we're here.

5 **WHAT OTHER PARENTING BOOKS DO YOU PUBLISH?** Yes, we do have two other best-selling parenting books: *Baby 411* and *Toddler 411*. Co-authored by an award-winning pediatrician, these books answer your questions about sleep, nutrition, growth and more. See the back of this book for details.

Let's Go Shopping!

Now that all the formal introductions are done, let's move on to the good stuff. As your tour guides to BabyLand, we'd like to remind you of one key rule: the Baby Biz is just that—business.

The juvenile products industry is a $8.9 BILLION DOLLAR business. While all those baby stores may want to help you, they are first and foremost in business to make a profit. As a consumer, you should arm yourself with the knowledge necessary to make smart decisions. If you do, you won't be taken for a ride.

What's New in This Edition?

Welcome to the 8th edition—this marks our 15th year in covering the baby biz. Wow, our book will soon get a driver's license.

As always, we've added dozens of brand reviews for cribs, car seats and strollers. New this year: eco-friendly baby products. We focus on green cribs and nursery furniture, plus cover the latest controversies regarding baby bottles and car seats that outgas chemicals like bromine.

What's the best (and most affordable) knock-off of the popular Bugaboo stroller? We've got the scoop in our updated feature, *Bugaboo Smackdown*. This handy comparison chart rates and reviews the best Bugaboo imitators. Also new in strollers: reviews of ten new stroller brands, including the latest European imports like Teutonia.

Potty seats are new to the 8th edition—we've also got more toddler product recommendations, including a large section on car seat boosters and kitchen booster.

New this year, we cover new hybrid diapers that are the latest eco-craze: cloth diapers with flushable liners.

We've increased our coverage of video baby monitors, with new reviews of models that are much better than in years' past.

Car seats that work beyond 40 lbs. with a five-point harness are a growth area and we have complete coverage with reviews, analysis and recommendations.

Of course, we've kept the features you love about *Baby Bargains*, including those nifty comparison charts that sum up our picks and our ever-popular baby registry at-a-glance (Appendix B).

Don't forget to check out our extensive online offerings, including an updated blog that covers breaking news and safety recalls. Surf our message boards for a listing of coupons, sales and deals—updated several times a week. And read reviews of baby products posted by our readers.

So, buckle your seat belts and secure all loose items like sunglasses and your sanity. We're off to Baby Gear Land.

Coming soon: iPhone apps, Kindle ebook

Baby Bargains is more than a book—soon we will be rolling out an ebook version for the Amazon Kindle as well as other ebook readers. And if you own an iPhone, look for our iPhone app that will let you look up the latest reviews on the fly.

Want to get an updated chapter from this book? You can download a PDF of our latest research direct from our web page (click Order Online button). That way if you just want to read about the latest strollers, you can get just that chapter for much less than buying the entire book again.

Check our web page at BabyBargains.com for the latest news on all these new versions of *Baby Bargains*. Or email us at authors@ BabyBargains.com if you have a question or suggestion.

CHAPTER 2

Nursery Necessities: Cribs, Dressers & More

Inside this chapter

H ow can you save 20% to 50% off cribs, dressers, and other furniture for your baby's room? In this chapter, you'll learn these secrets, plus discover smart shopper tips that help clarify all those confusing crib options and features. Then, you'll learn which juvenile furniture has safety problems and where to go online to find the latest recall info. Next, we'll rate and review over three dozen top brands of cribs, focusing on quality and value. Finally, you'll learn which crib mattress is best, how to get a deal on a dresser, and several more items to consider for your baby's room.

Getting Started: When Do You Need This Stuff?

So, you want to buy a crib for Junior? And, what the heck, why not some other furniture, like a dresser to store all those baby gifts and a changing table for, well, you know. Just pop down to the store, pick out the colors, and set a delivery date, right?

Not so fast, o' new parental one. Once you get to that baby store, you'll discover that most don't have all those nice cribs and furniture *in stock*. No, that would be too easy, wouldn't it? You will quickly learn that you have to *special order* much of that booty.

To be fair, we should note that in-stock items vary from shop to shop. Some (especially the larger chain stores) may stock a fair number of cribs. Yet Murphy's Law says the last in-stock crib you want was just sold five minutes ago. And while stores may stock a good number of cribs, dressers are another story—these bulky items almost always must be special-ordered.

So, let's cut to chase: when should you order nursery furniture?

The answer depends on WHERE you plan to buy furniture. *If you choose an independent baby store, order at your 20th week of pregnancy.* Yes, it really takes 10-14 weeks on average to have specialty-store nursery furniture ordered and delivered (we figured you want it there a few weeks before baby arrives!).

Major caveat: some brands take as long as 16 weeks to order . . . ask your local retailer for advice, as lead times for brands can shift.

What about chain stores like Babies R Us? You need less time than specialty stores, but it isn't lighting quick either. Babies R Us says IF the furniture is in stock at their warehouse, it takes seven to 21 business days to be delivered to a store. If the furniture is NOT in stock, you can cool your heels for four to six weeks. Bottom line: *if you choose a chain store, order at your 25th week of pregnancy.* That you have left plenty of time, even if the furniture is on a six week delay.

Why does it take so long to get nursery furniture? Most furniture today is made in China. Manufacturers wait until they receive enough orders of a certain collection before they go into production. Then the furniture is loaded into a shipping container and sent on a four-to-six week ocean journey to the U.S. Assuming all goes well (no hurricanes, port strikes, etc.), the furniture is delivered to a manufacture's distribution center. From there, it is trucked to the retailer.

Yes, you might get lucky and have your nursery furniture be in stock at a manufacturer or retailer's warehouse. But don't bet on it.

We should note that some parents wait until after a baby is born to take delivery of nursery furniture. Why? Certain religious and ethnic customs say it is bad luck to have any baby gear in the house before baby is born. These families will order baby furniture, but not have it delivered until baby is born—needless to say, if you go this route, you have to find a retailer willing to store your furniture until that time.

First-time parent question: so, how long will baby use a crib? Answer: it depends (and you thought we always had the answer). Seriously, most babies can use a crib for two or three years. Yes, some babies are out of the crib by 18 months, while others may be pushing four years. One key factor: when does baby learn they can climb out of the crib? Once that happens, the crib days are numbered, as you can understand. Of course, there may be other factors that push baby out of a crib—if you are planning to have a second child and want the crib for the new baby, it may be time to transition to a "big boy/girl" bed. We discuss more about the transition out of a crib in our other book, *Toddler 411.* See the back of this book for more info.

Cribs: Sources to Find

This year, more than one million households plan to buy infant/nursery furniture, according to a survey by *Kids Today*. That translates into $1.5 billion in sales of infant furniture—yes, this is big business. In their quest for the right nursery, parents have five basic sources for finding a crib, each with its own advantages and drawbacks:

1 INDEPENDENT BABY SPECIALTY STORES. Indie baby specialty stores are pretty self-explanatory—shops that specialize in the retailing of baby furniture, strollers, and accessories. Independents come in all sizes: some are small boutiques; others are as large as a chain superstore. A good number of indie retailers have joined together in "buying groups" to get volume discounts on items from suppliers—these groups include Baby Furniture Plus (babyfurniture-plus.com), Baby News (BabyNewsStores.com), NINFRA (ninfra.com) and USA Baby (USAbaby.com). Another good resource to find a specialty store near you is AllBabyAndChildStores.com.

Like other independent stores, many baby specialty shops have been hard hit by the expansion of national chains like Babies R Us. Yet, those that have survived do so by emphasizing service and products you can't find at the chains. Of course, quality of service can vary widely from store to store . . . but just having a breathing human to ask a question of is a nice plus.

The problems with specialty stores? Readers complain the stores only carry expensive brands. One parent told us the only baby specialty store in her town doesn't carry any cribs under $600. We understand the dilemma faced by mom and pop retailers—in order to provide all that service, they have to make a certain profit margin on furniture and other products. And that margin is easier to get on high-end goods. That's all well and good, but failing to carry products in entry-level price points only drives parents to the chains.

Another gripe with some indie stores: some shops can be downright hostile to you if they think you are price-shopping. A reader said she found this out when comparing high-end nursery furniture in her town. "When I asked to price cribs and dressers at two baby stores, I met with resistance and hostility. At one store, I was asked if I was a 'spy' for their competition! The store managers at both baby stores I visited said they didn't want people to comparison shop them on price, yet both advertise they will 'meet or beat' the competition's prices."

The bottom line: despite the hassles, if you have a locally owned baby store in your town, give them a shot. Don't assume chains always have lower prices and better selection. See the box on the next page for our picks of the top indie baby stores in the U.S.

The 21 best baby stores in America

Who are the 21 best independent baby stores in America? In researching this book, we have visited hundreds of baby stores from coast to coast during the past 15 years. Along the way, we've met some of the smartest retailers in the USA—folks we often turn to to find out what's REALLY happening in the baby gear biz. Which cribs, strollers and car seats are selling and winning raves from parents . . . and what are the bombs.

Readers often tell us they want to support indie stores—but which ones are most reputable? If you are tired of the chains, we offer our list of stores to check out.

A few notes: just in case you are wondering, NO retailers paid us to be on this list. We don't take advertising, commissions or fees to recommend stores in our book or blog. The retailers we think are best earned it the old fashioned way—by focusing on their customers.

We compiled this list from reader feedback and store visits; we also asked baby gear manufacturers to name their top retailers. This list focuses on baby stores in major metro areas (with a few exceptions). Most of these stores sell baby furniture/products in a wide range of prices; these aren't expensive boutiques, but mainstream retailers.

So . . . drum roll . . . here are the 21 Best Baby Stores in America (in alphabetical order):

Baby Furniture Warehouse (Boston)
Baby Love (Ft. Lauderdale)
Baby Super Mart (Broomall, PA)
Baby Town (Reseda, CA)
Baby's Room (Detroit)
Baby's 1st (Houston)
Behr's (Metro NY)
Berg's (Cleveland, OH)
Georgia Baby (Atlanta)
Goores (Sacramento, CA)
Great Beginnings (Washington DC area/Maryland)
Ideal Baby & Kids (Miami); also known as La Ideal.
Karl's (Philadelphia)
Kids Stuff Superstores (South Dakota, Nebraska)
Lazar's (Chicago)
Li'l Deb-N-Heir (Chicago)
Lone Star Baby (Dallas/Ft. Worth)
Lullaby Lane (San Francisco)
Tiny Totland (Manchester, NH)
Treasures Room (St Louis)
USA Baby (Milwaukee, WI location only)

2 **THE CHAINS.** There are two types of chains that sell baby products: specialty chains like Babies R Us who focus on juvenile products and discounters like Wal-Mart, Target, and K-Mart that have small baby departments. We'll discuss each in-depth later in this chapter. The selection at chains can vary widely—some carry more premium brands, but most concentrate on mass-market names to appeal to price-conscious shoppers. Service? Fuggedaboutit—often, you'll be lucky to find someone to help you check out, much less answer questions.

In recent years, we've seen a third type of chain enter the baby market: specialty chains such as Pottery Barn Kids (PBK) and Restoration Hardware. The former has stores that sell some baby furniture; the latter (Restoration Hardware) has a online-only baby boutique.

3 **DEPARTMENT STORES.** A few department stores still have baby departments that carry clothing and some gear; most furniture and nursery items are relegated to their web sites. Prices aren't typically as low as the discounters, but occasional sales sometimes bring bargains.

4 **ONLINE.** Long before the web, companies tried to sell furniture via mail order, albeit with mixed results. Perhaps the best example is JCPenney (jcpenney.com), whose mail-order catalog (and now web site specializes in affordable cribs and dressers. Despite the challenge of shipping bulky items like dressers, web sites and specialty retailers are still piling into the online nursery niche. We'll discuss the options and caveats more in depth later in this chapter.

Even if you decide to order your entire nursery online, there are several roadblocks. Given the weight and bulk of cribs and dressers, only a few (mostly lower-end) brands are typically sold online. Shipping charges can be exorbitant—and that assumes you can get items shipped at all (most sites don't ship furniture to Hawaii, Alaska, Canada or military addresses). With shipping, you then have the issue of damage, delays and worse. Given the limitations of the web as it is today, it is more realistic to use online sites to buy accessories (lamps, rockers, décor) for your nursery rather than an entire furniture suite.

5 **REGULAR FURNITURE STORES.** You don't have to go to a "baby store" to buy juvenile furniture. Many regular furniture stores sell name-brand cribs, dressers and other nursery items. Since these stores have frequent sales, you may be able to get a better price than at a juvenile specialty store. On the other hand, the salespeople may not be as knowledgeable about brand and safety issues.

What Are You Buying?

Ok, let's break this down. Outfitting a nursery usually means buying three basic furniture items: a crib, dresser (which doubles as a place to change baby's diaper) and rocker. Here's a quick discussion of each.

◆ **Crib.** Crib prices start at $100 for an inexpensive crib at a discounter like Wal-Mart. The mid-range for cribs is probably best typified by what you see at chains stores such as Babies R Us and Baby Depot—most of their cribs are in the $200 to $400 range (the stores seem to be a bit more pricey while their online sites offer more lower price options). Specialty stores and catalogs tend to carry upper-end cribs that run $400 to $700. And what about the top end? We'd be remiss not to mention the modern-design cribs, which run $1000 to $2000.

Surprise! The vast majority of cribs don't come with mattresses; those are sold separately ($60 to $200). Bedding is also extra ($50 to $500). We'll discuss mattresses later in this chapter; bedding gets its own entire chapter (Chapter 3).

◆ **Dresser.** Most nurseries need a place to store clothes, diapers, supplies and so on. Known in the baby biz as case pieces (because they are, uh, a case), dressers range from simple, ready-to-assemble four-drawer chests to elaborate armoires (and their smaller cousins, chiffarobes).

Now, there is no federal law that says you MUST buy a dresser or armoire that exactly matches the finish of your crib. Some folks simply re-purpose a dresser from another room to baby's nursery—or pick up a dresser second-hand or at a discount from a regular furniture store. That's fine, of course.

But . . . we realize the allure of matching nursery furniture convinces many new parents to pony up the bucks. So here are some general price guidelines: a ready-to-assemble dresser from IKEA or a discount store runs $150 to $200.

Now, if you'd like to have something fancier (and already assembled), prices for dressers range from $300 to $500 in chain stores. Step into a specialty store and you'll find plenty of fancy dressers, armoires and chiffarobes . . . for $500 to $1000 and higher.

Most dressers also double as a place to change baby—some have tops specifically designed for that purpose. These changer tops remove after baby is done with diapers (usually right before college). So most parents today do not need to buy a separate changing table.

◆ **Rocker.** A place to sit and nurse baby is an important part of any nursery's function—so the next question is . . . where to sit? Again, you can re-purpose a rocker from grandma's house or pick up one secondhand. If you have the room, a small loveseat or over-sized chair is a workable solution for nursing baby.

Brand new "glider-rockers" run the gamut from wooden chairs with thin pads to fully upholstered models. And the price range reflects this: you can spend as little as $100 to $200 for a rocker from Target or Wal-Mart . . . as much as $1300 for a tricked out leather model from a specialty store. Most folks probably buy a basic model from chain stores like Babies R Us for about $300. Yes, ottomans are a nice extra—but cost $100 to $300 more.

Glider rockers get their own section later in this chapter.

The Grand Total. As you can see, the bare-bones budget for a nursery would be $600 (simple crib, mattress, basic dresser and rock-er). The mid-range would run about $900 . . . and on the designer end, you could easily spend $2000 to $3000 on nursery furniture.

And these figures are BEFORE you get to any of the other décor items: bedding, lamps, paint, artwork, curtains, etc.

More Money Buys You . . .

Here's a little secret expensive crib makers don't want you to hear: ALL new cribs (no matter what price) sold in the U.S. or Canada must meet federal safety standards. Yes, the governments of both the U.S. and Canada strictly regulate crib safety and features—that's one reason why most cribs have the same basic design, no matter the brand or price. So, whether you buy a $100 crib special at K-Mart or a $1500 wrought iron crib at a posh specialty boutique, either way you get a crib that meets federal safety requirements.

Now, that said, when you spend more money, there are some perks. The higher the price tag of the crib (generally), the fancier the design (thicker corner posts, designer colors, etc.). That's all nice, but is it really necessary? No—a basic, safe crib in a simple fin-ish is all babies need.

The biggest sales pitch for cribs is convertibility: more expensive cribs are convertible. They morph into beds for older kids: toddler bed (basically, a crib with the sides removed), day bed and (finally) full-sized bed. That latter uses the sides of the crib to become a headboard and footboard—some cribs even transform into queen-size adult beds.

Convertible cribs are pitched to parents as "lifetime cribs" (your child will take the bed to college with them, we suppose) and smart investments, because it "grows with your child." Here's what the pitch leaves out: to convert the crib, you have to buy a conversion kit (sold separately, naturally). And think about the SIZE of the average kids' bedroom these days: most can barely squeeze in a TWIN

Three Golden Rules of Buying Nursery Furniture

◆ **Don't over buy**—think about your needs first. Here's a common first time parent mistake: rushing out to a local baby store and ogling that fancy cognac finish on a chiffarobe. Instead, think about what you really NEED. Start with the size of your baby's nursery—most secondary bedrooms in a typical suburban home are 10 x12 (some are smaller). That barely leaves room for a crib, dresser and rocker. Don't let a baby store sell you on a double dresser PLUS an armoire when you don't have room. For urban apartment dwellers, space is critical. Closets need to be tricked out to provide maximum storage. Expect furniture to do double duty.

◆ **Three words: set a budget.** Don't waste your time falling in love with a designer look if you haven't done the math. As you saw from the discussion on the last few pages, a three-piece nursery set (crib, dresser, rocker) runs anywhere from $450 . . . up to $3000. Pick a budget and stick with it. Then read the brand reviews later in this chapter—you'll quickly realize which ones are in your budget and which aren't! Again, it pays to think outside the box: can you re-purpose a dresser from another room? Get a hand-me-down rocker from a friend or off Craigslist?

◆ **Decide on nursery style.** There are two theories of nursery design: either a baby's room should look, well, baby-ish . . . or it should be more adult-looking, able to adapt as the child grows. Neither is right or wrong. If you subscribe to the baby-theme, then go with a simple (non-convertible) crib and dresser that will be later swapped out for a twin bed and computer desk/hutch. If you prefer the other path, then buy a convertible crib (which converts to a full size bed) and dresser that can do double duty. Some brands have dressers that are first a changing area for diapers . . . and then convert to a computer area complete with pull out keyboard drawer.

bed and dresser . . . a full or queen size bed is often impossible. We'll discuss this issue more later in the chapter

Some crib extras also have dubious value—take the under-crib storage drawer. Often seen on cribs that run $500 or more, this feature appeals to parents who have a storage crunch in their home (you can put blankets, extra clothes in the drawer). The problem? The drawer usually doesn't have a top. So, anything inside will be a dust magnet.

Ok, so now you know the typical prices of nursery furniture . . . and what more money really buys you. How do you decide what is best for your baby's nursery? See the following box for our Three Golden Rules of Buying Nursery Furniture.

Safe & Sound

Here's a fact to keep you up at night: cribs are the third-biggest cause of injuries and deaths among all nursery products. In the latest year for which statistics are available, 11,300 injuries and 32 deaths were blamed on cribs and mattresses.

And you couldn't click on a news web site in the past year without seeing another crib recall: since September 2007, over three MILLION cribs were recalled. The recalls involved both cribs sold in posh specialty stores and lower-end models sold in Babies R Us and Wal-Mart. The problems? Lead paint, defective slats that could break, poor side rail design and more.

Government safety regulators have been scrambling to tighten safety standards to stop the flow of recalls . . . but those efforts could take years. So, let's talk crib safety here and now. Here are our tips for buying a safe crib—and keeping your baby safe while using it.

◆ **Don't buy a used or old crib.** Let's put that into bold caps: **DON'T BUY A USED OR OLD CRIB.** And don't take a hand-me-down from a well-meaning friend or relative. Why? Because old cribs account for most of the injuries and deaths when it comes to cribs. Surprisingly, these old cribs may not be as old as you think—cribs made before 1999 don't meet current standards.

Most folks realize that cribs made in the 70's and 80's aren't safe . . . but that never seems to stop a well-meaning relative to bring down a "family heirloom" crib from the attic. These are death traps: spindles that are too far apart, cutouts in the headboard, and other hazards that could entrap your baby. Decorative trim (like turned posts) that looks great on adult beds are a major no-no for cribs—they present a strangulation hazard. (Note: cribs with TALL posts are fine; it is the shorter posts that are prohibited—see the graphic on the next page).

Some old cribs have lead paint, a dangerous peril for a teething baby. Another hazard to hand-me-down cribs (regardless of age): missing parts and directions. It only takes one missing screw or bolt to make an otherwise safe crib into a danger. Without directions, you can incorrectly assemble the crib and create additional safety hazards. So, even if your friend wants to give/sell you a recent model crib, you could still have problems if parts or directions are missing.

It may seem somewhat ironic that a book on baby bargains would advise you to go out and spend your hard-earned money on a new crib. True, we find great bargains on Craigslist and second-hand stores. However, you have to draw the line at your baby's safety. Certain second-hand items are great deals—toys and clothes come to mind. However, cribs (and, as you'll read later, car seats) are no-no's, no matter how tempting the bargains.

And second hand stores have a spotty record when it comes to selling safe products. A recent report from the CPSC said that a whopping two-thirds of all U.S. thrift/second-hand stores sell baby products that have been recalled, banned or do not meet current safety standards (specifically 12% of stores stocked old cribs). Amazingly, federal law does not prohibit the sale of cribs (or other dangerous products like jackets with drawstring hoods, recalled playpens or car seats) at second-hand stores.

Readers often ask us why we don't give tips for evaluating old or hand-me-down cribs. The reason is simple: it's hard to tell whether an old crib is dangerous just by looking at it. Cribs don't always have

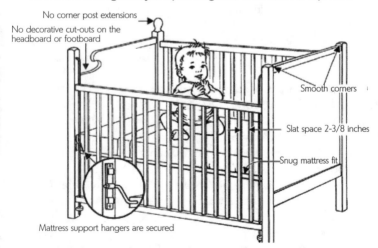

Older cribs typically have many hazards. Here's a graphic of what is dangerous. Note: all new cribs sold today are required by law to NOT have any of these features.

"freshness dates"—some manufacturers don't stamp the date of manufacture on their cribs. Was the crib made before or after the current safety standards went into effect in 1999? Often, you can't tell.

Today's safety regulations are so specific (like the allowable width for spindles) that you just can't judge a crib's safety with a cursory examination. Cribs made before the 1970's might contain lead paint, which is difficult to detect unless you get the crib tested. Another problem: if the brand name is rubbed off, it will be hard to tell if the crib has been involved in a recall. Obtaining replacement parts is also difficult for a no-name crib.

What about floor model cribs? Is it safe to buy a crib that has been used as a floor sample in a baby store? Yes—as long as it is in good working condition, has no missing/broken parts, etc. Floor model cribs CAN take a tremendous amount of abuse from parents, who shake them to check stability and so on. As a result, the bolts that hold the crib together can loosen. Obviously, that can be fixed (just have the store tighten the bolts) . . . and as a result, we think floor model cribs are fine. That isn't what we mean by avoiding a "used" crib!

What if a relative insists you should use that "family heirloom" crib we mentioned earlier? We've spoken to dozens of parents who felt pressured into using an old crib by a well-meaning relative. There's a simple answer: don't do it. As a parent, you sometimes have to make unpopular decisions that are best for your child's safety. This is just the beginning.

♦ **Cribs with fold-down rails.** A handful of drop-side cribs have fold-down rails—the upper one-third of the railing is hinged and folds down. These are also called swing gate cribs (see picture).

One major crib maker uses these rails for some of their models: Baby's Dream. While we like the quality of Baby's Dream's furniture overall, we do not recommend any crib with a fold-down rail. Why? Older babies who can stand (which happens around a year of age) can get a foothold on the hinged rail to climb out of the crib, injuring themselves as they fall to the floor.

A reader in Seattle, WA recently emailed us with exactly that story: her 13 month old son fractured his fibula after falling out of his Baby's Dream drop-gate crib. "We liked how the drop gate was easy to operate and worked better for a shorter person," she said. "However, we didn't foresee that the drop gate would provide a ledge for him to prop his foot on and fall out."

◆ **Cribs with drop-side rails should be regularly inspected.** Many cribs that were recalled in the past year had defective hardware or spindles that broke. Drop-side cribs are especially vulnerable—all that moving up and down can loosen hardware or spindles over time.

The CPSC has proposed tougher rules for these cribs, but that process can take years. Meanwhile, parents can take simple steps to avoid problems: first, inspect your crib from time to time. Make sure the bolts are secured, no spindles/slats are loose, etc. A drop-side rail should move smoothly on its track.

If something has broken on your crib, immediately stop using it. Don't attempt to repair it yourself—and never use a crib with missing, broken or loose parts.

◆ **Lead paint & formaldehyde.** The lead paint scare of 2007 is still fresh in the minds of many consumers—and that concern has translated into fears of cribs made in China. So, here's the scoop:

While there have been numerous toys and other children's products recalled for lead paint, there was only one nursery furniture recall for this reason (Munire recalled 3000 cribs and 5000 matching dressers for lead paint in 2008). Most nursery furniture companies have their paint and stains independently tested to verify they are lead-free—one (Sorelle) even posts its test results online. Yet, as the Munire recall shows, even a diligent company can have lapses.

Still, we realize some folks still don't trust China and want to avoid Chinese-made furniture. To help, we have a box on page 49 that lists all the nursery furniture makers who make their furniture in countries other than China.

What about formaldehyde? This chemical was in the news recently when the state of California sued five baby furniture makers for unsafe levels of formaldehyde. The suit was prompted by a report from Environment California, which found certain furniture items from Child Craft, Delta, Stork Craft, South Shore and Jardine had unsafe levels of the chemical.

Formaldehyde is found in particle board, glue and other parts of furniture—it's no surprise that the items flagged as being unsafe had composite wood or particle board components. For example, a Child Craft oak crib with high formaldehyde levels had a drawer made from composite wood. We've put the entire Environment California report on our web site (BabyBargains.com, click on Bonus Materials).

Here's our quick take on this controversy: yes, baby furniture is made with toxic chemicals—paint, glue, varnish, and manufactured wood products . . . all of which can give off toxic emissions. Experts can argue about safe levels of chemical X or Y, but it makes sense to try to limit exposure.

cribs

Our advice: stick with solid wood cribs and dressers. Avoid composite wood products—these are often seen in under-crib drawers, for example. Another idea: choose a crib with a more eco-friendly finish: Romina (reviewed later) offers an organic beeswax finish for some of its collections, for example.

◆ *Stripped screws.* Cheap cribs often have screws that attach directly to the wood of the headboard. The problem? The screws can strip over time (especially if the crib is assembled several times) and that can weaken the crib's support . . . which is very dangerous. If you ever discover you are not able to tighten the screws or bolts used to hold your crib together, immediately stop using it. When you are crib shopping, look at how the mattress support is attached to the headboards—look for metal screwed into metal.

◆ *Be aware of the hazards of putting a baby in an adult bed.* Co-sleeping is where a baby shares a bed with adults. While common in other parts of the world, co-sleeping is controversial here in the US—on one side are attachment parenting advocates, who insist it is safe, a big convenience for nursing moms and an important part of parent/child emotional bonds.

On the other side are safety advocates, including the Consumer Product Safety Commission and the American Academy of Pediatrics. A CPSC report released in 2002 blamed 122 infant deaths in a previous three year period on co-sleeping. Of those deaths, many were caused when a child's head became entrapped between the adult bed and another object (a headboard, footboard, wall, etc). Other deaths were caused by falls or suffocation in bedding. The American Academy of Pediatrics agreed with the CPSC's concerns, issuing a recommendation against co-sleeping in 2005.

We have an expanded discussion of this debate in our other book, *Baby 411.* Since this book focuses on gear, here is our quick take: whatever sleep routine you choose (co-sleeping in a family bed or solitary sleep in a crib), make sure you set up a SAFE sleeping environment. One compromise to this debate is to keep a newborn in a product like the Arm's Reach Co-Sleeper (we'll discuss this more in-depth later in the chapter). In a nutshell, the Arm's Reach is a bassinet that attaches to the adult bed, providing easy access for nursing, but a separate sleep space.

◆ *Some stylish cribs can make bumper tying a challenge.* Those thick corner posts on expensive cribs sure look pretty, but they can create problems—using a bumper pad (a bedding item discussed in the next chapter) on these cribs can be darn near impossible. Why? Many bumper pads have short ties that simply don't fit around thick corner posts. And other cribs have solid head-boards or footboards—this prevents the tying of a bumper. We'll discuss bumpers in the next chapter (our position: they're optional) . . . but if you decide you want to use them, be sure to get a crib that is bumper-compatible.

◆ **When assembling a crib, make sure ALL the bolts and screws are tightened**. A recent report on *Good Morning America* pointed out how dangerous it can be to put your baby in a miss-assembled crib—a child died in a Child Craft crib when he became trapped in a side rail that wasn't properly attached to the crib. How did that happen? The parent didn't tighten the screws that held the side rail to the crib. All cribs (including the Child Craft one here in question) are safe when assembled correctly; just be sure to tighten those screws! A smart safety tip: check your crib once a month to make sure all screws and bolts are firmly attached.

◆ **Recalls: where to find information.** The U.S. Consumer Product Safety Commission has a toll-free hotline at (800) 638-2772 and web site (cpsc.gov) for the latest recall information on cribs and other juvenile items. Both are easy to use—you can also report any potential hazard you've discovered or an injury to your child caused by a product. Write to the U.S. Consumer Products Safety Commission, Washington, D.C. 20207 or file a complaint online at cpsc.gov. FYI: The CPSC takes care of all juvenile product recalls, except for car seats—that's the purview of the National Highway Traffic Safety Administration (nhtsa.gov).

A great "all-in-one" site for recalls is Recalls.gov. Also: subscribe to our blog—we will send you an email or text message when a product is recalled. Go to BabyBargains.com/blog and enter your email at the box at the right and hit subscribe. It's free!

◆ **Safety is more than a crib.** Be sure to have a smoke and carbon monoxide detector for your baby's nursery. And if you haven't had your home tested for radon yet, this would be a good time. (We discuss radon and other environmental hazards in our book, *Toddler 411*. See the back of this book for details).

Smart Shopper Tips

Smart Shopper Tip #1
The Art and Science of Selecting the Right Crib.
"How do you evaluate a crib? They all look the same to me. What really makes one different from another?"

Selecting a good crib is more than just picking out the style and finish. You should look under the hood, so to speak. Here are our nine key points to look for when shopping for a crib:

◆ **Brand reputation.** Later in this chapter, we will rate and review the biggest crib brands. Our advice: stick with a brand that gets a B or better rating. We formulate these ratings from parent feedback (some of which is posted on our web site, where readers rate and review various crib brands) as well as our analysis of a brand's track record. We look at recall history, customer service, delivery reliability and overall quality to assign a rating.

◆ **Mattress support.** Look underneath that mattress and see what is holding it up. The best cribs use a metal spring platform or a grid of wooden slats. Other cribs use cheap vinyl straps or a piece of particle board. We think the last two are inferior—vinyl straps aren't as secure as metal springs or wood slats; and concerns have been raised over formaldehyde emissions with particle board (see earlier discussion).

◆ **Drop side or stationary?** Cribs come in two flavors today: those with drop sides (where one side lowers to give access to the baby) and those that don't. Here's a brief discussion of the differences:

1 STATIC/STATIONARY. As the name implies, these cribs have rails that do NOT lower. Why would crib designers do this? Well, these crib styles are easier to convert to full-size beds (the side rails become the head and footboards). The advantage to this design: there are no moving parts to break and these cribs seem much more stable/solid than other models. The downside: for shorter parents, it can be a long reach to put a sleeping infant down on the mattress when set in its lowest position. Our advice: try these cribs out in the store before buying.

2 DROP-SIDE. Knee-push drop-side cribs are the most common—by lifting the side rail and pushing against it with your knee, the drop side releases. The hardware for drop-sides can either be hidden (inside the crib posts) or exposed (the rail glides on tracks are screwed to the crib posts).

We should note there are two additional, less common drop-side releases still on the market today: double trigger and fold down rails. Used on low-price cribs from Delta, double trigger drop-sides are released by simultaneously pulling on two plastic triggers on either side of the rail. Crib makers that use this type of release tout its safety (only an adult can release the rail) and the lack of exposed hardware like that used on foot-bar releases. There is one major drawback: first, you need *two* hands to operate the release, not really possible if you have a baby in your arms (unless you can grow extras!). Clearly, this isn't a popular release since even Delta only makes one crib with the double triggers.

Fold-down rails are rarely used today (Baby's Dream still has a few in their line). Instead of lowering, the rail has a hinge that allows the top portion to fold down. We think fold-down rails are dangerous (see Safe & Sound section later in this chapter).

So, which kind should you get? Well, drop-side cribs have had a rough run of late: several recalls of drop-side cribs in 2008 were blamed on faulty hardware and broken slats. While the CPSC has promised tougher standards for these cribs in coming years, some safety advocates (notably Consumer Reports) have recommended parents buy stationary-side cribs instead.

Here's our take: we don't think ALL drop-side cribs should be avoided. Note that the 2008 recalls were focused on low-end cribs (Delta, for example sold at Wal-Mart for under $200) and a private-label line (Jardine) at Babies R Us ($150 to $300). We still think a drop-side crib from one of our top-rated furniture makers can be a safe option for your baby.

That said, it may be a moot point in coming years: many manufacturers are dropping drop-side cribs altogether, some as a result of the recent bad publicity. Therefore your choice may soon come down to stationary or stationary.

◆ **Hardware/bolts: hidden or exposed?** As we noted above, some cribs with drop-side releases have hardware that is hidden; others have exposed hardware. For static cribs, some have visible bolts that attach the crib rails to the headboard; others are hidden. Is there a difference in safety or durability? No, it's just aesthetics. The more money you spend, the more likely the hardware/bolts will be hidden.

◆ **How stable is the crib?** Stationary-side cribs tend to be more stable than drop-sides. Yes, sturdiness is often related to price: the higher price models tend to have stabilizer bars and more solid construction.

◆ **How do you move the crib?** In years past, most cribs came on wheels (casters). This made it easier to vacuum or clean behind a crib. Yet in recent years, most stationary-side cribs have jettisoned the wheels. Today, we see wheels/casters only on a few crib models, typically low-end brands sold at discount stores. The only caveat to going wheel-less: it is hard to move a heavy crib to vacuum behind it. Without wheels, it is a two person job to move a crib—and dragging it on the carpet can break it.

◆ ***How easy is it to assemble?*** Ask to see those instructions—most stores should have a copy lying around. Make sure they are not indecipherable. Yes, some stores offer set-up and delivery, but with chain superstores, you are typically on your own. Sadly, some crib makers don't put a high priority on easy-to-understand assembly instructions—check first before you buy! The good news: some crib makers now have instructions you can download from their web sites.

◆ ***Compare the overall safety features of the crib.*** In a section earlier in this book, we discuss crib safety in more detail.

◆ ***Which wood is best?*** Most cribs are made of hardwoods: birch, beech, oak, etc. In recent years, crib makers have also made some models in pine. The problem? Pine is a softwood that tends to nick, scratch and damage. Of course, not all pine is the same. North American pine is the softest, but pine grown in really cold climates (Northern Europe, for example) is harder.

Another recent trend: modern furniture made of medium-density fiberboard (MDF) with a glossy lacquer finish. Made of wood fibers and resin, MDF has a smooth, grain-free surface, which enables manufacturers to add that high-gloss finish.

So, which wood is best? We recommend you go with a hardwood crib—it doesn't matter whether it is birch, beech, mahogany or even ramin (also called rubber wood). The latter is an Asian hardwood that is often seen in low-price cribs.

We caution against pine furniture—even "hardwood pine" can be more susceptible to nicks, scratches and damage than other woods like birch or beech. If you decide to buy pine baby furniture, just prepare yourself for the inevitable ding here or there.

What about MDF? We aren't fans of composite wood—MDF simply isn't as durable as hardwood. Yes, we realize fans of modern furniture are more sold on the aesthetic here . . . MDF with a glossy lacquer makes for a sleek look. But you'll be paying through the nose for this (some modern cribs run $1000+) for a crib that isn't made from solid wood.

Another quick point: don't confuse finish with wood. Some stores and web sites tout "cherry" cribs when they are actually referring to the finish, not the actual wood. It may be a "cherry" stain, but the wood is probably not.

Smart Shopper Tip #2
Cyber-Nursery: Ordering furniture online

"We don't have any good baby stores nearby, so I want to order furniture online. How do you buy items sight unseen and make sure they arrive in one piece?"

Sure, you can buy just about everything today online, but when it comes to nursery furniture, we have one word of advice: don't. Despite the fact that most stores selling nursery items have online sites offering furniture, our readers report that the actual experience of buying a crib or dresser online leaves them frustrated.

You probably guessed the reason: bulk. Cribs and dressers are heavy and bulky—this makes them expensive to ship and susceptible to damage. If there is a problem, you have to deal with a customer service agent half way across the country.

Our advice: order from a local store and have the items delivered/set-up. If the store doesn't have items in stock, see if they have a "site to store" shipping option—you order online, but the item is delivered to a local store where you pick it up. This helps eliminate shipping damage.

Wastes of Money

1 **LOW QUALITY "BABY" FURNITURE THAT WON'T LAST.** Baby furniture stores (both chains and independents) are sometimes guilty of selling very poor quality furniture. Take a dresser, for example. Many dressers made by juvenile furniture companies have stapled drawers, veneer construction (instead of solid wood), cheap drawer glides and worse. Now, that wouldn't be so bad if such dressers were low in price. But often you see these dressers going for $500 and up in baby stores—it's as if you are paying a premium to merely match the color of your crib. While we don't see a problem buying low-end "disposable" furniture at a good price (IKEA is a prime example), paying a fortune for a poorly-made dresser is ridiculous. In this chapter, we will point out brand names that provide more quality for the dollar. Look for solid wood construction, dove-tail drawers, and smooth drawer glides if you want that dresser to last.

2 **UNDER-CRIB DRAWERS.** It sounds like a great way to squeeze out a bit more storage in a nursery—the drawer that slides out from under a crib. Getting a crib with such a feature usually costs an extra $100 or $150. The problem? Most of these drawers do NOT have tops . . . therefore anything kept in there will get

E-Mail from The Real World
Spending $385 for a $50 dresser

A reader in Ohio shared this bad experience with shopping for a dresser online:

"I ordered a three drawer combo dresser from a well-known baby gear web site. It had all of the things suggested in your book and was $385 (the Rumble Tuff line around here was $700 for the same thing). The manufacturer is Angel Line. The item arrived with split wood on the corner, a knob missing, a missing wall strap and one of the drawers didn't shut completely and was crooked. I called the site and they said I had to contact the manufacturer directly to get the problem resolved. It took four calls and the best I could get was another knob and drawer sent to me with corners that did not fit together. So, I essentially paid $400 for something that looks like a dresser that's $50 at a garage sale."

dusty in a hurry. So that nixes storing extra blankets or clothes. We say skip the extra expense of an under-crib drawer.

3 **THE TODDLER BED.** Some crib makers tout cribs that convert to toddler beds. Smaller than a twin bed, a toddler bed uses the crib mattress and is pitched as a transition between the crib and a big boy/girl bed. But, guess what? Most kids can go straight from a crib to a regular twin bed with no problem whatsoever. So, the toddler bed business is really a joke.

4 **CRADLE.** Most pediatricians recommend "rooming in" with your newborn to help with breastfeeding. But where will the baby sleep? Cradles and bassinets are one option, but can be pricey. Cradles (basically a mini crib that rocks) run up to $400, while separate bassinets (a basket on a stand) can cost $200. A more affordable solution: just set up the crib in your room. After you establish that breastfeeding rhythm, the baby and crib can move to the nursery. If you don't have room in your master bedroom to set up the crib, consider a playpen with bassinet feature like the Graco Pack N Play. A co-sleeper like the Arm's Reach (discussed later in this chapter) is another option. We'll discuss the best buys on bassinets later in this chapter; playpens like the Pack N Play are reviewed in Chapter 7, Around the House.

5 **CRIBS WITH "SPECIAL FEATURES."** Some stores carry unique styles of cribs and that might be tempting for parents looking to make a statement for their nursery. An example: round cribs. The only problem: special cribs like this may require additional expenses, such as custom-designed mattresses or bedding. And since few companies make bedding for round cribs, your choices are limited. The best advice: make sure you price out the total investment (crib, mattress, bedding) before falling in love with an unusual style.

6 **CHANGING TABLES.** Separate changing tables are a big waste of money. Don't spend $90 to $200 on a piece of furniture you won't use again after your baby gives up diapers. A better bet: buy a dresser that can do double duty as a changing table. Many dressers you'll see in baby stores are designed with this extra feature—just make sure the height is comfortable for both you and your spouse. Other parents we interviewed did away with the changing area altogether—they used a crib, couch or countertop to do diaper changes.

Top 9 Things Baby Stores Won't Tell You About Buying Nursery Furniture

◆ *Our store may disappear before your nursery furniture arrives.* It's a sad fact: baby stores come and go. Most retailers that close do so reputably—they don't take special orders for merchandise they can't fill. A handful are not so honest . . . they take deposits up until the day the landlord padlocks their doors. Our advice: always charge your purchase to a credit card. If the store disappears, you can dispute the charge with your credit card company and (most likely) get your money back. Another red flag: stores that ask for payment up front on a special order. The typical deal is half down with the balance due upon delivery. Stores that are desperate for cash might demand the entire purchase price upfront. Be suspicious. Another piece of advice: keep a close eye on what's going on with your furniture maker. How? Read our blog or surf our message boards at BabyBargains.com. Over the years, we've seen it all—strikes, floods, fires, port shutdowns and more. You name it, it can happen to the factory that makes your furniture. When we get a whiff of a problem, we send out the news to our readers via our e-newsletter, blog or on our message boards. That way you can switch to another brand if you've haven't placed an order yet . . . or formulate a plan B if your furniture is caught by a delivery delay.

◆ *Never assume something in a sealed box is undamaged.* Always OPEN boxes and inspect furniture before taking it out of a

cribs

store. Yes, that is a hassle, but we've had numerous complains about boxed furniture that someone has driven 50 miles home, only to discover a major gash or other damage. Or the wrong color is in the right box. Or a major piece is missing. A word to the wise: inspect it BEFORE going home.

◆ *If it is in stock, BUY IT.* Let's say you see a crib that is in stock, but the matching dresser is on back order. Do you get the crib now and wait on the dresser? Or special order both? Our advice: if an item is sitting there in a store (even if it is a floor sample), it is ALWAYS better to take the in-stock item now.

◆ *Your special order merchandise will be backordered until 2012, despite our promise to get it to you before your baby is born.* Almost all furniture today is imported . . . we are not talking from close-by countries like Canada or Mexico. Nope, odds are your furniture will be made in China, Vietnam,. Eastern Europe or South America. And a myriad of problems (labor strikes, port shutdowns, Latvian Independence Day) can delay the shipment of your nursery furniture. Our advice: ORDER EARLY. If the furniture store says it will take six weeks, plan on 12. Or 15.

◆ *Just because the crib maker has an Italian name doesn't mean your furniture is made in, say, Italy.* Not long ago, you had domestic makers of cribs (Child Craft, Simmons) and the imports, most of which were from Italy. Those days are long gone—today almost all nursery furniture is imported from Asia (specifically, China).

Here's where it gets confusing: sometimes the very same brand will import furniture from different countries. Sorelle, for example, started out as an Italian importer. Today, Sorelle imports most of its cribs and furniture from China, Brazil and Latvia in Eastern Europe. Ditto for Bonavita, which despite the Italian sounding name, imports most of its furniture from Vietnam and China. Natart makes some cribs in Canada and others are imported from China.

Bottom line: key on the brand's reputation for quality and customer service, not so much the country the crib is made in. Yes, we realize some folks are nervous about Chinese-made products. To address those concerns, we have a box later in the chapter that points out the brands not made in China. However, we don't think a crib or dresser made in China is inherently dangerous—again, it is the company's reputation for quality and customer service that is key, not the country of origin.

◆ *That special mattress we insist you buy isn't necessary.* Some baby stores are trying a new tactic to sell their pricey in-house brand of crib mattress: scaring the pants off new parents. We've heard all the stories—only OUR mattress fits OUR crib, a simpler foam mattress is DANGEROUS for your baby and so on. Please! Government standards require both cribs and mattresses to be within standard measurements. Yes, fancy boutiques might make their mattress a bit larger to give a tighter fit . . . but that doesn't mean a regular mattress won't work just as well (and is just as safe). It's no wonder stores push the in-house mattress—it can cost $250 or more. Our advice: save your money and get a plain crib mattress for half the price at another store.

◆ *Just because we say this item is discontinued does NOT mean you can't find it anywhere else.* This is especially true for chain stores—just because Babies R Us says the crib you've fallen in love with is now discontinued does NOT mean you can't find it from another store. That's because chains discontinue items all the time . . . and not just because the manufacturer is discontinuing it. Chains replace slow moving merchandise or just make way for something new. Meanwhile, the very same furniture (or for that matter, any baby gear) is sold down the street at another store.

◆ *The stain on your expensive nursery furniture may match . . . or not.* Here's something baby stores don't advertise: the finishes on that expensive nursery furniture you special ordered may not match. Why? Many furniture companies use different wood for different pieces—say birch for a crib, but pine for a dresser. The problem: each takes stain differently. As a result, a birch crib in cherry may not match a pine dresser in the same cherry stain. While the difference may be small, it bugs some folks more than others. The take home message: if matching stain is important to you, confirm all the pieces of your furniture are made of the same wood—and try to see a sample of the stain on a real piece of furniture to confirm colors (don't rely on online photos).

Money Saving Secrets

I CHECK OUT REGULAR FURNITURE STORES FOR ROCKERS, DRESSERS, ETC. Think about it—most juvenile furniture looks very similar to regular adult furniture. Rockers, dressers, and bookcases are, well, just rockers, dressers, and bookcases. And don't you wonder if companies slap the word "baby" on an item just to raise the price 20%? To test this theory, we visited a local discount furniture store. The prices were incredibly low. A basic four-drawer pine dresser was $200. Even maple or oak four-drawer dressers were just $350. The same quality dresser at a baby store by a "juvenile furniture" manufacturer would set you back at least $500, if not twice that. We even saw cribs by such mainstream names as Bassett at decent prices in regular furniture stores. What's the disadvantage to shopping there? Well, if you have to buy the crib and dresser at different places, the colors might not match exactly. But, considering the savings, it might be worth it.

2 THINK TWICE ABOUT MOD. Modern furniture is the rage in high-end boutiques, but what do you get for that ultra-mod look? Many "modern" cribs and furniture are made of MDF, particle board and laminates . . . and for this you're supposed to shell out $800 for a crib and $1600 for a dresser? Can someone explain to us why modern furniture costs TWICE as much as "regular" cribs and dressers that are made of all wood? Sure that mod furniture has a few extra coats of lacquer and looks all shiny. But we still don't get it—especially since nearly all nursery furniture (yes, even the mod stuff) is imported from Asia. Our advice: If you decide to go mod, stick with the more affordable options like IKEA (even Wal-Mart now sports a modern furniture collection at reasonable prices).

3 COMPARE ONLINE PRICES. Do you wonder if that local baby store has jacked up the price of nursery furniture? We know some of you live in towns or communities with little or no local competition for nursery items. One obvious solution: hit the web. Now, we realize we listed all sorts of caveats for online orders earlier in the book (high shipping fees, problems with damage, etc)—but let's face it. In some parts of the country, this is really your best option. As always, don't ASSUME local stores will be higher in price than the web. Do your homework first. And always ask local retailers if they will price match what you see online. Many quietly do! One good source to compare crib prices: BabyCribCentral.com doesn't sell cribs, but provides a handy price comparison engine.

A caveat to online shopping: if you live in Alaska or Hawaii (or are overseas military with an APO address), you may be out of luck. While Wal-Mart and Target will ship some items to Alaska and Hawaii, other sites refuse.

4 ONE WORD: IKEA. Sure, it's basic and no frills . . . but it's hard to beat the price! IKEA's ultra affordable cribs and dressers make even Wal-Mart look expensive. Example: the HENSVIK crib for $139 and matching wardrobe for $149. Yes, you will have to assemble it yourself. And no, it won't last through three kids. But hey—it's hard to beat the price. (See the brand reviews later for more on IKEA, including some key things to know before you buy).

5 **GO NAKED**. Naked furniture, that is. An increasing number of stores sell unfinished (or naked) furniture at great prices. Such places even sell the finishing supplies and give you directions (make sure to use a non-toxic finish). The prices are hard to beat. At a local unfinished furniture store, we found a three-drawer pine dresser (23″ wide) for $100, while a four-drawer dresser (38″ wide) was $175. Compare that to baby store prices, which can top $400 to $700 for a similar size dresser. A reader in California e-mailed us with a great example of this trend in the Bay Area: "Hoot Judkins" has two locations (Redwood City and Millbrae; hootjudkins.com) that sell unfinished furniture. She found a five-drawer dresser in solid birch for just $229 and other good deals on nursery accessories. Another idea: Million Dollar Baby/Da Vinci (see review later in this chapter) is one of the few crib makers to offer unfinished crib models (Jenny Lind, M0391). While unfinished cribs are somewhat rare, naked furniture stores at least offer affordable alternatives for dressers, bookcases, and more.

6 **SKIP THE SLEIGH CRIB.** Lots of folks fall in love with the look of a sleigh-style crib, which looks like (you guessed it) a sleigh. The only problem? Most sleigh cribs have solid foot and headboards. All that extra wood means higher prices, as much as $100 to $300 more than non-sleigh styles. If you have your heart set on a sleigh style, look for one with slats on the headboard instead of solid wood.

7 **CONSIDER AN AFFORDABLE CONVERTIBLE CRIB.** Now, the key word here is "affordable." In past editions of our book, we derided most convertible cribs for their high prices and expensive conversion kits. Fortunately, prices have come down in recent years. But there is key question here: do you have room in the nursery for the crib to convert to a full-size bed? If the answer is yes, then consider an affordable convertible. At chains stores like Babies R Us convertible cribs run $300 to $500. At specialty stores, brands like Munire and Westwood offer convertibles in the $400 to $600 range. Don't factor in the price of the kit to convert the crib to a twin or full-size bed—this is another $60 to $200. One tip: make sure the design has a true headboard and shorter footboard (many low-end convertible cribs cheat on this point by having the same size head and foot boards). This looks much better when converted to a double bed.

8 **TRY CRAIGSLIST.ORG.** As you probably know, Craigslist's popular online classified site has versions for dozens of cities, with a special "for sale" section for baby/kids stuff. Use Craigslist to find a local family that is unloading unneeded nursery furniture, gear and other items (but do NOT buy a used crib, as we've discussed earlier).

9 **DON'T WAIT ON THE CONVERSION KIT OR NIGHTSTAND.** Many parents like the concept of a convertible crib that can grow with your child from crib to twin or full-size bed. But to make that transition, you often need to buy a conversion kit (bedrails and other hardware). We recommend buying this (and other matching items like a nightstand) when you order your nursery furniture, instead of waiting until your child needs the crib converted. Why? Styles and colors can be discontinued at the drop of a hat; some manufacturers disappear altogether. If you wait and the conversion kit is no longer available, you've just spent a fortune on a convertible crib that can't be converted!

Baby Superstore Reviews: The Good, Bad & Ugly

There's good news and bad news when it comes to shopping for baby. Good news: there are an amazing number of stores to shop for baby gear. Bad news: there are an amazing number of

How to snag the best deals on Craigslist

Sure there are great deals on Craigslist, but how do you use this online wonder to save the most? Here are a few tips:

◆ **Be patient.** When you first go on Craigslist, you will be amazed at the prices and think you have to snap up deals quickly. But take some time to see what really are the *best* prices. A reader says she thought she got a good deal when she hastily bought a Baby Bjorn carrier off Craigslist for 50% retail—until she noticed the going rate is more like 75% off.

◆ **Use Craigslist list to find garage sales.** On Friday night or Saturday morning, just do a quick search in the garage sale listings for "baby."

◆ **Deals are even better than they look.** That's because there is no shipping or sales tax. Examples from our readers: a Dutailier rocker and ottoman for $260 (retail $600+), Boppy pillow for $5 (retail $35), cradle swing for $60 (retail: $140).

stores to shop for baby gear.

And as a first-time parent, you probably have never been in these stores (except for that time you bought a gift for a pregnant co-worker). Walking into a baby superstore for the first time can give even the most levelheaded mom or dad-to-be a case of the willies. It is a blizzard of pacifiers, strollers, cribs and more in a mind-numbing assortment of colors, features and options. So, as a public service, here's our overview of the major players in the baby store biz.

Babies R Us *(888-BABYRUS; web: babiesrus.com).* The 800-pound gorilla of baby stores, Babies R Us has 260+ stores nationwide and is the country's leading baby gear retailer. Love 'em or hate 'em, you'll probably find yourself in a BRU at some point—in some communities, BRU is the only game in town.

For the uninitiated, Babies R Us is your typical chain store—big on selection, decent prices . . . but service? That's not the point. Sure, our readers occasionally report they found a knowledgeable sales clerk. But other times, you are lucky to find a person to check you out, much less give advice on a car seat.

In the furniture section, Babies R Us carries brands that are exclusive to the chain: Jardine cribs (made by Dorel), Baby Cache (Munire), Amy Coe and Carter's (Butterfly Living). BRU's strategy is to price its cribs higher than discounters like Target but less than specialty stores. And since you can't find Jardine in any other stores, you can't price shop that specific model.

Unfortunately, this strategy came back to bite BRU in the butt in 2008 after a massive recall of a 375,000 Jardine cribs. The way BRU handled this recall sparked a large number of complaints (we covered this story on our blog), tarnishing the chain's image among parents.

While we aren't wild about most of BRU's furniture offerings, the rest of the store is better: you'll see Britax in the car seat section and Maclaren in strollers, both better brands. And BRU wins kudos for their web site, which was recently upgraded to include a gift-finding tool, store inventory levels and wish lists. The web site features additional brands not sold in BRU's stores (Bugaboo strollers, for example).

Babies R Us' ace in the hole is their gift registry, which now has a quick start option and other online tools. While no gift registry is perfect (and BRU's registry has seen its fair share of complaints on our message boards), we have noted that readers lately seem happier with BRU's registry after the company divorced itself from a disastrous partnership with Amazon over a year ago.

So, how to grade Babies R Us? For selection, make it an A-, service gets a C, pricing a B+ and the registry, an A. Overall, let's call it a B. ***Rating: B***

Baby Depot *(800-444-COAT; web: burlingtoncoatfactory.com).* Baby Depot is a store-within-a-store concept. Tucked inside the cavernous Burlington Coat Factory, Baby Depot is a nook stuffed with nursery furniture, strollers and a smattering of other gear.

Even though there are more Baby Depots than Babies R Us stores (370+ at last count), Baby Depot has always played second-fiddle to BRU. Part of the problem has been marketing strategy: Baby Depot could use one. Burlington/Baby Depot operates in a wide range of locations, some in shiny new suburban power centers and others in dingy warehouses. The company has experimented with free-standing baby superstores but now runs only one "Super Baby Depots" in Moorestown, New Jersey.

The selection of brands at Baby Depot is decent, but merchandising isn't exactly Baby Depot's strong suite. The aisles of the stores are often disorganized and cluttered.

The service at Baby Depot makes Babies R Us look like Nordstrom's. We get frequent letters from Baby Depot furniture customers, complaining about late orders, botched orders and worse.

On the plus side, Baby Depot has changed their draconian return policy—now you can return items within 30 days and get cash back (as long as you have a receipt and the tags are still attached).

So, here's our advice: if you see something here that is in stock and the price is right, go for it. But forget about special ordering anything such as furniture. ***Rating: C-***

Buy Buy Baby *Web: BuyBuyBaby.com.* Owned by the Bed, Bath & Beyond chain, Buy Buy Baby is our top pick in this category. Yes, they only have a dozen locations (mostly in the East), but the chain is expanding and may be worth a trip if one is nearby.

Service is the strong point here—folks at Buy Buy Baby know their stuff. Now, we realize that this might not be a fair fight—can Babies R Us (with 230+ stores) ever compete on service with a much smaller rival? It will be interesting to see if Buy Buy Baby can maintain that advantage as it expands from its Eastern base.

Given the urban slant to its locations, the brands and selection skew toward the expensive. Yes, there are Graco travel systems here . . . but also Bugaboo's $900 models. Ditto for the furniture, with Million Dollar Baby sharing floor space with more pricey options from Young America (by Stanley), Berg and Westwood.

The stores are merchandised a bit like Bed Bath and Beyond—that is crowded, with stacks of merchandise rising to the ceiling. While Babies R Us is a bit easier to navigate, Buy Buy Baby has more selection in several categories.

If we had to pick one point on which Buy Buy could improve, it would have to be their lackluster web site. No user reviews, poor organization and little in the way of buying advice—Buy Buy Baby's web site might have done the trick five years ago, but now it is among the weakest online entries. When you click on a category like strollers, you get a long list of links . . . for both stroller types and brands. A better brand search engine would be most helpful.

Despite their web site, we still give Buy Buy Baby our top rating among chain stores—if you happen to be near one, this store is a keeper. *Rating: A*

The Discounters: Target, Wal-Mart, K-Mart

What's Cool: Any discussion of national stores that sell baby items wouldn't be complete without a mention of the discounters: Target, Wal-Mart, K-Mart and their ilk. In recent years, the discounters have realized one sure-fire way to drive store traffic—discount baby supplies! As a result, you'll often see formula, diapers and other baby essentials at rock-bottom prices. And there are even better deals on "in-house" brands. The goal is to have you drop by to pick up some diapers . . . and then walk out with a big-screen TV.

Of all the discounters, we think Target is best (with one big caveat—their ruthless return policy, see below for a discussion). Target's baby department is a notch above Wal-Mart and K-Mart when it comes to brand names and selection. Yes, sometimes Wal-Mart has lower prices—but usually that's on lower-quality brands. Target, by contrast, carries Perego high chairs and a wider selection of products like baby monitors. The best bet: Super Targets, which have expanded baby products sections.

One important trend: discounters have bulked up their web sites with brands, products and models that are NOT carried in their stores. Sometimes you'll even find an upscale brand online at discount prices. We'll discuss the discounter web sites specifically below.

Needs work: If you're looking for premium brand names, forget it. Most discounters only stock the so-called mass-market brands: Graco strollers, Cosco car seats, Gerber sheets, etc. And the baby departments always seem to be in chaos when we visit, with items strewn about hither and yon. K-Mart is probably the worst when it comes to organization, Wal-Mart the best. We like Target's selection (especially of feeding items and baby monitors), but their prices are somewhat higher than Wal-Mart. What about service? Forget it—no matter which store you're in, you're on your own.

While we do recommend Target, we should warn readers about their return policy. Once among the most generous, Target now requires a receipt for just about any return. A raft of new rules and restrictions greet customers (sample: exchanges now must be made for items within the same department). This has understandably ticked off a fair number of our readers, especially those who have unfortunately chosen to register at Target for their baby gifts. Among the biggest roadblocks: Target won't let you exchange duplicate baby gifts if you don't have a gift receipt (and there are numerous other rules/restrictions as well). Of course, your friends may forget to ask for a gift receipt or throw it away. And watch out: gift receipts have expiration dates; be sure to return any item before that date. Target also limits the number of returns you can do in one year.

After receiving a fair amount of consumer complaints about this, Target now allows returns of registry gifts without a gift receipt IF the item is listed on your registry. The rub: you will get the lowest sales price in the last 90 days, not necessarily what your guest paid for it. That's a special gotcha for new parents—many baby products and clothes go on sale frequently, rendering your gift almost worthless on an exchange. This and other beefs with Target have spawned many complaints about their registry and even blogs dedicated to dissing the chain.

Our advice: think twice about registering at Target. While we get complaints about all baby registries (even industry leader Babies R Us), be sure to read the fine print for ANY baby registry before signing up. Ask about returns and exchange policies, including specifically what happens if you have to return/exchange a duplicate item without a gift receipt. And check for limits on the number of returns you can do within a certain time period. Finally, ask about HOW the store integrates your registry with the web site— if someone buys an item online instead of at a store, will this be reflected on your registry? Check our blog and message boards for the latest buzz on baby registries.

Web: Each of the major discounters sells baby products online. Here's an overview of each site:

◆ *WalMart.com:* Hit the baby tab and you'll find yourself in Wal-Mart's extensive online baby gear department. We like how the chain has expanded online offerings in recent years—there's much more on the web site than in the stores (particularly strollers). Wal-Mart has steadily improved the site over the last year or so— now you can search by brand, read product reviews and get a product delivered to a nearby store at no charge. And, of course, the prices are excellent.

◆ *Kmart.com*: K-Mart's online outpost is a winner—we liked the graphics and easy navigation. You can search by brand, price and more. We also liked the "This Just In" section for new arrivals. The only bummer: unlike Target, K-Mart's online selection brand-wise is much the same as the store—heavy on low-end brands like Baby Trend. The depth of merchandise on Kmart.com is also quite thin: go to convertible car seats and you'll see only a half dozen choices. Compare that to Target, which posts 15+ options online.

◆ *Target.com* is our pick as the best discounter web site—their online offerings go way beyond what's in the stores. We also like the user reviews, as well as the ability to sort any category by brand, price or best-sellers. Perhaps the biggest drawback with Target.com (as with other sites) is the rather skimpy product descriptions. You can often find more about a product by reading the user reviews than Target's own descriptions. Example: for a $200 crib, Target neglects to mention the crib's antiquated double-trigger rail release . . . something a buyer complained about in a review posted online.

Specialty Chains: More Baby Stores To Shop!

Inspired by the success of Pottery Barn Kids, several chains have ventured into the nursery business. An example: Room & Board (web: RoomandBoard.com), a ten-store chain (plus an outlet) with locations in California, Colorado, Illinois, Minnesota, Georgia and the New York City area. Their well-designed web site has a nursery section with a couple of cribs ($600 to $900), dressers and accessories. Quality is good, say our readers who've ordered from them.

And that's just the beginning: Land of Nod, a subsidiary of Crate & Barrel, has an extensive website (landofnod.com) with nursery offerings (10 cribs as of press time) as well as four stores plus an outlet in Northbrook, IL.

What's driving this is a boom in babies, especially to older moms and dads. Tired of the cutesy baby stuff in chain stores, many parents are looking for something more sophisticated and hip. Of course, it remains to be seen what this means for bargain shoppers. On one hand, more competition is always good—having a wide diversity of places to buy nursery furniture and accessories is always a plus. On the downside, most of these chains are chasing that "upscale" customer with outrageously priced cribs and bedding. "As much as parents love the furniture at Pottery Barn Kids, some wince at the prices," said the *Wall Street Journal* in a recent article on this trend. And we agree—while we love the PBK look, our goal in life is to try to find that same look . . . at half the price!

Outlets

There are dozens of outlets that sell kids' clothing, but when it comes to furniture the pickings are slim. In fact, we found just a handful of nursery furniture outlets out there. Here's a round up:

Pottery Barn Kids has eight outlets for their kids catalog, scattered around the country (go to outletbound.com and search for Pottery Barn to see if there is one near you). Readers report some good deals there, including a changing table for $100 (regularly $200) and a rocker for $200 (down from $700). The outlet also carries the PBK bedding line at good discounts. A reader in Georgia said the PBK outlet there features 75% off deals on furniture and you can get a coupon book at the food court for an additional 10% discount. "The best time to shop is during the week—they run more specials then," she said. "And bring a truck—they don't deliver." One final tip: call AHEAD before you go. The selection of nursery furniture can vary widely from outlet to outlet . . . some may have no stock during certain months.

Live in the Northeast? Check out ***Baby Boudoir Outlet,*** an offshoot of a baby store in New Bedford, MA (babyboudoiroutlet. com, 800-272-2293, 508-998-2166) that is also authorized by Child Craft to sell their discontinued furniture at wholesale prices or below. The Baby Boudoir Outlet has 1000 cribs in stock at any one time at prices that start under $200 (most are $250 to $400). The store also carries glider rockers, bedding and other baby products at 30% to 70% off retail. FYI: There is both a Baby Boudoir store and a warehouse outlet—you want to visit the outlet for the best deals. The outlet is around the corner from the main store. Of course, Baby Boudoir sells more than just Child Craft—they also sell discontinued Sorelle cribs (30% to 70% off) and certain discontinued Munire styles, as well as factory seconds from such bedding lines as Kids Line, Lambs & Ivy and more. A caveat to this outlet: a reader who recently visited the outlet described it as a "rusty warehouse in a bad neighborhood. I would put a HUGE disclaimer on this outlet to warn folks it is very bare bones."

Along the same lines, ***Baby Furniture Warehouse***, with stores in Reading and Braintree, MA (781-942-7978 or 781-843-5353; web: BabyFurnitureWarehouse.com, see below), specializes in selling overstock and discontinued cribs from Pali, Bonavita, Sorelle and Baby's Dream. You can save up to 30% off regular retail prices here—cribs run $260 to $500 and case pieces are also available. The store sells many furniture sets, including a three-piece package (crib plus two dressers) from Baby's Dream for $1150 or Pali for $1300. Reader feedback on this outlet has been mixed—folks tell us the customer service is either "helpful" or "leaves much to be desired."

Considering how great the deals are (where else can you find a package with Pali crib, dresser and Dutailier glider for $1500?), we still think it is worth a look if you are near Boston.

Bassett sells its cribs and nursery furniture from its namesake outlet in Bassett, Virginia (276) 629-6446. A reader recently visited the outlet for a good selection of cribs. She snagged a $500 retail crib at the Bassett outlet for $157 (new and in the box)!

Don't forget that **JCPenney** has seven outlet stores nationwide. The stores carry a wide variety of items, including children's and baby products (always call before you go to confirm selection). Check out the web site Outlet Bound (outletbound.com) for a current listing of locations.

Baby Gift Registries: Disappointing

We have a plea for tomorrow's computer science college graduates: fix the gift registries at chain stores—please!

Sure, computers can pilot a spaceship to Pluto or solve the most complex microbiology problem . . . but for some reason, such computer smarts elude the baby gift registry programmers at chains stores.

No matter how sweet the promises are about computerized registries ("Look Ma! I'm changing an item on the registry at 2am!") the reality falls WAY short of utopia. Judging from our reader mail and message boards, folks are steamed when they must deal with registry snafus . . . and who can blame them.

While the process of registering at any chain is relatively straightforward (you can scan items in the store or pick them off a web site), USING the registry is where things start to fall apart. You name it, we've heard it: duplicate gifts, out of stock items (with no notice to the parent), endless backorders and other goofs.

Here are the frustrations:

◆ *Online versus offline.* Many stores carry items online that aren't in stores. And in some cases, items can only be found in stores, not online. So if you register online at a major retailer, your friends who visit the retailer's stores may find a large chunk of your registry can't be purchased in the store. Another frustration: at Babies R Us, online-only items can't be returned to BRU stores—they can only be returned via the mail. And then the gift-giver receives the credit, not you.

◆ *Returns*. Stores have Byzantine return policies that can frustrate the seemingly simple task of returning a duplicate gift

Finally, for our Canadian readers in Ontario (or Buffalo, NY), check out the **Mother Hubbard** factory outlet in Toronto (416) 572-0486. This outlet sells the company's namesake cribs and dressers—discontinued styles, samples and more at 20% to 60% off retail. The outlet also offers bedding from Bebe Chic.

The Name Game: Reviews of Selected Manufacturers

Here's a look at crib brands sold in the U.S. and Canada. Our focus is on the most common nursery furniture brands you see in

---

(which shouldn't happen with registries, right?). Many stores require a gift receipt for returns—but whoops! Your gift-giver forgot to include that. No problem, just print out a copy of your registry from the web site? Whoops! The store deleted your registry 14 days after your baby was born. And so on.

◆ **Discontinued items.** You try to be smart and register early for that baby shower—but now several items are discontinued. Does the registry email you with notice? Are you kidding? Registries expect you to monitor your registry and replace items as needed. And product may disappear from an online registry, but still be available in stores.

Some of the problems with a gift registry only become apparent AFTER you've received a gift. Example: Pottery Barn's policy on gift certificates. If you want to use a gift certificate for an online or telephone purchase at Pottery Barn Kids, you must MAIL the certificate in and cool your heels for a two to three week processing period. How convenient.

Babies R Us runs the country's biggest gift registry—and comes in for a regular barbequing from our readers. To its credit, BRU has fixed many of the glitches that were apparent in recent years . . . but still hear from readers who have problems with returns, discontinued items and more.

Bottom line: take a second and read the gift registry feedback from recent parents on our web site (hang out in the "Lounge" forum or do a search on the site). Always READ the return policies of any gift registry BEFORE you sign up—is there a time limit for returns? Must you have a gift receipt? Are you limited to X number of returns or exchanges? Know ALL the fine print before you plunge in!

chains stores, independents and other furniture outlets. If you've discovered a brand that we didn't review, feel free to share your discovery by calling or emailing us (see our contact info at the end of the book).

How did we evaluate the brands? First, we inspected samples of cribs at stores and industry trade shows. With the help of veteran juvenile furniture retailers, we checked construction, release mechanisms, mattress supports, and overall fit and finish. Yes, we did compare styling among the brands but this was only a minor factor in our ratings (we figure you can decide what looks best for your nursery).

Readers of previous editions have asked us how we assign ratings to these manufacturers—what makes one an "A" vs. "B"? The bottom line is quality *and* value. Sure, anyone can make a high-quality crib for $800. The trick is getting that price down to $400 or less while maintaining high-quality standards. Hence, we give more bonus points to brands that give more value for the dollar.

What about the crib makers who got the lowest ratings? Are their cribs unsafe? No, of course not. ALL new cribs sold in the U.S. and Canada must meet minimum federal safety standards. As we mentioned earlier in this chapter, a $100 crib sold at Wal-Mart is just as safe as a $1500 designer brand sold at a posh boutique. The only difference is styling, features and durability—more expensive cribs have thick wood posts, fancy finishes and durability to last through two or more kids. The best companies have the best customer service, taking care of both their retailers and consumers.

Brands that got our lowest rating have poor quality control and abysmal customer service. Serious safety recalls also impacts a brand's rating.

The Ratings

- **A** **EXCELLENT**—*our top pick!*
- **B** **GOOD**— *above average quality, prices, and creativity.*
- **C** **FAIR**—*could stand some improvement.*
- **D** **POOR**—*yuck! could stand some major improvement.*

ABC. *See Million Dollar Baby. Sold exclusively at JCPenney.*

AFG Furniture. *This crib brand is reviewed on our free web site, BabyBargains.com (click on Bonus Material).*

Alta Baby *This crib brand is reviewed on our free web site, BabyBargains.com (click on Bonus Material).*

Amby Baby Motion Bed *Call 1-866-519-2229 for a dealer near you. Web: AmbyBaby.com* Invented by an Australian dad for his colicky daughter, the Amby baby hammock is just that—a hammock that is designed as a safe sleep environment to replace a bassinet, cradle or even crib. It looks like a swing, with a wide base (18") and comes with a mattress, pair of sheets, frame, spring and cross bar. The basic version runs $237, while a couple of deluxe versions (which include accessories like a mosquito net and more sheets) can cost up to $307.

So, should you get one? Well, we agree with the science behind this idea—a cocooned environment like a hammock mimics the womb, which soothes colicky babies. So, is it safe? Yes, we think it is—the exception would be preemies. We don't recommend a baby hammock for preemies (despite the fact the company sells an accessory to better accommodate smaller infants). If you have a preemie, discuss your baby's sleeping arrangement with your pediatrician. And, while Amby says you can use the hammock up to 59 lbs. with a second spring (the first spring that comes with the unit is good up to 29 lbs), we suggest you transition your baby out of the hammock around three months. Why? First, that's when colic usually ends (it starts around three weeks and can continue until three months. For more about colic, which affects 15% of babies, see our other book *Baby 411*).

Second, around three to four months of age, babies become more aware of their surroundings and that's why most pediatricians suggest this is the right time to transition a baby out of a cradle or bassinet (or in this case, a hammock). After four months, babies start to establish a permanent sleep routine. A crib would be best then. Why? Babies need to roll over and learn how to pull themselves up—something that can't be done in a hammock. Yes, Amby dismisses this concern by saying baby can learn these developmental milestones during the daytime on the floor, but considering how much time a baby spends in a "sleep environment," that seems a bit misguided.

Another caveat to the Amby: getting baby in and out of the Amby requires a bit of effort, not fun for sleeping parents. One reader who otherwise loved her Amby wished for a co-sleeper at night. Another reader noted you can pick up an used Amby's on Craigslist (we saw one for $150). Since the Amby isn't sold in many stores, it does have good resale value.

The take home message: if you have a history of colic in your family or your baby develops colic, consider the Amby Baby

Motion Bed hammock (after consulting with your pediatrician first). Use it until around three months. No, Amby does NOT cure colic, but it could help lessen it. ***Rating: A***

Amy Coe. *See Butterfly Living. Sold exclusively at Babies R Us.*

Angel Line *This crib brand is reviewed on our free web site, BabyBargains.com/cribs*

A.P. Industries *Call (800) 463-0145 or (418) 728-2145. Web site: apindustries.com.* Quebec-based crib maker A.P. Industries (also known as Generations) offers stylish cribs and case pieces, which are available in a dozen different collections. A.P. has survived the recent shake-out of Canadian crib makers, but not without some serious changes: all of A.P.'s cribs are imported from China. Most dressers are made in Canada, but some are imported from Vietnam. Prices are quite high: $700 for a crib, $1000 to $1200 for a dresser. At this point, you might be saying whoa! $700 for a Chinese-made crib? Yes, we had the same reaction—but A.P.'s key feature is a choice of 31 different finishes and knob styles. It's that level of customization that makes this brand unique. And A.P's take on modern (the Element) has been a good seller. As for customer service, A.P. has been up and down in recent years. Overall, this brand earns a thumbs up for those that can afford it. ***Rating: B***

Argington. *Web: Argington.com* Argington puts a green spin on their modern furniture: New York-based designers Andrew Thornton and Jenny Argie strive to use only solid wood ("virtually no MDF, particle board other similar engineered wood products.") All Argington's wood is FSC certified as part of its "sustainable manufacturing" (glues are low-emission, etc). The brand only has one crib offering (the two-toned Sahara for $700) with matching dresser for $800. Argington also offers a limited selection of organic cotton crib bedding. Early reports on this line are encouraging: quality is good and the pricing is slightly more reasonable when compared to the $1000+ modern cribs Argington competes against. ***Rating: B+***

Babee Tenda *See box on page 54-55.*

Baby Appleseed *Web: babyappleseed.com. See Nursery Smart.*

Baby Cache *This Babies R Us exclusive is made by Munire (see review later in this chapter).*

Not made in China

From lead paint in toys to tainted baby formula, China has had its share of, uh, quality control issues lately. And some of our readers have asked us, not surprisingly, how to furnish a nursery with products NOT made in China. While that sounds simple, it isn't: 90% or more of baby furniture sold in the U.S. is made in China—so avoiding Chinese-made items takes some effort.

But there is good news: there ARE a handful of companies that make their furniture somewhere other than China. And yes, there are still firms that make furniture in the U.S.A.: Newport Cottages and ducduc are examples, as is El Greco (which sells cribs via the Land of Nod chain) and modern crib designer ducduc. Oak Designs (oakdesigns.com) makes dressers and twin beds domestically.

Other furniture makers import goods from countries *other* than China: Romina makes furniture in Romania; Munire imports from Indonesia. Creations, Westwood and Bratt Décor have factories in Vietnam.

Some companies make PART of their furniture line in China— and the rest in other factories. Natart is a good example: it splits production between Canada and China. Dutailier makes dressers in Canada (but its cribs are imported from China). Capretti plans to debut a green collection (Verde) made in the USA in 2009. Sorelle makes some items in Brazil and Latvia while the rest is made in China.

A few caveats to this advice: first, production often shifts, so before you order, reconfirm with the manufacturer or retailer where the furniture is being made. Second, manufacturers that split production between China and other countries often don't publicize which furniture is made where. You have to ask.

Baby Trilogy Corner Cribs *This crib brand is reviewed on our free web site, BabyBargains.com/cribs*

Baby Gap *dorelfinefurnishings.com* Baby Gap's nursery furniture is made by Dorel, the Canadian conglomerate reviewed later in this section. The two crib offerings are pricey: $700 for a 3-in-1 sleigh crib and $550 for a "beadboard crib." Matching three drawer dressers are $550 as well. We have mixed feelings about this furniture. While shipping is included, paying $700 for a Dorel crib is like paying $70,000 for a Toyota Camry . . . you can, but why? Dorel sells similar models under their Jardine alias at Babies R Us: the $700

Baby Gap sleigh crib is very similar to the Jardine Madison crib for $380 at BRU. Another disappointment: the cribs are made of poplar, MDF and veneers. At this price, we'd expect to see all solid wood. And Dorel's safety track record has been mixed, to say the least: 320,000 Jardine/Dorel cribs were recalled in 2008 for defective spindles. Bottom line: if you like the look, save yourself big bucks and buy the Jardine BRU version. Or better yet, skip it and buy a brand that has a better reputation. **Rating: F**

Baby Mod. *This contemporary-style furniture is sold at Wal-Mart. It is made by Million Dollar Baby—see review later in this chapter.*

Baby's Dream *Call (800) TEL-CRIB or (229) 649-4404 for a dealer near you. Web: BabysDream.com; ForerverCocoon.com.* Georgia-based Baby's Dream's claim to fame is convertible cribs. The company was among the first to launch the trend in 1990—they were convertible before convertible was cool.

The company divides its offerings into two brands: Baby's Dream and Cocoon. Design-wise, there isn't much difference between the two. But there is one key difference: Baby's Dream is made in Chile, while Cocoon is imported from China. Each brand has its own web site.

Baby's Dream offers both static and fold-down rails on their cribs and a raft of accessories (armoires, mirrors, toy chests, etc). Prices are moderate: $370 to $550 for cribs; $500 to $700 for most dressers. New this year, Baby's Dream debuted the Chinese-made "Cube," their first modern collection with a $600 crib and $700 changer that morphs into a desk. (FYI: The Cube is an exception to the Baby's Dream line; the rest is imported from Chile).

New this year from Baby's Dream: the Easy Riser, a lift that raises

Who Is Jenny Lind?

You can't shop for cribs and not hear the name "Jenny Lind." Here's an important point to remember: Jenny Lind isn't a brand name; it refers to a particular *style* of crib. But how did it get this name? Jenny Lind was a popular Swedish soprano living in the 19th century. During her triumphal U.S. tour, it was said that Lind slept in a "spool bed." Hence, cribs that featured turned spindles (which look like stacked spools of thread) became known as Jenny Lind cribs. All this begs the question—what if today we still named juvenile furniture after famous singers? Could we have Hanna Montana cribs and Jessica Simpson dressers?

or lowers the mattress with a touch of a foot petal. A $200 extra, this addresses the concerns of smaller parents who find it hard to pick up baby in a static-side crib when the mattress is in its lowest position. It can be used with other brands of cribs as well.

Perhaps the biggest difference between Baby's Dream and Cocoon is the wood: you're more likely to see pine in Baby's Dream; Cocoon is made from birch.

So, how's the quality and customer service? Well, Baby's Dream has been up and down in recent years—two plant fires in Chile delayed deliveries in 2007 (and generated many complaints) . . . but the company turned a corner in the past year. Despite the 2007 hiccups, Baby's Dream generally gets good marks on deliveries and customer service.

Cocoon earns slightly lowers marks, however. While most readers are pleased, we did receive several reports of furniture that arrived damaged and other quality woes (uneven stains, drawers with glide problems, etc). So we'll give Cocoon a slightly lower rating than the main line.

One major caveat: we do NOT recommend Baby's Dream's cribs with fold-down rails. As we discussed earlier in the Safe & Sound section, these rails are dangerous in our opinion. Fortunately, Baby's Dream also offers models with static rails—go for that option if you like this brand.

FYI: Be sure to check out Baby's Dream's web site—the company occasionally offers coupons online and has a free pregnancy calendar and nursery guide, as of this writing. Also new: you can actually buy a crib online and pick it up at a local store. What a concept! *Rating: Baby's Dream (dressers and static cribs only): A; Cocoon: B+*

Babi Italia *This is a special brand made by Bonavita for chain stores. See the Bonavita review later in this section for more info.*

Babies Love by Delta *See the review of Delta later in this section.*

Bambino *See Ragazzi.*

Bassettbaby *Call (276) 629-6000 for a dealer near you. Web: bassettbaby.com.* Sold in mostly big box stores, Bassett divides its line into three brands: First Choice, Bassettbaby and Prestige.

First Choice is Bassett's most affordable line and features simple cribs and smaller-size dressers that are ready-to-be-assembled. The brand offers four crib styles (three drop-side and one convertible with a static rail). You'll find these in Wal-Mart and Target, with cribs running $250 to $300 and dressers $225 to $300.

Bassettbaby offers an upgrade in both styling and features: fancier finishes and fully assembled dressers with French dovetail drawer construction. Example: the Bassettbaby Pine Cottage 3-in-1 crib is $350 at Target with spring mattress platform; matching three-drawer dresser is $350 as well.

Bassett offers an exclusive version of its furniture to Babies R Us

Babee Tenda's "safety" seminar: Anatomy of a Hard Sell

We got an interesting invitation in the mail during our second pregnancy—a company called "Babee Tenda" invited us to a free "Getting Ready For Baby" safety seminar at a local hotel. The seminar was described as "brief, light and enjoyable while handing out information on preventing baby injuries." Our curiosity piqued, we joined a couple dozen other expectant parents on a Saturday afternoon to learn their expert safety tips.

What followed was a good lesson for all parents—beware of companies that want to exploit parents' fears of their children being injured in order to sell their expensive safety "solutions." Sure enough, there was safety information dispensed at the seminar. The speaker started his talk with horrific tales of how many children are injured and killed each year. The culprit? Cheap juvenile equipment products like high chairs and cribs, he claimed. It was quite a performance—the speaker entranced the crowd with endless statistics on kids getting hurt and then demonstrated hazards with sample products from major manufacturers.

The seminar then segued into a thinly veiled pitch for their products: the Babee Tenda high chair/feeding table and crib. The speaker (really a salesperson) spent what seemed like an eternity trying to establish the company's credibility, claiming Babee Tenda has been in business for 60 years and only sells its products to hospitals and other institutions. We can see why—these products are far too ugly and expensive to sell in retail stores.

How expensive? The crib sells for $600+ and the feeding table for about $400.

We found Babee Tenda's sales pitch to be disgusting. They used misleading statistics and outright lies to scare parents into thinking they were putting their children in imminent danger if they used store-bought high chairs or cribs. Many of the statistics and "props" used to demonstrate hazards were as much as 20 years old and under the name of BRU's in-house stylist Wendy Bellissimo. BRU has lowered the prices on this furniture in recent months: now a Wendy B pine crib is $400; a matching double dresser in pine is $400. What do you get for the money? Well, the crib features fancy turned spindles and converts into a full-size bed with headboard and footboard (the cheaper Bassett cribs just come with a head-board).

Generally, Bassett's strategy is to add a bit more bling to the BRU

long since removed from the market! Even more reprehensible were claims that certain popular juvenile products were about to be recalled. Specifically, Babee Tenda's salesperson claimed the Evenflo Exersaucer was "unsafe and will be off the market in six months," an accusation that clearly wasn't true.

The fact that Babee Tenda had to use such bogus assertions raised our suspicions about whether they were telling the truth about their own products. Sadly, the high-pressure sales tactics did win over some parents at the seminar we attended—some forked over nearly $800 for Babee Tenda's items. Since then, we've heard from other parents who've attended Babee Tenda's "safety semi-nars," purchased the products and then suffered a case of "buyer's remorse." Did they spend too much, they ask?

Yes, in our opinion. While we see nothing wrong per se with Babee Tenda's "feeding table" (besides the fact it's god-awful ugly), you should note it costs nearly four times as much as our top rec-ommended high chair, the very well made Fisher Price Healthy Care. There's nothing wrong with the crib either—and yes, Babee Tenda, throws in a mattress and two sheets. But you can find all this for much less than the $600 or so Babee Tenda asks.

A new twist to the Babee Tenda pitch: invitations sent by a Babee Tenda distributor in Virginia in 2004 carried a line that their seminar is sponsored "in conjunction with the Consumer Product Safety Commission and the National Highway Traffic Safety Administration." Whoa, sounds official! Except it isn't true—neither the CPSC nor NHTSA have anything to do with Babee Tenda's seminars . . . in fact, the federal government successfully sued Babee Tenda to stop the practice. In 2007, a federal judge ruled Babee Tenda committed mail fraud, calling their sales tactics "deceit-ful and reprehensible."

So, we say watch out for Babee Tenda (and other similar compa-nies like Babyhood, who pitches their "Baby Sitter" in hotel safety sem-inars). We found their "safety seminar" to be bogus, their high-pres-sure sales tactics reprehensible and their products grossly overpriced.

version of its furniture to justify the prices that are $100 or more than competing imports.

New this year, Bassett is debuting Prestige, a line for specialty stores that features $600 cribs and $700 dressers. We saw their first attempt and weren't impressed . . .yes, the dresser drawers are lined with cedar, but we don't see any real upgrade here. Compared to similarly priced lines Munire and Westwood, Bassett simply can't compete on features and finish.

All Bassett furniture is imported from China. How's the quality? We like Bassett's cribs, which we think are a good value. Yes, Bassett has had two recent recalls for its Wendy B cribs (one for defective bolts; another for spindles that were too far apart), but overall, Basset has a good quality record.

While we like Bassett's cribs, the case pieces are another story. Comparing Bassett's First Choice line, you can find better ready-to-assemble furniture at a lower price at IKEA. And Bassett's assembled dressers didn't impress us with their overall fit and finish.

Bottom line: Bassett's cribs in chain stores (not counting Babies R Us) are a good value, but skip the dressers. ***Rating: B+***

Bedford Baby *See Westwood.*

Bella D'Este *See Dorel.*

Bellini *Call (805) 520-0974, (800) 332-BABY or (516) 234-7716 for a store location near you. Web: bellini.com.* Bellini is an odd duck in the world of baby retailers: it is a franchised chain with some three dozen locations, mostly on the East and West Coasts that rack up $70 million in sales annually. While most baby retailers are either big-box chains (Babies R Us) or small mom-and-pop stores, Bellini occupy the middle ground (stores average 5000 square feet).

Bellini had its heyday in the 80's and 90's—then its business model of importing Italian furniture was unique. Selling $700 private-label cribs and other Bellini-exclusive furniture and linens, the chain's offerings were nicer than anything you could find in big-box stores.

However, the competition soon caught up with Bellini. Italian crib importers flooded the market in the 90's and then came the wave of low-cost Asian imports in recent years . . . at prices that were 20% to 40% less than Bellini. Competitors such as Pottery Barn and online luxe baby gear sellers further eroded Bellini's position. As a result, the chain has shrunk, losing both stores (down to 36 locations from 48 in years past) and sales.

Bellini's sagging fortunes have hit the chain's reputation—as stores have closed (some of whom disappeared with customer's deposits), parents have posted numerous negative reviews on our site. The chain has been its own worst enemy here—by not helping out stranded customers, Bellini's corporate owners have ensured more negative publicity. That reflects poorly on the remaining franchisees, many of whom still provide good customer service.

How's the quality? Inconsistent, say our readers. Given the premium prices, we shouldn't hear reports of peeling paint on $800 dressers (but we do). While most of their furniture is still imported from Italy and Canada, it's clear the quality isn't what it used to be.

JUVENILE PRODUCTS MANUFACTURERS ASSOCIATION

CERTIFIED

THIS MODEL TESTED BY AN INDEPENDENT LABORATORY FOR COMPLIANCE TO ASTM

Certifications: Do they really matter?

As you shop for cribs and other products for your baby, you'll no doubt run into "JPMA-Certified" products sporting a special seal. But who is the JPMA and what does its certification mean?

The Juvenile Products Manufacturers Association (JPMA) is a group of over 300 companies that make juvenile products, both in the United States and Canada. Over twenty-five years ago, the group started a volunteer testing program to head off government regulation of baby products. The JPMA enlisted the support of the Consumer Products Safety Commission and the American Society of Testing and Materials (ASTM) to develop standards for products in several categories, including cribs, high chairs and more.

Manufacturers must have their product tested in an independent testing lab and, if it passes, they can use the JPMA seal. The JPMA touts its seal as "added assurance the product was built with safety in mind."

So is a product like a crib safer if it has the JPMA seal? No, not in our opinion. In fact, the biggest crib recall in history (one million Simplicity cribs in 2007 after three deaths) involved cribs that were JPMA certified. How did that happen?

Well, the JPMA certification is a MINIMUM set of standards that mostly address adequate warning labels. While detailed warning labels for products are helpful, it doesn't stop defective design or faulty instructions (the problem in the Simplicity recall).

The Simplicity recall tarnished the JPMA's certification program— and the JPMA's actions in the past year (accusations of misleading the public on the safety of crib bumpers and lobbying against baby bottle regulations) have undermined the association's safety message. See our blog at BabyBargains.com (click on news/updates) for details about these stories on bedding and bottles.

The take-home message: the JPMA seal is no guarantee of safety.

Given the disappearing act of some of the franchisees, we still have serious reservations about this chain.

New for 2009, we notice Bellini is trumpeting a $500 drop-side crib on their web site, which otherwise doesn't look like it has been updated for a couple of years. ***Rating: C+***

Berg *(908) 354-5252. Web: bergfurniture.com.* In business since 1984, Berg branched out into juvenile furniture in the late 90's. Sold in stores like Buy Buy Baby, Berg offers several different crib models. Solid pine cribs (made in Russia and China) run $450 to $600, while convertible cribs (that convert to twin beds) are $650 to $800. Yes, that is pricey, but the convertible models do include the conversion kit. New this year, Berg has expanded its modern collections, including the two-toned Copenhagen. As for dressers, Berg case goods feature smooth glides and quality detailing. Feedback from parents on Berg has been quite positive. One caveat: Berg's pine groupings. Berg uses a soft pine, which is susceptible to nicks and scratches. As a result, Berg's pine furniture in baby stores often looks beaten up. . . obviously, this is less of an issue in a nursery, as long as you're careful. Or just skip the pine groups and get a different Berg style. ***Rating: A-***

Bethany James Collection *See Dorel. Sold exclusively at Wal-Mart.*

Bonavita *Call (888) 266-2848 or (732) 346-5150 for a dealer near you. Web site: LaJobi.com.* Bonavita's theme song must be that disco chestnut, "I Will Survive." What else could explain this company's history, which has had more ups and downs than a Six Flags thrill ride?

A brief history: La Jobi (Bonavita's parent) started as an importer of Italian furniture, sold to both chain stores like Babies R Us and indie retailers. To avoid raising the ire of specialty stores, Bonavita has marketed its wares under a plethora of aliases—it currently uses Babi Italia and Scandi in Babies R Us, Europa Baby in Baby Depot and its own moniker (Bonavita) in specialty channels. (Each brand has its own web site—go to LaJobi.com to access these sites).

When the Euro rose sharply against the dollar (making Italian furniture costly to import), Bonavita switched to Asian imports (Vietnam, Thailand and China). This transition was bumpy—quality glitches and delivery problems dogged this line for several years earlier in this decade. Yet the company survived (again) and now has put most of that behind it.

Bonavita's main market niche is value—and unlike their competitors, they've always been aggressive about marketing their goods in chain stores. While Bonavita typically is the most expensive price point for chains, the company gives you more style and features for the buck. Look at their $300 Scandi drop-side crib at Babies R Us. This modern crib (in a two-tone finish) is a good value, considering other similar styles run twice as much. The Scandi earns raves from our readers, happy to find a modern crib without a $1000 price tag.

Compared to other brands sold in chain stores, Bonavita not only out-does these other competitors style-wise, but also with quality touches like fit and finish. A typical Babi Italia crib at BRU is $300—a good buy for parents who want something better than a $200 Delta crib, but can't afford the $500 cribs sold in specialty stores.

In the past year, Bonavita licensed the Graco name and began selling cribs, gliders, cradles and dressers under that moniker in chains like Target and Wal-Mart. A simple Graco crib at Wal-Mart is $140 to $200, although a few online styles run up to $260. Target has similar prices. FYI: Bonavita plans to phase out drop-side cribs in the Graco line; all new models will be static.

For a regular Bonavita crib, expect to shell out $500 to $600 for a convertible style. Dressers from this line can be pricey, with prices ranging from $500 for a simple chest to $900 for an armoire. New at Bonavita: eco-nursery furniture. The company is debuting its first "eco-friendly" collection (Madre) which has water-based finishes and is made from wood from certified "sustainable" forests.

How's the quality? Overall, we like Bonavita. Even the low-end Graco line gets generally good marks from our readers who cite the great value. However, we did notice a smattering of negative reviews: mis-matched screw holes and other quality miscues dog some Graco cribs. We'll chalk this up to the start-up of the Graco operation—more recent reviews have been generally positive.

Quality-wise, Babi Italia at BRU is consistent winner. Even Bonavita's specialty store line can hold its own against the top competitors.

Customer service at Bonavita has been uneven, however. Readers of past editions of our book may recall Bonavita customer service meltdowns; but in the past year, we noticed things have improved. FYI: Bonavita parent La Jobi Industries was recently acquired by Russ Berrie, the baby gift company that also recently bought Kids Line and CoCaLo bedding. Hopefully, the new owners can improve the consistency of Bonavita's customer service. ***Rating: A-***

Bratt Décor *Call (888)-24-BRATT or (410) 327-4600 for a dealer near you. Web: brattdecor.com.* Well, at least you have to give this company bonus points for creativity—Bratt Decor made their name with offerings like the "Casablanca Plume" crib that was topped with (and we're not making this up) ostrich feathers. That (and the $1050 price tag) enabled Bratt Décor to earn a distinguished place on our list of the most ridiculous baby products in a previous edition of this book. In the past year, Bratt has expanded their line to include a series of wood cribs in various "vintage" and whimsical looks. Their Heritage Four Poster Crib with Stars is a take-off of a 1940's design with four finials that can be changed from stars to bunnies, flowers, planes or balls. Price: $800. All in all, we've noticed Bratt Décor's prices have drifted downward in recent years—most cribs now sell for $700 to $1000.

Bratt Décor's wood cribs are made in Vietnam; the metal models are imported from China. New this year, the Blu line of modern cribs features interchangeable micro-suede end panels for a custom look. Cool, but pricey at $1050 for the crib ($330 more for matching panels). A coordinating dresser is $1162.

What parents seem to like here is the style and colors of the cribs (Bratt Décor is one of the few crib makers out there today that does a navy blue or bright red finish). They also have matching accessories such as night stands, mirrors, bookcases and other decorative options. FYI: Bratt Décor is one of the few crib brands that sells direct via their web site. Bratt also has a company store in Baltimore, in addition to regular retail dealers. All in all, we'll give Bratt Décor thumbs up for style—but you're going to pay for it. *Rating: B*

Bright Future *See JCPenney.*

Butterfly Living New kid on the block Butterfly Living started shipping nursery furniture in late 2007 under various names: Carter's and Amy Coe at Babies R Us, Child of Mind (COM) at Wal-Mart and its own name at Target and Amazon. Prices are roughly $300 for a convertible crib and $170 for a changing table. Dressers are either ready-to-assemble ($250 at Target) or fully assembled ($400 at Babies R Us). So who is Butterfly Living? Started by a group of former Graco alums, Butterfly Living imports most of its furniture from Asia (Indonesia, China and Vietnam). Owner Ken Hopkins told us they are aiming to make stylish furniture at an affordable price point. Example: Butterfly Living cribs have all hidden hardware and no exposed bolts . . . and the furniture styles (the "casual" crib has a beadboard motif) echo the simple Pottery Barn aesthetic. The Amy Coe WestPort crib ($350) is Butterfly Living's take on modern, with a two-tone finish and under-crib drawer. Parent feedback on the brand has been mostly positive: fans like the sturdy construction, easy assembly and included conversion kit. Detractors point out the mattress support is an MDF board, many models do not have dropsides and the ready-to-assemble dressers are nothing special, quality-wise. We also were a bit surprised that despite being up and running for a year, Butterfly Living doesn't have a working web site. All in all, we will recommend Butterfly Living with this caveat: we'd like to see a bit more track record on this newcomer before we give them our top rating. *Rating: B*

Organic baby furniture

What makes nursery furniture green? As with many products marketed as organic or natural, there isn't a consensus as to what that means—and that's true with baby furniture as well.

Furniture, by its very nature, isn't the most green product on earth. A toxic brew of chemicals is used to manufacture and finish most items. Example: most furniture isn't made of solid wood but veneers (a think strip of wood over particle board). Glue is often used to adhere the veneer on particle board for dresser tops and sides. Some glues contain formaldehyde—as we discussed earlier on page 24, some baby furniture makers have been sued by the state of California for unsafe levels of this chemical.

For many folks, green means sustainable. So green baby furniture should be made from sustainable wood. But which wood is more eco-friendly? Some say bamboo is the most green (Natart's new Tulip line of furniture is made from bamboo, but is very pricey). Others say rubber wood (ramin) since the tree it comes from (Para rubber tree) is usually cut down anyway after it is used to produce latex.

Given all the confusion, here is our advice for green nursery furniture shoppers:

◆ *Look for solid wood furniture that is certified.* There are a handful of non-profit environmental organizations that certify wood as sustainable: the Forest Stewardship Council (FSC) is among the best known. FSC-certified crib makers include Argington, Ouef and Romina (all are reviewed in this chapter).

◆ *Consider a water-based paint or stain.* Romina offers a "Bees wax" finish that is about as organic as it gets. Pacific Rim also has a similar option: 100% pure tung oil with a beeswax sealant. Stokke's Sleepi crib features a formaldehyde-free varnish.

◆ *Avoid dressers made entirely of MDF or particle board.* The more solid wood, the better.

◆ *Consider an organic mattress.* We review mattresses later in this chapter.

C&T International *This company is the same as Sorelle; see their review later in this section.*

Canalli This private label furniture is made by Munire (see review later) and sold in a small number of stores in New Jersey and New York, most notably the Crib & Teen City chain (cribteencity.com).

Capretti Home *Web: CaprettiHome.com.* Launched in 2007, Capretti Home is the brainchild of Mitchell Schwartz, one of the key players who worked at the old Ragazzi label. After Ragazzi was sold to Stork Craft, Schwartz launched Capretti Home as his own label. It's perhaps no big surprise that the furniture takes design cues from the old Ragazzi—but Capretti tries to up the quality quotient with solid poplar construction, cribs that include a toddler guard rail and conversion kit to a full-size bed and more. Among the most popular features: self-closing drawer glides that prevent pinching.

Prices are high—$800 for a convertible crib, $600 for a drop-

---

E-MAIL FROM THE REAL WORLD
Leg got stuck in crib slats

"Yesterday, my nine month old somehow wedged his leg between two slats of the crib. I heard him scream shortly after I put him to bed for his afternoon nap and found his leg entrapped up to the thigh. I couldn't pull the slats apart and get his leg out myself, so I called 911. A police officer was able to pull the slats apart just enough so I could gently guide by son's leg back through. I took him to the doctor and he's fine, other than a bruise on his leg. Any tips on how we can avoid this in the future?"

Crib slats are required by federal law to be a certain maximum distance apart (2 3/8"). This is done to prevent babies from getting their heads trapped by the crib spindles or slats, a common problem with cribs made before 1973 when the rule was enacted. Of course, just because baby can't get a head stuck in there doesn't mean an arm or leg can't be wedged between the slats. A solution: Breathable Baby (CribShield.com) makes a "Crib Shield System" ($30) and "Breathable Crib Bumper" ($25 to $30) that uses Velcro to attach to a crib (it is compatible with most, but not all cribs). It is made of breathable mesh and is sold online at BabiesRUs.com and OneStepAhead.com. New this year: a bumper for cribs with solid ends Does everyone need this? No—it is rather uncommon for a baby to get their arms or legs wedged in the slats. But if you do discover this is a problem, that's one solution.

---

side model. A double dresser can run $1100. While Capretti did drop prices a smidge after its debut (cribs at one point were $900), we still find the line to be a bit out of sync with the rest of the market (compare a Capretti to Munire and you'll notice the price premium). Another criticism: Capretti only offers a handful of finishes and the accessories selection (mirrors, other accents) is thin compared to say, Stanley.

So, how's the quality? In our last edition, we gave Capretti an A . . . they started out strong in 2007, with initial shipments that justified their price premium. Yet in the past year, quality has slipped as Capretti has struggled with consistency. Other furniture start-ups have had similar hiccups (see Creations, screw-ups of) . . . but if you want to sell $800 cribs and $1100 dressers, you better be darn near prefect. And Capretti has disappointed.

Capretti told us that some recent problems were caused by improper packing at their China plant, particularly of their new Roma and Milano collections. Capretti said they are redoubling their quality control procedures to fix the problems. We'll have to wait and see.

New for 2009, Capretti plans to debut an eco-friendly collection made in the USA (Capretti's other lines are imported from China). The new Verti grouping has water-based finishes and other eco touches. At $1300 for a crib and $1900 for a dresser, it remains to be seen if China-phobic parents will be willing to pony up the big bucks for this furniture.

Capretti is a brand at a crossroads. Either its prices will have to come down or the quality must match that of its key competitors. Like its moniker (Capretti is Italian for "kids"), the company must decide what it wants to be once it grows up. ***Rating: B***

Caramia *Call (877) 728-0342 or (705) 328-0342 for a dealer near you. Web: CaramiaFurniture.com.* Ontario-based Caramia imports its cribs from Croatia and dressers from Vietnam. The styling is conservative and prices are moderate (most cribs are $400 to $550). The new Elena collection is Caramia's first stab at eco-friendly furniture: the crib is made from FSC-certified wood, water-based finish, natural glue, etc. Delivery is six to eight weeks on average, which is rather zippy in this industry. How about the quality? We consider Caramia to be in the middle of the pack—not the best, but not the worst. The dressers are probably the least-impressive part of this line: while the Elena is made of solid beech, other collections feature more MDF than you'd expect at this price. ***Rating: B-***

Carter's *See Butterfly Living.*

Chanderic This crib brand is reviewed on our free web site, BabyBargains.com/cribs.

Child Craft Call (812) 206-2200 for a dealer near you. Web: child-craftind.com. Here's a sad case study of American business. Child Craft, the Indiana-based crib maker that traces its roots back to 1911, was once among the top brands of nursery furniture. In recent years, however, the company has had a slow, painful slide into obscurity. Some of this has been bad luck (a 2004 flood knocked the company offline for several months) . . . while most of the blame can be laid at the company's leadership, which never fully adapted to the flood of Asian-produced nursery furniture, both on the high and low end of the market.

As a result, you rarely see Child Craft (or its sister brand, Legacy) in stores these days. Sure, Coscto.com has a collection of their furniture ($980 for a three-piece set). And yes, you can see Child Craft cribs online at Wal-Mart for $300. But you rarely see CC in person at chain stores like Babies R Us . . . and Child Craft's "upper-end" line Legacy has all but disappeared from specialty stores.

Into this bleak picture comes a new owner: Gateway Manufacturing, a Kentucky-based firm that is best known for its baby gates. Gateway's turnaround plan for Child Craft includes a new web site that allows consumers to customize their nursery furniture, order online and have it delivered to a local dealer.

That's a good idea, except Child Craft barely has any dealers left. And Gateway's other major initiative—turning the former upper-end Legacy label into a cheap ready-to-assemble brand—might go down as the most bone-headed decision in juvenile product history.

Child Craft still imports most of its furniture from Honduras, but the company plans to launch a new made-in-America set with a $650 convertible crib and $730 dresser.

So, how's the quality? Sadly, this line is a shadow of its former self. Child Craft used to be known for affordable yet decent quality furniture. Over time, quality has slipped and the workmanship now disappoints. It's unclear if the made-in-America set Child Craft plans for 2009 will reverse this trend. Overall, we still like Child Craft's cribs, but just about everything else (dressers, accessories) isn't up to snuff.

Bottom line: our rating for this brand continues to drift downward. We're not sure the new owner of Child Craft are up to the challenge of bringing the brand around—the company needs a heart transplant, not Botox. **Rating: C+**

Child of Mine by Carter's See Butterfly Living.

Childesigns *This company went out of business in 2005.*

Chris Madden *See Bassett.*

Cocoon *See Baby's Dream*

Concord *This crib brand is reviewed on our free web site, BabyBargains.com/cribs*

Corsican Kids *Call (800) 421-6247 or (323) 587-3101 for a dealer near you. Web: Corsican.com.* Looking for a wrought iron crib? California-based Corsican Kids specializes in iron cribs that have a vintage feel, with detailed headboard and footboard decoration. Before you fall in love with the look, however, be sure to turn over the price tag. Most Corsican Kids iron cribs sell for a whopping $1300 to $3000! Yes, you can choose from a variety of cool finishes like pewter and antique bronze but these prices are hard to swallow. And there are some downsides to wrought iron cribs: first, they are darn noisy when raising or lowering the side rail. Corsican's drop-sides are those exposed (rod/cane) hardware foot bar releases that most of the market abandoned long ago. And

Rug Burn: How to save on nursery rug prices

Yes, it's always exciting to get that new Pottery Barn Kids catalog in the mail here at the home office in Boulder, CO. Among our favorites are those oh-so-cute rugs Pottery Barn finds to match their collections. But the prices? Whoa! $300 for a puny 5′ by 8′ rug! $600 for an 8′ by 10′ design! Time to take out a second mortgage on the house. We figured there had to be a much less expensive alternative out there to the PBK options. To the rescue, we found **Fun Rugs** by General Industries (funrugs.com; 800-4FUNRUGS). This giant kids' rug maker has literally hundreds of options to choose from in a variety of sizes. Fun Rugs makes matching rugs for such well-known bedding lines as California Kids and Olive Kids. Now, their web site lets you see their entire collection, but you can't order direct from Fun Rugs. Instead, go to one of their dealers like **American Blind & Wallpaper** (American Blinds.com), **RugsUSA** (RugsUSA.com) and **NetKidsWear** (netkidswear.com search for rugs). All of those web sites sell Fun Rugs at prices that are significantly below similar rugs at PBK. Example: a 5′ by 8′ log cabin quilt design rug is only $138; PBK's price is $300 for a similar size rug. We found most of those web sites sell rugs for 40% less than PBK or posh specialty stores.

those side rails (made out of solid metal) are heavy. So, it's a mixed review for these guys. Yes, they are cool to look at but the practical drawbacks of wrought iron cribs (as well as the stratospheric prices) score only an average rating in our book. ***Rating: C+***

Cosco *See Dorel.*

Creations *Web: CreationsBaby.com. 602-269-5811.* Sometimes even nursery furniture companies need a do-over.

Such was the case with Creations, one of several new upper-end lines to debut in recent years with the goal of "taking quality to the next level." Industry veteran Michael Schaffer (Child Craft, Baby's Dream) teamed with adult furniture maker SLF, Inc. to launch the new line, which promised quality touches like multi-step finishes on cribs and dressers, armoires with double hinges, hutches with three-light settings, etc. The goal is nursery furniture that is more like adult furniture—Creation's dressers are 21" deep (as are most adult dressers) versus the 18" seen in most juvenile furniture.

Unfortunately, the line's launch was a disaster, with quality problems, delivery delays and worse.

So Creations hit the reset button, switching factories (from China to Vietnam) and rebooting the entire operation. The result? Quality is good and deliveries are on time (eight to ten weeks is the goal).

Prices are $500 to $700 for a crib or dresser; Creations ten collections are conservatively styled, with the over-the-top Venezia as perhaps the only exception. New for 2009, Creations plans to launch two new metal cribs in a brushed nickel finish for $700.

If we were to criticize anything with Creations, it would have to be the limited finishes—most groupings only have one or two options. And the lack of any modern grouping is an obvious missing piece in Creations' lineup.

All in all, we will recommend Creations and up their rating from last time. Compared to peers Munire and Ragazzi, Creations can hold its own. ***Rating: A***

Cub. *See NettoCollection.*

DaVinci *See Million Dollar Baby.*

Delta *Call (212) 736-7000 for a dealer near you. Web: deltaenterprise.com.* Imported from China and Indonesia, Delta (also known as Delta Luv and Babies Love by Delta) is perhaps best known for their low-price cribs sold in big box stores.

Unfortunately, the company became known for something else in 2008: one the biggest crib recalls in history. Nearly 1.6 million

Co-sleepers

If you can't borrow a bassinet or cradle from a friend, there is an alternative: the ***Arm's Reach Bedside Co-Sleeper*** (call 800-954-9353 for a dealer near you; web: armsreach.com). This innovative product is essentially a bassinet that attaches to your bed under the mattress and is secured in place. The three-sided co-sleeper is open on the bed side. The result: you can easily reach the baby for feedings without ever leaving your bed, a boon for all mothers but especially those recuperating from Caesarean births. Best of all, the unit converts to a regular playpen when baby gets older (and goes into a regular crib). You can also use the co-sleeper as a diaper changing station. The cost for the basic model? $210 to $245, which is a bit pricey, considering a plain playpen with bassinet feature is about $130. But the unique design and safety aspect of the Arm's Reach product may make it worth the extra cash layout.

In recent years, Arm's Reach has rolled out several variations on its co-sleeper. The "Universal" model ($40 to $250) is re-designed to fit futons, platform and European beds. The removable sidebar and new liner can also be positioned at the top level of the play yard to create a four-sided freestanding bassinet.

One of Arm's Reach most popular models is the "Mini Co-Sleeper Bassinet," which does not convert to a playpen ($160), even a sleigh-style wooden co-sleeper for $370.

If you like the functionality of a co-sleeper but not the look, there is good news. Arm's Reach web site (see above; click on accessories) now sells 13 floor-length liners in various colors to camouflage the co-sleeper.

Of course, Arm's Reach isn't the only co-sleeper on the mar-ket. ***The Baby Bunk*** (BabyBunk.com) is a wood co-sleeper that is either purchased for $300 or rented by the month. That's right, you can rent one for just $40 a month (with a refundable deposit) in case you want to see if this is for you. That might be the best bargain of all when it comes to co-sleepers. Baby Bunk also sells a series of accessories for their co-sleepers, including sheets, mattresses, bumpers and more.

While we like the co-sleeper, let us point out that we are not endorsing the concept of co-sleeping in general. Co-sleeping (where baby sleeps with you *in your bed*) is a controversial topic that's beyond the scope of this book. We discuss co-sleeping (along with other hot parenting issues) in our other book, *Baby 411* (see back of this book for details).

Delta cribs were recalled by the CPSC for defective hardware—two babies suffocated to death in their Delta cribs after the cribs' side rails detached. The 2008 recall comes on the heels of two smaller recalls in 2004 (Delta cribs had high levels of lead paint) and 2005 (defective slats).

In the past, we suggested low-end Delta cribs might be a good bet for Grandma's house (they can be assembled without tools). But given the safety problems, we wouldn't even recommend a Delta crib for occasional use. FYI: Delta also owns the Simmons brand, reviewed later in this chapter. **Rating: F**

Disney *The Disney Pooh crib sold at Wal-Mart is made by Delta; see review above.*

Domusindo *Web: domusindo.com. See JCPenney.*

Dorel *Web: djgusa.com* Canadian conglomerate Dorel is best known for their Eddie Bauer car seats and Safety 1st gadgets—but the company is also a big player in the nursery furniture biz. Just don't look for them under the name Dorel.

Dorel employs a blizzard of aliases in the furniture market: Jardine (Babies R Us), Bella D'Este (Babies R Us), Vintage Estate (Sears), Heritage Collection (K-Mart), Bethany James/Secure Reach (Wal-Mart) and so on. Baby Gap even launched its own Dorel-made crib line (under the moniker Dorel Fine Furnishings).

Why more aliases than a Jason Bourne movie? Perhaps it has to do with the numerous recalls that Dorel endured during the 1990's under their main Cosco label. In fact, Dorel/Cosco was fined nearly $2 million for failure to report product defects to the government at the start of this decade.

So, if you were the marketing whiz at Dorel, what would you do? Start calling your furniture anything but Dorel or Cosco.

Unfortunately, the company's safety woes didn't end with the name change. Jardine suffered one of the biggest crib recalls in history in 2008 when 320,000 cribs were yanked from Babies R Us for defective slats. Readers flooded our blog with complaints about how the recall was handled (Jardine and Babies R Us set up a byzantine process to replace the defective cribs, with multiple steps and long waits).

Given Dorel's longstanding troubles with safety in this segment, we don't recommend their nursery furniture, no matter what name they use. **Rating: F**

Dream on Me *Web: DreamOnMe.com.* The portable/folding crib market has been rife with problems in recent years, with major players like Evenflo and Delta recalling their models for safety rea-

Two guys, a container and a prayer

Back in ancient times (say, the 1970's), if you wanted to make and sell cribs, you needed a factory. This required a significant amount of capital, as well as the know-how to engineer cribs to comply with safety standards, finish cribs to match dressers and market the resulting furniture nationwide.

Fast forward to today: most start-up nursery furniture companies today are two guys, a shipping container from China . . . and a prayer.

We realize the days of domestic manufacturing are long gone for many basic items like furniture . . . yet the stark new reality of imported goods creates challenges for new parents—which brands can a parent trust to make safe furniture for their baby's nursery? Will their special ordered furniture arrive sometime before the child goes to college? Will the company be around in a few years to fill a parts or service request?

But the biggest question remains: will the furniture ever ship? Since nearly all furniture is imported from China or other Asian countries, it can take 12 weeks or more to land a container of nursery furniture at a West Coast port. Then it must be trucked to a distribution center and finally, out to stores (and consumers). And that doesn't count any disruptions (Chinese New Year, port strikes, bad weather, etc). It's no surprise that delayed shipments are a common complaint in our reader email and message boards.

Quality control is a problem that dogs many of today's new furniture brands. Why? The smaller companies often do NOT have a person there at the factory in Vietnam or China, watching out for quality problems. Hence problems are only discovered once items are shipped to retailers or consumers.

Customer service is another issue for today's furniture importers. Let's be honest: customer service in the baby business ranges from grossly inadequate to merely abysmal. And that's being charitable. When you are talking about small furniture importer, customer service often means one lone person sitting at a phone or answering emails. You are lucky to get a reply to an email (beyond a canned response) or a returned phone call.

The take home message for new parents: go into this process with your eyes open. Don't wait until the last minute to place an order—leave PLENTY of lead time. Stick to the better brands reviewed in this chapter. And once your furniture arrives, carefully inspect items for damage or incorrect assembly.

sons. Yet small player Dream on Me has a winner with their "3 in 1 Folding and Adjustable crib." Sold online for about $160, this crib is a good bet for Grandma's house. This might be the best choice in a category with limited options. (We should note Dream On Me also makes full-size cribs; we have not reviewed those models yet. Our rating applies only to the portable crib model). **Rating: B**

ducduc *For a dealer near you, call 212-226-1868. Web: ducduc-nyc.com.* New York-based ducduc was among the first entrants into the modern nursery category with an eco twist: all furniture is made in the USA (their plant is in Connecticut), contains no MDF or particle board and features finishes that are hazardous air pollutant-free. Of course, all this eco-fabulousness is going to cost you: a ducduc crib is about $1500; matching dressers can push $1800. No wonder this company's distribution is limited to pricey boutiques on the coasts. New for 2009, ducduc is debuting a crib collection with customizable fabric panels (you provide the fabric or chose one of theirs). The Parker crib is $1300 to $1545. Quality is good. **Rating: B**

Dutailier *Web: dutailier.com. 800-363-9817 or 450-772-2403.* Canadian rocker-glider maker Dutailier launched its furniture line in 2004 after acquiring fellow Canuck crib maker EG. The new line features a dozen collections of conservatively designed furniture. Cribs are made in China; dressers in Canada. Typical prices are $500 to $700 for a crib, while a dressers runs $800 to $1100. You can choose from 32 finish choices—Dutailier's "Design Center" web site lets you morph the color of any collection, which is a neat touch.

New this year, Dutailier jumps into the modern nursery trend with the Zoom collection: a $900 crib is paired with a matching three-drawer dresser ($760) or double dresser ($1050).

How's the quality? All in all, we like Dutailier—the company's attention to detail in its dressers and accessories is evident. Examples: the drawer casings are made of solid wood and drawers use French dovetail assembly. The only disappoint: the new modern line lacks corner blocks in the dresser drawers.

A couple of caveats: waits can be long for some items (up to 18 weeks, reported on reader who ordered a Dutailier crib). And, inexplicably, Dutailier does NOT show nursery furniture on its web site (which is focused on their glider-rockers). Yes, you can find it on retailer sites, but come on.

Overall, we recommend Dutailier. Perhaps the biggest negative here is the price—a three-piece nursery set can easily top $2500. **Rating: B+**

EA Kids *See Ethan Allen below.*

Bait and Switch with Floor Samples

Readers of our first book, *Bridal Bargains,* may remember all the amazing scams and rip-offs when it came to buying a wedding gown. As you read this book, you'll notice many of the shenanigans that happen in the wedding biz are thankfully absent in the world of baby products.

Of course, that doesn't mean there aren't ANY scams or rip-offs to be concerned about. One problem that does crop up from time to time is the old "bait and switch scheme," this time as it applies to floor samples of baby furniture. A reader in New York sent us this story about a bait and switch they encountered at a local store:

"We ordered our baby furniture in August for November delivery. When it all arrived, the crib was damaged and both the side rails were missing paint. We were suspicious they were trying to pass off floor samples on us—when we opened the drawer on a dresser, we found a price tag from the store. The armoire's top was damaged and loose and the entire piece was dirty. There was even a sticky substance on the door front where a price tag once was placed. Another sign: both the changing table and ottoman were not in their original boxes when they were delivered."

The store's manager was adamant that the items were new, not floor samples. Then the consumer noticed the specific pieces they ordered were no longer on the sales floor. After some more haggling, the store agreed to re-order the furniture from their supplier.

Why would a store do this? In a tough economy, a store's inventory may balloon as sales stall. The temptation among some baby storeowners may be to try to pass off used floor samples as new goods, in order to clear out a backlog at the warehouse. Of course, you'd expect them to be smarter about this than the above story—the least they could have done was clean/repair items and make sure the price tags were removed! But some merchants' dishonesty is only matched by their stupidity.

Obviously, when you buy brand new, special-order furniture that is exactly what you deserve to get. While this is not an everyday occurrence in the baby biz, you should take steps to protect yourself. First, pay for any deposits on furniture with a credit card—if the merchant fails to deliver what they promise, you can dispute the charge. Second, carefully inspect any order when it arrives. Items should arrive in their original boxes and be free of dirt/damage or other telltale signs of wear. If you suspect a special-order item is really a used sample, don't accept delivery and immediately contact the store.

Eden *Web: EdenBaby.com.* This LA-based crib importer sells a small collection of traditional and convertible cribs to a handful of independent stores nationwide (including USA Baby stores). Along with cribs, Eden also has five collections of furniture with matching dressers, armoires, hutches and combo dressers. The styling is very plain vanilla, with prices running $300 to $450 for a regular crib, $500 or more for convertible models. A three-drawer dresser is about $400. Imported from China. New for 2009, Eden has debuted a modern collection (Moderno) for $450 (crib) to $500 (dresser).

As for Eden's quality, we are not impressed (some dressers featured stapled drawers that lacked a smooth glide). Given the competition on the market, Eden needs to step up the styling, features and quality in order to better compete. **Rating: C+**

EG Furniture *See Petite Cheris.*

El Greco *Web: ElGrecoFurniture.com; Paintboxdesigns.com. An archived review of El Greco and Paintbox is on our free web site, BabyBargains.com/cribs*

Ethan Allen *(888) EAHELP1; web: ethanallen.com. See our web page BabyBargains.com/cribs for a review.*

Europa Baby *See Bonavita.*

An Amish Paradise

They may shun electricity, but the Amish do make some darn good furniture—and the quality puts most other juvenile makers to shame. But how do you buy Amish furniture if you don't live in, say, Amish country? The web, of course. Reader Andrea L. bought all her nursery furniture from the Amish and gave us the lowdown. First, consider going to SimplyAmish.com for an overview of the buying process. Most Amish do not sell direct to the public; they sell through mom and pop dealers who have small showrooms (and web sites).

Among the best Amish furniture web sites are AmishOak.com, AmishEtc.com, StoneBarnFunishings.com, AmishOakInTexas.com and PureOak.com. Our reader's advice: compare prices and beware of some dealers who take huge mark-ups. "Be leery of any dealer who can't give you a quick price quote," she said. "Research prices online to get an idea of usual pricing so you can spot any gouging." Another tip for do-it-yourselfers: you can often buy Amish nursery furniture unfinished.

Evenflo *See our web page BabyBargains.com/cribs for a review.*

First Choice *See Bassettbaby.*

Fisher Price *See Stork Craft.*

Golden Baby *See Sorelle.*

Graco *See Bonavita.*

Hart *See Westwood.*

Heritage Collection *See Dorel. Sold exclusively at Kmart.*

IKEA *Web: ikea.com.* European mega-store Ikea's nursery furniture is much like the rest of Ikea's product offerings: very simple and very affordable. Six crib styles range from the $80 Sniglar to the $160 Leksvik. Matching storage pieces run $150 (chests) to $230 (wardrobes).

In a past edition of this book, we recommended IKEA as an affordable option for parents on tight budgets—there aren't many ways to furnish an entire nursery for under $500. However, in the past year, we began receiving reports of a design flaw in some IKEA cribs: even when correctly fitted with a mattress, there is a large gap between the mattress and rail. While there hasn't been a recall on these crib as of this writing, we think this is obviously dangerous.

The affected crib models with the mattress gap are the Hensvik and Leksvik; the new Gulliver does NOT seem to have this problem, report our readers.

Another major caveat to IKEA: shipping charges. Readers report that if a crib or dresser isn't in stock at their local IKEA, ordering it online requires paying exorbitant shipping fees. How exorbitant? How about $300 in shipping for a $160 crib? Another reader reported $1777 in shipping and handling for $350 worth of furniture. Short of hand-delivering each item via a Swedish reindeer team, we're not sure how IKEA can justify this expense.

And assembling most IKEA items (dressers are ready-to-assemble, natch) can be frustrating for even the most ardent do-it-yourselfer, requiring long hours and lots of patience.

How's the quality? While the crib slats are solid beech, end panels tend to be made of fiberboard/MDF. And we weren't thrilled with IKEA's thin and insubstantial crib mattress (get a standard mattress from another source). However, most readers are satisfied with their IKEA purchases, based on our research.

So, it is a mixed review for IKEA. If you go for the Gulliver model, buy an item that is in stock and schedule lots of free time for assembly. IKEA can be a good solution for those who need nursery furniture on a tight budget. *Rating: A (Gulliver crib only); other models not recommended.*

Issi *See Bonavita.*

Jardine *See Dorel.*

Jenny Lind *This is a generic crib style, not a brand name. We explain what a Jenny Lind crib is in the box on page 50.*

Jesse. *See Natart.*

Jessica McClintock. *See Simmons.*

JCPenney *(800) 222-6161, web: jcpenney.com.* JCPenney is a big player in the online/mail-order crib business—their site has nearly three-dozen crib styles to choose from, along with a raft of other nursery furniture and accessories.

Penney's takes a curious approach to brands: it uses aliases to make the furniture look exclusive the site. The truth: most furniture sold here is made by major manufacturers under assumed names. Example: Bedford Baby is really Westwood, ABC is Million Dollar Baby and Sweet Pea is Delta. Only the Rockland and Savanna furniture are Penney's private label.

Despite having some brand names listed in their catalog, the company doesn't reveal the manufacturer for about 20% of its furniture and that is troubling (talk about buying a pig in a poke). As for Rockland, most readers tell us they are happy with the quality. A typical convertible crib runs $300 to $400; most of the dressers are $200 to $400.

On the upside, Penney's has a good reputation for safety. You'll note the recalls that dog competitors have largely bypassed Penney's (at least as far as their private label furniture is concerned),

Penney's customer service has been up and down in recent years. In our last edition, we noted a large number of complaints about late deliveries, backorder nightmares, the wrong style/color shipped—you name it. In the past year, Penney must have cleaned up its act because the negative feedback is down. So we will raise their rating a bit this time out. Bottom line: we only recommend Penney's if you live in a place with few other retail baby store alternatives. *Rating: C+*

LA Baby *Web: LABabyCo.com.* Importer LA Baby's main business is commercial-grade, less-than-full-size cribs sold to hotels and day care centers. In addition, LA Baby also has a line of full-size convertible cribs made in China for $350, with matching dressers (also $350). We saw LA Baby's furniture at a recent trade show and weren't impressed. Drawers on the dressers are stapled, not dovetailed. The $350 cribs are simple, but we expect more than exposed bolts and basic finishes at this price level. **Rating: C**

La Jobi *This is the parent company for Babi Italia and Bonavita. See their review earlier in this section.*

Land of Nod *Web: landofnod.com.* An off shoot of the Crate and Barrel chain, the Land of Nod (LON) catalog and web site offers nine cribs and a selection of matching accessories (including bedding, bassinets, and other gear.) Nope, this stuff ain't cheap: cribs range from $330 to $740. LON also sells the Stokke Sleepi crib (see review later).

The company has shifted its furniture strategy over the years. For a while, they sold Million Dollar Baby cribs with custom finishes. After a China safety scare (LON recalled 2000 cribs in 2006 for lead paint), the catalog now offers cribs from El Greco, a U.S.-based manufacturer better known for their commercial cribs.

As for Land of Nod's customer service and quality, readers give the brand high marks. But one reader was upset that her furniture order arrived damaged—twice. Land of Nod was accommodating in shipping out replacement pieces, but getting it right in the first place would be nice for a brand that sells such pricey items.

All in all, we like Land of Nod—the El Greco-made cribs are safe and sturdy. And while the prices aren't a bargain, many readers say the custom finishes and other coordinating accessories make it worth the investment. **Rating B**

Lea *These cribs are made by Simmons, see review later this chapter.*

Legacy *See Child Craft.*

Li'l Angels. *This crib brand is reviewed on our free web site, BabyBargains.com/cribs*

Little Miss Liberty *This crib brand is reviewed on our free web site, BabyBargains.com/cribs*

Litto 310-798-1788; *Web: LIttoKids.com.* Asian-influenced design marks Litto's first efforts, including an $950 crib covered in zebra wood and accented by a polished steel frame. The matching three-drawer dresser is $950 as well. New for 2009, Litto plans to debut a maple veneer crib with chrome feet for $750. The company also offers matching retro bedding for about $300 a set.

Litto joins a crowded modern field with many players peddling $1000 cribs. We're not quite sure what Litto's key advantage is . . . the line is small, so there are very few accessories or finish options. Given its limited availability, we've had little parent feedback on quality. The samples we've inspected at trade show were ok—but we are hard pressed to see why this furniture is worth the lofty price tags. If you want modern, you can find it elsewhere for much lower prices. **Rating C**

Luna *This crib brand is reviewed on our free web site, BabyBargains.com/cribs*

Million Dollar Baby *Call (323) 728-9988 for a dealer near you. Web: milliondollarbaby.com.* Million Dollar Baby is one of the industry's best survival stories—among the first to jump on the import bandwagon (the company launched in 1989), MDB has thrived by selling its wares in a large variety of stores under a series of aliases. It also didn't hurt that the company was the first to see the potential of the Internet to sell furniture.

Even though this company got its start selling low-price Jenny Lind cribs to discount stores, you'll now find MDB everywhere from

Hotel cribs: hazardous at $200 a night?

Sure, your nursery at home is a monument to safety, but what happens when you take that act on the road? Sadly, many hotels are still in the dark ages when it comes to crib safety. A recent survey by the CPSC found unsafe cribs in a whopping 80% of hotels and motels checked by inspectors. Even worse: when the CPSC invited hotel chains to join a new safety effort to fix the problem, only the Bass Hotel chain (Inter-Continental, Holiday Inn, Crowne Plaza) agreed to join. That chain pledged to have their staff inspect all cribs, making sure they meet current safety standards. We urge other hotels to join this effort, as research shows children under age two spend more than seven MILLION nights per year in hotels and motels. And if you find yourself in a hotel with your baby, don't assume the crib you request is safe—check carefully for loose hardware, inadequate size sheets and other problems. Another tip: consider bringing your own sheets to ensure safety.

specialty stores to Wal-Mart. MDB is sold under ABC in JCPenney and Baby Mod at Wal-Mart.

Overall, MDB divides its line into three parts. Da Vinci is MDB's online alias and entry-level price point—you'll see it online only at Babies R Us and other sites. Da Vinci cribs are $200 to $300; matching dressers are ready to assemble.

At specialty stores, the company uses the Million Dollar Baby brand and offers assembled dressers and cribs with a bit more detailing and design. Finally, MDB offers modern groupings in two price points: Baby Mod (at Wal-Mart) and Baby Miro. The latter is designed for specialty stores and will debut in 2009 with cribs and dressers priced around $500.

So, how's the quality? The cribs are good; the case goods are average. Our biggest beef with MDB: their heavy use of Asian pine, which is softer than other pine on the market and more susceptible to damage. We wish MDB had more hardwood groupings in their line and less pine.

Even MDB's upper-end line (Baby Miro) cuts corners on quality: dressers lack corner blocks and the basic metal glides don't stack up well to the competition.

How is MDB's customer service? We've heard mixed reports. Retailers seem happy with MDB's customer service and deliveries. Consumers are less enthusiastic, telling us about unreturned emails, poor assembly instructions and overall lackluster customer service.

Safety is a bright spot for this brand: as of this writing, Million Dollar Baby has never had a safety recall. That's impressive, considering the past year was marked by major recalls of other low-end brands (ahem, Delta, Dorel).

What are the best bets? We like the Baby Mod furniture sold on WalMart.com. These two-tone cribs ($300) and dressers ($250) aim for that contempo/sleek look (glossy "espresso" finish matched with antique white) at a fraction of the price of other modern nursery furniture. And the quality? It's much the same as MDB's other furniture—no one will mistake Baby Mod as heirloom-quality furniture, but you are getting decent value for the dollar. The caveats: most of the pieces are made of composites (not solid wood) . . . and what solid wood there is is soft pine. And like all MDB furniture, the instructions are poor and confusing.

We also think MDB's entry level Jenny Lind cribs ($200) would be a good bet for Grandma's house.

So it's a mixed review for Million Dollar Baby—this brand is definitely better than other low-end competitors like Delta or Simplicity. But be aware of the caveats to MDB (soft pine wood, poor instructions, etc) before purchasing. ***Rating: B-***

Morigeau/Lepine *This company closed in 2008.*

Mother Hubbard's Cupboard *This crib brand is reviewed on our free web site, BabyBargains.com/cribs*

Munire *For a dealer near you, call 732-339-6070. Web: MunireFurniture.com.* Munire is on a roll. This New-Jersey based importer has zoomed to the front of the pack of nursery furniture makers in the past year, thanks to a strong line-up of stylish furniture at middling to high prices.

After making furniture under contract for other companies for fifteen years, Munire launched their own brand in 2002. Munire's niche is adult-looking nursery furniture (with an emphasis on style and quality) at prices that are few notches below the other players on the market.

A typical offering: the Urban with its clean lines ($600 crib, $750 for a double dresser). While a couple of Munire collections are less expensive (the Essex crib is $400; the new Madison is $475), Most Munire cribs are in the upper $500's; all are imported from Indonesia.

Overall, a three-piece Munire furniture collection (crib, dresser, armoire) runs about $2000. Yes, that's more than some lower-end competitors, but you do get quality touches like dove-tail drawers and architectural details such as bun feet on the dressers. In fact, it is the quality that most impressed us about Munire: drawers feature a double-track, ball-bearing system for smooth glides, center supports, corner blocks and more. Most of Munire's collections are made of solid wood, although a few have painted MDF veneers.

Finish options are a bit limited—most collections come in four or five choices. Munire is conservative in its styling (you'll see cherry, white or espresso, but no funky colors) . . . and the company has decided to sit out the modern furniture trend for now.

If you like the Munire look but can't spend $500 for a crib, check out the brand's sister line at Babies R Us under the name Baby

Metal: it's the new black

While wood cribs are most common in the market today, some furniture makers will introduce new metal models in 2009. Creations, Natart and Simmons will give the metal market a try this year. The advantages to metal: metal cribs are very stable and can't be easily gnawed by a teething toddler. The downside: weight and a limited number matching accessories.

Cache. Basically, this is Munire Lite—similar design, but less fancy detailing. Baby Cache's five collections start at $400 for a crib, $530 for a dresser/changer combo. Hence, a three-piece Baby Cache nursery is about $1500. The downside? Baby Cache doesn't have the accessories Munire offers (such as night stands) and finishes are very limited.

How's the quality? Munire is like the Toyota Camry of nursery furniture brands: well-made, solid value but not top-of-the-line. Yes, other brands might have better quality, but you're going to pay more. Ragazzi's drawer glides are nicer . . . but a comparable dresser is $100 or $200 more than Munire. And Romina uses 100% solid beech wood . . . but its cribs and dressers are 30% to 40% more than Munire.

So, what's not to like about Munire? Well, detractors say some Munire cribs styles need to be completely disassembled to adjust the mattress height. Others complaint that Munire's cribs with static rails make it difficult to put down a sleeping baby (it's a long reach when the mattress is in its lowest position). Of course, that is a problem with most static cribs—but since Munire doesn't offer any drop-side models, it is an issue to consider here.

Munire suffered a black eye with an embarrassing recall in late 2008 for lead paint in one finish of one collection: 3000 Newport cribs in "rubbed black" had a red paint undercoat that contained lead. While the company vows to toughen its testing of paint, this was still a major lapse.

Finally, readers of our blog may remember the numerous delays in deliveries and quality woes that Munire suffered in 2007 (the company shifted plants that year). While the company is caught up on shipments now, it is probably prudent to leave an extra cushion of time when ordering this brand.

Despite the lead paint recall and Munire's past delivery owes, we still recommend Munire—their overall value and design outweigh the bumps they've had with delivery and recalls. **_Rating: A_**

Natart Call (819) 364-3189 for a dealer near you. Web: natart-furniture.com. Quebec-based Natart debuted in 2001 with a well made, if pricey collection of nursery furniture that won over fans for its attention to detail. We liked its creative design touches that squeezed extra use out of items (like a changing table that morphed into a computer desk).

Unfortunately, the company has faced the same choppy waters that sunk other French Canadian juvenile furniture makers. Natart's response was to shift half its production to China and Vietnam in 2007—that transition didn't go so well, as folks complained to us that Chinese-made Natart wasn't up to the same quality standards as Canada-made Natart.

Prices for Natart's furniture also rose, as the design became even more out there. Example: Tulip, new for 2009, is modern with an eco twist. Made of bamboo and MDF with water-based finish, a two-toned Tulip sleigh crib is $1100 with a matching $900 armoire. Even Natart's "entry-level" crib (the Emily) clocks in at close to $600.

Bottom line: this line has become too expensive. If you want to order it, we'd stick with the Canada-made collections (ask a retailer for the latest update on this, as production can shift).. **Rating: B-**

NettoCollection Web: NettoCollection.com; cubkids.com. New York designer David Netto helped launch the modern/minimalist design wave with his NettoCollection in 2002. An interior designer by trade, Netto's furniture comes in two collections: Netto (which is more expensive) and an entry-level line, Cub.

On the upper end, the "Modern Crib" ($1690) is typical of the Netto aesthetic with solid white lacquer panels and natural ash side rails. A shelf under the crib can hold optional $115 linen boxes. A matching dresser is $1730. Yes, a two-piece Netto nursery will set you back close to $3500.

If that's way too much, Netto's Cub line is designed as a slightly less-expensive alternative. The Cub 2.0 crib is $890, as is the matching three-drawer dresser. You get the same two-toned, minimalist aesthetic, but Cub is made in Vietnam (Netto is imported from Poland). And Cub is clearly a scaled down version of Netto (the end panels aren't as thick, etc).

So, how's the quality? With all the MDF in this line, it's hard to justify these prices. Yes, Netto is a style leader (the new curvy Louis crib has a whimsical touch . . . for $1600), but you can find many of these looks for much less elsewhere. Another caveat: Cub dressers are ready-to-assemble (Netto is fully assembled). FYI for New York City parents: Netto's Soho store runs occasional sample sales with prices 60% off. **Rating: C+**

Newport Cottage Web: NewportCottages.com. When it comes to over-the-top furniture, Newport Cottage turns the knob to 11. With their trademark look of two-toned case pieces with distressed finishes, Newport Cottage is a mix of both vintage and contemporary aesthetics. But this will cost you: a simple, colorful crib is $1200 to $1400. A dresser will set you back $1500. Yep, that is pricey . . . but at least the furniture is manufactured in the U.S. (which makes Newport Cottage one of the last domestic makers of nursery furniture). Quality is a mixed bag—the samples we saw at trade show looked fine, but this company has struggled with consistency when it comes to quality and shipping. And at that these prices, we'd expect perfection. One bummer: while Newport Cottage has a couple pictures of some furniture online, the entire catalog is not available. ***Rating: C***

Nursery Smart *Web: nurserysmart.com; babyappleseed.com.* *626-333-1919.* Newcomer Nursery Smart injects a bit of eco-activism into their Baby Appleseed furniture collection: when you buy one of their cribs, the company will plant ten trees in your baby's name, thanks to a partnership with the non-profit American Forests.

Cribs run $700 to $800; dressers are $600 to $700; armoires $900. The company offers four finishes. While there are just two collections as of press time, Baby Appleseed plans two new lines for 2009.

In a previous printing of this book, we recommended this brand after its successful test run in Buy Buy Baby (where it is sold under the name Nursery Smart). But then things went downhill. Like many young furniture companies, Baby Appleseed had serious teething problems: quality woes at their China plant led to a switch to Vietnam. This caused serious delays and more complaints. Finally, the company had a safety recall in 2008.

Given all the drama for this brand, we'll take a pass at recommending it this time out. ***Rating: C***

Nurseryworks *Web: Nurseryworks.net* Describing its furniture as "mid-century inspired baby furniture and bedding designed to fit a modern home," Nurseryworks is a LA-based company that adds a bit of a twist to the modernist trend: color. Their Aerial crib enables to you to customize the colors for the end panels, rails and slats—you can pick from cotton candy, citrus, lime, navy and something called slumber (a pale yellow). All yours for $990, plus $300 for an optional drawer. Nurseryworks' Studio crib features zebra wood laminate (apparently a popular trend today in modernist circles) and a built-in changing table for $2100. If all this is too much, Nurseryworks budget option (the Loom crib) runs $590 but only has a fixed side rail. For 2009, the company will introduce a new spindle crib for $1450.

Nurseryworks cleverly markets a line of complimentary bedding for its cribs—a six-piece set runs $350. Of all the modern crib designers, Nurseryworks has the biggest distribution, both in stores and online. We also liked the wide range of accessories. So, if your heart's desire is a modernist nursery (and you have the bank account to drop $3000+), Nurseryworks is probably the best bet. But we still find it hard to justify these prices ($1350 for a dresser? $1000 for a crib?), given that most of the furniture (imported from Asia) is MDF, veneers and laminate. ***Rating: B+***

Oeuf *Web: Oeufnyc.com.* Oeuf (literally, egg in French and pronounced like the "uff" in stuff) traces its roots to 2002, when French-American designers Sophie Demenge and Michael Ryan launched the company (and a family) in Brooklyn, New York. Their goal: pair eco-consciousness with modernist design elements. The result: the Oeuf crib, which takes its cues from minimalist Euro styling. The Oeuf crib's fixed side rails, headboard and footboard remove, converting the whole unit to a toddler bed. Like many modern cribs, the Oeuf crib has a wood base (in this case, birch) and MDF panels covered in a white lacquer finish. Price: $890. A matching three-drawer dresser is $900 to $1000. Oeuf also makes a "baby lounger" (bouncer) for $100 and has a knit clothing line ($60 mittens, anyone?). In the past year, Oeuf debuted a slightly less expensive line of furniture (Sparrow), with cribs at $650 and dressers for $740. Sparrow features more natural wood accents, paired with a grayish/brown MDF. All in all, we liked Oeuf—their prices are a bit lower than their modernist peers and the quality (considering all the items are made of MDF with just a dash of solid wood) is good. ***Rating: B***

Pacific Rim Woodworking *This crib brand is reviewed on our free web site, BabyBargains.com/cribs*

Paintbox *See El Greco.*

Pali *For a dealer near you, call (877) 725-4772. Web: pali-design.com.* Italian furniture maker Pali traces its roots to 1919, when the Pali family started out making chairs in Northern Italy. The company switched gears and focused on juvenile furniture in 1962 and then rode a wave of popularity in the 90's, when its Italian-made cribs and dressers won fans for their craftsmanship and stylish looks.

Unfortunately, the last decade hasn't been kind to Pali. The company blundered by keeping prices too high, a result of a stubborn insistence on keeping production in Europe when every other competitor switched to Asia. By shunning most big box stores and Internet sales, the company placed its bets on selling furniture through a dwindling base of specialty stores.

The result: Pali is a shadow of itself former self. Yes, the company belatedly switched production to Asia (most Pali furniture is now made in Thailand and Vietnam; a few dressers are still made in Canada), but the prices are very high. Most cribs are $600 to $800. A five-drawer dresser is $800.

Fortunately, Pali is also addressing its distribution woes—the brand is now sold online at some sites (CSNBaby.com, AlbeeBaby.com). And as we were going to press, Babies R Us was testing a Pali nursery set in a handful of stores (the Karla crib is $429). FYI: Pali is also sold in Buy Buy Baby.

How's the quality? It's still good, but the Asian-imported furniture lacks the polish we found in the old Italian-made Pali. Our biggest beef is value: Munire has about the same or better quality, but charges 20% less than Pali. And other upper-end furniture makers Romina and Ragazzi charge similar prices as Pali, but their quality is clearly better. Example: Romina uses solid beech wood their furniture; Pali uses rubber wood and birch veneers in some collections. We don't have a problem with rubber wood in sub-$500 cribs; but Pali wants $700 for its Arezzo convertible crib made of rubber wood.

So, after several years of earning a top rating in our book, we are dropping Pali's grade this time. If you can find it on sale, Pali can still be a good buy (example: older styles like the April crib for $370 on CSNBaby). And we are happy that Pali has opened a new distribution center in Montreal, which has helped reduce previously long waits for delivery. But Pali has to decide where it goes from here: either lower prices to compete with other mid-tier brands, or up the quality to compete with the top dogs. **Rating: B**

Pamela Scurry See Bassett.

Petite Cheris. See Dutailier.

True Colors: Swatches and samples

What's the difference between oak and pecan? When you order baby furniture, those terms don't refer to a species of wood, but the color of the stain. And many parents have been frustrated when their expensive nursery furniture arrives and it looks nothing like the "cherry" furniture they expected. Here's our advice: when ordering furniture, be sure to see ACTUAL wood samples stained with the hue you want. Don't rely on a web site picture or even a printed catalog. And remember that different types of wood take stain, well, differently. If you order your furniture in a pecan finish, but the crib is made of beech wood and the dresser is pine, they may NOT match. That's because beech and pine would look slightly different even when stained with the exact same finish.

Ordering online makes this more of a challenge. Most sites don't offer wood samples—you have to rely on a online picture (and how that is displayed on your monitor). Bottom line: you'll have to be flexible when it comes to what the final stain looks like. But if you have your heart set on a particular hue for your nursery furniture, it might be best to order off-line . . . and see a stained wood sample first.

Pottery Barn Kids *(800) 430-7373 or potterybarnkids.com.* It's rare that one retailer/catalog can change an entire industry. Pottery Barn Kids (PBK) scored that coup earlier this decade when their contemporary nursery décor (accented by vintage motifs and a bright color palette) literally changed the rules. Out went cutesy baby-ish décor; in came a more modern yet still whimsical look, thanks to PBK.

Despite its success, we are still put off by PBK's sky-high prices—cribs run $600 to $900, with one sleigh style running a whopping $1000. Imported from Asia as their own private label, PBK's cribs are convertible. . . but you can find the same looks/quality elsewhere for $200 to $300 less. Several of the cribs have MDF end panels—yes, the MDF is covered with a wood veneer, but for $900 you'd expect solid wood. Ditto for the mattress platform: some of the styles have fiberboard or masonite supports—for this price, we'd prefer solid wood or springs.

Watch out for shipping charges—PBK charges a "delivery charge" ($50) and then a shipping and processing charge ($60) for most cribs; or a total of $110 on a $700 crib.

While most parents are happy with PBK (they sell a wide variety of accessories, including glider rockers, changing tables and dressers), we've had more than one parent tell us about quality woes with PBK furniture: peeling paint on a crib, splintering wood on a dresser, etc. To PBK's credit, the web site or store usually takes care of the problem and replaces the defective item. But as one reader, who told us PBK's home delivery service miss-assembled her crib, described it, "it's always a canned apology with a pipe dream solution—we'll send someone out, but they never show up."

Bottom line: use this catalog for décor items like bedding or lamps and order the furniture elsewhere. **Rating (furniture): C**

Rachael Ashwell *See Shabby Chic.*

Ragazzi *Web: ragazzi.com.* We once compared Ragazzi to the Lexus of the baby furniture market—expensive, stylish, and exclusive. Well, Ragazzi ended its 34-year run as a Quebec nursery furniture maker in May 2006, when it suddenly shuttered its Canadian plant. In a terse fax to retailers, Ragazzi blamed the company's collapse on "today's economic realities." That news pretty much stunned Ragazzi's dealers and customers, who had little warning of the company's demise.

Enter Stork Craft, the Vancouver, Canada-based furniture importer best known for its low-end cribs sold in Wal-Mart. For an undisclosed figure, Stork Craft bought the rights to the Ragazzi name and re-launched the brand as an upper-end line in 2008.

We were skeptical when this deal was announced, but Stork

Craft surprised us—they actually shipped what they promised: a high-quality nursery furniture collection.

Actually, there are nine collections, all of which feature two crib options—a drop-side model and a "stages" crib, which are convertibles. Crib prices run $700 to $1100. As for dresser options, Ragazzi offers the gamut, from three/five drawer chests to armoires, night tables and combo dressers. A double dresser is $850.

We liked all the accessory options, although the available finishes (five for each collection) are somewhat limited. All the furniture is imported from China.

Quality is impressive: top drawers feature felt-lining, dove-tail joints, self-closing drawers and more. How does that stack up against its other competitors in the premium segment? Compared to Munire, Ragazzi has nicer drawer hardware. But Ragazzi pales a bit next to Romina, which uses 100% solid beech wood (Ragazzi has some veneers). Of course, Romina charges $1200 for a double dresser . . . almost 50% more than Ragazzi.

In a past edition of this book, we criticized Stork Craft's decision NOT to honor any warranties from past Ragazzi furniture—the new owners argued they just bought the name rights. That rightfully enraged former Ragazzi furniture owners, who found their warranties were worthless and requests for parts or conversion rails would not be honored.

That decision still upsets us . . . but we will give the new Ragazzi a rating based on the quality of their furniture shipping now (and not their past mis-steps). **Rating: A**

Relics Furniture *This crib brand is reviewed on our free web site, BabyBargains.com/cribs*

Restoration Hardware. *Web: RHBabyandChild.com* Restoration Hardware in the past year joined fellow chains Pottery Barn and Garnet Hill in rolling out a luxe kids line, complete with furniture, linens, lighting, apparel, gifts and more. Sold online only, Restoration Hardware's neo-classical nursery furniture is arranged in eight collections, each with crib, dresser, bookcase and armoire. Available in two finishes, RH's furniture appears to be custom-made for the chain by Million Dollar Baby with such upgrades as distressed finishes, hardwood construction with birch veneers and hidden hardware/bolts. Dressers include English dovetail joints, cedar-lined drawers and tip guards. Our hats are off: RH did a good job transforming Million Dollar Baby's Chinese-imported furniture into a luxury offering.

So, what's not to like? Well, the prices are outrageous: $900 for a drop-side crib, $1000 for a static sleigh model. And that doesn't include "shipping surcharges" ($100 for a crib, $150 for a dresser), hotel mini-bar prices for accessories ($350 nightstand, anyone?) and $130 for the crib conversion kit. And here's the kicker: cribs only convert to toddler beds (and goofy looking ones at that), not twin or full size beds as most convertible cribs. Hard to imagine, but Restoration Hardware has managed to make even the most expensive nursery brands such as Ragazzi and Stanley look like a bargain. So it is a mixed review for RH: we liked the coordinated collections and the upgraded Million Dollar Baby furniture . . . but at these prices, we are hard pressed to give RH anything higher than an average rating. The value just isn't there—you can spend HALF the price of these cribs and dressers and get BETTER quality and durability. **Rating: C**

Restore & Restyle *Web: target.com. Target's in-house brand of baby furniture is reviewed on our free web site, BabyBargains.com/cribs*

Rockland *See JcPenney.*

Romina *Web: RominaKidsFurniture.com.* The collapse of Canadian premium furniture maker Ragazzi in 2006 produced two surprising results: first, Stork Craft successfully re-launched the brand as an Asian import (see review above). And second, Ragazzi's former crib supplier, Romina, decided to enter the U.S. market on their own.

Yes, Romina used to supply Ragazzi with unfinished cribs . . . but could Romania-based Romina successfully launch their own line in the U.S.? As it turns out, the answer is yes.

Romina's success here could be attributed to two factors: first, good timing. Romina launched in the midst of the Chinese recall crisis—with furniture made in Romania, Romina is one of the few non-China options out there.

Second, Romina doesn't cut corners when it comes to quality—the line features 100% solid beech wood construction. No MDF, no rubberwood, no veneers over particle board, etc. Romina dressers feature dove-tail joints, corner blocks and drawer glides that are smooth "like butter," as one retailer described them.

Of course, this isn't cheap—and if you want Romina, you're going to pay for it. Cribs run $700 to $1100; a double dresser is $1200 to $1300. Yes, that's $400 to $500 more than Munire or Ragazzi charges for a similar dresser—you'll have to decide if avoiding an Asian import is worth that premium.

Romina's other major emphasis is their eco-friendly "Bees Wax" finish, which as the name implies is all-natural. Romina touts it as the ultimate organic finish. If you prefer a darker stain or painted look, Romina also offers eight other finishes, including a navy, white and a brown metallic.

Design-wise, Romina furniture is traditionally styled; the Ventianni

cribs

group is the company's only stab at the modern look. We liked all the available accessories: each collection features night stands, armoires, book cases and the like. Romina offers both drop-side and convertible (static) cribs.

All in all, this is one of the best nursery furniture lines on the market . . . if you can afford it. **Rating: A**

Room & Board *Web: roomandboard.com. This nine-store chain with locations in Chicago, San Francisco and New York is reviewed on our free web site, BabyBargains.com/cribs*

Rumble Tuff. *See RT Furniture.*

RT Furniture (aka Rumble Tuff). *Web: rtfurnitureusa.com.* RT Furniture is a Utah-based maker and importer of nursery furniture that got its start by popularizing the "hi-lo" combo dresser in the 90's. (A quick word on RT and Rumble Tuff–RT is the furniture maker; Rumble Tuff makes changing pads and other soft goods. Both companies used to have the same owners, but Rumble Tuff spun off on its own in 2006. Confusingly, some stores still refer to the furniture by the brand name Rumble Tuff, although it really is RT).

RT is in a state of flux as we write this. The company staked its success on affordable dressers made in Utah, but then the company switched gears and started importing from Asia. That didn't go so well–quality suffered and the company lost market share. So, RT hit the reset button: the company plans to re-launch with a collection of made-in-the-USA furniture in 2009. We'll wait and see how that turns out before issuing a rating. **Rating: Not Yet.**

Sauder *This brand is reviewed on our free web site, BabyBargains.com/cribs*

Savanna *A private label brand sold by JcPenney; see review earlier.*

Secure Reach by Bethany James *See Dorel. Sold exclusively at Wal-Mart.*

Scandi. *See Bonavita.*

Shabby Chic. *Web: ShabbyChic.com* Santa Monica designer Rachael Ashwell's Shabby Chic has turned the vintage look into a mini design empire that encompasses everything from couches to bedding, lighting to cribs. For the nursery, Ashwell offers a simple Jenny Lind-style crib for $375, changing table for $315 and three-drawer dresser for $900. Despite the bold vintage prints employed

in her adult bedding, Ashwell's crib bedding is much more sub-
dued. While we liked Ashwell's overall approach to design, we
wish she'd offer more coordinating accessories (lamp, rug, bookcase with hutch, etc). And while the prices aren't outrageous, we
note that you can find practically the same Jenny Lind crib from Da
Vinci/Million Dollar Baby for $230 with free shipping (davinci-
onlineretailer.com) Since we've had little feedback from readers on
the quality of this furniture, we'll wait and see on a rating for this
company. ***Rating: Not Yet.***

Shermag *See Chanderic.*

Simmons *Web: simmonskids.com.* Here's a sad story about the fall
of an American company. Simmons Juvenile was once one of the
country's biggest nursery furniture makers, selling cribs and dressers
to many generations of parents. Started in 1917 by Thomas Alva
Edison to provide wooden cabinets for one of his recent inventions
(the phonograph), Simmons morphed into a furniture company that
also made mattresses. The company spun off its juvenile division in
the 1980's (just to confuse you, there is still a Simmons company that
makes mattresses).

Then the company began its slow decline. Simmons made a couple major mistakes, chief among them a decision in the 90's to concentrate on selling its furniture in chain stores (forsaking the independent stores that built its business over the decades). The biggest
goof: Simmons never adapted to the changing nursery furniture
market, which soon became flooded with low-price imports from
Asia. Simmons stuck to making its cribs and dressers in plants in
Wisconsin and Canada.

By 2004, the company's deteriorating fortunes prompted the
management to sell their crib mattress biz back to Simmons and then
shutter the Wisconsin plant. Simmons sold the rights to their name
to Delta, which then relaunched Simmons as a separate, upscale division aimed at specialty stores. Ironic, no? Delta's first Simmons collection (imported from China and Vietnam) was a bust–$800 cribs,
$700 dressers were met with little enthusiasm among consumers.

Yes, you can find Simmons in chain stores like Babies R Us and
Baby Depot–last we looked, a Simmons crib was $400 to $500,
with matching five-drawer chest for $470. This is a much more real-
istic price point for Simmons. FYI: Simmons also sells cribs to Lea
Industries (owned by La-Z Boy Furniture Company).

New for 2009, Simmons is debuting a Jessica McClintock line of
furniture, with $900 cribs and $1000 dressers. Also new: Olympia,
a new low-price pine collection with cribs in the $400 range; a six-
drawer dresser is $530.

How's the quality? Well, Simmons has tweaked the line in recent years, adding some good features. We like the self-closing drawers on the dressers, which feature dove-tail construction and corner blocks. But the cheap drawer glides belong more in Delta's dressers sold in Wal-Mart than here—and the rubberwood and veneer construction isn't what we'd expect to see in dressers that run $650 to $1000. If Simmons really wants to compete with the Munires and Ragazzis of the world, then it needs turn in a better performance than this. ***Rating: C***

Simplicity *(800) 448-4308. Web: simplicityforchildren.com.* This brand has been involved in several major recalls, including one million defective cribs in 2007 and 900,000 dangerous bassinets in 2008.

The first recall was so disastrous for Simplicity that the company nearly went bankrupt; its assets were bought at auction by SFCA, a hedge fund that continued to market the company's cribs and bassinets under the Simplicity brand.

Unfortunately, the new owners of Simplicity said they weren't responsible for the defective bassinets—so the company refused to cooperate with the safety recall. This forced the Consumer Product Safety Commission to take an unprecedented step—it recalled the products without the help of the manufacturer.

In October 2008, the Illinois state attorney general sued Simplicity, alleging it "continued to sell dangerous bassinets despite knowledge of a design flaw that led to a baby's death in 2007," reported the Chicago Tribune.

Bottom line: we don't recommend buying anything from this company. ***Rating: F***

Sorelle *Call 201) 531-1919 for a dealer near you. Web: sorellefurniture.com.* Sorelle is the main brand for C&T, an importer that has been in the market since 1977 (FYI: Sorelle cribs are sold under the name Golden Baby or C&T at Babies R Us and Baby Depot).

Sorelle started out as an Italian importer, but in recent years, the company has begun importing cribs from Brazil and Latvia (in addition to Italy). Case pieces are made in all those locales, as well as Canada. Sorelle also imports three furniture collections from China. A good example of the line: the popular Lana crib sold at Baby Depot (and elsewhere) for $220—that's a great value for a birch crib with hidden hardware, knee push rail release and under crib drawer. Other Sorelle models run $250 to $500, which is affordable in today's market. Sorelle's dressers run $600 for a combo to $700 for an armoire.

New for 2009, Sorelle plans to roll out several new collections that copy the looks of high-end competitors. One stand out was a two-tone modern grouping, priced about 30% below similar modern offerings.

So, how's the quality? If you take a look at the two-dozen reviews of Sorelle posted to our web site, you'll note the opinions are all over the board. For every parent who tells us they are pleased with the quality and finish of their Sorelle furniture, another will write to blast a series of problems—defective side rails, "non-existent and rude" customer service, poor assembly instructions, missing parts and more.

It's the lack of customer service that bothers us most here: the attitude at Sorelle seems to be "you're getting a good price on this furniture, so don't complain if we don't return your call for parts." Sorry, but that doesn't cut it for us. ***Rating: C+***

Stanley *See Young America.*

Status. Stork Craft's new mid-price line is positioned as a step up from Stork Craft's wares sold in chain stores, yet less expensive than their premium Ragazzi brand. Sold in specialty stores and made in China, Status offers 12 collections. Each feature a static convertible crib and two dresser options (combo or double dresser and armoire). Each is available in five different finishes. Cribs run $500 to $600; a combo dresser is $680; armoires are around $900.

Unlike Stork Craft's ready-to-assemble dressers, Status comes fully assembled and features all hardwood construction (pine). The downside? The drawers lack dove-tail construction and feature basic wood-on-wood glides (most upper-end nursery furniture has metal glides). We also noticed visible bolts on the cribs, which is something you'd see on a $250 crib at Babies R Us . . . but not at this price.

All in all, this line is a head scratcher. What is the point? At these prices, Status competes directly with Munire and Westwood—but the quality and design isn't up to par. ***Rating: C***

Stokke/Sleepi *Call (877) 978-6553 for a dealer near you. Web: stokkeusa.com.* Color us skeptical when we first heard about this Norwegian company's ultra-expensive crib "system:" The Sleepi morphs from a bassinet to a crib, then a toddler bed and finally two chairs . . . for a cool $1000. A separate changing table (the Care) converts to a play table and desk for $500. As with all these funky European products, you'll have to buy specially made bedding with limited choices ($40 for a sheet; $320 for a set).

Yet the parent feedback on the Sleepi has been very positive—fans love its clever oval shape (fits through narrow doorways) and overall ease of use. The Sleepi is perhaps best suited to urban apartment dwellers with little space for a standard-size crib. Given positive reader reviews, we will up the rating of the Stokke Sleepi—yes, it is outrageously expensive and a niche product, but for those who are space-deprived, this is a good solution. ***Rating: A-***

Stork Craft *For a dealer near you, call (604) 274-5121. Web: storkcraft.com.* Stork Craft is probably best known as an entry-level brand that's sold in chain stores like Wal-Mart and Target, as well as in Babies R Us, Costco, JCPenney, and Burlington's Baby Depot.

Stork Craft's cribs start at $120 online at Wal-Mart, although most offerings are in the $200 to $300 range. At the top end, the $300 crib model features sleigh styling and the ability to convert to a full-size bed. All Stork Craft furniture is imported from Asia.

Stork Craft also makes a wide array of matching accessories, including dressers, rocker gliders and other items—the dressers are an affordable $180 to $300. All of the furniture is ready-to-assemble; readers report assembly ranges from difficult to frustrating, thanks to minimal directions and a lack of labeling for screws and parts. A significant amount of patience is necessary, say most readers.

So, let's talk quality. Parents generally give Stork Craft low marks, based on reviews posted to our web site. Fans like the affordable pricing and the fact you can order most of this furniture online. But detractors say items often arrive damaged, with missing parts and worse. One parent who paid $450 for a Stork Craft crib said she was extremely disappointed in the poor finish which looked very cheap—and the under-crib drawer's bottom constantly fell off its track when moved. Another parent who bought a $300 Stork Craft dresser said it arrived severely damaged and "looks as if it were purchased at a garage sale." Stork Craft's customer service also came in for criticism, with delays in fixing defective merchandise and parts among the top gripes.

Finally, Stork Craft has downgraded the quality of its cribs in recent years, in our opinion. Example: gone are the spring mattress supports. Now Stork Craft uses a MDF board to support the mattress, which is not our preferred choice.

Stork Craft competes against Million Dollar Baby (Baby Mod), Graco (made by Bonavita) and Butterfly Living in this price range. We'd recommend any of those companies over Stork Craft.

Bottom line: if you have your heart set on this brand, stick with the low-price items (the $150 cribs at Wal-Mart are a good bet). Skip the dressers, glider rockers and anything expensive (those $250+ cribs). And be sure to set your expectations accordingly. ***Rating: C***

Sweet Pea *See Delta. Sold at JCPenney.*

Today's Baby *This crib brand is reviewed on our free web site, BabyBargains.com/cribs*

Vermont Precision *This company exited the nursery furniture biz in 2006; an archive of our previous review of this brand appears on our free web site, BabyBargains.com/cribs*

Vintage Estate *See Dorel; this brand is sold at Sears.*

Wendy Bellissimo. These cribs sold at Babies R Us are made by Bassett (see review earlier).

8 tips to lower the risk of SIDS

Sudden Infant Death Syndrome (SIDS) is the sudden death of an infant under one of year of age due to unexplained causes. Sadly, SIDS is still the number one killer of infants under age one—over 2500 babies die each year.

So, what causes SIDS? Scientists don't know, despite studying the problem for two decades. We do know that SIDS is a threat during the first year of life, with a peak occurrence between one and six months. SIDS also affects more boys than girls; and the SIDS rate in African American babies is twice that of Caucasians. Despite the mystery surrounding SIDS, researchers have discovered several factors that dramatically lower the risk of SIDS. Here is what you can do:

Put your baby to sleep on her back. Infants should be placed on their back (not side or tummy) each time they go to sleep. Since the campaign to get parents to put baby to sleep on their backs began in 1992, the SIDS rate has fallen by 50%. That's the good news. The bad news: while parents are heeding this message, other care givers (that is, grandma or day care centers) are less vigilant. Be sure to tell all your baby's caregivers that baby is to sleep on his back, never his tummy.

Encourage tummy time. When awake, baby should spend some time on their tummy. This helps prevent flat heads caused by lying on their backs (positional plagiocephaly). Vary your child's head position while sleeping (such as, turning his head to the right during one nap and then the left during the next nap). Minimize time spent in car seats (unless baby is in a car, of course!), swings, bouncer seats or carriers—any place baby is kept in a semi-upright position. A good goal: no more than an hour or two a day. To learn more about plagiocephaly, go online to plagiocephaly.org.

Forget gadgets. Special mattresses, sleep positioners, breathing monitors—none have been able to reduce the risk of SIDS, says the American Academy of Pediatrics. Just put baby to sleep on her back.

Use a pacifier. Consider giving baby a pacifier, which has been shown in studies to reduce the rate of SIDS. Why? Scientists don't

Westwood Design *For a dealer near you, call 908-719-4707. Web: westwoodbaby.com.* Westwood Design was launched in 2005 by several veteran nursery furniture executives who partnered with an adult furniture company for distribution expertise. The company has found success in a crowded market by offering a high-quality product at affordable prices.

Westwood is sold in a variety of outlets, from specialty stores to chains like Buy Buy Baby. You'll find the brand under the aliases

know exactly, but some speculate pacifiers help keep the airway open. Okay, we should acknowledge that pacifiers are controversial—key concerns include breastfeeding interference, tooth development and ear infections. But if you introduce the pacifier after breast-feeding is well-established (around one month), there are few problems. Stop using the pacifier after one year (when the SIDS risk declines) to prevent any dental problems. While pacifiers do increase the risk of ear infections, ear infections are rare in babies when the risk of SIDS is highest (under six months old). Bottom line: Use pacifiers at the time of sleep starting at one month of life for breastfed babies. If the pacifier falls out once the baby is asleep, don't re-insert it. Stop using pacifiers once the risk of SIDS is over (about a year of life).

Don't smoke or overheat the baby's room. Smoking during pregnancy or after the baby is born has shown to increase the risk of SIDS. Keep baby's room at a comfortable temperature, but don't overheat (do not exceed 70 degrees in the winter; 78 in the summer). Use a sleep sack or swaddle baby with a blanket.

Bed sharing: bad. Room sharing: good. Why does bed sharing increase the risk of SIDS? Scientists say the risk of suffocation in adult linens (pillows, etc) or entrapment between bed frame and mattress, or by family members is a major contributor to SIDS. That said, *room sharing* (having baby in the same room as the parents, either in a bassinet or a product like the Arm's Reach Bedside co-sleeper) is shown to reduce the rate of SIDS. Again, researchers don't know exactly why, but it's possible parents are more attuned to their baby's breathing when baby is nearby.

No soft bedding. Baby's crib or bassinet should have a firm mattress and no soft bedding (quilts, pillows, stuffed animals, etc). Bumpers are optional—we will discuss this topic in the next chapter.

Make sure all other caregivers follow these instructions. Again, you might be vigilant about back-sleeping . . . but if another caregiver doesn't follow the rules, your baby could be at risk. Make sure your day care provider, grandma or other caregiver is on board.

Bedford Baby at JCPenney and Hart at Baby Depot. At the chains, a Westwood crib runs about $400. Dressers are $340 to $450. In specialty stores, Westwood tends to be a bit fancier in style and higher in price. Example: a new modern two-tone grouping in 2009 will feature a $600 crib; dressers are in the $500 to $700 range. Westwood's entry-level crib (the Jonesport) is about $500; most other styles are in the upper $500 range. All furniture is made in Vietnam.

New for 2009, Westwood plans to introduce several scaled-down furniture pieces (the company calls them "euro-sized") for folks trying to fit furniture in a small nursery.

Quality-wise, Westwood is a good value. Most of the cribs and dressers are made from solid hardwood (pine is most common), although the company does use some cherry veneers and painted MDF (in their modern grouping). You'll see some adult furniture touches here and there (hutches with built-in lights; dressers with height-adjustable feet)., which is unusual in the nursery furniture market.

We also like how transparent the company is—Westwood even posts pictures of their Vietnam factory to their company blog. That's unusual: most companies don't like talking about their factories, treating their locations like a national security secret.

The downsides? Well, the company only offers a limited number of finishes. And Westwood probably uses more veneers and MDF than its competitors in this price range. That said, parent feedback on Westwood has been very positive—readers love the sturdy construction, ease of assembly on the cribs and overall finished look. Another plus: customer service at Westwood is excellent. ***Rating: A***

Young America by Stanley *Call 888-839-6822 for a dealer. Web: youngamerica.com.* Adult furniture maker Stanley entered the juvenile market in 2003 with "Young America," a collection of a dozen styles with sculpted headboards and other high-end details. Despite the domestic moniker, Stanley's cribs are actually imported from China (although dressers are still made in the U.S.).

Stanley's mojo is their "built to grow" theme—cribs that can turn into full-size beds, added accessories like desks/study areas for older kids, trundle storage options and more. It's the plethora of accessories that sets Stanley's Young America apart from its competitors, where offering a matching nightstand is about as creative as they get.

Yet, Stanley has struggled to get a foothold in the youth market. One big reason: price. A Young America crib starts at $730—most are in the $800 range. A double dresser runs $1000 to $1500. Armoires are $1250 to $1700. Heck, a Young America nightstand can set you back $600.

Quality-wise, Young America doesn't stack up well against competitors like Romina, which offers solid wood construction (Stanley's dressers are more often veneers) and better drawer glides. Yes, Stanley offers felt-lined top drawers and dove-tail construction, but that doesn't justify these prices. And Stanley has struggled with consistency when it comes to quality, readers report.

And design-wise, Stanley has missed the mark, designing some dressers with odd sizes (some dressers were only 30″ tall—that's too short to use as a diaper changing station). To fix that problem, Stanley recently hired a former Pali sales manger to upgrade their line to better match their competitors. Hence, this line is in a transition year, as they hope to upgrade designs and features.

So, the basic choice here is this: does the wide range of options/accessories (Stanley offers 30 different items in a stunning 40 different finishes) and made in the USA label (at least for dressers) outweigh Young America's high prices and somewhat iffy quality? **Rating: B**

Vintage Estates See Dorel. Sold exclusively at Sears.

See the chart on the following pages for a summary of the major crib brands.

Brand Recommendations: Our Picks

Good. The best budget crib is made by Graco (actually, Bonavita). Specifically, we like the Graco Sarah ($160) or Lauren ($145; pictured). Both are simple, all-wood, single drop-side cribs. Another option: IKEA's Gulliver crib ($100 white, $140 birch). This simple static crib is a good buy as well.

Better. Step up to the $300 to $400 range and you'll find more convertible models that turn from a crib to full-size bed. Our favorites here include Baby Cache's Heritage crib (made by Munire, $400, Babies R Us exclusive; pictured) and Bedford Baby's Monterrey crib (made by Westwood, $400, JCPenney.com). Another good choice in this category is Baby's Dream—their Serenity convertible crib is $350.

Best. Who's got the very best quality when it comes to cribs and dressers? In the $400 to $600 range, we like Munire, Westwood and Creations. Each makes excellent convertible cribs and very good dressers.

Continued on page 96

NURSERY NECESSITIES

CRIB RATINGS

NAME	RATING	COST	WHERE MADE?
A.P. INDUSTRIES	B	$$$	CANADA/CHINA
ARGINGTON	B+	$$$	CHINA
BABYS DREAM/COCOON	A/B+	$$ TO $$$	CHILE/CHINA
BASSETTBABY	B+	$$ TO $$$	CHINA
BELLINI	C+	$$$	ITALY
BERG	A-	$$$	RUSSIA/CHINA
BONAVITA/BABI ITALIA	A-	$ TO $$$	VIETNAM/CHINA
BRATT DECOR	B	$$$	VIETNAM/CHINA
BUTTERFLY LIVING	B	$$	VIETNAM/CHINA
CAPRETTI HOME	B	$$$	CHINA/USA
CARAMIA	B-	$$ TO $$$	CROATIA
CHILD CRAFT	C+	$ TO $$	HONDURAS
CORSICAN KIDS	C+	$$$	USA
CREATIONS	A	$$$	VIETNAM
DELTA	F	$	ASIA
DUCDUC	B	$$$	USA
DUTAILIER	B+	$$$	CHINA
EDEN BABY	C+	$$ TO $$$	CHINA
IKEA	A	$	ASIA
JARDINE	F	$ TO $$	ASIA
JCPENNEY	C+	$$	ASIA
LAND OF NOD	B	$$ TO $$$	ASIA
LITTO	C	$$$	ASIA
MILLION $ BABY/DA VINCI	B-	$ TO $$$	ASIA
MUNIRE	A	$$$	INDONESIA
NATART	B-	$$$	CANADA/CHINA
NETTOCOLLECTION	C+	$$$	POLAND/VIETNAM (CU
NEWPORT COTTAGE	C	$$$	USA
NURSERY SMART	C	$$$	VIETNAM
NURSERYWORKS	B+	$$$	ASIA
OEUF	B	$$$	ASIA
PALI	B	$$$	ITALY/THAILAND
POTTERY BARN KIDS	C	$$$	ASIA
RAGAZZI	A	$$$	CHINA
RESTORATION HARDWARE	C	$$$	ASIA
ROMINA	A	$$$	ROMANIA
SIMMONS	C	$$$	ASIA
SIMPLICITY	F	$ TO $$	ASIA
SORELLE	C+	$$ TO $$$	ITALY/BRAZIL/ASIA
STOKKE/SLEEPI	A-	$$$	NORWAY
STORK CRAFT	C	$ TO $$	ASIA
WESTWOOD	A	$$$	VIETNAM
YOUNG AMERICA	B	$$$	ASIA/USA

Key: **Rating:** Our opinion of the manufacturer's quality and value.
Cost: $=under $200, $$=$200-400, $$$=over $400.
Jpma: Are these cribs JPMA-certified? See page 55 for details.

JPMA	Comments
	Good quality; lots of color choices.
	Green spin on modern furniture.
◆	Still have some folding rails; very good quality.
◆	Cribs good; case pieces bad. Big at Babies R Us.
◆	Sold only in namesake pricey boutiques.
	Big on pine groupings, but watch out for scratches.
◆	Graco line starts at just $140 at chain stores.
	Vintage looks, bright colors. Sells direct via own site.
	Markets cribs under Amy Coe and Carter's brands.
	New eco collection with water-based finishes made in USA
	Average quality, but watch out for MDF dressers.
◆	Affordable, but quality/service has slipped.
	Very pricey wrought-iron cribs; vintage feel.
◆	Conservative styling, good quality, adult looks.
◆	Low prices but low quality; major safety recall in 2008.
	Retro, modernist furniture; high gloss finish. Expensive.
	Quality has improved; expensive but two dozen finishes.
	Unimpressive quality, especially for dressers.
	Do-it-yourself assembly; low prices; very simple styling.
◆	Exclusive at Babies R Us. Major safety recall in 2008.
◆	Good quality; offers several private label brands.
	Stylish but pricey; good customer service, custom finishes.
	Limited availability; matching bedding line.
◆	Makes cribs for Restoration Hardware; sold online.
◆	Excellent quality; adult looks. Sold as Baby Cache in BRU.
	Innovative storage; whimsical touches but very pricey.
◆	Modern/minimalist; Cub line: do-it-yourself assembly.
	Two-tone, distressed finishes; quality/service inconsistent.
◆	Adult looks; struggles with delivery and quality issues.
◆	Can customize colors; mix and max. Modernist looks.
	Eco-style meets modernism; lowest price of modern group.
	Thai line lacks polish of Italy offerings; pricey.
	Design leader but overpriced; high shipping charges.
	High quality; lots of accessories. Adult looks.
◆	Upgraded line made by Million Dollar Baby; very pricey.
	Pricey, but very well-made furniture.
◆	Owned by Delta; average quality, high prices.
◆	Serious safety recalls in past year.
	Decent prices; mixed customer service reputation.
	Pricey crib "system" best for those with little space.
◆	Quality has slipped; poor customer service.
◆	Traditional looks; high quality. Pricey but worth it.
◆	40 color finishes; many accessories. Cribs made in China.

Got more money to burn? Ragazzi and Romina are two of the top picks when it comes to the luxury segment—each sell cribs in the $700 to $1100 range. The difference? While both offer top-of-the-line quality, Ragazzi offers a wider range of accessories and somewhat less pricey dressers—but Romina features solid-wood construction and is made in Europe (versus Ragazzi, which is imported from China).

If space is tight (yes, we are talking to you, New Yorkers), we'd suggest the Stokke Sleepi system. Ok, it isn't cheap ($1000), but when your urban lifestyle requires a compact crib/bassinet, the Sleepi is the answer.

Green. Romina wins the crown in the green nursery race—their uber-natural "Bees Wax" finish is offered on any of their five furniture collections. Romina also earns green points for their 100% solid beech wood and formaldehyde-free construction (no particle board or MDF). Another plus: all furniture is made in Romania.

Grandma's house. If you need a secondary crib for Grandma's house, consider a portable crib from Dream on Me for $160, which folds for easy storage or transport.

Bassinets/Cradles

A newborn infant can immediately sleep in a full size crib, but some parents like the convenience of bassinets or cradles to use for the first few weeks or months. Why? These smaller baby beds can be kept in the parents' bedroom, making for convenient midnight feedings.

What's the difference between a bassinet and a cradle? Although most stores use the terms interchangeably, we think of bassinets as small baskets that are typically put onto a stationery stand (pictured at top right). Cradles, on the other hand, are usually made of wood and rock back and forth.

A third option in this category is "Moses baskets," basically woven baskets (bottom right) with handles that you can use to carry a newborn from room to room. (Moses-Baskets.com has a good selection; but you

can even find Moses baskets on sites like Target.com). Moses baskets can only be used for a few weeks, while you can typically use a bassinet or cradle for a couple of months.

As for bassinets, we noticed a Badger Basket bassinet (a rather common brand, badgerbasket.com) start $80 at chain stores including the "soft goods" (sheets, liners, skirts and hoods). They've added fancier round and oval bassinets with pleated skirts and height adjustable drape canopies go for as much as $200. Cradles, on the other hand, run about $120 to $400 but don't need that many soft goods (just a mattress and a sheet). Moses baskets run $50 to $200 and include all the soft goods.

So, which should you buy? We say none of the above. As we mentioned at the beginning of this section, a newborn will do just fine in a full-size crib. If you need the convenience of a bassinet, we'd suggest skipping the ones you see in chain stores. Why? Most are very poorly made (stapled together cardboard, etc) and won't last for more than one child. The bedding is also low-quality. One reader said the sheets with her chain store-bought bassinet "were falling apart at the seams even before it went into the wash" for the first time. And the function of these products is somewhat questionable. For example, the functionality of a Moses basket, while pretty to look at, can be easily duplicated by an infant car seat carrier, which most folks buy anyway.

Instead, we suggest you borrow a bassinet or cradle from a friend. . . or buy a portable playpen with a bassinet feature. We'll review specific models of playpens in Chapter 7, but basic choices like the Graco Pack 'N Play run $60 to $300 in most stores. The bassinet feature in most playpens (basically, an insert that creates a small bed area at the top of the playpen) can be used up to 15 pounds, which is about all most folks would need. Then, you simply remove the bassinet attachment and voila! You have a standard size playpen. Since many parents get a playpen anyway, going for a model that has a bassinet attachment doesn't add much to the cost and eliminates the separate $80 to $200 expense of a bassinet. (See the next chapter for a discussion of bassinet sheets).

Another way to save: check out second-hand stores and garage sales. Just make sure the bassinet or cradle is in good repair and not missing any pieces. You'll need a new mattress for your second-hand cradle or bassinet—sites like BabyCatalog.com are a good source.

Of course, you can also go for the Arm's Reach Co-Sleeper (reviewed earlier) as an alternative to the bassinet as well.

Mattresses

Now that you've just spent several hundred dollars on a crib, you're done, right? Wrong. Despite their hefty price tags, most cribs don't come with mattresses. So, here's our guide to buying the best quality mattress for the lowest price.

The key issue in mattress safety is Sudden Infant Death Syndrome (SIDS), the leading cause of death among infants under one year of age, claiming over 2000 lives per year. We have a detailed discussion of SIDS in our book, *Baby 411* (see back of this book for info), but here is the take-home message when it comes to SIDS and mattresses: buy a FIRM mattress that correctly fits your crib, bassinet or cradle. See the box on page 90 for more tips on preventing SIDS.

Another point to remember: while mattresses come in a standard size for a full-size crib, the depth can vary from maker to maker. Some mattresses are just four inches deep; others are six. Some crib sheets won't fit the six-inch thick mattresses; it's unsafe to use a sheet that doesn't snugly fit OVER the corner of a mattress and tuck beneath it.

Mattresses should fit your crib snugly with no more than two finger's width between the mattress and all sides of the crib when *centered* on the mattress platform. Since most cribs and mattresses are made to a standard size, this is usually not a major problem. Occasionally, we hear from a parent who has purchased a crib in Europe only to find that they can't find a mattress here that fits (Europe has a different standard for crib sizes).

Smart Shopper Tip #1
Foam or Coil?

"It seems the choice for a crib mattress comes down to foam or coil? Which is better? Does it matter?"

Yes, it does matter. After researching this issue, we've come down on the foam side of the debate. Why? Foam mattresses are lighter than those with coils, making it easier to change the sheets in the middle of the night when Junior reenacts the Great Flood in his crib. Foam mattresses typically weigh less than eight pounds, while coil mattresses can top 20 or 30 pounds! Another plus: foam mattresses are less expensive, usually $100 to $160. Coil mattresses can be pricey, with some models running $200+.

Sounds easy, right? Just buy a foam mattress? Well, as always, life can be complicated—many baby stores (and even chains like Babies R Us) only sell coil mattresses, claiming that coil is superior to foam. One salesperson even told a parent that foam mattresses aren't safe for babies older than six months! Another salesperson actually told a parent they should expect to replace a foam mattress two to three times during the two years a baby uses a crib. Neither of these claims are true.

We've consulted with pediatricians and industry experts on this issue and have come to the conclusion that the best course is to choose a *firm* mattress for baby—it doesn't matter whether it's a firm coil mattress or a firm foam one. What about the claim that foam mattresses need to be replaced constantly? In the 15 years we've been researching this topic, we've never heard from even one parent whose foam mattress had to be replaced!

What's going on here? Many baby stores try to make up for the thin profit margins they make on furniture by pitching parents to buy an ultra-expensive mattress. The latest rage are so-called "2 in 1" mattresses that combine foam *and* coil (foam on one side; coil on the other). These can run $170 or more! While these mattresses are nice, they are totally unnecessary. A $100 foam mattress will do just as well.

So why all the pressure to get the fancy-shmancy double dip mattress? Such mattresses cost stores just $40 at wholesale, yet they sell for $200 or more!

Bottom line: foam mattresses are the best deal, but can be hard to find (hint: web sites like BabyCatalog.com sell foam mattresses). As a result, we'll recommend mattresses in both the coil and foam categories just in case the baby stores near you only stock coil.

Smart Shopper Tip #2
Coil Overkill and Cheap Foam Mattresses
"How do you tell a cheap-quality coil mattress from a better one? How about foam mattresses—what makes one better than the next?"

Evaluating different crib mattresses isn't easy. Even the cheap ones claim they are "firm" and comparing apples to apples is difficult. When it comes to coil mattresses, the number of coils seems like a good way to compare them, but even that can be deceiving. For example, is a 150-coil mattress better than an 80-coil mattress?

Well, yes and no. While an 80-coil mattress probably won't be as firm as one with 150 coils, it's important to remember that a large number of coils do not necessarily mean the mattress is superior. Factors such as the wire gauge, number of turns per coil and the temper of the wire contribute to the firmness, durability and strength of the mattress. Unfortunately, most mattresses only note the coil count (and no other details). Hence, the best bet would be to buy a good brand that has a solid quality reputation (we'll recommend specific choices after this section).

What about foam mattresses? The cheapest foam mattresses are made of low-density foam (about .9 pounds per cubic foot). The better foam mattresses are high-density with 1.5 pounds per cubic foot. Easy for us to say, right? Once again, foam mattresses don't list density on their packaging, leaving consumers to wonder whether they're getting high or low density. As with coil mattresses, you have to rely on a reputable brand name to get a good foam mattress (see the next section for more details).

Smart Shopper Tip #3
New crib mattress = dangerous fumes?

"I read on the 'net that some crib mattresses give off dangerous fumes that can cause SIDS."

This internet myth has its roots in New Zealand. In the mid 90's, a New Zealand chemist launched a web site that claimed Sudden Infant Death Syndrome was caused by toxic gasses given off by crib mattresses. His solution: wrap the mattress in a gas-impenetrable cover, which naturally, was sold on the same web site.

This theory has been discredited by SIDS researchers and scientists, who have studied SIDS causes for years and have found no link between mattress chemicals and infant deaths. Yet, there is still much online buzz about this theory, amid general concern over exposure of infants to household chemicals.

Is true that conventional crib mattresses (whether foam or coil) are made from scary-sounding chemicals. Most mattresses have these chemicals to meet fire retardant standards, which are mandated by both federal and state rules. *Bottom line: to date, there is no research that links sleeping on traditional crib mattresses to any disease or illness.*

That said, we can understand why new parents want to limit their newborns exposure to environmental hazards—you can't control all chemical exposure, but one place you do have some say is your child's nursery. In recent years, an entire industry of organic crib mattresses have sprung up to meet this concern.

Here's the take-home message: we think conventional crib mattresses (foam or coil) are safe. If you decide you want to go the organic route, however, we will provide some recommendations in that category later in this section.

Here are a few more shopping tips/myths about crib mattresses:

◆ *What's the best way to test the firmness of a crib mattress?*
Test the center of the mattress (not the sides or corners)—place the palm of one hand flat on one side of the mattress and then put your other hand on the opposite side. The greater the pressure needed to press your hands together, the more firm the mattress.

◆ *Are all crib mattresses the same size?* No, they can vary a small amount—both in length/width and thickness. Most coil mattresses are 4″ to 6″ in depth. What's the best thickness? It doesn't matter, but 5″ should be fine. FYI: 5″ mattresses are often less expensive then 6″ mattresses.

Remember the safest crib mattress is the one that snugly fits your crib—you shouldn't be able to fit more than two fingers between the headboard/side rails and the mattress. A tip: the mattress should be CENTERED on the crib mattress platform, not jammed up to one side or the other!

FYI: For the curious, full-size cribs sold in the US and Canada must be between 27 5/8″ and 28 5/8″ wide (and 51 3/4″ to 53″ in length). Hence most crib *mattresses* are about 27 1/4″ to 28 5/8″ in width.

◆ *All foam mattresses look alike—what separates the better ones from the cheaper options?* Test for firmness (see above). The more firm, the better. Another clue: weight. A slightly heavier foam mattress usually means they used a better-quality foam to make the product. Finally, look at the cover: three layers of laminated/rein-forced vinyl are better than a single or double layer. What about quilted covers? They are a waste of money, in our opinion.

Top Picks: Brand Recommendations

◆ **Foam Mattresses.** *Top pick:* the **Colgate** "Classica I" mattress ($100, colgatekids.com) is our top pick in this category—this five-inch thick mattress has top-quality foam and a reasonable price.

We should note that Colgate makes about a dozen foam crib mattresses and they are quite similar—some have fancier covers, others have "dual firmness" (a firmer side for infants; less firm for toddlers). While these are all acceptable, we still think the basic Classica I does the trick at an economical price. FYI: Colgate is sold in specialty stores only (no chains). Check their web site for a cur-rent list of dealers.

Runner up: Moonlight Slumber's "Starlight Support" foam mattress ($245; moonlightslumber.com) is more expensive than Colgate, but gets very good marks form our readers. Folks love the dual-zone firmness, with a less-firm side for toddlers. FYI: Moonlight Slumber makes a standard and supreme version of its mattress—the latter ($270) has a layer of memory foam. And the company makes a more affordable version of their foam mattress (the Little Dreamer, $170), which is five inches thick (the Starlight is 6").

◆ **Coil Mattresses.** *Top Picks:* the *Sealy* Baby Soft Ultra Crib Mattress features 150 coils for $85 at Babies R Us. Also good at BRU: The **Simmons** Super Maxipedic 160 coil mattress for $115.

Also worth a recommendation: **Sealy's** Natural Rest Mattress ($80 at Target) features 204 coils and a double laminated cover.

If you can find the Colgate brand, they too make a decent coil mattress—a 150-coil model is about $175.

Yes, most major crib makers also have mattress lines, most notably Child Craft and Pali. Prices typically run $150 to $350. Are they any better than the Sealy or Simmons coil mattresses found in chain stores? No. Save your money and get a basic mattress.

What about those fancy vibrating mattresses? Kolcraft makes a "Tender Vibes" mattress for $150 to $230 which features 150 coils, a vibrating feature and an automatic timer that gradually turns off the vibration after 15 minutes. Is this necessary? Unless you have a history of colic (that never-ending crying that afflicts some babies) in your family, it's overkill. Nothing wrong with it, but save your money and get a regular non-vibrating mattress.

Bottom line: there isn't much difference between coil mattress brands—each does a good job. Stick with the ones at 150 coils (80 is too little; 250 is overkill).

Still can't decide between foam or coil? Well, Colgate has a solution—a "2 in 1" mattress that is half foam and half coil. The company suggests the extra-firm foam side for infants. When your baby reaches toddler hood, you flip the mattress over to the coil side. The price: $190. As we pointed out earlier, the "2 in 1" mattress isn't something we'd recommend (it really isn't necessary), but we realize some readers have a tough time choosing between foam and coil!

◆ **Organic Mattresses.** Let's be honest: there is no evidence that organic crib mattresses are safer for babies than conventional mattresses. Yes, there is concern about environmental exposure of babies to toxic chemicals—and yes, most conventional mattresses are made of vinyl (PVC), polyurethane foam and chemical fire retardants. But the scientific research and evidence does NOT support the conclusion that babies are at any risk for sleeping on conventional mattresses.

Despite that, there is growing interest in organic mattresses—so here are our top picks if you plan to go this route.

Top pick: NaturePedic's "No-Compromise" coil mattress (web: naturepedic.com) comes in both natural ($260) and organic cotton versions ($300). These mattresses feature 252 coils and a food-grade polyethylene cover. If you want to go entirely organic, NaturePedic's Organic Cotton Ultra coil mattress ($360) has a quilted organic cotton cover. Between the two, we think the No Compromise mattress balances the best of both worlds: organic cotton filling, a firm coil innerspring AND a waterproof cover. All of NaturePedic's mattresses contain no PVC's, polyurethane foam or chemical fire retardants.

Runners-up: *Natura's* Naturlatex crib mattress ($300, web: NaturaWorld.com) is made from a natural form of latex and has an unbleached cotton cover. No, the cover isn't water-proof—the company sells a wool "puddle pad" that repels moisture.

Looking for an eco foam mattress? *Colgate's* new Eco Classica I mattress is the organic version of their conventional foam mattress. The Eco version replaces most of the petroleum-based foam with planet-based materials and features a cloth cover woven from bamboo fibers. Price: $170.

Wal-Mart.com sells an eco-foam mattress as well: the *Sealy* Posturepedic Springfree mattress features soy and latex-based foam; it weighs less than 12 pounds. At $150, it is a great value.

Also recommended: Devon, England-based *NaturalMat* (naturalmat.com) offers three organic mattress made of coir (the husk of a coconut), latex or mohair. Prices range from $375 to $625.

If you like the concept of an organic coil mattress but are on a tight budget, consider the *LA Baby* Organic Cotton 2-in-1 mattress at Costco.com for just $130—this 260 coil mattress features two 100% organic cotton layers covering the springs. Readers give this mattress a big thumbs up for its quality and value.

Dressers & Changing Tables

Now that you've got a place for the baby to sleep (and a mattress for her to sleep on), where are you going to put all those cute outfits that you'll get as gifts from Aunt Bertha? The juvenile trade refers to dressers, armoires, and the like as "case pieces" since they are essentially furniture made out of a large case (pretty inventive, huh?).

Of course, a dresser is more than just a place to store clothes and supplies. Let's not forget that all-too-important activity that will occupy so many of your hours after the baby is born: changing diapers. The other day we calculated that by our baby's first birthday, we had changed over 2400 diapers! Wow! To first-time parents, that may seem like an unreal number, but we're not exaggerating. On average, that is about SEVEN diaper changes a day during the first year . . . but for a newborn, expect up to 15 diaper changes a day. So, where are you going to change all those diapers? Most parents use the dresser top, but we'll also discuss changing tables in this section.

What are You Buying

DRESSERS. As you shop for baby furniture, you'll note a wide variety of dressers—three drawer, four drawer, armoires, combination dresser/changing tables, and more. No matter which type you choose, we do have three general tips for getting the most for your money.

First, choose a model whose drawers glide easily. Test this in the store—drawers with an easy glide typically have tracks on BOTH sides of the drawer. Cheaper dressers have drawers that simply sit on a track at the bottom center of the drawer. As a result, they don't roll out as smoothly and are prone to coming off the track.

Our second piece of advice: look at the drawer sides—the best furniture makers use "dove-tailed" drawer joints. There are two types of dove-tail drawers: English and French (see pictures at right). Either is OK; the cheapest dressers do not have dove-tailed drawers. Instead, the drawer and drawer front are merely stapled together.

A third quality indicator: drawers with corner blocks (pictured below). Pull the drawer out and turn it over to look at the corners—if there is a small block that braces the corner, that's good. Cheaper dressers omit this feature, which adds to the stability of the drawer. Also check the sides of the drawers: are they solid wood? Or particle board?

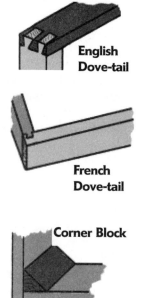

English Dove-tail

French Dove-tail

Corner Block

Step back a moment and look at the entire dresser—do the drawers fit? Are the hinges for an armoire adjustable (like what you'd see in good kitchen cabinets)? Is the back of the dresser a flimsy piece of chipboard that is stapled?

dressers

We've been amazed to see the quality (or lack thereof) when it comes to dressers in chain stores.

Let's take about wood for a second. Unlike cribs (most of which are made of solid wood), dressers are usually a compromise—solid wood on the parts you see (drawer fronts, front panels) and wood substitutes for the parts you don't see (basically, everything else).

Most dresser makers use fiberboard (sometimes referred to as MDF, medium density fiberboard) and particleboard as well as veneers (thin strips of wood glued over particleboard).

The key shopping tip: how much solid wood is there in the dresser? The better quality the dresser, the more solid wood. While one furniture maker (Romina) uses all solid wood that is the exception. The better quality furniture makers use solid wood drawer boxes, drawer fronts, tops and sometimes even sides. Or if veneers are used, they are over less expensive solid hardwood instead of MDF (Pali uses birch veneers over rubber wood, for example).

In recent years, we've seen more MDF used in baby furniture. Why? It is cheap, ease to sculpt and smooth (there is no wood grain or knots). Many modern/minimalist furniture designers are using MDF (usually coated with a high-gloss lacquer) as a design statement. While we don't see anything wrong with that, we do object to the sky-high prices for this—paying $1500 for a dresser made of MDF is like spending four-figures for a fake-leather jacket.

What are the concerns with MDF and other wood substitutes? In general, fake wood isn't as durable as solid wood, which means more possible warping in very humid or dry climates. Why? MDF is made by compressing/gluing together wood waste fibers. That compression/gluing can be affected by the moisture content in the air—and hence your expensive MDF dresser can warp.

Another concern with MDF: formaldehyde. This chemical can be found in high concentrations in MDF and particle board, thanks to that glue that binds the fibers together. The more MDF or particle board, the more possible formaldehyde, which can lead to unhealthy indoor air. In high concentrations, formaldehyde can cause a burning sensation and nausea . . . as well as a possible link to cancer.

But there is good news on this front: a new California law that went into effect in 2009 limits the amount of formaldehyde emissions from furniture. Since California is a big furniture market, manufacturers will have to adjust their entire production to limit use of these glues (and substitute them for soy-based glue).

The take-home message: when evaluating a dresser, look beyond the pretty espresso finish. Evaluate drawer construction, glides, corner blocks and the amount of solid wood.

2 **CHANGING AREA.** Basically, you have two options here. You can buy a separate changing table or use your dresser as a changing area. As mentioned earlier, we think a separate changing table is a waste of money (as well as a waste of space).

So most folks look for dressers to do double duty: not only a place to store clothes, but also change diapers. Basically, you need a changing area of the right height to do this—evaluate your and your spouse's heights to see what you'd need.

Where do you keep the diaper changing supplies? Well, you can use a drawer in the dresser or chiffarobe. Or, a rolling storage cart is another solution (cost: about $25 in many catalogs and stores such as Container Store web: containerstore.com. One disadvantage to changing baby in the crib: if you have a boy, he could spray the crib sheets, bumper pads, and just about anything else in the crib with his little "water pistol." Hence, you might find yourself doing more laundry. If you have back problems, leaning over into the crib to change a diaper may also be uncomfortable.

Safe & Sound

Safety doesn't stop at the crib—consider these items:

◆ **Anchor dressers to the wall.** Why? When baby starts exploring his nursery, she can tip over dressers, bookcases or shelves—no matter how heavy they are. Some furniture brands include anchor straps; in other cases, you'll need to visit a local hardware store.

◆ **Baby proof the diaper station.** If your diaper changing area has open shelves, you may have to baby proof the bottom shelves. As your baby begins to climb, you must remove any dangerous medicines or supplies from easily accessible shelves.

◆ **Air out all that new nursery paint, furniture and decor.** A University of Maryland study suggests new parents should air out freshly painted or wallpapered rooms before baby arrives. New furniture and mattresses also "out-gas" fumes for a brief time, so consider ventilating the nursery when they arrive as well. How much ventilation? The study suggested four to eight weeks of open window ventilation. Even if you can't go for that long, it makes sense to do some air-out of the nursery before baby arrives. Another idea: look for environmentally friendly paints that have lower out-gas emissions. If you install new carpet in the house, leave during the installation and open the windows (and turn on fans) for two days.

Our Picks: Brand Recommendations

Our picks for dressers mirror what we picked for cribs. For contact information on these brands, refer to the reviews earlier in this chapter. Here's a round up:

Good. Just as in cribs, *IKEA's* affordable dressers (about $130 to $250) are our top pick if money (or space) is tight. Let's be honest: IKEA's dressers aren't for the long haul and are nothing to fancy to look at. Plus you have to assemble everything yourself, which can be challenging. But if you need something on a temporary basis (and plan to swap out all the nursery furniture as your child grows older), IKEA is the answer.

Better. The dressers from brands like *Babi Italia/Scandi (Bonavita)* and *Baby Cache (Munire)* are better quality than what you'd see in discount stores like Wal-Mart. A simple four-drawer dresser from Scandi is $300 to $500; Baby Cache runs in the $500 to $600 range.

Best. Our top picks for nursery dressers and other case pieces are *Munire*, *Westwood* and *Creations*. Each sells dressers in the $500 to $700 range, although Munire and Westwood sell less-expensive options in the chains under names Baby Cache and Bedford Baby/Hart, respectively.

If you've got more cash to burn, the very best quality in dressers can be found in *Ragazzi* and *Romina*. A double dresser from Ragazzi is $850 and features felt-lined top drawers and top notch construction. Romina is even better, with all solid-wood construction—but a double dresser from this brand runs a whopping $1200.

E-MAIL FROM THE REAL WORLD
Antique bargains

A reader reminds us that antique stores can be great sources for dressers and storage units for baby's room.

"You might remind readers not to overlook the local antique store when shopping for nursery furniture. We found a great English dresser from the 1930s with ample drawer and cupboard space for $325 that has a lot more character than anything we've seen in baby stores, plus it can be easily moved to another room/use when our baby outgrows it."

Yet Even More Nursery Stuff

Just because to this point you have spent an amount equivalent to the gross national product of Peru on baby furniture doesn't mean you're done, of course. Nope, we've got six more items to consider for your baby's room:

ROCKER-GLIDER. We're not talking about the rocking chair you've seen at grandma's house. No, we're referring to the high-tech modern-day rockers that are so fancy they aren't mere rockers—they're "glider-rockers." Thanks to a hi-tech ball-bearing system, these rockers "glide" with little or no effort.

Is a glider-rocker a waste of money? Some parents have written to us with that question, assuming you'd just use the item for the baby's first couple of years. Actually, a glider-rocker can have a much longer life. You can swap the cushions after a couple of years (most makers let you order these items separately) and move the glider-rocker to a family room. Making this transition even easier is the trend toward all upholstered gliders (earlier models had exposed wood; the newer ones are all fabric). Yep, they are more expensive, but they can go from the nursery to the family room in a single bound.

Here are some shopping tips when looking at rocker gliders:

a) Go for padded armrests. You'll be cradling a newborn and spending many hours here—go for the padded armrests . . . and while you're at it, get the best padded chair overall.

b) Consider a chair with a locking mechanism. Some brands (notably Shermag) have an auto-locking feature; when you stand up, the chair can no longer rock. Very helpful if you have a curious toddler who might end up with pinched fingers.

c) Extra width is always smart. Some of the cheapest glider rockers are quite narrow, which might not seem bad if you are a small person. But remember you will most likely be using a nursing pillow with your newborn . . . and having the extra width to accommodate this pillow is most helpful!

Here is an overview of the biggest players:

◆ *Best Chair* Call 812-367-1761 web: bestchair.com This Indiana-based rocking chair maker just entered the baby biz in 2002, although they trace their roots to the 1960's. We were very impressed with their quality and offerings. Basically, Best specializes in upholstered chairs with over 100+ fabric choices. Delivery is four weeks and prices are decent for an all-upholstered look: most are $500 to $700. A matching ottoman is $200. Best is only sold in specialty stores. **Rating: A**

◆ **Brooks** Call 800-427-6657 or 423-626-1111 Tennessee-based Brooks sells glider-rockers that lack the style or pizzazz of Dutailier—these traditional chairs feature basic fabrics and exposed wood. Prices run $300 to $550 for the glider rockers, while the ottomans are $125-$200. One plus: all Brooks fabrics are available on any style chair. Brooks chairs feature solid base panels (Dutailier has an open base), which the company touts as more safe. While we liked Brooks' quality, one baby storeowner told us he found the company very disorganized with poor customer service. **Rating: B**

◆ **Crypton** Call 248-432-5718; web: cryptonfurniture.com Crypton is one of the more exciting new entrants to the glider category. A textile company that specializes in stain-resistant, hi-tech fabrics, Crypton has two offerings: the Aanabelle rocker and the Charlotte Glider. Both are $800 to $900, feature dozens of fabrics and take six weeks for delivery. We were amazed at the comfort of the chairs—and the stain, water and bacterial-resistant fabric is impressive. **Rating: A**

◆ **Dutailier** Call 800-363-9817 or 450-772-2403; web: dutailier.com. Quebec-based **Dutailier** is to glider-rockers what eBay is to online auctions—basically, they own the market. Thanks to superior quality and quick delivery, Dutailier probably sells one out of every two glider rockers purchased in the U.S. and Canada each year.

Dutailier has an incredible selection of 45 models, seven finishes, and 80 different fabrics. The result: over 37,000 possible combinations. All wood is solid maple or oak and features non-toxic finishes. You have to try real hard to avoid seeing Dutailier—the company has 3500 retail dealers, from small specialty stores to major retail chains.

Prices for Dutailier start at about $300 for their "Ultramotion" line sold at discount stores like Target.com. The Ultramotion gliders are entry-level: you get basic fabric cushions and exposed wood accents.

Dutailier's mid-price line (about $400) sold at chains like Babies R Us and feature upgraded fabric and more fabric choices. Of course, the price can soar quickly from there—Dutailier's specialty store line lets you customize a glider-rocker to your heart's content . . . add a swivel base, plush cushions or leather fabric and you can spend $600. Or $1000. The latest rage: all upholstered glider rockers (Prestige) run $1000 to $1200.

If you like the upholstered look but don't have that much coin, Dutailier offers a new option: the Grand Modern chairs, with fully upholstered arms (but open bases) for $425 chair, $175 ottoman in six fabrics and five finishes. Basically, much the same look, half the price.

Dutailier's Matrix line of ergonomic gliders echoes the look of those high-end office chairs with mesh backs ($800 to $1000). The Matrix gliders have memory-foam seats and are aimed at the modern nursery market. New for 2009, Matrix Too gliders is a lower-price version of the Matrix for $600 to $700 (ottoman $250); it omits the mesh seat and height adjustments.

If we had to criticize Dutailier on something, it would have to be their cushions. Most are not machine washable (the covers can't be zipped off and put into the washing machine). As a result, you'll have to take them to a dry cleaner and pay big bucks to get them looking like new. A few of our readers have solved this problem by sewing slipcovers for their glider-rockers (most fabric stores carry pattern books for such items). Of course, if the cushions are shot, you can always order different ones when you move the glider-rocker into a family room—but that can be expensive, as replacement cushions are $150 to $300.

It can take 10-12 weeks to order a custom Dutailier rocker (more for leather options), but the company does offer a "Quick Ship" program—a selection of 17 chair styles in two or three different fabric choices that are in stock for shipment in two weeks. We have received occasional complaints about how long it takes to order a Dutailier—one reader special-ordered a Dutailier from Babies R Us, only to find out some weeks later that the fabric was discontinued (Dutailier "forgot" to tell Babies R Us, who, to their credit, tried to fix the problem immediately). Other readers complain about fabric backorders, which cause more delays in delivery. Our advice: make sure the store double checks the order with Dutailier.

While Dutailier's web site lacks a product catalog, this is one of those products that is easy to research (and buy) online. Several sites

Upholstered chairs at a discount

The all upholstered rocking chair is the rage for nurseries—but the prices for these models can be exorbitant. $1200 for a chair, anyone? Yet, we've found some ways to save.

First, consider Wal-Mart—the chain sells online an un-upholstered Rocker Frame for $166 (ottoman is $50); add a $53 slipcover and poof! You've got a complete look at a fraction of the designer price. Another option: adult furniture stores and web sites, many of which sell upholstered rockers in the $400 range. Finally, try the Dutailier Versatile Upholstered Glider Rocker ($425 from BabyCatalog,com)—this glider lets you swap out fabrics as your baby grows.

carry the brand at a discount, including BabyCatalog.com—much of the Dutailier line (both wood and metal) is on that site. So, who's got the best deals on Dutailier? At the moment, we'd have to give the crown to Target. At both their Super Target locations and online (target.com), you can get a Dutailier for about $300. Yes, Target only carries one or two styles, so your choices are limited. If you want a discount on a Dutailier you saw online or at another store, check out the above mentioned sources like BabyCatalog.com or CSNBaby.com.

An optional accessory for glider rockers is the ottoman that glides too. These start at $130 at discounters like Target, but most cost about $170 to $300. We suggest forgetting the ottoman and ordering an inexpensive "nursing" footstool (about $30 to $40 from sites like Motherwear.com, 800-950-2500). Why? Some moms claim the ottoman's height puts additional strain on their backs while breastfeeding. While the nursing footstool doesn't rock, it's lower height puts less strain on your back. (That said, we should note that some ottoman fans point out that once their mom/baby get the hang of nursing, that gliding ottoman is a nice luxury).

One safety note: don't leave an older child sitting in a glider-rocker. Many can be tipped over by a toddler when they climb out of it. (Hint: some glider rockers have a lever that locks it in position when not in use). ***Rating: A***

◆ ***Jardine*** Made by Dorel Asia, Jardine's rocker gliders are sold at Babies R Us for about $250 chair, $100 ottoman. The quality is disappointing—these chairs don't rock as easily as a Dutailier or Shermag. We say pass on this one. ***Rating: D***

◆ ***Little Castle*** Web: LittleCastleInc.com. Expensive, but high quality is how we'd describe Little Castle's glider rockers. Little Castle specializes in all-upholstered, swivel gliders made in California. An example is their Cottage Chase, a soft, over-stuffed chair for $800. Other styles start at $600 and go up to $1000. As you'd expect for that price level, you get a wide choice of fabrics (all of which are online at Little Castle's web site) and other perks like a hidden release button to recline the chair. While Little Castle has two chair styles in five colors available for quick shipping, most custom chair orders take six to eight weeks (and sometimes, up to 12 weeks). So plan in advance. ***Rating: A***

◆ ***Shermag/Chanderic*** In the U.S., call 800-363-2635 for dealer near you or 800-556-1515 Canada. Web: shermag.com. Canada-based Shermag's strategy is to under-price Dutailier. Their $130 to $200 gliders (which include an ottoman) are sold online at Wal-Mart and in Target stores. Shermag's focus is the entry glider market, similar to Dutailier's Ultramotion rockers.

So what's the catch with Shermag's affordable line? First, these styles are a bit smaller in size than other glider-rockers—they fit most moms fine, but those six-foot dads may be uncomfortable. The color choices are also limited (just one or two, in most cases). And you should try to sit in these first to make sure you like the cushions (no, they aren't as super comfy as more expensive options but most parents think they're just fine).

Shermag's pricier options are found at stores like Babies R Us, where one $300 (including ottoman) is the average price point. For that extra money, you'll get a bigger chair, more fabric and frame color options.

How's the quality of Shermag gliders? While the low-end glider rockers get good marks from our readers, we did hear more complaints about Shermag's mid and upper price models. Perhaps the expectations are much higher here, but we were disappointed to note that readers thought the quality and durability of these $300 to $500 was not as good as Dutailier. As a result, we've dropped Shermag's rating in this edition. ***Rating: B***

◆ ***Stork Craft*** Like their cribs and dressers, Stork Craft's glider rockers are priced for the entry-level part of the market: about $140 to $240. The quality here is only average. Bottom line: there are better options than Stork Craft when it comes to gliders. ***Rating: C***

◆ ***And more ideas.*** What about plain rocking chairs (without cushions)? Almost all the glider-rockers we recommend above can be ordered without cushions. Of course, just about any furniture store also sells plain rocking chairs. We don't have any preference on these items—to be honest, if you think you want a rocker, we'd go for the glider-rocker with cushions. Considering the time you'll spend in it, that would be much more comfortable than a plain rocking chair with no padding.

2 **CLOSET ORGANIZERS.** Most closets are a terrible waste of space. While a simple rod and shelf might be fine for adults, the basic closet doesn't work well for babies. Wouldn't it be better to have small shelves to store baby clothing, equipment and shoes? Or wire baskets for blankets and t-shirts? What about three more additional rods at varying heights to allow for more storage? The solution is closet organizers and you can go one of two routes. For the do-it-yourself crowd, consider a storage kit from such brands as Closet Maid (call 800-874-0008 for a store near you; web: closet-maid.com) and Schulte's freedomRail. Closet Maid's web site is particularly helpful, with a useful "Design Selector" and how-to guide.

rockers

Schulte appears to be geared toward builders, but do-it-yourselfers can find their products at lumber yards. Another favorite source for storage items is Container Store (web: containerstore.com).

What if you'd rather leave it to the professionals? For those parents who don't have the time or inclination to install a closet organizer themselves, consider calling Closet Factory (web: closetfactory.com) or California Closets (californiaclosets. com). You can also check Craigslist.org for local companies that install closet organizers. Professionals charge about $500 to $1000 for a typical closet.

While a closet organizer works well for most folks, it may be especially helpful in cases where baby's room is small. Instead of buying a separate dresser or bookshelves, you can build-in drawer stacks and shelves in a closet to squeeze out every possible inch of storage. Another idea: a deep shelf added to a closet can double as a changing area.

3 **STEREO.** During those sleep deprivation experiments, it's sure nice to have some soothing music to make those hours just whiz by. A clock radio that let's you plug in an iPod is a worthwhile investment. An  example is the iHome clock radio (see right) for $80 to $100.

4 **DIAPER PAIL.** Well, those diapers have to go somewhere. We'll review our top picks for diaper pails in Chapter 7, Around the House.

5 **A CUTE LAMP.** What nursery would be complete without a cute lamp for Junior's dresser? A good web site for this is BabyCenter.com, which has a decent selection of lamps and nightlights.

6 **MORE FUN STUFF.** Need a small light to see baby during 2am diaper changes? We like the BabeeBrite, a hands-free mobile light source with an automatic on/off timer. $15; web: MommyBeeHappy.com.

If you have a preemie and your doctor wants you to track feedings and diaper changes, the Itzbeen Baby Care Timer is a good solution. The handheld timer tracks when baby last napped, ate or had a diaper change. Optional alarms will remind you if a time limit has been reached. Cost: $50; Web: Itzbeen.com.

The Bottom Line: A Wrap-Up of Our Best Buy Picks

For cribs, you've got two basic choices: a simple model that is,

well, just a crib or a convertible model that eventually morphs into a twin or full size bed.

For a basic crib, the Graco Lauren ($145) or Sarah ($160) are good choices. FYI: These cribs are marketed under the Babi Italia name at Babies R Us.

If you want a drop-side crib, look for models with hidden hardware and a quiet rail release—and check under the hood to look at the mattress support. We like metal springs or wood slats; avoid cheap boards made of MDF. Choose a crib made of hard wood that will resist scratches and nicks—avoid pine for that reason.

If a convertible crib makes sense to you, look at Baby's Dream, Munire (Baby Cache), Creations or Westwood. These models run $350 to $600. Yep, it costs more money up-front but you get a crib that converts to a full-size bed.

The best mattress? We like the foam mattresses from Colgate ($100 for the Classica I). Or, for coil, go for a Simmons Super Maxipedic 160 coil mattress at Babies R Us for $115. For organic mattresses, we liked the NaturePedic "No Compromise" coil mattress in natural cotton ($260).

The best dressers for your baby's nursery should have dove-tail drawers and smooth glides; the more solid wood, the better. Avoid pine and other soft woods, since these show scratches and other damage. The best dressers are the same as our crib picks: Baby's Dream, Munire, Creations or Westwood.

For glider rockers, Dutailier and Little Castle earn our top marks. A simple glider rocker runs $300, but fancy all-upholstered styles can push $1000.

So, here's a sample budget for an affordable nursery

Graco Sarah crib	$160
Simmons 160 coil mattress	$115
Baby Cache (Munire) dresser	$500
Dutailier Ultramotion glider-rocker	$300
Miscellaneous	$200

TOTAL $1275

By contrast, if you bought a designer modern crib ($1500) and paired it with a high-end dresser (plus mattress, glider rocker and miscellaneous items), you'd be out $3500 by this point. So by following our budget, you will have a safe yet affordable nursery . . . and saved $2225.

Of course, you don't have any sheets for your baby's crib yet. Nor any clothes for Junior to wear. So, next we'll explore those topics and save more of your money.

CHAPTER 3
Baby Bedding & Decor

Inside this chapter

H ow can you find brand new, designer-label bedding for as much as 50% off the retail price? We've got the answer in this chapter, plus you'll find nine smart shopper tips to help get the most for your money. We'll share the best web sites and mail-order catalogs for baby linens. Then, we'll reveal nine important tips that will keep your baby safe and sound. Finally, we've got reviews of the best bedding designers and a must-read list of seven top money-wasters.

Getting Started:
When Do You Need This Stuff?

Begin shopping for your baby's linen pattern in the sixth month of your pregnancy, if not earlier. Why? If you're purchasing these items from a baby specialty store, they usually must be special-ordered—allow at least four to eight weeks for delivery. If you leave a few weeks for shopping, you can order the bedding in your seventh month to be assured it arrives before the baby does.

If you're buying bedding from a store or catalog that has the desired pattern in stock, you can wait until your eighth month. It still takes time to comparison shop, and some stores may only have certain pieces you need in stock, while other accessories (like wall hangings, etc.) may need to be special ordered.

No matter where you buy your baby's bedding, make sure you take the time to wash it (perhaps more than once) to make sure it doesn't shrink, pill or fall apart. You'll want to return it as soon as possible if there is a problem with the quality.

Sources

There are six basic sources for baby bedding:

1 BABY SPECIALTY STORES. These stores tend to have a limited selection of bedding in stock. Typically, you're expected to choose the bedding by seeing what you like on sample cribs or by looking through manufacturers' catalogs. Then you have to special-order your choices and wait four to eight weeks for arrival. And that's the main disadvantage to buying linens at a specialty store: THE WAIT. On the upside, most specialty stores do carry high-quality brand names you can't find at discounters or baby superstores. But you'll pay for it—most specialty stores mark such items at full retail.

2 DISCOUNTERS. The sheer variety of discount stores that carry baby bedding is amazing—you can find it everywhere from Wal-Mart to Target, Marshall's to TJ Maxx. Even Toys R Us sells baby bedding and accessories. As you'd expect, everything is cash and carry at these stores—most carry a decent selection of items in stock. You pick out what you like and that's it; there are no special orders. The downside? Prices are cheap, but so is the quality. Most discounters only carry low-end brands whose synthetic fabrics and cheap construction may not withstand repeated washings. There are exceptions to this rule, which we'll review later in this chapter.

Most of our readers shop for their bedding online. Two favorite discount sites are BabyCatalog.com and OverStock.com. For hip bedding, try RestorationHardware.com and LandofNod.com. For hip bedding at a discount, readers give Target's Dwell Studio and Amy Coe brands good marks (much is sold online only at Target.com).

Bed Bath & Beyond sells contemporary bedding as well that isn't overly cutesy. Readers also like BabySuperMall.com, which has hundreds of bedding sets available. We also like BabySuperMall's suggested paint colors that match certain sets. And, as you'll read later in this chapter, we think Lands End has affordable crib sheets.

3 DEPARTMENT STORES. The selection of baby bedding at department stores is all over the board. Some chains have great baby departments and others need help. For example, JCPenney carries linen sets by such nearly ten manufacturers like Cocalo and Bananafish (see the reviews of these brands later in this chapter), while Macy's seems to only have a couple designers. Prices at department stores vary as widely as selection; however, you can guarantee that department stores will hold occasional sales, making them a better deal.

4 **BABY SUPERSTORES.** The superstores reviewed in the last chapter (Babies R Us, Baby Depot, etc.) combine the best of both worlds: decent prices AND quality brands. Best of all, most items are in stock. Unlike Wal-Mart or K-Mart, you're more likely to see 100% cotton bedding and better construction. Yet, the superstores aren't perfect: they are often beaten on price by online sources (reviewed later in this chapter). And superstores are more likely to sell bedding in sets (rather than a la carte), forcing you to buy frivolous items.

5 **THE WEB.** If there were a perfect baby product to be sold on-line, it would have to be crib bedding and linens. The web's full-color graphics let you see exactly what you'll get. And bedding is lightweight, which minimizes shipping costs. The only bummer: you can't feel the fabric or inspect the stitching. As a result, we recommend sticking to well-known brand names when ordering online. See above for our picks of top online discounters of baby bedding.

6 **MAIL-ORDER CATALOGS.** In the last few years, there's been a marked increase in the number of catalog sellers who offer baby linens, and that's great news for parents. Catalogs like Pottery Barn Kids, Land's End and Company Kids offer high quality bedding (100% cotton, high thread counts). Best of all, you can buy the pieces a la carte (eliminating unnecessary items found in sets) while at the same time, mixing and matching to your heart's content. If you want "traditional" bedding sets, JCPenney's catalog won't disappoint. We'll review these and more catalogs later in this chapter.

Parents in Cyberspace: What's on the Web?

Baby Catalog of America

Web: babycatalog.com

What it is: One of the best online baby gear web sites.

What's cool: Whatever bedding item or brand you want, this site has it. Want sheets and bumpers for a cradle? Need a custom-sized bassinet mattress? How about comfortable, good quality portable crib sheets? BabyCatalog.com has got it. As for bedding, you'll find lines like Kids Line, Sumersault, and Lams & Ivy to name a few. All these items are priced 20% to 50% off retail. And you can get another 10% off with the purchase of an annual membership ($25 per year or $50 for three years). If you're active duty military, you qualify for free membership for one year.

Needs work: The site is not fancy, but functional. User reviews of products would be a nice addition.

Baby Supermarket

Web: babysupermarket.com
What it is: Online outlet for Jackson, MS baby store
What's cool: At least 20 bedding lines, including some of our top picks (Cotton Tale, P.J. Kids and Sweet Kyla). Prices are good. Example: a four-piece set from Glenna Jean for $292 (regular price $335). Baby Supermarket does have a decent selection of separates including the Ultimate Crib Sheet. Free shipping on orders over $250.
Needs work: We found the navigation of the site very confusing. It takes a couple of clicks to get to a brand listing for bedding. But some of the brand links are empty. Separates aren't easy to find either. Click on bedding (don't look for it alphabetically) to find the link.

Baby Universe

Web: babyuniverse.com
What it is: The web's largest selection of bedding, 231 at last count.
What's cool: Over 18 bedding brands are here—best of all, you can buy many designs a la carte (including extra fabric). The site is easy to navigate. We liked the ability to search by gender, nursery theme or brand name. The shop-by-theme section included categories like Animals & Nature, Gardens & Flowers, Sports and more. Brand names include Picci, Glenna Jean, DwellStudio, Sleeping Partners and more. On a recent visit, we noted many free shipping offers and other discounts. FYI: Toys R Us bought Baby Universe in 2009.
Needs work: Some bedding items are special order—leave six weeks or more.

Overstock

Web: overstock.com
What it is: A huge resource for overstocked and discontinued items.
What's cool: It's hit or miss, but some bargains are amazing. For example, we saw a Sweet Kayla 12 piece crib set for $150 (regularly $300). You can sort crib sets by price and top sellers among other options. And we definitely like the candid reader reviews of the sets. Savings is about 50% off retail.
Needs work: This time around it's a bit easier to find the baby bedding section, although you'll need to go to the Other category to find Baby. Tip: use the search function to go straight to crib sets. A big frustration Overstock.com often omits brand names from their product listings, making it hard to tell if you are scoring a real deal. Also, many styles come in 12 piece sets with things like toy bags, diaper stackers and decorative pillows that you don't need.

◆ *Other web sites to check out:* Most bedding companies have their entire catalogs online. The best include California Kids (calkids.com), Kids Line (kidslineinc.com), Lambs & Ivy (lambsivy. com), and Glenna Jean (glennajean.com).

For parents looking for accessories and bedding with a Beatrix Potter or Winnie the Pooh themes, check out **Country Lane** (countrylane.com). This site sells 750 different accessories and bedding pieces available in both Pooh and Beatrix Potter line. Country Lane also carries Precious Moments. Discounts are up to 40% off.

What Are You Buying?

Walk into any baby store, announce you're having a baby, and stand back: the eager salespeople will probably pitch you on all types of bedding items that you MUST buy. We call this the "Diaper Stacker Syndrome," named in honor of that useless (but expensive) linen item that allegedly provides a convenient place to store diapers. But what do you really need? Here's our list of the absolute necessities for your baby's linen layette:

◆ **Fitted sheets**—at least three to four. This is the workhorse of your baby's linens. When it comes to crib sheets, you have three choices: woven, knit and flannel. Woven (also called percale) sheets are available in all cotton or cotton blend fabrics, while knit and flannel sheets are almost always all cotton. As to which is best, it's up to you. Some folks like flannel sheets, especially in colder climates. Others find woven or knit sheets work fine. One tip: look for sheets that have elastic all-around the edges (cheaper ones just have elastic on the corners). See the "Safe & Sound" section for more info on crib sheet safety issues.

If you plan to use a bassinet/cradle, you'll need a few of these special-size sheets as well . . . but your choices here are pretty limited. You'll usually find solid color pastels or white. Some specialty linen manufacturers do sell bassinet sheets, but they can get rather pricey. And you may find complete bassinet sets that come with all the linens for your baby. Just be sure to check the fabric content (all cotton is best) and washing instructions. By the way, one mom improvised bassinet sheets by putting the bassinet mattress inside a king size pillowcase. You may want to secure the excess fabric under the mattress so it doesn't un-tuck.

◆ **Mattress Pads/Sheet Protector.** While most baby mattresses have waterproof vinyl covers, many parents use either a mattress pad or sheet protector to protect the mattress or sheet from leaky diapers. A mattress pad is the traditional way of dealing with this problem and is placed between the mattress and the crib sheet. A more recent invention, the sheet protector, goes on top of the crib sheet.

A sheet protector has a waterproof vinyl backing to protect against leaking. And here's the cool part: it Velcro's to the crib's posts, making for easy removal. If the baby's diaper leaks, simply pop off the sheet protector and throw it in the wash (instead of the fitted crib sheets). You can buy sheet protectors in most baby stores or catalogs. See an "Email from the Real World" on the next page for information on sheet savers.

◆ **Blanket?** Baby stores love to pitch expensive quilts to parents and many bedding sets include them as part of the package. But remember this: *all babies need is a simple, thin cotton blanket.* Not only are thick quilts overkill for most climates, they can also be dangerous. The latest report from the Consumer Product Safety Commission on Sudden Infant Death Syndrome (SIDS) concluded that putting babies face down on such soft bedding may contribute to as many as 30% of SIDS deaths each year in the U.S. (As a side note, there is no explanation for the other 70% of SIDS cases, although environmental factors like smoking near the baby and a too-hot room are suspected). Some baby bedding companies have responded to these concerns by rolling out decorative flannel-backed blankets (instead of quilts) in their collections.

But what if you live in a cold climate and think a cotton blanket won't cut it? Consider crib blankets made from fleece (a lightweight 100% polyester fabric brushed to a soft finish) available in most stores and catalogs. For example, **Lands End** sells a micro fleece crib blanket (called the Bunny Belly blanket) for $20. Of course, polar fleece blankets are also available from mainstream bedding companies like **California Kids** (reviewed later in this chapter). Or how about a "coverlet," which is lighter than a quilt but more substantial than a blanket? Lightweight quilts (instead of the traditional thick and fluffy version) are another option for as little as $30 in catalogs.

We found a great product to keep baby warm and avoid a blanket altogether. **Halo Innovations** (halosleep.com), the manufacturer of a crib mattress reviewed in the last chapter, also makes a product called the SleepSack. This "wearable blanket" helps baby avoid creeping under a blanket and suffocating. Available in three sizes and fabrics, the SleepSack is $20 to $33. A portion of the sale price goes to First Candle/SIDS Alliance. **Kiddopotamus** (web: kiddopotamus.com) also has another option: the BeddieBye Zip-Around Safety Blanket for $14 to $16.

Swaddling blankets are now the rage (although most folks can figure out how to swaddle a baby without much effort). Examples include the **Miracle Blanket** ($30; miracleblanket.com) and the Kiddopotamus Swaddle Me ($10).

E-MAIL FROM THE REAL WORLD
Sheet savers make for easy changes

Baby bedding sure looks cute, but the real work is changing all those sheets. Karen Naide found a solution:

"One of our best buys was 'The Ultimate Crib Sheet.' I bought one regular crib sheet that matched the bedding set, and two Ultimate Crib Sheets. This product is waterproof (vinyl on the bottom, and soft white poly/cotton on the top) and lies on top of your regular crib sheet. It has six elastic straps that snap around the bars of your crib. When it gets dirty or the baby soils it, all you have to do is unsnap the straps, lift it off, put a clean one on, and that's it! No taking the entire crib sheet off (which usually entails wrestling with the mattress and bumper pads). It's really quick and easy! While the white sheet may not exactly match your pattern, it can only be seen from inside the crib, and as you have so often stated, it's not like the baby cares about what it looks like. From the outside of the crib, you can still see the crib sheet that matches your bedding. Anyway, I think it's a wonderful product, and really a must."

*Basic Comfort makes the **Ultimate Crib Sheet** (web: basic-comfort.com). It sells for $20 and is available at Babies R Us, Target and other baby web sites..*

Of course, there are several other companies that sell similar sheets; we've seen them in general catalogs like One Step Ahead and Baby Catalog of America.

*One of the coolest new products we found was the **Quick Zip** crib sheet from Clouds and Stars (cloudsandstars.com). Here's how it works: the sheet base covers the bottom of the mattress and stays in place. The top of the sheet is secured via a plastic zipper. Baby's diaper leaks at two in the morning, you zip off the top of the sheet and zip on a spare. No lifting of the mattress (except when you first set it up) and no untying bumpers. The white or ecru sheet sets are $35 and additional top sheets are about $20. They even make a version for portable cribs and organic cotton sheets are now available.*

◆ **Bumper Pads.** Bumpers are fabric pads designed to go around a crib to prevent an infant from knocking their head against the crib sides. Once considered a "must have" for new parents, crib bumper pads have become ensnared in controversy in recent years. Why? Numerous warnings about SIDS and soft bedding (see previous section) have led some safety advocates to advise against bumpers.

For example, the CPSC "recommends that infants under 12 months be put to sleep in a crib with no soft bedding of any kind under or on top of the baby." Note the CPSC doesn't specifically say anything about banning bumpers, but some safety experts have extrapolated their warning to include crib bumpers.

As you would guess, that warning didn't sit well with crib bedding makers, who felt bumpers were getting a bad wrap. The industry's trade association (the JPMA) asked the CPSC to examine the data on infant injuries and deaths due to bedding in order to better determine if bumpers were the culprits. The CPSC released a report in 2004 which found that 94 infant deaths between 1995 and 2003 were caused by bedding . . . but here's the rub: in most cases, authorities didn't specify exactly WHICH bedding item caused the death. In a third of the cases, the "sleep environment was cluttered with adult sized blankets, quilts and pillows." The bottom line: the CPSC concluded "although bumper pads and stuffed toys were mentioned as being in the crib in some of the other deaths, there was insufficient detail to conclude these were the causative agents in the infants' deaths."

Now that clears it up, doesn't it?

One important point for this study: the CPSC excluded any SIDS deaths from their examination of crib bumpers, for reasons unknown. Yet it stands to reason that if you want to decide whether bumpers are safe or dangerous, you should include ALL the data (both SIDS and other deaths due to bedding).

Adding more fuel to this debate: a study in the *Journal of Pediatrics* (September 2007) found 27 cases of infant death involving bumper pads in a 20 year period. The study concluded that bumpers were dangerous and any benefit (preventing minor injuries when baby rolls in the side of the crib) was outweighed by the risk of suffocation. The study's authors said the JPMA specifically mislead the public about crib bumper safety.

Here's the take-home message: *you do NOT need crib bumpers,* which we believe can be dangerous. However, if you decide to use bumpers (say, your baby starts banging into the side of the crib or gets her arms/legs stuck), consider a bumper alternative like the *CribShield,* which we will discuss in detail later this chapter. The CribShield is a breathable, thin mesh that attaches with Velcro to the crib rail—this avoids the entrapment or suffocation risk of traditional bumpers. Another alternative is a wedge-shaped foam bumper called the *Cozy Wedge* also discussed later.

If you still insist on using traditional bumpers, don't buy the ultra-thick or pillow-like bumpers. Instead choose firm bumpers that are made to properly and securely fit the crib (that means no overlapping sections or wide gaps between the ends at the corner sections). We recommend machine-washable bumpers with ties on the top *and* bottom, which let you attach the bumper more securely to a crib. Avoid any bumpers that are dry-clean only.

We'll have more comments on the safety aspects of bumpers in the Safe & Sounds section later in this chapter.

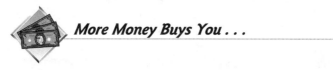

More Money Buys You . . .

Baby bedding sets vary from as little as $40 in discount stores up to nearly $1000 in specialty stores. The basic difference: fabric quality and construction. The cheapest bedding is typically made of 50/50 cotton-poly blends with low thread counts (120 threads per inch). To mask the low quality, many bedding companies splash cutesy licensed cartoon characters on their offerings. So what does more money buy you? First, better fabric. Usually, you'll find 100% cotton with 200 thread counts or more. Better quality bedding sets include more substantial bumpers with more ties. Some may even have slipcovers removable for easy cleaning. Cheap quality crib sheets often lack elastic all the way around and some shrink dangerously when washed (see Safe and Sound next for details).

Beyond the $300 price point, you're most likely paying for a designer name and frilly accessories (coordinating lamp shade, anyone?). At the upper end of the crib bedding market, you find luxury fabrics—silks, brocades, matte lasse, etc.

Safe & Sound

When it comes to baby safety, most folks think of outlet covers and coffee table bumpers—but your baby's crib bedding should be a key priority. Why? Your baby will be spending more time in a crib than any other place in the house. Here are several safety points to remember:

♦ **Make sure the crib sheets snugly fit the mattress.**
Let's talk about crib sheets. As you might guess, it is the elastic on

a sheet that helps it fit snugly to a mattress. But not all sheets have the same amount of elastic.

One quality sign: check to make sure the sheet's elastic extends around the ENTIRE sheet (cheaper quality crib sheets only have elastic on the ends, making a good fit more difficult to achieve).

Another issue to consider with crib sheets: shrinkage. *Never use a sheet that has shrunk so much it no longer can be completely pulled over the bottom corners of the mattress.*

Unfortunately, some sheets shrink more than others. Generally, the cheapest sheets sold in discount stores shrink the most. We will review and rate bedding brands later in this chapter—those brands we recommend have sheets that are pre-shrunk.

Our advice: for any crib sheet you buy, be sure to wash it several times according to the directions and see if it correctly fits your crib. If not, return it to the store.

In response to concerns about ill-fitting cribs sheets, a few new crib sheet alternatives have come on the market. Example: The *Stay Put* safety sheet (babysheets.com; $20 each) works like a pillowcase on your  mattress. The only downside: the fabric is 50% poly, 50% cotton. Another option to consider: "pocket" sheets wrap around the crib mattress and close easily with Velcro manufactured by *Halo* (halosleep.com), the makers of the SleepSack. Also consider the Ultimate Crib Sheet and the QuickZip sheet discussed earlier in this book as another safe sheet option.

Finally, if you want a safety sheet that is customized to your nursery décor, take a look at *Sweet Pea's Heirlooms* (sweetpeasheirlooms.com). These sheets completely encase the mattress (like a pillowcase) then snap on the end. And, best of all, you can get the sheet

Sheets with All Around Elastic

Here is a partial list of manufacturers who make their crib sheets with elastic all around the sheet:

Amy Coe	Garnet Hill	Nurseryworks
BB Basics	Hoohobbers	Pitter Patter
Baby Basics	Kidsline	Restoration
Baby Gap	Lands End	Hardware
Beautiful Baby	Luv Stuff	Sweet Kyla
Carousel	Maddie Boo	Wamsutta
Circo (Target)	Mr Bobbles	
Cottontale	Blankets	
Fleece Baby	Nava's Designs	

made-to-order (with a print on one side and a solid on the other, or any combination of fabric). A 200-thread count cotton sheet from Sweet Pea starts at $25, with flannel and fleece options as well.

◆ **No soft bedding in the crib.** Yes, we've said it before and here it is again: studies on Sudden Infant Death Syndrome (SIDS, also known as crib death) have linked SIDS to infants sleeping on fluffy bedding, lambskins, or pillows. A pocket can form around the baby's face if she is placed face down in fluffy bedding, and she can slowly suffocate while breathing in her own carbon dioxide. The best advice: put your infant on her back when she sleeps. And don't put pillows, comforters or other soft bedding or toys inside a crib.

In the late 90's, the Consumer Product Safety Commission issued new guidelines regarding SIDS and soft bed linens. The CPSC now recommends that parents not use ANY soft bedding around, on top of, or under baby. If you want to use a blanket, tuck a very thin blanket under the mattress at one end of the crib to keep it from moving around. The blanket should then only come up to baby's chest. Safest of all: avoid using any blankets in a crib and put baby in a blanket sleeper (basically, a thick set of pajamas) and t-shirt for warmth. (More on blanket sleepers in the next chapter). See the picture bellow for an example of the correct way to use a blanket.

One mom wrote to tell us about a scary incident in her nursery. She had left a blanket hanging over the side of the crib when she put her son down for a nap. He managed to pull the blanket down and get wrapped up in it, nearly suffocating. Stories like that convince us that putting any soft bedding in or near a crib is risky.

How much bedding is too much? A new father emailed us this question: "With all the waterproof liners, fitted sheets and ultimate crib sheets we're worried that our firm mattress is now becoming soft and squishy. How many layers are safe?"

Good point. We know that some parents figure it is easier to change crib sheets at 2 am if they simply pile on several layers of sheets on the crib mattress. (This way, you simply remove the top wet layer when changing the sheets). While we admire the creative thinking, we suggest NOT doing this. One sheet over a water-proof liner is enough. Or use an Ultimate Crib Sheet over your sheet—you won't need an additional liner since the Ultimate Crib Sheet is waterproof. The take-home message: any more than TWO layers on top of a mattress is dangerous.

E-MAIL FROM THE REAL WORLD
Lack of Bumper Ties Causes a Scare for Parents

Nicole Morely of Chicago wrote to tell us of a frightening incident with borrowed bedding that did not have ties on the bottom of the bumper. (Keep in mind, there is no requirement for bumpers to have ties top and bottom. We recommend it highly, however.)

"We were spending the holidays with grandparents who bought a crib and borrowed bedding so that our five-month-old would sleep comfortably. We failed to check the crib bumpers for ties at the top and bottom and woke up in the middle of the night to shrieking—we found our baby's head and arms trapped under the crib bumper! Scary and unbelievable! Fortunately, we got there in time. I can't believe that so many manufacturers still make them that way. We've called nearby stores and all the bumpers they sell only tie at the top. The one our daughter was trapped under is Classic Pooh made by Red Calliope. I can't imagine that it doesn't happen more often!"

◆ **Beware of ribbons and long fringe.** These are possible choking hazards if they are not attached properly. Remove any questionable decoration.

◆ **We do not recommend crib bumpers** for safety reasons discussed earlier. If you wish to ignore this advice, purchase bumpers with well-sewn ties at the top *and* bottom (at least 12 to 16 total). Ties should be between seven and nine inches in length. That's the industry's voluntary standard for safety—ties that are too short can't be tied correctly around a crib post. If ties exceed nine inches, they can be a strangulation hazard.

We should note that while there is a voluntary standard on bumper ties, our investigation of baby bedding found many manufacturers exceed the limit—one even had ties that were 14″ in length! In their defense, expensive bedding makers claim their customers put their bedding on high-price cribs, whose thick corner posts require longer ties. We think that's a weak excuse—14″ is too long, even for cribs with the thickest posts. If you buy bumpers with ties that exceed nine inches, we recommend cutting off any excess length after you install them on the crib.

A related issue to the length of the ties is their location: some companies have ties ONLY on the top of bumpers. In this case, we've had many reports of babies scooting under the bumper and getting trapped (see our Email from the Real World on the previous page). If you fall in love with bedding that has ties only on the top, consider adding additional ties yourself. Just be sure to sew them on securely. A chart later in this chapter will compare the tie length and location among different brands.

As we noted earlier, make sure the bumpers fit well with no overlapping and no gaps at the ends. And avoid bumpers that are too thick and fluffy. They pose the same kind of risk as pillows. Look for firm, flat bumpers. Before you decide to use bumpers, read the section earlier in this chapter for the latest research on bumper safety.

As a side note, Canada heavily discourages the use of bumpers. A Canadian reader emailed: "We are not supposed to use bumper pads due to the increased risk of SIDS. No one I know uses them. When the health nurse comes to visit you in the home, she checks to make sure you don't have bumper pads." You can find out more on Canada's crib bedding recommendations on the Health Canada web site: www.hc-sc.gc.ca.

◆ *If you use bumpers, remove them immediately when your child starts to pull up or stand.* Why? Bumpers make a great step stool that lets baby launch herself out of the crib! This usually happens around six months of age.

◆ *Never use an electric blanket/heating pad.* Babies can dangerously overheat, plus any moisture, such as urine, can cause electric shock.

◆ *Avoid blankets that use nylon thread.* Nylon thread melts in the dryer and then breaks. These loose threads can wrap around your baby's neck, fingers or toes or break off and become a choking hazard. Cotton thread is best.

◆ *Watch out for chenille.* It's popularity has waned in recent years, but we still see some chenille accents on baby bedding and in luxe items like blankets. The problem? With some chenille, you can actually pull out fibers from the fabric backing with little effort. And that might be a choking hazard for baby.

◆ *Travel.* Now that you've created a safe nursery at home, what about when you travel? Parents who frequently travel are often frustrated by hotels, which not only have unsafe cribs (see previous chapter) but also questionable sheets. At one hotel, we were given queen size bed sheets to use in a crib! A solution: one reader recommended bringing a crib sheet from home. That way you know your baby will be safe and sound. (When you reserve a crib at a hotel, find out if it is a portable crib or a standard crib so you know what size sheet to bring.) Check with some of our recommended safety sheet manufacturers listed earlier in this chapter and consider buying their port-a-crib versions for travel.

◆ *All linens should have a tag* indicating the manufacturer's name and address. That's the only way you would know if the linens were recalled. You can also contact the manufacturer if you have a problem or question. While this is the law, some stores may sell discounted or imported linens that do not have tags. Our advice: DON'T buy them.

Smart Shopper Tips

Smart Shopper Tip
Pillow Talk: Looking for Mr. Good Bedding
   "Cartoons or more cartoons—that seems to be the basic choice in crib bedding at our local baby store. Since it all looks alike, is the pattern the only difference?"
   There's more to it than that. And buying baby bedding isn't the same as purchasing linens for your own bed—you'll be washing these pieces much more frequently, so they must be made to withstand the extra abuse. Since baby bedding is more than just another set of sheets, here are nine quality points to look for:

1 **RUFFLES SHOULD BE FOLDED OVER FOR DOUBLE THICKNESS— INSTEAD OF A SINGLE THICKNESS RUFFLE WITH HEMMED EDGE.** Double ruffles hold up better in the wash.

2 **COLORED DESIGNS ON THE BEDDING SHOULD BE PRINTED OR WOVEN INTO THE FABRIC, NOT STAMPED** (like you'd see on a screen-printed t-shirt). Stamped designs on sheets can fade with only a few washings. The problem: the pieces you wash less frequently (like dust ruffles and bumpers) will fade at different rates, spoiling the coordinated look you paid big money for. In case you're wondering how to determine whether the design is printed rather than stamped, printed fabrics have color that goes through the fabric to the other side. Stamped patterns are merely applied onto the top of the fabric.

3 **MAKE SURE THE PIECES ARE SEWN WITH COTTON/POLY THREAD, NOT NYLON.** While nylon threads can be a safety

problem (see earlier discussion), they also are a quality issue. When nylon threads break in a dryer, the filling in bumpers and quilts can bunch up.

4 **CHECK FOR TIGHT, SMOOTH STITCHING ON APPLIQUÉS.** If you can see the edge of the fabric through the appliqué thread, the work is too skimpy. Poor quality appliqués will probably unravel after only a few washings. We've seen some appliqués that were actually fraying in the store—check before you buy.

5 **HIGH THREAD-COUNT SHEETS.** Unlike adult linens, many packages of baby bedding do not list the thread count. But, if you can count the individual threads when you hold a sheet up to the light, you know the thread count is too low. High thread-count sheets (200 threads per inch or more) are preferred since they are softer and smoother against baby's skin, last longer and wear better. Unfortunately, most affordable baby bedding has low thread counts (80 to 120 thread counts are common)—traditionally, it's the design (not the quality) that sells bedding in the baby biz. But there is good news on this front: several upstart brands (reviewed later) actually tout high thread counts for their sheets.

Another telltale sign of a quality sheet is the elastic. The best sheets will have elastic that encircles the entire sheet.

6 **FEEL THE FILLING IN THE BUMPER PADS.** If the filling feels gritty, it's not the best quality. Look for bumpers that are firm when you squeeze them (Dacron-brand filling is a good bet).

7 **THE TIES THAT ATTACH THE BUMPER TO THE CRIB SHOULD BE BETWEEN SEVEN AND NINE INCHES IN LENGTH.** Another tip: make sure the bumper has ties on both the top and bottom and are securely sewn. For more discussion on this issue, see "Safe & Sound" earlier in this chapter.

8 **THE DUST RUFFLE PLATFORM SHOULD BE OF GOOD QUALITY FABRIC**—or else it will tear. Longer, full ruffles are more preferable to shorter ones. As a side note, the dust ruffle is sometimes referred to as a crib skirt.

9 **REMEMBER THAT CRIB SHEETS COME IN DIFFERENT SIZES**— bassinet/cradle, portable crib, and full-size crib. Always use the correct size sheet.

CHAPTER 3: BEDDING   **129**

Wastes of Money/Worthless Items

"I have a very limited budget for bedding, and I want to avoid spending money on stuff that I won't need. What are some items I should stay away from?"

It may be tempting to buy every matching bedding accessory. And you'll get a lot of sales pressure at some stores to go for the entire "coordinated" look. Yet many baby-bedding items are a complete waste of money—here's our list of the worst offenders:

1 **DIAPER STACKER.** This is basically a bag (in coordinating fabric, of course) used to store diapers—you hang it on the side of a changing table. Apparently, bedding makers must think stacking diapers on the shelf of your changing table or storing them in a drawer is a major etiquette breach. Take my word for it: babies are not worried if their diapers are out in plain sight. Save the $30 to $50 that bedding makers charge for diaper stackers and stack your own. By the way, we've even seen $100 diaper stackers—these typically coordinate with equally expensive bedding sets.

2 **PILLOWS.** Some bedding sets still include pillows or pillowcases. Are the bedding designers nuts, or what? Haven't they heard that it's dangerous to put your baby to sleep on a pillow? What a terrible safety hazard, not to mention a waste of your money. We don't even think a decorative pillow is a good idea—what if another caretaker puts your baby to sleep in her crib and forgets to remove the decorative pillow? Forget the pillow and save $30 to $50.

3 **SETS OF LINENS.** Sets may include useless or under-used items like those listed above as well as dust ruffles and window valances. Another problem: sets are often a mixed bag when it comes to quality. Some items are good, while others are lacking. A better bet: many baby stores or even chains now sell bedding items a la carte. That way you can pick and choose just the items you need—at a substantial savings over the all-inclusive sets.

4 **CANOPIES.** Parents-to-be of girls are often pressured to buy frilly accessories like canopies. The pitch is a feminine look for her nursery. Don't buy into it. The whole set-up for a canopy is going to be more expensive (you'll need a special crib, etc.)—it'll set you back $60 to $175 for the linens alone. And enclosing your baby's crib in a canopy won't do much for her visual stimulation or health (canopies are dust collectors).

5 **ALL-WHITE LINENS**. If you think of babies as pristine and unspoiled, you've never had to change a poopy diaper or clean spit-up from the front of an outfit. We're amazed that anyone would consider all-white bedding, since keeping it clean will probably be a full-time job. Stick with colors, preferably bright ones. If you buy all-white linens and then have to go back to buy colored ones, you'll be out another $100 to $200. (Yes, some folks argue that white linens are easier to bleach clean, but extensive bleaching over time can yellow fabric.)

6 **HEADBOARD BUMPERS**. Whatever side you come down on in the bumper debate (some parents think they're a good safety item; we don't recommend them because of the suffocation risk), there is a certain bumper that definitely is a waste of money—the headboard bumper. This bumper is designed to cover the entire headboard of the crib. Regular bumpers are just a six to nine-inch tall strip of padding that goes around the crib . . . and that's all you need if you want bumpers. Headboard bumpers are more expensive than regular bumpers, running another $25 to $100, depending on the maker. Skip them and save the money.

7 **SLEEP POSITIONERS**. These $10 to $20 blocks of foam are supposed to hold baby in place on their back, but they are unnecessary. The current recommendation is to put baby to sleep on her back . . . and nearly all infants will stay right there through out the night until they reach six months of age (when they are strong enough to roll over on their own). Positioners are a waste of money.

Money Saving Secrets

1 **IF YOU'RE ON A TIGHT BUDGET, GO FOR A GOOD BLANKET AND A NICE SET OF HIGH THREAD-COUNT SHEETS.** What does that cost? A good cotton or fleece blanket runs $10 to $15, while a fitted sheet runs $10 to $20. Forget all the fancy items like embroidered comforters, duvet covers, window valances, diaper stackers and dust ruffles. After all, your baby won't care if she doesn't have perfectly coordinated accessories.

2 **DON'T BUY A QUILT.** Sure, they look pretty, but do you really need one? Go for a nice cotton blanket, instead—and save the $50 to $200. Better yet, hint to your friends that you'd like receiving blankets as shower gifts.

3 **SKIP EXPENSIVE WALL HANGINGS—DO DECOR ON THE CHEAP.**
One of the best new products we've discovered for this is Wall Nutz (wallnutz.com). These innovative iron-on transfers let you create paint-by-number masterpieces in your baby's room. Paint a six-by-eight foot mural or just add some decorative borders. Cost: $40 (plus the cost of paints).

A new idea: wall decals. These creative graphic "stickers" can be positioned and repositioned, removed and replaced. Choose from animals, flowers, abstract designs and more. Two companies offer these cool décor options: *Blik Re-Stik* (whatisblik.com; eight decals for $20) and *WallPops!* (wall-pops.com; $12 to $24). While these are reusable, take care when removing them as they may fray along the edges. *Wallies* (wallies.com) are similar to decals except that they are pre-pasted shapes. You wet the backing and stick wherever you like. FYI: Some Wallies aren't reusable—you have to strip them off like wallpaper. A pack of 20 small flowers runs about $13. They now offer bigger, mural size Wallies for about $40.

Of course, crafts stores are another great source for do-it-yourself inspiration. Michaels Arts & Crafts (800-MICHAELS; web: michaels.com) sells stencils and supplies for nursery decor.

4 **MAKE YOUR OWN SHEETS, DUST RUFFLES AND OTHER LINEN ITEMS.** Think that's too complicated? A mom in Georgia called in this great tip on curtain valances—she bought an extra dust ruffle, sewed a curtain valance from the material and saved $70. All you need to do is remove the ruffle from the fabric platform and sew a pocket along one edge. I managed to do this simple procedure on my sewing machine without killing myself, so it's quite possible you could do it too. A good place for inspiration is your local fabric store—most carry pattern books like Butterick, Simplicity and McCalls, all of which have baby bedding patterns that are under $10. There are other pattern books you can purchase that specialize in baby quilts—some of these books also have patterns for other linen items like bumpers. Even if you buy good quality fabric at $10 per yard, your total savings will be 75% or more compared to "premade" items.

5 **SHOP AT OUTLETS.** Scattered across the country, we found a few outlets that discount linens. Among the better ones Garnet Hill and Carousel (also known as babybeddingonline.com)—see their reviews in this chapter. Another reader praised the Pottery Barn Outlet. They have six locations at the time of this writing. The discounts start at 50% on bedding and furniture from their catalog and retail stores. Other outlets: Carter's, Baby Gap, and Nautica. Check Outlet Bound (www.outletbound.com) for locations.

6 **DON'T PICK AN OBSCURE BEDDING THEME.** Sure, that "Exploding Kiwi Fruit" bedding is cute, but where will you find any matching accessories to decorate your baby's room? Chances are they'll only be available "exclusively" from the bedding's manufacturer—at exclusively high prices. A better bet is to choose a more common theme with lots of accessories (wall decor, lamps, rugs, etc.). The more plentiful the options, the lower the prices. Winnie the Pooh is a good example, although you'll find quite a few accessories for other common themes like Noah's Ark, teddy bears, rocking horses, etc.

7 **GO FOR SOLID COLOR SHEETS AND USE THEMED ACCESSORIES.** Just because you want to have a Disney-themed nursery doesn't mean you have to buy Disney *bedding*. A great money-saving strategy: use low-cost solid color sheets, blankets and other linen items in the crib. Get these in colors that match/compliment theme accessories like a lamp, clock, poster, wallpaper, rugs, etc. (Hint: register for these items, which make nice shower gifts). You still have the Disney look, but without the hefty tag for Disney bedding. Many of the mail-order catalogs we review later in this chapter are excellent sources for affordable, solid-color bedding. Another bonus: solid color sheets/linens from the catalogs we recommend are often much higher quality (yet at a lower price) than theme bedding.

8 **SURF THE WEB.** Earlier in this chapter, we discussed the best web sites for baby bedding deals. Later in this chapter you'll find additional mail-order sources for bedding on a budget. The savings can be as much as 50% off retail prices. Even simple items like crib sheets can be affordably mail ordered.

The Name Game: Reviews of Selected Manufacturers

Here are reviews of some of the brand names you'll encounter on your shopping adventures for baby bedding. Note: we include the phone numbers, web sites and addresses of each manufacturer—this is so you can find a local dealer near you (most do not sell directly to the public, nor send catalogs to consumers). We rated the companies on overall quality, price, and creativity, based on an evaluation of sample items we viewed at retail stores. We'd love to hear from you—tell us what you think about different brands and how they held up in the real world by emailing authors@BabyBargains.com.

The Ratings

A **EXCELLENT**—*our top pick!*

B **GOOD**— *above average quality, prices, and creativity.*

C **FAIR**—*could stand some improvement.*

D **POOR**—*yuck! could stand some major improvement.*

Amy Coe *For a dealer near you, call (203) 227-9900. Web: amy-coe.com.* Designer Amy Coe turned her hobby of collecting vintage fabrics into a business when she launched her eponymous baby bedding line in 1993. The result is a linen collection with a flair for nostalgia: Coe takes fabrics that replicate patterns from the 1930's to the 1950's and crafts a full line of bedding items.

Coe has two lines: one for specialty stores (Amy Coe) and another for Babies R Us (amy coe). While both play off the same design inspiration, as you might expect, there are some major differences. The Amy Coe in specialty stores features more sumptuous fabrics and (no surprise) bigger price tags. The more expensive line runs $400 to $500 for a set and accessories are pricey too (chenille throws for $115, velour blankets for $80 and so on). Quality is high and most fabrics are all cotton.

At Babies R US, you get a more muted version of Amy's designs, although the fabric is still all-cotton and the sheets boast 200-thread counts and all-around elastic. Four-piece sets run just $170, extra sheets are $13 to $15 and velour blankets $22. How's the quality? Reviews are overall positive. Most parents noted that the sheets washed well and one mom thought the quality was as good as Pottery Barn Kids. ***Rating (Babies R Us version): B+ (Specialty stores version): A-***

BB Basics Online *Web: buybuybaby.com.* Private-label brands of bedding are commonplace among the chains. Target has it's Circo brand while Babies R Us has Koala Baby . . . so it's no surprise that Buy Buy Baby now has its own line, BB Basics (or BB Couture). This label offer three types of sheets: 200 and 400-thread count cotton percale and 180-thread count cotton jersey knit. Sheets are available in three sizes: crib, play yard and bassinet. All sheets have all around elastic and prices are rather affordable. A percale crib sheet is $8 each for 200-thread count and $15 for 400-thread count. Knit crib sheets are $9. So how's the quality? Feedback is mixed. One mom complained that the fit was too loose and the stitching came undone after the first washing. But another reader praised the knit sheets: "they're pretty good quality for the dollar." ***Rating: B-***

Baby Bedding Online *See Carousel.*

Baby Basics *See Carter's.*

Baby Gap *Web: babygap.com.* Baby Gap has five bedding collections as well as a la carte options. New this year: all crib sheets are organic cotton and 200 thread count with elastic all around. Bedding sets are priced at $250 for a four-piece set, although we saw some sets on sale for 25% off. Sheets run $19 while fleece blankets are $30. Reader feedback on this brand has been positive. One parent noted that the sheets were super soft and their fit "awesome." **Rating: A-**

Baby Martex *CoCaLo distributes this brand. See their review later in this section.*

BananaFish *For a dealer near you, call (800) 899-8689 or (818) 727-1645. Web: bananafishinc.com.* "Sophisticated" and "tailored" is how we'd describe this California-based bedding maker. BananaFish's emphasis is on all-cotton fabric with adult-like finishes (such as pique) and muted color palettes. New this year, they've added a new line (MiGi) and acquired the license to the Skip Hop brand. The Skip Hop bedding is ultra modern with a polkadot or lollipop floral design; MiGi is more of a minimalist aesthetic.

How's the quality? Overall, excellent, say readers. FYI: Part of BananaFish's line is made in China; the balance is still produced in the U.S. Fair warning: it's not cheap—prices range from $240 to $600 at retail for a four-piece set. The exception: the MiGi line starts at $160. **Rating: B**

Affordable Artwork

Framed artwork for baby's room has to be very expensive, right? Nope, not if you buy a framed print from **Creative Images** (call 800-784-5415 or 904-825-6700 for a store near you; web: www.crimages.com). This Florida-based company sells prints, growth charts, wall hangings and more at very affordable prices—just $30 to $100. Each print is mounted on wood and laminated (no glass frame) so baby can enjoy it at eye-level (just sponge it off if it gets dirty). Best of all, there are hundreds of images in any theme to choose from: Pooh, bunnies, Noah's Ark, plus other collections of animals, sports and pastels. Check out their web site for samples.

Beautiful Baby *For a dealer near you, call (903) 295-2229. Web: bbaby.com.* Next to Nava's (reviewed later), this is probably the most over-the-top bedding in the market today. There's nothing subtle about Beautiful Baby's linens, which feature satin, lace and tulle. The bumpers are so huge they're like king-size pillows sewn together (okay, that's an exaggeration, but trust us, they are BIG), but they do have the most bumper ties of any manufacturer (26). Good news, though, you can customize the bumper thickness. In fact, you can custom change just about anything in this line. Another plus: their sheets all have safety straps, an added feature we applaud. With over 1300 fabrics to choose from, Beautiful Baby says it takes four to six weeks to ship most orders. Prices are high: expect to shell out $400 to $800 for a three-piece set. Most but not all fabrics are 100% cotton. Bottom line: this line isn't cheap, but if you're looking for bedding you can customize with an over-the-top style, this is the brand for you. **Rating: B**

Bedtime Originals *Lambs & Ivy make this brand. See their review later in this section.*

Brandee Danielle *For a dealer near you, call (800) 720-5656, (714) 957-1240. Web: brandeedanielle.com.* Brandee Danielle has simplified its line in the past year—gone are the former sub-collections (BD Baby, Poshy Baby and Brandee B); now it all is Brandee Danielle.

The brand's web site highlights a few modern looks, but most of the collection is separated by gender. Also new: you can buy direct from the company, with a free shipping option for orders over $99. Prices overall run $100 to $300 for a four-piece set.

Designs are typically simple looks with some embroidery and appliqué. Sheets are 100% cotton. Overall, parents are pleased with the quality of embroidery and appliqué. One reader described the embroidery as "prettier in real-life than in the photos on the web site." And the machine washable pieces seem to stand up well to repeated washings.

So what's the problem? Some readers have complained that sets have elastic only on the corners of sheets. Some items (namely, quilts) are spot-clean only while other items are hand-wash only. And some sets have ties on the top of bumpers but only bottom ties on the corners.

Brandee Danielle seems to have corrected some of their customer service problems of the past. Parents report the company is more responsive to complaints. They also now offer free fabric samples so you don't have to visit a retailer to see the quality and colors. We'll boost their rating a bit this time to reflect the improvements. **Rating: B-**

bedding

LICENSE TRANSLATOR

Who makes what brand of bedding

One of the hottest trends in crib bedding is licensed characters—just about every cartoon character imaginable has been licensed to one of the big bedding makers for use in juvenile bedding. But how can tell you tell who makes what? Here is a list of popular licensed characters and their bedding makers:

LICENSE	SEE BEDDING MAKER
BABY BLASS	QUILTEX
BABY LOONEY TUNES	SPRINGS
BABY MARTEX	COCALO
CARE BARES	BABY BOOM
DISNEY BABY	CROWN CRAFTS
DORA THE EXPLORER	BABY BOOM
EDDIE BAUER	CROWN CRAFTS
HELLO KITTY	LAMBS & IVY
HOLLY HOBBIE BABY	CROWN CRAFTS
J. GARCIA	QUILTEX
KELLY B RIGHTSELL DESIGNS	CROWN CRAFTS
LAURA ASHLEY	SUMERSAULT
NAUTICAKIDS	CROWN CRAFTS
NOJO	CROWN CRAFTS
PRECIOUS MOMENTS	CROWN CRAFTS
SESAME STREET	CROWN CRAFTS
SNOOPY	LAMBS & IVY
THOMAS AND FRIENDS	BABY BOOM
WAMSUTTA	SPRINGS
WAVERLY BABY	CROWN CRAFTS
WINNIE THE POOH	CROWN CRAFTS

California Kids For a dealer near you, call (800) 548-5214, (650) 637-9054. Web: calkids.com. One of our favorite bedding lines, California Kids specializes in bright and upbeat looks. In the past few years, they've added more girl-oriented themes as well as a line of coordinating lamps. The quality is excellent; everything is 100% cotton.

California Kids used to make all their bedding in (you guessed it) California. Today, about 5% of the total line (or six collections out of 80) are made in India. Prices run $250 to $550 for a three-piece set (the average is about $300). Most of California Kids past sets included four-pieces, but more now come only as a three-piece with the bumper, sheet and quilt. It's a clever way to raise prices since they don't include that fourth piece, but charge the same price. With an amazing array of options (60+ patterns at last count), California Kids is sold in specialty stores and upper-end department stores. Available accessories include wall hangings, lampshades and fabric by the yard. Their web site has improved somewhat with more information on accessories and options. But we'd like to see a bit more info about fabrics. *Rating: A*

Carousel/Baby Bedding Online Web: *babybedding.com.* Carousel/ Baby Bedding Online use to sell its line of bedding exclusively through retail stores at about $250 to $450 per set. Several years ago, however, they decided to change to an Internet-only sales model online at BabyBeddingOnline.com. Selling directly to consumers resulted in lower prices—today their sets run $150 to $350. Can't beat those prices for an all cotton, 200+ thread count bedding line (with elastic all around). And best of all, Carousel doesn't do this half way. The web site offers free fabric swatches and other goodies. Looking for quality portable crib sheets or matching cradle sheets? How about rocking chair pads and high chair pads? They've got them. Lastly, Baby Bedding has an online outlet store with the same great deals (up to 75% off) as their old physical outlet in Atlanta, but you don't have to live near Atlanta to get them.

What do parents think about Carousel? Universally parents praise Carousel's great prices and quality. One mom noted that not only were the prices great, but even after repeated washing the crib set "still looks new!" Overall, we recommend Carousel—good designs, great quality and affordable prices. *Rating: A*

Celebrations Call (310) 532-2499 for a dealer near you. Web: *baby-celebrations.com.* Celebrations specializes in feminine, sophisticated looks—patchwork motifs, eyelet laces, lovely embroidery and layered dust ruffles. The all-cotton linens range from $335 to $500. Quality is excellent; we noticed the bumpers sported ties on the top and bottom (16 total). Most fabrics are all cotton. New this year, Celebrations has added a sub-line called Baby Brooklyn. The company refers to this line as "more affordable"—but the prices ($256 to $380) aren't exactly a steal. *Rating: B+*

Circo See Target

Classic Pooh *See Crown Craft*

CoCaLo *Call (714) 434-7200 for a dealer near you. Web: coca-lo.com.* You could say baby bedding runs in the family at CoCaLo. Owner Renee Pepys Lowe's mother (Shirley) founded Nojo in 1970 and Renee worked at the family business before it was sold to Crown Crafts. Since then, Renee has branched out on her own, launching the CoCaLo line in 1999 (the name comes from the first two letters of Renee's daughters, Courtenay and Catherine Lowe).

CoCaLo originally included four lines: Osh Kosh, Baby Martex, an eponymous collection and Kimberly Grant (reviewed later), which is now made by Crown Crafts. The company is dropping the Osh Kosh license and de-emphasizing Baby Martex in order to concentrate on their in-house lines Cocalo Baby, Cocalo Naturals and Cocalo Couture. The lowest priced (and largest) group is Cocalo Baby, ranging from $180 to $210 for a four-piece set. Unfortunately, not all of this collection is all-cotton, although the sheets are. CoCaLo Couture is a bit more upscale with prices in the $250 to $350 range. This line is more tailored with sophisticated color pallets. The Naturals line was not available for review as of press time, so no pricing info yet. Cocalo tells us this new collection will feature organically grown cotton.

Overall, CoCaLo is a good value, with decent quality for the price. ***Rating: B+***

Company Kids *Call (800) 323-8000 for a catalog or to place an order. Web: companykids.com.* A subsidiary of the Company Store, Company Kids offers a selection of sheets and blankets plus a crib comforter cover in a variety of patterns and solids. Everything is priced a la carte. Sheets run $14 each while comforter covers are about $60 each. You have a choice of either down comforters or down free for 460 each. Not a bad deal at all for 100% cotton percale fabrics.

While the prices are decent, we've received complaints about Company Kids' poor customer service and quality. Backordered items are a common gripe. Another reader was frustrated when her sheets ripped after several washings while another complained that the sheet shrunk after washing. Overall, quality reviews were mixed—some fans say the brand is good, comparable to Pottery Barn Kids. Others are less generous.

Given the mixed reviews, we'll tick down the Company Kids rating this time out. While the web site is easy to navigate and the prices are decent, quality and customer woes drag down this brand. ***Rating: B-***

Cotton Tale *Call (800) 628-2621 or (714) 435-9558 for a dealer near you. Web: cottontaledesigns.com.* Cotton Tale has been one of our favorite bedding lines for a long time and for good reason: originality and quality. There are no licensed cartoon characters or trendy fabrics like chenille here. Instead, you'll see beautiful soft pastels, whimsical animal prints and adorable appliqués. Best of all, Cotton Tale's prices are affordable—most range from $200 to $300 for a four piece set. Most of the fabrics are 100% cotton, although some trim may be a blend.

Cotton Tale's sub-line N. Selby Designs line kicks up the sophistication a notch with more luxurious looks. You'll find more bold colors as well as fun accents like tiers of ruffles and lots of polka dots. A four-piece set of N. Selby Designs sells for $250 to $500.

All in all, we'll give Cotton Tale a big thumbs up for the innovative designs and beautiful patterns. ***Rating: A***

CozyWedge *Made by Inspired Ideas. Web: cozywedge.com.* As we've discussed earlier in this chapter, traditional crib bumpers are controversial. But if you've got an active baby who keeps bonking his head against the crib, is there a safe solution? The CozyWedge is an option: this bumper is made from very firm foam with a removable, washable cotton slipcover. Unlike other bumpers that are soft and pose a suffocation risk if baby gets trapped up against or below the bumper, the CozyWedge is hard foam . . . sort of like a swimming noodle. Only a few inches tall, babies also can't use it to boost themselves out of the crib once they start standing. So the CozyWedge provides protection for babies without the concerns of traditional crib bumpers. The CozyWedge costs $60 (about the same as a regular bumper) and the organic cotton cover comes in eight solid colors. Bottom line: you don't need to rush out and get this product—but it is a future solution if you have a little head banger in the house. ***Rating: A***

CribShield & Breathable Bumper *Made by Trend-Lab. Call 866-873-6352 for a dealer near you. Web: cribshield.com.* Here's a mom-invented product that is a simple solution to babies who get their arms or legs caught in the crib spindles: a "breathable" bumper made of mesh that Velcros on to the crib. Unlike other thicker bumpers, this one allows for airflow and baby can't get trapped between it and the mattress. And it's affordable: $30 to $35 and available in stores or online (Wal-Mart.com carries it). The company makes two versions of the product: the Breathable Bumper (one style for beds with slats all around and one for cribs with solid ends) and the CribShield. The latter covers the entire crib from bottom rail to top rail, while the bumper is just a bumper (11″ deep). Detractors of these products say they don't fit all cribs (given the wide variety of models out there, that isn't a big surprise) and older babies can rip them off the crib. The web site addresses the fit problem with a Crib Fit Guide. And the manufacturer recommends using these products only until your baby reaches nine months of age. Bottom line: we think this a good solution if you have a baby who keeps getting stuck. Like the CozyWedge (reviewed above), there's no need to get this product before baby is born. Only a small percentage of babies will get their arms or legs caught in a crib's spindles. But if that is you, this might be a solution. ***Rating: A***

Crown Crafts *Call (800) 421-0526 or (714) 895-9200 for a dealer near you. Web: www.ccipinc.com or www.nojo.com.* Baby bedding behemoth Crown Crafts seems to have snapped up every possible character license you can imagine. Their current line up includes Eddie Bauer Baby, Disney Baby, Classic Pooh, Kelly B. Rightsell, Precious Moments, Holly Hobby, Nojo, Waverly, Nautica Kids, Sesame Street, Fisher Price, Little Bedding and Kimberly Grant

Tips on green bedding

Like many organic products today, there is no standard for organic baby bedding. This leaves it up to bedding manufacturers to determine for themselves what's organic. So, let's review some terms you'll see.

Organic cotton simply means cotton that's been grown with a minimum amount of toxic pesticides or fertilizers. That's right, there is no guarantee that organic cotton is completely pesticide- and fertilizer- free. But it is as close as you can get!

So, you want to go for organic cotton sheets—but what about the sheet's color? Since conventional sheets are dyed with synthetic chemicals, can an organic sheet be colored anything than the natural shade of cotton (that is, an off-white)?

Turns out, the answer is yes. Organic cotton can be grown in a few colors. Yes, that's right, just like you can buy naturally orange or purple cauliflower, you can buy colored cotton. Three colors are available: pink, light brown and green. Nature's Purest by Summer Infant Products is one bedding option that uses grown-in colors (SummerInfant.com, click on Organic; a four-piece set for $230).

Another solution: vegetable dyes. Kids Line (Kidsline.com; $160 for six-piece set) and Gap Baby (GapBaby.com; $19 for an organic crib sheet) sell baby bedding made of low-impact vegetable dyed cotton.

(reviewed separately). Crown Craft also makes Koala Baby sold exclusively in Babies R Us and reviewed separately later. Depending on the brand, sets run $70 to $300 and are sold at chain stores like Target, Babies R Us, Baby Depot and other chains.

For the most part, Crown Craft makes basic bedding sold in chain stores . . . and the quality of those lines is typically equal to the price. For the best overall quality for the dollar, we like the mid-priced lines like the Nojo or Eddie Bauer lines ($100 to $270). Most of Crown Crafts' sheets are 100% cotton, which is better than many of their competitors. Bottom line: you get what you pay for with this manufacturer. Stick with the better quality sets (Nojo, Eddie Bauer) and avoid the cheap-o character-theme sets (Disney Baby). **Rating: C+**

Disney Baby See Crown Craft

Dwell Web: dwellshop.com. When modern style cribs first emerged as a new style aesthetic, there weren't many bedding options that matched the look. Dwell Studio aimed to fill that niche, albeit at a rather high price.

Made of 210 to 320-thread count and 100% cotton, Dwell offers a simple, yet sophisticated look. Example: Motif is a '60's flashback with aqua, green and yellow hues. The price: $384 (we saw it for $320 online) for a set that includes a fitted sheet, padded bumper, crib skirt and blanket (items are also available a la carte). Dwell even makes oval bedding to fit the Stokke crib. We should note that the prices on Dwell's web site are significantly higher than you can find from other online resellers.

Parent reviews have been positive on this brand—readers laud the softness and fit. One summed it up as "expensive, but worth it."

What about Dwell Studio for Target bedding? It features 100% cotton, 200-thread count sheets and is priced at $80 for a three-piece set. That's the same look at a fraction of the regular Dwell price. The sheets were surprisingly soft with all around elastic; bumpers have top and bottom ties. Parent feedback has been positive. **Rating: B+ (for both the regular line and the Target line)**

Eddie Bauer. See Crown Craft

Fleece Baby Web: fleecebaby.com. So, you live in a part of the country where winter is colder than (fill in your own punch line here)? Given all the warnings about soft bedding and heavy quilts, how do you keep baby warm during those cold winter months? One solution is fleece baby sheets. Fleece Baby makes a wide variety of crib sheets, blankets, play yard sheets and more . . . all of 100% polar fleece. Crib sheets run $25 and are sold online at BabyCenter.com and various other sites. We had a reader road test the play yard version of the Fleece Baby sheet ($22) and she gave it two thumbs up. The only concern: after washing, the sheet lost a bit of its softness, but still overall it was a winner. One tip: use unscented dryer sheets on this bedding to retain softness. *Rating: A*

Garnet Hill *Call (800) 622-6212 for a catalog or to place an order. Web: garnethill.com.* Garnet Hill sells a small selection of all-cotton percale and flannel crib bedding. In addition a few themed sets, the catalog sells basics like the Dot-To-Dot sheets in flannel ($15) and percale $18). Quality is high: all sheets are 200-thread count with elastic all around. *Rating: B*

George *See Wal-Mart.*

Gerber *For a dealer near you, call (800) 4GERBER Web: gerber.com.* While Gerber offers some cute patterns in their bedding line and they're available almost everywhere, the bedding's quality leaves much to be desired. One reader emailed us this typical story: "I bought several of the Gerber Everyday Basics knit sheets. They fit my 5" thick Sealy mattress well when I bought them, they were super soft, and had elastic all the way around for safety. But then . . . I washed them on the delicate cycle in cold water and dried on low/delicate as instructed in the package. They shrunk so much I couldn't even get them on the mattress anymore!". We can't recommend this brand. *Rating: D*

Glenna Jean *(800) 446-6018 or (804) 561-0687. Web: glennajean.com.* Glenna Jean has notched 30 years in the bedding biz by adapting to the times—their current line features dressed-up designs with velvets, brocades, and bright color palettes.

Overall, Glenna Jean sets start at $225 and go up to $450. Most of the designs are 100% cotton with the exception of some of the trim. Our only caution: Glenna Jean's bumpers have top and bottom ties at the corners—the center of the bumper has top ties only. As you know, we aren't big fans of bumpers—but if you use one, make sure entire bumper has ties on the top and bottom. Glenna Jean's bumpers fail that test.

New this year from Glenna Jean: Sweet Potato, a lower-priced line (starting at $200) with a more mod look. Yes, this departs a bit from Glenna Jean's traditional look, but we liked the geometric designs and brighter colors—and the prices are certainly more reasonable than other mod bedding brands.

FYI: Glenna Jean is one of the last bedding manufacturers who makes nearly all its bedding in the US. *Rating: B+*

Graham Kracker *Call (800) 489-2820 for a catalog or to place an order. Web: grahamkracker.com.* This mail order company specializes in custom bedding. You can mix and match your own selections from nearly 100 different fabrics or you can provide your own fabric. The price? A whopping $495 for a five-piece set, which includes a headboard bumper and baby pillow (don't use this in the crib, please!). Everything is 100% cotton and there are all sorts of matching accessories. Most of the fabrics are bright, cheerful designs, but not too cutesy. Shipping time is two to three weeks. **Rating: B**

Holly Hobby *See Crown Craft.*

Hoohobbers *For a dealer near you, call (773) 890-1466. Web: hoohobbers.com.* The quality of this brand is impressive—all of the bumpers are made duvet-style with zippers. The result: it's easy to remove the covers for washing. Hoohobbers' 19 designs tend to have interesting color combinations in both bright jewel tones and pastels. Prices for all their four-piece collections are $380; that's expensive, but everything is 100% cotton and well constructed (the sheets feature all-around elastic, and the bumpers have top and bottom ties, for example). You can see and purchase any of their patterns on their web site. All bedding is made at Hoohobbers' Chicago factory (they have a factory outlet store in Chicago too). FYI: Hoohobbers' bassinets and Moses baskets come in coordinating fabrics as well. In fact, the company makes a wide range of accessories including furniture, bouncer seat covers and more. **Rating: B+**

Jessica McClintock *For a dealer near you, call (719) 947- 1170. Web: PacificCoastHomeFurnishings.com* Remember those lacy Jessica McClintock homecoming and prom dresses? Or her old-fashioned wedding gowns? We do (maybe we're showing our age), so it's not surprising that Jessica McClintock is bringing that lacy, Victorian look to crib bedding. Made by Pacific Coast Home Furnishings (which licensed the name), the designs are 100% cotton with satin, silk, and plush accents. Good news: even with the fancy fabrics and lace, the whole line is machine-washable and they have top and bottom ties on the bumpers. Prices range from $250 to $400 for a five-piece set. New this year, a lower priced collection will run $120 to $180. **Rating: B-**

JoJo Designs *Web: BeyondBedding.com.* JoJo Designs offers a rather amazing bedding deal: a nine-piece bedding set for only $110 to $200. What does that include? You get a comforter, bumper (ties on top only), sheet, skirt, two valances, diaper stacker, toy bag and throw pillow (never use this in your crib!). The 100% cotton sets come in all the popular themes plus some new modern styles this year. JoJo is not available in specialty stores or chain stores—only online at their website, Amazon.com and a few other e-tailers. By the way, all the bedding is dry clean only, although readers tell us they have washed and hung it dry with good results.

But how's the quality? Well, you're not getting top of the line fabric and designs here, but readers tell us the sets hold up well in the wash; they don't fade or fall apart. For a low price line, the quality here beats Gerber or Crown Craft's low price line. ***Rating: B***

Kelly B. Rightsell *See Crown Craft*

Kids Line *151 W. 135th St., Los Angeles, CA 90061. Call (310) 660-0110 for a dealer near you. Web: Kidslineinc.com.* Kids Line has been on a roll in recent years, designing sets with luxury touches while keeping prices affordable ($100 to $200 for a six-piece set). New in the past year they've added organic cotton sets that use eco-friendly vegetable dyes. Check out Bunney Meadows, for example with a mod brown and green motif including a cute green bunny silhouette. Price: $180 for a six piece set.

Kids Line has expanded their accessories line to include bath coordinates as well as blankets, wall hangings, lamps and more. And that seems to have resonated with our readers: parents tell us they love all the accessory options with Kids Line's patterns. How's the quality? Well, reviews are mixed. Some items are cotton-poly blends and parents have reported that shrinkage is sometimes a problem. On the plus side, colors hold up well in the wash, Kids Line has ties on both the tops and bottoms of bumpers and their sheets have elastic all around.

FYI: Kids Line also makes the Tiddliwinks line of bedding available mostly at Target. This lower-end line runs $70 to $90 for a three-piece set. While it has 100% cotton sheets with all around elastic, we found the overall quality of Tiddliwinks to be disappointing. And we suspect these sheets will shrink, since the washing instructions are cold-water only. Our advice: avoid Tiddliwinks.

Overall it is a mixed review for Kids Line—nice designs and great accessories . . . but a bit iffy on the quality (especially Tiddliwinks, the Target-exclusive). The Carter's separates are a better bet, quality wise. ***Rating: B***

Kimberly Grant *Call (714) 546-4411 for a dealer near you. Web: kimberlygrant.com.* If you're looking for bedding designs that are a bit lower key and not too cutesy, Kimberly Grant is a great option. Now produced by Crown Crafts (see review above), Grant continues to create sophisticated looks (floral prints, plaids) using luxe fabrics (velvets, satins, cotton), all in a warm palette. Prices run $150 to $400 for a four-piece set. Overall, we like the quality. ***Rating: A-***

Koala Baby *Available exclusively at Babies R Us.* Koala Baby is Babies R Us' attempt at establishing an in-house brand of bedding (Koala Baby is actually made by Crown Craft). The is sold a la carte. Bumpers cost $18 to $25 and bed skirts are $18, a two pack of sheets or blanket is $17. That's affordable. So what's the downside? Quality, for one. As one reader put it, "This brand is TERRIBLE! I washed the fitted sheet before putting it on my crib mattress and it shrunk about 6" in length! I wouldn't recommend these sheets to anyone." Another reader knocked the Koala Baby dust ruffle she bought, which was very poor quality and didn't wash well. While the concept is admirable (private-label bedding at affordable prices), Babies R Us has a loser with their Koala Baby line. ***Rating: D+***

Lambs & Ivy *For a dealer near you, call (800) 345-2627 or (310) 839-5155. Web: lambsivy.com.* Barbara Lainken and Cathy Ravdin founded this LA-based bedding company in 1979. Their specialty: cutesy baby bedding that is sold in discount and mass market stores (you'll also see them sold in JCPenney's catalog and on many web sites). This year they've added some whimsical looks along with vintage prints and licensed characters including Snoopy and Hello Kitty. Quality of the Snoopy line is actually good. Instead of using stamp printing, Lambs & Ivy uses photo-quality heat transfer technology. This is a clever way of achieving a nicer look without big cost (you have to see the bedding in person to note the difference). Prices are still reasonable at $150 to $285 for a six-piece set. Bedtime Originals, a sub-line of Lambs & Ivy, is lower in price (around $60 to $85 for a three piece set) and quality. We'd rank the overall quality of Lambs & Ivy a bit ahead of other mass-market bedding brands. Yes, some of the fabrics are blends (50-50 cotton/poly), but the stitching and construction is a cut above. ***Rating: B+***

Land of Nod *Call (800) 933-9904 for a catalog or to place an order. Web: landofnod.com.* This stunning catalog (owned by Crate & Barrel) features attractive layouts of baby's and kid's rooms, replete with cute linens and accessories. Even if you don't buy anything, the Land of Nod is a great place to get decorating ideas.

Land of Nod's in-house bedding is sold a la carte. Some designs only have a quilt, bed skirt and bumpers available. The fabric is 100% cotton, 200-thread count. And bumpers have ties on the top and bottom. A four-piece set runs $200 to $236, while a single sheet can cost $19. New this year: bedding sets from Skip Hop

$220 for a three-piece set (see Bananafish for review of these designs). We loved the color palettes, which ranged from patchwork denim to bright pastels. Check out the whimsical lamps and other accessories. **Rating: A-**

Lands End *Call (800) 345-3696 for a catalog or to place an order. Web: landsend.com.* Lands' End changes their options so frequently, it's tough to nail them down for you. While they've always made great quality sheets with all-around elastic, availability of specific colors and fabrics can vary. This year, they are showing seven crib bedding sets, ranging from a 220 count solid colored cotton percale set to a couple knit sets to an elegant matelasse grouping. They even have flannel sets. Priced a la carte, you'll find sheets for $20 to $30, bumpers from $50 to $100 and coverlets at $40 to $70. Not cheap, but they often have sales. (Blankets are a big seller at Lands End and come in a variety of options: fleece, cotton, lace and cashmere. Parent comments are universally positive on Lands End crib bedding: "incredibly soft, yet durable," "soft fabric, washes great" and "minimal shrinkage."

While the offerings change each season, Land's End designs have tended toward simple prints and pastels, with no cartoons or appliqués to clutter up the basic look. Another bonus: Lands' End web site has fantastic overstock deals, posted twice weekly. **Rating: A**

Laura Ashley *This is a licensed line of Sumersault. See their review later in this section.*

Little Bedding *See Crown Crafts.*

Little House *Web: HouseInc.com.* Designed by Annette Tatum, Little House bedding is part of the shabby chic trend, sold exclusively in baby boutiques and their own company stores in Santa Monica, CA. At $360 for a three-piece set, Little House is not as expensive as some designer brands. The fabric is 100% cotton poplin in a wide array of pastel mix and match patterns. Quality is good. **Rating: B**

Luv Stuff *Call (903) 450-1300 for a dealer near you. Web: luvstuffbaby.com.* Texas-based Luv Stuff's claim to fame is their unique, hand-trimmed wall hangings, which match their custom bedding. You can mix and match to your heart's content (all items are sold a la carte). The quality is high: the company's exclusive fabrics are mostly 100% cotton with high-thread count, plus all their collections are made in-house in Texas and they have ties both top and bottom and elastic around the whole sheet. As you might expect, however, all this quality isn't free—a four-piece ensemble (sheet, comforter, bumper, dust ruffle) runs $550 to $750. And Luv Stuff's bumpers aren't very consumer friendly—they are surface clean (with a mild detergent) or dry-clean only. Despite this, we liked the brand's unique and bold styles. This bedding is a tour de force of color and contrast. **Rating: B**

Maddie Boo *Web: maddieboobedding.com.* You can just imagine seeing Maddie Boo baby bedding in an *Architectural Digest* spread. And we will give this line bonus points for sophistication—some of their designs would look great on adult beds! Of course, you'll be paying *Architectural Digest* prices. Four-piece sets run $350 to $750.

Made in Houston, Texas, the sets are 100% cotton with high thread counts, and the accent fabrics include silk and linen. Ties are both top and bottom and sheets have all around elastic.

Surprisingly, Maddie Boo bedding can be found on sites like Amazon as well as in specialty stores. That doesn't mean you'll be able to find it at a discount, however, but the wide distribution is a nice surprise. Quality of the samples we viewed was high; but the prices drag down their overall rating. **Rating: B**

Mr. Bobbles Blankets *Web: MrBobblesBlankets.com.* We love the Graco Pak N Play and other playpens for their convenience . . . with one exception: those darn cheap sheets! Active babies easily pull off the sheets that come with most playpens and the thin, low-thread count cotton makes them a cold place for baby during winter months. To the rescue comes Mr. Bobbles Blankets, which besides its namesake blankets, also makes a No-Slip Play Yard Sheet for $20. We had a reader give this product a test-run and the verdict was positive. Made of 100% cotton flannel, the "very soft" sheets come in "cute fabrics" and "held up well after several washings," said our reviewer. And true to its claims, the sheet does not slip off the mattress—it is designed like a pillow sham so it doesn't easily pull off the corners. **Rating: A**

My Baby Sam *Web: MyBabySam.com.* This bedding line is an off-shoot of a baby gift dot-com (NewArrivalsInc.com) and is widely available, both in specialty stores and online at sites like Target.com, BabiesRUs.com and JCPenney. Three piece sets run about $150 while four-piece sets go up to $240, a decent value for an all-cotton set (bumpers have ties on the top and bottom). But . . . we noticed the set is cold-water wash only, which is not a good sign when it comes to shrinkage.

My Baby Sam's specialty store offerings are more elaborate looks than you see in discount stores and start at around $240 for a four-piece set. Quality is good—readers praise the soft fabrics and over-all construction. ***Rating: B+***

NauticaKids *See Crown Craft*

Nava's Designs *For a dealer near you, call (818) 988-9050. Web: navasdesigns.com.* Okay, Warren Buffet is your uncle . . . and he wants to give you a gift of baby bedding. Who you gonna call? Try Nava's, the most over-the-top bedding on the market today. The fabrics in this line are simply amazing—damask, silk dupioni, matte lasse and so on. Owner Nava Shoham has been designing nurseries since 1986 and her credits include numerous celebrities such as (and we are not making this up) Slash's nursery. Yes, that Slash. Fill in your own joke here. So, how much does this cost? Are you sitting down? Nava's bedding runs $800 to $1100 for a set. And, yes, some of the fabrics have to be dry-cleaned. But seriously, we dare you to find more sumptuous bedding on the market. We're impressed with Nava. . . making it over 20 years in this biz by selling these linens at these prices, well, that's an achievement in its own right. New this year: Nava is selling direct through her own online store. ***Rating: B***

NoJo *See Crown Craft.*

N. Selby Designs *See Cotton Tale.*

Nurseryworks *For a dealer near you, call (626)676-6287; web: NurseryWorks.net.* Modern crib maker Nurseryworks has a matching bedding line that features nine sets of 100% cotton bedding. Price are $330 to $400 for a six-piece set—pricey, yes, but not as high as some modernist bedding makers. Nurseryworks' design inspiration is the "use of uncommon visual vocabularies derived from common objects, nature and everyday things." Translation: interesting graphics of flowers, macaroni and, oddly, sugar cubes. Bumpers have top and bottom ties and sheets have elastic all around. Quality of this bedding is above average. ***Rating: B+***

OshKosh B'Gosh *See CoCaLo.*

Patchkraft *This crib brand is reviewed on our free web site, www.BabyBargains.com (click on Bonus Material).*

Picci *Imported by Mutsy. Web: picci.com.* Picci is a high-end bedding line imported from Italy. Here's an oddity of the baby market here: many European-made products are a big hit in the U.S. (Baby Bjorn, Perego strollers), but bedding is not among them. Why? Part of the blame is that what sells well in Europe for nurseries (garish colors, frilly treatments like canopies) just doesn't translate well across the Atlantic. To solve that dilemma, Picci researched American design sensibilities and went with a more toned down look. The result is impressive. In a market stuffed with cheaply made imports from Asia, Picci actually pulls off a tasteful line with a high-end feel. The only caveat is the prices: $280 to $400 for a set. Their new "Contemporary" line (mod florals and circles) runs $300 to $350. And they've added Natura organic bedding to the line—100% organic with the stuffing derived from corn. A three-piece set runs $450. That contrasts with their silk groups which can top $900. Expensive, but we give Picci bonus points for creativity and quality. **Rating: B+**

Pine Creek *Call (503) 266-6275 for a dealer near you. Web: pinecreekbedding.com.* Oregon-based Pine Creek Bedding has come back to their signature look with more flannel options, while offering sets with a new vintage feel. Look for old-fashioned graphics and soft colors. All the fabrics are 100% cotton and bumpers are slip covered with ties both top and bottom. Considering the quality, we thought Pine Creek's prices were pricey at $280 to $450 for a four-piece set. Pine Creek also sells accessories like lampshades and curtain valances, plus fabric is available by the yard. **Rating: A-**

Pitter Patter *For a dealer near you, call 505-751-9067 Web: pitterpattercollections.com.* Taos, New Mexico-based Pitter Patter has a unique take on baby bedding. Independent artists design their Hawaiian themed nursery linens, so many of the patterns and designs are one-of-a-kind. We loved the embroidered accents and playful prints. And yes, you can get a fabric-covered surfboard as an accessory. Quality is high, but the price is as well—this might be a suggestion for grandma to buy. A four-piece set runs $398 to $580 and features all cotton and some linen-cotton blends. New this year, a couple sets made with organic bamboo jersey knit ($580) as well as a set with organic soy sheets. All of Pitter Patter's bumpers include zip off slipcovers for easy cleaning with top and bottom ties; the sheets have all0around elastic. All in all, we liked Pitter Patter. It's refreshing to see a newcomer like Pitter Patter offer a different twist on baby bedding. **Rating: B+**

Pooh *Classic Pooh/Disney Pooh bedding are made by Crown Craft.*

Pottery Barn Kids *Call (800) 430-7373 for a catalog or to place an order. Web: potterybarnkids.com.* No catalog has shaken up the baby bedding and décor business in recent years like the

Pottery Barn Kids (PBK) catalog. Their cheerful baby bedding, whimsical accessories and furniture blew past competitors. PBK isn't cutesy-babyish or overly adult. It's playful, fun and bright. And hot. We get more questions about this catalog than any other.

So let's answer a few of those questions. PBK's bedding is 100% cotton, 200-thread count. The sheets have 10" corner pockets . . . and they *used* to have elastic that went all the way around the edge. We're disappointed to say that they now only make their crib sheets with elastic on the ends. And that elastic is the source of frustration among some parents we talked to—one PBK customer said she had to exchange several sheets after the elastic popped off or simply wore out after only one washing. By the way, PBK's spin on why they don't have elastic all the way around is that it is "for safety purposes." We'd bet that your child will find it harder to pull off a sheet with all around elastic than one with elastic only on the ends. So which one is really safer?

Several readers have also complained about the bumpers, which are knocked as "thin and insubstantial." One reader wrote saying "they are very thin and my child can get his arms and legs out of the slats of the crib because the bumpers smush down so easily!" Another reader complained that the ties kept pulling off her bumper. On the plus side, recent parent feedback has consistently praised the softness of PBK sheets. Their "chamois" sheets ($29; polyester fleece) have also come in for great praise. Moms say PBK's fleece sheets stay softer than Fleece Baby's sheets.

New this year: organic crib bedding. The catch—it isn't very organic. Some sheets note they have 5% organic cotton fabric. Wowie. They do offer a quilt and bumper that are 100% organic cotton for $100 to $110.

Prices for quilts range from $80 to $110, bumper sets are $70 to $100 and sheets are $16 to $19. While the prices are affordable, the nagging quality issues give us pause in recommending PBK's crib bedding. On the plus side, frequent sales make more expensive items like lamps and rugs even more affordable. The best deal: PBK's outlet stores. One reader saw sheets on sale for $8, duvet covers for $15 and even a crib for $175 at the outlet (see earlier in the chapter for locations). What really seems to be PBK's strong suit is accessories. The catalog is stuffed with so many rugs, lamps, storage options and toys, you can shop one place for a complete look.

So, it is a mixed bag for PBK: kudos to this retailer for shaking up the staid baby bedding biz. But poor quality gives us pause in recommending this brand, unless you get an unbelievable deal at their outlet store. *Rating:* **C+**

Precious Moments See Crown Craft

Quiltex *For a dealer near you, call (800) 237-3636 or (212) 594-2205. Web: quiltex.com.* Quiltex is famous for their licensed bedding items, including Hello Kitty, Precious Moments and Thomas the Tank Engine. Style-wise, we'd put Quiltex into the "cutesy, baby-ish" category—the groupings are heavy on the pastel colors and frilly ruffles. Unfortunately, most of the line is blends (50/50 cotton-poly fabric). The quality of the Quiltex designs is middle-of-the-road: some appliqué work leaves a bit to be desired, while other designs are merely stamped on the fabric. Their prices ($60 to $150 for a three-piece set) are a bit more reasonable. **Rating: C-**

Restoration Hardware *Call (800) 762-1751 for a catalog or to place an order. Web: rhbabyandchild.com.* Tipped corduroy, matelasse, sateen, jersey, damask. Right off the bat, you know Restoration Hardware's Baby & Child bedding selection is a bit different.

Take the "European tipped corduroy bumper and Italian medallion sheeting" set, for example. This set sports pin-wale chocolate corduroy with contrasting piping (blue, pink or mint). The matching sheet is 210-thread count organic cotton . . . and is actually made in Italy. The price: $140 for the bumper and $40 for the sheet. A matching bed skirt runs $70, as does the duvet. Hence, a four-piece set will set you back $316. Other sets feature 600-thread count Italian sateen sheets for $60. One has to wonder: does baby really need to sleep on 600-thread count sheets?

All the bedding collections are sold a la carte (and only online). Most have the same color accents (brown plus pink, green or blue). Hence, the limited color palette is one of the main downsides to Restoration Hardware. Yet, overall, we think the quality is impressive (all the sheets have elastic all around and ties on bumpers are top and bottom) so we'll give Restoration Hardware's Baby & Child bedding our recommendation. **Rating: A-**

Red Calliope *See Crown Craft.*

Sesame Street *See Crown Craft*

Skip Hop *See Bananafish*

Sleeping Partners *Call (212) 254-1515 for a dealer near you. Web: sleepingpartners.com.* Sleeping Partners' mojo is embroidered bedding sets. This year, they've lowered prices and added an organic line.

Tadpoles is Sleeping Partners flagship line. We noticed a simple five-piece set was $115 to $250 online (Sleeping Partners is sold on sites like BabyUniverse.com and in some stores like Buy Buy Baby). Tadpole

Organics sets are made of organic cotton in brown, sage and pink. It's affordable too: only $170 for a four-piece set. The Tadpole Basics line (mostly solid colors) sells at Target for as little as $120 to $150 for five pieces. Both lines are all cotton, 200 thread count with top and bottom bumper ties. Overall, the line washes well. Another plus: we spied a 15% coupon on their web site. **Rating: B-**

Springs *Web: springs.com.* Springs Industries sells five different bedding lines, including Wamsutta and Little Tikes. At the high end, Wamsutta has two options (one for boys, the other for girls). With 230-thread count, 100% cotton sheets and elastic all around, Wamsutta offers decent quality for the dollar (a set runs $150). Springs other bedding options are less impressive, however: the Little Tikes line features cheap-o poly/cotton blends (but prices are only $60 for set).

Springs is sold in discounters like Wal-Mart. With the exception of the Wamsutta line, we found the overall quality disappointing. **Rating C-**

Sumersault *Call (800) 232-3006 or (201) 768-7890 for a dealer near you. Web: sumersault.com.* Veteran bedding designer Patti Sumergrade has an eye for beautiful fabrics—the results are Sumersault's whimsical bedding collection. We loved the plaids and patchwork, all done with a sophisticated spin. Compared to other lines, Sumersault leaves most of the cutesy touches to optional wall hangings. A four-piece set retails for $150 to $300. FYI: Sumersault also makes the Laura Ashley Mother and Child bedding collection. We like the touches of embroidery and a few mixed-texture sets, which were winners design-wise. Their bumpers have ties top and bottom. Overall, the quality of Sumersault is excellent. **Rating: A**

Sweet Kyla *Call 800-265-2229 for a dealer near you. Web: sweetkyla.com.* Canadian bedding maker Sweet Kyla has popped up stateside in USA Baby Stores among other outlets. We liked their take on crib bedding, which often uses mixed textures (a touch of faux suede, for example) and patchwork motifs. Most fabrics are all-cotton and customer service and delivery is excellent. Readers who have purchased this line have been impressed with the quality (bumper ties top and bottom, elastic all around sheets. One caveat: all items must be washed in cold water on delicate settings. Only the sheets can be dried in the dryer. Sets are around $220 to $330 or you can order pieces a la carte. You can also buy their fabric by the yard. One parent who bought this brand for her son's nursery raved about their excellent fabric, saying the sheets in particular were "very soft and cozy." New this year: organic bedding called

Wee Organics. Made of 100% cotton knit, this bedding uses low impact dies or sets are available in natural. Prices for a three-piece bumper-less set were unavailable at press time. ***Rating: A-***

Tadpole *See Sleeping Partners.*

Target *Web: target.com.* Target not only sells bedding lines like Dwell Studio for Target (see more in the Dwell review), Tadpole (by Sleeping Partners) and Tiddliwinks (by Kids Line), they even have their own in-house line of basics called Circo. Quality is so-so; Circo gets mixed reviews from our readers. Folks love the prices—$63 for a three-piece set—and the cute prints. Yes, it is all-cotton and the sheets feature elastic all around, but many readers complain of shrinkage and thin thread counts. Our advice: buy a sheet or two to test before investing much in this brand. ***Rating: B***

Tiddliwinks *See Kids Line.*

Trend Lab Baby *Web: trend-lab.com.* Trend Lab may sound more like a chemical beaker maker than a bedding designer, but this brand is a hit in the under-$150 crib bedding market. Sold on Target.com and other discounters, Trend Lab offered (mostly) 100% cotton bedding in the $50 to $150 range for a four-piece set. In the past year, however prices have started to creep closer to $200.

So what does Trend-Lab offer? You'll see design elements like textured fabric (waffle weave and knit jersey, for example) as well as attractive embroidery and appliqué. The look is reminiscent of Wendy Bellissimo. And parents love their sheets. As one parent noted on our web site: "the crib sheets from Trend Lab are big enough to fit the mattress perfectly . . . and the quality is high." The downside: some items may shrink (note the cold-water washing instructions) and a few items are poly/cotton blends. But for the price, parents tell us Trend Lab is still a decent value. ***Rating: B***

Wal-Mart *Web: Walmart.com.* Wal-Mart has been busy expanding it online baby bedding offerings, including several brands like Trend Lab and My Baby Sam (which are reviewed separately above).

George is Wal-Mart's in-house brand. Quality is rather impressive—100% cotton and 200-thread count sheets on a four-piece set we inspected. And the cost? A mere $80 per set. The bumpers do have top and bottom ties. Parent feedback is positive; we'll give the line a thumbs-up. ***Rating: A-***

Wamsutta *See Springs.*

Waverly *See Crown Crafts.*

Wendy Bellissimo Baby N Kids *(818) 348-3682. Web: wendy-bellissimo.com or babiesrus.com.* Once upon a time, hotshot designer Wendy Bellissimo hawked her pricey bedding at specialty boutiques. But in 2004, when she abruptly shifted gears to partner with Babies R Us. Now a BRU exclusive, Bellissimo has expanded her horizons beyond bedding to include all sorts of décor accessories, diaper bags, mobiles, even a crib by Bassett. As for the bedding, the designs look much the same as before: the typical Bellissimo look is a simple block pattern with a touch of embroidery or chenille. Prices seem to have come down into a more realistic price range than in the past. For example, a three-piece set will run under $100 while a four-piece set is in the $180 to $220 range. All the designs have ties both top and bottom. But while we thought the look was a notch above what is normally sold at BRU, we were unimpressed with the quality of the crib sheet, which seemed thin and low in thread count. And the reviews for this bedding have been similarly mixed to downright hostile (several folks knocked the bedding for low quality). One reader wrote that her set "was so carelessly pieced together that it is it unbelievable." Take your $200 and buy a better quality bedding set from any of the above-mentioned designers. **Rating: C-**

Whistle & Wink *Call (212) 279-1616 for a dealer near you. Web: whistleandwink.com.* One of your lovely authors' (Denise's, actually) mothers, Helen, is a big fan of needlework. From childhood, Denise has been leafing through needlecraft books and magazines. So when she opened the Whistle & Wink catalog (a new designer that debuted in 2007), her first thought was how the embroidery reminded her of those old patterns from childhood. Truly, the look of many of W & W's designs are vintage motifs you might have seen in the mid-20th century. Beyond embroidery, the line also showcases toile fabrics and fun accents like rick rack, tassels and more. The cost for this 100% cotton, 240 count bedding is $400 for a three-piece set (bumper, sheet and bed skirt). That's definitely pretty expensive. Reader feedback on this new line has been limited, but what we've heard so far is positive. **Rating: B+**

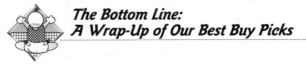

The Bottom Line:
A Wrap-Up of Our Best Buy Picks

For bedding, we think Cotton Tale, Amy Coe (at Target) and George (Wal-Mart) combine good quality at a low price. If you can afford to spend more, check out the offerings from Picci, Sumersault,

Continued on page 158

BEDDING RATINGS

Name	Rating	Cost
AMY COE	A-/B+	$ TO $$$
BABY GAP	A-	$$
BANANA FISH	B	$ TO $$$
BRANDEE DANIELLE	B-	$ TO $$
CALIFORNIA KIDS	A	$$ TO $$$
CAROUSEL	A	$ TO $$
CELEBRATIONS	B+	$$ TO $$$
COCALO	B+	$ TO $$
COMPANY KIDS	B-	$ TO $$$
COTTON TALE	A	$$ TO $$$
CROWN CRAFTS	C+	$ TO $$
DWELL	B+	$ TO $$
GERBER	D	$
GLENNA JEAN	B+	$$ TO $$$
HOOHOBBERS	B+	$$
JESSICA MCCLINTOCK	B-	$$
JOJO DESIGNS	B	$
KIDS LINE	B	$ TO $$
KIMBERLY GRANT	A-	$ TO $$
KOALA BABY	D+	$
LAMBS & IVY	B+	$ TO $$
LAND OF NOD	A-	$$
LANDS END	A	$
LUV STUFF	B	$$$
MADDIE BOO	B	$$ TO $$$
NAVA'S DESIGNS	B	$$$
NURSERYWORKS	B+	$$
PICCI	B+	$$
PINE CREEK	A-	$$ TO $$$
PITTER PATTER	B+	$$$
POTTERY BARN	C+	$$
QUILTEX	C-	$
RESTORATION HARDWARE	A-	$$ TO $$$
SLEEPING PARTNERS	B-	$ TO $$
SUMERSAULT	A	$ TO $$
SWEET KYLA	A-	$$
TARGET (CIRCO)	B	$
TREND LAB	B	$
WENDY BELLISSIMO	C-	$ TO $$
WHISTLE & WINK	B+	$$

KEY *See next page*

A quick look at some top crib bedding brands:

Fiber Content	Bumper Ties	Tie Length	Organic
100% cotton	Top/Bottom	10″	
100% cotton	Top/Bottom	*	◆
100% cotton	Top/Bottom	6″	
Mix	Top/Bottom	7″	
100% cotton	Top/Bottom	10″	
100% cotton	Top/Bottom	*	
100% cotton	Top/Bottom	9″	
Mix	Top/Bottom	6.5″	◆
100% cotton	Top/Bottom	*	
100% cotton	Top/Bottom	7.5″	
Mix	Varies	8″	
100% cotton	Top/Bottom	*	
Poly/Cotton	*	*	
Mix	** (see key)	10″	
100% cotton	Top/Bottom	6″	
100% cotton	Top/Bottom	*	
100% cotton	Top		
Mix	Top/Bottom	7″ to 9″	◆
100% cotton	Top/Bottom	6.5″	
100% cotton	Top	*	
Poly/cotton	Top	10″	
100% cotton	Top/Bottom	*	
100% cotton	Top/Bottom	*	
100% cotton	Top	11″	
100% cotton	Top/Bottom	*	
100% cotton	Top/Bottom	14″	
100% cotton	Top/Bottom	*	
100% cotton	Top/Bottom	*	◆
100% cotton	Top/Bottom	8″	
100% cotton	Top/Bottom	*	◆
100% cotton	Top/Bottom	*	◆
Poly/cotton	Top	7″	
100% cotton	Top/Bottom	*	◆
100% cotton	Top/Bottom	10″	
100% cotton	Top/Bottom	7″-9″	
100% cotton	Top/Bottom	9.5″	◆
100% cotton	Top	*	
Mix	Top/Bottom	*	
100% cotton	Top/Bottom	*	
100% cotton	Top/Bottom	*	

bedding

KEY

* N/A. In some cases, we didn't have this information by press time.
** Glenna Jean has bumpers with top and bottom ties only on the corners; the center section has top ties only.
COST: Cost of a four-piece set (comforter, sheet, dust ruffle/bed skirt, bumpers) $=under $200; $$=$200 to $400; $$$=over $400
FIBER CONTENT: Some lines have both all-cotton and poly/cotton blends—these are noted with the word "Mix."
BUMPER TIES: refers to the location of bumper ties, top and bottom or top only.
TIE LENGTHS: the length of the bumper ties; these are approximate estimates and may vary from style to style.
ORGANIC: Does the bedding maker offer any organic options? Yes/No. Note: this does not mean that ALL of the maker's offerings are organic.

---

and California Kids. And if money is no object, try Nava's.

Of course, there's no law that says you have to buy an entire bedding set for your nursery—we found that all baby really needs is a set of sheets and a good cotton blanket. Catalogs/web sites like Lands End and Baby Gap sell affordable (yet high-quality) basics like sheets ($19 to $32) and blankets ($15 to $30). Instead of spending $300 to $500 on bedding sets with ridiculous items like pillows and diaper stackers, use creative solutions (like wall decals) to decorate the nursery affordably and leave the crib simple.

And if you fall in love with a licensed cartoon character like Pooh, don't shell out $300 on a fancy bedding set. Instead, we recommend buying solid color sheets and accessorizing with affordable Pooh items like lamps, posters, rugs, etc.

Who's got the best deals on bedding? Web sites like BabyCatalog.com, BabySuperMall.com, and Overstock.com have the best bargains. If you're lucky to be near a manufacturer's outlet, search these stores for discontinued patterns.

Let's take a look at the savings:

Baby Gap cotton fitted sheets (two)	$38
Sleep sack (instead of a blanket)	$20
Miscellaneous (lamp, other decor)	$100
TOTAL	**$158**

In contrast, if you go for a designer brand and buy all those silly extras like diaper stackers, you could be out as much as $800 on bedding alone—add in wall paper, accessories like wall hangings, matching lamps and you'll be out $1100 or more. So, the total savings from following the tips in this chapter could be nearly $1000. Now that your baby's room is outfitted, what about the baby? Flip to the next chapter to get the lowdown on those little clothes.

CHAPTER 4

The Reality Layette:
Little Clothes for Little Prices

Inside this chapter

What the heck is a "Onesie"? How many clothes does your baby need? How come such little clothes have such big price tags? These and other mysteries are unraveled in this chapter as we take you on a guided tour of baby clothes land. We'll reveal our secret sources for finding name brand clothes at half off retail prices. Which brands are best? Check out our picks and our nine tips from smart shoppers on getting the best deals. Next, read about the many outlets for children's apparel that have been popping up all over the country. At the end of this chapter, we'll even show you how to save big bucks on diapers.

When Do You Need This Stuff?

◆ **Baby Clothing.** You'll need basic baby clothing like t-shirts and sleepers as soon as you're ready to leave the hospital. Depending on the weather, you may need a bunting (a snug-fitting, hooded sleeping bag of heavy material) at that time as well.

You'll probably want to start stocking up on baby clothing around the seventh month of your pregnancy—if you deliver early, you will need some basics. However, you may want to wait to do major shopping until after any baby showers to see what clothing your friends and family give as gifts.

Be sure to keep a running list of your acquisitions so you won't buy too much of one item. Thanks to gifts and our own buying, we had about two thousand teeny, side-snap shirts by the time our baby was born. In the end, our son didn't wear the shirts much (he grew out of the newborn sizes quickly and wasn't really wild about them anyway), and we ended up wasting money.

◆ **Diapers.** How many diapers do you need for starters? Are you sitting down? If you're going with disposables, we recommend 600 diapers for the first six weeks (about 14 diapers a day). Yes, that's six packages of 100 diapers each (purchase them in your eighth month of pregnancy, just in case Junior arrives early). You may think this is a lot, but believe us, we bought that much and we still had to do another diaper run by the time our son was a month old. Newborns go through many more diapers than older infants because they feed more frequently. Also, remember that as a new parent, you'll find yourself taking off diapers that turn out to be dry. Or worse, you may change a diaper three times in a row because baby wasn't really finished.

Now that you know how many diapers you need for the first six weeks, what sizes should you buy? We recommend 100 newborn-size diapers and 500 "size one" (or Step 1) diapers. This assumes an average-size baby (about seven pounds at birth). But remember to keep the receipts—if your baby is larger, you might have to exchange the newborns for size one's (and some of the one's for two's). Note for parents-to-be of multiples: your babies tend to be smaller at birth, so buy all newborn diapers to start. And double or triple our recommended quantity!

If you plan to use a diaper service to supply cloth diapers, sign up in your eighth month. Some diaper services will give you an initial batch of diapers (so you're ready when baby arrives) and then await your call to start up regular service. If you plan to wash your own cloth diapers, buy two to five dozen diapers about two months before your due date. You'll also probably want to buy diaper covers (six to ten) at that time. We'll discuss cloth diapers in depth later in this chapter.

Even if you plan to use disposable diapers, you should pick up one package of high-quality, flat-fold cloth diapers. Why? You'll need them as spit-up rags, spot cleaners and other assorted uses you'd never imagined before becoming a parent.

Sources

There are ten basic sources for baby clothing and diapers:

I **BABY SPECIALTY STORES.** Specialty stores typically carry 100% cotton, high-quality clothes, but you won't usually find them affordably priced. While you may find attractive dressy clothes, play clothes are typically a better deal elsewhere. Because the stores themselves are frequently small, selection is limited. On the upside, you can still find old-fashioned service at specialty stores—and that's helpful when buying items like shoes. In that case, the extra help with sizing may be worth the higher price.

As for diapers, you can forget about it—most specialty baby stores long ago ceded the diaper market to discounters and grocery stores (who sell disposables), as well as mail-order/online companies (who dominate the cloth diaper and supply business). Occasionally, we see specialty stores carry an offbeat product like Tushies, an eco-friendly disposable diaper. And some may have diaper covers, but the selection is typically limited.

2 DEPARTMENT STORES. Clothing is a department store's bread and butter, so it's not surprising to see many of these stores excel at merchandising baby clothes. Everyone from Sears to Nordstrom sells baby clothes and frequent sales often make the selection more affordable.

3 SPECIALTY CHAINS. Our readers love Old Navy (see money-saving tips section) and Gap Kids. Both sell 100% cotton, high-quality clothes that are stylish and durable. Not to mention their price adjustment policies—if you buy an item at Gap/Old Navy and it goes on sale within seven days, you get the new price. Old Navy's selection of baby clothes is somewhat limited compared to Gap Kids. Other chains to check out include Gymboree, and Children's Place. All are reviewed later in this chapter.

4 DISCOUNTERS. Wal-Mart, Target and K-Mart have moved aggressively into baby clothes in the last decade. Instead of cheap, polyester outfits that were once common at these stores, most discounters now emphasize 100% cotton clothing in fashionable styles.

Target has vastly expanded their baby clothes with their in-store brand, Cherokee. Not only have they expanded, but also the quality is terrific in most cases. We shop Target for all cotton play clothes and day care clothes. Durability is good.

Diapers are another discounter strong suit—you'll find both name brand and generic disposables at most stores; some even carry a selection of cloth diaper supplies like diaper covers (although they are the cheaper brands; see the diaper section later in this book for more details). Discounters seem to be locked into an endless price battle with warehouse clubs on baby items, so you can usually find deals.

REALITY
LAYETTE

5 **BABY SUPERSTORES.** Babies R Us, Baby Depot and Buy Buy Baby carry a decent selection of name-brand clothing at low prices. Most of the selection focuses on basics, however. You'll see more Carter's and Little Me than the fancy brands common at department stores. Over the years, Babies R Us has tried to upgrade their clothing options with a bit of embroidery here or an embellishment there. They've added sporty lines too like Nike track suits and more.

Diapers are a mixed bag at superstores. Babies R Us carries them, but Baby Depot doesn't. When you find them, though, the prices are comparable to discounters. We've seen diapers priced 20% to 30% lower at Babies R Us than grocery stores.

6 **WAREHOUSE CLUBS.** Members-only warehouse clubs like Sam's, Costco and BJ's sell diapers at rock-bottom prices. The selection is often hit-or-miss—sometimes you'll see brand names like Huggies and Pampers; other times it is an in-house brand. While you won't find the range of sizes that you'd see in grocery stores, the prices will be hard to beat. The downside? You have to buy them in "bulk," huge cases of multiple diaper packs that might require a forklift to get home.

Check out clubs' infant and toddler clothing as well. We'll talk later about some of the bargains we've found.

7 **WEB/MAIL-ORDER.** There are a zillion catalogs and web sites that offer clothing for infants. The choices can be quite overwhelming, and the prices can range from reasonable to ridiculous (don't worry, we'll give you the best bets). It's undeniably a great

CPSC Issues Thrift Shop Warning

Do second-hand stores sell dangerous goods? To answer that question, the Consumer Product Safety Commission randomly surveyed 301 thrift stores a few years ago, looking for recalled or banned products like clothing with drawstrings (an entanglement and strangulation hazard). The results: 51% of stores were selling clothing (mostly outerwear) with drawstrings at the waist or neck. This is particularly disturbing since 22 deaths and 48 non-fatal accidents since 1985 have been attributed to drawstrings. If you buy clothing at a consignment or thrift store or from a garage sale, be sure to avoid clothes with drawstrings. Another disturbing finding: about two-thirds of the stores surveyed had at least one recalled or banned product on the shelves.

way to shop when you have a newborn and just don't want to drag your baby out to the mall. Another strength of the web: cloth diapers and related supplies. Chains and specialty stores have abandoned these items, so mail order suppliers have picked up the slack. Check out "Do it By Mail" later in this chapter for the complete low-down on catalogs that sell clothing. Cloth diaper web sites are discussed later in the diaper section of the chapter.

8 **CONSIGNMENT OR THRIFT STORES.** You might think of these stores as dingy shops with musty smells—purveyors of old, used clothes that aren't in great shape. Think again—many consignment stores today are bright and attractive, with name brand clothes at a fraction of the retail price. Yes, the clothes have been worn before, but most stores only stock high-quality brands that are in excellent condition. And stores that specialize in children's apparel are popping up everywhere, from coast to coast. Later in this chapter, we'll tell you how to find a consignment store near you.

9 **GARAGE/YARD SALES.** Check out the box on the next page for tips on how to shop garage sales like the pros.

Baby Clothing

So you thought all the big-ticket items were taken care of when you bought the crib and other furniture? Ha! It's time to prepare for your baby's "layette," a French word that translated literally means "spending large sums of cash on baby clothes and other such items, as required by Federal Baby Law." But, of course, there are some creative (dare we say, sneaky?) ways of keeping your layette bills down.

At this point, you may be wondering just what does your baby need? Sure you've seen those cute ruffled dresses and sailor suits in department stores—but what does your baby *really* wear everyday?

Meet the layette, a collection of clothes and accessories that your baby will use daily. While your baby's birthday suit was free, outfitting him in something more "traditional" will cost some bucks. In fact, a recent study estimated that parents spend $13,000 on clothes for a child by the time he or she hits 18 years of age—and that sounds like a conservative estimate to us. Baby clothes translate into a $20 *billion* business for children's clothing retailers. Follow our tips, and we estimate that you'll save 20% or more on your baby's wardrobe.

Forget Me Not Kids

Web: ForgetMeNotKids.com

What it is: Designer brand baby and kid clothing.

What's cool: Selection here is amazing, including Baby Lulu and Jack & Lily as well as Tralala. And they've got shoes, baby blankets,

---

Garage & Yard Sales
Eight Tips to Get The Best Bargains

It's an American bargain institution—the garage sale.

Sure you can save money on baby clothes online or get a deal at a department store sale. But there's no comparing to the steals you can get at your neighbor's garage sale.

We love getting email from readers who've found great deals at garage sales. How about 25¢ onesies, a snowsuit for $1, barely used high chairs for $5? But getting the most out of garage sales requires some pre-planning. Here are the insider tips from our readers:

1 **CHECK THE NEWSPAPER/CRAIGSLIST FIRST.** Many folks advertise their garage sales a few days before the event—zero in on the ads/posts that mention kids/baby items to keep from wasting time on sales that won't be fruitful.

2 **GET A GOOD MAP OF THE AREA.** You've got to find obscure cul-de-sacs and hidden side streets.

3 **START EARLY.** The professional bargain hunters get going at the crack of dawn. If you wait until mid-day, all the good stuff will be gone. An even better bet: if you know the family, ask if you can drop by the day before the sale. That way you have a first shot before the competition arrives. One trick: if it's a neighbor, offer to help set-up for the sale. That's a great way to get those "early bird" deals.

4 **DO THE "BOX DIVE."** Many garage sale hosts will just dump kids clothes into a big box, all jumbled together in different sizes, styles, etc. Figuring out how to get the best picks while three other moms are digging through the same box is a challenge. The best advice: familiarize yourself with the better name brands in this chapter and then pluck out the best bets as fast as possible. Then evaluate the clothes away from the melee.

---

hair bows. They do seem to have a lot more for girls, but that's no surprise. The boys section included hats, dress up clothes and even boy themed gifts. It's definitely worth a look.

Needs work: Prices on new arrivals can be rather stiff: stick to the sale section with 75% off for the best deals.

Patsy Aiken

Web: patsyaiken.com or chezami.com
What it is: The only source now for this well-liked brand.

---

5 **CONCENTRATE ON "FAMILY AREAS."** A mom here in Colorado told us she found garage sales in Boulder (a college town) were mostly students getting rid of stereos, clothes and other junk. A better bet was nearby Louisville, a suburban bedroom community with lots of growing families.

6 **HAGGLE.** Prices on big-ticket items (that is, anything over $5) are usually negotiable. Another great tip we read in the newsletter *Cheapskate Monthly*—to test out products, carry a few "C" and "D" batteries with you to garage sales. Why? Most swings, bouncers and other gear use such batteries. Pop in your test batteries to make sure items are in good working order!

7 **SMALL BILLS.** Take small bills with you to sales—lots of $1's and a few $5's. Why? When negotiating over price, slowly counting out small bills makes the seller feel like they are getting more money. A wad of 20 $1's for a high chair feels like a more substantial offer than a $20 bill.

8 **DON'T BUY A USED CRIB OR CAR SEAT.** Old cribs may not meet current safety standards. It's also difficult to get replacement parts for obscure brands. Car seats are also a second-hand no-no—you can't be sure it wasn't in an accident, weakening its safety and effectiveness. And watch out for clothing with drawstrings, loose buttons or other safety hazards.

9 **BE CREATIVE.** See a great stroller but the fabric is dirty? And non-removable so you can't throw it in the washing machine? Take a cue from one dad we interviewed. He takes dirty second-hand strollers or high chairs to a car wash and blasts them with a high-pressure hose! Voila! Clean and useable items are the result. For a small investment, you can rehabilitate a dingy stroller into a showpiece.

What's cool: We've always loved Patsy Aiken's clothes, but their distribution used to be limited to fancy baby boutiques. The good news: their site now sells the entire collection online. The US-made clothes are all 100% cotton with amazing embroidery and appliqué. You'll find beautiful bright colors with fun accents. They've cut out a lot of the super dressy designs and seem to be concentrating on casual clothes. Prices average around $30 to $50 for the typical dress or overall. Not cheap but the quality is terrific. This is a great site for grandmas looking for a cute shower gift.

Since they've decided to discontinue selling their line in stores, they've added a new method of buying their designs. Called Chez Ami, it's a take off on the old Tupperware parties. You get a group of your friends together and have a Patsy Aiken clothing party. Check out the web site for more details.

Needs work: Patsy Aiken has upgraded their site so it's easier to use, but it seems like there are fewer infant sized clothes now.

One of a Kind Kid

Web: oneofakindkid.com, see Figure 1 on the next page.

What it is: Web site with extensive selection of high-quality kids clothes.

What's cool: This site specializes in the upper-end clothes you see in Nordstrom and Neiman Marcus. We saw brands like Mulberibush, Skivvydoodles and Lily Pulitzer among others. One of a Kind Kids has a great "sales rack" with clothes up to 70% off. New items appear weekly so check back frequently.

Needs work: Unfortunately, the site notes that many of the items on their site are "one of a kind." This means if you see something you like, you may have to order it on the spot. While the thumbnails of the clothes are expandable, their tiny size makes it hard to get a quick read on what's available.

TrendiTikes

Web: trenditikes.com

What it is: Trendy kids clothes as well as seasonal items.

What's cool: Looking for something really specific for your child? Here's a site that allows you to shop by designer, price, style and size. Organization seems to be their forte. We're impressed with the brands as well: Sara's Prints, Junk Food (love their t-shirts), Monkey Bar, Mim Pi and more. Diaper bags are a major focus. On our last visit, the site had a major sale on Petunia Pickle Bottom bags.

Needs work: Navigation is a bit confusing—clicking on "Trends" on the home page brings you to a blank page.

◆ *Other great sites. Preemie.com* (preemie.com) is a wonderful oasis for parents of preemies. You'll find items like hospital shirts, basics, sleepwear, caps and booties and diapers. Not to mention, they have a selection of diaries and books as well as calendars. If you've got a preemie, this is the site for you.

Kid Surplus (kidsurplus.com) is another discounter/closeout store. They've expanded their layette to include Zutano, Lil' Jellybean and Kushies. We also saw sleep sacks and Tic Tac Toe socks and slippers. The site is a bit of a jumble and you'll have to scroll through lots of different stuff, but the prices are great.

A reader recommended ***BargainChildrensClothing.com***, noting that it offers name brand kids clothes at 20 to 70% off. We checked it out and found clothes options from preemie sizes up to 16. Brands included Mulberribush, Flapdoodle and Calvin Klein.

We'd be remiss if we didn't also mention *eBay* (web: ebay.com) in this section. Their baby area is often stuffed with great deals on baby clothes. One tip: look for listings that say NWT—that's eBay-speak for "New With Tags." Obviously, these items are worth the most, yet often still sell for 50% off retail. Other eBay jargon to look for: NWOT (new without tags), NIB (new in box) and EUC (excellent used condition). EBay has just about everything it comes to baby clothes, from basic items to luxury goods.

A bit of eBay strategy: one of our readers recommended shopping at an expensive baby boutique in town, noting the high-end brands and looking for them when you shop eBay. In fact, when looking on eBay for samples to show off on NBC's Today Show, we did just that. We located a snazzy, high end Geisswein jacket on eBay for only $122. The regular retail on the jacket was $225 in boutiques. (Of course, we'd never spend $100+ on a winter jacket for our child, but if you have to have that Geisswein look, eBay is da bomb).

What Are You Buying?

Figuring out what your baby should wear is hardly intuitive to first-time parents. We had no earthly idea what types of (and how many) clothes a newborn needed, so we did what we normally do—we went to the bookstore to do research. We found three-dozen books on "childcare and parenting"—with three-dozen different lists of items that you *must* have for your baby and without which you're a very bad parent. Speaking of guilt, we also heard from relatives, who had their own opinions as to what was best for baby.

All of this begs the question: what do you *really* need? And how much? We learned that the answer to that last, age-old question was the age-old answer, "It depends." That's right, nobody really knows. In fact, we surveyed several department stores, interviewed dozens of parents, and consulted several "experts," only to find no consensus whatsoever. So, in order to better serve humanity, we have developed THE OFFICIAL FIELDS' LIST OF ALMOST EVERY ITEM YOU NEED FOR YOUR BABY IF YOU LIVE ON PLANET EARTH. We hope this clears up the confusion. (For those living on another planet, please consult our *Baby Bargains* edition for Mars and beyond).

Feel free to now ignore those lists of "suggested layette items" provided by retail stores. Many of the "suggestions" are self-serving, to say the least.

Of course, even when you decide what and how much to buy for your baby, you still need to know what *sizes* to buy. Fortunately, we have this covered, too. First, recognize that most baby clothes come in a range of sizes rather than one specific size ("newborn to 3 months" or "3-6 months"). For first time parents buying for a newborn, *we recommend you buy "3-6 month" sizes (instead of newborn sizes).* Why? That's because the average size newborn will grow out of "newborn" sizes way too fast. The exception to this rule: preemies and multiples, which also tend to be on the small side. (We'll list resources for preemie clothing shortly).

No matter how big or small your newborn, a smart piece of advice: keep all receipts and tags so you can exchange clothes for larger sizes—you may find you're into six-month sizes by the time your baby hits one month old! (Along the same lines, don't wash *all* those new baby clothes immediately. Wash just a few items for the initial few weeks. Keep all the other items in their original packaging to make returns easier).

Ever wonder how fast your baby will grow? *Babies double their birth weight by five months . . . and triple it by one year!* On average, babies grow ten inches in their first year of life. (Just an FYI: your child will average four inches of growth in her second year, then three inches a year from ages 3 to 5 and two inches a year until puberty.) Given those stats, you can understand why we don't recommend stocking up on "newborn" size clothes.

Also: remember, you can always buy more later if you need them. In fact, this is a good way to make use of those close friends and relatives who stop by and offer to "help" right after you've suffered through 36 hours of hard labor—send them to the store!

We should point out that this layette list is just to get you started. This supply should last for the first month or two of your baby's life. Also along these lines, we received a question from a mom-to-be who wondered, given these quantities, how often do we assume you'll do laundry. The answer is in the next box.

The "Baby Bargains" Layette

Let's talk quality when it comes to baby clothes.

First, you want clothing that doesn't shrink. Look at the washing instructions. "Cold water wash/low dryer setting" is your clue that this item has NOT been pre-shrunk. Also, do the instructions tell you to wash with "like colors?" This may be a clue that the color will run. Next check the detailing. Are the seams sewn straight? Are they reinforced, particularly on the diaper area?

Go online and check message boards for posts on different brands. On our boards (Babybargains.com), parents comment frequently on whether a brand shrinks, has plenty of diaper room, falls apart after a few washings, etc. Spend a little time online to get some intel on the best brands—and which ones to avoid.

Now, let's get to the list:

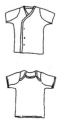

◆ *T-Shirts.* Oh sure, a t-shirt is a t-shirt, right? Not when it comes to baby t-shirts. These t-shirts could have side snaps, snaps at the crotch (also known as Onesies or creepers) or over-the-head openings. If you have a child who is allergic to metal snaps (they leave a red ring on their skin), you might want to consider over-the-head t-shirts.

E-MAIL FROM THE REAL WORLD
How Much Laundry Will I Do?

Anna B. of Brooklyn, NY had a good question about baby's layette and laundry:

"You have a list of clothes a new baby needs, but you don't say how often I would need to do laundry if I go with the list. I work full time and would like to have enough for a week. Is the list too short for me?"

Our answer: there is no answer. Factors such as whether you use cloth or disposable diapers (cloth can leak more; hence more laundry) and how much your baby spits up will greatly determine the laundry load. Another factor: breast versus bottle-feeding. Bottle-fed babies have fewer poops (and hence, less laundry from possible leaks). An "average" laundry cycle with our layette list would be every two to three days, assuming breast feeding, disposable diapers and an average amount of spit-up.

(FYI: While some folks refer to Onesies as a generic item, the term Onesie is a trademarked clothing item from Gerber.)

By the way, is a Onesie t-shirt an outfit or an undergarment? Answer: it's both. In the summer, you'll find Onesies with printed patterns that are intended as outfits. In the winter, most stores just sell white Onesies, intended as undergarments.

HOW MANY? T-shirts usually come in packs of three. Our recommendation is to buy two packages of three (or a total of six shirts) of the side-snap variety. We also suggest buying two packs of over-the-head t-shirts. This way, if your baby does have an allergy to the snaps, you have a backup. Later you'll find the snap-at-the-crouch t-shirts to be most convenient since they don't ride up under clothes.

◆ **Gowns**. These are one-piece gowns with elastic at the bottom. They are used as sleeping garments in most cases. (We'll discuss more pros/cons of gowns later in this chapter.)

HOW MANY? This is a toss-up. If you want to experiment, go for one or two of these items. If they work well, you can always go back and get more later.

◆ **Sleepers**. This is the real workhorse of your infant's wardrobe, since babies usually sleep most of the day in the first months. Also known as stretchies, sleepers are most commonly used as pajamas for infants. They have feet, are often made of flame-retardant polyester, and snap up the front. As a side note, we've seen an increase in the numbers of cotton sleepers in recent years. Another related item: cotton long johns for baby. These are similar to sleepers, but don't have feet (and hence, may necessitate the use of socks in winter months).

One parent emailed us asking if she was supposed to dress her baby in pants, shirts, etc. or if it was OK to keep her daughter in sleepers all day long. She noted the baby was quite comfortable and happy. Of course, you can use sleepers exclusively for the first few months. We certainly did. As we've said all along, a comfortable baby is a happy parent!

HOW MANY? Because of their heavy use, we recommend parents buy at least four to eight sleepers.

◆ **Blanket Sleepers.** These are heavyweight, footed one-piece garments made of polyester. Used often in winter, blanket sleepers usually have a zipper down the front. In recent years, we've also seen quite a few fleece blanket sleepers, their key advantage being a softer fabric and a resistance to pilling.

HOW MANY? If you live in a cold climate or your baby is born in the winter, you may want to purchase two to four of these items. As an alternative to buying blanket sleepers, you could put a t-shirt on underneath a sleeper or stretchie for extra warmth.

Another option is a new product: the sleep sack. A couple manufacturers, Halo (halosleep.com) and Kiddopatomus (kiddopatomus.com) market these, which take the place of a blanket (in a sense, these are wearable blankets). Typically made of light-weight fleece, they are worn over t-shirts or light sleepers (see picture of the Halo at right).

Finally, swaddling has seen a resurgence in popularity. Most folks use a receiving blanket, but if you have trouble doing the "burrito wrap" with a blanket, you can try the Swaddleaze Startlefree Sleeper (www.summerinfant.com). This $28 fleece sack has a swad-dling wing that wraps around your baby and Velcros in the back. And we just had to mention the Cozy Cocoon baby bunting (cozy-cocoon.com). What a simple and adorable concept. Basically a body sock made of organic cotton knit, this bunting simply rolls up over your baby. These would be especially cool for a preemie and are well priced starting at $20 each.

◆ *Coveralls*. One-piece play outfits, coveralls (also known as rompers) are usually cotton or cotton/poly blends. Small sizes (under 6 months) may have feet, while larger sizes don't.

HOW MANY? Since these are really play clothes and small infants don't do a lot of playing, we recommend you only buy two to four coveralls for babies less than four months of age. However, if your child will be going into daycare at an early age, you may need to start with four to six coveralls.

◆ *Booties/socks*. These are necessary for outfits that don't have feet (like gowns and coveralls). As your child gets older (at about six months), look for the kind of socks that have rubber skids on the bottom (they keep baby from slipping when learning to walk).

HOW MANY? Three to four pairs are all you'll need at first, since baby will probably be dressed in footed sleepers most of the time.

◆ *Sweaters*. HOW MANY? Most parents will find one sweater is plenty (they're nice for holiday picture sessions). Avoid all-white sweaters for obvious reasons!

♦ **Hats**. Believe it or not, you'll still want a light cap for your baby in the early months of life, even if you live in a hot climate. Babies lose a large amount of heat from their heads, so protecting them with a cap or bonnet is a good idea. And don't expect to go out for a walk in the park without the baby's sun hat either.

HOW MANY? A couple of hats would be a good idea—sun hats in summer, warmer caps for winter. We like the safari-style hats best (they have flaps to protect the ears and neck).

♦ **Snowsuit/bunting.** Similar to the type of fabric used for blanket sleepers, buntings also have hoods and covers for the hands. Most buntings are like a sack and don't have leg openings, while snowsuits do. Both versions usually have zippered fronts.

FYI: Snowsuits and buntings should NOT be worn by infants when they ride in a car seat. Why? Thick fabric on these items can compress in an accident, compromising the infant's safety in the seat. So how can you keep your baby warm in an infant car seat? Check out Chapter 7, Car seats—we'll discuss several car seat cover-ups/warmers that keep baby toasty without compromising the safety of the seat.

HOW MANY? Only buy one of these if you live in a climate where you need it. Even with a Colorado winter, we got away with layering clothes on our baby, then wrapping him in a blanket for the walk out to a warmed-up car. If you live in a city without a car, you might need two or three snowsuits for those stroller rides to the market.

♦ **Kimonos**. Just like the adult version. Some are zippered sacks with a hood and terry-cloth lining. You use them after a bath.

HOW MANY? Are you kidding? What a joke! These items are one of our "wastes of money." We recommend you pass on the kimonos and instead invest in good quality towels.

♦ **Saque Sets**. Two-piece outfits with a shirt and diaper cover.

HOW MANY? Forget buying these as well.

♦ **Bibs**. These come in two versions, believe it or not. The little, tiny bibs are for the baby that occasionally drools. The larger versions are used when you begin feeding her solid foods (at about six months). Don't expect to be able to use the drool bibs later for feedings, unless you plan to change her carrot-stained outfit frequently.

HOW MANY? Skip the drool bibs (we'll discuss why later in this chapter under Wastes of Money). When baby starts eating solid foods, you'll need at least three or four large bibs. One option: plastic bibs for feeding so you can just sponge them off after a meal.

 ◆ **Washcloths and Hooded Towels**. OK, so these aren't actually clothes, but baby washcloths and hooded towels are a necessity. Why? Because they are small and easier to use . . . plus they're softer than adult towels and washcloths.

HOW MANY? At first, you'll probably need only three sets of towels and washcloths (you get one of each per set). But as baby gets older and dirtier, invest in a few more washcloths to spot clean during the day.

◆ **Receiving Blankets**. You'll need these small, cotton blankets for all kinds of uses: to swaddle the baby, as a play quilt, or even for an extra layer of warmth on a cold day.

Clothing: What you need, when

If you're new to this baby thing, you may be wondering how to pair the right clothing with your baby's developmental stage (if you're back for another round, think of this as a refresher). Here's a little primer on ages and stages.

◆ **0-3 months:** Newborns aren't even lifting their heads and they aren't able to do much besides eat, sleep and poop. Stick with sleepers, sleep sacks, and nightgowns for these guys. They don't need overalls or shirts and pants. Look for items sized by weight if possible since 0-3 month sizes can be all over the board.

◆ **3-6 months:** By the end of this stage your little one will be rolling over, sitting up and sleeping somewhat less. Still need those sleepers, but you're probably going to expand the wardrobe to include a few more play clothes. Two new items you will need now: bibs and socks. Depending on your baby's growth, you may find that you're buying nine and 12-month sizes.

◆ **6-12 months:** Finally, your baby is crawling, standing, maybe even cruising. At the end of a year she's likely tried those first tentative steps! Play clothes are a layette mainstay during these months. You'll also need good, no-skid socks that stay on (or very flexible shoes). Again, you may find you're buying into the 18-month sizes.

How many? We believe you can never have too many of these blankets, but since you'll probably get a few as gifts, you'll only need to buy two or three yourself. A total of seven to eight is probably optimal.

What about the future? While our layette list only addresses clothes to buy for a newborn, you will want to plan for your child's future wardrobe as well. For the today's baby, clothes come in two categories: play clothes (to be used in daycare situations) and dress-up clothes. Later in this chapter, we'll discuss more money-saving tips and list several recommended brands of play and dress-up clothes.

More Money Buys You . . .

Even the biggest discounters now offer good quality clothing. But with more money you tend to get heavier weight cottons, nicer fasteners, better quality embellishments and more generous sizing. At some point, however, considering how fast your little one is growing, it's a waste to spend top dollar on baby clothes!

Safe & Sound

Should your baby's sleepwear (that is, the items he'll wear almost non-stop for the first several months of life) be flame retardant? What the heck does "flame retardant" mean anyway?

According to the Consumer Product Safety Commission (CPSC), items made of flame retardant fabric will not burn under a direct flame. Huh? Doesn't "flame retardant" mean it won't burn at all? No—that's a common myth among parents who think such clothes are a Superman-style second skin that will protect baby against any and all fire hazards.

Prior to 1996, the CPSC mandated that an item labeled as sleep-wear be made of "flame retardant fabric." More often than not, that meant polyester because the alternative (untreated cotton fabric) DOES burn under direct flame. While there are a few companies that make cotton sleepwear that is chemically treated to be fire retardant, the prices of such items were so high that the de facto standard for children's sleepwear for many years was polyester.

Then the government changed its mind. The CPSC noticed that many parents were rebelling against the rules and putting their babies in all-cotton items at bedtime. After an investigation, the CPSC revised the rules to more closely fit reality.

clothes

First, pajamas for babies nine months and under were totally exempt from the flame-retardant rules. Why? Since these babies aren't mobile, the odds they'll come in contact with a fire hazard that would catch their clothes on fire is slim. What if the whole house catches fire? Well, the smoke is much more dangerous than the flames—hence, a good smoke detector in the nursery and every other major room of your house is a much better investment than fire-retardant clothes.

What about sleepwear for older babies? Well, the government admits that "close-fitting" all-cotton items don't pose a risk either. Only flowing nightgowns or pajamas that are loose fitting must meet the flame retardant rules today.

If you still want to go with "flame retardant" baby items, there are a couple of options beyond plain polyester. Look for fleece PJ's—the Lands' End catalog now sells "Angel Fleece" pajamas for babies and young children ($26.50). The fabric, while polyester, is specially woven to breathe and be more comfortable. Another option: some catalogs listed later in this chapter sell cotton PJ's treated to be flame retardant.

Finally, one last myth to dispel on this topic: does washing flame-retardant clothing reduce its ability to retard flames? Nope—fabrics like polyester are *naturally* flame retardant (that is, there is no magic chemical they've been doused with that can wash out in the laundry). What about those expensive treated all-cotton clothes? We don't think that's a problem either.

There is one exception to the laundry rule: if you do choose to buy flame-retardant clothing, be sure to avoid washing such clothing in soap flakes. Soap flakes actually add a flammable chemical residue to clothes. And so do dryer sheets and liquid softeners. For more advice on washing baby clothes, see the discussion on page 177.

What about other safety hazards with children's clothing? Here are a few more to consider:

◆ **Check for loose threads.** These could become a choking hazard, or the threads could wrap around fingers or toes, cutting off circulation. Be careful about appliqués as well. "Heat-welded" plastic appliqués on clothes can come off and cause choking. Poorly sewn appliqués can also be a hazard.

◆ *Avoid outfits with easy-to-detach, decorative buttons or bows—these may also be a choking hazard.* If you have any doubts, cut the decorations off.

◆ *Watch out for drawstrings.* In recent years, most manufacturers have voluntarily eliminated such drawstrings. But if you get hand-me-downs or buy second-hand clothes, be sure to remove any strings.

One Size Does Not Fit All

A six month-size t-shirt is a six-month-size t-shirt, right? Wrong. For some reason, baby clothing companies have yet to synchronize their watches when it comes to sizes. Hence, a clothing item that says "six-month size" from one manufacturer can be just the same dimensions as a "twelve-month size" from another. All this begs the question: how can you avoid widespread confusion? First, open packages to check out actual dimensions. Take your baby along and hold items up to her to gauge whether they'd fit. Second, note whether items are pre-shrunk—you'll probably have to ask (if not, allow for shrinkage). Third, don't key on length from head to foot. Instead, focus on the length from neck to crotch—a common problem is items that seem roomy but are too tight in the crotch. Finally, forget age ranges and pay more attention to labels that specify an infant's size in weight and height, which are much more accurate. To show how widely sizing can vary, check out the following chart. We compared "six-month" t-shirts from six major clothing makers plus three popular catalogs, Hanna Andersson, Lands' End and Baby Gap. Here's what these six-month t-shirts really translated to in terms of a baby's weight and height:

What a six month t-shirt really means

MAKER	WEIGHT	HEIGHT
BABY GAP	17-22 LBS.	27-29"
CARTER'S	16.5-20.5 LBS.	26.5-28.5"
GYMBOREE	17-23 LBS.	25-29"
HANNA ANDERSSON	14-21 LBS.	26-30"
HEALTH-TEX	13-17 LBS.	25-28"
LANDS' END	18-23 LBS.	27-29"
LITTLE ME	12-16 LBS.	24-27"
OSHKOSH	16.5-18 LBS.	27-28.5"

Here's another secret from the baby clothing trade: the more expensive the brand, the more roomy the clothes. Conversely, cheap items usually have the skimpiest sizing. What about the old wives' tale that you should just double your baby's age to find the right size (that is, buying twelve-month clothes for a six-month old?). That's bogus—as you can see, sizing is so all over the board that this rule just doesn't work.

◆ *Lead in jewelry.* Cheap jewelry from China has consistently turned up on the Consumer Product Safety Commission's recall list. These items are sold in mall stores and from vending machines. Best bet: never purchase jewelry for infants and toddlers. Items like necklaces are likely to end up in their mouths and can be a potential lead and choking hazard. If you choose to pierce your child's ears, stick with high-quality hypoallergenic metals like gold.

Laundry Conundrum: What's Best for Baby's Clothes?

Ever since Dr. Spock's best-selling tome on taking care of baby, most parenting authors have advised washing baby's clothes and linens in mild soap or detergents. The implication is that baby's skin is delicate and could be irritated by harsh chemicals.

Yet, it helps to take a second to talk about just WHAT we are washing our clothes, hands and hair with these days. Until World War II, most soaps were made of animal or vegetable products. After the war, new synthetic "detergents" debuted, which were chemical compounds that cleaned better and cost less than soap. Detergent use skyrocketed, while soaps languished. Today nearly all products we think of as "soap" are really detergents.

Over the past 20 years, we've seen an explosion in personal care detergents, including soft soaps, bath gels, anti-bacterial liquids, hair products and more. In the nursery, just look at the huge use of baby wipes (which often contain alcohol and crude detergents) instead of the washcloths of old. At the same time, however the number of children with severe eczema has climbed sharply, from the 3% in the 1950's to nearly 10% today. That's right, one out of ten children today suffers from eczema.

Is it possible the high-tech detergents we use today to wash our skin, clothes and dishes are contributing to the eczema epidemic? While there is no scientific data to prove this link, researchers in England have been actively studying this for the past decade. Dr. Michael Cork, a dermatologist at Sheffield University, suggests detergents strip the fat between cells, making the skin more susceptible to conditions like eczema.

Unfortunately, there is no known cure for childhood eczema, which can be painful in its most severe form. It is often treated with steroid creams, which may have harmful long-term side effects.

So, what should new parents do? First, look at your family's history of eczema and other skin diseases. If you DO have a family history of eczema, we'd suggest going on a detergent-free diet for your household. Why the entire house? That's because baby will be touching your hair, clothes and sheets and those of your family as well. It's not enough to wash your baby's clothes in non-detergent soap. The entire family will have to sign on to this. See below for specific suggestions of detergent-free products.

Even if you have no such history in your family, consider using the mildest soaps or detergents for your baby: products like Cetaphil and Dove bar soap among the best options. Stick with laundry products that are dye and fragrance free as well. No, you don't have to use Dreft—any perfume and dye-free mild detergent will do. And consider a second rinse cycle—this helps remove detergent residue. Finally, if you use bleach in the laundry, add some distilled vinegar to the rinse cycle to remove some of the odor and help clothes last longer.

In our family, we've had success removing detergents from our house, where our youngest son suffers from severe eczema. We noticed a sharp improvement in his skin after banishing detergents. Here are our tips for families with severe skin allergies:

◆ **Wash baby's clothes** in pure soap. Consider **Cal-Ben's Seafoam Liquid** laundry soap, which is made from natural soap (web: CalBenPureSoap.com). Another source for traditional soap flakes is soap-flakes.com. You may also find other pure soaps in natural food stores. Read the labels carefully, however, since some items still contain detergents and others may have allergenic fruit or vegetable ingredients. Do not use fabric softeners, drier sheets or other laundry products. WARNING: if you plan to use soap or soap flakes, only buy untreated cotton sleepers for your child. Polyester sleepers as well as fire retardant-treated cotton sleeper will lose their fire retardancy when washed in soap. Check the label on your sleepers for any warnings on this.

◆ **Baby's hair and skin** should be washed with Dove or Cetaphil bar soap. Never use bubble baths, oils or kid's shampoo. For hand soap in the kitchen and bath, we've used Cal-Ben's Seafoam liquid soap or the bar soap mentioned above. Yes, that means everyone in the house. We chucked our old shampoo and use a pure soap shampoo (Cal Ben's Gold Star shampoo) as well. Stay away from anti-bacterial soaps. They can cause painful flair ups for eczema sufferers. Wash hands frequently to avoid germs and follow with a good emollient moisturizer.

◆ **Dishes.** Yes, babies can be exposed to detergent residue by handling cups or dishes. Consider a detergent-free dishwashing gel (again, Cal-Ben makes an option, Seafoam Dish Glow).

A few caveats to this: pure soap products are hard to find and expensive—we order ours from the web site mentioned above, although some natural food stores carry these brands as well.

And, true enough, soap does NOT clean as well as detergent, especially in the laundry. That said, we are willing to put up with this hassle in order to see improvement in our son.

We understand this is quite a commitment—having mom or dad give up a favorite shampoo or hair gel isn't fun. But remember, baby is running her hands through your hair and touching your skin. Even a small detergent residue can cause a reaction in some kids.

While we follow this detergent-free diet and it seems to be offering huge relief for our son's eczema, we realize it may just be part of the puzzle. Some kids have eczema that is triggered by a food allergy . . . and drier times of the year (winter, for example) can aggravate the skin, even in a detergent-free house. For our son, allergy shots (plus cutting back on detergents) helped get his eczema under control. If your baby or toddler develops eczema, consult with a pediatrician, allergist or dermatologist for the best treatment course.

Someday we hope science is able to positively link eczema with environmental factors, then we as parents can take positive steps so our children don't have to suffer.

Smart Shopper Tips

Smart Shopper Tip
Tips and Tricks to Get the Best Quality

"I've received several outfits from friends for my daughter, but I'm not sure she'll like all the scratchy lace and the poly/cotton blends. What should she wear, and what can I buy that will last through dozens of washings?"

Generally, we recommend dressing your child for comfort. At the same time, you need clothes that can withstand frequent washings. With this in mind, here are our suggestions for baby clothing:

1 **SEE WHAT YOUR BABY LIKES BEFORE INVESTING IN MANY GARMENTS.** Don't spend $90 on fancy sweaters, only to find baby prefers cotton Onesies.

2 **WE GENERALLY RECOMMEND 100% COTTON CLOTHING.** Babies are most comfortable in clothing that breathes.

3 **IF YOUR CHILD DEVELOPS A RED, ITCHY RASH, IT COULD BE AN ALLERGY.** Culprits could include metal snaps on a t-shirt, zippers or even the ink on tagless labels. One idea: consider alternatives such as shirts that have ties or that pull over the head. Stick with clothes that have plastic snaps and zippers.

4 **IN GENERAL, BETTER-MADE CLOTHES WILL HAVE THEIR SNAPS ON A REINFORCED FABRIC BAND.** Snaps attached directly to the body of the fabric may tear the garment or rip off.

5 **IF YOU'RE BUYING 100% COTTON CLOTHES, MAKE SURE THEY'RE PRE-SHRUNK.** Some stores, like Gymboree (see review later in this chapter), pre-wash their clothes to prevent shrinkage. With other brands, it's hard to tell. Our advice: read the label. If it says, "wash in cold water" or " tumble dry low," assume the garment will shrink (and hence buy a larger size). On the other hand, care instructions that advise "washing in warm water and tumble dry" usually indicate that the garment is already preshrunk.

6 **GO FOR OUTFITS WITH SNAPS AND ZIPPERS ON BOTH LEGS, NOT JUST ONE.** Dual-leg snaps or zippers make it much easier to change a diaper. Always check a garment for diaper accessibility—some brands actually have no snaps or zippers, meaning you would have to completely undress your baby for a diaper change! Another pet peeve: garments that have snaps up the back also make diaper changes a big hassle.

7 **BE AWARE THAT EACH COMPANY HAS ITS OWN WARPED IDEA ABOUT HOW TO SIZE BABY CLOTHES.** See the box "One Size Does Not Fit All" earlier in this chapter for more details.

8 **BEWARE OF APPLIQUES.** Some appliqué work can be quite scratchy on the inside of the outfit (it rubs against baby's skin).

9 **KEEP THE TAGS AND RECEIPTS.** A reader emailed us her strategy for dealing with baby clothes that shrink: until she has a chance to wash the item, she keeps all packaging, tags and receipts. If it shrinks, she returns it immediately.

Wastes of Money

Waste of Money #1
Clothing that Leads to Diaper Changing Gymnastics
"My aunt sent me an adorable outfit for my little girl. The only problem: it snaps up the back making diaper changes a real pain.

In fact, I don't dress her in it often because it's so inconvenient. Shouldn't clothing like this be outlawed?"

It's pretty obvious that some designers of baby clothing have never had children of their own. What else could explain outfits that snap up the back, have super tiny head, leg and arm openings, and snaps in inconvenient places (or worse, no snaps at all)? One mother we spoke with was furious about outfits that have snaps only down one leg, requiring her baby to be a contortionist to get into and out of the outfit.

Our advice: stay away from outfits that don't have easy access to the diaper. Look instead for snaps or zippers down the front of the outfit or on the crotch. If your baby doesn't like having things pulled over his head, look for shirts with wide, stretchie necklines.

Waste of Money #2
The Fuzz Factor

"My friend's daughter has several outfits that aren't very old but are already pilling and fuzzing. They look awful and my friend is thinking of throwing them out. What causes this?"

Your friend has managed to have a close encounter with that miracle fabric known as polyester. Synthetics such as polyester will often pill or fuzz after washing, making your baby look a little rag-tag. Of course, this is less of a concern with sleepwear—the flame retardancy of polyester fabric outweighs the garment's appearance.

However, when you're talking about a play outfit, we recommend sticking to all-cotton clothes. They wash better, usually last longer, and generally look nicer—not to mention they feel better to your baby. Cotton allergies are rare, unlike sensitivities to the chemicals used to make synthetic fabrics. You will pay more for all-cotton clothing, but in this case, the extra expense is worth it. Remember, just because you find the cheapest price on a polyester outfit doesn't mean you're getting a bargain. The best deal is not wasting money on outfits that you have to throw away after two washings.

If you get polyester outfits as gifts, here's a laundry tip: wash the items inside out. That helps lessen pilling/fuzzing. And some polyester items are better than others—polar fleece sweatshirts and pajamas are still made of polyester, but are softer and more durable.

Waste of Money #3
Do I Really Need These?

"My mother bought me a zillion gowns before my baby was born, and I haven't used a single one. What the heck are they for?"

"The list of layette items recommended by my local department store includes something called a saque set. I've never seen one,

and no one seems to know what it is. Do I really need one?"

"A bath robe with matching towel and washcloth seems like a neat baby gift for my pregnant friend. But another friend told me it probably wouldn't get used. What do you think?"

All of these items come under the heading "Do I Really Need These?" Heck, we didn't even know what some of these were when we were shopping for our baby's layette. For example, what in the world is a saque set? Well, it turns out it's just a two-piece outfit with a shirt and diaper cover. Although they sound rather benign, saque

---

Baby Needs a New Pair of Shoes

As your baby gets older, you may find she's kicking off her socks every five minutes. And at some point she's going to start standing, crawling and even walking. While we suggest waiting to buy shoes until walking is firmly established, there will come a day when you will need to buy that first set of shoes. Here are some suggestions:

First, look for shoes that have the most flexible soles. You'll also want fabrics that breath and stretch, like canvas and leather—stay away from vinyl shoes. The best brands we found were recommended by readers. Reader Teri D. wrote us about Canadian-made **Robeez** (800) 929-2649; web: robeez.com. (See picture at right). "They are the most AWESOME shoes—I highly recommend them," she said in an email. And Teri wasn't the only one who loves them. Our email has been blitzed by fans. Robeez are made of leather, have soft, skid-resistant soles and are machine washable. They start at $28 for a basic pair. Another reader recommended New Zealand-made **Bobux** shoes ($26.50, web: bobuxusa.com). These cute leather soft soles "do the trick by staying on extremely well," according to a reader. Finally, we also like **PediPeds** (pedipeds.com). The soft-soled shoes are hand stitched and made of leather. They are sized from 0 to five years and sell for around $32 to $40.

What about shoes for one or two year olds? We've found great deals at Target, where a wide selection of sizes and offerings was impressive. Another good source: Gap Kids/Baby Gap. Their affordable line of sneakers are very good quality. Parents have also told us they've had success with Babies R Us' in-house brand; others like Stride Rite shoes, which are often on sale at department stores. If none of these stores are convenient, consider the web or mail order—see the Do It By Mail section later in this chapter for possibilities..

sets are a waste of money. Whenever you pick up a baby under the arms, it's a sure bet her clothes will ride up. In order to avoid having to constantly pull down the baby's shirt, most parents find they use one-piece garments much more often than two-piece ones.

As for gowns, the jury is still out on whether these items are useful. We thought they were a waste of money, but a parent we interviewed did mention that she used the gowns when her baby had colic (that persistent crying condition; see our other book *Baby 411* for a discussion). She believed that the extra room in the gown made her baby more comfortable. Other parents like how gowns make diaper changes easy, especially in the middle of the night. Finally, parents in hot climates say gowns keep their infants more comfortable. So, you can see there's a wide range of opinions on this item.

There is no question in our minds about the usefulness of a baby bathrobe, however. Don't buy it. For a baby who will only wear it for a few minutes after a bath, it seems like the quintessential waste of your money (we saw a monogrammed options for a whopping $90!). Instead, invest in some good quality towels and washcloths and forget those cute (but useless) kimonos.

Waste of Money #4
Covering Up Those Little Piggies
"I was looking at baby shoes the other day and I saw a $40 pair of Nike Little Huarache sneakers! This is highway robbery! I can't believe babies' shoes are so expensive. Are they worth it?"

Developmentally, babies don't need shoes until after they become quite proficient at walking. In fact, it's better for their muscle development to go barefoot or wear socks. While those expensive Merrells might look cute, they're really a waste of time and money. Of course, at some point, your baby will need some shoes. See the box on the opposite page for our tips on how to buy babies' first shoes.

Waste of Money #5
To Drool or Not to Drool
"I received a few bibs from my mother-in-law as gifts. I know my baby won't need them until she's at least four to six months old when I start feeding her solids. Plus, they seem so small!"

What you actually received was a supply of *drool* bibs. Drool bibs are tiny bibs intended for small infants who drool all over everything. Or infants who spit-up frequently. Our opinion: they're pretty useless—they're too small to catch much drool or spit-up.

When you do buy bibs, stay away from the ones that tie. Bibs that snap or have Velcro are much easier to get on and off. Another good bet: bibs that go on over the head (and have no snaps or Velcro). Why? Older babies can't pull them off by themselves.

Stay away from the super-size vinyl bibs that cover the arms, since babies who wear them can get too hot. However, we do recommend you buy a few regular-style vinyl bibs for travel. You can wash them off much more easily than the standard terry-cloth bibs. As for sources of bibs, many of the catalogs we review in this book carry such items. Readers have also recommended the long sleeve bib from *A Better Bib* (abetterbib.com). Made of soft, breathable fabrics, these bibs run $17.

Reader Sharon F. from Chicago wrote in to praise Pelican bibs: "I want to strongly recommend Pelican bibs! They really protect clothing and catch dropped food" better than other bibs. Pelican bibs have a wide lip for catching spills. Cost: $,5 online at Amazon.com and other sites.

Another bib we like: the *SnugEase* ($8, snugease.com; pictured), a mom-designed terry cloth bib with a clever design—it doesn't require Velcro or snaps to stay on baby. Instead, "memory arms" keep it in place. And the SnugEase has extra gathered fabric at the neck to prevent food from dribbling down onto baby's clothes (which seems to happen with regular bibs). Two thumbs up for SnugEase.

Money Saving Secrets

1 REMEMBER THESE TWO STORES: OLD NAVY AND THE CHILDREN'S PLACE. Old Navy (oldnavy.com) is the hip, discount offshoot of the Gap (gap.com) with 700+ stores nationwide. Readers rave about the buys they find at Old Navy (sample: "adorable" 100% cotton Onesies for just $12 per 3-pack; gripper socks, 8 to $10), although most admit the selection is limited. The options change rapidly and Old Navy's sales and clearance racks are "bargain heaven," say our spies. An insider tip to Old Navy and Gap Kids: the stores change out their merchandise every six weeks, moving the "old" stuff to the clearance racks rather quickly. Ask your local Old Navy or Gap Kids which day they do their markdowns (typically it is Tuesday night, effective Wednesday).

Here's another tip for folks who shop Old Navy or the Gap regularly: check to see if your recent purchases have been marked down. You may be able to get a refund if items you've bought are marked down even more. One reader emailed us her great deal:

"Last month I found a hooded sweatshirt for baby on clearance. It was originally $15 marked down to $10.50. The next week, I went back and the same sweatshirt had been marked down from $10.50 to $1.99. So they refunded me $8.60!" Both Old Navy and the Gap allow you a price adjustment within 14 days of purchase. But you don't have to bring the clothes back, just your receipt.

A Gap employee emailed us the inside scoop on their markdowns. She told us that prices ending in $.97 are the lowest price you'll see on the markdown rack. After 14 days at the $.97 price, the stores have the authority to cut the price in half to "kill" the item. Finally, if you have a Gap credit card, you can get an additional 10% off everything on the first Tuesday of every month. And our source says don't forget to take the register surveys—they'll save you 10% as well.

The Children's Place (childrensplace.com) has over 851 stores in the US and Canada. They're about as ubiquitous as Old Navy, and the prices are just as good. They offer their clothing in sizes newborn to 4T. One reader wrote: "I found that this chain has really great looking and durable clothes for extremely reasonable prices." She did note that sizes run a bit small, so buy up a size. An example of their offerings: we saw a white, ruffled girl's cardigan for a mere $14.50. If you order online, the site offers a flat $5 shipping fee plus you can make returns at their stores.

E-MAIL FROM THE REAL WORLD
Second-hand bargains easy to find

Shelley Bayer of Connecticut raved about Once Upon A Child, a nationwide chain of resale stores with well over 100 locations in the US and Canada (web: www.OUAC.com).

"We have seven locations of Once Upon A Child in Connecticut and I love them! The clothes and toys are of great quality and very affordable. The good thing about these stores is that when you take something in to be sold, they pay you cash. You do not have wait for something to be sold and keep checking your account like a traditional consignment shop."

One caution about second-hand stores—if you buy an item like a stroller or high chair at a resale shop, you may not be able to get replacement parts. One mom told us she got a great deal on a stroller that was missing a front bar . . . that is, it was a great deal until she discovered the model was discontinued and she couldn't get a replacement part from the manufacturer.

2 **WAIT UNTIL AFTER SHOWERS AND PARTIES TO PURCHASE CLOTHES.** Clothing is a popular gift item—you may not need to buy much yourself.

3 **STICK WITH BASICS—T-SHIRTS, SLEEPERS, CAPS, SOCKS AND BLANKETS.** For the first month or more, that's all you need since you won't be taking Junior to the opera.

4 **SALES!** The baby area in most department stores is definitely SALE LAND. At one chain we researched, the baby section has at least some items that are on sale every week! Big baby sales occur throughout the year, but especially in January. You can often snag bargains at up to 50% off the retail price. Another tip: consider buying for the future during end-of-season sales. If you're pregnant during the fall, for example, shop the end-of-summer sales for next summer's baby clothes. Hint: our research shows the sale prices at department stores are often better deals than the "discounted" prices you see at outlets.

5 **CHOOSE QUALITY OVER LOW PRICE FOR PLAYCLOTHES AND BASICS.** Sure that polyester outfit is 20% cheaper than the cotton alternative. HOWEVER, beware of the revenge of the washing machine! You don't realize how many times you'll be doing laundry—that play outfit may get washed every couple of days. Cheap polyester clothes pill or fuzz up after just a few washings—making you more likely to chuck them. Quality clothes have longer lives, making them less expensive over time.

6 **FOR SLEEPWEAR, TRY THE AFFORDABLE BRANDS.** Let's get real here: babies pee and poop in their sleepers. Hence, fancy designer brands are a money-waster. A friend of ours who lives in Texas uses affordable all-cotton Onesies as sleepwear in the hot summer months. For the winter here in Colorado, we use thermal underwear, which we've found for as little as $15 in Target.

7 **CAN'T RETURN IT?** Did you get gifts of clothing you don't want but can't return? Consign it at a local thrift store. We took a basketful of clothes that we couldn't use or didn't like and placed them on consignment. We turned these duplicates into $40 cash.

8 **SPEAKING OF CONSIGNMENT STORES, HERE IS A WONDERFUL WAY TO SAVE MONEY:** Buy barely used, consigned clothing for your baby. We found outfits ranging from $5 to $7 from high quality designers like Alexis. How can you find a consignment or thrift shop in your area specializing in high-quality children's clothes? Besides looking in the phone book, check out web sites like the National Association of Resale & Thrift Shops (narts.com, click on the shopping guide icon). Here are two tips for getting the best bargains at second-hand stores: First, shop the resale stores in the richest part of town. Why? They are most likely to stock the best brands with steep discounts off retail prices. Such stores also have clothes with the least wear (we guess rich kids have so many clothes they don't have time to wear them all out)! Second: ask the consignment store which day is best to shop. Some stores accept new consignments on certain days; others tell us that days like Tuesday and Wednesday offer the best selection of newly consigned items.

9 CHECK OUT DISCOUNTERS. In the past, discount stores like Target, Wal-Mart and Marshall's typically carried cheap baby clothes that were mostly polyester. Well, there's good news for bargain shoppers: in recent years, these chains have upgraded their offerings, adding more all-cotton clothes and even some brand names. We've been especially impressed with Target. For basic items like t-shirts and play clothes that will be trashed at day care, these stores are good bets. Wal-Mart sure impressed one of our readers: "I spent $25 for a baby bathing suit in a specialty store, and for a little over twice that (about $60) I bought my daughter's entire

For basic items like t-shirts and play clothes that will be trashed at day care, these stores are good bets. Wal-Mart sure impressed one of our readers: "I spent $25 for a baby bathing suit in a specialty store, and for a little over twice that (about $60) I bought my daughter's entire summer wardrobe at Wal-Mart—shorts, t-shirts, leggings, Capri pants, overalls and matching socks. Some of the pieces were as low as $2.88." And don't forget other discounters like Marshalls, TJ Maxx and Ross. Bargain tip: ask the manager when they get in new shipments—that's when selection is best.

By the way, Carter's makes Child of Mine brand clothing sold at Wal-Mart and Just One Year brand at Target.

10 WAREHOUSE CLUBS. Warehouse clubs like Sam's, BJ's and Costco carry baby clothes at prices far below retail. On a recent visit to Costco we saw Carter's fleece sleepers for only $7.29. All-cotton play clothes were a mere $13 while all-cotton pajamas (2T-10) were $12. Even baby Halloween costumes and kids outerwear (raincoats, fleece jackets) are terrific seasonal deals.

11 DON'T FORGET ABOUT CHARITY SALES. Readers tell us they've found great deals on baby clothes and equipment at church-sponsored charity sales. Essentially, these sales are like large garage/yard sales where multiple families donate kids' items as a fund-raiser for a church or other charity.

Outlets

Here's a round up of our favorite outlet stores for baby and kids clothes. Remember: outlet locations open and close frequently—always call before you go.

CARTER'S

Locations: Over 219 outlets.
Call (888) 782-9548 or (770) 961-8722 for the location nearest you.

It shows you how widespread the outlet craze is when you realize that Carter's has over 150 outlets in the U.S. That's right, 150. If you don't have one near you, you probably live in Bolivia.

We visited a Carter's outlet and found a huge selection of infant clothes, bedding, and accessories. Prices were generally marked 50% off retail although sharp-eyed readers noted that department store sale prices are often just as good.

The best deals, however, are at the outlet's yearly clearance sale in January when they knock an additional 25% to 30% off their already discounted prices. A store manager at the Carter's outlet we visited said that they also have two other sales: back-to-school and a "pajama sale." In the past, we noted that all the goods in their outlet stores were first quality. However, they have added a couple "seconds" racks (called "Oops" racks) in most of their stores with flawed merchandise. Our readers report that most seconds have only minor problems and the savings are worth it.

HANNA ANDERSSON

Outlets Stores: Lakewood, CO; Michigan City, IN; Albertville, MN; Kittery, ME; Woodinville, WA; Williamsburg, VA

If you like Hanna Anderson's catalog, you'll love their outlet stores, which feature overstocks, returned items and factory seconds. For more information on Hanna Anderson, see "Do It By Mail" later in this chapter.

HARTSTRINGS

Locations: 27 outlets, mostly in the eastern U.S. Call (610) 687-6900.

Hartstrings' 27 outlet stores specialize in first-quality apparel for infants, boys, and girls and even have some mother/child outfits. Infant sizes start at three months and go up to 24 months. The savings range from 30% to 50%.

Health-Tex

Locations: Over 80 outlets. Web: VFOutlet.net.

Health-Tex children's clothing is owned by Vanity Fair Corporation, which also produces such famous brands as Lee jeans, Wrangler, and Jantzen. The company operates over four-dozen outlets under the name VF Factory Outlet. They sell first-quality merchandise; most are discontinued items. Most of the VF outlets carry the Health-Tex brand at discounts up to 70% off retail.

JCPenney

Locations: 20 outlets; call (800) 222-6161, Web: JCPenney.com

A reader in Columbus, Ohio emailed her high praise for the Penney's outlet there. She snagged one-piece rompers for $5 (regularly $25) and hand-loomed coveralls for $2.99 (compared to $28 in stores). She also found satin christening outfits for both boys and girls for just $5 that regularly sell for as much as $70! The outlet carries everything from layette to play clothes, at discounts of 50% or more. (Hint: the outlet stores also have maternity clothes).

OshKosh

Locations: 157 outlets. Call (920) 231-8800 for the nearest location.

OshKosh, the maker of all those cute little overalls worn by just about every kid, sells their clothes direct at over 154 outlet stores. With prices that are 30% to 70% off retail, buying these play clothes staples is even easier on the pocketbook. For example, footed sleepers were $7.70 (regularly $11), and receiving blankets were $18.20 (regularly $24).

We visited our local OshKosh store and found outfits from infant sizes up to size 16. They split the store up by gender, as well as by size. Infant and toddler clothes are usually in the back of the store.

The outlet also carries OshKosh shoes, socks, hats, and even stuffed bears dressed in overalls and engineer hats. Seasonal ensembles are available, including shorts outfits in the summer and snowsuits ($42) in the winter. Some clothes are irregulars, so inspect the garments carefully before you buy.

One complaint: a parent wrote telling us she was disappointed that OshKosh had cheap elastic around the legs and didn't wash well. In her opinion, the quality of Carter's was much better in comparison.

FYI: OshKosh was purchased by Carter's in 2005.

◆ *Other outlets.* A great source for outlet info is **Outlet Bound** magazine, which is published by Outlet Marketing Group (web: outletbound.com). Outlet Bound has an excellent web site with the most up-to-date info on outlets in the U.S. and Canada. We did a search on children's clothing outlets (you can search by location, store, brand or product category) and found several additional interesting outlets. These included outlets for Little Me (11 outlets), the Disney catalog outlet (21 locations) and the Oilily catalog (two outlets).

If you can't get enough of the *Gap*, check out their outlet stores (they have 159) (650) 952-4400 (web: gap.com). With several locations nationwide, most Gap outlets have a baby/kid's clothing section and great deals (50% off and more).

Did you discover an outlet that you'd like to share with our readers? Call us at our office at 303-442-8792 or e-mail authors@ BabyBargains.com.

The Name Game: Our Picks for the Best Brands

Walk into any department store and you'll see a blizzard of brand names for baby clothes. Which ones stand up to frequent washings? Which ones have snaps that stay snapped? Which are a good value for the dollar? We asked our readers to divide their favorite clothing brands/stores into three categories: best bets, good but not great and skip it.

The Best Bets tend to be clothes that were not only stylish but also held up in the wash. The fabric was usually softer and pilled less. Customer service also comes into play with the best brands. Hanna Andersson is a great example of a company that bends over backwards for their customers. Gymboree, on the other hand, seems to be less than satisfactory for many parents, souring them on the brand. Keep in mind, some brands are pricey, so look for sales and second hand deals. Or just point Grandma to these sites!

Good but not Great clothes were pretty good, just not as soft or as stylish as Best Bets. The Skip-It brands were most likely the poorest quality: they shrunk in the wash, pilled up or fell apart. Inconsistent sizing was also a problem with brands like Babies R Us' Koala Kids.

Check these brands web sites to find local stores; some brands sell direct, of course.

Best Bets

AMERICAN APPAREL		AMERICANAPPAREL.NET
BABY GAP	(800) GAP-STYLE	BABYGAP.COM
BABY LULU		BABYLULU.COM
CARTER'S	(770) 961-8722	CARTERS.COM
COZY TOES		COZYTOES.COM
FLAP HAPPY	(800) 234-3527	FLAPHAPPY.COM
FLAPDOODLES	(302) 731-9793	FLAPDOODLES.COM
FUNTASIA! TOO	(214) 634-7770	FUNTASIATOO.COM
H & M		HM.COM
HANNA ANDERSSON		HANNAANDERSSON.COM
HARTSTRINGS/KITESTRINGS	(212) 868-0950	HARTSTRINGS.COM
HEDGEHOG		HEDGEHOGUSA.COM
JAKE AND ME	(970) 352-8802	JAKEANDME.COM
JANIE AND JACK		JANIEANDJACK.COM
KISSY KISSY		KISSYKISSYONLINE.COM
LITTLE LUBBALOO		LITTLELUBBALOO.COM
LITTLE ME	(800) 533-5497	LITTLEME.COM
LL BEAN		LLBEAN.COM
MINIBODEN		MINIBODEN.COM
MULBERRIBUSH (TUMBLEWEED TOO)		MULBERRIBUSH.COM
NAARTJIE		NAARTJIE.COM
OLD NAVY		OLDNAVY.COM
OSHKOSH B'GOSH	(800) 692-4674	OSHKOSHBGOSH.COM
PATSY AIKEN	(919) 872-8789	PATSYAIKEN.COM
PUMPKIN PATCH		PUMPKINPATCHUSA.COM
SARAH'S PRINTS	(888) 477-4687	SARASPRINTS.COM
SWEET POTATOES/SPUDZ	(800) 634-2584	SWEETPOTATOESINC.COM
TEA COLLECTION		TEACOLLECTION.COM
WES & WILLY		WESANDWILLY.COM
ZUTANO		ZUTANO.COM

Good But Not Great

CHILDREN'S PLACE		CHILDRENSPLACE.COM
GOOD LAD OF PHILA.	(215) 739-0200	GOODLAD.COM
GYMBOREE	(877) 449-6932	GYMBOREE.COM
LANDS END		LANDSEND.COM
LE TOP	(800) 333-2257	LETOP-USA.COM
TARGET (LITTLE ME, CLASSIC POOH, HALO, TYKES, CIRCO)		TARGET.COM
WAL-MART (FADED GLORY)		WALMART.COM

Skip It: GERBER, HANES, KOALA KIDS (BABIES R US), DISNEY, HEALTH-TEX, CARTER'S JUST ONE YEAR AT TARGET, GEORGE BY WALMART

Do it by Mail

CHILDREN'S WEAR DIGEST (CWD)

To Order Call: (800) 242-5437; Fax (800) 863-3395.
Web: cwdkids.com.
Outlet: Two outlets in Richmond, VA.

If you're looking for name brands, check out Children's Wear Digest (CWD), a catalog that features clothes in sizes newborn to 14 years for both boys and girls. In a recent catalog, we saw clothes by Sweet Potatoes, Mulberribush, Wes and Willie, Lacoste, and Hartstrings. Unlike other catalogs that de-emphasize brand names, CWD prominently displays manufacturer info.

Children's Wear Digest doesn't offer much of a discount off regular retail, but it does have a selection of sale clothes from time to time with savings of 15% to 25%. A best buy: CWD's web site (cwdkids.com) has online bargains, with savings of up to 50% on quite a few items. They have two outlet centers in Richmond, VA.

CREWCUTS BY J. CREW

To Order Call: (800) 562-0258
Web: Jcrew.com
Discount Outlets: Yes, nearly 60, check the web site for locations.

J Crew's new kids line is remarkably similar to their adult offerings, from bright colored hoodies to cashmere sweaters and cool t-shirts. But don't expect to find anything for infants. This line is strictly for the two years and up crowd. Too bad—you can see how cute a mom and daughter hoodie set would be for Christmas. But hold on to your seat . . . a corduroy jumper will set you back $40. And a cotton cable sweater was a whopping $50. Not for the faint of wallet. This might be the site for Grandma presents or special occasion wear rather than daycare items.

HANNA ANDERSSON

To Order Call: (800) 222-0544; Fax (503) 321-5289.
Web: hannaandersson.com.
Discount Outlets: Yes. Check outlet section earlier in the chapter.

Hanna Andersson says it offers "Swedish quality" 100% cotton clothes. Unfortunately, Swedish quality is going to set you back some big American bucks. For example, a simple romper styled like a rugby shirt was a whopping $40. At that price, it's hard to imagine buying a complete wardrobe here no matter how cute their clothes are.

These aren't clothes you'd have your baby trash at daycare–Hanna Andersson's outfits are more suitable for weekend wear or going to Grandma's house. One note of caution: while the quality is very high, some items have difficult diaper access (or none at all). Another negative: Hanna Andersson uses "European sizing," which can be confusing. (Yes, there is an explanation of this in the catalog and on the website, but we still found it difficult to follow). Furthermore, some items (like dresses) are cut in a boxy, unstructured way.

On the plus side, we liked their web site (hannaandersson.com), which features an online store, sizing info and more. The site has a sale page that offers 20% to 40% off on overstock items; you can quickly glance at the specials by category.

GARNET HILL

To Order Call: (800) 870-3513.
Web: GarnetHill.com.
Discount Outlets: Two outlets: Manchester, VT and Franconia, NH. Check their web site for locations and hours.

We mentioned Garnet Hill in our bedding chapter as a good place to find 100% cotton crib bedding. The same web site also has a decent selection of clothes for kids sizes six months to 3T. Like Crewcuts reviewed above, prices aren't cheap. T-shirts start at $18, cute, roll neck sweaters are $30 and jeans run $44. Certainly there are some unique items here that may justify a little splurge like the cool polka dot flamenco pants ($46) . . . but this catalog is probably best for grandparents looking for gift ideas.

LANDS' END

To Order Call: (800) 963-4816; Fax (800) 332-0103.
Web: landsend.com.
Discount Outlets: They also have a dozen or so outlet stores in Iowa, Illinois and Wisconsin–call the number above for the nearest location.

Lands' End children's catalog features a complete layette line– and it's darn cute. The clothes are typically 100% cotton although you'll see some fleece as well as velour. Choose from playsuits, Onesies, hat/bib sets, even cashmere sweaters and pants–all in sizes birth to 24 months. Most items were $10 to $30 (cashmere sweater $75). Don't look for fancy dress clothes from this catalog; instead Lands' End specializes in casual playwear basics like sweat pants, overalls and cute caps (for toddlers no doubt).

Lands' End web site is a continuation of the catalog's easy-to-use layout—you can buy items online, find an outlet store and more. Best bet for deals: check the great overstock deals, posted twice weekly.

LL BEAN

To Order Call: (800) 441-5713; Fax (207) 552-3080
Web: llbean.com
Retail store: Freeport, ME

LL Bean has now added a LL Bean Baby collection with . fleece items, a cashmere sweater, booties and diaper bag. The selection is limited, but we thought the Bean Booties that looked like duck shoes were cut. Prices were $35 for a fleece hoodie with ears on the hood. Matching fleece pants were $20. Infant sizes range from 1 to 18 months. Check for sales on baby items.

NAARTJIE

Web: Naartjie.com
Outlets: One outlet in Phoenix, AZ. Regular stores in California, Arizona, Colorado, Oregon, Utah and Washington.

Naartje is a western US chain that originally started in South Africa. In fact, a "naartjie" (pronounced nar chee) is an Afrikaans word for small, sweet citrus fruit. Sounds delish! Anyway, we first heard about this chain from one of our readers and were excited to have a store near us we could visit. We agree with our reader: the quality is comparable to Gymboree and Hanna Andersson. And yes, this line is full of cute stuff. We saw embroidered tunics for $13, corduroy patch pants for $13 and even. some great dress up clothes. We loved the outfit ideas section on their web site with those adorable baby models. Very inspiring if you're just too tired to make decisions.

PATAGONIA KIDS

To Order Call: (800) 638-6464; Fax (800) 543-5522
Web: patagonia.com
Outlets: Four outlet stores: Santa Cruz, CA; Freeport, ME; Dillon, MT; Salt Lake City, UT

Outdoor enthusiasts all over the country swear by Patagonia's scientifically engineered clothes and outerwear. They make clothing for skiing, mountain climbing, and kayaking—and for kids. That's right, Patagonia has a just-for-kids catalog of outdoor wear. In their recent kids' section on line, we found a few pages of clothes for babies and toddlers. Now if you are dying for a baby version of

Patagonia's overprice down jackets they've got it. At $100, the Baby Puff Rider is one of the most expensive winter coats we've seen for baby. Remember, these little guys grow so fast they have a meal and a nap and wake up a size or two bigger. Do you really want to spend this kind of dough only to have them outgrow it before winter is over?

While they may make some of the best winter gear around, unless you're taking Junior to the top of Mt. Everest, look elsewhere for your baby.

WOODEN SOLDIER

To Order Call: (800) 375-6002;
Web: WoodenSoldier.com
Outlets: Two located in New Hampshire. Call for more information.

If you really need a formal outfit for your child, Wooden Soldier has the most expansive selection of children's formalwear we've ever seen. Unfortunately, the prices are quite expensive—a girls' silk plaid dress with velvet collar is $124; a boy's vest and pant set with shirt is $98. And those are for infant sized clothes (6 to 24 months)!

On the plus side, the quality of the clothes is certainly impressive. And you won't find a bigger selection of dressy clothes around. They even offer some matching adult outfits. Wooden Soldier also continues to expand their casual offerings, which now include overalls, jumpsuits and cotton sweaters.

Finally, Wood Soldier entered the Internet Age with a web site (WoodenSoldier.com). We've been complaining for years that they didn't offer online shopping, so we're really happy to see they finally got their act together. And now you can actually order online—you don't have to call or download their order blank and mail it in. Hurray! Welcome to the 21st century!

◆ *Other catalogs.* Looking for Disney cartoon clothing and accessories? *Disney's* Catalog (800) 237-5751 (web: disneyshopping.com) has a few infant options. We liked the too-cute Halloween costumes as well as the winter gear. We found the quality from the Disney catalog to be quite good; most items wash and wear well.

If you need outdoor gear, check out *Campmor* (800) 226-7667 (web: campmor.com) or *Sierra Trading Post* (800) 713-4534 (web: sierratradingpost.com). Both heavily discount infant and children's outerwear, including snowsuits. Campmor even had some Sarah's Prints PJs for 50% off last we looked. They both also have backpacks. Since these items are closeouts, the selection varies from issue to issue.

Our Picks: Brand Recommendations

What clothing brands/catalogs are best? Well, there is no one correct answer. An outfit that's perfect for day care (that is, to be trashed in Junior's first painting experiment) is different from an outfit for a weekend outing with friends. And dress-up occasions may require an entirely different set of clothing criteria. Hence, we've divided our clothing brand recommendations into three areas: good (day care), better (weekend wear) and best (special occasions). While some brands make items in two or even three categories, here's how we see it:

Good. For everyday comfort (and day-care situations), basic brands like Carter's, Little Me, and OshKosh are your best bets. We also like the basics (when on sale) at Baby Gap (Gap Kids) for day-care wardrobes. For great price to value, take a look at Old Navy and Target. As for catalogs, most tend to specialize in fancier clothes.

Better. What if you have a miniature golf outing planned with friends? Or a visit to Grandma's house? The brands of better-made casual wear we like best include Baby Gap, Flapdoodles, and Gymboree. Also recommended: Jake and Me, MulberriBush, and Sweet Potatoes. For catalogs, we like the clothes in Hanna Andersson and Talbot's Kids as good brands.

Best. Holidays and other special occasions call for special outfits. We like Patsy Aiken, and the dressier items at Baby Gap. Of course, department stores are great sources for these outfits, as are consignment shops. As for catalogs, check out Wooden Soldier.

Note: For more on finding these brands, check out the Name Game earlier in this chapter. See "Do it By Mail" for more information on the catalogs mentioned above.

Diapers

The great diaper debate still rages on: should you use cloth or disposable? On one side are environmentalists, who argue cloth is better for the planet. On the other hand, those disposable diapers are darn convenient.

Considering the average baby will go through 2300 diaper changes in the first year of life, this isn't a moot issue—you'll be dealing with diapers until your baby is three or four years old (the average girl potty trains at 35 months; a boy at 39 months). Yes, you read that last sentence right . . . you will be diapering for the next

35 to 39 MONTHS.

Now, in this section, we've decided NOT to rehash all the environmental arguments pro or con for cloth versus disposable. Fire up your web browser and you'll find plenty of diaper debate on parenting sites like BabyCenter.com or ParentsPlace.com. Instead, we'll focus here on the FINANCIAL and PRACTICAL impacts of your decision.

Let's look at each option:

Cloth. Prior to the 1960's, this was the only diaper option available to parents. Fans of cloth diapering point to babies that had less diaper rash and toilet trained faster. From a practical point of view, cloth diapers have improved in the design over the years, offering more absorbency and fewer leaks. They aren't perfect, but the advent of diaper covers (no more plastic pants) has helped as well.

Another practical point: laundry. You've got to decide if you will use a cloth diaper service or launder at home. Obviously, the latter requires more effort on your part. We'll have laundry tips for cloth diapers later in this chapter. Meanwhile, we'll discuss the financial costs of cloth in general at the end of this section.

Final practical point about cloth: most day care centers don't allow them. This may be a sanitation requirement governed by state day care regulators and not a negotiating point. Check with local day care centers or your state board.

Disposables. Disposable diapers were first introduced in 1961 and now hold an overwhelming lead over cloth—about 95% of all households that have kids in diapers use disposables. Today's diapers have super-absorbent gels that lower the number of needed diaper changes, especially at night (which helps baby sleep through the night sooner). Even many parents who swear cloth diapers are best often use disposables at night. The downside? All that super-absorbency means babies are in no rush to potty train—they simply don't feel as wet or uncomfortable as babies in cloth diapers.

The jury on diaper rash is still out—disposable diaper users generally don't experience any more diaper rash than cloth diaper users.

Besides the eco-arguments about disposables, there is one other disadvantage—higher trash costs. In some communities, the more trash you put out, the higher the bill.

The financial bottom line: Surprisingly, there is no clear winner when you factor financial costs into the diaper equation.

Cloth diapers may seem cheap at first, but consider the hidden costs. Besides the diapers themselves ($100 for the basic varieties; $200 to $300 for the fancy ones), you also have to buy diaper covers. Like everything you buy with baby, there is a wide cost variation. The cheap stuff (like Dappi covers) will set you back $3 to $6 each. And you've got to buy several in different sizes as your child grows, so the total investment could be nearly $100. If you're lucky, you can find diaper covers second-hand for $1 to $3. Of course, some parents find low-cost covers leak and quickly wear out. As a result, they turn to the more expensive covers—a single Mother-Ease (see later for more info on this brand) is $12.25. Invest in a half dozen of those covers (in various sizes, of course) and you've spent another $240 to $480 (if you buy them new).

What about laundry? Well, washing your own cloth diapers at home may be the most economical way to go, but often folks don't have the time or energy. Instead, some parents use a cloth diaper service. In a recent cost survey of such services across the U.S., we found that the average is about $750 a year. While each service does supply you with diapers (relieving you of that expense), you're still on the hook for the diaper covers. Some services also don't provide enough diapers each month. You'll make an average of eight changes a day (more when a baby is newborn, less as they grow older), so be sure you're getting about 60 diapers a week from your service.

Proponents of cloth diapers argue that if you plan to have more than one child, you can reuse those covers, spreading out the cost. You may also not need as many sizes depending on the brands you use and the way your child grows.

So, what's the bottom line cost for cloth diapers? We estimate the total financial damage for cloth diapers (using a cloth diaper service and buying diaper covers) for just the first year is $850 to $1200.

By contrast, let's take a look at disposables. If you buy disposable diapers from the most expensive source in town (typically, a grocery store), you'd spend about $650 to $750 for the first year. Yet, we've found discount sources (mentioned later in this chapter) that sell disposables in bulk at a discount. By shopping at these sources, we figure you'd spend $400 to $500 per year (the lowest figure is for private label diapers, the highest is for brand names).

The bottom line: the cheapest way to go is cloth diapers laundered at home. The next best bet is disposables. Finally, cloth diapers from a diaper service are the most expensive.

Parents in Cyberspace: What's on the Web?

All Together Diaper Company

Web: clothdiaper.com
What it is: Home of the all-in-one cloth diaper made in house by the All Together Diaper Company.

What's cool: We loved the simplicity of this site. In business since 1990, the All Together Diaper Company sells its own cloth diaper system in various packages. The accompanying FAQ, washing instructions and analysis of diaper costs are really helpful. While some of their price comparisons between cloth and disposable are a bit inaccurate (slanted toward cloth, of course), the information on the cost of home washing was helpful.

What about the diapers? We were impressed with the cool design—the all-in-one (AIO) system has cotton inside against baby's skin, a waterproof outer shell, adjustable snaps and elastic leg openings. These diapers are $9 to $15 each or $96 to $180 per dozen. They now offer unbleached AIO's. Less expensive are the prefold diapers, which do not have the waterproof shell. Price: $11 to $30 per dozen (quantity discounts available). Packages are another plus on the All Together Diaper Company site. You can even buy a package called All the Cloth Diapers Your Baby Will Ever Need! This includes 48 small, 42 medium, 42 large and 36 toddler diapers. Cost: $999 (priced separately this would cost $1500).

Needs work: The web site seems to load a bit slowly.

The Baby Lane

Web: thebabylane.com

What it is: A comprehensive baby product and information site with a selection of cloth diapers and accessories.

What's cool: This is really the Mother of All Cloth Diaper sites. You'll find offerings from Under the Nile, Bumkins, Kushies, Plushies, Imse Vimse, Bummis and Kissaluv. Kushies Ultras were $9 for infant sizes (discounts available for five packs).

Needs work: While the site has made it a bit easier to find diaper products, it's a bit busy. You'll want to read all tiny the boxes on the opening since they have many discount offers you might miss otherwise.

Diapers 4 Less

Web: diapers4less.com

What it is: The web site for Diaper Factory Plus, a manufacturer of generic disposable diapers.

What's cool: Even with shipping costs, this site's diapers are about 20% less than any other discount diaper sites. And their diapers have Velcro closures, a foam waistband and a cloth-like cover like national brands. Shipping is free.

Small (8-16 lbs) size diapers run 24¢ per diaper. You have to buy 4 packs of 64 each (256 diapers) for a total of $62. Not bad, especially because shipping is free. In the chart following this section, you'll see this price (24¢ per diaper) compares well with grocery stores (which of course don't usually deliver to your home). Sample packs are available if you want to check out the quality (free except for shipping). Note: they will accept unopened packages as returns for refund or exchange.

Needs work: Plan ahead since UPS ground shipping can take seven to ten days to get to you.

Baby Works

Web: babyworks.com

What it is: Cloth diapers and a range of other eco friendly baby gear.

What's cool: You'll find diaper covers like Nikkys and Bummis, all-in-one diaper systems, cotton diapers, laundry products, and accessories. We saw the Bumkins all-in-one system for $16-18 per diaper. We liked all the washing instructions included on each page for the different items. Other nice features: Baby Works has a recommended layette for cloth diapers, you can order samples and they can troubleshoot leaking problems for you. By the way, they have a store in Portland, OR if you're visiting or live in the area.

Needs work: Prices aren't anything to shout about, but the selection is good.

◆ Other sites to consider:

Disposables: We found several more sites that sell disposable diapers on line. Among the best: **CVS Pharmacy** (cvspharmacy.com) and **Diaper Site** (diapersite.com).

Cloth: Noel Howell, one of our readers, emailed us with great suggestions for sites to help newbee moms interested in using cloth diapers. **Diaperpin.com** is good for parents still trying to decide whether cloth is for them. **Mothering.com** is another site with advice on specific brands of cloth diapers. There are also plenty of articles on cloth diapering but be prepared for some preaching!

Check out any of the following web sites as well: **kellyscloset. com, cottonbabies.com, aunaturalbaby.com** and **babybunz. com**. Reader Sherri Wormstead noted that all three of these sites are competitively priced and have a wide variety of supplies. Another reader noted that her favorite source for cloth diapers is **Wee Bunz** (WeeBunz.com) because they carry just about every brand. They have a bricks and mortar store in Portland, OR too. Finally, check out **Baby Because** (babybecause.com). They carry a huge assortment of folded diapers, all-in-one systems and diaper covers. Samples are available as well as diaper bags and accessories.

Our Picks: Brand Recommendations

Disposables. The evolution of disposable diapers is rather amazing. They started out in the 1960's as bulky and ineffective at stopping leaks. In 40 years, disposables morphed into ultra-thin, super-absorbent miracle workers that command 95% of the market.

And writing about disposable diaper brands is like trying to nail Jell-O to a wall—every five minutes, the diaper makers come out with new features and new gimmicks as they jostle for a piece of the nearly $27 billion worldwide diaper market. In the 11 years since the first edition of this book came out, the constant innovation in this category is amazing. We used to talk about three types of diapers: basic (thick, tape tabs), ultrathin (with the gel and tape tabs) and supreme (fabric-like outer layer, Velcro tabs). But in recent years, almost all diapers have added Velcro tabs, nicer outer layers and the ubiquitous super absorbent gels. So what separates the good from the bad diapers? *The key is good fit, no leaks and comfort for baby.*

Who's got the cheapest diapers?

What's the best place to buy disposable diapers? We did a price comparison among several major sources, listed here from least to most expensive:

STORE OR WEB SITE	DIAPER TYPE	COUNT	PRICE	PER DIAPER
SAM'S CLUB	HUGGIES #1-2	264	$37.62	14¢
COSTCO	HUGGIES #2	258	$42.86	16¢
DIAPERS.COM	HUGGIES #1-2	228	$36.99	16¢
AMAZON	HUGGIES #1-2	228	$36.99	16¢
BABIES R US	HUGGIES #1	192	$33.99	18¢
WAL-MART	HUGGIES #1	100	$19.47	19¢
GROCERY STORE*	HUGGIES #1	56	$10.69	19¢
TARGET	HUGGIES #1	100	$20.00	20¢
DIAPERS4LESS.COM**	HOUSE BRAND	256	$61.95	24¢

Price: Includes shipping.
Per Diaper: The cost per diaper.

* Checked at Kroger (King Soopers).
** Free shipping.
† Flat shipping fee regardless how many you order.

Note: Prices checked as of 2009.

No matter what brand you try, remember that sizing of diapers is all over the board. The "size two" diaper in one brand may be cut totally different than the "medium" of another, even though the weight guidelines on the package are similar. Finding a diaper that fits is critical to you and your baby's happiness.

Now, let's answer some common questions about disposables:

Q. What makes one brand different from another?

A. Surprisingly, the absorbency of diapers varies little from brand to brand. A *Consumer Reports* test of 14 families with infants and toddlers is a case in point. They tested seven types of disposable diapers. Five of them tested "very good" or "excellent" for leak protection. No matter what brand you choose, you'll probably have a diaper that fits well and doesn't leak. Yes, the premium/supreme diapers scored highest in CR's tests, but the difference between them and the cheaper options was minimal (except for the price, of course).

Besides absorbency, gimmicks and marketing ploys are the only differences between brands. This market goes through fads faster than Madison Avenue. We remember gender-specific diapers, which were on the market for about five minutes. That was more hype than real benefit and now they're gone (we're back to unisex versions). Another fad that came and went: "Pampers Rash Care," a premium diaper which "contains the same active ingredients as many diaper rash creams" to prevent diaper rash. Now Pampers offers "Go Baby Grips" while Huggies touts their Natural Fit feature. Next week we expect Luvs to come out with a brand that promises higher college entrance scores. Call it Luvs "Ultra SAT Boosters."

Q. What about store brands like Babies R Us and others? Is there much difference?

A. Although store diapers used to be less impressive than name brands, in the last few years they've caught up in terms of cloth like covers, Velcro fasteners and ultra absorbency. And they cost as much as 30% less too.

Q. Do certain brands work better for boys or girls?

A. We used to hear anecdotal evidence from our readers that Huggies were better for boys and Pampers better for girls. In recent years, however, parents tell us there doesn't seem to be a gender difference at all.

Q. How many diapers of each size is a good starting point?

A. Most babies go through 12 to 14 diapers *per day* for the first few months. That translates into about 500 to 600 diapers for the first six weeks. As you read at the beginning of the chapter we recommend buying 100 "newborn" size diapers and 400 to 500 "size one" diapers before baby is born. Caveat: some families have large babies, so keep the receipts just in case you have to exchange some of those newborns for size 1.

So how many do you need of the larger sizes? Starting with a case of each size as you transition to larger diapers is a good idea. There are typically 100 diapers or more in a case. As you near a transition to a larger size, scale back the amount of smaller size diapers you buy so you don't have any half opened packs lying around.

Finally, remember that as your baby grows, she will require fewer diaper changes. Once you add solid foods to her feeding schedule you may only be doing eight to ten changes a day (we know—eight to ten a day still seems like a ton of changes; but it will feel much less than baby's first few weeks). Plus you'll be much more experienced about when a diaper really is wet.

So which diaper brand is best? While Consumer Reports says there isn't much difference between brands, our readers have different ideas. We'll include comments from our Reader Poll in the reviews below.

◆ **Huggies.** Huggies has been a strong brand for years. They now offer four diaper options: Huggies Newborn Gentle Care, Huggies Supreme Gentle Care with Cuddleweave (we kid you not) Fit, Huggies Natural Fit, Huggies Snug & Dry, and Huggies Overnights. While parents weren't crazy for regular Huggies, many were full of praise for the Supremes.

The Gentle Care version is for newborns, with a u-shaped waistband for umbilical cords. They come in newborn up to size 2. Supreme Gentle Care are available in sizes 1 and 2. "Cuddleweave is supposed to make them the "softest ever."

The Natural Fit diapers are intended for older babies. They claim their hourglass shape fits babies better. These are available in sizes 3 to 6. Snug & Dry diapers have LeakLock, which is supposed to create "unbeatable leakage protection. They are also extra stretchy which promises a better fit in sizes 1 to 6.

Overnights are made to be even more absorbent so babies can actually sleep through the night (and parents too!). And they still have their "Little Swimmers" swim diapers—great for the pool or beach.

As for wipes, Huggies offers six varieties from Extra Sensitive to Natural Care to Soft Skin. Feedback from parents was a thumbs up on the wipes, no matter the type.

Huggies web site (huggies.com) has become a little bit confusing to use. Once you get the "happy baby" section, you'll find it confusing to find actual product info. We suggest clicking on one of the side windows rather than going to "Products." You'll avoid lots of video ads that way. The website also offers parenting advice on both pregnancy and child development with expert interviews and articles.

◆ **Pampers.** Pampers continues to offer an extensive line of diapers to cover baby's stages of development and growth. Swaddlers New Baby are intended for newborns to size 2-3. Claiming to "wrap your baby in ultra comfort" these diapers are for very young, inactive babies. Pampers claims they have soft, stretchy sides for a "flexible fit." Swaddlers Sensitive (sizes newborn to 2) have "Air Dry" breathable fabric, a wetness indicator and special liner. They also claim these diapers are hypoallergenic, hence the "Sensitive" part of the name.

For the next stage when babies begin to kick, roll over, crawl and stand, Pampers has introduced their Cruisers. These are supposed to have more elasticity and give for active babies as well as less bulk. They also promise stronger fasteners. Cruisers are sized from 3 to 7. Baby Dry diapers are yet another line of diapers in sizes from newborn to toddler targeted for nighttime use. They've added "caterpillar-flex" (sizes 1-6) to allow the waistband to expand and contract giving the diaper a better fit.

Readers who responded to our disposable diaper poll gave both Swaddlers and Cruisers high ratings over all. The Baby Dry line came in for lots of criticism, however—parents complained that these diaper leak. As for Pampers wipes, again parents seemed to like them although some complained that the wipes were too wet. Pampers offer seven versions of their wipes including sensitive, unscented and lavender scented plus a flushable wipe for older kids.

Pampers' easy to use web site (pampers.com) explains the new offerings pretty well, and there is an easy-to use search engine that helps you figure out what's available for your baby at any particular stage or weight. Pampers also has a coupon program and will send out free samples if you sign up as a member.

◆ **Luvs.** Made by Procter & Gamble, the company that also makes Pampers, Luvs are marketed as a lower-price brand. All in all, based on reader feedback, we didn't see much difference between Luvs and Pampers . . . or Huggies.

New this year, Luvs includes a blue Leakguard Core that is supposed to improve leak protection. Like the more expensive diapers, Luvs have an hourglass shape, fabric-like outer layer, reusable fasteners and range from newborn to size 6. Luvs is also offering a money-back guarantee—if you're not satisfied with their diapers, they offer your money back on a pack of Luvs. But there is some fine print (you'll have to send in your original receipt, it's limited to one refund per household, they deduct a dollar for postage and it take six to eight weeks to get the refund). Still, no one else is offering a guarantee.

Readers were mixed in their appraisal of Luvs. Some said they leaked, but others praised the low price and thought they worked fine.

Luvs' web site (luvs.com) has a simple layout. Besides products info, you can find message boards and other advice online.

◆ **White Cloud by Wal-Mart.** We mentioned White Cloud (Wal-Mart's private label brand) in our last edition, but we think it deserves a full-blown recommendation this time around. Parents seem universally pleased with the quality and impressed with the price of White Cloud (112 size 2 diapers for $15.97—14 cents each). Parents told us these diapers don't leak, nor any strange chemical or perfume smell. But price was the biggest reason parents gave for trying White Cloud—they're affordable everyday, not just when they're on sale.

◆ **Store brands**. We've received numerous emails from parents who love store-brand diapers at Target, K-Mart, Walgreens and CVS Pharmacy. Even grocery stores are getting into the game with private label diapers at prices to rival the discounters. Generally, these diapers are 20% to 50% cheaper than name brands—Wal-Mart's "Parents Choice" run just 10¢ each (size 1). In the past, generic diapers were inferior in terms of features and quality but no more—most have the same ultrathin design, cloth-like covers and reusable tabs.

Who's got the best store-brand diapers? Target and CVS brands got mixed reviews, while Walgreens had a few thumbs up from our readers. Recently a mom reported that Publix store brand was so good, she stopped buying Pampers Cruisers. Bottom line: give store brand diapers a try. If you find one that works, you can find significant savings over the name brands.

Eco-friendly Disposables. Are there diapers that combine the convenience of disposables with the ecological benefits of cloth diapers? Yes—here's an overview of so-called eco-friendly disposables:

Tushies, first invented by a Denver pediatrician in the late 1980's, bills its diapers as a gel-free, latex-free, perfume-free alternative to name brand disposables. Made with non-chlorine bleached wood pulp surrounding an absorbent cotton core, Tushies also has a "cloth-like" cover. Tushies mentions that without the gel, their diapers won't "explode" in the swimming pool. The disadvantages to Tushies? They are considerably thicker than regular diapers. And like most "all-natural" versions of consumer goods, Tushies ain't cheap. They sell a case of 160 size small diapers for $68.04. That's 42¢ per diaper. Compare that to grocery store prices of 19¢ per diaper and warehouse clubs of 14¢ per diaper. Prices are slightly lower if you join their online club at www.tushies.com. They are also sold in health food stores like Whole Foods and Wild Oats.

Seventh Generation (seventhgeneration.com) is another website offering a chlorine-free disposable diaper with a thinner design. The diapers have a cloth like outer layer, reusable tabs, and are latex and fragrance free. Made of wood pulp, a polyolefin backing and a polyolefin outer cover, Seventh Generation also includes an absorbent polymer gel. They are careful to explain that the gel they use is non-toxic, non-carcinogenic and non-irritating. In fact, you can view a list of all the ingredients and see material safety data sheets too. A reader also recommends the company's wipes saying they are "free of chemicals and full of good stuff for my baby's skin."

You can find these diapers online at Amazon or in stores such as Whole Foods and Vitamin Cottage. On Amazon.com, a pack of 176 stage 1 Seventh Generation diapers was $42.99 (24¢ per diaper). Coupons are available on Seventh Generation's web site.

Here's a popular new diaper that isn't quite a disposable, nor a cloth diaper—*gDiapers* are flushable diapers. Yep, you read it right. Flushable. To be precise, part of a gDiaper is flushable.

A gDiaper starter kit comes with two reusable "little g" pants (like cloth diaper covers) and ten diaper refills for $27. Once you are ready to dispose of the diaper refills, you have a choice: flush them, compost the wet diapers or throw them in the garbage. GDiapers notes you never compost a poopy diaper, only flush it. But what about throwing them out? Isn't that the same as disposables? Not necessarily since there is no plastic in gDiapers, so they degrade fast (supposedly 50 to 150 days) . . . if you don't put them in a plastic trash back, of course.

GDiapers' web site has several videos showing their product at work. And we've heard from several moms who love this idea. It is a nice compromise in the cloth versus disposable debate. One caveat: you'll find gDiapers aren't as absorbent as disposables, simply because they use only wood pulp (fluffed for extra absorbency) rather than that super absorbent gel. Price is really going to be the issue with gDiapers. Additional washable "little g" pants range from $17 to $19. Refills start at 32¢ each for a 160 of the small size. Ouch!—that's twice the price of disposables when bought at discount stores!

Another newcomer to the eco-friendly disposable is *Nature Babycare* diapers. Like gDiapers, these are chlorine free and use no plastics (corn-based materials). They were designed by a Swedish mom and are compostable. They are slightly less expensive that the gDiapers (27¢ per diaper) for the small size, but still considerably more than standard disposables. You'll find them on web sites like Diapers.com and BetterBabyBuns.com.

Ultimately, while these products are promising options for parents looking for a natural alternative to mainstream disposables, the price is certainly going to be a factor in getting parents to use them. And there is still an issue of where these diapers will go. Until recycling centers with composting options become more widely available, there's a question as to whether these diapers won't still end up buried under tons of earth and trash waiting to decompose.

Cloth Diapers. If you ask 100 parents for their recommendations on cloth diapers (as we recently did on our web site), you're likely to get 100 different opinions—it seems everyone has their special system or favorite brand! Unlike disposable diapers, there aren't three or four brands that everyone uses or recognizes. Instead, there are at least 20 different options from simple prefold diapers with pins to fancy all-in-one diapers. And prices are all over the board too. So what's an aspiring CD'er (cloth diaperer) to do? First let's take you through the basics with Karen F., our CD guru from our message boards:

A cloth diaper has three basic functions. Working from the inside out:

1. Wick it away. This layer is intended to keep baby from sitting in her pee. This layer lets moisture through in one direction but not back towards the skin. In cloth diapers, this layer is fleece or suede-cloth, but only certain kinds of fleece will do this. Some people just cut rectangles of fleece and lay them inside the diaper. Some diapers are lined with fleece, sewn in place while others are pocket diapers with the fleece next to the skin. And there are some people who skip this layer and change the diaper as soon as baby pees.

2. Soak it up. Typically, the absorbent layer in cloth diapers is made of cotton or hemp and is sewn in layers. There are also some diapers with a micro fiber towel for the absorbent layer. Some people add an extra layer called a "doubler" which is just layers of cloth sewn together. This allows parents to increase absorption when needed (overnight, for example). See below for a discussion of the different options for this layer.

3. Keep the rest of the world dry. Remember those awful plastic/rubber pants of yesteryear? Uncomfortable for baby and noisy too! Today's options are much more comfortable to wear and touch. Cloth diaper covers can be polyurethane laminate (PUL) over cotton or polyester, nylon, wool or fleece. Wool is naturally water repellent when it has natural lanolin in it. (Otherwise sheep would bulk up like a sponge in a rainstorm!). The type of fleece that is used as diaper covers is water repellent."

Okay, now that you know the mechanics of cloth diapering, what should you use for your little guy or gal? First, here's the lingo you'll need to master:

1 **PREFOLDS** (CPF for Chinese prefolds or DSQ for diaper-service quality). These are what most parents think of when they envision cloth diapers. They are heavyweight 100% cotton cloths that have been prefolded (so that there is extra padding in the middle) and sewn down. This process leads to a diaper with six to eight layers in the middle and two to four layers on the sides. They can then be pinned onto your baby (not our favorite idea) or folded into a diaper cover. Avoid flat fold diapers—these are really just burp pads and great dust cloths!

2 **FITTED DIAPER:** Sometimes called pre-fitteds, these are pre-fold diapers that have elastic sewn in for the leg openings. They don't have snaps or Velcro so they have to be secured with pins or in a cover. You'll get a more snug fit around the leg openings with these.

E-MAIL FROM THE REAL WORLD
Cloth diaper laundry tips

Once you make the decision to use cloth diapers, you'll want to research the "art" of cleaning them. Too many harsh chemicals can damage and fade cloth diapers and covers, not enough will leave diapers looking less than pristine. So what's a parent to do? Here's some advice from readers who've experienced lots of diaper cleaning.

Rowan Cerrelli writes:
"I do not like to use chlorine bleach to wash out diapers since they are expensive and the chlorine ruins them. There are some products out there that use natural enzymes to predigest 'stuff' out of the diapers, therefore eliminating the need for bleach. Companies that have these products include Seventh Generation and Ecover. They are also available in natural food grocery stores."

Catherine Advocate-Ross recommends:
"I use Bio-Kleen laundry powder on the diapers. Works great and you need very little."

Bio-Kleen's web site bi-o-kleen.com explains their products and directs consumers to stores or web sites that carry them. They have an extensive line including liquid as well as powder detergent and stain and odor eliminator. The main ingredient in the line is grapefruit seed and pulp extract.

Kelly Small, from Wallingford, CT emailed us to say:
"I highly recommend OxyClean— it is great on the poop stains!!!"

---

3 **DOUBLER (ALSO CALLED LINER).** Available in paper, cotton or even silk, doublers are used when you need extra absorbency. They are inserted between the diaper and baby's bottom. These would be a great option at night or on a long car trip.

4 **DIAPER COVER/WRAP.** This item is placed over the diaper to stop leaks. One style of diaper cover is called a wrap—think of it as baby origami. You'll wrap your baby up and secure the Velcro tabs to the front strip. Some covers snap in place and there are other pants that can be pulled on (elastic waist).

5 **ALL-IN-ONE.** Just what you'd think, an all-in-one (AIO) is a diaper and cover sewn together. There are pluses and minuses to this design. Yes, the convenience of grabbing one item and snapping or velcroing it on your baby is great, but if your baby makes a mess, you have to wash the whole thing. With a tradition-

---

Finally, Rebecca Parish has some practical advice on cloth diapers:
"We (my friends and I) have run across a shortcut that I had not heard about before we attempted cloth diapering. Mainly, we have found it entirely unnecessary to rinse diapers out at all before laundering them. We own a four-day supply of pre-fold diapers and wraps. When our baby poops, we take an extra diaper wipe with us to the toilet, and use it to scrape what easily comes off into the toilet. Then we throw the dirty diaper into our diaper pail, right along with all the other dirty diapers. There's no liquid in the pail for soaking—they just sit in there dry. About every three or four days we throw the entire contents of the diaper pail into the laundry machine, add regular detergent (we use Cheer) and two capfuls of bleach (about 4 teaspoons), and run the machine. The diapers and wraps all come out clean. Just two extra loads of laundry a week (which is nothing compared to the extra loads of clothes we now wash), and no dipping our hands into toilet water. I generally use about five diaper wipes every time I change a messy diaper as it is, so using one extra one for scraping poop into the toilet seems like no big deal.

I think washer technology has improved significantly enough in recent years to allow for this much easier diaper cleaning. We own a fairly new front-loader washer. I don't think the brand name is important; we have a friend who owns a different brand of front-loader, and gets equally good results. However, one of our friends with an older top-loader uses our same system but ends up with stains; she doesn't care but I would. "

Bottom line: new technologies (detergents, additives and washers) have led to great improvements in the cleaning of cloth diapers.

al diaper/cover combination, you won't have to wash the cover every time unless baby gets poop on it. So you'll end up buying more all-in-ones to keep yourself from doing laundry constantly.

6 **POCKET DIAPER.** Made famous by Fuzzi Bunz, the pocket diaper is an all-in-one with a pocket sewn into the lining. You can then customize the diaper for more absorbency by adding an insert or a prefolded diaper.

7 **SNAPPI FASTENERS.** Made in South Africa, these cutting-edge diaper fasteners replace the traditional (and potentially painful) diaper pin. Check out their website at snappibaby.com for a look at how they work.

Whew! That's a lot to remember. So anyway, what's the bottom line? What should you buy? Great question. Here's what our cloth diaper guru recommends if you're just starting out and have a new-born: Buy two to three dozen prefold diapers and four to six diaper covers. You may also want to get a few pocket diapers or all-in-ones and a couple Snappis.

Now you probably want to know which brands to buy. So we polled our readers to find out their favorites. Right off the bat, they told us "it depends." Depends on your baby's body type, whether you're looking for nighttime leak protection and many other factors. A couple of the brands readers *could* agree on were Fuzzi Bunz and Snap-EZ Fleece Pocket diapers. Here is a list of the many other brands parents mentioned:

◆ *Fitted Diapers:*
Sugar Plum Babies (monkeytoediapers.com/sugarplumbaby)
Bizzy B Hive (hyenacart.com/bizzybhive)
Bijou Baby Gear (bijoubabygear.com)

◆ *Diaper Covers:*
AngelDry (wool) (angeldrydiapers.com)
Aristocrat (wool) (aristocratsbabyproducts.com)
Bummis (bummis.com)
Windro (wool)
Imse Vimse Bumpy (imsevimse.us/)
Luxe (wool) (luxebabydiapers.com)
Bizzy B Hive (wool) (hyenacart.com/bizzybhive)

◆ *All-In–Ones:*
Girl Woman Goddess (girlwomangoddess.com)
Lullaby Diapers (lullabydiapers.com)
Bum Genius (bumgenius.com)

Daisy Doodles (daisy-doodles.com)
Cuddlebuns (cuddlebunsdiapers.com)
DryBees (drybees.com)

◆ *Pockets:*
Fuzzi Bunz (they license their pocket design to those companies below)
Happy Heiny's (happyheinys.com)
Olive Branch Baby Marathon (olivebranchbaby.com)

◆ *A source for all of the above:*
Swaddlebees (swaddlebees.com)

Notes: Keep in mind that many of these companies are small, run by a couple friends or by a family. We've noticed that they often don't have fancy web sites and occasionally run out of stock for a while. Some websites sell directly to customers, others do not. And still others don't have their own websites but do sell online through retailers.

Need more information? A good book on using cloth diapers is *Diaper Changes* by Theresa Rodriquez (M. Evans and Co., publisher; $15). Also, check out our online message boards on our web site at babybargains.com. They have extensive commentary from cloth diaper parents with tips and recommendations.

Wipes. Like diapers, you have a basic choice with wipes: name brand or generic. Our advice: stick to the name brands. We polled our readers and their top picks were: **Huggies Natural Care** and **Target Sensitive Skin** brands. The reviews were more mixed with Pampers wipes: some parents thought they were too wet and too expensive.

We found most cheap generic wipes to be inferior. With less water and thinner construction, store brand wipes we sampled were losers. There is one exception to this rule, however: Costco's Kirkland brand wipes, which many readers have said are fantastic. One mom emailed: "They are not as rigid as Huggies or Pampers, have a lighter scent and are stronger than any other wipe we tried." And it's hard to beat the price: $16 for 704 (that's 2¢ per wipe). Another mom really loves BJ's Berkely and Jensen brand of wipes. She thought they were softer than Costco, more like Huggies. And the price is great: $15 for 720 wipes.

Money Saving Secrets

Here are some tips for saving on disposable diapers (cloth diaper bargain advice is at the end of this section):

1 **BUY IN BULK.** Don't buy those little packs of 20 diapers—look for the 80 or 100 count packs instead. You'll find the price per diaper goes down when you buy larger packs.

2 **GO FOR WAREHOUSE CLUBS.** Both Sam's (samsclub.com) and Costco (costco.com) wholesale clubs sell diapers at incredibly low prices. For example, Costco sells a 258-count package of Huggies stage 2 for just $42.80 or about 17¢ per diaper. We also found great deals on wipes at the wholesale clubs. Another warehouse club is BJ's (bjs.com), which has over 100 locations in 16 states, most in the Eastern U.S. By the way, one reader noted that the size 1-2 diapers she's seeing in warehouse clubs are really size 1. She's been frustrated with this sizing issue since the size 3 diapers are too big but there isn't anything in between the 1-2 and the 3 sizes.

3 **BUY STORE BRANDS.** As mentioned earlier, many parents find store brand diapers to be equal to the name brands. And the prices can't be beat—many are 20% to 30% cheaper. Chains like Target, Wal-Mart and Toys R Us/Babies R Us carry in-house diaper brands, as do many grocery stores. In fact, Wal-Mart's White Cloud brand is a favorite among our readers.

4 **CONSIDER TOYS R US.** You may not have a wholesale club nearby, but you're bound to be close to a Toys R Us (or their sister division, Babies R Us). And we found them to be a great source for affordable name-brand diapers. The best bet: buy in bulk. You can often buy diapers (both name brand and generic) by the case at Toys R Us, saving you about 20% or more over grocery store prices. As you might have noted in the earlier diaper cost comparison, Babies R Us was one of the lowest-priced sources for diapers we found. Don't forget to check the front of the store for copies of Toys R Us' latest catalog. Occasionally, they offer in-store coupons for additional diaper savings—you can even combine these with manufacturer's coupons for double savings.

5 **WHEN BABY IS NEARING A TRANSITION POINT, DON'T STOCK UP.** Quick growing babies may move into another size faster than you think, leaving you with an excess supply of too-small diapers.

6 **DON'T BUY DIAPERS IN GROCERY STORES.** We compared prices at grocery stores and usually found them to be sky-high. Most were selling diapers in packages that worked out to 20¢ per diaper. We should note there are exceptions to this rule, however: some grocery chains (especially in the South) use diapers as a "loss-leader." They'll sell diapers at attractive prices in order to entice shoppers into the store. Also, store brands can be more attractively priced, even at grocery stores. Use coupons (see below) to save even more.

7 **USE COUPONS.** You'll be amazed at how many coupons you receive in the mail, usually for 75¢ off diapers and 50¢ off wipes. One tip: to keep those "introductory" packages of coupons coming, continue signing up to be on the mailing lists of the maternity chain stores (apparently, these chains sell your name to diaper manufacturers, formula companies, etc.) or online at diaper manufacturers' web sites.

8 **ASK FOR GIFT CERTIFICATES.** When friends ask you what you'd like as a shower gift, you can drop hints for gift certificates/cards from stores that sell a wide variety of baby items— including diapers and wipes. That way you can get what you really need, instead of cute accessories of marginal value. You'd be surprised at how many stores offer gift certificate programs.

9 **FOR CLOTH DIAPER USERS, GO FOR "INTRODUCTORY PACKAGES."** Many suppliers have special introductory deals (Mother-Ease offers their One-Size diaper, a liner and cover for $22 which includes shipping). Before you invest hundreds of dollars in one brand, give it a test drive first.

10 **BUY USED CLOTH DIAPERS.** Many of the best brands of cloth diapers last and last and last. So you may see them on eBay or cloth-diaper message boards. Buy them—you can get some brands for as little a buck or two. As long as you know the quality and age of the diapers you're buying, this tip can really be a money saver.

11 **REUSE THEM.** Okay, we know this may be obvious, but hang onto your cloth diapers and use them for your next child. Every child is different, so even if you buy a brand and it doesn't fit your baby well, it may work on your next child. And of course, you can always sell them on eBay when you're all finished.

The Bottom Line: A Wrap-Up of Our Best Buy Picks

In summary, we recommend you buy the following layette items for your baby (see chart on next page).

Quantity	Item	Cost
6	T-shirts/onesies (over the head)	$18
6	T-shirts (side snap)	$20
4-6	Sleepers	$64-$96
1	Blanket Sleeper	$12.50
2-4	Coveralls	$50-$100
3-4	Booties/socks	$10-$12
1	Sweater	$16.50
2	Hats (safari and caps)	$20
1	Snowsuit/bunting	$20
4	Large bibs (for feeding)	$24
3 sets	Wash cloths and towels	$36
7-8	Receiving blankets	$20
TOTAL		**$311 to $395**

These prices are from discounters, outlet stores, or sale prices at department stores. What would all these clothes cost at full retail? $500 to $600, at least. The bottom line: follow our tips and you'll save $100 to $300 on your baby's layette alone. (Of course, you may receive some of these items as gifts, so your actual outlay may be less.)

Which brands are best? See "Our Picks: Brand Recommendations" earlier in this chapter. In general, we found that 100% cotton clothes are best. Yes, you'll pay a little more for cotton, but it lasts longer and looks better than clothes made of polyester blends (the exception: fleece outerwear and sleepwear). Other wastes of money for infants include kimonos, saque sets, and shoes.

What about diapers? We found little financial difference between cloth and disposable, especially when you use a cloth diaper service. Cloth does have several hidden costs, however—diaper covers can add hundreds of dollars to the expense of this option although the cost can be spread out among additional children.

For disposables, we found that brand choice was more of a personal preference—all the majors did a good job at stopping leaks. The best way to save money on disposable diapers is to skip the grocery store and buy in bulk (100+ diaper packages) from a warehouse club. Diapers from discount sources run about $300 to $375. The same diapers from grocery stores could be $600 or more. Another great money-saver: generic, store-brand diapers from Wal-Mart, Target, K-Mart and the like. These diapers performed just as well as the name brands at a 20% to 30% discount.

CHAPTER 5

Maternity & Nursing

Inside this chapter

Love 'em or hate 'em, every mother-to-be needs maternity clothes at some point in her pregnancy. Still, you don't have to break the bank to get comfortable, and, yes, fashionable maternity items. In this chapter, we tell you which sources sell all-cotton, casual clothes at unbelievably low prices. Then, we'll review the biggest maternity chains and reveal our list of top wastes of money. Finally, you'll learn which nursing clothes moms prefer most.

Maternity & Nursing Clothes

Getting Started: When Do You Need This Stuff?

It may seem obvious that you'll need to buy maternity clothes when you get pregnant, but the truth is you don't actually need all of them immediately. The first thing you'll notice is the need for a new bra. At least, that was my first clue that my body was changing. Breast changes occur as early as the first month and you may find yourself going through several different bra sizes along the way.

Next, it's time for the bump. Yes, the baby is making its presence known by making you feel a bit bigger around the middle. Skirts and pants feel tight as early as your third month. Maternity clothes at this point may seem like overkill, but some women do begin to "show" enough that they find it necessary to head out to the maternity shop.

If you have decided to breastfeed, you'll need to consider what type of nursing bras you'll want. Buy two or three in your eighth month so you'll be prepared. You may find it necessary to buy more nursing bras after the baby is born, but this will get you started. As for other nursing clothes, you may or may not find these worth the money. Don't go out and buy a whole new wardrobe right off the bat. Some women find nursing shirts and tops to be helpful while others manage quite well with regular clothes. More on this topic later in the book.

Sources

1 MATERNITY WEAR CHAINS. Not surprisingly, there are a few nationwide maternity clothing chains. Visit any mall and you'll likely see the names Pea in the Pod, Destination Maternity and Motherhood, to mention a few. More on these chains later in the chapter.

2 MOM AND POP MATERNITY SHOPS. These small, independent stores sell a wide variety of maternity clothes, from affordable weekend wear to high-priced career wear. Some baby specialty stores carry maternity clothes as well. The chief advantage to the smaller stores is personalized service—we usually found salespeople who were knowledgeable about the different brands. In addition, these stores may offer other services. For example, some rent formal wear for special occasions, saving you big bucks. Of course, you may pay for the extra service with higher prices. While you're shopping at the independents look for lines from manufacturers like Meet Me in Miami, Juicy Maternity and Olian (olianmaternity.com). Readers have been pleased with the quality and style of these brands.

3 CONSIGNMENT STORES. Many consignment or thrift stores that specialize in children's clothing may also have a rack of maternity clothes. In visits to several such stores, we found some incredible bargains (at least 50% off retail) on maternity clothes that were in good to excellent condition. Of course, the selection varies widely, but we strongly advise you to check out any second-hand stores for deals.

4 DISCOUNTERS. When we talk about discounters, we're referring to chains like Target, Wal-Mart and K-Mart. Now, let's be honest here—these discounters probably aren't the first place you'd think of to outfit your maternity wardrobe. Yet, each has a surprisingly nice selection of maternity clothes, especially casual wear. Later, we'll tell you about the incredible prices on these all-cotton clothes

5 DEPARTMENT STORES. As you might guess, most department stores carry some maternity fashions. The big disadvantage:

the selection is usually rather small. Selection is much greater, how-ever, on store websites. And department stores like Penney's and Sears often have end-of-the-season sales with decent maternity bargains. Look for maternity sections at Kohl's, JCPenney, Sears, Macy's, Nordstrom, Neiman Marcus and other

6 **WEB/MAIL-ORDER.** Even if you don't have any big-time maternity chains nearby, you can still buy the clothes they sell. Many chains offer a mail-order service, either from printed catalogs or online stores. In the "Do It By Mail" section of this chapter, we'll give you the run-down on these options.

7 **NON-MATERNITY STORES.** Maternity stores don't have a monopoly on large-size clothes—and you can save big bucks by shopping at stores that don't have the word "maternity" in their name. One of our favorites: Old Navy & the Gap. Their maternity clothes are both stylish and affordable.

8 **YOUR HUSBAND'S CLOSET.** What's a good source for comfy weekend wear? Look no further than the other side of your closet, where your husband's clothes can often double as mater-nity wear.

9 **OUTLETS.** Yes, there are several outlets that sell maternity clothes and the prices can be a steal. We'll discuss some alternatives later in this chapter.

10 **YOUR FRIENDS.** It's a time-honored tradition—handing down "old" maternity clothes to the newly pregnant. Of course, maternity styles don't change that much from year to year and since outfits aren't worn for a long time, they are usually in great shape. Just be sure to pass on the favor when you are through with your pregnancy.

Parents in Cyberspace: What's on the Web?

eBay
Web: ebay.com
What it is: A surprising source of maternity bargains.
What's cool: Here are the deals just one of our readers, Alison Lewis of Winston-Salem, NC found: "I got five long sleeve cotton maternity shirts and two pairs of corduroy pant (mostly Motherhood brand) for a total of $21.50 and the shipping was $4." She notes too that the selection on eBay is "pretty much endless."

Needs work: Expect to find some real duds in the fashion department here. There's bound to be a lot of junk you'll have to sift through to find the jewels.

Expressiva

Web: expressiva.com
What it is: Terrific source for nursing clothes.
What's cool: Wow! That's all we could say when we took a look at Expressiva's designs. You really never would know they were nursing clothes. And they don't make you look like a sack of potatoes. Tops, dresses, casual clothes, bras and sleepwear are available here. Sizes range from extra small to 3X and the site includes hints about sizing for specific outfits. We love the special collection for plus sizes. Eight styles of nursing openings are available and the site shows you exactly how each type works. Prices are reasonable for the quality. If you want to look good and still offer the best first food for your baby, this is a site to check out.

Lane Bryant

Web: lanebryant.com
What it is: A great source for plus-size maternity clothes.
What's cool: Plus-size moms often email us to complain about the lack of selection of plus-size maternity clothes at traditional stores. Good news: Lane Bryant to the rescue. With sizes that go from 14 to 28, plus petites and talls, the depth of offerings is impressive. They offer dresses, swimsuits, even cocktail dresses. Prices are moderate—jeans for $50, a poplin stretch shirt for $35, etc.
Needs work: Fashion is often hit or miss, but at least the wide selection makes finding suitable items easier.

Motherwear

Web: motherwear.com
What it is: More nursing clothes.
What's cool: "This catalog makes the best clothes for nursing!" gushed one mom in an email to us and we have to agree—this is a great catalog and web site. The quality is excellent with prices in the reasonable range (a special occasion dress for $69). They have a clearance section as well and don't forget to check their weekly specials. A cool feature: want to see what the nursing openings look like on each garment? Just click on "How Does it Work?" and see clear photos of each opening. Motherwear has a satisfaction guarantee and easy return policy.

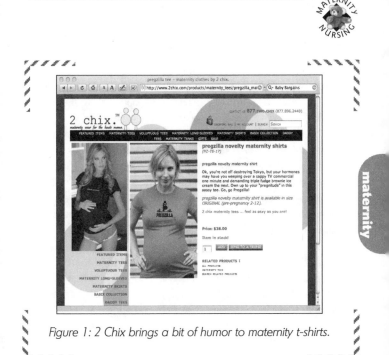

Figure 1: 2 Chix brings a bit of humor to maternity t-shirts.

maternity

◆ **Other sites:** Years ago, maternity clothes were meant to cover up a pregnancy. Women were encouraged to wear the fashion equivalent of a burlap sack. But no more. Check out the sassy maternity t-shirts on **2 Chix** (2chix.com; pictured above). Potato sacks these are not. Form fitting tank tops as well as short and long sleeved T's are the rule here, many with cutesy sayings like "Pregzilla" and "knocked up." Prices ranged from $38 to $50. We also chuckled at the dad shirts with sayings like "he shoots, he scores." Not that you'd want him to wear this around your dad, but his friends would be amused.

While most folks know the **Gap** as a great place for kids' clothes, did you know Gap also does maternity? While most moms will only be able to find Gap Maternity online (gap.com), some BabyGap bricks and mortar stores offer maternity in store as well. You'll find classics like cardigans and jeans as well as stretch shirts, swim suits and more. Nice feature: photos showcase their four different types of waistbands for pants. And sizes range from 0 to 20 plus inseams go up to 34." Check frequently for sale items—they seem to offer more sales than most maternity retailers. Readers have been impressed with the quality of Gap maternity, according to our email. By the way, GapMaternity has added a new Medela store-within-a-store on their web site. Find bras, pumps, lanolin and breast pads here. Sign up for email special sales and get these items at a discount.

Old Navy, Gap's low price sister chain is also selling maternity on line (oldnavy.com). As with other Old Navy clothes, the quality is a bit less but then so are the prices. The Gap and Old Navy now share a web site (with Banana Republic and Piperlime—sister chains) and return policies. Used to be you could return online purchases to the stores. No more. But to make up for it, all online returns are free.

Another bricks and mortar store with a decent online maternity selection is **Ann Taylor Loft**. Styles and fabrics are very similar to the typical non-maternity options from the store. We saw great details like ruffles and gathers as well as business-ready designs. Prices are reasonable . . . and especially affordable during sales. We saw a woven wrap blouse by Olian for $50, regularly $80. Another big advantage is their excellent size and fit guide—a chart shows your pre-maternity size and the correlating pregnancy size you should buy. Nifty! Their return policy echoes Old Navy and the Gap—no in-store returns of online items, but mailing back is free.

Chatter on our message boards has mentioned the website **Due Maternity** (duematernity.com) as a great place for maternity clothing. You'll see many fashion-forward brands on this site, including Chiarakruza, Momzee and their own Due Designs. The prices are in the upper range, but they have an extensive sale section.

Maternity 4 Less (maternity4less.com) received a parent recommendation for speedy delivery. Our reader reported that they exchanged a pair of maternity pants for her in only a matter of days, not the usual weeks other mail-order sources take. They carry the gamut of maternity and nursing clothes and accessories. Maternity 4 Less also has a section of the site for plus sizes. The site isn't much to look at but the prices are darned reasonable.

One of our readers raved about the jeans on **Fashion Bug's** web site (fashionbug.com). "They were awesome!" she wrote. Prices ranged from $20 to $45 and plus sizes are available.

For a wide range of styles and sizes (up to 3X plus talls and petites), check out **Mom Shop** (momshop.com). With great full size photos and an easy to use site, we think MomShop.com is a top site.

Nursing clothes are where **One Hot Mama** (onehotmama.com) got their start, but they have expanded into maternity clothes as well. Either way, they attempt to showcase hip styles from manufacturers like Rebel Jeans and Jolie Bebe. Just don't read the long-winded sermons on nursing from the site's owners.

Isabella Oliver (isabellaoliver.com) is a great site we stumbled upon when researching this book. This stylish site offers the usual categories like work and casual, but also includes 4th trimester clothes, resort wear and even bridal. While the designs are very hip they are expensive. Sale items however, are a great deal. And we like the attitude on this site. The designers have a blog, they offer good fashion advice and interesting "style notes." It's more than just clothes.

For our Canadian readers, check out **Thyme Maternity** (thymematernity.com), recommended by a reader in Ontario. She thought the styles were more "real world," the sizing was great and prices were reasonable. They no longer offer mail order, but their web site has a directory of stores in Canada. As a side note, another Canadian mom wrote to recommend that her countrywomen consider going to Buffalo or other US cities to shop for maternity clothes.

We could go on and on with all these maternity/nursing web sites, but let's condense it a bit for you. The following are yet more options to check out for maternity and nursing clothing:

Birth and Baby	birthandbaby.com
Mommy Gear	mommygear.com
Fit Maternity	fitmaternity.com
Naissance Maternity	naissancematernity.com
Twinkle Little Star	twinklelittlestar.com

What Are You Buying?

What will you need when you get pregnant? There is no shortage of advice on this topic, especially from the folks trying to sell you stuff. But here's what real moms advise you to buy (divided into two topic areas, maternity clothes and then nursing clothes):

Maternity Clothes

◆ **Maternity Bras.** Maternity bras are designed to grow with you as your pregnancy progresses; these bras also offer extra support (you'll need it). Maternity bras are available just about everywhere, from specialty maternity shops to department stores, mail order catalogs and discount chains. More on this topic later in this chapter; look for our recommendations for maternity underwear.

HOW MANY? Two in each size as your bust line expands. I found that I went through three different sizes during my pregnancy, and buying two in each size allowed me to wear one while the other was washed.

◆ **Sleep Bras.** Why a sleep bra, you ask? Well, some women find it more comfortable to have a little extra support at night as their breasts change. Toward the end of pregnancy, some women also start to leak breast milk (to be technical, this is actually colostrum). Sleep bras hold breast pads in place to soak up any leaks. And once the baby arrives, a sleeping bra (about $10-$20) also keeps you from leaking when you inadvertently roll onto your

Plus-size Maternity Clothing

What's the number one frustration with maternity wear? Finding decent plus-size maternity clothes, say our readers. Some maternity clothing manufacturers think only women with supermodel bodies get pregnant. But what to do if you want to look attractive and your dress size starts at 16 or above? Our readers have recommended the following sites:

Baby Becoming	babybecoming.com
JCPenney	jcpenney.com
MomShop	momshop.com
Motherhood	maternitymall.com
Expressiva	expressiva.com
Plus Maternity	plusmaternity.com

stomach—yes, there will come a day when you can do that again. Some women just need light support, while others find a full-featured bra a necessity.

HOW MANY? Two sleep bras—one to wear while one is in the wash.

◆ **Underpants.** In the past, our recommendation for maternity underpants extolled the virtues of traditional maternity underwear. But time rolls on—and fashion has changed. Most women today are wearing bikini-style underpants as standard gear. And, readers note, you can continue to wear those same styles when you're pregnant. So, save yourself some money and forget the maternity underpants. If you're already wearing bikini styles, stick with them. But, now is a good time to consider upgrading your underpants wardrobe in case you've let your skivvies wear out a bit. After all, you'll be going to lots of check ups and eventually the hospital—your mom would be embarrassed if your unmentionables were full of holes!

HOW MANY? If you need new underpants or plan to ignore our advice and buy maternity underpants, we recommend at least eight pairs.

◆ **Maternity belts and support items.** Pregnancy support belts can be critical for some moms. For example, Pam A., one of our readers sent the following email when she was 7 1/2 months along:

"Last week I got the worst pain/cramp that I have ever had in my life. It kept coming and going while I was walking, but it was so bad that I doubled over in pain when it hit. I went to my doctor and she said that the baby was pushing on a ligament that goes between the abdomen and the leg. She recommended that I get a "Prenatal Cradle" (prenatalcradle.com). I'll tell you what—it is the most wonderful purchase I have ever made in my life. It was about $70, but it works wonders. It does not totally eliminate the pain, but it gives enough support that it drastically reduces the pain and even gives me time to change positions so that it does not get worse. I have even found that wearing it at night helps to alleviate the pain at night rolling over in bed."

Your best bet, if you find you need some support, is to check with your doctor as Pam did. Many of these belts are available on general web sites like OneStepAhead.com, BuyBuyBaby.com and some drugstore sites. If you're a plus-size mom and need a maternity support belt, check out your local medical supply store for larger sizes. Maternity shops don't seem to carry many plus-size belts.

How many? Kind of obvious, but one should be enough. And most likely you'll need this late in your pregnancy unless you are carrying multiples.

◆ **Career Clothing.** Our best advice about career clothing for the pregnant mom is to stick with basics. Buy yourself a coordinating outfit with a skirt, jacket, and pair of pants and then accessorize.

Now, we know what you're saying. You'd love to follow this advice, but you don't want to wear the same old thing several times a week—even if it is beautifully accessorized. I don't blame you. So, go for a couple dresses and sweaters too. The good news is you don't have to pay full price. We've got several money-saving tips and even an outlet or two coming up later in this chapter.

Thanks to casual office wear trends, pregnant woman can spend hundreds of dollars LESS than they might have had to ten or twenty years ago. Today, you can pair a pencil skirt with a sweater set for most office situations.

◆ **Casual Clothes.** Your best bet here is to stick with simple basics, like jeans and cords. You don't necessarily have to buy these from maternity stores. In fact, later in this chapter, we'll talk about less-expensive alternatives. If you're pregnant in the summer, dresses can be a cooler alternative to pants and shorts.

◆ **Dress or Formal Clothes.** Forget them unless you have a full social calendar or have many social engagements associated with your job. Sometimes, you can find a local store that rents maternity formalwear for the one or two occasions when you might need it.

Nursing Clothes

◆ **Nursing Bras.** The one piece of advice every nursing mom gives is: buy a well-made, high quality, nursing bra *that fits you*. Easier said than done you say? Maybe. But here are some tips we gleaned from a reader poll we took.

First, what's the difference between a nursing bra and a maternity bra? Nursing bras have special flaps that fold down to give baby easy access to the breast. Access is usually with a hook or snaps either in the middle or on top of the bra near the straps. Readers insist new moms should look for the easiest access they can find. You'll need to be able to open your nursing bra quickly with only one hand in most cases.

Next, avoid under wire bras at all cost. They can cause plugged ducts, a very painful condition. If you sport a large cup size, you'll need a bra that is ultra supportive. Check out Motherhood Maternity bras. Some of our readers told us they have a good selec-

News from Down Under: Maternity Bras for the Real World

What makes a great maternity bra? Consider the following points while shopping:

◆ *Support—part I*. How much support do you need? Some women we interviewed liked the heavy-duty construction of some maternity bras. For others, that was overkill.

◆ *Support—part II* Once you decide how much support you need, consider the *type* of support you like. The basic choices: under wire bras versus those that use fabric bands and panels. Some moms-to-be liked stretchy knit fabric while others preferred stiffer, woven fabric.

◆ *Appearance*. Let's be honest: some maternity bras can be darn ugly. And what about the bras that claim they'll grow with you during your pregnancy? Yes, they may stretch some—but one bra won't work for the entire nine months of pregnancy.

◆ *Price*. Yes, the best maternity bras can be pricey. But I've found it doesn't pay to scrimp on underwear like bras and panties. Save money on other items in your maternity wardrobe and invest in comfortable undergarments.

tion of large cup sizes. And in most cases, nursing moms require a sleep bra too—some for support, some just to hold nursing pads.

Mothers living near a locally owned maternity shop or specialized lingerie store recommended going in and having a nursing bra fitted to you. One reader reported that "I was wearing a bra at least three cup sizes too small. The consultant fitted me properly and I couldn't believe how comfortable I was!" If you don't have the luxury of a shop full of specialists, Motherwear (motherwear. com) has good online tips and information (click the link for "how does it work") and Bravado (bravadodesigns.com) offers extensive sizing tips for different models.

If you plan to nurse, you should probably buy at least two bras during your eighth month (they cost about $30 to $45 each). Why then? Theoretically, your breast size won't change much once your baby is born and your milk comes in. I'd suggest buying one with a little larger cup size (than your eighth month size) so you can compensate for the engorgement phase. You can always buy more later and, if your size changes once the baby is born, you won't have invested too much in the wrong size. If you want more advice on nursing bras, you can check out Playtex's cool web site at playtex.com. Click on the link to "Expectant Moments," their maternity brand.

How many? Buy one to two bras in your eighth month. After the baby is born, you may want to buy a couple more.

◆ **Nursing Pads.** There are two options with nursing pads: disposable and reusable. Common sense tells you that reusable breast pads make the most economical sense, particularly if you plan to have more children. Still, if you aren't a big leaker, don't plan to breast feed for long or just need something quick and easy when you're on the go, disposables are handy.

When we polled our readers, we were surprised to learn that the majority preferred disposables. Those by Lansinoh (lansinoh.com; $8.50 for 60 at drugstore.com) were by far the favorite followed by Johnson and Johnson ($5.40 per 60), Gerber (60 for $5.69) and Curity (12 for $1.44). What's the secret to these disposables? The same type of super absorbent polymer that makes your baby's diapers so absorbent. That makes them super thin too so you aren't embarrassed by telltale "bulls-eyes" in your bra. Moms also love the individually wrapped pads because they can just grab a couple and throw them in the diaper bag on the way out of the house. Interestingly, moms were divided on whether they like contoured or flat pads or those with adhesive strips or without.

While there wasn't one discount source mentioned for disposable breast pads, moms tell us when they see their favorite brands on sale at Wal-Mart, Target or Babies R Us, they snapped up multiple boxes.

For the minority who preferred reusable, washable pads, Medela ($6 per pair), Avent ($6.50 for three pair) and Gerber ($5 for three pair) made the top of the list. Some moms recommend Bravado's (bravadodesigns.com) Cool Max pads ($15 for three pair) for superior absorption. A few parents have raved about Danish Wool pads (danishwool.com). These soft, felted pads contain natural lanolin, a godsend for moms with sore, cracked nipples. They aren't cheap ($19 to $32 per pair) but we thought them worth the mention. Another pad recommended by a reader is LilyPadz by Lilypadz.com. She told us they are streamlined and reusable, can be

Reader Poll: Nursing clothes brands

When we polled our readers about nursing clothes we were immediately chastised by at least half the respondents for even considering recommending them. "A waste of money," "ugly!" and "useless" were a few of the more charitable comments from these readers. As many as one third had never even used a single nursing top. They preferred to wear button up shirts or t-shirts and loose tops that they just pulled up. One mom told us "I got pretty good at being discreet in public with my regular clothes and no one was the wiser."

But other moms loved nursing clothes. And their favorites were those from **Motherwear**, the catalog and web site we reviewed earlier in this chapter. In our poll over 100 respondents mentioned Motherwear as the best source for well-made, comfortable nursing clothes. The biggest complaint about Motherwear was that their clothes are expensive. Readers suggested buying them used from ebay.com. The next closest company was **One Hot Mama** (onehotmama.com) with 17 votes.

Other sites recommended by parents included **Expressiva** (expressiva.com), and **Birth and Baby** (birthandbaby.com).

Regardless of where nursing clothes were purchased, moms were universal in thinking that the best tops have two vertical openings over the breasts. Forget the single center opening! And no buttons either. Too hard, our moms said, to open with one hand while baby is screaming in your ear. Twin sets and cardigan sweaters were the preferred styles. Readers thought they looked least like nursing clothes. And lots of moms thought just having a few nursing camisoles and t-shirts to wear under a regular shirt was the way to go. Finally, several parents recommended the Super Secret Nursing Shirt from One Hot Mama ($64).

Want to make your own nursing clothes? Creative sewers will find great patterns on **Elizabeth Lee's** web site (elizabethlee.com).

worn with or without a bra and cost about $23 per pair.

If you have nipple soreness (you have our sympathies!), Jeri from Stoneham, MA recommended a product called Soothies (soothies.com). These reusable gel pads can be slipped into your bra to cool and soothe painful nipples. You can find them online or in drugstores for $12.

◆ **Nursing Clothes.** You may not think so (especially at 8 1/2 months), but there will come a day when you won't need to wear those maternity clothes. But what if you want to nurse in public after baby is born? Some women swear by nursing clothes as the best way to be discreet, but others do just fine with loose knit tops and button front shirts. Bottom line: one obvious way to save money with nursing clothes is not to buy any. If you want to experiment, buy one or two nursing tops and see how they work for you. By the way, parents of twins found it difficult if not impossible to use a nursing top when nursing both babies at the same time. See the previous box for more reader feedback on nursing clothes.

Reader Tracy G. suggested that working moms who are nursing or expressing milk might want to check into getting a nursing camisole or tank top. "I wear them under a regular shirt and don't feel so exposed when I pump at work or nurse in public." Her favorite: a Wal-Mart brand camisole. She thought it was softer than Motherhood Maternity options.

◆ **Nursing Pajamas.** Looking for something comfortable to sleep in that allows you to nurse easily? Nursing PJ's are one answer, although only a few moms we interviewed use them. Most hated nursing gowns and found it much simpler to sleep in pajamas with tops they could pull up or unbutton quickly

If you are interested in a specific nursing pajama, check out **Majamas** (majamas.com). One of our product testers tried out their cotton/lycra t-shirt with her newborn and thought it was great, worthy of a recommendation. It allowed her to sleep without wearing a nursing bra since it had pockets for holding breast pads and had easy nursing access. They have several pajama designs as well as t-shirts and have expanded the line to include maternity clothes.

More Money Buys You . . .

Like any clothing, the more you spend, the better quality fabric and construction you get. Of course, do you really need a cashmere maternity sweater you'll wear for only a few months? Besides fabric, you'll note more designer names as prices go up. For example, Lilly Pulitzer and Juicy Couture are making maternity clothes now.

Smart Shopper Tips

Smart Shopper Tip #1
Battling your wacky thermostat

"It's early in my pregnancy, and I'm finding that the lycra-blend blouses that I wear to work have become very uncomfortable. I'm starting to shop for maternity clothes—what should I look for that will be more comfortable?"

It's a fact of life for us pregnant folks—your body's thermostat has gone berserk. Thanks to those pregnancy hormones, it may be hard to regulate your body's temperature. And those lycra-blend clothes may not be so comfortable anymore.

Our advice: stick with natural fabrics as much as possible, especially cotton. Unfortunately, a lot of lower-priced maternity clothing is made of polyester/cotton blend fabrics.

Smart Shopper Tip #2
Seasons change

"Help! My baby is due in October, but I still need maternity clothes for the hot summer months! How can I buy my maternity wardrobe without investing a fortune?"

Unless you live in a place with endless summer, most women have to buy maternity clothes that will span both warm and cold seasons. The best bets are items that work in BOTH winter or summer—for example, lightweight long-sleeve shirts can be rolled up in the summer. Cropped pants can work in both spring and fall. Another tip: layer clothes to ward off cold. Of course, there's another obvious way to save: borrow items from friends. If you just need a few items to bridge the seasons (a coat, heavy sweater, etc), try to borrow before buying.

Smart Shopper Tip #3
Petites aren't always petite

"I'm only 5 feet 2 inches tall and obviously wear petite sizes. I ordered a pair of pants in a petite size from an online discounter, but they weren't really shorter in the leg. In fact, I'd have to have the pants reconstructed to get the right fit. What gives?"

Many maternity web sites advertise that they carry a wide range of sizes but in truth you may find the choices very limited. And in some cases, "petite" is really just sizes 2 to 4. Translation: these pants aren't really shorter in the leg. How can you tell without ordering and then having to return items? Your best bet is to try on items before you buy. That's not always easy, of course, especially when ordering online. In that case, check the size charts on each site to be sure they offer *real* petites. And if a manufacturer (like the Gap, for example) makes petites that fit you in their regular clothing, chances are their maternity line will be comparable.

Here are our readers recommendations for petite maternity: Kohl's, JCPenney, Old Navy, Gap, Japanese Weekend, Juicy Couture, Rebel jeans and Lands End.

Smart Shopper Tip #4
Tall isn't easy either

"At nearly six feet, I can't find any maternity pants that don't look dorky. Help!"

Just as with petites, we see lots of sites promising a wide range of sizes . . . only to find they have one style that comes in a 31" inseam. And you need a 34." I feel your pain. At 5'9" myself, I recall finding almost nothing in the right length for me. There are more choices today for tall women, but you may find yourself forced to wear more skirts and dresses than pants during your pregnancy.

Here's a partial list of sites that carry tall maternity: JC Penney, Eva Lillian (evalillian.com), Mom Shop (momshop.com), Isabella Oliver (isabellaoliver.com), Gap, and Old Navy, Tall Girl Shop (talllgirl-shop.com), and RG Maternity (rgmaternity.com), Mom's Maternity (momsmaternity.com). If you discover any new sites or stores with tall sizing, email us and we'll add them.

Our Picks: Brand Recommendations for Maternity Undergarments

Thank goodness for e-mail. Here at the home office in Boulder, CO our e-mail (authors@BabyBargains.com) has overflowed with great suggestions from readers on maternity undergarments.

God bless Canada—those Maple Leaf-heads make one of the best maternity bras in the world. Toronto-based **Bravado Designs** (for a brochure, call 800-590-7802 or 416-466-8652; web: bravadodesigns.com) makes a maternity/nursing bra of the same name that's just incredible. "A godsend!" raved one reader. "It's built like a sports bra with no under wire and supports better than any other bra I've tried . . . and this is my third pregnancy!" raved another. The Original Bravado bra comes in three support levels, sizes up to 42-46 with an F-G cup and seven colors/patterns (you

---

Fetal Monitors: Good idea?

If you're like us, you waited with baited breath to hear your baby's heartbeat at about ten to 12 weeks. Finally, a real indication that you're about to become parents (as if the morning sickness wasn't clue enough)!

Your doctor used a fetal heart monitor to listen to your baby's heartbeat. And now you've discovered you can buy your own fetal heart monitor online. So should you?

The *Wall Street Journal* recently asked this question of both doctors and the Food and Drug Administration (they regulate these monitors). In response, the FDA noted that fetal heart monitors are a medical device and, as such, require a prescription from a doctor. While some sites will not rent or sell a monitor to a parent without the prescription, others assume you have your doctor's okay.

Why do you need a prescription? After all, isn't a heart monitor just a Doppler ultrasound that checks the heartbeat? What's the big deal?

Doppler ultrasound devices use acoustical energy that is emitted continuously from the unit. It's the "continuous" part that has doctors and the FDA concerned. In your doctor's office, he or she will use a fetal heart monitor for a few minutes. But unsupervised parents at home may decide to use it every day for longer periods of time. The risk: the unit could heat up causing damage to the fetus.

Our advice: don't bother with a fetal heart monitor. If you want to use a fetal heart monitor to make sure your child doesn't have a defect or problem, don't bother. It's unlikely that an untrained person would be able to detect a defect. Doctors are trained to listen for and identify defects or disruptions in a baby's heartbeat; parents are not. And most likely you'll be seeing your doctor enough in the next several months to allow her to find any problems.

As for the "entertainment value" of hearing your baby's heartbeat and sharing it with others we'd recommend a simple option—consider buying a good stethoscope. Then have your doctor teach you how to use it to hear your baby's heartbeat. By about 18 weeks you can usually hear a heartbeat with a stethoscope. And you can buy one for as little as $100.

can also call them for custom sizing information). Available via mail order, the bra costs $35. Also available from Bravado: the Supreme design for fuller-breasted women and the Lifestyle bra, a microfiber design with a "cottonflex" lining for extra comfort. New this year: Body Silk Seamless bras and the Original design now in a bamboo blend fabric. And if a bra isn't enough, check out their nursing tank tops ($45 to $57).

Another plus: the Bravado salespeople are knowledgeable and quite helpful with sizing questions. In the past, some of our readers criticized the Bravado for not providing enough support, but the Supreme should answer those concerns. Our readers have noticed great prices on Bravado Bras at WearstheBaby.com ($32 including shipping).

Need more support? One reader recommended the **YES! Bra** from YES! Breastfeeding (yesbreastfeeding.com). She noted that "the chest elastic doesn't curl and it's much more supportive than (the original) Bravado." At $20, it's also very affordable.

Playtex Expectant Moments brand was mentioned by our readers as a good choice as well. They offer two nursing bra choices, an underwire and an underwire alternative. Sizes range from B to DDD cups and 34" to 44." A nice touch, they offer sizing advice specifically for maternity and nursing customers on their web site at playtex.com. You'll find these bras at stores like JCPenney. **Medela**, as you'd imagine, also has a big following for their bras. Five options are available: Comfort, Seamless Underwire, Seamless Soft Cup, Sleep Bra and a new Nursing Camisole. Some are also available in extended sizes from 36F to 46H. Prices average around $40 for the nursing bras.

Finally, many readers have recommended Leading Lady maternity and nursing bras. They are available widely in many department stores and maternity outlets. Their web site is leadinglady.com and they manufacturer quite a wide assortment of bras is a huge range of sizes.

Looking for maternity shorts/tights for working out? One of the best is **Fit Maternity** (fitmaternity.com; 800-961-9100). They offer an unbelievable assortment of workout clothes including unitards, tights, swimsuits, tennis clothes and more. Also check out their books and work out tapes. On the same subject, **Due Maternity** (duematernity.com) offers several yoga and workout pants as well as swimsuits.

Our Picks: Brand Recommendations for Nursing Bras, Pads and Clothes

Nursing pads are a passionate topic for many of our readers with disposables beating out reusables as moms' favorites. They loved both **Lansinoh** and **Johnson & Johnson** disposable by an overwhelming number. **Medela**, **Advent** and **Bravado** make great reusable nursing pads.

Bravado is also quite popular as a nursing bra for all but the largest of cup sizes as are **Playtex** and **Medela**. If you need a size larger than DD, consider **Motherhood Maternity's** brand as well as **Leading Lady**. The web is the best place to find bras on deal including **Decent Exposures** (decentexposures.com) and **Birth and Baby** (birthandbaby.com).

Most moms found that specialized nursing clothes weren't a necessity, but for those who want to try them, nearly everyone recommended **Motherwear** (motherwear.com). **One Hot Mama** (onehotmama.com) and **Expressiva** (expressiva.com) were other stylish sites to consider. Look for discounts on clearance pages or eBay.com.

Wastes of Money

Waste of Money #1
Maternity Bra Blues

"My old bras are getting very tight. I recently went to my local department store to check out larger sizes. The salesperson suggested I purchase a maternity bra because it would offer more comfort and support. Should I buy a regular bra in a larger size or plunk down the extra money for a maternity bra?

We've heard from quite a few readers who've complained that expensive maternity bras were very uncomfortable and/or fell apart after just a few washings. Our best advice: try on the bra before purchase and stick to the better brands. Compared to regular bras, the best maternity bras typically have thicker straps, more give on the sides and more hook and eye closures in back (so the bra can grow with you). Most of all, the bra should be comfortable and have no scratchy lace or detailing. Readers tell us that a good sports bra can also be a fine (and affordable) alternative.

Waste of Money #2
Over the Shoulder Tummy Holder

"I keep seeing those 'belly bras' advertised as the best option for a pregnant mom. What are they for and are they worth buying?"

Belly bras provide additional support for your back during your pregnancy. One style envelopes your whole torso and looks like a tight-fitting tank top. No one can argue that, in many cases, the strain of carrying a baby is tough even on women in great physical shape. So, if you find your back, hips, and/or legs are giving you trouble, consider buying a belly bra.

However, in our research, we noticed most moms don't seem to need or want a belly bra. The price for one of these puppies can range from $30 to $50. The bottom line: hold off buying a belly bra or support panty until you see how your body reacts to your pregnancy. Also, check with your doctor to see if she has any suggestions for back, hip, and leg problems.

Waste of Money #3
Overexposed Nursing Gowns/Tops

"I refuse to buy those awful nursing tops! Not only are they ugly, but those weird looking panels are like wearing a neon sign that says BREASTFEEDING MOM AHEAD!"

"I plan to nurse my baby and all my friends say I should buy nursing gowns for night feedings. Problem is, I've tried on a few and even though the slits are hidden, I still feel exposed. Not to mention they're the ugliest things I've ever seen. Can't I just wear a regular gown that buttons down the front?"

Of course you can. And considering how expensive some nursing gowns can be ($35 to $50 each), buying a regular button-up nightshirt or gown will certainly save you a few bucks. Every mother we interviewed about nursing gowns had the same complaint. There isn't a delicate way to put this: it's not easy to get a breast out of one of those teenie-weenie slits. Did the person who designed these ever breastfeed a baby? I always felt uncovered whenever I wore a nursing gown, like one gust of wind would have turned me into a centerfold for a nudist magazine.

And can we talk about nursing shirts with those "convenient button flaps for discreet breastfeeding"? Convenient, my fanny. There's so much work involved in lifting the flap up, unbuttoning it, and getting your baby positioned that you might as well forget it. My advice: stick with shirts you can pull up or unbutton down the front. These are just as discreet, easier to work with, and (best of all) you don't have to add some expensive nursing shirts (at $30 to $75 each) to your wardrobe. See box (Reader Poll) earlier for more feedback from real moms.

Another tip: if possible, try on any nursing clothing BEFORE you buy. See how easy they are to use. You might be surprised how easy (or difficult) an item can be. Imagine as you are doing this that you have an infant that is screaming his head off wanting to eat NOW, not five seconds from now. You can see why buying any nursing clothes sight unseen is a risk.

Waste of Money #4
New shoes

"Help! My feet have swollen and none of my shoes fit!"

Here's a little fact of pregnancy that no one tells you: your feet are going to swell and grow. And, sadly, after the baby is born, those tootsies won't be shrinking back to your pre-pregnancy size. A word to the wise: don't buy lots of new shoes at the start of your pregnancy. But no need to despair. After your baby is born, you'll likely have a built-in excuse to go shoe shopping!

Another suggestion from reader Gretchen C. of Rochester, WA: "It is never too early to buy shoes that don't tie! I go to the gym every morning, and it was getting to be a huge ordeal just to get my shoes tied. I bought some slip on shoes at 20 weeks and I still think it's one of the smartest things I've done."

Money-Saving Secrets

1 **CONSIDER BUYING "PLUS" SIZES FROM A REGULAR STORE.**
Thankfully, fashion lately has been heavy on casual looks . . . even for the office. This makes pregnancy a lot easier since you can buy the same styles in larger ladies' sizes to cover your belly without compromising your fashion sense or investing in expensive and often shoddy maternity clothes. We found the same fashions in plus-size stores for 20% to 35% less than maternity shops (and even more during sales).

One drawback to this strategy: by the end of your pregnancy, your hemlines may start to look a little "high-low"—your expanding belly will raise the hemline in front. This may be especially pronounced with dresses. Of course, that's the advantage of buying maternity clothes: the designers compensate with more fabric in front to balance the hemline. Nonetheless, we found that many moms we interviewed were able to get away with plus-size fashions for much (if not all) of their pregnancy. How much can you save? In many cases, from 25% to 50% off those high prices in maternity chains like Pea in the Pod.

2 **DON'T OVER-BUY BRAS.** As your pregnancy progresses, your bra size is going to change at least a couple times. Running out to buy five new bras when you hit a new cup size is probably foolish—in another month, all those bras may not fit. The best advice: buy the bare minimum (two or three).

3 **TRY BRA EXTENDERS, BELLA BAND.** You may be able to avoid buying lots of maternity bras by purchasing a few bra extenders. Available from fabric stores, OneHanesPlace.com and even Amazon.com among other sites, these little miracles cost as little as $1.50. You simply hook the extender onto the back of your bra and you can add up to two inches around the bust. You may still need to purchase new bras at some point, but with extenders, you can continue to use your pre-pregnancy bra for quite a while.

By the way, Candy from San Diego wrote to us about a similar product for pants called the Bella Band (bellaband.com).: "I bought the Bella Band early on in my pregnancy and love it so much that I recently bought another one. It was perfect for keeping my "normal" clothes on when I couldn't button them anymore. Then it helped me keep maternity pants on when they were still a little too big but I couldn't fit in my regular clothes anymore." Keep in mind the Bella Band is really for use in early pregnancy before you're big enough to buy true maternity pants and skirts. It will allow you to wear your regular pants during that stage where you're just not ready for maternity. Another, similar product is available from Baby Be Mine (on Amazon.com) a three pack was only $60 while a three pack of BellaBands was $74.

4 **BUT DON'T SKIMP ON QUALITY WHEN IT COMES TO MATERNITY BRAS AND UNDERWEAR.** Take some of the money you save from other parts of this book and invest in good maternity underwear. Yes, you can find cheap bras for $20 at discount stores, but don't be penny-wise and pound-foolish. We found the cheap stuff is very uncomfortable and falls apart, forcing you to go back and buy more. Investing in better-quality bras and underwear also makes sense if you plan to have more than one child—you can actually wear it again for subsequent pregnancies.

5 **CONSIDER DISCOUNTERS FOR CASUAL CLOTHES.** Okay, I admit that I don't normally shop at K-Mart or Target for my clothes. But I was surprised to discover these chains (and even department stores like Sears) carry casual maternity clothes in 100% cotton at very affordable prices. Let's repeat that—they have 100% cotton t-shirts, shorts, pants, and more at prices you won't believe. Most of these clothes are in basic solid colors—sorry, no fancy prints. At Target, for example, I found a 100% woven cotton maternity shirt (long sleeves) for $20. Jeans were only $30. Even a knit skirt was a mere $10. The best part: Liz Lange designs the Target line. Our readers say the quality is a bit less than Liz's regular, specialty store version, but the style is good and the prices can't be beat. Don't forget to check Target's sale rack too. One reader found items for as little as $4 on sale.

While the discounters don't carry much in the way of career wear, you'll save so much on casual/weekend clothes that you'll be ecstatic anyway. Witness this example. At A Pea in the Pod, we found a white, cotton-knit top and stretch twill pants. The price for the two pieces: a heart-stopping $185. A similar all-cotton tank top/shorts outfit from Target was $34. Whip out a calculator, and you'll note the savings is an amazing 80%. Need we say more?

By the way, don't forget to check out stores like Kohls, Marshall's, Ross and TJ MAXX. One reader told us she found maternity clothes at 60% off at TJ MAXX. Of course, as we've mentioned, readers like Old Navy and the Gap as well. Corrie, a reader from Chicago, did all her maternity shopping on line at Old Navy. She spent a total of $365 for eight pairs of pants, one pair of jeans, eleven sweaters, eight long sleeve tops, three button-down shirts, five sleeveless tops and two cardigans. This works out to less than $10 per piece!

For fans of the hip discounter H & M, there's great news: the chain has a maternity section in 20 of their stores! Granted most of them (11) are in New York, but if you live in a major metropolitan area and have an H & M, check to see if yours has a maternity section. Dubbed "Mama," our readers report these departments are selling tops for $12 to $16, camisoles for $8 and more. They carry pretty much everything except underwear. Prices are fantastic.

6 **RENT EVENING WEAR—DON'T BUY.** We found that some indie maternity stores rent eveningwear. For example, a local shop we visited had an entire rack of rental formalwear. An off-white lace dress (perfect for attending a wedding) rented for just $50. Compare that with the purchase price of $200+. Sadly, places that rent maternity wear are few and far between, but it might be worth a look-see in your local community.

7 **CHECK OUT CONSIGNMENT STORES.** You can find "gently worn" career and casual maternity clothes for 40% to 70% off the original retail! Many consignment or second-hand stores carry only designer-label clothing in good to excellent condition. If you don't want to buy used garments, consider recouping some of your investment in maternity clothes by consigning them after the baby is born. You can usually find listings for these stores in the phone book or online. (Don't forget to look under children's clothes as well. Some consignment stores that carry baby furniture and clothes also have a significant stock of maternity wear.) One web source to find consignment shops is narts.org.

8 **FIND AN OUTLET.** Check out the next section of this chapter for the low-down on maternity clothes outlets.

9 **BE CREATIVE.** Raid your husband's closet for over-sized shirts and pants.

10 **SEW IT YOURSELF.** A reader in California emailed in this recommendation: she loved the patterns for nursing clothes by Elizabeth Lee Designs (435-454-3350; web: elizabeth-lee.com). "I would think anyone with a bit of sewing experience could handle any of the patterns, which don't LOOK like nursing dresses or tops." In addition to patterns, Elizabeth Lee also sells ready-made dresses and tops. Another bonus: the company has one of the largest selections of nursing bras we've seen, including Bravado Bras.

Pattern companies like Simplicity (simplicity.com) and McCall (mccall.com; includes Butterick and Vogue as well) have their patterns online and in fabric stores. You'll find a limited selection of designs, but if you're a sewing maven, here's a way to avoid the high prices and frustrating return policies of retail maternity stores.

11 **BEG AND BORROW.** Unless you're the first of your friends to get pregnant you know someone who's already been through this. Check around to see if you can borrow old maternity clothes from other moms. In fact, we loaned out a big box after our second baby was born and it has made the rounds of the whole neighborhood. And don't forget to be generous after your baby making days are over too.

12 **CHECK OUT CLEARANCE AREAS IN CATALOGS AND ONLINE.** Many of our most devoted discount shopping readers have scored big deals on their favorite web sites' clearance pages. For example, on Motherwear.com we noticed a "Sweetheart" nursing dress, regularly marked at $59 but on sale for only $25. Old Navy had some pinstripe trousers marked down to $25 and the Gap had a cable crewneck sweater, regularly $48 on sale for $30.

13 **WHEN ORDERING MATERNITY CLOTHES FROM WEB SITES, POOL YOUR ORDERS!** Most web sites offer a free shipping option on orders of $75 to $100 or more (especially after holidays and during end of season sales). Check to see what deals they're offering when you visit. Also, chain stores like the Gap will let you return items to your local store, saving you the return-shipping fee.

Outlets

MOTHERHOOD MATERNITY OUTLETS

Locations: 81 Motherhood outlets and 10 Maternity Works outlets.

The offspring of the catalog and retail stores of maternity giant Motherhood Maternity (see review later in this chapter), these outlets have started springing up in outlet malls across the country. On a recent visit, the outlet featured markdowns from 20% to 75% on the same designs you see in their catalog or retail stores.

GAP

Location: 172 outlets. Some carry maternity while others don't. Check OutletBound.com for a listing and to call before you visit.

Readers tell us the maternity selection at some Gap outlets is pretty impressive. One reader wrote "On my last trip there, they had racks and racks of maternity jeans for $5 a piece! All pants, skirts, shorts, long sleeve and short sleeve shirts were also $5 a piece. Sweaters were a bit pricier at $10, but when you're saving all that money you don't feel bad about the splurge. My girlfriend was able to pick up a couple of maternity blazers at great prices as well. The store is usually jam packed but the staff runs a very orderly process in the dressing rooms and at the check out lines."

The Name Game:
Reviews of Selected Maternity Stores

Usually this section is intended to acquaint you with the clothing name brands you'll see in local stores. But now there is only one giant chain of maternity wear in North America—Destination Maternity Corp. (formally known as Mothers Work Inc.), which operates stores under three brand names. This company is the 800 pound gorilla of maternity clothes with over 1032 locations (278 leased departments in Kohl's—called Oh Baby by Motherhood) in the US, Canada and Puerto Rico. Destination Maternity has over a 40% share of the $1.2 billion maternity clothing market in the US.

FYI: keep in mind that these chains often offer a larger selection of maternity clothing online than what you see in the stores. This is, of course, frustrating since you can't try them on. On the upside, the draconian return policies of the bricks and mortar stores don't apply to online purchases. So you'll be able to return online purchases more easily.

So let's take a look at these three divisions, a new concept they've added, and their web site.

◆ **Motherhood.** Motherhood is the biggest sister in the chain. While most stores are located in malls and power centers, 232 are also leased departments within Kohl's (called Oh! Baby by Motherhood). Motherhood carries maternity clothes in the lowest price points. As an example, dresses at Motherhood range from $17 to $50.

◆ **Mimi Maternity.** The company re-branded all Mimi Maternity stores to be A Pea in the Pod stores or Destination Maternity in late 2008.

◆ **A Pea in the Pod.** A Pea in the Pod (APIP) is Destination Maternity's most expensive division. With dress prices ranging from $145 to $300, you can see what we mean. APIP has over 100 stores and is positioned to be more of a designer boutique. On their web site, they describe their target shopper to be someone with "closets filled with Prada, Gucci and Armani."

◆ **Destination Maternity Superstore.** These superstores (check their web site at destinationmaternity.com for locations) com-

Watch out for return policies!

Have you bought a maternity dress you don't like or that doesn't fit? Too bad—most maternity stores have draconian return policies that essentially say "tough!" Most don't accept returns and others will only offer store credit. A word to the wise: make sure you REALLY like that item (and it fits) before you give any maternity store your money. A reader in Brisbane, California emailed us with the most horrific story we've ever heard about maternity stores' return policies.

"I recently visited a Destination Maternity store in San Francisco and was shocked to find their return policy stands even when you haven't left their store yet! They overcharged me for a sale item that was miss marked and then said all they could give me was store credit for the difference! I hadn't stepped one foot outside the store! They refused to credit my charge card, so now I'm stuck with a $65 store credit for a place I despise!"

Remember: ALL Destination Maternity stores (including Motherhood and Pea in the Pod) share their appalling return/refund policies.

bine A Pea in the Pod and Motherhood Maternity under one roof. They also include a spa called Edamame Spa offering a wide range of classes with topics like yoga, scrap booking 101 and financial planning. Only the New York City location is open at this time.

All these stores carry mostly merchandise designed in house, exclusively for the different divisions.

Now that you know the basics, what do real moms think of Destination Maternity's stores? First and foremost, moms dislike, no, hate their return policy. The policy is pretty basic, once you've bought an item, you have ten days to return it for store credit or exchange only (you must have the tags and receipt too). No refunds. What if it falls apart in the wash on day 11? Too bad for you. By the way, if you order an item online from Mother Works web site, you'll find a more generous return policy: *Items can be returned for refund or exchange and you have 30 days to return the clothing.* You cannot return items bought online to the store or vice versa, but at least you get extra time and even the money back with an online return. Our advice, if you see it in the store, try it on. If you like it, go home and order it online.

And don't forget that Motherhood has in store "boutiques" in Kohl's department stores. In these cases, the leased stores have to comply with the same generous return policy of the department store where they lease space. Good news for you.

As for individual chains, most moms agreed that the quality at Motherhood is poor. Although some readers have praised their maternity and nursing bras, in general, most agree with the following: "I have found the quality to be inconsistent. I've bought shirts that have unraveled within a few months. . . trashy!" The consensus seems to be that if you buy at Motherhood, you should stick to the sale rack and don't expect high quality except for their bras.

On the other hand, A Pea in the Pod is just way too expensive. That's the general feeling among our readers about this store. Most moms don't feel the style of clothing at this chain is anything special. Certainly not to spend $85 for a cotton t-shirt. Considering how short a time a pregnancy is it's a huge waste of money to spend over $180 on a Pea in the Pod shorts outfit. And what about their "legendary" service, as Pea in the Pod likes to tout? It's a joke, say our readers. One mom summed it up best by saying: "For the price that one is paying, one expects a certain degree of customer service and satisfaction, both of which are lacking in this over-priced store. What a complete and utter disappointment!"

Consumer alert: one new mom warned us about giving personal info to a maternity chain when you make a purchase (clerks may ask you if you want to receive sales notices). The problem: you often end up on junk mailing lists. In the case of our reader, even though she specifically requested the chain not sell her information to third parties, they did so. Once on those lists, it's tough to stop the junk from arriving in your mailbox.

Do it By Mail

JCPENNEY

To Order Call: (800) 222-6161. Ask for "Maternity Collection" catalog.
Web: JCPenney.com/shopping

Perhaps the best aspect of Penney's maternity offerings is their wide range of sizes—you can find petites, talls, ultra-talls and women's petites and women's regular sizes. It's darn near impossible to find women's sizes in maternity wear today, but Penney's carries sizes up to 5X (or 32WE) and some styles are available in petites and talls.

Look for career separates, jeans, dresses even active wear and lingerie on their site. We noticed a lovely satin-tie knit cocktail dress for a mere $28. If you've got a formal occasion to go to, this is one of the most inexpensive options out there. They also have suit separates that would come to only $40 for a jacket and skirt. Wow! Yes, they are mostly polyester and rayon. And yes, the colors leave a bit to be desired, but they are a great option when you're on a budget.

One bargain hint: Penney's has quite a few unadvertised sales and discounts on maternity wear. When placing your order, inquire about any current deals.

E-MAIL FROM THE REAL WORLD
Stay fit with pregnancy workout videos

Sure, there are plenty of workout videos targeted at the preggo crowd. But which are the best? Readers give their top picks, starting with Margaret Griffin:

"As a former certified aerobics instructor, I have been trying out the video workouts for pregnancy. I have only found three videos available in my local stores, but I wanted to rate them for your readers.

"*Buns of Steel: Pregnancy & Post-Pregnancy Workouts* with Madeleine Lewis ($13) gets my top rating. Madeleine Lewis has excellent cueing, so the workout is easy to follow. Your heart rate and perceived exertion are both used to monitor your exertion.

There is an informative introduction. And I really like the fact that the toning segment utilizes a chair to help you keep your balance, which can be off a little during pregnancy. Most of the toning segment is done standing. This is a safe, effective workout led by a very capable instructor and I highly recommend it."

"A middle rating goes to **Denise Austin's: Fit & Firm Pregnancy** ($15). Denise has a good information segment during which she actually interviews a physician. She also provides heart rate checks during the workout. However, there are a couple of things about this workout that I don't particularly like. First, during the workout, there are times when safety information is provided regarding a particular move. This is fine and good, but instead of telling you to continue the movement and/or providing a picture-in-a-picture format, they actually change the screen to show the safety information and then cut back into the workout in progress. Surprise! You were supposed to keep doing the movement. Second, Denise Austin is a popular instructor, but I personally find that her cueing is not as sharp as I prefer and sometimes she seems to be a little offbeat with the music. My suggestion is get this video to use in addition to other videos if you are the type who gets easily bored with one workout."

Reader Laura McDowell recommended a few different workout DVDs. **Leisa Hart's FitMama** ($10) workout DVD was a favorite. "I loved it! Leisa has great energy and her peppy attitude made me smile through the whole workout. It has about 20 minutes of salsa dancing and then modified yoga." Laura also enjoyed **Kathy Smith's Pregnancy Workout** (discontinued by manufacturer, but still available used on Amazon). It was "a total 80s throwback; fun and energizing. She moves through the steps fast at times, but is always clear about offering ways to slow down if you need to. The hair, outfits and music are highly entertaining so the workout goes fast and feels great."

Another reader recommended **The Perfect Pregnancy Workout** DVD ($25). "It's by a former Cirque du Soleil acrobat, who leads the exercises with a French accent. It also offers beginner, intermediate and advanced options for each exercise."

Yoga is a terrific low impact exercise that does a wonderful job of stretching muscles you'll use while carrying and delivering your child. It's a terrific option for pregnant moms. And it's definitely become one of the most popular exercise options in North America. So it was only a matter of time before our readers began reviewing yoga DVDs. Here are some of their comments:

Sheri Gomez recommended Yoga Zone's video **Postures for**

Pregnancy ($15), calling it "wonderful for stretching and preventing back problems. It's beginner friendly and not too out there with the yoga thing." Her only complaint: there is no accompanying music, so she played her own CDs along with the tape.

Eufemia Campagna recommended Yoga Journal's **Prenatal Yoga** with Shiva Rea ($20). She noted that each segment of the tape is done using three women at different stages of pregnancy. "The segments are all accompanied by lovely, relaxing music and the instructor's directions are so clear that you don't even have to look at the TV to know what you need to do!"

Another reader, Carolyn Oliner, also complimented this DVD: "It's not so much of a traditional yoga workout but a great series of poses and stretches that work for pregnant women and leave you feeling warm and stretched and (more gently) exercised." Finally, another reader noted that this workout is "really gentle (pretty easy for experienced yogini)."

Finally, we should note that Pilates has also been adapted for pregnancy exercise. You'll find several options on DVD including **Pilates During Pregnancy, Jennifer Gianni's Fusion Pilates for Pregnancy**, and **Prenatal Pilates** as well as many others.

Note: Amazon.com is a great source to find these videos. If you have any favorite DVDs, email us your review of them and we'll add them to our collection. One of our readers noted that NetFlix (netflix.com) has a huge assortment of pregnancy DVDs for rent if you don't want to buy.

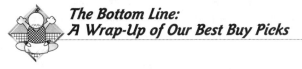

The Bottom Line: A Wrap-Up of Our Best Buy Picks

For career and casual maternity clothes, we thought the best deals were from the Old Navy, the Gap and H&M stores. Compared to retail maternity chains (where one outfit can run $200), you can buy your entire wardrobe from these places for a song.

If your place of work allows more casual dress, check out the prices at plus-size stores or alternatives like Old Navy. A simple pair of jeans that could cost $140 at a maternity shop are only $36 or less at Old Navy. And if you prefer the style at maternity shops, only hit them during sales, where you can find decent bargains. Another good idea: borrow from your husband's closet—many items can do double-duty as maternity clothes.

For weekend wear, we couldn't find a better deal than the 100% cotton shirts and shorts at discounters like Target, Wal-Mart and K-

Mart. Prices are as little as $10 per shirt—compare that to the $34 price tag at maternity chain stores for a simple cotton shirt.

Invited to a wedding? Rent that dress from a maternity store and save $100 or more. Don't forget to borrow all you can from friends who've already had babies. In fact, if you follow all our tips on maternity wear, bras, and underwear, you'll save $700 or more. Here's the breakdown:

1. Career Wear: $240. Old Navy featured cuffed stretch pants, a sweater and t-shirt for a mere $75. Buy two versions of these in different colors, add a couple nice dresses (another $60) and skirts ($50) and you're set.

2. Casual Clothes: $100. Five outfits of 100% cotton t-shirts and shorts/pants from Target run $100. Don't forget sale items on Gap Maternity as well as Old Navy's maternity line.

3. Underwear: $200 to $300. We strongly suggest investing in top-quality underwear for comfort and sanity purposes. For example, a Bravado bra is $35. Some readers have found good deals on affordable underwear at Target or online. Either way, you need eight pairs of underwear, plus six bras, including regular/nursing and sleep bras. One tip: see if you can wear your pre-pregnancy panties . . . this works for some moms, saving the $100 expense in "maternity" underwear.

Total damage: $540 to $640. If you think that's too much money for clothes you'll only wear for a few months, consider the cost if you outfit yourself at full-price maternity shops. The same selection of outfits would run $1300 to $1700.

CHAPTER 6

Feeding Baby

Inside this chapter

How much money can you save by breastfeeding? What are the best options for pumps? Which bottles are best? We'll discuss these topics as well as ways to get discount formula, including details on which places have the best deals. And of course, we'll have tips and reviews on the next step in feeding: solid food. Finally, let's talk about high chairs—who's got the best value? Durability? Looks?

Breastfeeding

As readers of past editions of this book know, we are big proponents of breastfeeding. The medical benefits of breast milk are well documented, but obviously the decision to breast or bottle-feed is a personal call for each new mom. In the past, we spent time in this chapter encouraging breast-feeding . . . but we realize now we are preaching to the choir. Our time is better spent discussing how to save on feeding your baby, no matter which way you go. So, we'll leave the discussion of breast versus bottle to our other book *Baby 411* (as well your doctor and family). Let's talk about the monetary impact of the decision, however.

Breastfeed Your Baby and Save $500

Since this is a book on bargains, we'd be remiss in not mentioning the tremendous amount of money you can save if you breast-feed. Just think about it: no bottles, no expensive formula to prepare, no special insulated carriers to keep bottles warm/cold, etc. So, how much money would you save? Obviously, NOT buying formula would be the biggest money-saver. Even if you were to use the less-expensive formula powder, you would still have to spend nearly $25 per 25.7-ounce can of powdered formula. Since each can makes about 188 ounces of formula, the cost per ounce of formula is about 13¢.

That doesn't sound too bad, does it? Unless you factor in that a baby will down 32 ounces of formula per day by 12 weeks of age. Your cost per day would be $4.16. Assuming you breastfeed for at least the first six months, you would save a grand total of $759 *just on formula alone*. The American Academy of Pediatrics recommends breastfeeding for 12 months (with solid foods added to the mix at six months), so in that case your savings could be as much as $1500! That doesn't include the expense of bottles, nipples and accessories! By the way, statistically speaking, nearly 74% of American moms breastfeed their babies at birth. By six months, however, the number of breastfeeding moms drops to nearly 43% (although this is an improvement up from 33% in 2007).

To be fair, there are some optional expenses that might go along with breastfeeding. The biggest dollar item: you might decide to buy a breast pump. Costs for this item range from $60 for a manual pump to $350 for a professional-grade breast pump. Or you can rent a pump for $45 a month (plus a kit—one time cost of about $50 to $60). And of course, you'll also need some bottles—but arguably fewer than if you formula-feed.

If $759 doesn't sound like a lot of money, consider the savings if you had to buy formula in the concentrated liquid form instead of the cheaper powder. A 32-ounce can of Enfamil ready-to-eat liquid costs about $6.69 at a grocery store and makes up only eight 4-ounce bottles. The bottom line: you could spend over $1000 on formula for your baby in the first six months alone!

Of course, we realize that some moms will decide to use formula because of a personal, medical or work situation—to help out, we have a section later in this chapter on how to save on formula, bottle systems and other necessary accessories.

Sources: Where to Find Breast Feeding Help

The basis of breastfeeding is attachment. Getting your new little one to latch onto your breast properly is not a matter of instinct. Some babies have no trouble figuring it out, while many others need your help and guidance. In fact, problems with attachment can lead to sore nipples and painful engorgement. Of course, you should be able to turn to your pediatrician or the nurses at the hospital for breastfeeding advice. However, if you find that they do not offer you the support you need, consider the following sources for breastfeeding help:

1 **LA LECHE LEAGUE** (800) LA LECHE or web: lalecheleague. org. Started in 1956 years ago by a group of moms in Chicago, La Leche League has traditionally been the most vocal supporter of breastfeeding in this country. You've got to imagine the amount of chutzpah these women had to have to buck the bottle trend and promote breastfeeding at a time when it wasn't fashionable (to say the least).

In recent years, La Leche has established branches in many communities, providing support groups for new moms interested in trying to nurse their children. They also offer a catalog full of books and videotapes on nursing, as well as other child care topics. Their famous book *The Womanly Art of Breastfeeding* is the bible for huge numbers of breastfeeding advocates. All in all, La Leche provides an important service and, coupled with their support groups and catalog of publications, is a valuable resource.

2 **NURSING MOTHERS' COUNCIL** (408) 272-1448, (web: nursingmothers.org). Similar in mission to La Leche League, the Nursing Mothers' Council differs on one point: the group emphasizes working moms and their unique needs and problems.

3 **LACTATION CONSULTANTS.** Lactation consultants are usually nurses who specialize in breastfeeding education and problem solving. You can find them through your pediatrician, hospital, or the International Lactation Consultants Association (703) 560-7330 web: iblce.org. Members of this group must pass a written exam, complete 2500 hours of clinical practice and 30 hours of continuing education before they can be certified. At some hospitals, resident lactation consultants are available to answer questions by phone at no charge. If a problem persists, you can set up an in-person consultation for a minimal fee (about $65 to $90 per hour, although your health insurance provider may pick up the tab).

Unfortunately, the availability and cost of lactation consultants seems to vary from region to region. Our advice: call area hospitals before you give birth to determine the availability of breastfeeding support. Another good source for a referral to a lactation consultant is your pediatrician.

4 **HOSPITALS.** Look for a hospital in your area that has breastfeeding-friendly policies. These include 24-hour rooming in (where your baby can stay with you instead of in a nursery) and breastfeeding on demand. Pro-nursing hospitals do not supplement babies with a bottle and don't push free formula samples.

5 **Books.** Although they aren't a substitute for support from your doctor, hospital, and family, many books provide plenty of info and encouragement. Check the La Leche League web site for titles.

6 **The web.** We found several great sites with breastfeeding information and tips. Our favorite was *Medela* (medela.com), which is a leading manufacturer of breast pumps. Medela's site features extensive information, resources and articles on breastfeeding, as well as advice on how to choose the right breast pump.

The catalog **Bosom Buddies** (bosombuddies.com or call 888-860-0041) has a web site with a good selection of breastfeeding articles, product information and links to other breastfeeding sites on the web.

Of course, our message boards are also a good place to find help—we have a special board on feeding where you can ask other moms for advice, tips and support. Hint: use our boards to find a discount web site that has the lowest price on a breast pump you want; there's always lots of discussion on who's the cheapest, who's offering free shipping and more. Go to BabyBargains.com and click on message boards.

7 **Your Health Insurance Provider.** Contact your health insurance provider as soon as you become pregnant. They often have a variety of services available to policyholders, but you have to ask.

8 **DVDs.** The "Real Deal on Breastfeeding" ($23; RealDealVideos. com) covers issues like latching on, how to position your baby, different holds, trouble shooting and increasing your supply of milk. They've also included a selection of experiences from real breastfeeding moms to help remind you that you aren't alone in this.

Stephanie Neurohr is the mother of seven children (hence her company name: Mother of 7, Inc.), so you can't say she doesn't have experience. And with a film degree as well, it seems natural that she would produce a series of baby care videos. As part of her video series, Stephanie offers four breastfeeding DVDs (most of which are $37 to $47). These DVDs include interviews with 28 experts, as well as moms from around the world plus 3-D animation to help moms understand the mechanics of breastfeeding. You can see a trailer for one of the videos on her web site at MotherOf7.com.

Parents in Cyberspace:
What's on the Web?

Medela

Web: medela.com

What it is: A treasure trove of info on breastfeeding.

What's cool. Medela's web site is a great example of what makes the 'net so helpful—instead of just a thinly veiled pitch for their products, Medela stuffs their site with reams of useful info, tips and advice. Yeah, you can read about their different breast pumps, but the site is full of general breastfeeding tips, links to other sites and more. "Tips and Solutions" is an excellent FAQ for nursing moms. You can even submit questions to an online lactation consultants. You'll also find instructions for all their products on line in case you misplace them!

Needs work: Although they've improved the site, you'll find it takes a lot of clicks to get where you want to go. And we'd still like to see approximate retail prices for Medela's products on the site.

Nursing Mother Supplies

Web: nursingmothersupplies.com

What it is: An extensive nursing supply resource.

What's cool: Not only does this site carry breast pumps and supplies from Medela and Ameda Egnell , they offer support to customers after they buy. They have extensive FAQs on the site and even a breast pump comparison chart. They claim they discount all their pumps off regular retail, although we found the same prices elsewhere. Nursing pillows, storage options (Milk Mate Storage bottles are $13-$26), Medela bottles and pads are also available. Funniest name for a new product: Hooter Hiders. These fancy nursing cover ups cost about $35 and come in a large selection of patterns. They're almost as funny as the My Breast Friend nursing pillow.

Needs work: Not much to complain about here. The site is a bit primitive in design, but it does the job—loads fast, has a shopping cart feature, clear photos, etc. We also like the gentle approach to encouraging breast-feeding. These guys aren't too preachy.

Breast Pumps Direct

Web: breastpumpsdirect.com

What it is: A discount nursing supply resource.

What's cool: The prices. You can buy a Medela Pump in Style Advanced Backpack for $90 off retail. And that's not all. Breast Pumps Direct has Avent's iQ, Ameda's Purely Yours and other pumps as well—all on sale. Manual pumps and accessories are also sold on the site. And you can find reviews of pumps, comparison charts, tips on breastfeeding and more.

◆ **Other web sites:** Here is a couple sites with a name that speaks for itself: ***Affordable-medela-pumps.com***. Readers have mentioned it as great sites for pumps from Medela, Ameda, and Avent to name a few. ***Mommy's Own*** (mommysown.com) carries nearly every brand of recommended pump, bottle, breast pad and more. You'll find Boppy pillows, Majamas nursing clothes and LilyPadz breast pads at decent prices plus advice and forums you can join. Finally, a reader, Cherie Kannarr, thought that ***BreastFeeding.com*** "is a wonderful site, filled with facts, stories, humor, and support for nursing mothers."

What Are You Buying?

Even if you exclusively breastfeed, you probably will find yourself needing to pump a bottle from time to time. After all, you might want to go out to dinner without the baby. Maybe you'll have an overnight trip for your job or just need to get back to work full or part time. Your spouse might even be interested in relieving you of a night feeding. The solution? Pumping milk. Whether you want to pump occasionally or every day, you have a wide range of options. Here's our take on them:

◆ **Manual Expression:** OK, technically, this isn't a breast pump in the sense we're talking about. But it is an option. There are several good breastfeeding books that describe how to express milk manually. Most women find that the amount of milk expressed, compared to the time and trouble involved, hardly makes it worth using this method. A few women (we think they are modern miracle workers) can manage to express enough for an occasional bottle; for the majority of women, however, using a breast pump is a more practical alternative. Manual expression is typically used only to relieve engorgement.

◆ **Manual Pumps**: Non-electric, hand-held pumps are operated by squeezing on a handle. While the most affordable option, manual pumps are generally also the least efficient—you simply can't duplicate your baby's sucking action by hand. Therefore, these pumps are best for moms who only need an occasional bottle or who need to relieve engorgement.

◆ **Mini-Electrics:** These battery-operated breast pumps are designed to express an occasional bottle. Unfortunately, the sucking action is so weak that it often takes twenty minutes *per side* to

BREAST PUMPS

Which pump works best in which situation?

	Manual	Mini-Elec.	Piston Elec.	Rental*
Do you need a pump for:				
A missed feeding?	■	◆		
Evening out from baby?	■	◆		
Working part-time.	■	◆		
Occasional use, a few times a week.	■	◆		
Daily use; full-time work			●	●
Premature or hospitalized baby?			●	●
Low milk supply?			●	●
Sore nipples/engorgement?	■		●	●
Latch-on problems or breast infection?			■	●
Drawing out flat or inverted nipples?	■	◆	●	●

Key: ■ = Good ◆ = Better ● = Best
*Rental refers to renting a hospital-grade pump. These can usually be rented on a monthly basis.
Source: Medela.

express a significant amount of milk. And doing so is not very comfortable. Why is it so slow? Most models only cycle nine to fifteen times per minute—compare that to a baby who sucks the equivalent of 50 cycles per minute!

◆ **High-End Double Pumps:** The Mercedes of breast pumps—we can't sing the praises of these work horses enough. In just ten to twenty minutes, you can pump *both* breasts. And high-end double pumps are much more comfortable than mini-electrics. In fact, at first I didn't think a high-end pump I rented was working well because it was *so* comfortable. The bottom line: there is no better option for a working woman who wants to provide her baby with breast milk.

Today, you have two options when it comes to these pumps: rent a hospital-grade pump (which often is called a piston-electric) or buy a high-end consumer grade double-pump.

Rental Pumps. These are what the industry refers to as hospital-grade or piston electric pumps. They are built to withstand continuous use of up to eight to ten times a day for many years. Often they are much heavier than personal use pumps like the Medela Pump-In-Style. And all the interior parts are sealed to prevent contamination from one renter to the next. *In fact, the Food and Drug Administration (FDA) certifies rental pumps for multiple use.* The only item each renter must buy is a new collection kit.

Where to find: Pediatricians, lactation consultants, doulas, midwives, hospitals, maternity stores and home medical care companies

The best milk storage options

Once you've decided to express breast milk for your child, you'll need to consider how to store it. Freezer bags are the most common method and most major pump manufactures and bottle makers sell bags. So, who's got the best storage bags? **Lansinoh** (sold in Target; 50 pack for $10)) is the hands-down winner. "They are sturdy, stand on their own and have an excellent double lock seal closure," said one mom. Others echoed that recommendation. Lansinoh also sells BPA-free storage bottles that fit most breast pumps ($10 for four at Target.com).

Another good choice is **Medela**, the king of breast pumps. Their recently improved bags attach to any Medela pump and feature a zipper-top. Amazon.com sells a box of 50 for $18. Medela also sells 80 ml. breast milk containers and lids (12-pack is $14) and plastic collection bottles ($3 each). Both options are compatible with Medela breast pumps and are BPA free.

A completely different alternative is **Mothers Milk Mate** (www.mothersmilkmate.com). For $30, you get a ten-bottle storage system with rack. The 5 oz. bottles are BPA free and the set comes with freshness dating labels. Some parents complained in the past that there are no nipples that will attach directly to the storage bottles.

As you can see, bottles are making a lot of headway in the breast milk storage department. Used to be we saw only storage bags. Why the change? All those great antibodies in mom's milk stick to some types of bags and don't get to baby's mouth. That's why most lactation professionals prefer the hard polypropylene bottles (frosted plastic) for breast milk storage.

And finally, a great option for freezer storage: **Milk Trays** by Sensible Lines (SensibleLines.com). It's hard to believe no one has thought of this before—Milk Trays are like old-fashioned ice cube trays but with a twist. The tray's 16 one-ounce capacity cubes are shaped like skinny cylinders, small enough to fit into any baby bottle. It comes with a sealed lid to block freezer burn and is made from BPA-free plastic. The trays sell for $16 for two.

are sources to find rental pumps. You can also call La Leche League (800-LALECHE; web: lalecheleague.org) or other lactation support groups for a referral to a company that rents pumps.

How much: Prices generally average about $45 to $65 per month to rent a breast pump. Common brands of hospital-grade pumps include Egnell and White River Concepts, although consumer brands Medela and Ameda also make hospital versions. Collection kits cost about $45 to $60 for the bottles, shields and tubes.

Professional-Grade Electric Pumps. These electric pumps are available for sale to consumers and are intended to be used no more than three or four times a day. Unlike rental pumps, they are lighter weight and easier to carry around (to work or elsewhere). Examples of these pumps include the Medela Pump-In-Style and the Ameda Purely Yours.

These pumps have an open system without sealed parts and are therefore only recommended as a single-use item. *The FDA, lactation consultants, pediatricians and manufacturers DO NOT recommend using a second-hand personal pump.* Even if you change the tubes and shields, there is a possibility of cross contamination. (The exception is the Bailey Nurture III breast pump, which is one of the very few pumps certified by the FDA for multiple users).

Where to find: Online is a primary source. Also: most independent baby stores and Babies R Us carry a selection of electric breast pumps. See earlier in the chapter for some of our favorite sources.

How much: Prices range from about $150 to $350 depending on the brand and accessories included. We will review pumps next and include prices.

Breast Pumps (model by model reviews)

Manual Pumps

AVENT ISIS (SCF300)
Web: AventAmerica.com
Price: $45.
Type: Manual.
Comments: The best manual pump on the market. Our readers love this pump, which Avent claims is as efficient as a mini-electric (it takes about eight to ten minutes to empty a breast). You can buy the Isis by itself, or as part of a kit that includes extra bottles, cooler packs and more ($50 to $60).
Rating: A

Breastfeeding in public: Exposing yourself for onlookers' fun and your baby's health

Here's a controversial topic to discuss around the office water cooler: breastfeeding in public. Since our society tends to see a woman's breasts as sexual objects rather than as utilitarian milk delivery systems, you will occasionally hear stories of moms who run into problems when they nurse their babies in public. Ironically, one of the chief advantages of breastfeeding is its portability. No hauling and cleaning bottles, mixing formula, and your child gets nourishment exactly when he needs it.

Amazingly, some parts of the developed world still manage to equate breastfeeding in public with indecent exposure. Every now and again, a story will appear on news sites featuring breastfeeding moms having a nurse-in to protest an anti-breastfeeding policy or to remind busy bodies that the law allows breastfeeding in public.

The irony is that breastfeeding in public actually involves very little flashing. As an admitted public breast feeder, I can attest to the fact that it can be done discreetly. Here are some suggestions:

1 **USE EXPRESSED MILK.** If the thought of breastfeeding in public is not your cup of tea, consider bringing a bottle of expressed milk with you.

2 **USE THE SHAWL METHOD.** Many women breastfeed in public with a shawl or blanket covering the baby and breasts. While this works well, you must start practicing this early and often with your baby. Otherwise, you'll find that as she gets more alert and interested in her surroundings, she won't stay under the shawl.

MEDELA HARMONY
Web: Medela.com
Price: $30 to $35.
Type: Manual.
Comments: The Harmony is a winner. Similar to the Avent Isis, it has fewer parts to wash than the Avent and is easier to assemble. One mom with larger breasts found this pump worked better for her than the Isis. The Harmony is also a few dollars cheaper than the Isis.
Rating: A

3 **FIND ALL THE CONVENIENT REST ROOM LOUNGES IN YOUR TOWN.** Whenever we visited the local mall, I nursed in one of the big department store's lounge areas. This is a great way to meet other breastfeeding moms as well. Of course, not every public rest room features a lounge with couches or comfy chairs, but it's worth seeking out the ones that do. We applaud stores like Babies R Us for having "breastfeeding rooms" with glider-rockers and changing tables for easy nursing.

Wonder where to find the best spots to nurse? Nursing Room Locator (http://nursingrooms.wordpress.com) is a fantastic blog that posts reviews of nursing rooms all over the country. In the postings for our home state, we noticed there were two for our local mall with information on how clean they were, what amenities were offered and even details on the lighting! Great for moms who don't feel comfortable nursing in public or who want a quite, comfy place to relax.

Another creative alternative: stores will usually let you use a dressing room to breastfeed. Of course, some stores are not as "breastfeeding friendly" as others. New York City, for example, has 10 million people and about seven public rest rooms. In such places, I've even breastfed in a chair strategically placed facing a wall or corner in the back of a store. Not the best view, but it gets the job done.

4 **TRY YOUR CAR.** Yep, the backseat of a parked car is a good place to nurse. I found it easier and more comfortable to feed my child there, especially when he started to become distracted in restaurants and stores. The car held no fascination for him, so he tended to concentrate on eating instead of checking out the scenery. I suggest you keep some magazines in the car since you may get bored.

DR. BROWNS NATURAL FLOW MANUAL BREAST PUMP
Web: Handi-Craft.com
Price: $50.
Type: Manual.
Comments: This pump's claim to fame is its honeycomb filter, which is supposed to stimulate more milk production. But readers have been universally negative on this pump, saying it simply doesn't work as well as the Isis or Harmony. So, we say pass.
Rating: D

Other manual pumps: Ameda makes two manual pumps: one under its own name and another under a license from Lansinoh. Both are similar and cost about $30, although the Ameda One-Hand manual pump has a different handle design. We've had little feedback on these pumps; and since they are sold only online, spare parts are harder to find.

Mini Electric Pumps

EVENFLO COMFORT SELECT SINGLE ELECTRIC BREAST PUMP
Web: Evenflo.com
Price: $40.
Type: Mini-electric.
Comments: It's not nicknamed the Evil-Flo for nothing—this one hurts. Yep, it's cheap and that's about the only thing going for it.
Rating: D+

MEDELA SINGLE DELUXE BREAST PUMP
Web: Medela.com
Price: $50.
Type: Mini electric.
Comments:
While Medela is among the top brands for breast pumps, the brand's entry in the mini-electric category receives decidedly mixed reviews from readers. For every mom who loved this pump, another complained about motors that burned out right after the warranty period was up and other woes. Yes, the Medela Swing (see below) costs more than twice this pump, but it is a much better choice.
Rating: D

MEDELA SWING BREAST PUMP
Web: Medela.com
Price: $130-$150.
Type: Mini electric.
Comments: This single electric pump offers Medela's 2-Phase Expression (the same system as the Medela's more expensive pumps), which is supposed to copy baby's natural sucking rhythm. The pump has two different modes: first to stimulate letdown and then to simulate baby's normal sucking pattern. Moms applaud this pump's ease of use and comfort. The only negative: it's a single pump and hence is best for occa-

sional use. In fact, some moms wished it came as a double version. Despite that, we will give it our highest rating. **Rating: A**

More mini-electrics: You'll see several other brands of mini-electric breast pumps on market today (most notably, First Years and Playtex among others). With the exception of the Medela Swing, most of these pumps fair poorly according to our reader feedback. For occasional use, you are better off getting a simple manual pump. Or if you need a serious pump for daily pumping, the professional-grade options (reviewed below) are the best bets.

Professional-Grade Pumps

AMEDA PURELY YOURS
Web: Ameda.com
Price: $150 for the pump only; $200 for the Carry All version; $230 for the Backpack
Type: Professional.

Comments: It's smaller! It's lighter! And its less expensive—the Ameda Purely Yours has won a legion of fans for its Purely Yours Pump, which comes in three versions: pump only (use your own bag), Carry All and Backpack. Each weighs about five pounds and has the same number of suction settings (eight) and speeds (nine), but the backpack includes a car adapter (that is optional with the CarryAll). The Ameda has a built-in AA battery pack, versus the Medela, which has a separate battery pack. Best of all, the Ameda is easy to maintain (milk can't get into the tubes, which means less cleaning than the Medela). The downside? Medela is sold in many more retail outlets than Ameda meaning you can get spare parts and supplies easier (although to its credit, Ameda has great customer service). The Lansinoh is a branded version of the same pump for $150. *FYI: In the past year, Ameda was purchased by Evenflo. So far, there haven't been any changes to the line as a result of this change in ownership.* **Rating: A**

AVENT ISIS iQ
Web: AventAmerica.com
Price: $100 for the Uno and $200 to $300 for the Duo (pictured).
Type: Professional.
Comments: Perhaps the coolest thing about Avent's ISIS iQ is the customization feature. Moms can adjust the suction strength, the length of suction time and the rest period—that's fantastic.

So how does it work? You start by pumping manually, then the pump "copies" your preferences (that's explains the iQ moniker). You can continue to tweak the settings with "infinite variable controls" and it remembers your latest settings.

So what's the downside to the ISIS iQ? Not much. There are a lot of parts to assemble, but most moms noted that with practice it's pretty easy. We did hear from one mom who complained that when set up on a desk, the Isis iQ can be rather tippy to use. She also noted that milk gets stuck in the diaphragm and has to be emptied at the end.

And finally, the price is a big stumbling block. Although you can find it discounted online to $200 for the double version, the price in some stores is close to $300 . . . that is twice the Ameda Purely Yours. At least Avent doesn't skimp on what comes with the pump: besides the pump itself, you get two Avent feeding bottles, two breast milk storage containers, two storage bags, eight gel packs, and an electric adapter in an insulated tote bag. Still, $300 is a chunk of change compared to the Ameda Purely Yours, but comparable to the top-of-the-line Pump In Style Advanced.

Our readers are generally split into two camps when it comes to pumps: Medela vs. Avent. Medela fans like the wide availability of parts and Medela's excellent customer service. Avent fans love the pump's overall quality and compatibility with Avent's very popular bottles—the pump connects directly to the bottles, etc.

Aside from the price, moms thought it was quiet, comfortable and easy to clean. And it does the job.

Rating: A

BAILEY MEDICAL NURTURE III
Web: BaileyMed.com
Price: $130 to $160.
Type: Professional

Comments: This pump comes in two versions—basic ($130) and deluxe ($160). It's claim to fame: the Nurture III is the only small pump approved for multiple users by the FDA. Hence you can buy this pump and hand it down to a friend or sell it online. The Nurture III features adjustable suction and manual cycling, where mom can control the cycling pattern. This feature takes some practice, say our readers—and isn't a plus for sleep-deprived moms. Fans say it does a great job at expressing milk, but others have a problem letting-down with the Nurture III. The deluxe version (which we've seen discounted to $135 online) includes an insulated carry bag with ice pack and four extra bottles. If resale is a key concern, then this is a good pump to consider.

Rating: B+

LANSINOH LIGHTWEIGHT DOUBLE ELECTRIC BREAST PUMP

Comments: This pump is a repackaged version of the Ameda Purely Yours reviewed above—basically the same pump, just in purple. Priced at $145 at most chain stores; $105 on Amazon.

MEDELA PUMP IN STYLE ADVANCED
Web: Medela.com
Price: $280 to $330.
Type: Professional

Comments: It's the 800-pound gorilla of the breast pump category: the Medela Pump In Style (PIS).

So what's all the fuss about? If you are serious about pumping every day, the Pump In Style allows you to carry a high quality pump with you to work. You can empty both breasts in a short amount of time with great comfort. As a nursing mom, I remember using the Original version and found it pretty comparable to a hospital-grade pump.

The PIS has evolved over the years—gone is the basic "Original" version and now we have the Advanced, which comes in three flavors: backpack ($280), shoulder bag ($280) and metro bag ($330).

In general, the Advanced features Medela's new "2-Phase Expression" technology that mimics the way infants nurse at the breast. At first, infants apparently nurse quickly to simulate let down. Then they settle into a deeper, slower sucking action—the Pump In Style Advance simulates this pattern.

The Advanced three versions are similar: they all have the same pump, just a different bag. The metro is slightly different (and $50 more expensive): it has a removable pump motor and storage bags.

So what's the disadvantage of the Pump In Styles? Cost is a biggie: the PIS is $100 or so more than the Ameda Purely Yours, which

Pumps: Have a Plan B

If you plan to return to work and will rely on pumping to feed your baby, make sure you have a Plan B in case your breast pump breaks. Yes, pumps are just machines and sometimes they break down—that means tracking down replacement parts at a store across town. Or waiting for parts to arrive by mail. The best advice: have a Plan B, like a back-up manual or mini-electric pump on hand. This is especially important if you choose a brand (like Ameda) that is mostly sold online—the only way to get replacement parts for such pumps is through the mail!

Nursing Extras

Many nursing moms find a nursing pillow makes breastfeeding easier and more comfortable. Our readers have emailed us positive comments for *My Brest Friend* by Zenoff Products (800-555-5522; web: zenoffproducts.com). Okay, it probably qualifies as the Most Stupid Name for a Baby Product Ever award, but it really works—it wraps around your waist and is secured with Velcro. It retails for about $40. An old favorite is the *Boppy* pillow. Sold for $25 online this perennial favorite doesn't have a waist strap, but many moms swear by it as a simple, affordable nursing pillow.

Got twins? Check out *EZ-2-NURSE's* pillow (800-584-TWIN; we saw it on www.nursingmothersupplies.com). A mom told us this was the "absolute best" for her twins, adding, "I could not successfully nurse my girls together without this pillow. It was wonderful." Cost: $60.

If you're not sold in the idea of a big, bulky nursing pillow, we did find an alternative. *Utterly Yours* (utterlyyours.com) makes a small, hand-sized pillow that you position directly under the breast. Cost: $22 to 30 (including pillow cover), depending on the size.

is smaller, lighter and has several other attractive features. Medela's higher price is no doubt attributable to their "minimum advertised price" policy, which prevents Internet discounters from selling their pumps below a certain price.

Fans of Medela love the availability of parts (sold in many retail stores) and Medela's excellent customer service. So, all in all, we will recommend the Pump in Style—it is an excellent pump.
Rating: A

MEDELA FREESTYLE BREAST PUMP
Web: Medela.com
Price: $380
Type: Professional
Comments: The Freestyle is Medela's latest pump and they pulled out all the stops: hands-free option, LED display, pumping session timer, memory function and more.

How does it differ from the Pump in Style (PIS)? Well, the Freestyle can be removed from its bag (unlike the PIS backpack or shoulder bag) and it features a rechargeable battery for three hours of pumping (the PIS can use AA batteries or a wall outlet).

Yet it is the hands-free option that is the killer app here: fans call it "life changing," especially for moms with another toddler at home (and hence the need to multi-task). Of course, at $380, this pump better be darn impressive. And it's amazing that all this comes from a pump that basically fits in the palm of your hand (ok, if you have big hands).

So why buy the Freestyle instead of the Pump In Style? Fans of the Freestyle say it is easier to use and clean than the PIS. Even the breast shields are softer and more comfortable. The downside? The Freestyle isn't exactly quiet, although no louder than the Pump In Style.

Rating: A

PLAYTEX EMBRACE DELUXE

Web: playtex.com
Price: $180 to $200
Type: Professional.
Comments: Playtex entered the breast pump market with both a professional grade and manual pump in the past year. The Embrace Deluxe features soft silicone breast shields, a closed system design and the included accessories (car adapter, etc) that are often extra with other brands. The downsides? Since Playtex is a new player, it's harder to find accessories (like extra breast shields) at retail—you'll have to order them online and wait for shipment. And the Playtex breast shields have multiple parts to assemble and clean, which is frustrating. Reader feedback on this pump is much more limited than on Medela or Avent, as Playtex is a much smaller player. Overall, we'd describe the feedback as mixed: fans like the breast shields (which are softer than Medela's) and the included accessories, such as a car charger. Detractors point out the pump is NOISY and very slow (about 50% slower than Medela or Ameda). The weak suction is a deal-killer—we don't recommend this pump. **Rating: D**

Bisphenol-A (BPA) and breast pumps

Bisphenol-A is a chemical used in the production of polycarbonate bottles. After health concerns were raised about BPA in 2008, most major bottle makers phased out BPA—this includes in the collection bottles used in breast pumps. Specifically, all of Avent's breast pumps are BPA-free. Medela, the other major breast pump maker, has always been BPA-free (their collection bottles were not made of polycarbonate).

Before buying a breast-pump, check to the make sure the collection bottles are BPA-free. There still might be old stock for sale online that uses the old BPA-laden polycarbonate bottles.

Our Picks: Brand Recommendations

◆ ***Manual Pump:*** The best manual pumps are the Avent Isis (SCF300) $45 and Medela Harmony ($30 to $35). Between the two, the Medela Harmony has the slight edge, given its lower price and easier-to-clean design.

◆ ***Mini Electric Pump:*** Medela's new Swing mini-electric is pricey ($130) but very good quality. Yes, you can find other brands of mini-electric pumps in discount stores for $40 and $50, but we have one word of advice: don't.

◆ ***Professional Grade Pump:*** You can't go wrong with either, so we'll make it a tie: the Medela Pump In Style ($280 to $330) and Ameda Purely Yours ($150 to $230) are the co-champs. For daily pumping, you can't go wrong with either one. If hands-free operation is important, then consider the excellent Medela Freestyle ($380).

Before you buy a pump, we suggest RENTING a hospital-grade pump first for a week or two (or a month). After you decide you're committed to pumping and you're comfortable with how double pumps work, then consider buying one of your own. Given the hefty retail prices, it makes sense to buy only if you plan to pump for several months or have a second child.

Bottom line: a hospital rental pump is probably best for most moms. But if you need portability and plan to have additional children, investing in a good quality pump from Medela or Ameda is worth it.

Safe and Sound

As we mentioned earlier in the What Are You Buying section, we don't recommend buying a used breast pump. Models like Medela's Pump In Style can actually collect milk in the pump mechanism. So, let's state it clearly: DO NOT PURCHASE A USED BREAST PUMP. The risk of exposing your baby to any pathogens in the previous user's breast milk is not worth it.

Of course, it is fine to re-use your own breast pump for another child down the road. Just replace the tubing and collection bottles to make sure there are no bacteria left over from previous uses.

One more safety tip: if it hurts stop. No kidding! Pumping to express milk for your baby should not be a painful experience. The last thing you want to do is damage breast tissue.

Smart Shopper Tip

Smart Shopper Tip #1
When to buy that pump.

"I don't know how long I want to breastfeed. And I'll be going back to work soon after my baby is born. When should I get a pump?"

We'd suggest waiting a bit before you invest in a breast pump or even nursing clothes. Many moms start with breast-feeding, but can't or don't want to continue it after a few weeks. For them investing in a pump would be a waste of money. If you aren't sure how long you want to breast feed, but you'd like to pump some extra bottles of milk anyway, consider renting a hospital grade pump first and trying it out before you invest a couple hundred dollars. You can often rent for as little as one month, which will be much cheaper than buying a pump that can run $200 to $350.

Waste of Money

Even Cows Opt for the Electric Kind
"I'm going back to work a couple of months after my baby is born. My co-worker who breastfeeds her baby thinks manual and mini-electrics pumps are a waste of money. Your thoughts?

While they may be useful to relieve engorgement, manual pumps aren't very practical for long-term pumping when you're at work. They are very slow, which makes it hard to get much milk. Mini-electric breast pumps are better but are really best only for occasional use—for example, expressing a small amount of milk to mix with cereal for a baby who's learning to eat solids. The problem with mini-electrics: some are painful and most are too slow.

Your best bet if you plan to do some serious pumping is to rent a hospital-grade pump. These monsters maintain a high rate of extraction with amazing comfort. A lactation consultant we interviewed said these pumps can empty both breasts in about ten to 15 minutes—contrast that with 20 to 30 minutes for mini-electrics and 45 minutes to an hour for manual pumps.

As mentioned earlier, the manual pump that received top rating from our readers is the Avent Isis—and even though it is a vast improvement over previous options, it still is a MANUAL pump. It may not work well for moms who plan to work part or full-time and still nurse their baby. That said, one solution is to use two pumps—

a mom we interviewed uses a Medela Pump In Style when she's tired (during the evening or night-time) and an Avent Isis at work (it's much quieter; doesn't need electricity, etc).

Money Saving Tips

1 **GET A FREE PUMP—COURTESY YOUR HEALTH INSURANCE.** One reader noted that her insurance provider would pay $50 toward the purchase of a breast pump; yet another reader found her medical insurance covered the *entire* cost of a $280 pump! You'll have to ask about this benefit; insurance companies don't always volunteer this info. And other insurance providers will only pay for a pump if there is a medical reason (premature birth, etc). You may have to get a "note from your doctor" to qualify. FYI: Medela has downloadable forms on their web site that are templates to request insurance reimbursement.

2 **CONSIDER EBAY.** Many readers have noted that breast pumps, including Medela's Pump In Style (PIS), are available for sale on eBay.com at huge discounts. We saw one, new in the box, for only $182. Some of them are older models or even used, so you'll need to educate yourself on what you're buying. Again, our advice: don't buy a used pump—only a new one.

3 **DON'T FEEL LIKE YOU HAVE TO BUY THE "TOP BRAND."** There are several manufacturers of breast pumps besides Medela. And our readers say their products work just as great for a lot less money (we discussed these alternative brands earlier in this chapter). For example, the Ameda Purely Yours pump averages only $200, while the Medela Pump in Style Advanced is a whopping $370 retail and the Avent ISIS iQ is $350. However, we recommend sticking with manufacturers who specialize in breastfeeding. The First Years, for example, makes a ton of other products from spoons to bath tubs as well as breast pumps. We aren't as impressed with the quality of their pumps compared to other brands, however.

Formula

Is there any nutritional difference between brands of formula? No—the federal government mandates that all formula have the same nutritional value (the amount of protein, etc). That's right— the "generic" formula sold at a discounter is nutritionally no different than pricey name brands.

How pricey? A 25-ounce can of name-brand powdered formula runs $25.50 today. Yep, 25 bucks a can. At these prices, you can see how buying formula can take a bite out of your baby budget in a hurry. Here's an overview how to save.

What Are You Buying?

Baby formula is just baby formula, right? Nope, it is more complicated that—formula comes in several versions (powdered, liquid concentrate, ready-to-drink) as well as types (cow's milk, soy, etc). Not to mention organic, specialty brands and more. Here's a quick overview:

◆ *Versions.* Formula comes in three different versions: powder, liquid concentrate and ready-to-drink. Powder is least expensive, followed by liquid concentrate. Ready-to-drink is the priciest. A recent grocery store pricey survey revealed the cost per ounce of powdered formula is 13¢. Compare that to liquid concentrate (17¢) and ready to drink (21¢) per ounce.

◆ *Types.* Beside cow's milk-based formula, there is also soy-based formula. Which is best? Cow's milk formula with iron—this formula is tolerated best by the most babies and recommended first by most doctors. Of course, there are many specialty formulas for babies with special problems—we call these the "gourmet" formulas, described in more detail below. Our advice in nut-shell: buy the cheapest cow's milk based formula you can find.

◆ *Organic.* These pricey formulas are certified "antibiotic, pesticide and growth hormone free." Here's an overview of the offerings:

Earth's Best Infant Formula (earthsbest.com) now offers organic infant formula with iron, a powdered formula made from organ-

The most popular formula brands

Market share by brand, 2009

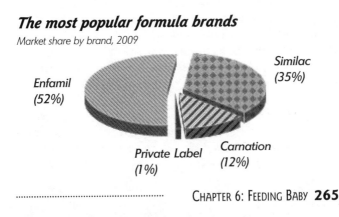

Similac (35%)

Enfamil (52%)

Private Label (1%)

Carnation (12%)

ic lactose with 27 other vitamins and minerals. Earth's Best sources it's milk from Horizon Organic (horizonorganic.com), which feeds its cows only organic grain and hay grown without fertilizers or insecticides, and they use no growth hormones or antibiotics.

We found this brand in Whole Foods Markets, although it may not yet be in every store. A 25.75 oz can runs $29 (that's 15¢ per ounce; 36% more than the cheapest store brand formula bought at a discount store). This formula is USDA certified organic. Earth's Best now makes a soy version of infant formula.

Baby's Only Organic baby formula (babyorganic.com) is manufactured by Nature's One, (naturesone.com). The product is made with no genetically engineered organisms, bovine growth hormones, antibiotics or steroids, insecticides or chemical fertilizers. Available only in a powder, Baby's own comes in regular, soy and a DHA/ARA option. FYI: Baby's Only is marketed as a "toddler" formula for babies 12 months and up. Why? The FDA has a strict certification program for infant formula, which the Baby's Only formula has not gone through. The concern: we fear some parents may give this to younger infants, missing the small disclaimer and "toddler" typeface. We would not feed an infant any formula that was not certified by the FDA.

Similac has released its own version of organic formula produced without growth hormones, antibiotics or chemicals and certified by the USDA. The cost: $31.50 for a 25.7 oz. can or 17¢ per fluid ounce. We also noticed **O Organic Formula** for sale at our local Safeway grocery store. This private label option was $26 for 25.7 oz (14¢ per fluid ounce). Finally, **Parent's Choice** (see later in the chapter) also sells an organic infant formula sold at Wal-Mart.

Just to wrap up, organic formula costs anywhere from 14¢ to 17¢ per ounce while regular formula like Enfamil Lipil runs from 11¢ per ounce at warehouse clubs to 14¢ per ounce in grocery stores.

FYI: At least one formula brand, Baby's Only Organic, is touting cans that have BPA free linings. For more information on BPA please see the discussion on page 261.

◆ *Gourmet formula.* Formula makers have been busy rolling out additional formula to accommodate a range of baby needs. For example, there is a lactose-intolerant formula (Enfamil LactoFree), Isomil DF for babies with a stomach virus and Enfamil AR for babies with gastro esophageal reflux. We discuss these formulas in greater detail in our other book, *Baby 411* (see our web site for more information).

◆ *Toddler formula.* First created by Carnation ("Follow Up" formula, now marketed under the Nestle name), then copied by other formula manufacturers, "toddler" formulas are intended to be used for older children (typically nine months old and up) instead of regular cows milk or soymilk. Most parents move to whole milk or soymilk when their child reaches one year of age. In order to hang on to consumers longer, formula manufacturers have developed these toddler formulas. So what's the big difference between baby formula and toddler formula? All these toddler formulas add calcium and iron as well as a variety of vitamins (E, C, D) depending on the brand.

That's just a brief overview of formula—we have an in-depth discussion of formula in our *411* book. Co-written with a pediatrician, Dr. Ari Brown, the book extensively discusses breastfeeding, formula and feeding challenges for all infants. It's all in a fun-filled chapter called "Liquids." Check our web site (Baby411.com) for Dr. Brown's blog, which covers breaking news items on infant feeding.

Safe and Sound

Formula is one of the most closely regulated food items in the US. The Food and Drug Administration has strict guidelines about what can and cannot go into baby formula. The FDA requires expiration dates, warning labels and so on. So what are the safety hazards you might run up against? Here are a couple:

1 ASK YOUR DOC FIRST. Never switch formula types or brands without discussing it with your pediatrician first. While our recommendation is to buy the cheapest cow's milk you can find, some babies have health problems that require special formula.

2 CONFUSING CANS CONFRONT SOY FORMULA USERS. Soy formula now accounts for 17% of the infant formula market. Yet, a case of mistaken identity has caused problems. Some parents mistakenly thought they were feeding their babies soy formula, when in fact they were using *soymilk*. The problem: soymilk is missing important nutrients and vitamins found in soy formula. As a result, babies fed soymilk were malnourished and some required hospitalization. Adding to the confusion, soymilk is often sold in cans that look very similar to soy formula. The government has asked soymilk makers to put warning labels on their products, so most should be labeled. If you use soy formula, be careful to choose the right can at the grocery store.

3 IRON. Another concern: low-iron formula. A myth among some parents is that the iron in standard formula causes constipation—it does not, says pediatrician Dr. Ari Brown, co-author of *Baby 411*. Yes, constipation can be a problem with ALL formulas.

formula

But, babies should NEVER be on low-iron formula unless instructed by a pediatrician.

4 EXPIRED FORMULA. We realize those cans of formula look like they could survive a nuclear attack (they remind us of the "bomb-proof" cans of Hawaiian Punch our moms used to buy in the '70's), but they do have expiration dates on them. And many of our readers have written to tell us that stores don't always remove expired formula from the shelves in a timely manner. That includes grocery stores, discounters and even warehouse clubs. So read the label carefully and check your own stores of formula before you open a can. Also, watch out for formula sold on auction sites. Be sure to ask about expiration dates.

5 DON'T BUY OFF BRAND FORMULA IN ETHNIC GROCERY STORES. While the 2008 melamine scare mainly affected families in China, a few cans did make it into the U.S. through ethnic grocery stores. Federal law bans such black market imports, but that doesn't mean they don't happen. Stick to name brand formula bought in mainstream stores.

Money Saving Tips

1 STAY AWAY FROM PRE-MIXED FORMULA. Liquid concentrate formula and ready-to-drink formula are 50% to 200% more expensive than powdered formula. Yes, it is more convenient but you pay big time for that. We priced name brand, ready to drink formula at a whopping 21¢ per ounce.

Guess what type of formula is given out as freebies in doctors' offices and hospitals? Yes, it's often the ready-to-drink liquid formula. These companies know babies get hooked on the particular texture of the expensive stuff, making it hard (if not impossible) to switch to the powdered formula later. Sneaky, eh?

What's the most popular type of formula in the US? Powder. Over 60% of the formula sold in the US is powdered while liquid concentrate accounts for only 27% of formula sales.

2 CONSIDER GENERIC FORMULA. Most grocery stores and discounters sell "private" label formula at considerable savings, at least 30% to 40%. At one grocery store chain, their generic powdered formula worked out to just 5¢ per fluid ounce, a 50% savings.

The largest maker of generic formula is PBM Products (PBMProducts.com). This company makes generic formula under several different brand names including Bright Beginnings (BrightBeginnings.com), Member's Mark (sold at Sam's Club) and Parent's Choice (sold at Wal-Mart). Generic formula has come a long way in recent years—now you can buy generic organic formula as well as several other special varieties.

We should note that some pediatricians are concerned about recommending generic formula—doctors fret that such low-cost formula might discourage breastfeeding. Ironic, when so many pediatricians hand out all those free samples of formula. We'd love to see them stop accepting samples from Similac, Enfamil and Carnation and start discouraging hospitals from doling them out to moms in the maternity wards.

3 **BUY IT ONLINE.** Yep, you can buy formula online from eBay. You can save big but watch out—some unscrupulous sellers try to pawn off expired formula on unsuspecting buyers. Be sure to confirm the expiration date before buying formula online. And watch out for shipping charges—formula is heavy and shipping can outweigh any deal, depending on the price you pay. We saw three cans of formula (12.9 oz. each) go for $22.94 with free shipping on eBay (about 8¢ per ounce).

4 **BUY IN BULK.** We found wholesale clubs had the best prices on name brand formula. For example, Costco (Costco.com) sells a 38 oz. can of Enfamil for $31.88 (11¢ per fluid oz.). That is 27% less than grocery stores. And generic formula at wholesale clubs is an even bigger bargain. Costco's Kirkland brand formula was $17.99 for two 25.7-ounce cans (5¢ per fluid ounce).

5 **ASK YOUR PEDIATRICIAN FOR FREE SAMPLES.** Just make sure you get the powdered formula (not the liquid concentrate or ready to pour). One reader in Arizona said she got several free cases from her doctor, who simply requested more from the formula makers.

6 **SHOP AROUND.** Yes, powdered formula at a grocery store can run $20 to $25 for a 28-ounce can (approximately)—but there's no federal law that says you must buy it at full retail. Readers of our book have noticed that formula prices vary widely, sometimes even at different locations of the same chain. In Chicago, a reader said they found one Toys R Us charged $1.20 less per can for the same Similac with Iron ready-to-feed formula than another TRU across town. "They actually have a price check book at the registers with the codes for each store in the Chicagoland area," the reader said. "At our last visit, we saved $13.20 for two cases (about 30% of the cost), just by mentioning we wanted to pay the lower price."

Another reader noticed a similar price discrepancy at Wal-Mart stores in Florida. When she priced Carnation Good Start powdered formula, she found one Wal-Mart that marked it at $6.61 per can. Another Wal-Mart (about 20 miles from the first location) sells the same can for $3.68! When the reader inquired about the price discrepancy, a customer service clerk admitted that each store independently sets the price for such items, based on nearby competition. That's a good lesson—many chains in more rural or poorer locations (with no nearby competition) often mark prices higher than suburban stores.

7 FORGET TODDLER FORMULA. When your child is ready for whole milk (usually at one year of age, according to most pediatricians), you can switch from formula (about 10¢ per ounce) to milk (about 2¢ per ounce). Yep, that is a savings of 80%! No, you don't need toddler formula.

What about the claim that toddler formulas have extra calcium, iron and vitamins? Nutritionists point out that toddlers should be getting most of their nutrition from solid foods, not formula. Toddlers should only be drinking about two cups a day of whole milk. Additional calcium can be found in foods as diverse as yogurt and broccoli; iron in red meat and spinach; vitamins in a wide variety of foods.

But what if you don't think your child is getting enough of those nutrients? Adding a vitamin and mineral supplement to your child's diet would *still* be less expensive than blowing your money on toddler formulas.

You may be wondering, in the day of increasing concern about obesity, why whole milk is recommended. Pediatricians tell us toddlers between 12 and 24 months of age need the fat in whole milk to foster brain development. At age two, you should switch to skim milk or 1%. For more on toddler development and nutrition, check out our *Toddler 411* book. See the back of this book for more information.

8 CHECK OUT AMAZON. Yep, Amazon sells formula (and even diapers) in their health and personal care store. Prices for formula were about 10% to 15% cheaper than full retail and if you order more than $25 (which is pretty easy), you may qualify free shipping. Compare Amazon's prices with the lowest discount source in your area to see if it makes sense.

9 JOIN A FORMULA CLUB. Several formula makers have frequent buyer clubs. Example: Enfamil's Family Beginnings offers checks for purchasing formula, a free diaper bag, and more. It's free (sign up at Enfamil.com) but be prepared to fill out lots of forms asking for information on where you live, when your baby is due and your attitudes toward breast and formula feeding. Bonus savings idea: Sam's Club accepts Enfamil's checks, which lets you stretch those freebies even farther! And you can find lots of checks for sale on eBay.com at great prices.

Bottles/Nipples

What's the best bottle for baby? Actually, it's more than just the bottle. The nipple—how the milk is delivered to baby is just as important as the container.

When it comes to nipples, there are a myriad of choices. At the low end, Playtex and Gerber are available in just about every grocery store in the U.S. and Canada. Mid-price options like Evenflo and Munchkin's Healthflow are also widely available. At the high end, brands such as Avent and Dr. Brown bottle systems are sold in baby specialty stores and chains like Target and Babies R Us.

So, which nipple (and bottle) system is best? This is like asking folks to name their favorite Thanksgiving dish—everyone will have a different opinion. For many parents, the bottle/nipple system they start with is the one they stick by. And the low-end options can work just as well as the premium brands.

That said, **Avent** and **Dr. Brown's** are the two brands with the most positive parent feedback, according to our research. Why? Avent gets a nod for its well-designed nipple, which is clinically proven to reduce colic (uncontrollable, extended crying that starts in some babies around one month of age). Ditto for Dr. Brown's Natural Flow bottle (handi-craft.com), which has a patented vent system that eliminates bubbles and nipple collapse. Avent and Dr. Brown's are pricey, however—they cost about $5 a bottle. That compares to $2 to $4 for other bottles from makers like Evenflo and Playtex.

In the past year, a controversy swirled around plastic baby bottles. After the government issued a report that questioned the safety of a chemical (Bisphenol-A or BPA) used in polycarbonate bottles, major retailers vowed to drop BPA-laden bottles. This forced bottle makers to formulate their bottles to be BPA-free. (We've posted a Q&A about BPA on our web site BabyBargains.com, click on Bonus Material).

The upshot: most plastic bottles sold today are BPA-free. While the government did not ban bottles that contain BPA, all the major bottle brands now use BPA-free plastic or offer other non-BPA options (such as glass, polyethylene or polypropylene). Of course, there may be older baby bottles still on the back of some store shelves—a word to the wise: make sure the package says BPA-free before buying any bottle, breast pump or sippy cup.

One quick note: in most cases, bottles and nipples aren't inter-changeable. You can't use an Avent nipple on a Gerber bottle and so on. The exception: Dr. Brown's nipples DO fit on Evenflo's glass bot-tles, report our readers (a bit of trimming on the vent tube is required).

Where can you find bottles at a discount? Chains like Target and Wal-Mart carry even premium bottle brands like Avent and Dr. Brown's at good prices. We also like Kid Surplus (kidsurplus.com), which also has great deals on bottles.

Bottle Warmers & Sterilizers

When you are a first-time parent, how do you know you will really need an item? Which ones are wastes of money? Take bottle sterilizers and warmers, for example. Will your child die from some bacterial agent if you don't sterilize your baby bottles? Will Junior scream bloody murder if his bottle isn't a perfect 85 degrees Fahrenheit? The answer to both questions is: probably not. In most cases washing baby bottles in the dishwasher cleans them just fine—and a room temperature bottle will make a hungry baby just as happy as a warmed bottle of formula or milk. But what if you decide you want a bottle sterilizer or warmer? Here are our recommendations:

Like the competition in bottles, Avent also seems to win the sterilizer war with their "Express II Microwave Steam Sterilizer." The Express II ($32) has a larger capacity than previous mod-els; it holds six bottles. If you prefer a plug in sterilizer, the iQ 24 Electronic Steam Sterilizer sterilizes six bottles in six minutes and keeps bottles sterile for up to 24 hours. It can also steril-ize up to two ISIS breast pumps or up to six 9 oz. bottles. Cost: a whopping $90.

While Avent makes a good sterilizer, we would suggest get-ting the matching sterilizer for your bottle brand. For example, if you decide to use Born Free bottles, then the Born Free ster-ilizer ($45) is a good bet. Why? Sterilizers for one brand can sometimes damage other brand's bottles—for example, we did receive a report that Medela's Quick Clean Micro-Steam bags can melt Born Free bottles.

What about bottle warmers? Avent makes a pretty good one, the "Express Bottle and Baby Food Warmer" ($46). It can heat a bottle in four minutes. It also fits baby food jars and all types of baby bottles (not just Avent). However, in general, bottle warm-ers are unnecessary for most parents—you can skip this purchase.

![Smart Shopper Tip icon]

Smart Shopper Tip

Smart Shopper Tip #1
Nipple confusion?

"When I check the catalogs and look in baby stores, I see bottles with all different shaped nipples. Which one is best for my baby? How do I avoid nipple confusion?"

Nipple confusion occurs when a baby learns to suck one way at the breast and another way from a bottle. This happens because the "human breast milk delivery system" (that is, the breast and nipple) forces babies to keep their sucking action forward in their mouths. The result: they have to work harder to get milk from a breast than from a conventional baby bottle.

So if you want to give an occasional bottle, what bottle is least likely to cause nipple confusion? Unfortunately, the answer is not clear—some parents swear that Avent's nipple is best. Fans of Dr. Brown's bottle say it is better. Others find less expensive options like the Playtex Nurser work just as well.

Are there really that many differences between nipples, besides shape? Not really. All major brands are dishwasher-safe, made of silicone and have very similar flow rates. The bottom line: you may have to experiment with different nipples/bottles to find one your baby likes.

Smart Shopper Tip #2
Bottle confusion?

"How many bottles will I need if I formula feed? What nipple sizes do I need? Do I need a bottle sterilizer?"

Yes, the questions about bottles and feeding baby can be rather endless! To help, on our web site, we've posted a great email from a mom who's been there, done that. This email actually appeared first as a thread on our message boards, but we thought it was the most comprehensive discussion of bottle-feeding we've ever seen. Since it is eight pages long, however, we didn't have room to reprint it here. Go to Babybargains.com and click on Bonus Material to read it online.

Baby Food

At the tender age of four to six months, you and your baby will depart on a magical journey to a new place filled with exciting adventures and never-before-seen wonders. Yes, you've entered the SOLID FOOD ZONE.

Parents in Cyberspace: What's on the Web?

Looking for a schedule of what foods to introduce when? Earth's Best's web site has a comprehensive chart with suggestions (earths-best.com, click on Health & Nutrition, then Doctor's Corner, then Infant Feeding Schedule). Gerber's slick web site (gerber.com) Unfortunately, you'll have to sign up on the site to get to information like recommended feeding schedules. Watch out for lots of spam from this site.

We also liked Beechnut's site (beechnut.com), which includes "suggested menus," and "feeding tips." Although it is designed for Canadian parents, Heinz's baby food web site, heinzbaby.com contains extensive nutritional advice and menu planners among other information. Canadians can take advantage of rebate offers and other deals on this site (hopefully, they'll add the rest of North America to the coupon deals soon).

Safe & Sound

1 **FEED FROM A BOWL, NOT FROM THE JAR.** Why? If you feed from a jar, bacteria from baby's mouth can find their way back to the jar, spoiling the food much more quickly. Also, saliva enzymes begin to break down the food's nutrients. The best strategy: pour the amount of baby food you need into a bowl and feed from there (unless it's the last serving from the jar). And be sure to refrigerate any unused portions.

2 **DON'T STORE FOOD IN PLASTIC BAGS.** If you leave plastic bags on the baby's high chair, they can be a suffocation hazard. A better solution: store leftover food in small, Tupperware-type containers.

3 **DO A TASTE TEST.** Make sure it isn't too hot, too cold, or spoiled. We know you aren't dying to taste the Creamed Ham Surprise from Gerber, but it is a necessary task.

4 **CHECK FOR EXPIRATION DATES.** Gerber's jarred food looks like it would last through the next Ice Age, but check that expiration date. Most unopened baby food is only good for a year or two. Use opened jars within one to two days.

5 **AVOID UNPASTEURIZED MILK, MILK PRODUCTS AND JUICES.**
Babies don't have the ability to fight off serious bacterium like
e. coli. Avoid these hazards by feeding your child only pasteurized
dairy and juice products.

Also steer clear of feeding honey to children less than one year
of age. Botulism spores can be found in honey—while not harmful
to adults and older kids, these spores can be fatal to infants.

6 **A FINAL WORD OF ADVICE ON FEEDING BABY:** The American
Academy of Pediatrics (AAP) recommends the following
regarding feeding peanuts, a highly allergenic food with lifelong
implications: For families with NO history of food allergies, your
baby can eat peanuts or peanut butter after one year of age. For
"high risk" families (that is, those with a history of food allergies), You
should avoid the top allergy foods (peanuts, egg whites, shellfish,
and tree nuts) until age three.

For a comprehensive discussion of food allergies and intoler-
ances, see our new book, Baby *411*. Dr. Ari Brown, an award winning pediatrician and mother includes the most up-to-date information on this topic as well as other feeding issues.

Smart Shopper Tips

Smart Shopper Tip #1
Tracking Down UFFOs (Unidentifiable Flying Food Objects)
*"We fed our baby rice cereal for the first time. It was really cute,
except for the part when the baby picked knocked the bowl to the
floor . . . multiple times! Should we have bought some special stuff
for this occasion?"*

Well, unless you want your kitchen to be redecorated in Early
Baby Food, we do have a few suggestions. First, a bowl with a bottom that suctions to the table is a great way to avoid flying saucers.
Plastic spoons that have a round handle are nice, so baby can't stick
the spoon handle in her eye (yes, that does happen—babies do try
to feed themselves even at a young age). Spoons with rubber coat-
ings are also recommended; they don't transfer the heat or cold of
the food to the baby's mouth and are easier on the gums. One
clever spoon is Munchkin's "White Hot Infant Spoon" (web:
munchkininc.com, four for $5). This spoon uses a special coating
that changes color when baby's food is too hot (over 110°).

Smart Shopper Tip #2
Avoiding Mealtime Baths

"Our baby loves to drink from a cup, except for one small problem. Most of the liquid ends up on her, instead of in her. Any tips?"

Congratulations! You have a child who is ready to join the rest of the world and give up the bottle or breast. You may have mixed feelings about this, especially when you have to wash all those additional bibs, the floor and yourself more frequently. But this is a cool milestone. Babies are developmentally able to use a cup between ten and 16 months.

So what's the solution to the inevitable mess your baby will make when learning to drink from a cup? Most parents turn to sippy cups. But we don't recommend them. Why? Sippy cups aren't exactly beloved by doctors and dentists. Turns out babies use the same sucking action to get milk from a sippy cup as they do when sucking from a baby bottle. Hence they are not learning how to drink from a cup. Plus, sippy cups direct the flow of liquid straight for the back of baby's top front teeth—this promotes tooth decay. That's why most dentists are no fans of sippy cups.

Is there an answer to this dilemma? When being clean and pristine aren't that important (say when eating at home in the kitchen with lots of clean up gear handy) let your baby practice with a regular plastic

Pacifiers: Good or Bad?

Should your baby use a pacifier? Surprisingly, this is a controversial topic.

Some experts argue that early use of pacifiers may interfere with breastfeeding. But new studies show that pacifier use in children actually reduces the risk of Sudden Infant Death Syndrome (SIDS). It's unclear why pacifiers work, but studies clearly show a lowered risk of SIDS.

So, here are our recommendations for pacifier use: wait to give your child a pacifier until breastfeeding is well established (about a month of age). Discontinue pacifier use by six months of age. Why? Ninety percent of SIDS deaths occur between one month and six months of age. For more on the health benefits of pacifiers, see our other book, *Baby 411*.

So, now that you know what's good about a pacifier, which type of pacifier is best? There are two types—regular pacifiers have round nipples, while "orthodontic" pacifiers have flat nipples. Either is fine—but consult with your pediatrician if you have concerns on this topic.

cup. But also try to teach her to use a straw. That way, when you're out at a restaurant, she won't be taking a bath in public.

Money-Saving Tips

1 MAKE YOUR OWN. Let's be honest: baby foods like mashed bananas are really just . . . mashed bananas. You can easily whip up this stuff with that common kitchen helper, the food processor. Many parents skip baby food altogether and make their own. One tip: make up a big batch at one time and freeze the leftovers in ice cube trays. Check the library for cookbooks that provide tips on making baby food at home. A reader suggestion: the "Super Baby Food" book ($19.95, F. J. Roberts Publishing, web: superbabyfood. com). This 590-page book is about as comprehensive as you can find on the subject.

2 FYI: TOYS R US AND BABIES R US SELL BABY FOOD. If you think your grocery store is gouging you on the price of baby food, you might want to check out the prices at Babies R Us. We found Gerber 1st Foods in a four-pack of 2.5-ounce jars for $2.09—that works out to about 50¢ per jar or about 15% less than grocery store prices. Toys R Us also sells four-packs of assorted dinners from Gerber's 2nd and 3rd Food collections.

E-MAIL FROM THE REAL WORLD
**Making your own baby food
isn't time consuming**

A mom in New Mexico told us she found making her own baby food isn't as difficult as it sounds:

"My husband and I watch what we eat, so we definitely watch what our baby eats. One of the things I do is buy organic carrots, quick boil them, throw them in a blender and then freeze them in an ice cube tray. Once they are frozen, I separate the cubes into freezer baggies (they would get freezer burn if left in the ice tray). When mealtime arrives, I just throw them in the microwave. Organic carrots taste great! This whole process might sound complicated, but it only takes me about 20 minutes to do, and then another five to ten minutes to put the cubes in baggies."

---

3 **COUPONS! COUPONS! COUPONS!** Yes, we've seen quite a few cents-off and buy-one-get-one-free coupons on baby food and formula—not just in the Sunday paper but also through the mail. Our advice: don't toss that junk mail until you've made sure you're not trashing valuable baby food coupons. Another coupon trick: look for "bounce-back" coupons. Those are the coupons put in packages of baby food to encourage you to bounce back to the store and buy more.

4 **GO FOR A LESSER-KNOWN BRAND.** Example: Bay Valley Foods' Nature's Goodness (formerly owned by Del Monte) makes good quality baby food, but is not as well known as Gerber or Earth's Best. It is priced about 20% less than the competition. The only drawback: it isn't available everywhere.

5 **SUBSTITUTE COMPARABLE ADULT FOODS.** What's the difference between adult applesauce and baby applesauce? Not much, except for the fact that applesauce in a jar with a cute baby on it costs several times more than the adult version. (One caveat: make sure the regular applesauce is NOT loaded with extra sugar). Another rip-off: "next step" foods for older babies. Gerber loves to tout its special toddler meals in its "Graduates" line. What's the point? When baby is ready to eat pasta, just serve him small bites of the adult stuff. Bottom line: babies should learn to eat the same (hopefully healthy) foods you are eating, with the same spices and flavors. Toddler or graduate foods are a waste of time and money.

6 **GO FOR THE BETTER QUALITY.** That's a strange money-saving tip, isn't it? Doesn't better quality baby food cost more? Yes, but look at it this way—the average baby eats 600 jars of baby food until they "graduate" to adult foods. Sounds like a lot of money, eh? Well, that only works out to $300 or so in total expenditures (using an average price of 89¢ per jar). Hence, if you go for the better-quality food and spend, say, 15% to 20% more, you're only out another $90. And feeding baby food that tastes more like the real thing makes transitions to adult foods easier.

How about organic baby food? Well, there is no scientific data that shows any health benefit for organic baby food. But, we think the key issue here is exposure to pesticides. Organic foods are certified pesticide-free; since pesticide residues affect the small bodies of infants and children more than adults, avoiding such exposure with organic food for infants makes sense.

"Toddler" foods: a waste of money?

When the number of births leveled off in recent years, the baby food companies began looking around for ways to grow their sales. One idea: make foods for older babies and toddlers who have abandoned the jarred mushy stuff! To boost sales in the $1 billion baby food market, Gerber rolled out "Gerber Graduates" while Heinz debuted "Toddler Cuisine," microwaveable meals for kids as old as 36 months. So, what do nutritionists and doctors think of these foods? Most say they are completely unnecessary. Yes, they are a convenience for parents but, besides that, so-called "toddler foods" offer no additional nutritional benefit. In their defense, the baby food companies argue that their toddler meals are meant to replace the junk food and unhealthy snacks parents give their babies. We guess we can see that point, but overall we think that toddler foods are a complete waste of money. Once your baby finishes with baby food, they can go straight to "adult food" without any problem—of course, that should be HEALTHY adult food. What's best: a mix of dairy products, fruits, vegetables, meat and eggs. And, no, McDonald's French fries don't count as a vegetable!

The Name Game: Reviews of Selected Manufacturers

Here's a round up of some of the best-known names in baby food. We should note that while we actually tried out each of the foods on our baby, you may reach different conclusions than we did. Unlike our brand name ratings for clothing or other baby products, food is a much trickier rating proposition. We rated the following brand names based on how healthy they are and how much they approximate real food (aroma, appearance, and, yes, taste). Our subjective opinions reflect our experience—always consult with your pediatrician or family doctor if you have any questions about feeding your baby. (Special thanks to Ben and Jack for their help in researching this topic.)

The Ratings

A **EXCELLENT**—*our top pick!*
B **GOOD**— *above average quality, prices, and creativity.*
C **FAIR**—*could stand some improvement.*
D **POOR**—*yuck! could stand some major improvement.*

Beech-Nut *(800) BEECHNUT; Web: beechnut.com.* Beech-Nut was one of the first baby food companies to eliminate fillers (starches, sugar, salt) or artificial colors/flavors in its 120 flavors. While Beech-Nut is not organic, the company claims to have "stringent pesticide standards." Our readers generally give Beech-Nut good marks (some like it better than Gerber). Recently, Beech-Nut started adding DHA and ARA (see the formula discussion above for more about these important lipids) to its DHA plus+ baby food. We've seen the DHA plus+ online at the outrageous cost of about 1.19¢ per 4 oz. jar.

The only bummer about Beech-Nut baby food: it can be hard to find (not every state has stores that carry it). You can use their where to buy function or order directly from the website. Look for online deals and coupons on the site as well. **Rating: B+**

Del Monte *See below for review of Natures Goodness.*

Earth's Best *(800) 442-4221. Web: earthsbest.com.* Earth's Best emphasis is organic baby food.. Started in (where else?) Vermont, Earth's Best has gone through several owners before landing in the lap of natural foods conglomerate Hain Celestial (parent of Celestial Tea). Despite all the changes in ownership, Earth's Best has maintained its focus, with the largest line of "natural" baby foods on the market—all vegetables and grains are certified organically grown (no pesticides are used), and meats are raised without antibiotics or steroids. Another advantage: Earth's Best never adds any salt, sugar or modified starches to its food. And the foods are only made from whole grains, fruits and vegetables (instead of concentrates). Yes, Earth's Best is more expensive (89¢ per four ounce jar; or 15% to 20% more than conventional baby food) but as we pointed out earlier, that's works out to only about $90 more per year. Reader feedback on Earth's Best has been positive—fans like the extensive choice and commitment to organic principals. All in all, Earth's Best is a much-needed natural alternative to the standard fare that babies have been fed for far too many years. **Rating: A**

Gerber *Web: gerber.com.* Dominating the baby food business with a whopping 79% market share (that's right, three out of every four baby food jars sold sport that familiar label), Gerber sure has come a long way from its humble beginnings. Back in 1907, Joseph Gerber (whose trade was canning) mashed up peas for his daughter, following the suggestion of a family doctor. Today Gerber sells $2 billion in baby food a year, having been acquired by European conglomerate Nestle in 2007.

Over the years, Gerber has tried to expand beyond jarred baby food. It launched microwavable toddler meals in 2002 and has licensed its name out for a variety of baby products, including cups, infant toys and even baby skincare items. Yet controversy has constantly dogged Gerber—in the 90's, consumer pressure forced the company to stop adding sugar and starch to its baby foods. The Federal Trade Commission has accused the company of deceptive advertising when it claimed a survey showed that four out of five pediatricians recommended the brand (the actual number was 16%).

On the upside, Gerber offers parents one key advantage: choice. The line boasts an amazing 200 different flavors. Gerber is sold in just about every grocery store on Earth. And we have to give Gerber credit: bowing to consumer interest in all things organic, Gerber rolled out "Tender Harvest" to compete with Earth's Best. The new line is made with "whole grains and certified organic fruits and vegetables" (note that Gerber's regular line still uses fruit and vegetable concentrates). Finally, we noticed that Gerber is now packing its first foods in plastic rather than glass. While we like the changes Gerber has made, we still have problems with the brand: we think their "Graduates" line of "toddler" foods is a waste of money. And their juice line is overpriced compared to others on the market. Quality-wise, we will give Gerber an average rating. **Rating: C**

Healthy Times Web: healthytimes.com. Healthy Times got its start selling one of the first health-food baby products back in 1980: a teething biscuit. Since then, the company has expanded their baby food offerings to include 22 jarred baby foods, baby cereal, snacks and toiletry items. The baby food line is certified organic and contains no soy, flour or other fillers. You'll find single fruits and vegetables (stage 1), fruit and veggie blends (stage 2) and dinners (combos of several veggies, and meat and veggies). You can buy Healthy Times online on the company's web site for 89¢ per 4 oz. jar for stage one foods—that's slightly less than Earth's Best stage-one foods. We also saw Healthy Times foods on Amazon.com and at Whole Foods, Trader Jo's and Vitamin Cottage. **Rating: A-**

Naturally Preferred Web: kroger.com. Launched in 2003, Kroger's own in-house brand of baby food is dubbed Naturally Preferred. You'll find it in grocery stores like Ralph's, Fry's, City Market and King Soopers to name a few. For a complete listing of stores in the Kroger chain, check their website. Like all private label brands, the big draw here is the price. Sample: a four-ounce jar of Naturally Preferred is 50¢, compared to Gerber Tender Harvest at 73¢ for the same size item.. **Rating: B**

Natures Goodness Web: naturesgoodness.com. Formerly owned by Heinz and then Del Monte, Nature's Goodness was sold to Baby Valley Foods in 2006. We like the fact that the company's website posts its nutritional labels online—and we noted the lack of added sugars or starches in most of the line. As for price, Nature's Goodness is priced about 15% to 20% less than Gerber, making it a good deal. A 2.5-ounce jar of bananas goes for 38¢ versus a similar Gerber natural fruit for 45¢ per 2.5 ounces. The feedback from parents on this line is positive; the only drawback is availability—Nature's Goodness isn't in as many stores as Gerber. **_Rating: A_**

◆ **_Frozen organic baby food._** This is a new category of baby food we're seeing in health food stores like Whole Foods. But the prices are astronomic: anywhere from $1.44 to $3.12 per 4 oz container. That's six times the cost of Gerber jarred food. There are even companies that will deliver fresh baby food or customize a menu of baby food for you (if you live in New York, Los Angeles, Boston and Seattle). Again, it's ridiculously expensive: up to $3.50 per jar plus delivery.

If you're still interested, here are some sources for frozen baby food: Evie's Organic Edibles (eviesorganicedibles.com), Plum Organics (plumorganics.com) Homemade Baby (homemadebaby. com), Bohemian Baby (bohemian-baby.com), Happy Baby (happy-babyfood.com).

High Chairs

As soon as Junior starts to eat solid food, you'll need this quintessential piece of baby furniture—the high chair. Surprisingly, this seemingly innocuous product generates over 9900 injuries each year. So, what are the safest high chairs? And how do you use them properly? We'll share these insights, as well as some money-saving tips and brand reviews in this section.

 ### Safe and Sound

| **STRAP ME IN.** *Most high chair injuries occur when babies are not strapped into their chairs.* Sadly, two to three deaths occur each year when babies "submarine" under the tray. To address these types of accidents new high chairs now feature a "passive restraint" (a plastic post) under the tray to prevent this. Note: some high chair makers attach this submarine protection to the tray; others have it on the seat. We prefer the seat. Why? If it is on the tray and the tray is removed, there is a risk a child might be able to squirm out of the safety belts (which is all that would

hold them in the chair). As a side note, some wooden high chairs only seem to have a crotch strap—no plastic post. This may mean it is easier for a baby to squirm out when the tray is removed.

FYI: Even if the high chair has a passive restraint, you STILL must strap in baby with the safety harness with EACH use. This prevents them from climbing out or otherwise hurting themselves.

2 **THE SAFETY STANDARDS FOR HIGH CHAIRS ARE VOLUNTARY.** This means not all high chairs on the market today meet all these voluntary standards. Perhaps the safest bet: look for JPMA-certified high chairs. The JPMA requires a battery of safety tests, including checks for stability, a locking device to prevent folding, a secure restraining system, no sharp edges, and so on.

3 **INSPECT THE SEAT—IS IT WELL UPHOLSTERED?** Make sure it won't tear or puncture easily.

4 **LOOK FOR STABILITY.** It's basic physics: the wider the base, the more stable the chair. Another tip: never put the high chair near a wall—babies have been injured in the past when they push off a wall or object, tipping over the chair. This problem is rare with the newest high chairs (as they have wide, stable bases), but you still can tip over older, hand-me-down models.

5 **CAREFULLY INSPECT THE RESTRAINING SYSTEM.** Straps around the hips and between the legs do the trick. The cheapest high chairs have only a single strap around the waist. Expensive models have "safety harnesses" with multiple straps.

6 **SOME HIGH CHAIRS OFFER DIFFERENT HEIGHT POSITIONS,** including a reclining position that supposedly makes it easier to feed a young infant. The problem? Feeding a baby solid foods in a reclining position is a choking hazard. If you want to use the reclining feature, it should be exclusively for bottle-feeding. We do think the recline feature is a plus for another reason, however: it is easier to move baby in and out of the high chair when it is reclined. And when babies start out with solid foods, they may go back and forth between the bottle and solid food during meals. Hence, the recline feature is helpful when they need to take a bottle break.

More Money Buys You

Whether you spend $30 or $500, most high chairs do one simple thing—provide you with a place to safely ensconce your baby while he eats. The more money you spend, however, the more comforts there are for both you and baby. As you go up in price, you find chairs with various height positions, reclining seats, larger trays, more padding, casters for mobility and more. From a safety point of view, some of the more expensive high chairs feature five-point restraint harnesses (instead of just a waist belt). As for usability, some high chairs are easier to clean than others, but that doesn't necessary correspond to price. Look for removable vinyl covers that are machine-washable (cloth covers are harder to clean).

Smart Shopper Tips for High Chairs

Smart Shopper Tip #1
High Chair Basics 101

"What's the difference between a $50 high chair and one that's $400? And does it matter what color you get? I like white best."

The high chair market is basically divided into two camps: the low-end chairs from companies like Graco and Cosco and high-end models from Peg Perego and Chicco. New in recent years are both ultra-modern high chairs (the Fresco, the Flair) and retro wood versions (Eddie Bauer, Graco). The key differences: styling (cutesy versus sleek/modern) and quality/durability.

Peg Perego's Prima Pappa, for example, became a runaway success, thanks to its stylish looks and compact fold for storage. At $200+, however, the Pappa is TWICE the price of Fisher Price's top-of-the-line high chair. And, as you'll read later, some readers gripe that the Pappa is a nightmare to clean.

There finally is good news to report on the high chair front, however. In recent years, several new competitors have debuted in the market in the "mid" price range (that is, between the $50 Cosco chairs and the $200 Peregos) with decent looks AND good features. While we will discuss some of these specific models later in the chapter, here are some basic features and new trends to keep an eye out for:

◆ **Tray release.** Nearly all high chairs now have a "one hand" tray release that enables you to easily remove the tray with a quick motion. The problem: not all releases are the same. The more expensive chairs generally have a release that's easier to operate. Our advice: take a second in the store and remove the tray a few times from sample models. You'll note some trays are sticky; other "one-hand" tray releases really require two hands.

◆ **Dishwasher-safe trays—NOT!** Most high chairs today come with a dishwasher-safe tray insert. This cover snaps off the main tray and pops in the dishwasher for clean-up . . . or does it? In the reviews in this section, we'll note some models whose dishwasher-safe trays are too big to fit in an actual dishwasher. A word of advice: measure the bottom rack of your dishwasher and take that dimension with you when high chair shopping.

◆ **Tray height.** Some parents complain the tray height of certain high chairs is too high—making it hard for smaller babies to use. A smart tip: take your baby with you when you go high chair shopping and actually sit them in the different options. You can evaluate the tray heights in person to make sure the chair will work for both you and baby. We'll note which chairs have the best/worst tray heights later in our reviews. Generally, a chair with a tray height of less than 8″ should work for most babies. A few models have tray heights over 8″—those can be a major problem since a child can't reach the food on the tray. Why is this important? Some day (we know it seems light years away), your baby will feed himself . . . and being able to see and reach the food is important!

◆ **Seat depth.** Most chairs have multiple tray positions and reclining seats. But what is the distance between the seat back when it is upright and the tray in its closest position? A distance of 5″ to 7″ is acceptable. Over 7″ and you run the risk that there will be a large gap between your baby and the tray—and all their food will end up in their lap. Again, take your baby with you when shopping for a chair, as smaller babies may be harder to fit.

◆ **Looks versus features** The kitchen is often the hub for most houses—and it's no surprise that guests gravitate there during visits. Hence, we can understand why folks would like their high chair to look nice, fitting in with the kitchen décor. Unfortunately, most high chairs are plastic and some feature cartoon motifs. So we know that some parents are tempted to go with one of those nice new wood hybrid chairs that look pretty. But watch out: most wood hybrid chairs are long on style but short on features—they don't adjust like a plastic high chair, nor are they as easy to clean. Bottom line: we suggest going for practical instead of pretty.

◆ **Washability.** Here's an obvious tip some first-time parents seem to miss: make sure the high chair you buy has a removable washable seat cover OR a seat that easily sponges clean. In the latter category, chairs with VINYL covers trump those made of cloth—vinyl can be wiped clean, while cloth typically has to be washed. This might be one of those first-time parent traps—seats with cloth covers sure look nicer than those made of vinyl. But the extra effort to machine wash a cloth cover is a pain . . and some cloth covers can't be thrown in the dryer! That means waiting a day or more for a cover to line dry.

Of course, the cloth/vinyl issue becomes somewhat confusing when you consider some vinyl seats have cloth edging/piping. Our advice: be careful of any seat with cloth accents, as it might be very hard to clean. (Make sure the seat is washable *and* machine dryable).

What color cover should you get? Answer: anything but white. Sure, that fancy white "leatherette" high chair looks all shiny and new at the baby store, but it will forever be a cleaning nightmare once you start using it. Darker colors and patterns are better. Another tip: avoid high chairs that have lots of cracks and crevices near the tray and seat, which makes cleaning difficult.

Smart Shopper Tip #2
Tray Chic and Other Restaurant Tips

"We have a great high chair at home, but we're always appalled at the lack of safe high chairs at restaurants. Our favorite cafe has a high chair that must date back to 1952—no straps, a metal tray with sharp edges, and a hard seat with no cushion. Have restaurateurs lost their minds?

We think so. People who run restaurants must search obscure foreign countries to find the world's most hazardous high chairs. The biggest problem? No straps, enabling babies to slide out of the chair, submarine-style. The solution? When the baby is young, keep her in her infant car seat; the safe harness keeps baby secure. When your baby is older (and if you eat out a lot), you may want to invest in a portable booster seat. We'll discuss and recommend hook on chairs and booster seats later in this chapter.

The Name Game: Reviews of Selected Manufacturers

Here's a round up of the best high chairs on the market today:

The Ratings

A **EXCELLENT**—*our top pick!*
B **GOOD**— *above average quality, prices, and creativity.*
C **FAIR**—*could stand some improvement.*
D **POOR**—*yuck! could stand some major improvement.*

Baby Trend *(800) 328-7363, (909) 902-5568, Web: babytrend. com.* Baby Trend's high chair was one of our top picks in a previous edition of this book, but our rating of this chair continues to drift down as complaints from readers stack up. Yes, it is a credible knock-off of the Perego and Chicco chairs, yet sells for 40% less ($80 to $100 in most stores).

You get all the standard features you'd expect: five-point harness, four-position reclining seat, three-position tray with one hand release, six height positions, compact fold and casters. Some models have a separate dishwasher-safe tray. And, yes, the Baby Trend high chair is generally easier to use than competitors (it requires little assembly and the seat recline is easy to adjust, for example).

For 2009, Baby Trend sells an $80 version (Trend 86) of their high chair at chains Babies R Us and Wal-Mart and a $100 version (Trend 88) elsewhere. The more expensive model has a fully reclining seat and is fully assembled (the cheaper one has a partial seat recline and requires assembly).

So, why all the complaints? The pad is this chair's Achilles' heel. We've received several reports that the cloth pad (which has a reversible vinyl side) fell apart or bunched up after machine washing. Even Baby Trend, in an email to us, admitted the pad "responds best to hand washing." Gee, that's nice—too bad the instructions for the chair say to machine wash the pad on the gentle cycle . . . with no mention of hand washing. Add that to the fact the pad has to be line dried and you have a deal-breaker here. Another major complaint centers on the tray height, which is way too high for average-size babies. Of course, not all the reviews are negative: some parents have had success with this high chair. And we give Baby Trend bonus points for improving the chair over the years. But Baby Trend's customer service stumbles and the pad washing issue have convinced us that this chair isn't worthy of a recommendation. ***Rating: C+***

Boon *(888) 376-4763, Web: booninc.com.* Boon's Flair high chair debuted in 2007, part of the modernist wave sweeping the baby products biz. At least this chair features something unique: a pneumatic lift, which gives the chair "effortless height adjustment." Basically, a button on the base will automatically lower the chair. We do like the seamless seat, which is easier to clean than other high chairs (where food finds its way into every last crack and crevice). The pad and harness remove for cleaning and a dishwasher-safe tray within a tray is easy to use. The Flair comes in two versions:

standard (which has a translucent frosted glass seat, white pad and plastic base) and elite (high-gloss white seat, orange pad, stainless steel base; pictured). The standard Flair is about $200, the Elite Flair $380. (We can't help but wonder if the folks at Boon were watching a DVD of *Office Space* when they named this chair).

For 2009, Boon told us they are phasing out the Elite Flair, although we still see it sold online as of press time. The standard Flair will continue on, with a new berry pink color.

The only negative for the Flair: the seat doesn't recline, making this chair inappropriate for smaller infants who are bottle-feeding. A reclining seat is a standard feature on almost all high chairs, so we wonder why Boon left this out. Reader feedback on the Flair is positive: fans love how easy it is to clean and the small footprint. The only negative: the straps should tighten a bit more for smaller babies. And the lack of a chest buckle means the harness can slide off the shoulders of some kids. Yet, most folks love this chair, whose sleek look is the big draw. ***Rating: A***

Bloom *Web: BloomBaby.com* Bloom's Fresco high chair is the latest entrant in the space-age, Jetsons-style high chair category. It's egg-shaped, seamless seat and circular base echo the Boon Flair with one big exception: the Bloom Fresco can recline, making it suitable for infants. And we liked the micro-suede seat upholstery (in nine colors) and pneumatic-assist height adjustment. But  the price? $400 is way too high, in our opinion. Since the Fresco is so new, we don't have much parent feedback—but one parent who did buy it was disappointed with the twisty straps that are hard to adjust. For $400, you'd think Bloom would get that right.

Bloom has a second high chair model: the Nano, which is tagged as an "iconic minimalist" model with a flat fold and "micro leather" seat in six colors. Price: $180—that's about three times the price of other simple high chairs that don't recline, lack wheels and fold up flat. In the past year, Bloom modified the Nano so it has a smaller footprint. Parent feedback on the Nano has been positive— folks like its flat fold and simple design.

New for 2009, Bloom plans to debut the Dina high chair, a $300 ultra-slim wood chair that weighs just ten lbs. The wood chair folds up to just two inches wide. For $300, you'd think Bloom would throw in a chair pad, but no . . . that's an extra $40.

It's hard to assign a rating for this brand—the prices are so high that few parents have purchased them. The little we have heard, however, is positive. But the prices drag down Bloom's overall rating—it's hard to justify spending this much on a high chair. ***Rating: B***

Calla Chair *Web: callachair.com.* This high chair is reviewed on our web site BabyBargains.com (click on Bonus Material).

Carter's. This high chair is made by Kolcraft, see review later.

Chicco *(877) 4CHICCO. Web: chiccousa.com.* Chicco's Polly high chair is the successor to the Mamma, a high chair we only gave a C in our last report. So is the Polly an improvement? Yes.

Retailing at $140, the Polly features an adjustable footrest, compact fold, three-position seat recline, seven height positions and removable dishwasher-safe tray. You also get two pads (one can be on the chair while the other is being cleaned. (FYI: an older model Polly with a single pad can still be found online for $80 or so).

New for 2009, Chicco is debuting a new version of the Polly, dubbed the Polly Magic. It will be similar to the regular Polly (same double pad, two trays, etc), but will add toys and a storage basket. Magically, the price of this high chair will hit $180.

Fans of this chair like the tray, which can be removed with one-hand and hung off pegs on the back of the frame. The compact fold is nice, but the chair doesn't stand well by itself. Readers who like the Polly also love the stylish look—it comes in one of 12 snazzy color combinations.

As for negatives, the Polly's pad is not machine washable, which is a bummer. You can't only spot clean it. Several readers complain that Chicco's dishwasher-safe tray insert is too large to fit in a dishwasher (as Homer would say, Doh!). And yes, this chair can be a bear to clean: crevices in the tray and chair collect food, plus the harness straps can't be removed to be washed. And the harness buckles often stick and are hard to undo, report readers.

A few older Polly's still have cloth pads—we'd avoid these and stick with the newer, vinyl seat versions (much easier to clean).

So it's a mixed review for the Chicco Polly: fans like the stylish design and easy fold. But the negatives are creeping up for this model, so we've lowered our rating a bit this time out. ***Rating: B***

Combi *(800) 992-6624, (803) 802-8416; Web: combi-intl.com.* Best known for its strollers, Combi has been trying to crack the high chair category but its efforts have met with little success. Typical Combi high chairs had some gimmick (at one point, they sold a "gliding" high chair that rocked back and forth), but for their current offering (the Hero), Combi has played it safe. This $150 high chair features a

washable pad, five-point harness, three-position recline and (here's the unique feature) the ability to attach to a kitchen chair as a booster chair for older kids. The price seems high to us—and we were turned off by the Hero's dinky dishwasher-tray insert. Sorry, the Hero looks like a zero. ***Rating: C***

Cosco *Web: djgusa.com.* Like most things Cosco makes, their high chairs define the entry-level price point in this market. The Cosco Convenience (also known as the Beginnings Simple Start) high chair (pictured) is a bare bones model ($35 at Wal-Mart). This would do the trick for grandma's house—the simple chair has a tray with one-hand  release, four-position seat recline and vinyl pad. Nothing too fancy to look at, but how many bells and whistles does Grandma need?

While these high chairs are fine for occasional use at Grandma's house, we aren't keen on these offerings as a primary high chair. Why? A lack of safety features (example: three-point harnesses instead of a five-point) make these chairs better for occasional use.

New for 2009, Cosco plans to debut the Feast & Fold high chair—this small $130 chair will features a slim standing fold (six and a half inches). This chair wasn't out as of press time, so no feedback yet. ***Rating: C-***

Eddie Bauer *Web: djgusa.com.* Cosco has had big success with their Eddie Bauer brand in car seats and strollers, so it's no big surprise they decided to bring the name to high chairs. We were impressed with their creative offering here: a hybrid wood chair with plastic tray. Yep, in the cat-  egory of "everything old is new again," The Eddie Bauer Newport Collection high chair ($120) combines the look of wood with the convenience of plastic (the tray has a removable dinner tray, like most competitors).

So, what are the trade-offs? Well, you can forget about many of the features you'll find in plastic chairs—Eddie Bauer's chair lacks wheels, height adjustments, seat recline and more.

Reader feedback on this chair has turned sharply negative over the past year. When it first debuted, the Eddie Bauer wood high chair had a full pad that covered the entire seat; in the past year, the pad design changed to a smaller size, showing more wood. We speculated last year this would make it harder to clean (more food would get on the wood) and we were right—the negative reviews shot up after the design change.

"It's pretty out of the box, but impossible to keep that way," said one reader, who summed up the frustrations of many parents. Food sticks to the dark wood finish, the slats on the side of the seat, just about anywhere—and it is impossible to clean. The finish also comes off, say others, indicating Cosco cut some corners here.

FYI: Cosco sells a similar version of this chair under the Safety 1st (Vineland) moniker.

In a past edition of this book, we gave this seat our recommendation and a high rating. That's all changed now, as we drop the rating to reflect poor consumer reviews after the design change. **Rating: D**

Evenflo *(800) 233-5921 or (937) 415-3300. Web: evenflo.com.* Evenflo has always been an also-ran in the high chair market, thanks to quality woes and designs that lack pizzazz. And that lackluster record continues with Evenflo's current high chair offerings: the Expressions and Majestic (pictured).

Evenflo prices its offerings in a niche between Cosco's bare-bones models sold at Wal-Mart and the more pricey stuff you see at specialty stores. Take the Expressions chair, for example. This chair ($55 to $70) looks good on paper: one-hand tray release, compact fold, seven height positions, reclining seat, wheels and so on. The Expressions comes in two versions, the base model and the Plus, which adds a dishwasher-safe tray.

The Majestic is an upgraded model includes a dishwasher-safe tray, swing-out removable snack tray, foot rest, machine washable pad, four position recline and storage in the base. The Majestic comes in several versions, from a basic model for $60 to a "Discovery" version with toys for $120.

Parent feedback on Evenflo's high chairs is a mixed bag. The Expressions gets better marks as a good, simple high chair (and a decent value at $55). But parents are more caustic when it comes to the Majestic—a too-high tray, a seat that doesn't fully adjust upright and difficult assembly are key gripes.

Overall, we've been unimpressed with Evenflo's quality control— we've heard many stories of parts that break, screws that come out of the seat and so on. That suspicion was verified in 2008 when Evenflo recalled nearly 100,000 Majestic high chairs because "plastic caps and metal screws can loosen and fall out, posing both a fall and choking hazards to children," reported the CPSC.

It seems that Evenflo cuts corners . . . and that comes back to bite you. So it is a tepid review for Evenflo: the Expressions is ok, but the Majestic is a loser. **Rating: C-**

Fisher-Price *(800) 828-4000 or (716) 687-3000. Web: fisher-price.com.* Folks, we have a winner! Fisher-Price finally has hit a home run with the Healthy Care high chair. It features a three-position seat recline, five-point restraint, one-hand tray removal, dishwasher-safe tray liner, and various height adjustments. All in all, a good value—the Healthy Care starts at $95 for a basic version at Wal-Mart and goes up to $110 for the Rainforest (pictured) or Precious Planet models. The basic model omits the one-hand tray release; the premium version has toys and an upgraded pad.

Parents universally praise the Healthy Care for its ease of use and cleanability (yep, those harness straps and toys can be thrown into the dishwasher). The only negative to this chair is the fashion—that cutesy color scheme on the chair turns parents off. Some complain the chair tends to collect food in crevices (the ruffles on the Aquarium model are food collectors; we suggest going for the ruffle-free Rainforest, Precious Planet or plain model). And the Healthy Care requires quite a bit of assembly. Despite that, this is the best bet in the high chair market and we give the Healthy Care our highest rating.

Fisher Price makes two other high chairs: Space Saver and the Zen Collection wood hybrid. The Space Saver ($55) is the first high chair that sits on a dining chair (sort of a souped-up booster). This model features a full-size tray and three-position recline—plus it converts to a toddler booster. If you are short of space (think New York City apartment), this might be a great option. Detractors point out that once you strap this thing to a chair, you can't push the chair under the table—hence defeating the space saving concept. We see that point, but still think this is a great solution for urban condos with little space to store a bulky high chair.

Fisher Price's first wood hybrid chair, the Zen, debuted in the past year. This $150 high-chair features a plastic seat with three-position recline, a tray with dishwasher-safe insert and three-position height adjustment. The Zen is actually a combination of plastic, wood and metal—the chair is plastic (with a vinyl cover), the legs are metal and the footrest and support bars are wood.

The Zen is quite a departure for Fisher Price—this company is not exactly known for its design aesthetic. Most folks have to hide their Fisher Price chairs when guests come over; this one you can leave out and it will fit most contemporary kitchens.

Reader feedback on the Zen has been positive: fans love the easy assembly and overall quality—yes, the Zen's looks factor into why folks are willing to spend $50 more than a Healthy Care chair. The negatives: while the legs fold up, the chair is NOT compact when folded. Some moms have complained the seat is a bit snug for bigger babies

(Fisher Price's claim that it will hold 50 pound kids seems a stretch).

Bottom line: Fisher Price's high chairs are the best of breed. If you are on a tight budget and don't mind the bright fashion, the basic Healthy Care is a great value. If the cutesy pattern is too much, try the Zen. ***Rating: A***

Graco *(800) 345-4109, (610) 286-5951. Web: gracobaby.com.* Graco has had mixed results in the high chair category. For every innovation (the Graco Contempo high chair, pictured, featured the most compact fold on the market), the company seems to also take a step backward. Graco had to recall 100,000 Contempo high chairs in 2006 after the chair collapsed when not fully opened and locked into place (Graco received 18 reports of the chair collapsing).

high chairs

Graco divides its high chairs in two categories: standard and full-featured. The standard chairs include the Easy Chair, a bare-bones model that sells for as little as $50 in big box stores (a good buy for Grandma's house) with a simple tray, three-position recline and vinyl pad.

As for full-featured chairs, Graco offers the Harmony, Meal Time and the aforementioned Contempo. The Harmony comes in several versions, ranging from a stripped-down version for $70 at Amazon to a $110 "deluxe" model with toys. The Harmony's key selling point: a contoured design lets you pull baby up to the table easier than other models. The Harmony also features a one-hand height adjustment and seat recline, plus a "baby booster" insert that provides head and neck support for younger babies. The cushy padded vinyl seat and storage basket are nice features, as is the snap-off dinner tray.

What's the quality like? Parents give the Harmony mixed marks. Detractors point to the difficult assembly and a chair that doesn't adjust fully upright. Fans of the Harmony point out that the chair's many features make it a good value for the price. Overall, the Harmony isn't bad . . . but doesn't have the same positive feedback as Fisher Price's offerings.

The Graco Contempo ($100 to $130) lives on, despite the recall. Feedback on this model has been much more positive, with folks loving the ultra compact fold and extra seat pad. You also get six position height adjustment, a three-position recline and dishwasher-safe tray insert.

On the more affordable end, the Graco Meal Time high chair ($60 to $90) features a one-hand, three-position recline, dishwasher-safe tray, four height adjustments, casters and one-hand tray release. Feedback on this model has been sparse (it isn't as popular as the Contempo or Harmony), but what little we've heard has been positive—folks like the easy assembly and cleanability. It doesn't fold up as compact as the Contempo, however.

After watching their competition roll out wood high chairs to great success, Graco joined the market in the past year with their Classic Wood offering ($125 to $150). Graco's spin: their chair is all wood, except for the seat pad and clear plastic tray cover, which is dishwasher safe. Fans like the Classic Wood chair's easy assembly and machine washable pad—this chair is much easier to clean than the comparable Eddie Bauer model. But . . . this is a wood high chair, so you don't get a seat that reclines or adjusts in height, nor a tray that removes with one hand. And some parents told us the under-tray wood bar that prevents a child from sliding out is not adjustable and hence too tight for older babies/toddlers.

New for 2009, the Blossom high chair cuts a much more modern pose than most Graco chairs. It will have all the standard features you expect from today's chairs (three-position recline, six position height adjustment, dishwasher safe tray insert) plus a few surprises: an adjustable footrest and a parent tray under the chair. The Blossom's key feature: it converts to a toddler booster with a seat back insert that adjusts in size. Whether this is worth the $180 price tag remains to be seen—the Blossom wasn't out as of press time, so no parent feedback yet.

Also new for 2009: the Graco Cozy Dinette, a $100 high chair with a flip-open third tray and seat recline indicator. Again, no feedback yet on this one as it is too new.

Overall, we think Graco does a good job with its high chairs. While we still think Fisher Price is a step or two ahead of them quality-wise, Graco is close. The Contempo is our top pick in this line. **Rating: B**

IKEA. *Web: ikea.com.* IKEA has two simple high chairs: the Antilop ($20; pictured) is a plastic chair with metal legs . . . but lacks a tray and doesn't fold up. You can purchase a tray for the Antilop for an additional $5. The Agam ($35) is a simple wood high chair that includes a removable center support, but lacks a tray or safety harness. Obviously, this chair is more appropriate for an older toddler that needs a boost to a table (but doesn't need a safety harness or tray). We would not recommend these chairs for babies (unless you purchase the Antilop tray). **Rating: C**

Inglesina *Web: inglesina.com.* Italian stroller company Inglesina jumped into the high chair market in the past year with the pricey

Zuma, which attempts to be both high style and practical. The rounded seat echoes modern seats by Bloom and Boom, but the more traditional base echoes a bit of Pali. The Zuma has eight height positions, three-position seat recline and a whopper of a price tag: $300. As a newcomer to the high chair market, Inglesina has made a few mistakes: the tray requires two hands to remove and the dishwasher-safe tray insert doesn't cover the entire main tray. The gap between baby and the tray is too far, in our opinion (as a result, food ends up in baby's lap). We've had little actual feedback on this chair—the high price means very few have sold.

FYI: also has a second, simpler high chair: the Club for $109. This chair doesn't really do anything but look pretty. The Club is probably best for toddlers who aren't ready for a booster seat yet. ***Rating: C***

Kolcraft *(773) 247-4494. Web: kolcraft.com.* Kolcraft's emphasis in this category is on being the low price leader and their current offerings are a case in point. The Recline N Dine is just $50. What do you get for that? Well, a rather basic high chair with one-hand tray release, vinyl pad and storage basket (but no wheels).

Kolcraft also sells a fancier high chair under their Sesame Street license (Sesame Beginnings, $65). This chair adds wheels, toys, and three-position seat recline. But the chair doesn't fold, which is an odd omission for a $65 chair.

The Kolcraft Contours Perfect Fit High Chair ($120; pictured) is a new model with a soft foam seat that is easy to clean (no crevices for food to hide). Cool feature: a clever under-seat crumb catcher. The Perfect Fit has a three-position seat recline, seven height positions and an adjustable foot rest. Yes, there is a dishwasher-safe tray insert,

but the tray itself is rather dinky compared to the competition. This chair is one of the best chairs Kolcraft has made in years, but it is in so few stores, there is little way to see it in person.

What about the quality? Let's be honest: these would be great for grandma's house, where occasional use wouldn't tax them too much, but not as an everyday high chair. In the past, we heard many gripes about Kolcraft's previous high chairs . . . seat pads that ripped too easily, straps that were hard to adjust and more. While the Contours Perfect Fit is an exception to the rule, most of Kolcraft's chairs only merit an average rating. ***Rating: C+***

high chairs

Peg Perego *(260) 482-8191. Web: perego. com.* Yes, the Prima Pappa has been a best seller but its day has come and gone. Sure, it looks stylish and features a four-position reclining seat, seven height adjustments, a dishwasher-safe dinner tray, five-point restraint and compact fold. And the fabrics! Very chic. But let's look at the chair's key flaw: the tray. It sits a whopping 8.5″ above the seat, making it too tall except perhaps for Shaq's kids. Another problem: the tray sits 7″ from the back seat, creating a gap the size of the Grand Canyon between your baby and her food. Then let's talk about this chair's cleanability—it's notorious for collecting food in every little nook and cranny. And the dishwasher-safe tray insert is too big to fit in most dishwashers. All this for $265! Wow, what a deal.

Perego hasn't really changed this chair much in recent years. There are currently two version of the Prima Pappa: the Best and the Diner. The Best features an upgraded, tailored seat cushion. The Diner has a seat pad made of microfiber. Otherwise, the chairs are basically the same.

We should note that you can occasionally find Peg high chairs (especially last year's models) for as little as $130 online.

Perhaps the best thing about the Perego high chair is how it looks—the fabrics are gorgeous. And this chair is made in Italy. But when you actually use the chair, the design flaws (it lacks a compact fold, the tray is sticky and tough to remove with one hand, lack of cleanability, etc.) quickly outweigh how pretty it looks.

Bottom line: we're not wild on this brand for high chairs. Instead of innovating in this category, Perego has been content to rest on its laurels . . . while competitors have knocked it off with better products at a lower price. Bottom line: if you like the looks of the Perego, save yourself $70 and get the Chicco Polly instead—same styling, just easier to use and clean.

New for 2009, Perego plans to debut a new high chair, the Tatamia ($350)—this chair is billed as a "multi-purpose baby seat" since it also functions as a swing and bouncer. This chair wasn't out as of press time, so no reader feedback yet. **Rating: C+**

Rochelle *Web: carom.com.* If plastic high chairs seem, well, too plastic-y, there is an alternative: a wooden high chair. Yes, kiddos, in the day before injection-molded plastic, this was how babies sat at the dinner table—in a high chair made of wood.

Rochelle has been making wooden high chairs in Michigan for 30 years. The company offers a half dozen models, most of which retail for $180 to $210. Example:

the Charlotte ($200; pictured), which comes with a slide-on tray and safety harness. But let's be real: these chairs lack most of the modern features you see in plastic chairs—obviously, there is no seat recline, the wood tray can't be popped into the dishwasher and the chair lacks submarine protection (the simple harness isn't a match for modern five-point harnesses). Most parents add a foam pad, as the hard wood doesn't exactly make for comfortable seating.

While these high chairs are fine, the lack of safety features is the major negative. We understand why some folks like the look of wood . . . but the Graco and Fisher Price wood hybrid high chair are probably a more practical (and safe) alternative to the wood high chair. ***Rating: C***

Safety 1st. *Web: Safety1st.com* While parent Cosco sells bare-bones high chairs to the discount chains, Safety 1st focuses on a slightly more upscale market. Example: Safety 1st has a hybrid wood model, much like their sister-brand Eddie Bauer. The Safety 1st Vineland wood high chair ($70 at Wal-Mart) has a plastic tray with one-hand release and dishwasher-safe insert. This chair comes with a  three-point harness and a pad that only partially covers the chair.

Safety 1st offers two plastic models: the PlaySafe and Serve 'n Store LX. The PlaySafe ($70) is your basic high chair with seven height positions, dishwasher-safe insert and compact fold. What's missing: the safety harness doesn't adjust well for smaller babies. And there is a huge gap between the tray and baby.

The Serve 'n Store LX ($80 to $90) is almost identical to the PlaySafe, but costs about $10 to $20 more. There is a Disney version of this chair at Sears for $65.

Overall, the quality of Safety 1st's high chairs is only average. They are neither innovative nor affordable. If you want a bare bones chair for Grandma, you're better off with one of Cosco's offerings for $30 less. If you want a full feature high chair, you're better off with Fisher Price or Graco, which are priced the same or $10 more than Safety 1st. ***Rating: C+***

Sesame Beginnings. *Kolcraft makes this high chair, see review earlier in this chapter..*

Slex. Imported from Europe by Sorelle (yes, the same company as reviewed in the crib chapter), Slex high chairs are similar to the Stokke Tripp Trapp (reviewed below). They morph from high chair to toddler chair to adult chair. The difference: while the

Tripp Trapp is (mostly) wood, the Slex is steel and plastic. And expensive—most web sites sell it for $400, although oddly, we saw it for just $200 on BabyDepot.com as of press time. There is little to no parent feedback on this model, which isn't widely sold in stores in the U.S. ***Rating: Not Yet.***

Stokke *Web: stokkeUSA.com.* The Stokke Tripp Trapp is the revised version of the Kinderzeat, which we recommended in a previous edition. This $250 chair has a seat and footrest that adjusts to multiple positions—the result is you can use it from six months (once baby can sit up) to age eight or beyond. The downsides? Well, the baby rail ($40) and seat cushion ($40-$55) are extras—making this a very pricey investment. And the Tripp Trapp doesn't come with a tray . . . so baby will be making a mess on your table, not his high chair tray. Our view: the Tripp Trapp is probably best for older toddlers who have outgrown a regular high chair (as an alternative to a booster seat). The quality of the Stokke Tripp Trapp is excellent. ***Rating: A-***

Summer *(866) 782-6222; web: summerin-fant.com.* Better known for their baby monitors, Summer tip-toed into the high chair market in the last year with a unique offering: the Newborn to Toddler High chair ($110). While this chair looks like an ordinary high chair (three-position seat recline, four position height adjustment, one-hand tray release, dishwasher-safe tray insert, five-point harness), it does have one unique feature: an infant mode that is akin to a bouncer seat. With a push of a button, it morphs into a regular high chair. Since Summer is so new to the market, we've had little reader feedback on this chair, but we will give Summer bonus points for trying something unique here. ***Rating: Not Yet.***

Svan of Sweden *(866) 782-6222; web: scichild.com.* Svan is a multi-function high chair imported from Europe, much like the Tripp Trapp (discussed earlier). The all-wood Svan (a plastic dishwasher tray cover is included) morphs from a high chair to a chair for toddlers and then older kids. Available in five finishes (including espresso), the Svan retails for $250 for the chair plus another $40 for cushions.

So is the Svan worth the nearly $300 price tag? Fans tell us they love how sturdy the chair is, yet still light enough to move around the

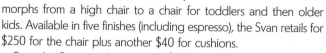

kitchen. The aesthetic and small footprint are the key selling points. On the other hand, this is a wood high chair, so there is no seat recline or other perks you find in plastic chairs. Adjusting the chair's height requires an Allen wrench, which is a pain—and several parents complained about the Svan's numerous nooks/crannies to clean. Overall, however, most of the reviews for the Swan are positive—this is a good chair if you can get past the drawbacks and price. FYI: Svan also makes a simple wood high chair (the Anka) for $180. **Rating: B+**

Valco *Web: valcobaby.com.* Stroller maker Valco plans to give the high chair market a try in 2009 with the $125 Astro, a basic high chair that folds flat (and comes with a travel bag). We saw a prototype of the chair and thought it was a work in progress; since it wasn't out as of press time, no rating yet. **Rating: Not Yet.**

Zooper *Web: zooperstrollers. com.* This high chair is reviewed on our web page BabyBargains. com, click on Bonus Material.

◆ **Other Brands**. *Kettler* is a brand better known in this country for their tricycles, but their Tipp Topp high chair has won fans for its simple design. We found it for $230 on web sites like AlbeeBaby.com. Similar wood chairs are also made by Geuther, a European import sold on HighChairs.com.

If you like those wood high chairs at restaurants, you can buy a similar model online: the *Lipper* wood high chair for $37 at Amazon.

Like the look of the Stokke Tripp Trapp but don't have $300? Hippo Smile (HippoSmile.com) sells a credible knock-off of the Tripp Trapp called the Happy Hippo high chair for $125—it is mostly sold in stores in Canada, but we also saw it on Amazon as of press time.

Our Picks: Brand Recommendations

Here is our round up of the best high chair bets.

Good. Is space tight in your kitchen? *The Fisher-Price Space Saver* ($55) lives up to its name—it straps to a regular chair and provides most of the features of a full-feature high chair, yet costs half as much. Another good option: the *Graco Contempo* ($100), which has the most compact fold of any high chair on the market and positive feedback.

Better. *Chicco's Polly* high chair lands a spot as number two on our recommended list. The Polly has all the standard adjustments you'd expect in a full feature high chair, plus two pads. Yep, the price is more than the Fisher Price pick we discuss next ($140) . . .

but we'd bet many folks will view this chair's styling and fashion as worthy of the upgrade. The only bummer: the Chicco Polly's dishwasher-safe tray is so big it doesn't fit in a dishwasher.

Best. The *Fisher-Price Healthy Care* has got it all—great safety features, ease of use, cleanability and more. We like the snap-off dishwasher-safe tray, good design and easy-to-clean vinyl pad. At $95 to $110, it is about 30% cheaper than the Polly depending on the version

HIGH CHAIRS

High chairs, compared

NAME	RATING	PRICE	TRAY HEIGHT	TRAY DEPTH
BABY TREND	C+	$80-$100	8.5″	8
BOON FLAIR	A	$200-$380	*	*
BLOOM FRESCO	B	$400	*	*
CHICCO POLLY	B	$140	7.5	7
COMBI HERO	C	$150	*	*
EDDIE BAUER WOOD	D	$120	8	5
EVENFLO EXPRESSIONS	C-	$55-$70	7	5
EVENFLO MAJESTIC	C-	$60-$120	8	6
FISHER PRICE HEALTHY CARE	A	$95-$110	7.5	6
FISHER PRICE SPACE SAVER	A	$55	7.5	5
GRACO CONTEMPO	B	$100-$130	7.5	6
GRACO HARMONY	B	$70-$110	7	7
GRACO BLOSSOM	B	$180	*	*
IKEA ANTILOP	C	$20	*	*
INGLESINA ZUMA	C	$300	*	*
KOLCRAFT CONTOURS	C+	$120	*	*
PEG PEREGO PRIMA PAPPA	C+	$265	8.5	7
SAFETY 1ST SERVE 'N STORE	C+	$80-$90	*	*
STOKKE TRIPP TRAPP	A-	$250	*	*

KEY

TRAY HEIGHT: Distance from the seat to the top of the tray. Any measurement under 8″ is acceptable. Above 8″ is too tall.

DEPTH (tray to seat): Distance from the back of the seat to the tray. 5″ to 7″ is acceptable.

SUB?: Most high chairs have a special guard to prevent a child from submarining under the tray. Some models attach this to the chair; others to the tray. A better bet: those that attach to the seat. See discussion earlier in this chapter.

(we suggest the Rainforest or Precious Planet models, as they omit the ruffled cushion found on the Aquarium). The only drawback to the Fisher Price high chair: you have to like the like the cutesy fashion. If you can't get past the look, try the **Fisher Price Zen** ($150), a wood hybrid chair with a muted green/brown palette and excellent features.

Grandma's house. For grandma's house, a simple *Cosco Convenience* (a.k.a. Beginnings Simple Start) ($35) should do the

Sub?	Pad	Comment
Seat	Cloth	Pad should be hand-washed, line dried.
Seat	Vinyl	Seamless seat; automatic height adjust.
Seat	Cloth	Seamless seat, auto height, seat reclines
Tray	Vinyl	New $180 version with toys, storage.
Seat	Vinyl	Converts to kitchen booster. Dinky tray.
Tray	Both	Wood with plastic tray; hard to clean.
Seat	Vinyl	Simple high chair, decent value.
Seat	Vinyl	Difficult assembly, tray is too high.
Seat	Vinyl	Better bet: version without seat ruffles.
Seat	Vinyl	Attaches to chair; great for little space.
Seat	Vinyl	Narrowest fold on market.
Seat	Vinyl	Contoured design; infant head support.
Seat	Vinyl	New; converts to toddler booster.
Seat	None	Tray is $5 extra; better for older toddlers.
Seat	Cloth	Seamless seat, mod look, very pricey.
Tray	Foam	Under seat crumb catcher. Dinky tray.
Seat	Vinyl	Style leader; many colors, hard to clean.
None	Cloth	Large gap between tray, baby. Compact fold
Seat	Cloth	Baby rail is $140 extra; no tray.

Pad: Is the seat made of cloth or vinyl? We prefer vinyl for easier clean up. Cloth seats must be laundered and some can't be thrown in the drier (requiring a long wait for it to line dry). Of course, this feature isn't black and white—some vinyl seats have cloth edging/piping.

* Not applicable or not available. Some of these models were new as of press time, so we didn't have these specs yet.

trick. No, it doesn't have casters or other fancy features, but Grandma doesn't need all that. *The Kolcraft Recline N Dine* ($50) is another good choice.

Hook-on Chairs and Boosters

Your toddler has outgrown his high chair, but doesn't quite fit into the adult chairs at the kitchen table. What to do? Consider a booster. There are three types of kitchen booster seats on the market today:

1 **HOOK-ON CHAIRS.** As the name implies, these seats hook on to a table, instead of attaching to a chair. Pros: Lightweight; yet most can hold toddlers up to 35 to 40 lbs. Very portable—many parents use these chairs as a sanitary alternative when they dine out since many restaurants seemed to have last cleaned their high chairs during the Carter administration. Cons: May not work with certain tables, like those with pedestal bases. Fear of tipping an unstable table leads some restaurants to prohibit these chairs. Hook-on chairs do not recline, a feature you see on regular boosters.

2 **BOOSTER SEATS WITH TRAYS.** These boosters strap to a chair and usually have a tray. Pros: Most fold flat for travel. Some have multiple seat levels. Can use with or without a tray. Cons: Child may not be sitting up at table height. Some brands have too-small trays and difficult to adjust straps make for a loose fit.

3 **PLAIN BOOSTERS (NO TRAY).** These chairs are just boosters— nothing fancy, no trays. Pros: Better bet for older toddlers (age four or five) who want to eat at the table. Cons: No restraint system or belt, so this isn't a choice for younger toddlers.

Our Picks: Brand Recommendations

◆ **Hook-on chair. Top pick:** *Graco Travel Lite Table Chair* (gracobaby.com). This simple, safe and affordable ($35) hook-on chair is a great option when you need a chair for baby at a restaurant, grandma's house or when traveling. It is very portable, weighing only ten pounds, and includes a tray. On the other hand, the padding isn't very cushy, the tray is small and you can only use it (or any hook-on) on a table with a flat underside. The weight limit is 37 pounds.

Runners Up: Chicco's two entrants in this category are also strong contenders. The *Caddy* ($40) has a compact fold, three

point harness and "quick grip" table clamps. The seat pad is removable and machine washable. The *Hippo Travel Seat* ($50; pictured) has added a double locking attachment for extra safety.

◆ *Kitchen booster seat with tray.*
Top pick: *Fisher Price Healthy Care Booster Seat* (fisher-price.com). Fisher Price has a winner here: we liked the snap-off feeding tray that can go into the dish-washer, easy fold and shoulder strap for

road trips plus three different height settings. When your child gets older, the tray removes so the seat becomes a basic booster. The only caveat: the back does not recline, so your baby must be able to sit up on his own to use it safely. (No biggie for most toddlers, but we know some folks consider these boosters as high-chair replacements—not a good idea unless your child can sit upright). Price: $25, making this a good value.

Runner Up: *Summer Infant Deluxe Comfort Booster* (summerinfant.com). This affordable ($22) booster is similar to our top pick, but adds one nice bonus: it features a compact fold for easy transport. No snack tray, but the full-size tray is dishwasher-safe. Be aware: this seat has a 33-

pound limit—as a result this one won't work for larger toddlers. (FYI: The Fisher Price Healthy Care booster is good up to 45 pounds).

◆ *Kitchen booster seat without tray.*
The BabySmart Cooshie Booster. This is our recommendation for older toddlers—the Cooshie Booster's super comfortable foam design is a winner. It's lightweight and non-

skid. No, there isn't a safety harness, but older kids don't really need it. How old? The manufacturer says this seat would work for babies as young as 12 months, but we think that is a stretch. The optimum time to use this booster would be between ages three and five, in our opinion. Yes, we think some toddlers as young as two would be mature enough but any younger would be pushing it. We used this booster with our youngest son and it got raves. The seat costs $30 to $40 although we saw it on ebay.com for less.

A brief warning: The *Bumbo Baby Sitter* ($40) is a popular seat designed for younger infants to sit upright. The problem? The Bumbo should ONLY be used on the floor (NOT on a raised surface like a chair or table). A report by a San Francisco TV station chronicled several cases of babies tipping out of their Bumbos . . . and toppling to the floor when the Bumbo was on a table. A 2007 recall focused on beefing up the warnings for how to use the Bumbo.

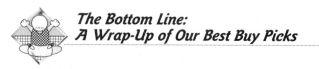

The Bottom Line:
A Wrap-Up of Our Best Buy Picks

What's the most affordable way to feed baby? Breastfeeding, by a mile. We estimate you can save $500 in just the first six months alone by choosing to breast-feed instead of bottle-feed.

Of course, that's easy for us to say—breastfeeding takes some practice, for both you and baby. One product that can help: a breast pump, to relieve engorgement or provide a long-term solution to baby's feeding if you go back to work. Which pumps are best? For manual pumps, we like the Avent Isis ($45) for that occasional bottle. If you plan to pump so you can go back to work, a professional-grade pump works best. Tip: rent one first before you buy. If you like it and decide you are serious about pumping, we liked the Medela Pump In Style ($280-$330) or Ameda Purely Yours (about $150 to $230).

If you decide to bottle feed or need to wean your baby off breast milk, the most affordable formulas are the generic brands sold in discount stores under various private-label names. You'll save up to 40% by choosing generic over name brands, but your baby gets the exact same nutrition.

Who makes the best bottles? Our readers say Avent and Dr. Brown's are tops, but others find cheaper options like Playtex work just was well at half the price.

Let's talk baby food—besides the ubiquitous Gerber, there are several other brands that are good alternatives. One of the best is Earth's Best, although it is more pricey than affordable brands like Nature's Goodness and Beechnut. How can you save? Make your own baby food for pennies or buy jarred baby food in bulk at discount stores. And skip the toddler meals, which are a waste of money.

Finally, consider that quintessential piece of baby gear—the high chair. We felt the best bets were those that were easiest to clean (go for a vinyl, not cloth pad) and had snap-off dishwasher-safe trays. Our top pick is the Fisher Price Healthy Care ($95 to $110), although the Chicco Polly ($140) is a stylish alternative.

Now that you've got the food and kitchen covered, what about the rest of your house? We'll explore all the other baby gear you might need for your home next.

CHAPTER 7

AROUND THE HOUSE

Around the House: Monitors, Diaper Pails, Safety & More

Inside this chapter

W hat's the best bathtub for baby? Which baby monitor can save you $40 a year in batteries? What's the best—and least stinky—diaper pail? In this chapter, we explore everything for baby that's around the house. From bouncer seats to the best baby monitors, we'll give you tricks and tips to saving money. You'll learn about play yards and swings. Finally, let's talk safety—we'll give you tips and advice on affordable baby proofing. So let's get cracking.

Getting Started: When Do You Need This Stuff?

The good news is you don't need all this stuff right away. While you'll probably purchase a monitor before the baby is born, other items like bouncer seats and even bath-time products aren't necessary immediately (you'll give the baby sponge baths for the first few weeks, until the belly button area heals). Of course, you still might want to register for these items before baby is born. In each section of this chapter, we'll be more specific about when you need certain items.

What Are You Buying?

Let's take a tour around the house to see what items you might consider for baby. Of course, these ideas are merely suggestions—none of these items are "mandatory." We've divided them into two categories: bath-time and the baby's room.

Bath

1 **TOYS/BOOKS.** What fun is taking a bath without toys? Many stores sell inexpensive plastic tub toys, but you can use other items like stacking cups in the tub as well. And don't forget about tub safety items, which can also double as toys. For example, Safety 1st (800) 739-7233 (safety1st.com) makes a *TempGuard Rubber Ducky or Froggy*, a yellow duck or frog with attached thermometer (to make sure the water isn't too hot) for $2.50 at Kmart. *Tubbly Bubbly* by Kel-Gar (972) 250-3838 (web: kelgar.com) is a $12 elephant or hippo spout cover that protects against scalding, bumps and bruises. In fact, Kel-Gar makes an entire line of innovative bath toys and accessories.

2 **TOILETRIES**. Basic baby shampoo like the famous brand made by Johnson & Johnson works just fine, and you'll probably need some lotion as well. The best tip: first try lotion that is unscented in case your baby has any allergies. Also, never use talcum powder on your baby—it's a health hazard. If you need to use an absorbent powder, good old cornstarch will do the trick.

What about those natural baby products that are all the rage, like Mustela or Calidou? We got a gift basket of an expensive boutique's natural baby potions and didn't see what the big deal was. Worse yet, the $20-a-bottle shampoo dried out our baby's scalp so much he had scratching fits. We suppose the biggest advantage of these products is that they don't contain extraneous chemicals or petroleum by-products. Also, most don't have perfumes, but then, many low-price products now come in unscented versions as well. The bottom line: it's your comfort level. If you want to try them out without making a big investment, register for them as a shower gift.

If you have a history of allergies or skin problems in your family, consider washing baby's skin and hair with Dove or Cetaphil bar soap. These do not contain detergents that you find in even the most basic baby shampoo. And remember, just because a product is "organic" or "all-natural" doesn't mean it's non-allergenic. In fact, ingredients like shea butter (made from a tree nut), calendula and chamomile all have potential for reactions including rashes, breathing problems (anaphylaxis) and eye irritation. See our other book, *Baby 411* for more on alternative ingredients and their potential side effects.

3 **BABY BATHTUB.** While not a necessity, a baby bathtub is a nice convenience (especially if you are bathing baby solo). See the next section of this chapter for more info on bathtubs.

4 **POTTY SEAT.** Potty seats come in two flavors: floor models and inserts. Inserts are molded (and sometimes padded) seats made for smaller bottoms. They are installed on top of the regular toilet seat. Floor models are traditional self-contained units with a base and seat.

Some potty seats start out as floor models and then the seat can be removed and used as an insert on the regular toilet. Our advice: go for the insert. Yes, you'll need a step stool for your little one to climb up, but it's much easier to transition to a regular toilet if your child is already using one. And think about how excited your child will be to use the same toilet as his parents (trust us, it is a big deal).

Our top picks for inserts are the **Contoured Cushie Tushie** ($11; MommysHelperInc.com; pictured), the **First Years Soft Trainer** ($13; TheFirstYears.com) and the **Flip-n-Flush** ($12; Kaplanco.com).

For floor potties, we recommend the **Baby Bjorn Potty Chair** ($25; BabyBjorn.com) and the **Fisher Price Fun to Learn Potty** ($35; Fisher-Price.com).

Safe & Sound

◆ **BATH SEATS SHOULD NOT BE USED.** It looks innocuous—the baby bath seat—but it can be a disaster waiting to happen. These seats suction to the bottom of a tub, holding baby in place while she takes a bath. The problem? Parents get a false sense of security from such items and often leave the bathroom to answer the phone, etc. We've seen several tragic reports of babies who've drowned when they fell out of the seats (or the seats became un-suctioned from the tub). The best advice: AVOID these seats and NEVER leave baby alone in the tub, even for just a few seconds.

◆ **TURN DOWN YOUR WATER HEATER.** Ideally, your water heater should be set at no more than 120° F. At 140° F it poses a safety hazard. You can also consider installing anti-scalding devices on your showers and faucets. One such device is called **ScaldShield** and sells at hardware stores for about $40.

◆ **NO SKID RUGS IN THE BATHROOM.** Invest in rugs that have rub-berized no skid bottoms. You don't want to slip carrying your baby, and you don't want your new walking toddler to bang his head on the toilet or tub.

◆ **Lock it up.** Install cabinet and toilet locks. This is just as important as safeguarding baby from dangers in the kitchen. And now is
a great time to retrain your husband to put the lid down on the
toilet seat. Locks don't work unless you actually use them.

Baby Bathtubs

Sometimes, it is the simplest products that are the best. Take baby
bathtubs—if you look at the offerings in this category, you'll note
some baby bathtubs convert to step stools and then, small compact
cars. Okay, just kidding on the car, but these products are a good
example of brand manager overkill—companies think the way to success with baby bath tubs is to make them work from birth to college.

So, it shouldn't be a surprise that our top pick
for a baby bathtub is, well, just a bathtub. The
EuroBath by Primo ($25; web: primobaby.com;
pictured right) is a sturdy tub for babies, age birth
to two. It weighs less than two pounds and is easy
to use—just add baby, water and poof! Clean
baby. The EuroBath is well designed, although it
is big—almost three feet from end to end. It may
be a tight fit if you have a small bathroom. In that
case, you might want to consider the ***Funtime***
Froggy Bath Center by Safety 1st ($15; pictured).
Nothing fancy, but it does have a foam liner and
(as the name implies) a "froggy" sling to cradle a newborn. This might
be a good choice for Grandma's house. A deluxe version is available
with rinse pitcher, spout cover and eight toys for $25.

Got a big baby? Some parents tell us regular bathtubs (like the
Safety 1st tub mentioned above) don't work as
well when Junior is a linebacker in training. So,
try out the ***First Years Sure Comfort Deluxe*** tub
($18; see at right). It's no frills but does have an
anti-slip backrest. One reader writes with kudos
for the ***EZ Bather Deluxe*** by Dex Products ($10,
800-546-1996; dexproducts.com), an L-shaped vinyl frame that
keeps babies head above water in the bathtub or kitchen sink.

What about tubs with bells and whistles like built-in thermometers? A waste of money, say our readers, who complain the thermometers often don't work.

A baby bathtub is a great item to pick up second-hand or at a
garage sale. Or borrow from a friend. Readers say they've snagged
baby bath tubs for $2 or so at garage sales—with a little cleaning,
they are just fine. What if you want to give baby a bath in a regu-

lar tub or kitchen sink? A bath sling like *Summer's Mother's Touch* ($15) will do the trick!

Now that we've finished with the bath, let's move on to baby's room: diaper pails, baby monitors and more.

Baby's Room

1   **A Diaper Pail.** Yes, there are dozens of diaper pails on the market. We'll review and rate the offerings in the next section.

2   **Baby Monitor.** Later in this chapter, we have a special section devoted to monitors, including some creative money-saving tips. Hint: if you have a small house or apartment, you may not even need a baby monitor!

3   **The Changing Area.** A well-stocked changing area features much more than just diapers. Nope, you need wipes and lots of them. We discussed our recommendations for wipe brands in Chapter 4, the Reality Layette. We should note that we've heard from some thrifty parents who've made their own diaper wipes— they use old washcloths or cut-up cloth diapers and warm water.

What about wipe warmers? In previous editions of this book, we've recommended these $20 devices, which keep wipes at 99 degrees (and lessen the cold shock on baby's bottom at three in the morning).

However, a series of safety recalls on wipe warmers in the past 10 years for fire hazards has led us to NOT recommend this product.

Other products to consider for the diaper changing station include diaper rash ointment (A & D, Desitin, etc.), lotion or cream, cotton swabs, petroleum jelly (for rectal thermometers) and rubbing alcohol to care for the belly button area (immediately remove this item from the changing area once you finish belly button care—it's poisonous!).

4   **Portable Cribs/play yards**. While this item doesn't necessarily go in your baby's room, many folks have found portable cribs/play yards to be indispensable in other parts of the house (or when visiting grandma). Later in this chapter, we have a special section devoted to this topic.

5   **White Noise**. In the past, we noted that some parents swear they'd never survive without the ceiling fan in their baby's room—the "white noise" made by a whirling fan soothed their fussy baby (and quieted sounds from the rest of the house). We even recommended a white noise generator for babies who needed calming. However, in a study published in the journal *Science* (April 18, 2003), researchers say using white noise can be dangerous to your

child's developing hearing. Our advice now is to avoid those white noise generators and find other ways to sooth your baby to sleep. (For the record, the slight hum of a ceiling fan or A/C unit is not a problem—the concern is noise generators put close to the crib).

While white noise generators are a no-no, ceiling fans are a good idea. A study in the *Archives of Pediatrics and Adolescent Medicine* published in 2008, showed that babies who sleep in a room with a ceiling fan have a much lower risk of dying of Sudden Infant Death Syndrome (SIDS). Why would a ceiling fan make a difference, you ask? Turns out that by circulating the air in your baby's room, you lower the chances that he or she will "rebreath" exhaled carbon dioxide. This rebreathing has been suggested as one cause of SIDS. So we definitely recommend a ceiling fan, both for that low hum in the background and the recirculation of the room's air.

6 HUMIDIFIER. See our web page (babybargains.com; click on bonus material) for advice on buying a humidifier for baby's room.

Diaper Pails

Pop quiz! Remember our discussion of how many diapers you will change in your baby's first year? What was the amount?

Pencils down—yes, it is 2300 diapers! A staggering figure . . . only made more staggering by figuring out what do with the dirty ones once you've changed baby. Yes, we can hear first-time parents raising their hands right now and saying "Duh! They go in the trash!"

Oh, not so fast, new parental one. Stick a dirty diaper in a regular trashcan and you may quickly perfume your entire home—not to mention draw a curious pet and we won't even go there.

So, most parents use a diaper pail, that specialized trashcan designed by trained scientists to limit stink and keep out babies, pets and stray relatives. But which diaper pail? Here's our Diaper Pail 411:

Diaper pails fall into two camps: those that use refill cartridges to wrap diapers in deodorized plastic and pails that use regular kitchen trash bags.

As you'd guess, pails that use special refills are more expensive (the refills cost about $6 each) and wrap about 140 or so diapers. The pail can hold 20-25 diapers at a time, which is about three days worth of diapers. Bottom line: you'll about need to buy 16 refill cartridges per year—or a $100. And that's on top of the $30 to $40 that the pails cost.

So, should you just get a diaper pail that uses regular kitchen trash bags? Yes, they are less expensive to use—but there is sometimes a major trade-off. Stink. These pails tend to stink more and hence, have to be emptied more frequently (perhaps daily or every other day) than the diaper pails that use special deodorized plastic.

Obviously, the decision on which diaper pail is right for you and your baby's nursery depends on several factors. What is the distance to the trash? If you live in a house with easy access to an outside trashcan, it might be easier to go with the lower-cost alternatives and just take out the diapers more frequently. If you live in an apartment where the nearest dumpster is down three flights of stairs and a long walk across a parking lot, well, it might make sense to go with an option that requires less work.

Another factor: how sensitive are you to the smell? Some folks don't have a major problem with this, while moms who are pregnant again with a second child may need an industrial strength diaper pail to keep from losing it when walking into baby's nursery. A great tip from our readers: dump the poop. Before tossing the diaper, dump the poop into the toilet. No matter what you use to contain used diapers, this simple step will largely mitigate odor.

Whatever your decision, remember you'll live with this diaper pail for three or more YEARS (that's how long before most children potty train). And it's a fact of life: diapers get stinkier as your baby gets older . . . so the diaper removal strategy that works for a newborn may have to be chucked for a toddler. Yes, you may be able to use a plain trashcan with liner when your newborn is breastfeeding . . . but after you start solid foods, it will be time to buy a more stink-free diaper pail.

Given those caveats, here is an overview of what's out there:

CLEAN AIR ODOR FREE DIAPER DISPOSAL BY FIRST YEARS

Type: Kitchen trash bag.
Price: $40. Extra carbon filters $15 for two.
Pros: Uses a fan and carbon filter to trap odors. Holds 40 diapers. Uses standard kitchen trash bags.
Cons: LOUD! Requires four D batteries. Smell escapes.

Comments: Like the Graco diaper pail reviewed below, First Years must have figured it needed some catchy gizmo to break into the diaper pail market. Voila! The first diaper pail with a fan and carbon filter! Readers have one universal complaint: it is too LOUD! When you put a diaper in, the pail cranks up the decibels like a 747 (ok, an exaggeration, but you get the idea). Other readers report diapers that jam and a general lack of stink control.

Bottom line: A loser.
Rating: F

DIAPER CHAMP BY BABY TREND

Type: Kitchen trash bag.

Price: $30-$35. Web: BabyTrend.com.

Pros: Did we mention no expensive refills? The Diaper Champ uses regular ol' kitchen bags, yet the contraption works to seal out odor by using a flip handle design. Easy to use. Taller design means it holds more diapers than the Genie.

Cons: Not as stink-free as the Genie or Dekor, especially when baby starts solid foods. Bigger footprint than other pails.

Comments: When you redesign a best-selling product, you're supposed to improve it, right? Yes, unless you are Baby Trend, a brand that seems to botch even the simplest task. Fans loved the original Diaper Champ, which began the idea of using regular kitchen trash bags (and hence, saved hundreds of dollars in refill cartridges). The new Diaper Champ, unfortunately, is a step backwards: yes it has a wider opening, but parents tell us it doesn't work as well (diapers get stuck, the smell can be atrocious, etc). And the diaper removal process may require an EPA HazMat Rapid Response team, given the stink level. Fans of this diaper pail seem to like it . . . until their baby starts solid foods. Then the smell can be overwhelming, forcing folks to buy Dekor or Genie. One tip: if you go with the Champ, put a fabric softener sheet in the pail with each load (this cuts down on the smell). And be prepared to scrub it every month or two with bleach, leaving it outside to air out. And the Champ probably isn't the best bet if you have an older toddler, who can put toys into the slot (trust us, not a pretty sight).

Bottom line: A mixed review: good for the first few months, not so good after baby starts solid food. A bargain—but beware the stink trade-offs.

Rating: C+

DIAPER DEKOR

Type: Refill canister

Price: $30 to $90. Refill packs are $5-$7.50 each and wrap 335 newborn diapers. Web: regal-lager.com

Pros: Hands free operation—you hit the foot petal and drop in a diaper. Comes in three sizes, largest can hold 5+ days of diapers. Converts to a regular trashcan after baby is done with diapers. Parents say it is much easier to use than the Diaper Genie, reviewed below.

Cons: New "biodegradable" refills are terrible at containing stink, readers report. Hinges on the "trap door" seem prone to breakage, as does the foot pedal.

Comments: The only serious competition for the Diaper Genie, the Diaper Dekor comes in three sizes: regular ($30, holds 30 diapers), Plus ($40, 40 diapers) and XL ($90, 50+ diapers). The regular Diaper Dekor is best for newborns; the Plus is pitched for larger families (where more than one child is in diapers) and the XL is best for multiple births or a daycare center . . . or the Octomom.

The Dekor was one of our top picks for diaper pails in our last edition—but then the company re-designed the refills . . . the result is a disaster. First, Regal Lager jacked the price: the new refills come in packs of two (the old ones had three), but the price stayed the same—clever! But the worst part is a change in the plastic: the new refills are now "biodegradable." And in case you missed the eco-friendly message, the plastic is now green. The problem? The new refills are horrible at blocking odor, the main reason why you'd part with the big bucks to buy one of these pails. Reader after reader has assailed the new refills; while you can order the original refills (that worked well) from Regal Lager's home page, they have just about disappeared from stores.

While we are all for saving the environment, ruining the effectiveness of a product in order to make it more green is a colossal mistake.
Bottom line: Re-designed refills are a disaster; avoid this pail.
Rating: F

DIAPER GENIE II / ELITE BY PLAYTEX

Type: Refill canister
Price: II: $25 II: $25; Elite: $40. Refill cartridges ($6) hold 180 diapers.
Web: diapergenie.com
Pros: Wraps each diaper in deodorized plastic. One-hand operation. Easy to remove diapers. Some say better at stink control than Diaper Champ.
Cons: Expensive, since you have to keep buying those refills.
Comments: The revised Diaper Genie II addresses some of the key gripes with the original version (the Twistaway, now discontinued): there's no more twisting when diapers go in, enabling one-hand operation. A clamp keeps the diapers (and the smell) inside the container. The Genie II also holds more diapers, since there are no more chains of sausages as with the original. The removal process has also been improved: Playtex actually designed a cutter that, well, cuts.

The Diaper Genie comes in two version: the II and the II Elite. The latter features a foot petal, is taller and has anti-microbial coated plastic (to control odor). Both versions use the same refills (in case you find an old Twistaway Genie at a garage sale, it uses different refills that are still sold in some stores).

There used to be a three-way competition in diaper pails

between the Genie, the Dekor and Baby Trend's Diaper Champ. But after Baby Trend muffed the re-design of the Champ and the Dekor did the same with their new biodegradable refills, the Diaper Genie now wins by default.

That doesn't mean the Genie doesn't have its detractors, many of whom cite the cost of refill cartridges as a major negative. Those parents think a steel trash can with tight fitting lid (with frequent emptying) is just as effective as the Genie. That is debatable, but others object to the process of putting a diaper in the Genie, which requires pushing it below a clamp (ew, we know).

Bottom line: The Genie is the best in its field—but that doesn't mean its perfect. There is probably no such thing as a stink-free diaper pail, especially when baby starts solid foods. But between the Champ, Dekor and Genie, the Genie is at the top.

Rating: A

TOUCH FREE DIAPER PAIL BY GRACO

Type: Kitchen trash bag.

Price: $50. Extra carbon filters $4.

Pros: Motion sensor activates lid—just drop in diaper, without ever touching the diaper pail. Can switch pail to manual as well. Uses standard 10 or 13-gallon trash bags.

Cons: Requires four D batteries—lots of them! Must replace carbon filters. Pricey. Small size only holds a few diapers. Poor stink control.

Comments: We love gizmos and gadgets as much as anyone, so Graco's new "Touch Free" Diaper Pail has that novelty appeal . . . but then our cynical side kicks in. Is it really worth spending $20 more than the Baby Trend Diaper Champ to get a motion-sensor activated lid? Sure, you can switch the pail to "manual mode" if you have dogs or older kids, but that kind of defeats the whole whiz-bang nature of the Touch Free. And the verdict from readers? Parents who've used the Touch Free tell us they aren't happy with it—it eats batteries (four D's every week, which must be replaced each time by removing three small screws). And the Touch Free fails at stink control. Plus it is too small, say readers.

Bottom line: The Touch Free violates the cardinal rule of baby products: keep it simple. We say pass on this diaper pail.

Rating: C-

VIPP DIAPER PAIL

Type: Refill canister.

Price: $295. Plastic liners: $4.

Pros: Uh . . . it's from Denmark?

Cons: Yes, the world's first $300 diaper pail!

Comments: We'll let one of our readers describe her experience with the Vipp: "So I gave in and bought the VIPP diaper pail from Giggle. I thought that despite the obscene price this would be a worthwhile investment that would fight smell, not take up too much space, and look attractive in my Manhattan apartment. I saw that it is made in Denmark, used in doctor's offices and has a steel liner. Basically no plastic to absorb smell. And despite the many debates about Dekor/Genie, it seemed that neither one is quite ideal.

"Well this story does not end well. For $300 I also wanted ease of use (special bags are needed)—but even their special VIPP bag is rather difficult to get in and out. Sadly, I took my 39 week pregnant self to return the trashcan and the woman at Giggle confirmed that although it is great at keeping the smell at bay, it is difficult to change the bag. I really was shocked to find that this 80-year-old Danish company did not have this down to more of a science. While this is not an official 'diaper pail' I think this is aggravating even if using this for regular trash."

Bottom line: You don't need to spend $300 on a trashcan.

Rating: F

More pails: There are several other basic diaper pails on the market today, such as the $15 Safety 1st Diaper Pail. Most are simple plastic trashcans with lids. Our suggestion: if you go this route, just get a stainless steel step-on trashcan ($40 to $80 at stores like Bed Bath &

Coupon deals cut the cost of online shopping

How do baby product web sites generate traffic and sales? One tried and true method is the online coupon—a special discount, either in dollars or percentage off deals. Sites offer these as come-ons for new customers, returning customers . . . just about anyone. Coupons enable sites to give discounts without actually lowering the prices of merchandise. You enter the coupon code when you place the order and zap! You've saved big.

Yes, there are sites that list coupon deals across the internet (FatWallet.com, eDealFinder.com), but how do you find the best coupons for baby stuff? Check out our message boards (BabyBargains.com, click on Message Boards). On the Bargain Alert board, we keep a pinned thread with all the latest coupon deals, all submitted by our readers (spam isn't allowed). Updated regularly, this thread has all the best deals. (And there's even a separate pinned thread for freebies).

Beyond). Why steel? They are easier to clean—and less likely to stink like plastic. And you are getting a real trashcan you can repurpose to another part of the house after baby is done with diapers.

What about "hands free pails"? Models like the Sassy Hands-Free Diaper Pail ($30) pitch their motion-activated, touch-free lid as the ultimate convenience. Well . . . any pail that runs on batteries should be avoided. First, many of these wonder pails break or jam. And why pay extra for motion-activation when a simple foot petal will do the trick (and won't break or run out of batteries)?

Bonus Material Online: Humidifiers, Toys, Pets

On our web site, BabyBargains.com, click on Bonus Material to read about humidifiers, toys (our top picks, including crib mobiles), and how to introduce your pet to a new baby. Plus a report on affordable baby announcements.

Bouncer Seat/Activity Gyms

◆ **ACTIVITY GYM.** Among our favorites is the *Gymini by Tiny Love* (for a dealer near you, call 800-843-6292; web: tinylove.com). The Gymini is a three-foot square blanket that has two criss-cross arches. You clip rattles, mirrors and other toys onto the arches, providing end-less fun for baby as she lies on her back and reaches for the toys. The Gymini comes in four different versions: a basic version in black, white and red is $35 and the "super deluxe" model (Lights & Music) is about $55. The more expensive versions have more toys. Another plus for the Gymini: it folds up quickly and easily for trips to Grandma's.

◆ **ACTIVITY SEAT/BOUNCER WITH TOY BAR.** An activity seat (also called a bouncer) provides a comfy place for baby to hang out while you eat dinner, and the toy bar adds some mild amusement. The lat-est twist to these products is a "Magic Fingers" vibration feature—the bouncer basically vibrates, simulating a car ride. Parents who have these bouncers tell us they'd rather have a kidney removed than give up their vibrating bouncer, as it appears the last line of defense in soothing a fussy baby, short of checking into a mental institution.

What features should you look for in a bouncer? Readers say a carrying handle is a big plus. Also: get a neutral fabric pattern, says another parent, since you'll probably be taking lots of photos of baby and a garish pattern may grate on your nerves.

What is the best brand for bouncers? Fisher Price (fisher-price.com) makes the most popular one in the category; most are about $20 to $60, depending on the version. A good choice: the *Fisher Price RainForest bouncer* ($40). Although some of sounds were a little loud, the toys and waterfall got high marks. Yes, other companies make similar products (Summer makes one for $50, Combi has some ranging in price from $40 to $80 version, etc.) but the feedback we get from parents is that Fisher-Price is the best.

The only caveat: most bouncer seats have a 25-pound weight limit. If you want something that will last longer, consider the *Baby Bjorn Babysitter 1-2-3*. Yes, it is more pricey than the Fisher-Price (about $100, depending on the store) and lacks a vibrating feature . . . but you can use it up to 29 lbs. Fisher-Price does have a bouncer that can even be used up to 40 lbs.–the *Infant-to-Toddler* rocker. It's a great deal at $28. Parent feedback on that model is very positive.

Graco has added a new sub-category to bouncers: a "soothing center." The *Graco Sweet Peace* ($135; pictured) provides four cradling motions, six speeds and the removable carrier doubles as a floor rocker (or you can use it with a Graco infant car seat). Feedback on the Sweet Peace has been mostly positive with only a few complaints that the motor is a bit loud. Parents really like that it plugs into the wall (battery-operation is optional) and is easy to put together.

In the category "what to buy when money is no object" is the *Oeuf Baby Lounger*. This $98 bouncer seat is merely a canvas seat covering a steel frame. Yep, that's it for nearly a 100 bucks. It's cute, but come on. Could it at least vibrate? But wait, *Svan* makes a seat for even more: $120. But this one does have a cool bent wood frame with canopy. Svan also claims it's ergonomic and easy to clean. We like that it folds for travel and is adjustable.

◆ **TOY BARS FOR YOUR CAR SEAT.** Here's another money-saving tip: turn your infant car seat into an activity center with an attachable toy bar. Manhattan Toy makes a *Whoozit Activity Spiral* with dangling toys that wraps around carrier handles for $20. Infantino also has a car seat toy that wraps around the seat handle. The *Happy Wrappy* includes crinkle and rattle toys, for $20. Another plus: your baby is safer in an infant car seat carrier than in other activity seats, thanks to that industrial-strength harness safety system. Safety warning: only use these toy bars when the car seat is NOT inside a vehicle (that is, at home, etc.). Toy bars are not safe in a vehicle as they can be a hazard/projectile in an accident.

One caveat: some parents and pediatricians believe that leaving an infant in a car seat for extended periods of time can contribute to breathing problems in very young infants. For older babies, excessive time in an infant seat could lead to flat head syndrome (plagiocephaly). Unfortunately, doctors don't agree on how much time in an infant seat is too much. Use your common sense and move your child out of the seat frequently.

Monitors

For her first nine months, your baby is tethered to you via the umbilical cord. After that, it's the baby monitor that becomes your surrogate umbilical cord—enabling you to work in the garden, wander about the house, and do many things that other, childless human beings do, while still keeping tabs on a sleeping baby. Hence, this is a pretty important piece of equipment you'll use every day—a good one will make your life easier . . . and a bad one will be a never-ending source of irritation.

 *Smart Shopper Tips for Monitors*

Smart Shopper Tip #1
Bugging your house
"My neighbor and I both have babies and baby monitors. No matter what we do, I can still pick up my neighbor's monitor on my receiver. Can they hear our conversations too?"

You better bet. Let's consider what a baby monitor really is: a radio transmitter. The base unit is the transmitter and the receiver is, well, a receiver. So anyone with another baby monitor on the same frequency can often pick up your monitor—not just the sound of your baby crying, but also *any* conversations you have with your mate in the nursery.

We should note that you can also pick up baby monitors on many cordless phones—even police scanners can pick up signals as far as one or two miles away. The best advice: remember that your house (or at least, your baby's room) is bugged. If you want to protect your privacy, don't have any sensitive conversations within earshot of the baby monitor. You never know who might be listening.

So are there any monitors that are private? Until just recently, the answer was no. But there is good news: several models feature "digital" (DECT) technology—their signals can't be intercepted, unlike older analog monitors. We'll discuss DECT later in this section and point out which models feature this technology in our product reviews.

The best advice: only turn on your monitor when baby is napping. Leaving it on all day means others can listen in to every noise and sound.

Smart Shopper Tip #2
Battery woes

"Boy, we should have bought stock in Duracell when our baby was born! We go through dozens of batteries each month to feed our very hungry baby monitor."

Most baby monitors have the option of running on batteries or regular current (by plugging it into a wall outlet). Our advice: use the wall outlet as often as possible. Batteries don't last long—as little as eight to ten hours with continual use. Another idea: you can buy another AC adapter from a source like Radio Shack for $10 or less—you can leave one AC adapter in your bedroom and have another one available in a different part of the house. (Warning: make sure you get the correct AC adapter for your monitor, in terms of voltage and polarity. Take your existing AC adapter to Radio Shack and ask for help to make sure you are getting the correct unit. If not, you can fry your monitor).

Another solution: several new baby monitors (reviewed later in this chapter) feature rechargeable receivers! You'll never buy a set of batteries for these units—you just plug them into an outlet to recharge.

Smart Shopper Tip #3
Cordless compatibility

"We have a cordless phone and a baby monitor. Boy, it took us two weeks to figure out how to use both without having a nervous breakdown."

If we could take a rocket launcher and zap one person in this world, it would have to be the idiot who decided that baby monitors and cordless phones should share the same radio frequency. What were they thinking? Gee, let's take two people who are already dangerously short of sleep and make them real angry!

So, here are our tips to avoid frustration:

First, realize the higher the frequency, the longer the range of the monitor. Basic baby monitors work on the 49 MHz frequency— these will work for a few hundred feet. Step up to a 900 MHz monitor and you can double the distance the monitor will work (some makers claim up to 1000 feet). Finally, there are baby monitors that work on the 2.4 GHz frequency, where you can pick up your baby in Brazil. Ok, not that far, but you get the idea. Of course, "range" estimates are just that—your real-life range will probably be much less than what's touted on the box.

Now here's the rub: cordless phones and WiFi networks can often interfere with your baby monitor. Old cordless phones worked on the 49 MHz frequency, but modern models are more likely to be found in the 900 MHz or the 2.4 GHz (or even 5.8 GHz) bands. If you've got a baby monitor at 900 MHz and a cordless phone on the same frequency, expect trouble. Ironically, as more and more devices use the higher frequency, the old 49 MHz for baby monitors now seems to be the most trouble free when it comes to interference.

Wifi networks work on the 2.4 GHz band—yep, the same frequency used some baby monitors. The same advice as above: don't get a baby monitor on the same frequency as your WiFi network. FYI: Baby VIDEO monitors work on either the 900 MHz or 2.4 GHz frequencies and can have the same interference issues as audio monitors.

New to the market are digital or DECT monitors, which work on the 1.9 GHz range. Since very few other electronics operate on this band, DECT phones are virtually interference-free and work at even longer range than 2.4 GHz monitors. Another plus: DECT monitors can't be monitored by noisy neighbors. Bottom line: if your house is buzzing with electronics, consider a DECT monitor (examples include Philips baby monitors and Safety 1st's High Def audio monitor).

So, to sum up, here is our advice: first, try to buy a baby monitor on a different frequency than your cordless phone or WiFi network. Second, always keep the receipt. Baby monitors have one of the biggest complaint rates of all products we review. We suspect all the electronic equipment in people's homes today (cell phones, Wi-Fi routers, fax machines, large-screen TVs the size of a Sony Jumbotrons), not to mention all the interference sources near your home (cell phone towers, etc.) must account for some of the problems folks have with baby monitors. Common complaints include static, lack of range, buzzing and worse—and those problems can happen with a baby monitor in any price range.

So, read our monitor recommendations later with a grain of salt. ANY monitor (even those we rate the highest) can still run into static and interference problems, based on what electronics are in your home.

Again, the best advice: always keep the receipt for any baby monitor you buy—you may have to take it back and exchange it for another brand if problems develop.

Smart Shopper Tip #4
The one-way dilemma

"Our baby monitor is nice, but it would be great to be able to buzz my husband so he could bring me something to drink while

I'm feeding the baby. Are there any monitors out there that let you communicate two ways?"

Yep, Philips has models that do just that (see reviews later in this chapter). Of course, there is another alternative: you can always go to Radio Shack and buy a basic intercom for about $50. Most also have a "lock" feature that you can leave on to listen to the baby when he's sleeping. Another advantage to intercoms: you can always deploy the unit to another part of your house after you're done monitoring the baby. Of course, the only disadvantage to intercoms is that they aren't portable—most must be plugged into a wall outlet.

Here are other features to consider when shopping for monitors:

◆ *Out of range indicators.* If you plan to wander from the house and visit your garden, you may want to go for a monitor that warns you when you've strayed too far from its transmitter. Some models have a visual out of range indicator, while others beep at you. Of course, even if your monitor doesn't offer this feature, you'll probably realize when you're out of range—the background noise you hear in your home will disappear from the receiver.

◆ *Low battery indicator.* Considering how quickly monitors can eat batteries, you'd think this would be a standard feature for monitors. Nope—very few current models actually warn you when you're running out of juice. Most units will just die. If you plan to heavily use your monitor on battery power (out in the garden, for example), look for this feature.

◆ *What's the frequency?* As we discussed above, the right or wrong frequency can make a world of difference. Before selecting a monitor, think about the wireless gadgets you have in your home (particularly cordless phones). Then look carefully at packages . . . not all monitors put that info up front.

◆ *Extra receivers.* It is convenient to leave one receiver in your bedroom and then tote around another receiver when wandering in the house.

◆ *Digital technology.* New models use digital technology to prevent eavesdropping by your neighbors. Digital monitors also avoid static and interference from other electronics in your home.

◆ *Great, but not necessary.* Some monitors have a temperature display, which might help you spot a nursery that's too warm.

monitors

Others have a base with nightlight or play lullabies to sooth baby. Nice, but most folks don't need this.

Smart Shopper Tip #5
The cordless phone trick
"A techie friend of mind mentioned that some of the new cordless phones can double as baby monitors. Which phone has that feature?"

Here's a clever way to avoid spending $50 on a baby monitor. Simply use your cordless phone to monitor the baby's room. Uniden (uniden.com), for example sells not one but 55 cordless phone models with a room monitor feature. One example is the DCT756-3 Compact Cordless Telephone (three handsets included for $70). Basically, you put one handset in the baby's room, turn on the room monitor feature and you can listen in on a second handset. One caveat: with some models you can't both monitor a room and receive a phone call at the same time. Make sure your model can receive a call when in monitor mode.

The bottom line: if you need a new cordless phone for your house, consider buying one with a room-monitoring feature.

More Money Buys You

Basic baby monitors are just that—an audio monitor and transmitter. No-frills monitors start at $20 or $25. More money buys you a sound/light display (helpful in noisy environments, since the lights indicate if your baby is crying) and rechargeable batteries (you can go through $50 a year in 9-volts with regular monitors). More expensive monitors even have transmitters that also work on batteries (so you could take it outside if you wish) or dual receivers (helpful if you want to leave the main unit inside the house and take the second one outside if you need to work in the garage, etc.). Finally, the top-end monitors either have digital technology or intercom features, where you can use the receiver to talk to your baby as you walk back to the room. The most expensive monitor on the market, Philips' $200 Digital Monitor, adds a room temperature thermometer, adjustable sound sensitivity, music and a night light.

And don't forget baby video monitors. Several models are available ranging in price from $100 to $150. They may not be very useful however, with poor picture clarity and excessive interference being the two most common complaints. Almost all have consistently bad parent reviews.

The Name Game: Reviews of Selected Manufacturers

Here's a look at the best baby monitors.

Major caveat to these reviews: ANY baby monitor, even those that earn our highest ratings, can have problems with static, poor reception or interference. Why? As we discussed earlier, houses today have a myriad of radio equipment (Wi-Fi, anyone?), cell phones and other interference-causing sources. The best advice: keep your receipt and buy a monitor from a store with a good return policy. You may have to try a few different models/brands before finding one that works.

The Ratings

A EXCELLENT—*our top pick!*

B GOOD— *above average quality, prices, and creativity.*

C FAIR—*could stand some improvement.*

D POOR—*yuck! could stand some major improvement.*

Angelcare *Web: angelcare-monitor.com.* Angelcare monitor ($70 single, $90 double receiver) preys on parents fear of Sudden Infant Death Syndrome—this "movement" monitor sounds an alarm if baby stops breathing (or moving) for 20 seconds. The problem? The American Academy of Pediatrics says monitors like Angelcare or Babysense don't work in preventing SIDS. And if you have a preemie whose breathing needs to be monitored, you need to get a *medical grade* monitor from your pediatrician. Bottom line: you don't need to spend big bucks on a breathing monitor; a simple audio monitor at half the price is fine.

FYI: Angelcare was recently bought by Graco and has expand-ed their monitor line to include audio and video monitors. We've received little feedback from readers; this grade reflects our opinion of the Angelcare movement monitor. ***Rating: F***

Axis *Web: axis.com.* Most baby video monitors come with both a camera and monitor—you can view baby via a handheld or small TV monitor. But what if you want to watch baby's nursery from your computer or smartphone? Axis makes excellent network cameras—small video cameras that connect to your home Internet network either via a wired or wireless connection. The 207MW is the small-est wireless megapixel network camera on the market today. Yes, it is expensive ($300 to $400, sold online at Amazon and other sites) but it works much better than other so-called baby video monitors. Out by the time you read this, Axis plans to release a new series of small network cameras (example: M1031-W) for about $280.

With an Axis camera, you can monitor the video from any computer on your home network—or remotely from the Internet via a smartphone such as the iPhone or Blackberry. Fair warning: setting up a network camera to view over the Internet requires a fair amount of tech knowledge. *Rating: A*

Babysense *Web:babysafeus.com.* Babysense V Movement Monitor ($130) is similar to the Angelcare—it detects baby's movements to prevent SIDS. We don't recommend monitors like the BabySense; see the Angelcare review above for our reasoning. *Rating: F*

BebeSounds. *See Angelcare.*

Evenflo *Web: evenflo.com. Evenflo has exited the monitor category as of this writing, but we still see some older models sold online. An archived review of Evenflo's monitor is on our web site, BabyBargains.com (Bonus Material).*

First Years *Web: thefirstyears.com. First Years has exited the monitor category as of this writing, but we still see some older models sold online. An archived review of First Year's monitor is on our web page, BabyBargains.com (Bonus Material).*

Fisher Price (800) 828-4000 or (716) 687-3000. *Web: fisher-price.com.* Fisher Price's success in this market is due to keeping things simple: their basic Sound 'n Lights monitor ($25 single, $35 double) is a study in simplicity—it is an analog, 49 MHz audio-only monitor with a sound and light display. That's it—and that will do the trick for most folks. Parent feedback on this monitor is good.

If your house is buzzing with electronics, the Fisher Price Private Connection monitor is a possible solution ($45 single, $60 dual). This 900 MHz monitor has ten switchable channels and rechargeable batteries. Despite the name, this monitor is not digital, nor does it scramble the signal between transmitter and base. Parent feedback has been mixed on this model—in the past year, more readers have complained of static issues with the Private Connection.

Fisher Price also offers another 900 MHz model: the Long Distance monitor ($40), with sound/light display and nightlight feature. Like the Private Connection, reader feedback here is mixed, although slightly more positive.

For 2009, Fisher Price plans to debut a new model: Mom

Response monitor, which will come in audio or video versions. The audio monitor ($60 single, $90 double) will work on the 900 MHz frequency and allow moms (we assume it only work for moms, since it isn't called Dad Response) to remotely trigger "soothing sounds and lights." These sounds include nature sounds and music.

The Remote Control Video Monitor will also be out by the time you read this; this 2.4 GHz video monitor ($180) features a night-vision camera, color LCD screen and remote activation of "soothing music," which we assume will not include a cut from the new AC/DC album.

We gave Fisher Price of one of our top ratings in this category in past editions of this book, but we've been disappointed with their lack of digital/DECT models as well as their meager offerings in the fast-growing video monitor market. The simple Sound N Lights is probably the best bet here, but it is showing its age.

Rating (Sound 'N Lights only): B

Graco *(800) 345-4109, (610) 286-5951. Web: gracobaby.com.* Graco has aggressively expanded in the monitor market in recent years, with offerings in the analog, digital and video segments. In 2008, Graco also bought BebeSounds, maker of the Angelcare movement monitors (reviewed earlier).

Graco's best-selling monitor is the imonitor ($60 single, $90 dual); it is pricey, but features digital signal, an (alleged) 2000-foot range and rechargeable battery. Feedback on this model has been positive—the only negative is the battery life (only about 90 minutes when not in the charging cradle). The digital feature on this model delivers as promised, with privacy and little to no interference. Feedback on this model has been generally positive, although complaints about too-short range and the aforementioned short battery life hold down the overall scores.

Graco also makes three other versions of the imonitor: the Vibe ($60-$90; which, as the name implies, adds a vibration feature like a cell phone), the Mini ($100, yep a smaller version of the imonitor) and a Duo Vibe. The latter is a "multi-child" version ($125) that can monitor two rooms at once—parents of multiples, take note.

FYI: In 2009, Graco is phasing out the regular imonitor; the imonitor vibe will be the flagship offering from here on.

Graco has been cutting back on its analog monitors—it now only offers the UltraClear II, which comes in regular ($30) and vibe ($40) versions. These simple 49 MHz monitors offer a sound/light display . . . and that's about it. This model gets very good parent reviews; unfortunately, the UltraClear lacks rechargeable batteries.

Graco offers two video monitors, one analog (Flat Panel monitor, $200) and the other digital (imonitor video vibe, $200). The Flat

Panel is a 900 MHz model with night vision, 5.5″ color screen, TV compatibility and two camera expansion capability. By contrast, the imonitor video monitor is a 2.4 GHz monitor with a small 2″ color screen, night vision, digital zoom and vibration feature.

Feedback on Graco's video monitors has been mostly negative: the Flat Panel is a re-packaged BebeSounds monitor, which receives poor marks for video quality.

The imonitor video monitor was a big disaster when it was first released in 2007—readers complained of poor resolution, a useless zoom feature, too short range and more. Graco went for a do-over with a 2.0 version in 2008, with better screen resolution, battery-saving mode and other software improvements. The verdict? While the

BABY MONITORS	*A quick look at various features and brands*	
NAME	**MODEL**	**PRICE**
FISHER PRICE	SOUND 'N LIGHTS	$25/$35
	PRIVATE CONNECTIONS	$45/$60
	LONG DISTANCE MONITOR	$40/$60
	MOM RESPONSE	$60/$90
	REMOTE CONTROL VIDEO	$180
GRACO	IMONITOR VIBE	$60/$90
	IMONITOR MINI	$100
	ULTRA CLEAR II	$30-$40
	ULTRA CLEAR II	$30-$40
	IMONITOR VIDEO VIBE	$200
PHILIPS	SCD 510	$100
	SCD 520	$120-$150
	SCD 530	$200
SAFETY 1ST	CRYSTAL CLEAR	$16
	GLOW & GO	$30/$33
	HIGH-DEF DIGITAL	$60
	HIGH-DEF DIGITAL VIDEO	$230
SONY	BABY CALL NTM-910	$40/$80
SUMMER	CLOSE2YOU	$30
	SECURE SOUNDS	$40/$60
	SECURESLEEP	$60
	DAY & NIGHT VIDEO HANDHELD	$180

reviews have been slightly more positive for the 2.0 model, the overall feedback is still disappointing. Perhaps wait for the 3.0 model?

Overall, we give Graco bonus points for trying innovative features here (vibration, multi-child models, etc). But the video monitors are poor; and the best audio monitor is probably the simplest (UltraClear). ***Rating: B+***

Mobicam *Web: getmobi.com.* Mobicam was among the first affordable video baby monitors ($85) with an LCD screen to score widespread distribution. You'd think after being on the market for five years, this company would have the video monitor thing down to a science. You'd think . . . but you'd be wrong.

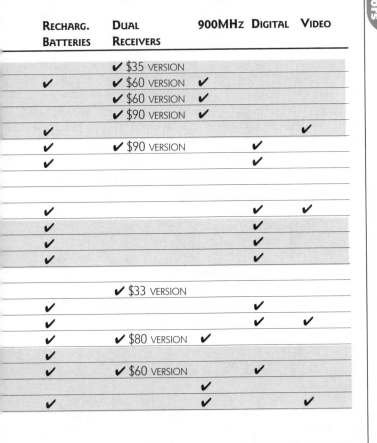

✔= Yes

900MHZ: A higher frequency that eliminates interference with cordless phones and extends a monitor's range.

DIGITAL: Does the monitor have digital technology?

RECHARG. BATTERIES	DUAL RECEIVERS	900MHz	DIGITAL	VIDEO
	✔ $35 VERSION			
✔	✔ $60 VERSION	✔		
	✔ $60 VERSION	✔		
	✔ $90 VERSION	✔		
✔				✔
✔	✔ $90 VERSION		✔	
✔			✔	
✔			✔	✔
✔			✔	
✔			✔	
✔			✔	
	✔ $33 VERSION			
✔			✔	
✔			✔	✔
✔	✔ $80 VERSION	✔		
✔				
✔	✔ $60 VERSION		✔	
		✔	✔	
✔		✔	✔	✔

monitors

Numerous quality woes have dogged Mobicam for years, including broken on/off switches, broken power cords, etc. Interference and static were other major issues for other users—some of this is caused by the 2.4 GHz frequency that Mobicam uses . . . the same as WiFi Internet routers.

Mobicam attempted to address these problems with an updated version dubbed Mobicam Ultra in 2006. The updated camera sports a larger display, voice activation and "new technology for clear sound and picture" (it now works on the 900 MHz frequency). And the verdict from consumers? Numerous gripes about constant static, poor night vision and poor customer service.

The latest version of Mobicam (AV, $150) features an Internet monitoring option that lets you view your camera online from any PC or Windows Media-enabled cell phone.

Given all the problems this product has had over the years, we don't recommend Mobicam. ***Rating: D***

Philips Avent *Web: Consumer.Philips.com.* Consumer products giant Philips is known for its innovative products . . . and, at the same time, monumentally inept marketing and poor customer service.

Case in point: Philips baby monitors. The European consumer products giant made a big push into the monitor market at the start of this decade with cutting-edge offerings that were way overpriced. No surprise, the monitors bombed, thanks in part to high prices and thin distribution (surprise, chain stores didn't want to stock $200 monitors). And when consumers had problems, their complaints fell on deaf ears at Philips' anemic customer service department.

So, Philips has hit the reset the button with three new monitors that are (dare we say it?) more affordable. At least, affordable for Philips.

Philips ace-in-the-hole is DECT technology: as we discussed earlier, this special frequency virtually guarantees interference-free reception. No static, no problem with cordless phones or WiFi networks, etc.

All three Philips monitors offer DECT: the basic SCD510 features rechargeable batteries, adjustable microphone sensitivity, sound/light display, intercom feature and out-of-range indicator. Price: $100.

The SCD520 ($120 to $150) adds a nightlight and temperature display on the parent unit—and you can set alerts if the temperature rises or falls below a certain point. The SCD530 ($200) has all the above, plus adds a humidity sensor.

Very few stores seem to be carrying the Philips monitors—Target carries them online, but as of press time, was priced quite a bit higher than Amazon.

Reader feedback has been positive on these new models—parents like the ability to adjust the microphone sensitivity to screen out background noise in baby's room. Fans also laud the interference-free reception and long battery life (about 24 hours on a charge). But some readers report the volume on the parent unit is way too low, even at the highest setting. Other gripes: the temperature sensor is off by five degrees and the screen on the parent unit is hard to read in dim light, even with the backlight on.

Bottom line: no one needs to spend $200 on a baby monitor. BUT . . . if you live in an area with lots of interference, a simple DECT monitor like the $100 SCD510 is a good buy. Skip the more pricey models with the temperature display and just get a $10 digital thermometer at the hardware store. ***Rating: B+***

Safety 1st *(800) 962-7233 or (781) 364-3100. Web: safety1st.com.* Like Graco, Safety 1st offers both audio and video monitors.

In the audio category, the company starts with a bare bones 49 MHz model with no sound and light display (Crystal Clear, $16). The Sound View Monitor ($20) is similar, but adds a sound/light display.

The Glow & Go also has a sound/light but adds a temperature display (on base) and comes in both single ($30) and dual receiver ($30) versions. The baby's unit has a glow light with a 15 minute auto-shut off.

Safety 1st has had a hit with their digital monitor, the oddly named High-Def Digital Monitor ($60). We're not sure what makes this monitor "high def," but it does offer rechargeable batteries and DECT technology so it is nearly interference-free and very sensitive. Readers have been very positive about this monitor, although a few complain you have to consult the manual often to decipher all the blinking lights (it has indicators for low batteries, out of range, etc).

As for video monitors, Safety 1st's best-seller is the High Def Digital Color Video Monitor ($230), which features night vision, low battery and out of range indicators. This camera uses H.264 video technology, which is a new tech standard that enables less interference and lower bandwidth usage. That probably explains why this video monitor gets much better marks compared to older-style monitors.

Safety 1st's other two video monitors (In-sight, $100; Close View, $150) use more traditional 900 MHz technology and generally get poor reviews from readers, who complain of poor video reception, static and worse.

Safety 1st's success with DECT audio and video monitors prompts us to raise their rating this time out. The best bets would be the very simple audio monitors (Crystal Clear or Sound View) or the DECT models (High-Def audio or video). ***Rating: B***

Sony *Web: sonystyle.com.* Sony has been a fringe player in the monitor market, thanks to prices that were always too high. But there is good news: Sony has woken up and lowered its prices. The Sony

monitors

BabyCall NTM-910 is a 27-channel model with rechargeable batteries for $40 single, $80 dual. Yes, you read that right—the BabyCall has 27 channels (most monitors have at most one or two). The result is less chance for interference and that's what parents seem to love about Sony's BabyCall—it works without static, buzzing, clicking and all the other complaints you read about monitors. The downside? Well, the receiver is rather bulky. And since this monitor isn't digital, it is possible to eavesdrop on the signal. And the 900 MHz frequency has less range than 2.4 GHz or DECT. But this model does have an out-of-range indicator and an optional sound-activated mode that silences the receiver until sufficient noise activates it. Given the positive reader feedback for Sony, we'll give them our highest rating. **Rating: A**

Summer *Web: summerinfant.com.* Summer has an impressive array of 11 video monitors—yep, you read right, 11 models. But the company also offers a plethora of audio monitors: the Secure Sounds 2.4 GHz digital audio monitor is a good example. Available in five iPod-esque colors, Secure Sounds ($40 single, $60 dual) features sound/light display, rechargeable batteries, and out-of-range indicator.

Summer offers two other simple monitors: the 49 MHz Close2You Cordless ($30, which features a transmitter that can operate on battery power) sold at BRU and 900 MHz SecureSleep monitor ($60), which features a temperature read-out on both the receiver and transmitter, and doubles as a nightlight. Cool feature: the nightlight changes color based on the temperature (red is too hot, blue too cold, yellow just right).

Summer's video monitors are this brand's key mojo—you'll find monitors with black and white TV displays (Baby's Quiet Sounds), color flat panel monitors (Day & Night), handheld models (Best View) and more. Prices start at $60 for a black and white TV model and go up to $200 for a handheld or color flat screen. The Best View Handheld Color Video Monitor is one of the few models on the market today that has the ability to pan, tilt and zoom . . . for $270.

So, how's the quality? Well, Summer's audio monitors get poor marks from readers, who complain about interference, static and other quality woes. Most of Summer's video monitors work on the 900 MHz frequency, which is prone to interference—and probably explains why many readers complain these models don't work well.

The models with the best reader feedback are the most expensive ones: the Baby's Quiet Sounds Color Handheld model ($180) and the similar Day & Night Handheld Color Video Monitor ($180). Most readers are happier with these models compared to the LCD screens.

Since the reader feedback splits sharply between the audio and video monitors, we'll divide our rating accordingly.
Ratings: Audio: C- Video: B+

Our Picks: Brand Recommendations

Here are our picks for baby monitors, with one BIG caveat: how well a monitor will work in your house depends on interference sources (like cordless phones, wireless internet routers), the presence of other monitors in the neighborhood, etc. Since we get so many complaints about this category, it is imperative you buy a monitor from a place with a good return policy. Keep the receipts in case you have to make an exchange.

Good. The *Graco UltraClear II* ($30; pictured) and *Safety 1st Crystal Clear* ($16) are very simple 49 MHz monitors. Nope, you don't get any fancy features with these models (no rechargeable batteries or two-way intercom), but these models do their job just fine. The Graco model includes two parent units.

Better. Are the neighbors a bit too nosy? If so, you may want to consider a new digital monitor. The *Philips Avent SCD510* ($100; pictured) features DECT digital technology to stop interfer- ence and eavesdropping. The SCD510 also has rechargeable batteries, out-of-range indicator and intercom feature. Another good choice with DECT technology: *Safety 1st's High-Def Digital Monitor* ($60). The difference? The Safety 1st model lacks rechargeable batteries and the intercom feature found in the Philips.

Best. If your house is buzzing with electronic equipment and you fear Baby Monitor Interference Hell, then it's time to check out our top-rated baby monitor, the *Sony BabyCall* *NTM-910*. For $40, you get a monitor with 27 selectable channels . . . odds are, one will work. Add in rechargeable batteries, an out-of-range indicator and very positive parent reviews and we've got a winner.

Video. *Summer's Day & Night Handheld Color Video Monitor* ($180) features night vision, rechargeable batteries, LED sound lights and 900 MHz technology. A video on/off but- ton turns the monitor into an audio-only monitor at night. In a field crowded by inferior video monitors, this one is the best of the field.

If you have some tech savvy and want to monitor baby's nursery over your home network or smartphone, go for an *Axis* camera such as the 207MW ($300 to $400) or M1031-W ($280).

monitors

Twins. Need to monitor two different rooms in your house at once? The *Graco imonitor Multi Child monitor* ($130) is pricey, but you do get digital technology (for better reception and privacy), and rechargeable batteries. With two receivers and two transmitters, you can monitor babies in two rooms. The receivers switch between the two rooms at preset intervals.

Swings

You can't talk to new parents without hearing the heated debate on swings, those battery-operated or wind-up surrogate parents. Some think they're a godsend, soothing a fussy baby when nothing else seems to work. Cynics refer to them as "neglect-o-matics," sinister devices that can become far too addictive for a society that thinks parenting is like a microwave meal—the quicker, the better.

Whatever side you come down on, we do have a few shopping tips. First, ALWAYS try a swing before you buy. Give it a whirl in the store or borrow one from a friend. Why? Some babies love swings. Others hate 'em. Don't spend $120 on a fancy swing only to discover your little one is a swing-hater.

When we last wrote on the topic of swings, you still had a choice between wind-up swings and battery-operated models. While you may still find some wind-up models at garage sales or on eBay, most swings sold in stores are battery-operated. On Craigslist, we've seen wind-up swings for as little as $20. Of course, check with the CPSC (cpsc.gov) to make sure a used swing hasn't been recalled. Good news: many swings now also include an AC adapter so you can plug the swing into a wall outlet. This saves tremendously on batteries. Fisher-Price has several options with adapters.

If you are in the market for a new swing, remember this rule: swings eat batteries faster than toddlers can scarf M&M's. Look for swings that use fewer batteries—some use as little as two or three (others up to four). See the email from the real world for more on this below.

New swings range in price from $50 to $140. The more money you spend the more bells and whistles you get—see below for brand picks.

Remember to observe safety warnings about swings, which are close to the top ten most dangerous products, as far as injuries go. You must always stay with your baby, use the safety belt, and stop using the swing once your baby reaches the weight limit (about 25 pounds in most cases). Always remember that a swing is not a baby-sitter.

Our picks: Brand recommendations

Swings today come in three flavors: full-size, compact or travel. As you might guess, the latter category folds up for easy transport. Each work fine—if you have the space, go for a full-size model. If not, try a compact or travel version.

Who makes the best swings? Both *Fisher Price* and *Graco* come out on top.

We like *Fisher-Price's Papasan Cradle Swing* ($100), which features two position seat recline, eight songs and "nature sounds" (with adjustable volume) and six speeds. It comes in several colors, including a neutral hue and a version that matches the Zen high chair (unfortunately, that one is $180).

Graco's top-selling swing is their *Sweet Peace "Newborn Soothing Center,"* which we discussed earlier in the bouncer section of this chapter. This one is a hybrid between a swing and bouncer and gets very good review from readers.

If you'd prefer a more standard swing, Graco's *Lovin' Hug Open Top* swing comes with or without vibration (both versions are around $90). These swings feature six speeds, five-point safety harness and various classical tunes and nature sounds.

Both Graco and Fisher Price have swings down to a science, minimizing battery usage and featuring quiet motors.

How about a swing for Grandma's house? We like the *Open Top Take-Along Swing*, again by Fisher-Price. This cool swing folds up for portability, making it a good bet for $65 to $80.

Baby Proofing

All parents want to create a safe environment for their baby. And safety begins at the place where baby spends the most time—your home.

First, let's discuss the biggest safety hazards . . . and what baby products cause the most injury. Next, we'll give you our picks for that ubiquitous safety item, the baby gate. Finally, we'll discuss our tips for making your baby's toys safe.

Getting Started: When Do You Need This Stuff?

Whatever you do, start early. It's never too soon to think about baby proofing your house. Many parents we interviewed admitted they waited until their baby "almost did something" (like playing with extension cords or dipping into the dog's dish) before they panicked and began childproofing.

Remember Murphy's Law of Baby Proofing: your baby will be instantly attracted to any object that can cause permanent harm. The more harm it will cause, the more attractive it will be to him or her. A word to the wise: start baby proofing as soon as your child begins to roll over.

Safe &Sound: Smart Baby Proofing Tips

The statistics are alarming—each year, over 100 children die and millions more are injured in avoidable household accidents. Obviously, no parent wants their child to be injured by a preventable accident, yet many folks are not aware of common dangers. Others think if they load up their house with safety gadgets, their baby will be safe. Yet, there is one basic truth about child safety: *safety devices are no substitute for adult supervision.* While this section is packed with safety must-haves like gates, you still have to watch your baby at all times.

Where do you start? Get down on your hands and knees and look at the house from your baby's point of view. Be sure to go room by room throughout the entire house. On our web site, BabyBargains.com (click on bonus material), we have room-by-room advice on how to baby proof on a shoestring.

Top 10 Baby Products That Should Be Banned

We asked Dr. Ari Brown, a pediatrician in Austin, TX and co-author of our book *Baby411* for a list of baby products that should be banned. Some are dangerous, others simply foolish and unnecessary. Here is her take:

1 **BABY WALKERS: NEVER!** There are so many cases of serious injury associated with these death traps on wheels that some countries (including Canada) ban of baby walkers. More on why walkers are dangerous later in this chapter.

2 **DON'T GET YOUR KIDS HOOKED ON BABY EINSTEIN.** TV and electronic media of any type, even "educational videos" designed for babies, are bad for developing brains. Babies need active, not passive learning, and getting them used to watching TV is a bad habit.

3 **THROW AWAY THE PACIFIER AT SIX MONTHS.** As we discussed in the feeding chapter, pacifiers are now recommended after breastfeeding is well established (about one month). But . . . remember to STOP the pacifier at six months! Your baby needs to learn to fall asleep and/or comfort herself without a crutch.

What are the most dangerous baby products?

The Consumer Product Safety Commission releases yearly figures for injuries and deaths for children under five years old related to juvenile products. The latest figures from the CPSC are for 2006 and show a slight decline in the number of injuries. The following chart details the statistics:

PRODUCT CATEGORY	INJURIES	DEATHS
WALKERS/JUMPERS	4,000	1
STROLLERS/CARRIAGES	11,100	1
INFANT CARRIES/CAR SEATS*	14,200	7
CRIBS, BASSINETS, CRADLES**	11,300	32
HIGH CHAIRS	9,900	2
BABY GATES/BARRIERS	2,000	<1
PLAY YARDS	1,100	11
CHANGING TABLES	3,800	<1
PORTABLE BABY SWINGS	1,600	1
BATH SEATS	***	12
OTHER	5,300	2
TOTAL	**66,400**	**241**

Key:
  Deaths: This figure is an annual average from 2002 to 2004, the latest figures available.
  *excludes motor vehicle incidents
  ** including crib mattresses and pads
  ***in the CPSC's latest report bath seat injuries were not tabulated due to a low sample size

Our Comments: The large number of deaths associated with cribs almost exclusively occurs in cribs that are so old they don't meet current safety standards. We encourage parents to avoid hand-me-down, antique and second hand cribs.

4 **AVOID EAR THERMOMETERS.** They are notoriously unreliable, and since fever in infants (over 100.3 degrees) could be serious, an inaccurate reading might give parents a false sense of security. Rectal thermometers are the most accurate.

5 **DON'T FALL FOR THE BABY TOOTHPASTE HYPE.** The best way to clean your baby's teeth is to wipe them with a wet washcloth, twice daily. The sweet taste of baby toothpaste encourages your baby to suck on the toothbrush once in his mouth and you can't maneuver it around well.

6 **BEWARE OF NATURAL BABY SKIN-CARE PRODUCTS.** Over 25% of "natural" infant products contain common allergens including peanuts, which can sensitize infants to permanent food allergy.

7 **YOU DON'T NEED TEETHING TABLETS** from the health food store. Some of these contain *caffeine* as an ingredient! Save the espresso for kindergarten!

8 **FORGET SIPPY CUPS.** They promote tooth decay because the flow of liquid heads straight to the back of the top front teeth. If your baby hasn't quite mastered drinking from a cup yet, offer her a straw instead.

9 **HANGING MOBILES ARE ONLY FOR NEWBORNS.** Remove all toys and decorations hanging over your baby's crib by the time he or she is five months old. They become hazardous when babies start to pull themselves up and grab for them.

10 **ENJOY THOSE BEAUTIFUL QUILTS AS WALL HANGINGS**, not in the crib.

Safety Gates: Our Picks

When you look at the options available in baby gates, you can get easily overwhelmed. KidCo, Safety 1st, Evenflo, SuperGate (North States) and First Years are just a few of the brands available. And you'll see metal, plastic, fabric padded, tall, short, wide, permanent mount, pressure mount and more. So, what to get? The temptation of many parents (including us) is to buy what's cheapest. But after buying and using at least six gates, here are our picks and tips:

Your best option from the start is to stick with the metal or wooden gates. Plastic never seems to hold up that well and looks dirty in short order from all those sticky fingerprints. Our favorite brand is **KidCo**. They make pressure-mounted (Gateway), hardware-mounted (Safeway) and extra-wide and odd-shape gates (Elongate, Hearthgate). We used the permanent mount gate (the Safeway $70), which expands from 24.5 inches to 43.5 inches. We thought it was fairly easy to install and simple to use. The Gateway ($80; pictured) is the pressure-mounted version. The Elongate ($85) fits spaces from 48 inches to 60 inches wide. All three gates can be expanded further with inexpensive extensions. Another winner: the Hearthgate ($180), a product that allows you to gate off your fireplace so you can have a fire but avoid bumps and burns.

A reader recommended a similar gate to the Safeway, the **Stairway Special** ($90) by Cardinal Gates (cardinalgates.com). The permanent mount metal gate was recommended to her by a professional baby proofer. She reports that they were easy to install and use.

Another excellent option for a pressure gate is the **First Years' Hands Free Gate** ($55). This metal gate has a foot pedal that adults can step on to open. If you have your hands full, this is a great way to get in and out.

Soft gates have recently entered the market including the **Soft n' Wide** from Evenflo ($45). It is a stationary gate (does not swing open) with nylon covered padding at the top and bottom to protect baby from the metal frame. This is useful if you don't want to move the gate often and don't need to open the gate for access. Otherwise swinging gates are a better bet.

Finally, check out the plastic **Supergate** from North States Industries ($40; northstatesind.com), a gate our readers have recommended. This gate expands up to 62 inches, slides together and swings out of the way so you can easily clear a path. It is a permanent-

mounted gate so it can be used at the top of stairs. Pictured at right is the Supergate Superyard ($60).

We give the **KiddyGuard Mesh Child Safety Gate** (web: kiddyguardgate.com) our award for "best thinking outside the box." This gate opens and retracts like a window blind. At $90, however, it's a bit on the expensive side and can only be used for kids up to 24 months of age.

Most of these gates can be found at Babies R Us and Baby Catalog (babycatalog.com).

Money-Saving Secrets

1 **OUTLET COVERS ARE EXPENSIVE.** Only use them where you will be plugging in items. For unused outlets, consider a cheaper option—moving heavy furniture in front to block access. What type of outlet cover should you buy? We like the *Safe-Plate* ($3 from babyguard.com), which requires you to slide a small plate over to access the receptacle. In contrast, those that require you to rotate a dial to access the outlet are more difficult to use.

2 **MANY DISCOUNTERS LIKE TARGET, K-MART, AND WAL-MART SELL A LIMITED SELECTION OF BABY SAFETY ITEMS.** We found products like gates, outlet covers, and more at prices about 5% to 20% less than baby stores.

3 **HOME IMPROVEMENT STORES SELL CHILD SAFETY PRODUCTS.** Yep, Home Depot, Lowe's and other hardware and home improvement stores carry cabinet locks, safety gates and more. Plus you'll find items like blank outlet plates for outlets you never use. We saw a KidKusion fireplace cushion at Lowe's for $39.

4 **SOME OF THE MOST EFFECTIVE BABY PROOFING IS FREE.** For example, moving items to top shelves, putting dangerous chemicals away, and other common sense ideas don't cost any money and are just as effective as high-tech gadgets.

5 **CRAIGSLIST.ORG.** A great source for used baby gear, including safety items. One reader scored a Safety 1st Swing N Lock Gate (in the box, never installed) for just $10. The gate was $30 in stores (it is now discontinued).

Bonus Material Online

For more safety tips and advice, go to our web site, BabyBargains.com (click on Bonus Material). There you'll find practical tips on baby proofing on a budget, as well as mail order sources for safety gadgets.

 **Safe & Sound for Toys**

Walk through any toy store and the sheer variety of toys will

E-MAIL FROM THE REAL WORLD
A solution for those coffee tables

Reader Jennifer K. came up with this affordable solution to expensive coffee table bumpers.

"When our son started to walk we were very worried about his head crashing into the glass top tables in our living room. We checked into the safety catalogs and found those fitted bumpers for about $60 just for the coffee table. Well, I guess being the self-ish person that I am, and already removing everything else dangerous from my living room. I just didn't want to give up my tables! Where do we put the lamps, and where do I fold the laundry?

"My mother-in-law had the perfect solution. FOAM PIPE WRAPPING!!! We bought it at a home improvement store for $3. You can cut it to fit any table. It is already sliced down the middle and has adhesive, (the gummy kind that rolls right off the glass if you need to replace it). The only disadvantage that we've come across is that our son has learned to pull it off. But at $3 a bag we keep extras in the closet for 'touch-ups.'

"Now the novelty has worn off, so I have NOT had to replace it as often. And I'm happy to report that we've had plenty of collisions, but not one stitch!"

safety

boggle your mind. Buying toys for an infant requires more careful planning than for older children. Here are nine tips to keep your baby safe and sound:

1 **CHECK FOR AGE APPROPRIATE LABELS.** Yes, that sounds like a no-brainer, but you'd be surprised how many times grand-parents try to give a six-month old infant a toy that is clearly marked "ages 3 and up." One common misunderstanding about these labels: the age range has NOTHING to do with the developmental ability of your baby; instead, the warning is intended to keep small parts out of the hands of infants because those parts can be a choking hazard. Be careful of toys bought at second-hand stores or hand-me-downs—a lack of packaging may mean you have to guess on the age-appropriate level. Another trouble area: "kids meal" toys from fast-food restaurants. Many are clearly labeled for kids three and up (although some fast food places do offer toys safe for the under-three crowd). One smart tip: use a toilet paper tube to see if small parts pose a choking hazard . . . anything that can fit through the tube can be swallowed by baby.

2 **MAKE SURE STUFFED ANIMALS HAVE SEWN EYES.** A popular gift from friends and relatives, stuffed animals can be a hazard if you don't take a few precautions. Buttons or other materials for eyes that could be easily removed present a choking hazard—make sure you give a stuffed animal the once over before you give it to baby. Keep all plush animals out of the crib except maybe one special toy (and that only after baby is able to roll over). While it is acceptable to have one or two stuffed animals in the crib with babies over one year of age, resist the urge to pile on. Once baby starts pulling himself up to a standing position, such stuffed animals can be used as steps to escape a crib.

3 **BEWARE OF RIBBONS.** Another common decoration on stuffed animals, remove these before giving the toy to your baby.

4 **MAKE SURE TOYS HAVE NO STRINGS LONGER THAN 12 INCHES**—another easily avoided strangulation hazard.

5 **WOODEN TOYS SHOULD HAVE NON-TOXIC FINISHES.** If in doubt, don't give such toys to your baby. The toy's packaging should specify the type of finish.

6 **BATTERY COMPARTMENTS SHOULD HAVE A SCREW CLOSURE.** Music players (and other battery-operated toys) should not give your baby easy access to batteries—a compartment that requires a screwdriver to open is a wise precaution.

7 **BE CAREFUL OF CRIB TOYS.** Some of these toys are designed to attach to the top or sides of the crib. The best advice: remove them after the baby is finished playing with them. Don't

---

Oppenheim Toy Portfolio

While we do have a few basic baby toy recommendations on our web page (BabyBargains.com; click on bonus material), our specialty is really baby gear, not toys. As a result, we recommend this source for reviews on toys, books, video and software: The Oppenheim Toy Portfolio (web: toyportfolio.com). The web site picks the best toys and books for infants, toddlers and preschoolers. Readers agree. Said one mom:

"Now I understood better what to look for in a toy and what was skill/age appropriate—not what the manufacturers listed on the boxes! We have made many fewer return-the-toy trips and I am a much happier person."

leave the baby to play with crib toys unsupervised, especially once she begins to pull or sit up.

8 **DO NOT USE WALKERS.** See the list of top 10 baby products that should be banned earlier in this chapter.

9 **STATIONARY PLAY CENTERS.** What about walker alternatives? So-called "stationary" play centers have made a big splash on the baby market, led by Evenflo's Exersaucer. Most stationary play centers run $40 to $150 and are basically the same—you stick the baby into a seat in the middle and there are a bunch of toys for them to play with. (The more money you spend, the better the toys, bells and whistles). While the unit rocks and swivels, it doesn't roll across the floor. And that's a boon to parents who need a few minutes to make dinner or take a shower.

So, should you get one? Well, our belief is these play centers are optional—and if overused, can be a problem. We're troubled by studies that have shown infants who use walkers and stationary play centers suffer from developmental delays when compared to babies who don't use them.

Bottom line: babies should spend a LIMITED time in a stationary play center. If you are going to use one of these items, your child should spend no more than 15 minutes a day in them (long enough for a quick shower). As for a brand of stationary play center, we recommend the *Evenflo ExerSaucer*, based on parent feedback.

And traditional walkers should never, ever be used in our opinion.

10 **JUMPERS.** These contraptions attach to a doorway and let baby bounce up and down, thanks to a large spring that acts like a bungee cord. Yet, we've been troubled by the large number of recalls and reported injuries attributed to jumpers. Unfortunately, the CPSC doesn't separately break out injuries for jumpers (it lumps them in the category with walkers—these products caused a total of 4000 injuries, according to a 2008 CPSC report). But given the large number of recalls, we would suggest parents avoid this item.

Wastes of Money

Waste of Money #1
Outlet plugs

"My friend thought she'd save a bundle by just using outlet plugs instead of fancy plate covers. Unfortunately, her toddler figured out how to remove the plugs and she had to buy the plates anyway."

safety

Tummy Time Toys: A Waste of Money?

"Friends keep telling me that Tummy Time for my baby is a must. I've heard that my daughter might suffer developmental delays if I don't include tummy time in her day. What is it and why is it so important?"

Do babies spend too much time on their backs? That's one concern parents and child development specialists have brought up in recent years. Before the advent of the Back to Sleep campaign, the SIDS awareness program that encourages parents to put their babies to bed on their backs, babies were more likely to be placed in a variety of positions. Nowadays, however, babies spend an inordinate amount of time on their backs. And some folks wonder if that is causing a delay in creeping, crawling and walking.

The solution is a simple one: just put your baby on her tummy for a few minutes a day when she is awake. Yes, there is research that shows that extra tummy time can help your child reach developmental milestones sooner. But keep in mind that normal babies who don't participate in increased periods of tummy time typically still meet developmental milestones within the normal time period. So there is no need to panic if your baby isn't getting "15 minutes of tummy time daily."

In fact, many parents have noted that their babies hate being on their stomachs. For those babies who object to being on their tummies, you simply don't have to force them. Of course, baby products manufacturers have jumped on this new craze to come up with more stuff you can buy to make Tummy Time more fun. For example, Camp Kazoo, the makers of Boppy pillows (boppy.com) make a Boppy Tummy Play pillow for $30. This smaller version of the famous Boppy has a few toys attached to entertain your baby.

Don't think you need to buy extra stuff to make tummy time successful in your house, however. Save your money and just get down on the floor with your baby face to face. After all, you're the thing in her life she finds most fun, so get down there and spend some quality tummy time with her.

It doesn't take an astrophysicist to figure out how to remove those cheap plastic outlet plugs. While the sliding outlet covers are pricier, they may be well worth the investment. Another problem: outlet plugs can be a choking hazard. If baby removes one (or an adult removes one and forgets to put it back), it can end up in baby's mouth. If you want to try plugs anyway, do a test—check your outlets to see how tight the plugs will fit. In newer homes, plugs may have a tighter fit than older homes. While we generally think the outlet cover plates are superior to plugs, we do recommend the

plugs for road trips to Grandma's house or a hotel room (because they are easier to carry and install).

Waste of Money #2
Plastic corner guards

"The other day I was looking through a safety catalog and saw some corner guards. It occurred to me that they don't look a whole lot softer than the actual corner they cover. Are they worth buying?"

You've hit (so to speak) on a problem we've noticed as well. Our advice: the plastic corner guards are a waste of money. They aren't very soft—and babies can easily pop them off a table. So what's the solution? If you're worried about Junior hitting the corner of your coffee table, you can either store it for a while or look into getting a soft bumper pad (up to $60—see our reader email earlier in the chapter for a more affordable alternative). Similar bumpers are available for your fireplace as well. On the other hand, you may decide that blocking off certain rooms is a more practical option.

Waste of Money #3
Appliance safety latches

"I can't imagine that my daughter is going to be able to open the refrigerator any time soon. So why do they sell those appliance latches in safety catalogs, anyway?"

There must be some super-strong kids out there who have enough torque to open a full-sized refrigerator. Most infants under a year of age don't seem to have the strength to open most appliances. However, toddlers will eventually acquire that skill. One point to remember: many appliances like stoves and dishwashers have built-in locking mechanisms so use them! And keep all chairs and stools away from the laundry room to prevent your baby from opening the washing machine and dryer.

A Baby First Aid Kit

Wonder what should be in your baby first aid kit? As a childless couple, we were probably lucky to find a couple of bandages and an ancient bottle of Bactine in our medicine cabinet. Now that you're Dr.

Mom (or Nurse Dad) it's time to take a crash course on baby medicine etiquette. By the way, do not administer any of the drugs mentioned here without first checking with your doctor. He/she will know the safest dosage for your infant. Here's a run-down of essentials.

◆ *Acetaminophen* (brand name: Tylenol). For pain relief and fever reduction. If you suspect your child may have an allergy to flavorings, you can buy a version without all the additives. You may also want to keep acetaminophen infant suppositories in your medicine cabinet in case your infant persists in vomiting up his drops. Or refuses to take them at all. Do NOT keep baby aspirin in your house. Aspirin has been linked to Reyes Syndrome in children and is no longer recommended by pediatricians. Warn grandparents about this issue, as some may take a baby aspirin daily for heart health.

◆ *Children's Ibuprofen* (brand name: Motrin). This is another great option for pain relief and fever reduction. Typically, Ibuprofen will be a bit longer lasting than Acetaminophen.

◆ *Children's Benadryl.* To relieve minor allergic reactions.

◆ *Antibiotic ointment* to help avoid bacterial infection from cuts.

◆ *Baking soda* is great for rashes.

◆ *Calamine lotion* to relieve itching. Some versions include Benedryl so check the label carefully.

◆ *A good lotion.* Unscented and non-medicated brands are best.

◆ *Measuring spoon or cup for liquid medicine.* For small infants, you may want a medicine dropper or syringe. Droppers often come in the box with some medications.

◆ *Petroleum jelly*, which is used to lubricate rectal thermometers.

◆ *Plastic bandages like Band-Aids.*

◆ *Saline nose drops* for stuffy noses.

◆ *Tweezers*. For all kinds of fun uses.

◆ *A card with the number for poison control.* The national number for poison control is (800) 222-1222. You can also get your local poison control number from the web site of the American Association of Poison Control Centers (aapcc.org).

◆ *Thermometer*. Remember the old mercury thermometers of our childhood? They were so simple and straightforward. Today, you'll find digital thermometers, ear thermometers, strip thermometers, pacifier thermometers and more. Some use infrared technology and even solar-powered alternatives to mercury and simple batteries. But in the end, the most important job of a thermometer is to take an accurate temperature. And it would be nice if it could do it fast.

According to pediatricians we've interviewed, the most accurate thermometer is a digital rectal thermometer ($5 to $10). We know . . . your first reaction is "Ewww!" But accuracy is important, perhaps life saving, in infants under three months of age. If you're concerned about doing it correctly, ask your doctor to show you at one of your child's exams. It doesn't hurt, so you can practice once with the doctor just to make sure.

After one year of age, you don't necessarily need to use a rectal thermometer to take your child's temperature. At that point, you can use a digital thermometer ($5 to $10) under your baby's arm pit. No need for ear thermometers (too big for tiny ear canals), pacifier thermometers, temporal artery scanners or skin strips. In this case, simple really is best.

◆ *Do not use: cough and cold meds.* These medicines are NOT to be used for kids under four years of age because of overdosing problems.

Top 11 Safety Must Haves

To sum up, here's our list of top safety items to have for your home (in no particular order).

◆ *Fire extinguishers* rated "ABC," which means they are appropriate for any type of fire.

◆ *Outlet covers.*

◆ *Baby monitor*—unless your house or apartment is very small, and you don't think it will be useful.

◆ *Smoke alarms.* The best smoke alarms have two systems for detecting fires—a photoelectric sensor for early detection of smoldering fires and a dual chamber ionization sensor for early detection of flaming fires. An example of this is the First Alert "Dual Sensor" ($25 to $35). We'd recommend one smoke alarm for every bedroom, plus main hallways, basement and living rooms. And don't forget to replace the batteries twice a year. Both smoke alarms and carbon monoxide detectors can be found in warehouse clubs like Sam's and Costco at low prices.

◆ *Carbon monoxide detectors.* These special detectors sniff out dangerous carbon monoxide (CO) gas, which can result from a malfunctioning furnace. Put one CO detector in your baby's room and another in the main hallway of your home.

◆ *Cabinet and drawer locks.* For cabinets and drawers containing harmful cleaning supplies or utensils like knives, these are an essential investment. For play time, designate at least one unsecured cabinet or drawer as "safe" and stock it with pots and pans for baby.

◆ *Spout cover for tub.*

◆ *Bath thermometer or anti-scald device.*

◆ *Toilet locks*—so your baby doesn't visit the Tidy Bowl Man. One of the best we've seen in years is KidCo's toilet lock ($15), an award-winning gizmo that does the trick. Check their web site at kidco-inc.com for a store that carries it.

◆ *Baby gates.* See the section earlier for recommendations.

◆ *Furniture wall straps.* Since 2000, over 100 deaths have been caused by TV's and furniture tipped over onto kids. We recommend you anchor all your large furniture to the wall, especially shelves and dressers in baby's room. Once your child becomes a climber, she'll climb anything so be prepared.

Play Yards

The portable play yard has been so popular in recent years that many parents consider it a necessity. Compared to rickety playpens of old, today's play yards fold compactly for portability and offer such handy features as bassinets, wheels and more. Some shopping tips:

◆ *Don't buy a second-hand play yard or use a hand-me-down.* Many models have been the subjects of recalls in recent years. Why? Those same features that make them convenient (the collapsibility to make the play yards "portable") worked too well in the past—some play yards collapsed with babies inside. Others had protruding rivets that caught some babies who wore pacifiers on a string (a BIG no-no, never have your baby wear a pacifier on a string). A slew of injuries and deaths have prompted the recall of ten million playpens over the years. Yes, you can search government recall lists (cpsc.gov) to see if that hand-me-down is recalled, but we'd skip the hassle and just buy new.

◆ *Go for the bassinet feature.* Some play yards feature bassinet inserts which can be used for babies under three months of age (always check the weight guidelines). This is a handy feature that we recommend. Other worthwhile features: wheels for mobility, side-rail storage compartments and a canopy (if you plan to take the play yard outside or to the beach). If you want a play yard with canopy, look for those models that have "aluminized fabric" canopies—they reflect the sun's heat and UV rays to keep baby cooler.

◆ **Check the weight limits.** Play yards have two weight limits: one for the bassinet and one for the entire play yard (without the bassinet). Graco and most other play yard versions have an overall weight limit of 30 lbs. and height limit of 35″ The exception is the Arms Reach Co-Sleeper which tops out at 50 lbs. However, there is more variation in the weight limits for the bassinet attachments. Here are the weight limits for the *bassinet attachments* on various play yards:

Arms Reach Co-Sleeper	30 lbs.
Graco Pack N Play	15 lbs.
Chicco Lullaby	15 lbs.
Compass Aluminum	18 lbs.
Combi Play Yard	15 lbs.

Our Picks: Brand Recommendations

What are the best brands for play yards? The crown goes to *Graco*—their **Pack 'n Play** play yards are the best designed and least-recalled. Last we looked, they had seven models that ranged from $60 to $200. Most fall in the $100 range, however.

So, which model should you get? We like the basic Pack 'n Play with bassinet attachment, which start at $60 to $80 in discount stores and on Amazon. More deluxe versions of the Pack 'n Play add canopies, vibrating mattresses, and so on—run $150 to $200.

A brief word on the Graco play yard with bassinet feature: we recommend this as a good alternative to a stand-alone bassinet or cradle in Chapter 2. However, some readers note that Graco advises the product is "intended for naps and play" and question whether a newborn should sleep full time in the bassinet. We understand the confusion, but here's our advice: when it comes to newborns, there isn't much of a distinction between "naps" and nighttime sleep—day or night, most newborns are sleeping only four hours at a stretch (they need to feed at roughly that interval). Hence, Graco's advice to only use the Pack N Play for "naps or play" applies more to older babies—the product shouldn't take the place of a full-size crib (but is fine for occasional use at Grandma's house or a hotel room). The bottom line: we believe the bassinet feature is fine for full-time use for newborns who are under the weight limits (typically 15 pounds).

What about the other brands? Yes, you can find play yards by Baby Trend, Evenflo, Kolcraft and Fisher Price, but we don't think their quality or features measure up to Graco's offerings.

So, what's new for play yards? In a word, extra padding. Graco has upgraded their Pack 'n Plays with quilted pads and bumpers. *Chicco* also jumped on this trend, debuting their first play yard with extra cushy padding (which is machine-washable). The Chicco Lullaby is a winner—it sells for $170 and includes toy gym, electronic music and vibrations with remote and bassinet.

Don't care about fancy features and just want a large square play yard? Joovy fills that niche with their new Room^2 for $150. The steel frame makes it heavy, but the square shape means 50% more room.

Finally, check out Baby Bjorn's *Travel Crib Light* ($200 to $280). Not cheap, but this ultra-light play yard folds up like an umbrella and fits in a smaller size carry case. Parent feedback has been universally positive.

If the Bjorn is out your price range and you still need something for trip's to Grandma's house that is light weight, try the Graco's *Travel Lite Crib* ($90). It is 20% smaller than a standard Pack N Play, but still has a bassinet attachment and canopy, wheels and push button fold.

FYI: Be sure to check out some of our recommendations for play yard sheets in Chapter 3. While most parents love their play yard, the cheap-o sheets that come with most are a pain (they slip off the mattress too easily, etc). We discuss alternatives like Mr. Bobbles Blankets and Fleece Baby in Chapter 3 that solve this problem.

The Bottom Line:
A Wrap-Up of Our Best Buy Picks

In the nursery, the Diaper Genie II gets the best marks from readers—but many find a simple can with regular kitchen trash bags will do the trick.

Stay away from wipe warmers, which have safety concerns.

An activity/bouncer seat with a toy bar is a good idea, with prices ranging from $20 to $60—we like the Fisher Price bouncers best. An affordable alternative: adding a $10 toy bar to an infant seat.

As for bathtubs, we thought the EuroBath ($25) by Primo was the best bet, although it is big. A good option for Grandma's house might be the simple First Years Sure Comfort Deluxe tube ($18).

For baby monitors, a simple Graco UltraClear II ($30) will work for most folks. If you are concerned about interference, consider the Phillips Avent SCD510 ($100) which has rechargeable batteries and DECT technology. Another great monitor with rechargeable batteries is the Sony BabyCall NTM-910 ($40.

For swings and play yards, Graco is the brand of choice. Graco's swings set the standard for quality and features, although Fisher-Price's cradle swings are a good second bet. For play yards, the Graco Pack 'n Play with bassinet feature is our pick.

CHAPTER 8

CAR

SEATS

Car Seats: Picking the right child safety seat

Inside this chapter

W hat's the best car seat for your baby? What is the difference between an infant, convertible or booster seat? We'll discuss these issues and more in this chapter. You'll find complete reviews and ratings of the major car seat brands as well as informative charts that compare the best choices.

Here's a sobering figure: in the most recent year's statistics, motor vehicle crashes killed 1,670 children under age 14 and injured another 200,000. And 100 infants under age one were killed in traffic accidents in 2007.

While the majority of those injuries and deaths occurred to children who were not in safety seats, the toll from vehicle accidents in this country is still a statistic that can keep you awake all night. Just to make you feel a tiny bit better, the lives of 367 children under age five were saved last year because they were in a child restraint.

By law, every state in the U.S. (and every province in Canada) requires infants and children to ride in child safety seats, so this is one of the few products that every parent must buy. In fact you may find yourself buying multiple car seats as your baby grows older—and for secondary cars, grandma's car, a caregiver's vehicle and more.

So, which seat is the safest? Easiest to use? One thing you'll learn in this chapter is that there is not one "safest" or "best" seat. Yes, we will review and rate the various car seat brands and examine their recall/safety history. BUT, *remember the best seat for your child is the one that correctly fits your child's weight and size—and can be correctly installed in your vehicle.*

And that's the rub: roadside safety checks reveal 80% to 90% of child safety seats are NOT installed or used properly. Although the exact figure isn't known, a large number of child fatalities and injuries from crashes are caused by improper use or installation of seats.

Realizing that many of today's child safety seats are a failure due to complex installation and other hurdles, the federal government has rolled out a safety standard (called LATCH) for child seats and vows to fix loopholes in current crash testing. The results so far are mixed—we'll discuss these issues later in this chapter.

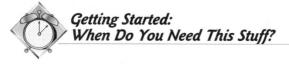

Getting Started: When Do You Need This Stuff?

You can't leave the hospital without a car seat. By law, all states require children to be restrained in a child safety seat. You'll want to get this item early (in your sixth to eighth month of pregnancy) so you can install it in your car before baby arrives.

Sources to Find Car Seats

1 DISCOUNTERS. Car seats have become a loss leader for many discount stores. Chains like Target and Wal-Mart sell these items at small mark-ups in hopes you'll spend money elsewhere in the store. The only caveat: most discounters only carry a limited

---

E-MAIL FROM THE REAL WORLD
Car seats save lives

"When I was expecting my first child, I used your book extensively. I followed your recommendation for a car seat for my baby. I'm so glad I did because we recently were involved in a potentially deadly accident. My car's left back-side (where my ten-month-old baby was sitting), hit a lamp post. To give you an idea how serious it was, the car door was pushed in nearly a foot and a half.

"My son was riding in his Graco SnugRide infant seat, installed rear facing and attached to its base. He was actually injured by the collision when the door was damaged and the air bag deployed. We rushed him to the hospital where he was found to have superficial skull fractures and minor bruises. Good news: he recovered quickly without any permanent damage. Later, when we showed the hospital staff the photos of the vehicle, they were amazed that our son survived the accident."

selection of seats, typically of the no-frills models.

2 **BABY SPECIALTY STORES.** Independent juvenile retailers carry car seats, but the selection is often limited by the size of the store (small boutiques may just have one or two brands).

3 **THE SUPERSTORES.** Chains like Babies R Us, Buy Buy Baby and Burlington Coat Factory's Baby Depot dominate the car seat business, thanks to a wider selection of models than discounters. Prices can be a few dollars higher than the discounters, but sales often bring better deals.

4 **ONLINE.** We'll discuss our favorite sites to buy a car seat online shortly, but remember this caveat: Prices are usually discounted, but watch out for shipping—the cost of shipping bulky items like car seats can outweigh the discount in some cases. Use an online coupon (see the previous chapter for coupon sites) to save and look for free shipping specials.

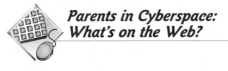

Parents in Cyberspace: What's on the Web?

The web is teeming with both information and bargains on car seats. Here's the best of what's out there.

◆ **NHTSA.** The National Highway Traffic Safety Administration site (nhtsa.gov) is a treasure trove of car seat info—you can read about recalls, the latest news on changing standards and installation tips. Confused about how to use your LATCH car seat? The web site offers instructional videos for both rear and forward facing seats. You can also contact the government's Auto Safety Hotline at 800-424-9393 to ask car seat related questions. Even better: NHTSA now ranks car seats on their *ease of use* (assembly, instructions, securing a child, etc). The most recent report covers over 90 seats, from infant to booster. Note: these ratings do NOT cover how well a seat does in crash tests or compatibility with different vehicles.

◆ *The American Academy of Pediatrics* (aap.org, go to "Parenting Corner") is an excellent resource for buying tips.

◆ *The National Safe Kids Campaign* (safekids.org; click on United States) has a helpful interactive "safety seat guide" that helps you determine which seat is right for the age and weight of the child.

CAR
SEATS

◆ *Safety Belt Safe USA* (carseat.org) has a good site with tips on picking the best seat for your child, as well as the latest recalls and info on child safety seats.

◆ *CarSeatData.org* has an "interactive compatibility database" that lets you search for which seats work in which vehicles. Very cool.

◆ *Our web site* has a message board dedicated to car seats. Plus: we have a brochure called "Buying a Better Car Seat Restraint" produced by a Canadian auto insurance company. This publication (downloadable as a PDF) has excellent advice on buying a seat. For a link to the brochure and the ratings web page, go to BabyBargains.com and click on the "Bonus Material" section.

◆ *Insurance Institute for Highway Safety* booster seat report is posted on our web site BabyBargains.com/boosters.

◆ *Where to buy online.* Our readers' favorite sites to buy car seats at a discount include BabyCatalog.com, Amazon, Bed Bath & Beyond (owners of Buy Buy Baby) and EliteCarSeats.com. As always, look for a coupon code for additional savings, free shipping and the like.. Check out the Bargain Alert message board on our site (BabyBargains.com/coupons) for a regularly updated list of coupon deals and discounts.

More Money Buys You . . .

As you'll read later in this chapter, all child safety seats are regulated by the federal government to meet minimum safety standards. So whether you buy a $50 seat from Wal-Mart or a $250 brand from a specialty store, your baby is equally covered. When you pay extra money, however, there are some perks. First, on the safety front, the more expensive seats have shock-absorbing foam that protects a child from side-impact collisions. The more expensive seats are also easier to use and adjust . . . and clearly that is a major safety benefit. For infant seats, when you spend more money, you get an adjustable base (which enables a better fit in vehicles), a canopy to block the sun and plush padding.

Speaking of padding, the more money you spend, the cushier the seat—some makers throw in infant head pillows, body cushions and more . . . all of which raises the price.. These are not marketed as a safety benefit, but more for the baby's "comfort." The problem? Newborns and infants don't really care. They are just fine in a seat with basic padding (versus the deluxe version). Of course, if you have a super long commute or an older child (say over two years), padding and comfort becomes more of a relevant issue. But for most babies, basic padding is just fine.

Smart Shopper Tips

Smart Shopper Tip #1
So many seats, so much confusion

"I'm so confused by all the car seat options out there. For example, are infant car seats a waste of money? Or should I go with a convertible seat? Or one of those models that is good from birth to college?

Children's car seats come in four flavors: "infant," "convertible," "boosters" and "hybrid." Let's break it down:

◆ **Infant** car seats are just that—these rear-facing seats are designed for infants up to 22 lbs. or so and 26"-29" in height (a couple models works up to 30 lbs. and 30" in height). On average, parents get about six months of use out of an infant seat (of course, that varies with the size/height of the child). Infant car seats have an internal harness (usually five-point) that holds the infant to the carrier, which is then snapped into a base. The base is secured to the car. Why the snap-in base? That way you can release the seat and use the carrier to tote your baby around.

◆ **Convertible** car seats (see right) can be used for both infants *and* older children (most seats go up to 40 or 65 lbs.)—infants ride rear facing; older kids over one year of age ride facing forward. Convertible seats have different harness options (more on this later); unlike infant seats, however, they do not have snap-in bases.

◆ **Booster** seats come in three types: hybrid/combo seats, high back and backless boosters. We'll discuss each in-depth in a special section on boosters later in this chapter. In a nutshell, here's how they work: after your child outgrows their convertible seat, the booster correctly positions the safety belt. Most states have laws that

require booster seat use until 60 or 80 lbs. (or up to age eight).

Of course, real life doesn't always fit neatly into these categories—some seats pitch their use from birth to 100 lbs. The most well known is the Cosco Alpha Omega (also called the Eddie Bauer Three in One)—the pitch here is one seat that can be used for an infant, toddler and then older child. The Alpha Omegas is used rear facing from 5 to 35 lbs., then forward-facing 22lbs. to 40 lbs. From 40 lbs. to 100 lbs. the Alpha Omega converts to a booster seat that uses the auto safety belt to restrain an older child. We'll review this seat later in this chapter. (There will be a quiz on this later as well).

So, does it make more sense to buy one car seat (that is a convertible model) and just skip the infant car seat? There is considerable debate on this subject. Some safety advocates think convertible car seats are safer, pointing to recalls of infant car seats. Others deride infant car seats for their overuse *outside* of a car (as a place for baby to nap), speculating that such babies are at risk for SIDS (Sudden Infant Death Syndrome, discussed in Chapter 2). Fuel was added to this fire in 2006, when a *British Medical Journal* study generated headlines, saying that babies in infant car seats are at risk for breathing problems.

But . . . we analyzed that study and found the researchers examined only nine babies in New Zealand to come up with that conclusion (see our *Baby 411* blog for a detailed discussion). And while babies born prematurely (less than 37 weeks in gestation) are at an increased risk for breathing problems while in a car seat, full term infants ARE NOT. Sure, you should always supervise a newborn in an infant seat (have someone ride in the back seat if possible). And limit your baby's time in an infant seat. But that doesn't mean infant seats are UNSAFE or dangerous for sleeping infants.

On the other side of the debate are advocates who say infant car seats fit newborns better—most are designed to accommodate a smaller body and baby travels in a semi-reclined position, which supports an infant's head and neck. Yes, some convertible seats recline—but the degree of recline can be affected by the angle of your vehicle's seat back. And certain convertible seats (those with bar shields instead of five-point restraints—more on this later) simply don't work well with infants.

Furthermore, most babies don't outgrow their infant car seats until six months (and some as late as 12 months, depending the baby's weight and seat's limits)—and that can be a very long period of time if you don't have an infant car seat.

Why? First, it's helpful to understand that an infant car seat is more than just a car seat—it's also an infant carrier when detached from its base. Big deal, you might say? Well, since infants spend much of their time sleeping (and often fall asleep in the car), this *is* a big deal.

By detaching the carrier from the auto base, you don't have to wake the baby when you leave the car. Buy a convertible car seat, and you'll have to unbuckle the baby and move her into another type of carrier or stroller (and most likely wake her in the process). Take it from us: let sleeping babies lie and spend the additional $100 for an infant car seat, even if you use it for just six months.

Remember: babies should be REAR-FACING until they reach one year of age, regardless of weight. If your child outgrows his infant car seat before one year of age, be sure to use a convertible seat in rear-facing mode for as long as possible. Most convertible seats can be used rear-facing until baby is 30 or 33 lbs.

Smart Shopper Tip #2
Infant seats: Are they safe?

"I heard that in a recent crash test, many infant car seats failed. Are they safe?"

You are referring to the now infamous *Consumer Reports* article from February 2007. Before we get into the details of how the *Consumer Reports* test went wrong, let's take a second to explain how car seat safety works. The federal government, through the National Highway Traffic Safety Administration (NHTSA), sets safety standards for car seats. You can't sell a car seat here in the U.S. that doesn't meet these safety requirements.

To be certified as meeting federal standards, car seat makers must crash test their seats. This is done either in an in-house facility or outside lab and reported to the government. Once a seat is on the market, the NHTSA performs spot checks, crash testing models from time to time.

While we won't delve into the technical details of federal standards, you should know that the basic crash test for a car seat is a frontal collision at 30 mph. Now, that number wasn't picked out of thin air—the vast majority of auto accidents occur at 30 mph or less. According to the Michigan Transportation Research Institute, the 30 mph test is "more severe than approximately 98% of frontal impact crashes nationwide."

Consumer Reports magazine independently crash test car seats—to confirm that seats actually meet standards These crash tests are proprietary—*Consumer Reports* hires an independent lab to run the test, but the results are not peer-reviewed (that is, independently verified).

So what happened with *Consumer Reports* in 2007? The magazine designed a new crash test that was flawed (the speeds were much higher than CR thought it was using). The results were dramatic—ten out of 12 infant car seats failed. Since CR didn't used outside experts to check its test design or results, this flawed report made it into the magazine . . . and the media.

After a series of mea culpas and pressure from the NHTSA, *Consumer Reports* withdrew their report and vowed to re-test the seats using correct protocol (that is, the current government standards). CR's re-test, which was reported in late 2007, showed that *all infant car seats sold on the market today pass government safety standards*.

Smart Shopper Tip #3
New standards, new problems?

"I hear there are problems with LATCH. What is LATCH anyway?"

Stop any ten cars on the road with child safety seats and we'll bet eight or nine are not installed or used correctly. That's what road-side checks by local law enforcement in many states have uncovered: a recent study by the National Highway Traffic Safety Administration stopped 4000 drivers in four states and found a whopping 80% made mistakes in installing or securing a child safety seat.

What's causing all the problems?

Many child safety seats have failed parents, in our opinion. Installation of a car seat is an exercise in frustration—even parents who spend hours with the instructions still made mistakes. The number one culprit: the auto seat belt—it is great at restraining adults, but not so good at child safety seats. And those seats simply won't work well if they aren't attached to a car correctly . . . that's the crux of the problem. Simply put, thanks to the quirkiness of auto safety belts (different auto makers have different systems), putting a child safety seat in a car is still like trying to fit a square peg into a round hole. Some seats wobble too much; others can't be secured tightly to the back seat.

The bottom line: some child safety seats simply DON'T FIT in some vehicles. Which cars? Which seats? It's hard to tell. There is one good web site with a car seat compatibility database (carseat-data.org), but it doesn't cover every seat and every vehicle. Often, parents find it's trial and error to see what works.

So, that's where LATCH comes in. The federal government rolled out a new, mandated "uniform" attachment (called LATCH or ISOFIX), required for all vehicles and safety seats made after 2002. LATCH stands for "Lower Anchors and Tethers for Children." ISOFIX stands for International Standards Organization FIX, which is the international version of LATCH. (More on ISOFIX later in this section).

What is LATCH? Instead of using the auto's seat belt, car seats attach to two

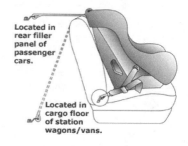

Located in rear filler panel of passenger cars.

Located in cargo floor of station wagons/vans.

anchor bars in the lower seatback. The result: fewer confusing installations, no more locking clips or other apparatus needed to make sure the seat is correctly attached. (Another part of the new standard: tether straps, which are discussed later in this section.) See picture of a LATCH-installed car seat at right.

Here is a sum up of frequent questions we get on LATCH seats:

◆ *Which manufacturers sell LATCH seats?* Answer: all. Every infant and convertible car seat sold now includes LATCH. However, booster car seats aren't required to us LATCH (although a few do).

◆ *Will I have to junk my old car seat?* Yes, car seat safety advocates do NOT recommend using a seat that is over five years old. Why? Belts, clips and interior parts in car seats wear out over time . . . hence, seats five years old or older may no longer be safe to use. (The last time a non-LATCH seat would have been manufactured was 2002—and that is now beyond the five-year guideline).

◆ *My car does not have LATCH. What is the safest seat I can buy?* All LATCH seats are backward compatible—that is, they can be safely installed and used in older vehicles that do NOT have LATCH anchors. Remember the safest seat is the one that best fits your car *and* your child. There is no one "safest" seat. Get the best seat you can afford (we'll have recommendations later in this chapter) and use it with a tether strap. And get your car seat safety checked to make sure you have the best installation and fit.

◆ *I need to move my LATCH seat to a second car that doesn't have the new attachments. Will it work?* Yes, see above.

◆ *I know the safest place for a baby is in the middle of the back seat. But my car doesn't have LATCH anchors there, just in the outboard positions! Where should I put the seat?* Our advice: use the LATCH positions, even if they are only on the side. Some car seat and vehicle makers say it is okay to use a LATCH seat in the middle of the back seat if you use the LATCH anchors in the outboard positions—check with your car seat and vehicle owner's manual to see if this is permissible.

◆ *I got a LATCH seat that doesn't fit in my vehicle! I thought this was supposed to be universal.* LATCH has been sold to the public as some kind of magic pill that will instantly make all seats fit all vehicles. Hardly. Because of the wide variety of vehicles and seats (a SUV versus a compact, minivan versus pickup), it is unreasonable to expect any system would make this happen. While LATCH helps, it is not the cure-all.

◆ **I find LATCH hard to use.** You're not alone: a recent survey showed that 40% of parents aren't using LATCH. Problems with LATCH include hard-to-reach anchors that are buried in the seat back, making installation a challenge. Some LATCH clips are also easier to use than others. Car seat makers are trying to respond to these issues. Example: Evenflo's new Symphony car seat has an improved LATCH clip that is easier to install.

Smart Shopper Tip #4
Strap Me In

"What is a tether strap? Do I want one?"

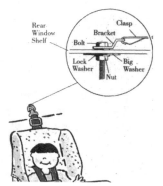

Back in 1999, the federal government mandated that all convertible child safety seats be sold with a tether strap—these prevent a car seat from moving forward in the event of a crash. How? One end of the tether strap attaches to the top of the car seat; the other is hooked to an "anchor bolt" that is permanently installed on the back of the rear seat or on the floor in your vehicle.

Most newer vehicles already have anchor bolts, making the use of a tether strap a snap. (Hint: check your vehicle's owner's manual to find instructions on using tether straps). Older vehicles may have pre-drilled anchorage points—just ask your car dealer for the "anchor bolt installation kit" (a part number that's listed in your owner's manual in the section on installing child safety seats). You can install the bolt or have the dealer do it.

Of course, really old cars are trickier since they lack anchor bolts or even pre-drilled holes—to install the anchor bolt, you may need to drill through your car's sub floor (a job for the car dealer, as you can guess). And just finding out the part number for the anchor bolt can be a challenge; some car dealers are clueless about this issue.

A side note: most seats can only use tether straps when FOR-WARD-FACING. Only four models (the Britax Roundabout, Marathon and Wizard and the Sunshine Kids Radian 65/80/XT) have a tether which can be used in either rear or forward-facing positions. Note: tether straps are typically not used with infant seats or booster seats (but always consult your seat's directions for specific advice on this).

So, is the tether strap worth all the hassle? Yes—crash tests show car seats are SAFER when used with a tether strap. The strap keeps the car seat (and hence, your baby's head) from moving forward in a crash, lowering the chance of injury. Unfortunately, parents don't seem to be getting this message: a 2006 survey from the NHTSA revealed that only 55% of parents are using a top tether.

Are seats used *without* tethers unsafe? No, the federal government requires seats to be safe even when a tether is not in use. Of course, the tether adds that extra measure of safety and is always preferable to a tether-less installation.

Smart Shopper Tip #5
One Size Does Not Fit All
"My friend has a car seat that just doesn't fit very well into her car. Does anyone put out a rating system that says which seats are most compatible? Easiest to use? Safest?"

There are two resources to check out: first, CarSeatData.org has a capability database—pick a vehicle or seat and read feedback from parents.

Also: the National Highway Traffic Safety Administration rates car seats on their ease of use and posts the results on the web at nhtsa.gov or call 888-327-4236.

Note these are not crash test results. NHTSA rates seats on how a seat assembles, installs and secures a child. In the latest report, over 90 seats were rated. The government updates the report every year.

Smart Shopper Tip #6
Recalls
"I saw online that a particular car seat is being recalled. Should I be skeptical of other seats by that manufacturer?"

Here's a sobering fact of car seat shopping: most major brands of car seats have had a recall over the past five years. We've seen recalls on cheap seats sold in Wal-Mart and $300 car seats sold in specialty stores, making recalls a reality no matter what brand you consider. So if all major brands have had recalls, how do you shop for the best seat?

First, understand that some recalls are more serious than others. Some car seats are recalled for minor problems, like incorrect warning labels. Other companies do voluntary recalls when their own testing reveals a problem. The key issue: look to see if there are any injuries associated with the defective product. Obviously, car seats that are so defective as to cause injury to babies are much more serious than minor labeling recalls.

Another issue: how does a company handle a recall? Do they fight the government, forcing regulators to order a recall? Or do they voluntarily recall the item and set up an efficient process to get replacements or retrofit kits to consumers? In the past, we have lowered our ratings for car seat manufacturers who bungled a recall effort.

When a company announces a recall, the product is typically removed from store shelves (if the recall is for the current production run). If the recall is for a product's previous production, you may still see it on store shelves (since the defect may have been corrected months before). That's why it is key to see WHEN the recalled product was manufactured. Of course, different car seats in the same manufacturer's line may be totally unaffected by a recall.

Another tip: make sure to fill out the registration card that comes with any car seat you buy . . . and send it in! In theory, this will get you expedited recall information and repair kits. Also: sign up for a recall email list on Recalls.gov. s

Unfortunately, with some car seat makers, even if you fill out a registration card you may not get a recall notice. For more on this problem, see the box on pages 362-3.

Smart Shopper Tip #7
Watch the height limit

"My son isn't anywhere near the 26 lb. limit for his infant seat, but he's so tall I don't think it is safe anymore—he has to bend his legs when we put him in!"

Here's a little known fact about most infant seats: in addition to WEIGHT limits, all infant car seats also have HEIGHT limits. And like everything in the car seat world, each seat has different limits (check the sticker on the side of the carrier—by law, the manufacturer must list both height and weight limits). Once your baby exceeds EITHER the height or weight limit, you should move him to a convertible seat.

One note on this: while the weight limit is important, do one other test if your child is approaching the height limit—is there less than an inch of seat left above baby's head? If so, then move your baby to a convertible seat (facing the rear of the vehicle until they pass one year of age).

With the bigger babies everyone seems to be having these days, this isn't a moot point. A large infant might exceed the height limit BEFORE he or she passes the weight limit. Here's the scoop: height limits range from 26" for the Evenflo Embrace to 30" for the Britax Companion infant car seat. Most infant seats have weight limits of 26 lbs, although a few seats (the Graco SafeSeat, the Britax Chaperone and the Chicco Key Fit 30) work to 30 lbs. Later in this section, we'll have a chart that lists the height and weight limits of all major infant car seats. See the box "How Big is Normal?" later in this chapter for more on this topic.

Smart Shopper Tip #8

Do I have to buy THREE seats?

"My baby has outgrown his infant seat. Can I buy a combo seat that converts to a booster?"

The short answer: yes. Do we recommend it? No. Why? We think the safest place for an infant who has outgrown an infant seat is in a CONVERTIBLE seat in rear-facing mode. Leave them there until they are AT LEAST a year of age—longer if they still are under the weight limit. Note: nearly all "combo" seats with five-point harnesses that convert to a belt-positioning booster are FORWARD-FACING only seats. Examples of combo seats include the Cosco Summit and Graco CarGo.

So, what is best? When your child outgrows her convertible seat, THEN we recommend a booster seat (combo or belt-positioning). Now, we realize what you are thinking: have we lost our minds? We are recommending you buy THREE seats for your child: infant, convertible, and then a booster. Wouldn't it be cheaper to get one of those all-in-one seats or at least one that combines the convertible/booster function? No, not in our opinion. The all-in-one-seats (like the Eddie Bauer Three-In-One or Cosco Alpha Omega) are a poor choice; see review later in this chapter.

And while those combo boosters are a good choice for a three or four year old child who has outgrown his convertible seat but is not mature enough to sit in a belt-positioning booster, combo seats are NOT good for infants—they often don't recline and have less sleeping support than convertibles.

Smart Shopper Tip #9

European seats

"I saw a cool European car seat online—is that safe or legal to use in the U.S.?

Short answer: no.

Thanks to the web, you can order a car seat from Switzerland . . . or South Africa. Making this more tempting: the belief among some safety advocates that Europe has better car seats than the U.S. or Canada.

But let's do a reality check: European standards are DIFFERENT than the U.S. or Canada. Different does not necessarily mean better, however. European seats are designed to work in European cars, which have different safety features compared to vehicles sold in North America.

Bottom line: it is ILLEGAL (and foolish) to use a seat from overseas here in the U.S. (Ditto for you Canadians—seats must be certi-

CAR SEATS

fied to meet Canadian standards before they can be sold or used in Canada. So if you are a Canadian reading this book, you can't buy a seat in the U.S. and use it legally in Canada).

Smart Shopper Tip #10
Holding Your Baby Back: Safety Harness Advice
"Which safety harness is best—the 5-point or bar-shield?"

Car Seat Lesson 101: understanding the different harness systems available on the market. For INFANT seats, you have two choices: three point or five-point belts (although nearly all infant seats now have five-point harnesses). For CONVERTIBLE seats, you have two choices: five-point or bar-shield.

Five point belts refer to the number of points in which the belt attaches to the car seat. A bar shield lowers over the baby's head and snaps into a buckle—bar-shield car seats are often sold at discount stores.

Registering a Complaint: Do Some Seat Makers Ignore Registered Users During Recalls?

As a new parent, you try to do everything you can to make sure your baby is safe. Besides researching which products are safe, many parents also diligently fill out warranty and registration cards with the expectation they will be contacted in case of a future safety recall.

Yet many parents are surprised to learn that baby product companies fail to mail out notices of defective products to registered users. Why? Companies complain that mailing costs are too high—instead they issue a press release to the media, hoping web sites, local newspapers, radio and TV will spread the word about a defective product. No wonder experts estimate the response rate for recalls is an abysmal 50%.

Hello? Is this insane or what? Parents take the time to fill out and mail those registration cards that manufacturers include in product boxes, but for what? Instead of receiving a courtesy email, call or postcard that the car seat you are using might be dangerous, you are supposed to be watching the local news at exactly the right moment to hear your car seat is recalled? Or see page 16A of the local paper? Last year, the Consumer Products Safety Commission (CPSC) issued 100+ recalls of baby products, including toys. That's almost two per week! So, what can a parent do to keep up with what's safe and what's recalled? Here are our tips:

Our recommendations: for INFANT seats, we recommend five-point harnesses, which have become the de facto standard. Yes, you will see an occasional three-point harness on a cheap infant car seat sold at a discounter, but that is the exception to the rule. Our advice: go for the five-point harness.

For CONVERTIBLE seats, we also recommend the five-point version. Why? Safety experts say it's the best choice because you can tighten the belts to securely hold your baby in her seat. Bar shields have several problems. The biggest: most don't adjust well to growing children. Even those expensive models that feature *adjustable* shields only adjust so much—if your child grows quickly, they still might outgrow the car seat. The result? You'll have to move them into a booster seat (making an extra purchase).

Another major problem with bar shields: wiggling toddlers can get out of them way too easily. One mom told us she was horrified to look in her rear view mirror one day and find her 18 month-old child STANDING in his car seat while the vehicle was moving. We

◆ **Track your purchases.** In order to know whether you have a recalled product, you first have to know what you've got to begin with. One parent told us she kept a spreadsheet with the following info for all her baby products: manufacturer, model, serial number, date manufactured, company phone number/web site, where purchased and price paid. Okay, perhaps that's a bit overboard for most parents. But at least put all your receipts and product manuals into a file or shoebox. The goal: create ONE place you go to when a recall is announced.

◆ **Stay informed.** Register for free email alerts about recalls. Our blog (BabyBargains.com/blog) tracks the latest recalls. We can send you a text message or email when a product is recalled—enter your email and click subscribe when you are on the blog page. Of course, the Consumer Products Safety Commission also emails out recall notices—sign up at Recalls.gov or CPSC.gov.

◆ **Consider buying products from web sites that will inform you of recalls.** Case in point: Amazon does a good job of letting customers know of recalled products. One reader was amazed when Amazon sent her a recall notice (with detailed instructions on what to do) for a bassinet she bought over a year ago.

◆ **Be careful with second-hand purchases.** We don't recommend buying a used car seat off Craigslist. But if you insist, do a search of the NHTSA's web site (nhtsa.dot.gov) to make sure the seat isn't recalled.

think five point harnesses are safer since it is very difficult for baby to wiggle out when the belts are tightened correctly.

Let's be honest, however: the five-point harness is the *least convenient* to use. You have to put each strap around baby's arms, find the lower buckle (which always seems to disappear under their rump) and then snap them in. Bar-shields slip over the baby's head in one motion and are easier to buckle.

The fact that the five-point harness is inconvenient is just the way it goes (you'll get the hang of it, trust us). Simply put, it's the safest choice for your baby. And sometimes as a parent you have to do what's best for your child, even if that makes your life less convenient.

Here are ten more shopping tips for car seats:

◆ *How easily does it recline?* Many convertible seats have a recline feature to make sure baby is at a proper angle. Of course, how easily the seat reclines varies from model to model—and reaching that lever in a rear-facing seat may be a challenge. Check it out in the store before you buy.

◆ *No-twist straps.* Better car seats have thicker straps that don't twist. The result: it is easier to get a child in and out of a seat. Cheaper seats have cheaper webbing that can be a nightmare— "twisty straps" are a key reason why parents hate their car seats. Later when we review specific car seat models, we'll note which ones have twisty straps.

◆ *Check the belt adjustments.* You don't merely adjust the car seat's belts just when your baby gets bigger—if you put Junior in a coat, you'll need to loosen the belts as well. As a result, it's important to check how easily belts adjust. Of course, every car seat maker seems to have a different idea on how to do this. The best car seats let you adjust the belts from the *front*. Those models that require you to access the back of the seat to adjust the belts are a big hassle. FYI: do not put your child in a bulky coat or snowsuit when sitting in a safety seat. In the case of an accident, the bulky coat might compress, compromising the safety of the seat. At most, only put a child in a thin coat (like a polar fleece) when they are riding in a child safety seat. (To keep an infant warm, consider a seat cover-up, which goes on the outside of the seat. We'll discuss examples of these products later in this chapter).

◆ *Change the harness height.* Some seats require you to re-thread the belts when you change harness heights. Try this in the store to see how easy/difficult it is. Note: the best seats have automatic harness height adjusters that require no re-threading.

◆ **Look at the chest clip.** The chest clip or harness tie holds the two belts in place. Lower-quality seats have a simple "slide-in" clip—you slip the belt under a tab. That's OK, but some older toddlers can slip out from this type of chest clip. A better bet: a chest clip that SNAPS the two belts together like a seat belt. This is more kid-proof.

◆ **Are the instructions in Greek?** Before you buy the car seat, take a minute to look at the set-up and use instructions. Make sure you can make sense of the seat's documentation. Another tip: if possible, ask the store for any installation tips and advice.

◆ **Is the pad cover machine-washable?** You'd think this would be a no-brainer, but a surprising number of seats (both convertible and infant) have covers that aren't removable or machine washable. Considering how grimy these covers can get, it's smart to look for this feature. Also check to see if you can wash the harness.

◆ **Will the seat be a sauna in the summer?** Speaking of the seat pad, check the material. Plush, velvet-like covers might seem nice in the store, but think about next August. Will your baby be sitting in a mini-sauna? Cotton or cotton-blend fabric pads are better than heavier weight, non-breathable fabrics.

◆ **Does the seat need to be installed with each use?** The best car seats are "permanently" installed in your car. When you put baby in, all you do is buckle them into the seat's harness system. Yet a few models need to be installed with each use—that means you have to belt the thing into your car every time you use it. Suffice it to say, that's a major drawback.

◆ **Watch out for hot buckles.** Some inexpensive car seats have exposed metal buckles and hardware. In the hot sun, these buckles can get toasty and possibly burn a child. Yes, you can cover these buckles with a blanket when you leave the car, but that's a hassle. A better bet is to buy a seat with a buckle cover or no exposed metal.

◆ **How heavy is it?** This is a critical factor for infant car seats, but also important for convertibles. Why? First, remember you are lugging that infant seat WITH a baby that will weigh seven to ten lbs. *to start.* When your baby outgrows the infant seat, she will weigh 22 to 30 lbs. *in addition to the seat weight!* To help you shop, we list the weights for major infant car seat brands later in this chapter. What about convertible seats? If you buy one seat and plan to move it from car to car, weight may be a factor here as well.

CAR SEATS

◆ *Buying a new car?* Consider getting a built-in (also called integrated) child safety seat, which is a $200 to $400 option on vehicles like minivans. This is an option for parents who have a child who is older than one of age and heavier than 20 lbs. The only caveat: most integrated seats lack side-impact protection and may not fit small children well. Of course, offerings vary by maker. For example, Volvo offers a integrated booster seat ($500 for two seats) that has won kudos for its innovative design.

Safe & Sound

1 **NEVER BUY A USED CAR SEAT.** If the seat has been in an accident, it may be damaged and no longer safe to use. Bottom line: used seats are a big risk unless you know their history. And the technology of car seats improves every year; a seat that is just five years old may lack important safety features compared to today's models. (And, as we discussed earlier, seats older than five years also have parts that may wear out and fail . . . a big reason not to use an old seat). Another tip: make sure the seat has not been recalled (see the contact info below for the National Highway Traffic Safety Administration). Safety seats made before 2000 may not meet current safety standards (unfortunately, most seats aren't stamped with their year of manufacture, so this may be difficult to determine). The bottom line: risky hand-me-downs aren't worth it. Brand new car seats (which start at $50) aren't that huge of an investment to ensure your child's safety.

2 **GET YOUR SEAT SAFETY CHECKED.** No matter how hard you try to buy and install the best seat for your child, mistakes with installation can still occur. There's nothing like the added peace of mind of having your car seat safety checked by an expert. Such checks are free and widely available. The National Highway Traffic Safety Administration's web site (nhtsa.dot.gov) has a national listing of fitting/inspection stations.

3 **DON'T TRUST THE LEVEL INDICATOR.** Yes, many infant car seats come with "level indicators" and instructions to make sure the seat is installed so the indicator is in the "green" area. When in the green, the seat is supposedly at the correct angle to protect your baby in case of a crash. Nice idea, but thanks to the myriad of back seat designs in dozens of cars, the seat may be incorrectly installed even if the indicator says it is fine. At car seat safety checks, many techs ignore the level indicator and instead use this test: They take a piece of paper

and fold one corner to form a 45-degree angle. Then they place the side of the paper against the back of the infant car seat where the baby's back would lie. When the folded corner is level with the horizon, the seat is at the correct angle—even if the indicator says it ain't so. If you aren't sure your seat is installed to the correct angle, take it to a car seat safety check.

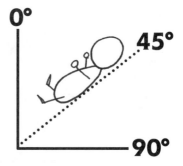

4 **FORGET CAR SEAT ADD-ONS.** We've seen all manner of travel "accessories" for kids in car seats, including bottle holders, activity trays and so on. The problem: all these objects are potential hazards in an accident, flying around the car and possibly striking you (the adult) or your child.

5 **HOW TALL IS TOO TALL?** You'll notice that most child safety seats utilize two types of limits: weight and height. It's the latter limit that creates some confusion among parents. Convertible seats have both a rear and forward facing height limit—this is required by federal law (for those inquiring minds, the standards are FMVSS 208, 213, 225). Most safety techs say the maximum height for a child is when their head is one inch below the top of the shell (the 1″ rule) or if your child's shoulders exceed the height of the top harness slot. The problem: some car seat makers have more strict height limits than the 1″ rule. Here's the frustrating part: kids often outgrow the seat's stated height limit *before* they reach that 1″ rule or their shoulders are taller than the top harness slot, leaving some parents to wonder if they should continue using the seat. The problem is one of interpretation: while the federal law requires every seat to have height limits, car seat makers are free to interpret this rule (and usage of the seat). Some seat makers just interpret the rules more strictly than others. Bottom line: while we understand seat makers might have their own take on federal safety standards, it is generally safe to use a seat until your child's head is 1″ below the top of the seat or their shoulders exceed the top harness slot—even if their height is slightly above the stated limit for the seat.

6 **READ THE DIRECTIONS VERY CAREFULLY.** Many car accidents end in tragedy because a car seat was installed improperly. If you have any questions about the directions, call the company or return the car seat for a model that is easier to use. Another tip: read your vehicle's owner's manual for any special installation instructions. Consult with your auto dealer if you have any additional questions.

What's the number-one problem with car seat installation? Getting a tight fit, say safety techs. Make sure the safety seat is held firmly against the back of the car seat and doesn't wobble from side to side (or front to back). One tip: put your knee on the seat and push down with your full weight while you tighten the seat belt or LATCH strap. This eliminates belt slack and ensures a snug installation.

7 KEEP YOUR CHILD REAR FACING AS LONG AS POSSIBLE. Safety experts agree that the longer a child is rear-facing, the safer the child is in an accident. Why? Newborns and even young toddlers have undeveloped neck muscles—this can lead to an injury, especially if a child is forward-facing in an accident. Good news: more and more seats have higher rear-facing limits. Several infant car seats now work to 30 or 32 lbs. rear-facing. And many convertibles also work to 33 or 35 lbs. rear-facing. The take home message: keep your child rear-facing as long as possible (to age two or three if you can).

8 PUT THE CAR SEAT IN THE BACK SEAT. Air bags and car seats don't mix—several reports of injuries and deaths have been attributed to passenger side air bags that deployed when a car seat was in the front seat. As a result, the safest place for kids is the back seat. In fact, whether the car has an air bag or not, the back is always safer—federal government statistics say putting a child in the back seat instead of the front reduces the risk of death by 27%.

And where is the safest part of the back seat? Safety experts say it's the middle—it is the furthest away from side-impact risks. The only problem with that advice is that some cars have a raised hump in the middle of the back seat that makes it difficult/impossible to safely install a car seat. Another problem: safety seats are best held against the car's back seat by a three-point belt—and some middle seats just have a two-point belt. Finally, consider the LATCH problem we noted above (where many vehicles have no LATCH anchors in the middle of the back seat, only the sides). Bottom line: while the middle of the back seat is the safest spot, sometimes you just can't install a seat there. The next best place is in an outboard position of the back seat with a lap/shoulder belt.

What about side curtain air bags you see in the back seats of some cars? Many new cars come equipped with side-impact air bags or curtains. These air bags are NOT as dangerous as front air bags, as they deploy with much less force in the event of a side impact crash. Therefore, putting a car seat next to a door that has a side curtain air bag is not a danger.

9 **REGISTER YOUR SEAT.** Don't forget to send the registration card back to the manufacturer. Yes, earlier we discussed how some manufacturers fail to send notices to registered users when a car seat is recalled (instead, relying on a media announcement) . . . but register your seat anyway just in case.

10 **PICKUP TRUCKS ARE OFTEN NOT SAFE FOR CAR SEATS.** "A pickup truck should not be considered a family vehicle," concluded an article by the Children's Hospital of Philadelphia on car seat safety—and we agree. Why? "Children in the rear seat of compact extended-cab pickups are nearly five times as likely to be injured as children seated in the back seat of other vehicles," according to a study by Partners for Child Passenger Safety, sponsored by the same hospital.

Of course, not all pickup trucks are alike. Some larger pickup trucks with full-size rear seats do allow car seats (check your vehicle manual for advice). Depending on the vehicle maker, pickup trucks with these seats are called SuperCrew, Double Cab, Crew Cab or Quad Cab. However, pickup trucks with jump seats should NEVER be used with car seats—these are often referred to as Extended Cab or SuperCab trucks. If your pickup truck does not have a rear seat and you must use the front seat (again, not recommended), you must disable the passenger-side air bag.

Even if your pickup truck has a full-size rear seat that allows for car seat installations, think twice about using this vehicle with car seats. Again, studies show that all passenger cars are generally safer in an accident (for kids in a car seat) compared to pickup trucks.

11 **CONSIDER SEATS WITH SIDE IMPACT PROTECTION.** About 25% of all vehicle accidents are side-impact collisions. Over the last few years, more and more seats have been adding side-impact protection. This would be especially important if your vehicle does not have rear-curtain airbags to protect rear occupants. Yes, these seats tend to cost a bit more than those without side-impact protection, but we think it is a wise investment.

Recalls

The National Highway Traffic Safety Administration (NHTSA) posts recalls online (nhtsa.dot.gov) and has a toll-free hot line to check for recalls or to report a safety problem. For info, call (800) 424-9393 or (202) 366-0123. You can have a list of recalled car seats automatically faxed to you at no charge (in case you don't have online access). Note that this is a different governmental agency than the Consumer Product Safety Commission, which regulates and recalls other juvenile products. (For Canadian recalls and safety seat rules, see the special section at the end of this book for more info).

Money-Saving Secrets

1 **BRITAX'S SEMI-ANNUAL SALES.** Britax prevents its car seats from being discounted below a fixed minimum price . . . except twice a year when the company allows sales. These sales are usually held in February and September—for one week, you can find great deals on Britax. Our car seat message board at BabyBargains.com tracks the best deals.

2 **GET A FREE SEAT!** A reader emailed in this great tip—her health insurance carrier provides free infant car seats to parents who complete a parenting class. No specific class is required . . . you just provide proof of completion. And health insurance providers aren't the only ones with car seat deals—check with your auto insurance provider as well. Of course, it is in the insurers best interest to hand out free seats or rebates—each child safety seat used today saves auto insurers $100, private health insurers $45 and the government $45 in costs that would otherwise be incurred from unrestrained kids in auto crashes. Insurers pay out a whopping $175 million in claims annually resulting from crashes in which children age birth to four were traveling unrestrained in motor vehicles (source: "Child Safety Seats: How Large are the Benefits and Who Should Pay?"; The Children's Safety Network). The take-home message: CALL your health and auto insurance providers to see what freebies, rebates and other deals they have for new parents. Another tip: check with your employer. Some companies sell discounted car seats as a family-friendly perk, so check that too.

3 **IF YOU HAVE TWO CARS, YOU DON'T NEED TO BUY TWO INFANT SEATS.** Instead, just buy one seat and then get an extra stay-in-the-car base. While it's not widely known, major infant seat makers sell their auto bases separately for $40 to $70. Stores rarely carry these bases; you'll probably have to buy an extra base online.

4 **COUPONS!** Use Froogle (Froogle.google.com) to compare prices on seats—but then how to get a deal? Find out the latest coupons and discounts by popping over to our Bargain Alert message boards (BabyBargains.com, then Message Boards, then Bargain Alert). Right at the top, we keep a pinned thread with a list of the best online coupon codes, discounts and deals. The thread is updated regularly, so come back to visit when you need a code.

How big is normal?

A quick glance at the "average" growth charts for infants makes you realize why kids outgrow their infant seats so quickly. Most infant seats are only rated for babies up to 22 lbs. and 29" in height. The average male infant hits 22 lbs. at about nine months (at the 50th percentile). But for boys at the top of the growth chart, that could happen at a mere six months! Girls are of course a bit behind that curve, hitting 22 lbs. on average at 12 months of age (at the 50th percentile). Girls at the top of the chart might hit 22 lbs. as soon as eight months.

When a child outgrows his infant seat, he must go into a convertible seat—and there is the rub. Safety advocates say babies should be rear facing to one year of age and AT LEAST 20 lbs. Our advice: make sure the convertible seat you buy is rear-facing to at least 30 lbs.

What about height? Boys hit 29" at around ten months (again the 50th percentile). But some really tall baby boys can hit 29" as soon as eight months. For girls, the average age when most infants hit 29" is 12 months, but it can happen as soon as eight months.

Bottom line: some kids may outgrow their seats by HEIGHT long before they hit the weight limit.

And here's the take home message: keep your child REAR-FACING as long as possible, given your seat's limits. It is the safest way for them to ride.

Source: National Center for Health Statistics, www.cdc.gov/ growthcharts.

5 EXPENSIVE MODELS AREN'T NECESSARILY BETTER. If you spend $100 on a car seat, are you getting one that's twice as safe as a seat that's $50? Not necessarily. Often, all you get for that additional money is plush padding and extras like pillows. Do infants notice the extra padding? No, not in our opinion. Sure, you need SOME padding, but the minimum is fine for most infants. We do agree that this becomes more of an issue as a baby gets older—toddlers may be uncomfortable in less-padded seats for longer car trips. But since infants sleep most of the time, we think babies under a year of age don't notice the quilted fabric you paid extra bucks for. Bottom line: the $50 seat may be just as safe and probably as comfortable for baby.

The Name Game: Reviews of Selected Manufacturers

Here are our reviews of the major car seat brands. FYI: many of the infant seats reviewed here are sold as travel systems that combine a car seat and stroller; the strollers are reviewed separately in the next chapter. Of course, you don't have to buy a travel system—nearly all infant seats are sold separately.

Special note: this section gives you an overview of each brand; we review each model seat separately later in this chapter! s

The Ratings

A **Excellent**—*our top pick!*
B **Good**— *above average quality, prices, and creativity.*
C **Fair**—*could stand some improvement.*
D **Poor**—*yuck! Could stand some major improvement.*

Baby Trend *For a dealer near you, call (800) 328-7363, (909) 902-5568, Web: babytrend.com.* Baby Trend scored a coup when its Flex-Loc infant car seat ($90-$100) won top honors as a Best Buy in a *Consumer Reports* 2007 report. And, new for 2009, the Flex Loc is rated to 30 lbs. Yet Baby Trend, the company, has been dogged by poor customer service and other glitches. Example: the availability of Baby Trend's car seats has been inconsistent in recent years. In a past edition, we recommended their infant seat, only to have Baby Trend stop selling the seat as a stand-alone model (you could only buy it as part of a travel system—with one of Baby Trend's inferior strollers). As of this writing, you can buy their infant seats as a stand-alone item, but not all chain stores stock it. And Baby Trend's customer service is among the worst in the business, further dampening our enthusiasm for this brand.

Safety Track Record. There have been no recalls on these seats as of this writing.

Baby Trend's infant seats are reviewed on page 382.

Britax *(888) 4-BRITAX or (704) 409-1700. Web: britax.com.* European-based Britax came to the U.S. car seat market in 1996 and changed the rules of the game: the company introduced several premium car seats that were packed with extra safety features . . . and sold at premium prices. Britax was the first seat maker to cross the $200 price level (and some of its seats now top $300).

Britax's success is due to both its innovation (side impact crash protection, a tether can that can be used in rear or forward facing position) and the seats' ease of use. On that latter score, Britax's seats are easy to install (they are a favorite of safety techs) and easy for parents to use (the harness adjustments, etc).

That said, Britax isn't perfect. The company has had a dozen safety recalls in the last ten years (most for minor issues) . . . and in the past couple of years, the company hasn't introduced many new models, instead content to sit on its big lead in the car seat biz. Britax has tried to launch a series of companion strollers to boost sales of its infant car seat—that effort has found little success. And a push to sell less-expensive (and scaled down) versions of its car seats in a deal with Fisher Price flopped in 2007.

That said, Britax still makes among the country's top-selling convertible seats (Roundabout, Marathon) and is one of the best-respected brands in this category.

For 2009, Britax will debut a replacement for its poor-selling infant seat, the Companion. The new model (the Chaperone) will correct several problems with the Companion: it will have a higher weight limit (30 lbs.) and feature an improved headrest and no re-thread harness. See a more detailed review of this new seat later in this chapter.

Safety track record: Despite its emphasis on safety, Britax hasn't been immune to recalls for production defects and other snafus—the company has had several major recalls in the past ten years. But the company has handled these responsibly, offering repair kits and fessing up to its mistakes in a timely manner. Yes, in a previous book, we complained about Britax's slow response to a past recall, but the company has improved its customer service in recent years.

Another plus: Britax has a replacement program if your seat has been in an accident.

Britax's infant seat is reviewed on page 383. Britax's convertible seat reviews begin on page 396. Britax's booster seat reviews begin on page 428.

EPP vs. EPS foam

When you take the fancy fabric cover off a car seat, you'll notice that many car seats are lined with foam for crash protection. Car seat makers use two types of foam: EPS and EPP. EPS (expanded polystyrene foam) is a hard yet lightweight foam used in bicycle helmets. EPP (expanded polypropylene foam) is similar to EPS but softer (and hence more comfortable) for older toddlers. The take-home message: either foam is fine, but more makers are using EPP foam as an upgrade..

Century. *This brand, owned by Graco, was discontinued in 2002.*

Combi *(800) 992-6624, (803) 802-8416; Web: combi-intl.com.* While better known for its strollers, Combi is a small player in the car seat market. The main emphasis here is on infant seats that pair with Combi strollers to form travel systems, although Combi does sell a couple of convertible and booster seats as well.

Combi's infant car seat line up includes the Shuttle (formerly referred to as the Centre) and the Connection (which is being phased out this year). All of Combi's strollers work with the Shuttle.

In the convertible seat category, Combi has a couple of niche offerings. The Zeus ($300), which rotates from rear to forward-facing without having to reinstall it, has an anti-rebound bar and side impact protection. New for 2009, the Coccoro ($200) is a compact convertible that can fit three seats across in most vehicles.

Safety track record. Combi has had two major recalls in recent years: the Avatar convertible seat in 2005 and the Centre/Shuttle infant seats in 2007.

Combi's infant seats are reviewed on page 385. Combi's convertible seats are reviewed on page 402; boosters are on page 430.

Cosco *(812) 372-0141 or 514-323-5701 for a dealer in Canada). Web: djgusa.com.* Owned by Canadian conglomerate Dorel Industries, Cosco is a big player in the car seat market with over six million seats sold each year. As one blogger once put it,

---

That new car seat smell?

Given all the toy recalls for lead paint and the general anxiety among parents regarding environmental hazards, it's no surprise that environmental groups have turned an eye toward that mandatory safety item everyone must buy: the car seat.

HealthyCar.org tested dozens of car seats for toxic chemicals, measuring the amount of bromine, chlorine and lead and assigning ratings from low to high concern.

The results showed some car seat makers do a better job at keeping toxic chemicals to a minimum. Example: Sunshine Kids scored at the top of the ratings for the "healthiest" car seats—that's probably thanks to the company's intentional efforts to use a unique flame-retardant treatment that nearly eliminates out-gassing.

Other companies had a mix of good and bad news: Britax generally scored well, but a couple of Britax fabrics (specifically Onyx) had high levels of bromine.

You can see the entire results at HealthyCar.org.

Dorel/Cosco puts the industrial in the Baby Industrial Complex.

Dorel/Cosco sells its seats under a variety of brand names: Eddie Bauer, Alpha Elite, Alpha Sport, Safety 1st and Maxi Cosi, which is Dorel's European subsidiary.

In previous years, Cosco would take the same basic seat, change the fabric pad and sell it under various brand names, depending on the outlet. Hence, you'd see the same seat sold in Wal-Mart under the Cosco brand, an upgraded version in Target sold under the Safety 1st nameplate and then a top-of-the-line model sold under the Eddie Bauer moniker at chains like Babies R Us.

Realizing parents aren't likely to be fooled by such small distinctions, Cosco told us they plan to make each brand more unique. So, you'll see basic seats under the Cosco name in discount stores . . . but Safety 1st car seats will now have brand-specific technology like "SecureTech" (to make sure a harness is latched correctly) and SofTech (foam cushions).

Perhaps Cosco's most unique brand is the Maxi Cosi line of car seats—since these are imported (and designed) by Cosco's European division, these seats aren't simply rehashes of Cosco's domestic seats. The Maxi Cosi car seats pair with a line of hot-selling strollers under the Quinny brand (another Dorel Euro import).

For 2009, Cosco has made only small, cosmetic changes to its line of car seats—there are no new major models. We'll review the specific seats later in this chapter.

Safety track record: Cosco's safety track record has been marred by recalls—20+ at last count since 1990. Now, you could point out that since Cosco is the largest seller of car seats in North America, it follows the company would have more recalls than a smaller competitor. True, but it is the *type* of safety lapses that bother us.

Example: Cosco allegedly sold hundreds of thousands of Touriva convertible seats AFTER the company knew a plastic notch in the seat caused skull fractures in low-speed crashes. That allegation came to light in an investigation by the *Chicago Tribune* (July 14, 2007, "When car-seat safety, commerce collide"). Despite Dorel's own engineers labeling the notch a "child safety concern," Dorel continued to make Tourivas with the notch for three years. Why? The Tribune alleges that Cosco didn't want to shut down its production lines (losing roughly $4 million in Touriva sales) to switch molds to a notch-less seat.

For the record, Dorel maintains it did investigate the notch allegation and its own testing confirmed "these recesses will not injure a child." When asked point blank if it delayed fixing the Touriva to rack up extra sales, the company replied: "The suggestion that Dorel would sacrifice the safety of children for a few extra dollars of profit is insulting and not worthy of further comment."

car seats

Yet, this isn't the first time Cosco allegedly put profits ahead of safety—in 1996, the American Academy of Pediatrics told parents NOT to use shield boosters (a type of booster seat that uses a shield to hold a child in place) because of numerous injuries. Yet Dorel/Cosco continued to sell shield boosters until 2004, selling ten million of the $20 boosters in a 20-year period. Cosco has settled dozens of shield-booster lawsuits (without admitting fault), according to the *Chicago Tribune*.

Reviews of Cosco's infant seats start on page 387, while Cosco's convertible seat reviews start on page 403. Cosco's booster seats are reviewed starting on page 431.

Eddie Bauer. *These seats are made by Cosco; see the previous review for details.*

Evenflo *(800) 233-5921 or (937) 415-3300. In Canada, PO Box 1598, Brantford, Ontario, N3T 5V7. (905) 337-2229. Web: evenflo.com.* Evenflo has struggled in this category, thanks to a string of disastrous recalls and other snafus. Yes, Evenflo has tried to add innovative features (mostly to their convertible seats), but the company has had a tough time overcoming its poor reputation in the marketplace. All in all, Evenflo often seems outflanked in the car seat market; Britax trumps them on safety features and Graco outguns them in infant seats and travel systems. Even downscale Cosco has a hotter license (Eddie Bauer).

Judging from parent reviews posted to our web site, Evenflo has a ways to go to win the hearts of car seat buyers. Ease of use (or lack thereof) is a common gripe, with seats that have difficult-to-adjust belts and other frustrations.

Evenflo's newest seat is the Symphony, a convertible seat that works up to 100 lbs. and features an easier-to-use LATCH connector. We'll review that seat and all Evenflo's models in depth later in this chapter.

Safety track record: Evenflo's safety track record is mixed, with many recalls for their infant car seats during the past 15 years. Example: the 2008 recall of one million Discovery infant seats that separated from their bases in a crash. This followed a 2006 recall of the Embrace infant seat for defective handles that unexpectedly released, causing some infants to tumble out of the seat. If that sounds familiar, you may remember the huge recalls of Evenflo infant car seats from the 1990's for a similar issue.

Reviews of Evenflo's infant seats start on page 389, while Evenflo's convertible seat reviews start on page 404. Evenflo's booster seats are reviewed on page 432.

First Years *Web: TheFirstYears.com.* When baby gear and toy maker Learning Curve acquired Compass in 2007, the company's First Years brand incorporated Compass' car seats into their baby gear line. Compass debuted in 2004 with a well-received booster seat, but the company lacked the marketing clout to compete with the big boys like Britax and Graco.

The First Years car seat line includes an infant seat (the Via), a convertible (True Fit) and a booster (the Folding Booster car seat). The company's niche seems to be car seats that are a step up in features, safety and design from the mass market brands like Dorel/Cosco . . . but priced below the premium that Britax charges.

Despite the new corporate parent, these seats are still hard to find at retail (but are sold online). And so far, The First Years hasn't introduced any new models, content to add features to existing seats. Example: in 2009, the company will debut a premium version of the True Fit (the C670) that will feature an anti-rebound bar.

Safety track record. First Years/Compass recalled the I420 infant car seat in 2006 because of a defective harness strap.

First Years' infant seat is reviewed on page 389; their booster seat is reviewed on page 434.

car seats

Seat cover-ups provide warmth

Okay, you aren't supposed to put baby in a car seat with a bulky coat. But what if you live in, say, Maine and its currently ten degrees outside as you read this? Try a cover-up that fits OVER the car seat and hence doesn't compromise the seat's safety. One of our favorites: **Kiddopotamus's**
"Poppit" ($28), a multi-purpose cover-up that can be used as a front carrier warmer. . . or on top of a car seat. The same company also offers several other innovative travel products, including the RayShade (a cover for strollers). For more details, call (800) 772-8339 or web: kiddopotamus.com.

What about other infant body pillows or warmers that fit between baby and the car seat? If it does not come in the box with your infant or convertible car seat, we wouldn't use it. Add-on or after-market products that are not manufacturer-tested may compromise the seat's safety. The same thing goes for car seat toy bars or special mirrors so you can see baby from the front seat. Don't use them in a vehicle—they could come loose in an accident, becoming a dangerous projectile.

Fisher-Price Fisher Price car seats were re-packaged Britax seats—scaled down with fewer features but with lower prices. These seats were discontinued in 2007.

Graco *(800) 345-4109, (610) 286-5951. Web: gracobaby.com.* Graco's success in the car seat market boils down to one model: its best-selling infant seat, the SnugRide. That gave Graco a major leg-up in the travel system market (travel systems combine both an infant car seat and stroller). As a result, when you walk into chain stores, you'll see many Graco car seats.

The SnugRide comes in two models: the basic version (that works up to 22 lbs.) and the new SnugRide 32, which (as you might guess) works up to 32 lbs.

Graco has had less success with its convertible seat line, which lacks the extra safety features seen in Britax seats. To compete, Graco offers seats that are $100 to $200 less expensive than Britax. Examples include a basic model (ComfortSport), a model that reclines (Cozy Cline, formerly the SafeSeat) and the unique Nautilus 3-in-1. The latter seat is forward-facing only, but works up to 65 lbs. with a five-point harness (like many Britax models) and then converts to a high back booster to 100 lbs. The same seat then becomes a backless booster for older kids (hence the 3 in 1 moniker).

Graco has more success with their booster line, which includes the TurboBooster and AirBooster.

What is the lightest infant car seat carrier?

Here at *Baby Bargains* we have Ivy League-trained scientists who help us determine important stuff like which infant car seat weighs the least (and hence, is easiest to lug around). Oh, we're just kidding. Actually, we the authors just went to our local baby store and stood there in the aisles lifting each infant seat and saying things like "Yep, this one is lighter!" For this edition, we actually employed a scale to get accurate readings (and you thought only the folks in lab coats *at Consumer Reports* got to play with such toys). Our official results: the lightest seat is the Evenflo Discovery (5.5 lbs.) followed by the Graco SnugRide (8 lbs.). The heaviest seats? That crown goes to the Peg Perego Primo Viaggio at a whopping 10 lbs. Weighing in at 9.9 lbs. is the Combi Shuttle and the Graco SnugRide 32 weights 9.75 lbs. while the Compass 1420, the Chicco KeyFit and Baby Trend Flex-Loc are 9 lbs. We list the weights for infant car seat carriers in a chart later in this chapter. Of course, the weight of an infant seat isn't the only factor we used to decide which was best, but it certainly is important.

Safety track record: Compared to brands like Dorel/Cosco and Evenflo, Graco's safety record is good. That doesn't mean Graco isn't perfect, of course. In 2007, Graco recalled 277,000 ComfortSports for a mis-assembled anchor belt. Four years prior to that recall, Graco recalled 650,000 SnugRide infant seats for missing hardware used to attach the carrier to the base. A recall for this same seat for a similar issue happened in 2002 as well.

Graco's infant seat is reviewed on page 390. Graco's convertible seat is reviewed on page 407. Graco's booster seats are reviewed starting on page 434.

IMMI. *See SafeGuard.*

Orbit *(650)704-0985. Web: OrbitBaby.com* "High style" aren't two words you'd normally associate with a travel system, that combination of infant car seat and stroller often sold in discount stores. Orbit aims to change that—their high-end travel system is the brainchild of two Palo Alto-based designers whose goal is to inject a bit of style into a bland market.

Orbit's car seat is, well, different. Described on a parenting blog as looking like a crockpot (bummer that we didn't think of that first), the Orbit infant seat has two soft carrying straps and is only sold as part of a system (base and stroller) for a whopping $900.

Orbit has slowly expanded its line in recent years, adding a toddler car seat ($360) that "docks" with its car base and fits on the stroller frame.

While we give Orbit bonus points for creativity, the high prices of this seat sharply limit its appeal.

Safety track record: No recalls as of this writing.
The Orbit infant seat is reviewed on page 393.

Peg Perego *(260) 482-8191. Web: perego.com.* Peg's single entry is an infant car seat, the Primo Viaggio. Launched to stop the loss of stroller sales to cheaper "travel systems," the Viaggio has gone on to be quite a hit, despite its relatively high price tag (about $100 more than Graco's popular seat). Chalk that up to Peg's sense of style (the Viaggio features luxury Italian fabrics) and pairing with Peg's popular strollers. In recent years, Perego has only made a few small modifications to the seat, most notably adding side impact protection.

Safety track record: While Peg had two early recalls on their infant seat (in 2001 and 2002), the company has been subsequently recall-free (as of this writing).

Peg Perego's Primo Viaggio is reviewed on page 394.

Radian. *See Sunshine Kids below.*

Recaro *(800) 8-RECARO; 248-364-3818. Web: recaro.com.* Recaro is a 100-year old German-based company well known in Europe for their racing seats and other safety gear. After watching Britax's success on this site of the Atlantic, Recaro decided to give the U.S. market a try. So far, Recaro has had limited success in cracking the market (their prices are too high), but we give them credit for persistence as well as rolling out innovative models. "These seats scream quality," said one of our readers—you can tell when you take a Recaro seat out of the box that the company does NOT skimp on construction details. So if you can afford it, we suggest giving these seats a look-see.

Recaro entered the U.S. market with three booster seat offerings (the current line-up includes the Young Sport, the SIP and the Vivo). In 2007, Recaro debuted its first convertible seat (the Como, $250), which has a five-point harness that works up to 70 lbs. The new Signo ($290) is similar to the Como, but adds an adjustable headrest.

In the past year, Recaro revised its booster seats and lowered prices—the Vivo and Vivo Lite sell for under $100 and work up to 100 lbs. Recaro's previous booster seats only worked up to 80 lbs. and often sold for more than $200.

Bottom line: Recaro makes impressive seats, but their thin distribution makes seeing one in person difficult.

Safety track record: Recaro had a recall on its convertible seats (Signo and Como) in 2007 for a defective harness.

Recaro's convertible seats are reviewed on page 410 and booster seats start on page 437.

Consumer Reports crash tests vs our ratings

Every time *Consumer Reports* comes out with a report on car seats, our phones and email light up—many readers want to know how we sometimes come to different conclusions as to which are the best car seats. It's quite simple: *Consumer Reports* actually crash tests car seats, something we don't have the budget to do here at *Baby Bargains*. When we rate a car seat, we look at the seat's overall features, ease of use and value based on parent feedback and our own hands-on inspections. We also look at the company's recall track record and (if available) any *Consumer Reports'* crash test reports. Even though we might use different rating methodologies, most of the time we agree with *Consumer Reports*. In the case of a major discrepancy, we'll often comment on this on our blog at BabyBargains.com.

SafeGuard *(317) 896-9531. Web: safeguardseat.com.* Safeguard is a new player in the car seat biz. Owned by IMMI, Safeguard's parent actually makes much of the hardware you see in other seats such as Britax. So why go into competition with your customers? IMMI has grown increasingly frustrated in recent years, as new innovations it pioneered went unused in car seats. So, it decided to roll out seats to demonstrate there is a market for advanced safety features.

SafeGuard's two offerings include the eponymous (and very expensive) SafeGuard, a forward-facing seat with five-point harness for toddlers weighing 22 to 65 lbs. SafeGuard's Go Booster works from 30 to 60 lbs. with a five-point harness and up to 100 lbs. as a booster.

While we're always happy to see more competition in the car seat market (there have been more players getting out than in recently), it's hard to really know whether IMMI wants to be a long term player as a manufacturer of car seats . . . or just convince other car seat makers to adopt its inventions. Time will tell, but meanwhile, at least parents have a new choice when it comes to upper-end seats.

Safety track record: No recalls as of this writing.

SafeGuard's forward-facing seat is reviewed on page 411. SafeGuard's booster seat is reviewed on page 439.

Safety 1st. *These seats are made by Cosco; see earlier review.*

Sunshine Kids *(888) 336-7909; skjp.com.* Sunshine Kids makes a variety of juvenile products, but it is their innovative Radian convertible car seats that stand out here. The Radian's (which comes in two versions, one that works up to 65 lbs. and another to 80) claim to fame is it is the only folding car seat. Sunshine accomplishes this by omitting the typical base you see on a convertible seat—this clever design trick makes the Radian perfect for car pools. The Radian 80 is also the only convertible seat that works up to 80 lbs. with a five-point harness—the highest capacity on the market.

New for 2009, Sunshine Kids will roll out a version of the Radian with side impact protection (dubbed the Radian XT) for $280.

In the past year, Sunshine Kids debuted the Monterrey ($130), the company's first booster seat offering. The Monterrey features a deep seat with width adjustment. The only bummer for Sunshine: its distribution is rather sparse. You won't see these seats in chain stores—instead, you'll probably have to hunt down a seat in a specialty store or online.

Safety track record: No recalls as of this writing.

Sunshine Kids convertible seat is reviewed on page 413.

Teutonia *teutoniausa.com.* Owned by Graco, this German brand of strollers has a matching infant car seat (the t-tario 32), which is the same as the Graco SnugRide 32.

Infant Car Seats (model by model reviews)

BABY TREND FLEX-LOC ADJUSTABLE BACK

Price: Latch-Lock Adjustable Back: $90-100. Extra bases $40.

Type: Infant seat, five-point harness.

Limits: 22 lbs. and 28.5″. New models will work up to 30 lbs.

Pros: Top rated seat in recent crash test.

Cons: Carrier is quite heavy; Hard to find in some stores—mostly sold as part of a travel system with an inferior stroller.

Comments: Baby Trend scored a coup when the Flex-Loc infant seat landed a "Best Buy" rating in a *Consumer Reports* 2007 report.

The seat itself has nice features . . . you get two harness slots, an adjustable crotch strap, EPS foam for head protection and a machine washable pad. The base is adjustable and uses an all-steel connection

Leaving On a Jet Plane

Which car seats can be taken on an airplane? Most of the infant and convertible seats reviewed in this section are certified for use in an airplane. But will they fit? That's a tougher question—each airline has different size seats. Hence, wide car seats like the Evenflo Triumph may not fit (especially if you're required to keep the armrests down for take-off). Check with the airline before you get to the airport if you have questions about car seat compatibility. A better bet: simple seats like the Graco ComfortSport (which is narrow and light in weight) usually do the trick.

Here's a listing of convertible car seats with the narrowest bases: Graco ComfortSport (17.0″), Safety 1st Intera (16.5″) and Cosco Touriva (16.3″). By comparison, a seat like the Britax Marathon is 19.5″ wide.

FYI: There is a way to avoid lugging your own car seat on a plane: the FAA has approved the first child safety harness for airlines, the ***AmSafe Aviation Cares*** (KidsFlySafe.com). This $75 seat can be purchased online and provides additional belt and shoulder harnesses for a child weighing 22 to 44 lbs.—perfect for infants that have outgrown their infant seat (and for parents who don't want to lug a heavy convertible seat in the airport).

for the seat—that provides a better measure of safety in case of an accident. You can use the seat with or without its base, another plus.

The downsides? Well, the carrier is quite heavy at 9.4 lbs. And while Baby Trend plans to release a 2009 update for the Flex-Loc that works up to 30 lbs., at press time, the seat is just 22. That's behind the curve of competitors like Chicco (30) and Graco's revised SnugRide (32). And that probably explains while parents with bigger babies complained their infants quickly outgrew this seat. More criticism: the handle release button can be hard to reach and stiff to release. And the strange triangle handle takes a bit of getting used to.

While we will recommend this seat, let us warn you that Baby Trend is a flakey company to deal with: despite winning good reviews from several sources (including this book), Baby Trend often lets its seats run out of stock. Or it suddenly makes the seat only available as part of a travel system, paired with one of Baby Trend's inferior strollers. Part of this stems from Baby Trend's poor distribution—this seat is only sold in a handful of chain stores (mainly, Babies R Us).

We have also lowered this seat's rating a bit to reflect Baby Trend's customer service, or lack thereof. Unanswered emails, unreturned phone calls and a general "we don't care" attitude mar Baby Trend's brand.

Rating: B

BABY TREND EZ-LOC ADJUSTABLE BACK

Comments: This seat is the same as the Flex-Loc above, but features a rigid or ISOFIX version of LATCH (the Flex-Loc has a flexible webbing-based LATCH like you see on most other seats). This seat is already referred to as the Rigid Latch-Loc. Fair warning: the rigid LATCH connection doesn't work well with some vehicles.

Rating: B

BRITAX CHAPERONE

Price: $200-$230

Type: Infant seat, five-point harness.

Limits: 30 lbs.

Pros: Anti-rebound bar, side-impact protection, EPS foam.

Cons: Price, not compatible with most strollers.

Comments: Britax's previous infant car seat, the Companion, was a critical success but commercial flop. The seat drew kudos from safety techs for its design, which included an anti-rebound bar, side impact protection and ease of installation. We gave it an A- in our last book.

But . . . at $200, the seat was nearly twice as expensive as competitors. And the low weight limit (22 lbs.) combined with the hefty carrier weight (it tipped the scales at 10+ lbs.) made the Companion a non-starter for most parents. Despite Britax's success

infant seats

in selling expensive convertible seats, the company couldn't transfer that magic to the infant seat category. One big reason: Britax's infant seats don't fit in many universal stroller frames . . . and Britax's own strollers have been flops.

So, back to the drawing board. The new Chaperone will work up to 30 lbs. and will be compatible with a new stroller (also dubbed the Chaperone). But the price will still be high, estimated to be $200 to $230. The Chaperone should be out by the time you read this. While we did see prototypes of both the Chaperone infant seat and stroller, we haven't seen the final production versions as of press time.

Will Britax's new infant seat break the company's streak of washouts in this category? Stay tuned to our blog for updates. **Rating: Not Yet.**

Chicco KeyFit 30

Price: $160-180, extra base $70.
Type: Infant seat, five-point harness.
Limits: 30 lbs., 30".
Pros: EPS foam, newborn insert, works with some Chicco strollers.
Cons: Doesn't work with most universal stroller frames. Skimpy sunshade. Heavy carrier.

Comments: The Chicco KeyFit scored at the top of *Consumer Reports* latest car seat report and that has helped propel the sales of this already popular seat into best-seller status. And it is well deserved.

The Chicco KeyFit boasts a nice list of features: a seat lined with EPS foam for improved side impact protection, thick seat padding, multi-position canopy and comfort grip handle. Chicco hired a former Graco engineer who worked on the SnugRide to design the KeyFit and it shows in the details . . . the base has a "single-pull" LATCH adjustment, a leveling foot to account for uneven back seats and even a smooth underside to keep from damaging your back seat upholstery. As you'd expect from Chicco, the fashion of this seat boasts Italian flair and there is even a newborn insert for a better fit.

FYI: Chicco makes two versions of the seat: the original KeyFit had a 22-pound limit. The KeyFit 30 has a (you guessed it) 30-pound limit. Between the two, we'd suggest the KeyFit 30 as it is only $10 more than the 22-pound version.

Our readers have been very positive about the KeyFit's ease of use, lauding the no-twist, easy-to-adjust straps, the ability to leave the handle in the up position when driving (most seats require it to be lowered), and overall ease of installation. Quibbles? The KeyFit carrier weighs nine lbs., a tad heavier than other seats. And the sunshade is too small. A few readers also report the fabric doesn't breathe, so the seat can get hot.

The KeyFit 30 can fit into both Chicco's Cortina and Trevi strollers. That's probably the KeyFit's key weakness: besides Chicco's own strollers, you can't fit the KeyFit into other strollers or stroller frames (which mostly work with Graco or Peg seats).

Overall, this is an excellent seat that is highly recommended.

Rating: A

COMBI CONNECTION & SHUTTLE

Price: $170 (Connection), $150-170 (Shuttle). Extra base: $60.

Type: Infant seat, five-point harness

Limits: 22 lbs., 29".

Pros: EPS foam, one-pull harness adjustment, nice padding.

Cons: Not easy to use. Shuttle doesn't work with Combi's stroller frame. Funky belt paths.

Comments: The Combi Connection and Shuttle (pictured) infant car seats have similar features: while the bases are slightly different,

The NYC Taxi Dilemma

Here's a common email we get from parents in New York and other urban areas: are there any portable car seats that can be used in taxis? Something that is lightweight, easy to install and collapses to fit inside a small purse when not in use? Well, the answer is no—there's no perfect solution. But we have a few ideas. Let's break out our advice for New Yorkers by age:

◆ *Infant (birth to six months).* The safest way for an infant to ride in a taxi is in an infant car seat. Most (but not all) can be strapped in without the stay-in-the-car base. However, always check the manual BEFORE buying any seat to confirm this feature.

◆ *Babies/toddlers (six months to four years).* Many infant car seats can be used up to 30 or 32 pounds—use the seat as long as you can. For older babies, there aren't many good options. If you use a car service to go to or from an airport, you can usually request a car seat in advance. Otherwise, using public transport is probably the safest option.

◆ *Older kids.* A booster seat is the safest way to go—and a simple backless booster such as the Graco TurboBooster (backless version) is lightweight and portable.

infant seats

both have carriers with EPS foam for crash protection, comfort pads on the harness and one-pull harness adjustment. The Connection costs about $20 more than the lower price Shuttle, but the Connection does add a bit more padding (Combi's "egg shock" foam in the head area) and an infant body pillow.

The biggest different between the Connection and Shuttle: the Shuttle has an anti-rebound bar, which keeps the seat more stable in the case of a crash.

The Shuttle comes in two trim levels, regular and EX. There isn't much difference except a bit more padding and a deluxe canopy on the EX model. For 2009, Combi has improved the Shuttle's base, making it smaller and easier to use, thanks to a new locking clip design. But the belt path on the new Shuttle base had us scratching our heads: it is way too complex compared to other seats.

Combi plans to discontinue the Connection some time in 2009, but it is still being sold as of press time.

FYI: All of Combi's strollers work with the Shuttle infant seats. This is a change from years past, when some strollers worked only with certain Combi infant car seats.

In their most recent car seat report, *Consumer Reports* only tested an older version of the Shuttle (called the Centre), which scored at the bottom of their rankings. Why? Ease of use, or lack thereof. And our readers agree: the Shuttle has a hard-to-adjust handle, making the seat difficult to get in and out of car. Others knocked the flimsy canopy and hard to adjust belts. The carrier is also heavy at ten lbs.

As for the Connection, (with the exception of installation issues) parents were generally more positive in their ratings, although several noted the fabric started to pill and fuzz after just a few months of use. Unfortunately, the Connection works only with Combi's most

Fabric vs. Model Names

When shopping for a car seat online, you'll note that some sites refer to seats by their fabric AND model name. For example, Amazon sells the Britax Roundabout Onyx. Britax is the manufacturer; Roundabout is the model name; Onyx is the fabric.

In this section, we refer to brands and models of car seats—since color or fabric patterns change frequently, we don't reference this. Just beware that a seat like the Graco Metropolitan SnugRide and Graco Family Tree SnugRide (as examples) are basically the same seat. Yes, the fabric might be fancier on one version, but you are talking the same basic seat! When we recommend a seat like the Graco SnugRide, our recommendation applies to all the fabrics/versions of that seat.

expensive strollers.

Regarding safety, Combi's track record has been mixed, with several major recalls in recent years. Example: a 2008 recall for 67,000 Shuttle and Centre seats after testing revealed the seats could separate from the base in a crash.

Combi's car seats are a prime example of what's wrong with this company: confusing, overlapping products that are overpriced and outmoded (note that Combi doesn't have an infant seat that goes to 30 lbs.).

Rating: C

COSCO DESIGNER 22 *See the Eddie Bauer Deluxe infant seat below. The Cosco Designer 22 is the same as this seat.*

EDDIE BAUER DELUXE (AKA DESIGNER 22, SAFETY 1ST STARTER)
Price: $90; extra base: $50.
Type: Infant seat, five-point harness
Limits: 22 lbs., 29".
Pros: Low price.
Cons: Recalled in 2006; problems with base.

Comments: Like most Cosco seats, the Eddie Bauer Deluxe infant seat is sold under a wide variety of aliases (the Designer 22, Safety 1st Starter, the Cosco Alpha Elite, etc.) . . . but the features are the same. Basically, this is a simple infant seat with the same features you see in most other seats on the market: an adjustable base, five-point harness, canopy, etc. The only difference: the Cosco version of this seat lacks a front adjustment to tighten the belts (that appears on all other models). What's missing? Side-impact protection, for one. EPS foam for additional crash protection (which is almost now a standard feature) isn't here either. Of course, this seat sells for $90—that's about 30% to 50% less than seats with those features, so we guess you can call that a trade-off.

FYI: A scaled down version of this infant seat is sold as the Safety 1st Starter for $80 online. A version of the Designer 22 with more padding is sold as the Safety 1st Designer for $73 on Amazon.

The Eddie Bauer Deluxe infant seat has seen its share of troubles in the past year. First, in 2006, Cosco recalled this seat for loose handle screws that were a choking hazard. Then Cosco launched a "customer satisfaction program" to handle complaints about the base not fitting in some vehicles. Notice we didn't say recall—Cosco changed the base and offered the fixed base to existing owners . . . but only if folks knew to call in and request it. Shame on Cosco—the company should have issued a formal recall and sent the new base to all registered owners.

Given Cosco's past safety record and troubles with this seat's base, we will take a pass on recommending this infant seat.

Rating: D+

EDDIE BAUER SUREFIT *See the Safety 1st OnBoard.*

EVENFLO DISCOVERY

Price: $50 to $70; extra base $25.

Type: Infant car seat, three-point harness.

Limits: 22 lbs., 26".

Pros: Lightweight carrier, low price. Z-shaped handle is easy to carry.

Cons: Not easy to use.

Comments: This bare-bones seat is sold in discount stores like Wal-Mart. The carrier (at 5.5 lbs.) is among the lightest on the market. And yes, Evenflo has added EPS foam to the seat (a few years after the competition). But . . . you don't get many features with this seat—the base doesn't adjust, there is just one crotch strap position and so on. Want to adjust the straps? You'll have to do that from the back of the seat, a major pain.

That probably explains why the Evenflo Discovery scored at the very bottom of *Consumer Reports* 2007 report on infant car seats—that report weighed ease of use heavily in their rankings. And our feedback from parents is similar: yes, this seat is cheap, but in this case, you get what you pay for.

Rating: D

SuddenStop

Driving around here in our home town of Boulder, CO, we have all manner of pedestrians and bicyclists who add new meaning to the word Kamikaze. Without warning, we'll have one of these daredevils throw themselves out in the street in the path of our car, forcing us to slam on our brakes. Of course, given the traffic in our town, this always puts us at risk of being rear-ended.

If this sounds familiar, one product we discovered may be a great solution: the **SuddenStop** license plate frame (web: SuddenStop.com). This $30 gizmo attaches to any license plate and rapidly flashes a bright red LED when you slam on your brakes. We saw a prototype of this product at a trade show and were impressed—the SuddenStop would make a great gift.

With over two million rear-end collisions a year in the U.S., we'd hope this technology would find its way into all vehicles.

EVENFLO EMBRACE
Price: $80 to $95; extra base $40.
Type: Infant car seat, five-point harness.
Pros: Three-position adjustable base, easier to release base and handle.
Cons: Recalled in 2007 for faulty handle.
Limits: 22 lbs., 29".

Comments: Here, in a nutshell, is why Evenflo is in last place in the car seat biz: the Embrace infant seat was supposed to be a fresh start for Evenflo, after their last major car seat (the PortAbout) was recalled for failing a *Consumer Reports* crash test in 2005. The Embrace features a new, easier release mechanism for the carrier (this was a gripe for past models). The seat also has a three-position adjustable base and Z-handle with the "Press 'n' Go" system that releases the handle with one hand.

Yet, Evenflo had to recall 450,000 Embrace infant seats in 2007 after 679 reports of the handle of the carrier unexpectedly releasing, causing 160 injuries to children. (As a side note, 679 reports? 160 injuries? At what point did Evenflo think it was time to pull the plug?).

If that sounds familiar, then you may remember the massive recalls Evenflo suffered in the late 90's for their On My Way infant car seat with a very similar problem.

About the best we can say for this seat is it is a bit easier to install and use than the Evenflo Discovery . . . but that's not saying much. Given the past safety issues with this seat and Evenflo's track record, we say pass.
Rating: D+

FIRST YEARS VIA
Price: $120
Type: Infant seat, five-point harness.
Limits: 22 lbs., 30".
Pros: Carrier is completely lined with foam. Widest, deepest carrier. Light weight.
Cons: Must use carrier with base. Doesn't fit into shopping carts or stroller frames.

Comments: The First Years Via is a very good infant seat . . . which is impossible to find in most retail stores.

That, in a nutshell, is what is wrong with The First Years and their efforts in this category. When the company bought out Compass in 2007, we had high hopes they'd expand distribution of Compass' innovative (yet under-marketed) seats. Yet two years later, the seats languish in no man's land.

Take the Via, which features a carrier entirely lined in EPS foam (yet still weighing only 8.4 lbs.), a padded handle, side impact protection, washable pad, height adjustable base and more. We liked the built-in belt lock-off for non-LATCH installations and steel-on-steel construction for latching the carrier to the base (some cheaper seats use plastic hooks, which can break and have led to past recalls). While not the cheapest seat on the market, the Via is about $100 less than similar high-end seats by Britax and Peg Perego.

The downside? The seat doesn't work without its base (hence this isn't the best choice for urban dwellers who want to use it on the go in a taxi), nor is it compatible with most stroller frames. And the Via is showing its age, only working up to 22 lbs. (most seats now go up to 30).

Amazon is one of the few places you can find this seat for sale.
Rating: A-

GRACO SAFESEAT STEP 1
Price: $130-140; extra base $50.
Limits: 30 lbs., 32".
Pros: Works up to 30 lbs. (great for bigger babies). EPS foam. Easy to use and install.
Cons: Heavy, bulky to carry.
Type: Infant car seat, five-point harness.
Comments: The Graco SafeSeat is part of Graco's SafeSeat line that

Chocolate donuts with sprinkles?

Here's a confusing thing about car seat shopping: most car seat makers offer their models in a plethora of versions. At one point a couple of years ago, one infant seat maker had FIVE different versions of the same seat: the Classic, Plus, Elite, Supreme and the Extra Crispy. Okay, there wasn't an Extra Crispy, but you get the point. The key thing to remember: the seat was basically the very same seat in each configuration, just with minor cosmetic variations (an extra bit of padding here, a pillow there, etc). Yes, sometimes there are more significant variations like a five-point harness (versus three-point) or an adjustable base. But often there isn't much difference. Think of it this way: car seat makers produce a chocolate donut and top it with different color sprinkles—the rainbow sprinkle version goes to Wal-Mart, the green sprinkle donut goes to Target, etc. That way the companies can offer "exclusives" on certain models to large retailers, so the chains don't have the same exact offerings. But remember this: basically, it's the same donut. Bottom line: don't get caught up in all the version stuff. If the basic seat has the features you want, it doesn't really matter whether you buy the Plus or the Elite. Or the Extra Crispy.

includes a forward-facing toddler seat and booster. The key feature of the SafeSeat is its ability to work up to 30 lbs., compared to some versions of Graco's other infant seat (the SnugRide) that just work to 22.

Why is that important? Well, babies are getting larger and heavier . . . and safety experts say it is best to keep a child rear facing as long as possible. With some larger babies outgrowing a typical 22-pound limit infant car seats as early as four months, the Graco SafeSeat will extend that time even for the largest of infants.

Our readers give the Graco SafeSeat high marks for ease of use: thanks to built-in safety belt lock offs, the SafeSeat is easy to install. And adjusting the harness is a snap. The SafeSeat features EPS foam lining and a base with a dial adjustment for the proper angle. The negatives? The sunshade/canopy is wimpy. And the Graco SafeSeat is HEAVY (9.75 lbs. empty) and somewhat bulky (which is an unfortunate byproduct of the design to accommodate larger infants). Most parents found it to be manageable, but keep this in mind if you are petite.

Another small consideration: The Graco SafeSeat does not work with as many strollers brands as Graco's other infant seat (the SnugRide reviewed below). The SafeSeat DOES work with many Graco strollers and a few other brands—double check this before you buy the seat if you have your heart set on a specific stroller.

FYI: Graco has scaled back the number of SafeSeat models as it launches a revamped SnugRide that works up to 32 lbs. (see below). The SafeSeat Step 1 and SnugRide 32 are basically the same seat.

In previous years, there were various versions of the SafeSeat, with more plush models running $160. It's unclear if the SafeSeat will continue beyond 2009 or be replaced with the SnugRide 32.

Rating: A

GRACO SNUGRIDE / SNUGRIDE 32

Also known as the Tuetonia t-tario 32
Price: $80 to $160; extra base $35-$50
Type: Infant seat; comes in both three-point and five-point harness versions.
Limits: Base: 22 lbs., 29"; SnugRide 32: 32 lbs, 32"
Pros: Lightweight carrier (for the base model), level indicator, canopy, easy to use. Front belt adjuster on some models. Works with many strollers.
Cons: Only one crotch position.
Comments: Here is the country's top-selling infant car seat—and it deserves to be. The Graco SnugRide is an affordable infant seat with excellent features: EPS foam lining, adjustable base and good fit in most vehicles.

2009 is a transition year for this seat: Graco has debuted a new version of the SnugRide (dubbed the SnugRide 32) that works up

CAR SEATS

to 32 lbs. and 32 inches. The original SnugRide works up to 22 lbs. and 29″ and is still sold in stores—so check the box carefully if you want the higher weight model.

Our feedback on the SnugRide is mostly from the 22 lb. version (the 32 model just came out as of press time). The overall verdict: thumbs up. For ease of use, the SnugRide earns good marks. The few complaints centered on the "annoying" handle, which must be lowered when driving (it takes two hands). And be aware of the harness adjuster: the cheapest SnugRides require you to adjust the harness from the back. Our advice: buy the models with a FRONT adjuster, which is much easier to use.

As always, Graco makes a zillion versions of the SnugRide with the main difference being the fabric. A simple SnugRide in discount stores runs $80, while plusher versions with boot can top out at $160. One tip: newborns don't really care how much padding there is in the seat—that's really an issue for older kids in convertible seats. Hence, the less-expensive SnugRides are just fine.

So which SnugRide should you get? Parents with bigger babies should consider the 32; otherwise the basic model should be ok. Again, we'd only suggest the models with the front harness adjuster. Be aware the SnugRide 32 is a heavier carrier (10 lbs. versus 8 lbs. for the basic version).

Are there trade-offs between the SnugRide and more expensive seats? Well, the SnugRide does lack extra side-impact protection like you see on the Peg Perego and Britax seats (and even Graco's SafeSeat). And the seat lacks an anti-rebound bar, seen on the Britax and Combi seats.

On the other hand, one advantage to getting the ever-popular SnugRide: it is compatible with a wide range of strollers and stroller frames, much more than the Graco SafeSeat. (Since the SnugRide 32 is new, we're not sure about its compatibility with strollers as of this writing).

So, overall, this seat is a winner—good crash test ratings, excellent ease of use and features. Add in the affordable price and we have a winner.

Rating: A

MAXI COSI MICO

Price: $150-180.

Limits: 22 lbs., 29″.

Pros: Works with Quinny strollers, EPP foam, four harness heights, deep side wings.

Cons: Canopy doesn't stay up, small seat means bigger babies outgrow it quickly.

Comments: Cosco imports this seat from their European subsidiary, adapted for the US market and designed to work with the hot-selling Quinny strollers. Availability is a bit limited: Babies R Us only sells it online; you can also find it in specialty stores and on Amazon.

Reader feedback has been mixed: fans say it is easy to use and install, plus the EPP foam is softer than the EPS foam you see on most other seats.

Detractors hate the canopy (which does not stay in place) and the Mico's low weight limit/small size—bigger babies just don't fit as well in the Mico and quickly outgrow the seat. Others tell us it is hard to use the Mico's buckle and adjust the straps.

Bottom line: there is a sharp difference of opinion on this seat. For every reader who tells us she loves her Mico, we have another one that curses the seat. As a result, we've dropped our rating on this seat for this book.

Rating: C

MIA MODA VIVA
Price: $100.
Limits: 22 lbs.
Comments: Stroller maker Mia Moda launched this basic infant seat in 2007. The Viva sells for $100, works up to 22 lbs. and has EPS foam, three harness heights and a three-positioning reclining base. The carrier weighs only 7.5 lbs. A new version of the Viva (Viva Supreme) will debut in 2009 with a better canopy and full body infant inset. While we did see a sample of the Mia Moda Viva at a trade show, there are few out there in the wild: we haven't heard any parent feedback on the Viva. Part of that may be the Viva's thin distribution: it is only sold online. Given the lack of real world feedback, we don't have a rating for this seat yet. **Rating: Not Yet.**

ORBIT
Price: $900, as part of a travel system with stroller frame.
Limits: 22 lbs., 29″.
Pros: Well, it is stylish.
Cons: Did we mention it is sold as part of a travel system that's $900?
Comments: Orbit is a start-up company that aims to inject a bit of cache into the travel system market. Their first offering, the Orbit Baby Infant System, includes an infant car seat, in-car base and stroller frame that attempts a Bugaboo-like vibe. The infant car seat is a bit strange looking (one parenting blog compared it to a crock pot), with an innovative soft-strap handle and rotating base. We liked Orbit's "SmartHub" base technology, that lets you "dock" the seat at any angle. The base also has a front knob that ensures a

infant seats

tight fit to the vehicle.

The feedback on the Orbit has been mixed. Fans love the Orbit's technology and ergonomic design. Tall parents particularly love the tall handles; others love how it is a conversation starter with other parents.

But . . . detractors point out the bulky 10 lb. carrier is HEAVY, which provides a serious upper body workout as baby gets bigger. The limited 22 lb. weight limit means larger babies are going to outgrow the Orbit seat quickly (the company does sell a toddler car seat, more on that later). The bulk of the Orbit seat makes for a tight fit in smaller cars.

And let's get real for a second: does anyone really need to spend $900 on an infant car seat and stroller frame? Most babies will outgrow the Orbit infant car seat at six months or earlier. Then you have to pony up another $200 for a toddler stroller seat. So that means you are now spending a total of $1100. (A new bassinet cradle that docks to the stroller frame is another $280).

So, it's a mixed review for the Orbit. Kudos to the company for their innovative features and design. But let's do the math. You could buy an Orbit for $900 . . . or buy a Graco SnugRide for $100 plus a stroller frame for $50 and take the $750 savings and start a college fund for your infant.

Rating: B

PEG PEREGO PRIMO VIAGGIO SIP 30/30

Price: $240-$275. extra base: $85.

Limits: 30 lbs., 30″

Pros: Matches Perego's hot-selling strollers. Side impact protection, auto harness adjustment, improved canopy, luxe fabrics.

Cons: Price.

Comments: Peg Perego has had much success in this category, despite the seat's high price tag.

Some of that success can be chalked up to Peg's slow but steady improvements to the Primo Viaggio. In recent years, the company has added side impact protection, an automatic adjustable harness and a better canopy to the seat, which now works up to 30 lbs. and can be used with or without the base.

Of course, a big part of Peg's mojo here is their Italian fabrics and style—plus the fact this seat mates with many of Peg's fashionable strollers. The luxe Italian fabrics are sharp, but most of Peg's competitors have caught up in the looks department in recent years.

As for ease of use, most of our readers give the Viaggio good marks, although not quite as high as the Graco SafeSeat or SnugRide. Negatives include a bulky, heavy carrier that exceeds 10 lbs.

Obviously, the price of the Viaggio is its biggest drawback—Peg has let the price of this seat creep dangerously close to $300. While it is a well-made, safe infant car seat, it's hard to justify the $100 to $200 price premium over similar seats from Chicco and Graco.

On the plus side, there are many bargain Primo Viaggio seats sold online—most are previous years' models that are in the $150 to $200 range. Be aware, however, that many earlier models only work to 22 lbs. and omit the side impact protection.

Rating: A-

QUINNY *See Maxi Cosi.*

SAFETY 1ST DESIGNER 22 *This is the same as the Eddie Bauer seat, reviewed earlier in this section.*

SAFETY 1ST ONBOARD

Also known as the Eddie Bauer SureFit
Price: $120. Extra base: $85.
Limits: 22 lbs, 22."
Pros:. One of the few seats designed to work with preemies.
Cons: 22 lbs. limit. No side impact protection.

Comments: This relatively new seat form Safety 1st features a special insert for preemies (you can use the OnBoard for babies from four lbs. and up). You also get EPP foam, four harness height positions and an adjustable base. Basically, the OnBoard is a plain Jane infant seat without any special bells or whistles.

The Safety 1st OnBoard is only sold in a handful of stores, which probably explains why we've had very little feedback on it. Safety 1st told us they were planning to bring out a version of the seat that works up to 30 lbs, but that wasn't available as of press time. FYI: The Eddie Bauer SureFit ($120) is the same as the Safety 1st OnBoard.
Rating: Not Yet.

SAFETY 1ST STARTER/DESIGNER
Price: $50-$75
Comments: This seat is the same as the Eddie Bauer Deluxe (Designer 22) reviewed earlier in this chapter.

TEUTONIA T-TARIO 32
Price: $225
Comments: This seat is the same as the Graco SnugRide 32, reviewed earlier.

◆ *Car beds.* How do you transport a preemie home from the hospital? The smallest infants may not be able to sit in a regular infant seat—in that case, a "car bed" enables an infant to travel lying down. Check with your hospital—some rent out car beds for preemies for free (one mom said she had to pay a $50 deposit, refundable when she returned the car bed). If you have to purchase a car bed, we'd recommend the **Cosco Dream Ride** ($70, rating: A). Also: EliteCarSeats.com sells the *Angel Guard AngelRide* infant car bed for $100—it can be used for premature infants up to nine lbs. FYI: ALL premature infants should be given a car seat test at the hospital to check for breathing problems—ask your pediatrician for details.

Convertible and Forward Facing-Only Car Seats (model by model reviews)

ALPHA SPORT/ALPHA OMEGA THREE IN ONE
See Eddie Bauer Three In One convertible seat.

BRITAX ADVOCATE
Price: $370
Type: Convertible, five-point harness.
Limits: 5 to 35 lbs. rear facing, 20 to 65 lbs. forward facing, 49" tall.
Pros: Same as Boulevard but with added side impact protection.

Cons: Price. Big seat—may not fit into smaller vehicles.
Comments: This seat is the same as the Britax Boulevard CS, reviewed below, with one major difference: the Advocate has added side impact protection cushions that compress to protect the child during a crash. Yep, think of these as side-impact air bags for your car seat. This seat should be out by the time you read this.
Rating: Not Yet.

BRITAX BOULEVARD
Price: $310-330.
Type: Convertible, five-point harness.
Limits: 5 to 35 lbs. rear facing, 20 to 65 lbs. forward facing, 49" tall.
Pros: Same as the Marathon (see page 398), but seat adds height-adjuster knob. Additional side impact protection with headrest.

Cons: Price. Big seat—may not fit into smaller vehicles. EPS foam only in headrest.
Comments: This seat is virtually the same as the Marathon (see later review), with two significant differences. First, you get a height adjuster knob that lets you make numerous adjustments to the harness heights (instead of being stuck with the four positions you see

in the Marathon). Hence, you don't have to re-thread the belts every time your child grows. The second difference is what Britax calls "true impact protection." Basically, this is a reinforced headrest lined with EPS foam that protects your child in a side-impact collision. The first version of this seat (called the Wizard) had a headrest that many felt was too restrictive, so Britax revised the headrest to make it wider. Britax also added an infant pillow, like the Decathlon.

New for 2009, Britax is coming out with a new version of the Boulevard, dubbed the Boulevard CS. The CS stands for Click and Safe—you hear a click when you adjust the harness to make sure it is as snug as possible. The Boulevard CS is $330, while the older Boulevards (still sold online) are $310.

According to reader feedback posted to our web site, parents give the Boulevard high marks for ease of use.

Rating: A-

BRITAX DECATHLON

Price: $295

Type: Convertible, five-point harness.

Limits: 5 to 35 lbs. rear facing, 20 to 65 lbs. forward facing. 49" tall.

Pros: Use up to 65 lbs., can be tethered rear- or forward-facing, adjustable crotch strap, plush padding.

Cons: Expensive. Very tall seat, which can block rear view in some cars. Some complain the harness is hard to adjust.

Comments: The Decathlon is a slight evolution of the more widely available Britax Marathon. Like the Marathon, the Decathlon works up to 65 lbs., can be tethered front or rear facing and has the HUGS strap system (read the Marathon review for the pros and cons of HUGS). So, what's different? And why is this seat about $30 more than the Marathon? Well, the Decathlon includes an infant body pillow, which the Marathon omits. So if you plan to use this seat from birth or you have a small infant that is graduating from their infant seat, the pillow may make for a better fit.

The other key difference: the Decathlon has an automatic harness adjustment—basically a button you push to adjust the straps. While that sounds like a plus (the Marathon has a manual strap you pull on), parents give mixed reviews to the push-button harness adjustment. Some find it difficult to use, while others say it is fine. Spend a few minutes with it in the store to see what you think before buying this seat.

Another advantage of the Marathon over the Decathlon: the Marathon is more widely available . . . as a result, you can often find one on sale for a low price. That can make the price difference $50 to $100 between the two models (although the official price differ-

convertible seats

ence is $30).

Other than that, the Decathlon and Marathon are twins—and that means the Decathlon is just as tall as the Marathon. It may not fit well into the back seat of a small car . . . or your rear-view may be obstructed by the seat (depending on the vehicle). One plus for the Decathlon: you can use a tether to 65 lbs. (if your vehicle allows this), unlike the Boulevard, which has a 50-pound limit.

Rating: B+

BRITAX DIPLOMAT

Price: $260

Type: Convertible, five-point harness.

Limits: 5 to 35 lbs. rear facing, 20 to 40 lbs. forward facing. 40″ tall.

Pros: Similar to the Roundabout, but adds side impact protection. Comfort foam, body pillow.

Cons: Can only use up to 40 lbs.

Comments: The Diplomat is basically the same as the Britax Roundabout—for an extra $40, you get side-impact protection wings and an infant body pillow. Realizing that its Marathon/Boulevard seats are too big to fit rear-facing in the back of smaller cars, the Diplomat offers a compromise: you get the side impact protection of the Boulevard . . . but the smaller size of the Roundabout. The big trade-off: this seat only works up to 40 lbs.

Bottom line: while this is a good seat, if your vehicle is roomy enough, we'd suggest a seat that goes to 65 lbs. (Marathon, Boulevard, etc).

Rating: A

BRITAX MARATHON

Price: $250-280.

Type: Convertible, five-point harness.

Limits: 5 to 35 lbs. rear facing, 20 to 65 lbs. forward facing, 49″ tall.

Pros: Up to 65 lbs. with a five-point harness. Plush pad, EPS foam, same pros as Roundabout.

Cons: Must re-thread harness manually. HUGS harness system gets mixed reviews.

Comments: The Marathon is Britax's best-selling seat and that's no wonder: this model was one of the first to work to 65 lbs. with a harness. Since its release, Britax has done a series of Marathon spin-offs that add side impact protection (Boulevard) or an infant body pillow (Decathlon). Despite being more old school, the Marathon is still worthy of consideration.

The Marathon has four harness heights (the top is 18″), Britax's

CAR SEATS

Britax seats, compared

Yep, the Britax car seat line can be confusing. Here's an overview:

	ADVOCATE	BOULEVARD	BOULEVARD CS	DECATHLON	MARATHON	DIPLOMAT	ROUNDABOUT	FRONTIER
Price	370	310	330	295	250	260	180	280
Rating	**	A-	A-	B+	A-	A	A	C
Weight	65	65	65	65	65	40	40	80/100
Height	49	49	49	49	49	40	40	52/60
Side Impact	◆	◆	◆		◆			◆
No-rethread	◆	◆	◆		◆			
HUGS		◆	◆	◆	◆			◆

** *Not yet—seat too new as of press time for rating.*

Key:
Weight—forward facing weight limit, in pounds.
Height: the seat's child height limit, in inches.
No rethread: does the seat have a no-rethread harness?
HUGS: Harness Ultra Guard System—pads that cushion the child's neck and chest and work to reduce forward head movement in the event of impact.

convertible seats

"Versa-Tether" (which means the seat can be tethered rear or forward facing) and EPS foam.

Thanks to its wide distribution, you can find the Marathon sold in many stores and online. That means you can often snag one on sale: as of this writing, Amazon had ten color options available. While most were $250 to $280, there was one pattern for just $187. And other sites offer free shipping specials from time to time on the seat.

So, what's not to like about the Marathon? Well, first, this is a big seat. It is bigger/wider (it's 19.5″ wide and 28″ tall) than the Roundabout and hence may not fit into some smaller cars (go to carseatdata.org to see which vehicles work and which ones don't).

And let's talk about the HUGS system, which appears on the Marathon. Britax says this harness system is designed to "better distribute webbing loads to reduce head movement and minimize the chance for webbing edge loading on the child's neck in the case of an impact. In addition, it is designed to reduce the chance of improper positioning of the chest clip."

The first version of HUGS generated many complaints from parents, who said it didn't fit larger children and was confusing to use.

Britax tweaked the system by coming out with larger HUGS straps and clarifying its use in the seat's instructions. But some folks still dislike HUGS and find it difficult to use. FYI: you must re-thread the harness on the Marathon to change the harness height.

And the Marathon omits any side impact protection (you have to upgrade to the Boulevard to get this). Side impact cushions have both fans and detractors. While the safety benefit is obvious, some kids don't like the wings around their heads, which limit vision and can make it difficult to use. Our advice: if your vehicle has side curtain air bags in the rear seats, extra side impact protection for the car seat may be unnecessary.

Despite these negatives, the overall reader feedback on this seat is very positive. All in all, we recommend the Marathon—IF you have a vehicle in which it can fit!

Rating: A-

BRITAX REGENT
Price: $220.
Type: Forward-facing harness seat.
Limits: 22 to 80 lbs. 53" tall.
Pros: One of the few seats that works with a five-point harness up to 80 lbs.
Cons: Very wide and heavy.

Comments: Ah, the power of YouTube.com—witness the case of the Britax Regent and its sudden popularity. In an emotional video posted to YouTube in 2006, a mother who lost her son in a car accident recounted the story of when their vehicle was broadsided and flipped upside down in a ditch. The child, who was sitting in a belt-positioning booster, died when he was ejected out of the car. The gist of the video: the parents believed the seat belt failed and their child would have survived if he was sitting in a harnessed seat, secured to the vehicle by LATCH. At the end of the video, the parents suggested the Britax Regent as just such a seat.

Well, a million views later, the video became legendary, sparking debate among car seat advocates as to its accuracy (we detail the debate on our blog). And faster than you can say YouTube, the sales of the Britax Regent zoomed into the stratosphere (selling out in some stores).

Despite the hype, the Regent is a basic forward-facing seat (that's right—it can NOT be used rear-facing for kids under a year). It works from 22 to 80 lbs. with a five-point harness . . . and that's the key feature that separates the Regent from other "toddler" seats—few have a harness that works up to 80 lbs.

There is a catch to this, however: the Regent's instructions prohibit securing the seat with LATCH over 48 lbs. That means you have to use the vehicle's safety belt to secure the seat. And some vehicles have even lower limits on the weight of a child in a seat when secured with LATCH (Honda is 40 lbs.). This sort of defeats the entire point of the YouTube video, which speculated LATCH is a safer way to secure a seat like the Regent.

And beware that the Regent requires the *use of a tether beyond 50 lbs.* That means you won't be able to use it in some older vehicles, which lack tether anchors.

Finally, be aware that the Regent is a monster, size-wise—at 28 inches tall, it is three inches taller than the Marathon. And it is 21.5″ wide, among the biggest on the market. Therefore, you can forget about squeezing this in a smaller (or even mid-size) vehicle. Bottom line: while we do recommend this seat, we like two other competitors (the SafeGuard Go and Radian 80) better for toddlers—and they're more affordable. These seats are reviewed later in this chapter.

Rating: B

BRITAX ROUNDABOUT

Price: $180-200.

Type: Convertible, five-point harness.

Limits: 5 to 35 lbs. rear facing, 20 to 40 lbs. forward facing. 40″ tall.

Pros: Excellent features—EPS foam, no-twist straps, can be tethered rear- or forward-facing, easy to adjust harness, double-strap LATCH, nice colors.

Cons: Harness slot a bit too high for smallest infants.

Comments: The Roundabout is our pick once again as one of the best convertible seats. Yes, it isn't the cheapest seat out there, but you get a boatload of extras that make the seat easy to use . . . if the seat is easy to use and adjust, odds are folks will use it correctly.

Britax sells the Roundabout (and all its seats) on its safety record. Part of that safety advantage is rock-solid installation and this is where Britax excels—the lock-off clips provide snug belt install and Britax's double-strap LATCH connectors are among the best in the business. We also found Britax's harness to be easy to use and the straps don't twist. Finally, we should mention that you can tether the Roundabout either rear or forward facing, a key safety advantage.

So, what are the downsides? These are mostly minor quibbles. The lowest harness slot (10″) is too tall for the smallest infants, even though this seat is rated for use from five lbs. and up. Other seats like the Evenflo Triumph (8.0″) and the Graco ComfortSport (8.5″) have lower harness slots and hence would be a better choice if you decide to forgo the infant seat and just buy one convertible. Another slight problem: the Roundabout is a bit wide—1″ to 3″ inches wider than other competing seats. Not a big deal . . . except if you try to take this seat on an airplane. While the FAA has approved the Roundabout for aircraft use, it may be a tight squeeze on some airlines.

Like the Marathon, the Roundabout is old school: you have to manually re-thread the harness to change the harness height. And the Roundabout doesn't have side impact protection (the Diplomat adds that feature).

One final caveat: the Roundabout has a 40 lb. limit. As we discussed in the Marathon review above, parents of babies who are at or above the 50th percentile of height/weight may want to consider a seat that goes to 65 lbs.—that would mean a Marathon, not a Roundabout.

All in all, this is an excellent seat. Parents laud its comfort features and safety (EPS foam lines the child's head and torso area, while the seat has an extra layer of "comfort foam"). We give the Britax Roundabout our highest rating.

Rating: A

COMBI COCCORO

Price: $200

Type: Convertible

Limits: 5 to 30 lbs. rear facing, 20 to 40 lbs. forward facing,

Comments: This new seat should be available by the time you read this—the Coccoro is a compact car seat (it weights just 11 lbs.) pitched for parents with small cars. Thanks to its small base size, Combi is suggesting this seat as a solution for parents who need to fit three car seats across the backseat. The top harness slot will be 15," which is impressive for a compact seat. Another plus: the Coccoro will have built-in lock off clips, a nice safety feature. And the Coccoro will come in a series of bright colors.

So, given all the indications, this might be a great seat for folks looking for a compact convertible to fit in a smaller car. The Coccoro could give the Britax Roundabout a run for its money.

Rating: Not Yet.

COMBI ZEUS

Price: $250-300

Type: Convertible

Limits: 5 to 22 lbs. rear facing, 20 to 40 lbs. forward facing,

Pros: Base rotates from rear to forward facing without reinstallation.

Cons: 22 lbs. rear facing is too low.

Comments: Combi's Zeus has a unique feature: a turnable base—you can flip the seat from rear to forward-facing without reinstallation. While that is nifty, the Zeus has a fatal flaw: it only works rear-facing to 22 lbs. Nearly every convertible seat on the market works to 30 or 35 lbs. rear-facing. That's important because safety advocates advise a baby should ride REAR-facing until one year of age—that 22 lb. limit will force parents to turn around their babies long before a year in most cases. So despite the fact that this seat has some nice features (an anti-rebound bar, for example), the 22 lb. rear-facing limit is a deal killer. And paying nearly $300 for a seat that only has a top forward-facing limit 40 lbs. also seems crazy.

FYI: Combi plans to come out with a new Zeus that has a higher rear-facing limit sometime in 2009.

Rating: F

COSCO ALPHA OMEGA *See Eddie Bauer Three in One.*

COSCO SCENERA
Price: $50
Type: Convertible, five-point harness.
Limits: 5 to 35 lbs. rear-facing, 22 to 40 lbs. front-facing.
Pros: Affordable car seat for a second car.
Cons: Avoid overhead bar shield
Comments: This simple seat is our top pick for that little-used second car or Grandma's vehicle. The Scenera isn't fancy: you get a five-point harness with four height positions and three crotch slots. The padding is very simple and there isn't any EPS foam, side-impact protection or other goodies. But then again, this seat is just $50—perfect when you need an affordable seat that is easy to install and use. FYI: We do NOT recommend the bar-shield version of this seat (Scenera Versa), as we think it doesn't offer the best crash protection compared to the five-point harness.

Rating: B+

EDDIE BAUER DELUXE 3-IN-1
(a.k.a. Alpha Omega Elite, Safety 1st Alpha Omega Elite, Alpha Echelon)
Price: $160 to $180.
Type: Convertible, five-point harness.
Limits: 5 to 35 lbs. rear-facing, 22 to 40 lbs. front-facing, 30 to 100 lbs. as a booster.
Pros: It's an infant seat! It's a convertible! It's a booster!
Cons: Twisty straps. Poor recline. And much more!
Comments: This best-selling seat is sold under a zillion aliases, as you'd expect from Cosco. It is marketed under the Eddie Bauer, Safety 1st, Cosco and Alpha brands in a variety of price points and

convertible seats

spin-offs. We've seen it in a stripped-down version for $100 at Costco . . . and deluxe version for $200 online. A typical offering is the tricked-out Eddie Bauer version sold for $170.

The pitch for this seat is simple: you can use it from birth to college. Ok, perhaps not college, but this seat aims for a triple play: rear-facing for infants up to 33 lbs., as a convertible with five-point harness up to 40 lbs. . . . and then as a belt-positioning booster up to a whopping 100 lbs. for toddlers and older kids.

The problem: it just doesn't live up to the hype. It is poorly designed, hard to use and expensive. Our reader feedback hasn't been kind to this seat: readers knock the instructions as "vague and confusing," the belts are hard to adjust in the rear-facing mode and the straps are so thin they constantly get twisted and snagged. Yet another problem: the highest harness slot in this seat (14.5") is a full inch lower than other seats like the Britax Roundabout. Why is this a problem? That low slot means some parents will be forced to convert this seat to booster mode too soon for larger children.

As for safety, this seat scored better in crash tests with LATCH than just with a safety belt. *Consumer Reports* latest tests pegged this seat as only "good" (most other seats in this price range scored "very good" or "excellent") for crash protection with a safety belt. And we're disappointed that this seat doesn't have EPS foam or side impact protection.

FYI: Cosco makes two versions of this seat: the Alpha Omega and the Alpha Omega Elite. While similar (both add EPP foam), the Elite goes to 50 lbs. with a five-point harness and 100 lbs. as a belt-positioning booster (the regular Omega is 80) and adds armrests and an adjustable headrest.

Bottom line: despite its pitch, this seat is too expensive and hard to use.

Rating: D

◆ *Other Cosco models:* The *Safety 1st Uptown* is a $100 convertible seat sold at Wal-Mart. The Uptown works up to 40 lbs. and has EPP-type foam for seat padding and crash protection.

EVENFLO SYMPHONY
Price: $200
Type: Convertible.
Limits: 5 to 35 lbs. rear-facing, 20 to 40 lbs. forward-facing with five-point harness, 30 to 100 lbs. as a belt-positioning booster.
Pros: Excellent harness adjuster. SureLATCH makes for quick and easy installs.
Cons: 40 lb. limit for harness.

Comments: The Symphony is Evenflo's answer to the Dorel/Eddie Bauer 3-in-1 seat . . . it aims to work with newborns to older kids up to 100 lbs.

SureLATCH is the headline here: Evenflo's new LATCH connectors that tout a "super-fast, tight and safe installation." SureLATCH features built-in retractors that eliminate belt slack—this makes the Symphony one of the easier to install with LATCH.

Although this seat is still relatively new, feedback on the seat has been positive. Fans like the removable padding for infants and excellent harness adjuster.

But we were puzzled by the lower harness limit (40 lbs.)—most new seats have higher harness limits. In fact, Evenflo's own Titan Elite and Triumph Advance have 50 lb. harness limits. The low limit may force parents to move to booster mode before their child is ready.

That said, the Symphony's booster mode is probably better than Dorel/Eddie Bauer's—it's easy to adjust and will provide a good fit for older kids. BUT, the Symphony is not a very tall booster . . . that means kids will probably outgrow it by height long before the stated 100 lb. limit.

Bottom line: this seat is probably one of the better attempts at an "all in one" seat. But the low harness limit means it is probably best for smaller kids who won't outgrow that harness too soon.

Rating: B+

EVENFLO TITAN ELITE

Price: $75 to $100

Type: Convertible; comes in five-point and bar-shield versions.

Limits: 5 to 30 lbs. rear-facing, 20 to 50 lbs. forward-facing.

Pros: Value, excellent crash tests.

Cons: Hard to clean cover and adjust straps.

Comments: Here's another seat to consider for grandma's car—the Evenflo Titan is a bare-bones seat where the price ($75) is right. Nothing fancy here: you get a five-point harness, four shoulder positions and simple padding. While we weren't wild about Evenflo's Triumph, the Titan shows how simpler is sometimes better.

FYI: Evenflo makes several versions of the Titan, including a Titan Elite (pictured) that adds more padding, a head pillow, cup holders and so on. But at $100, it is too pricey. If you plan to use this as a secondary car seat, save the $30 and just get the basic version.

Like the Cosco Scenera, the Evenflo Titan has no side-impact protection, fancy padding or EPS foam, but, hey, it's affordable. The big gripe we heard from parents on the Titan were the straps—some found the harness hard to adjust, especially when the seat is

rear facing. So we will caveat our review: the Titan is probably best as a seat for kids over a year (and not riding rear-facing).
Rating: B+

EVENFLO TRIUMPH ADVANCE
Price: $120 to $170.
Type: Convertible seat; five-point harness
Limits: 5 to 35 lbs. rear-facing, 20 to 50 lbs. forward-facing.
Pros: Special harness "remembers" last setting, EPP foam, up-front five-position recline and harness adjustment (no re-threading). Half the price of Britax.

Cons: Tension knob is hard to adjust when seat is in rear-facing mode. Wide base may not fit in smaller cars. Can only use the top harness slot when forward facing, making the seat difficult to use for larger (but young) infants.

Comments: Evenflo has made steady improvements to this seat over the years and that's a good thing. Older versions of the Triumphs garnered a large number of reader complaints about ease of use.

The latest Triumph is dubbed the Advance. Available in three trim levels (LX, DLX and Premier) the Advance works to 50 lbs. (older Triumphs only work to 40 lbs.). The difference in the models is just fabric and a bit more padding with the DLX version. Also new: EPP foam and improvements to harness adjustment system.

The Triumph's key features are the TensionRight knob that tightens the harness from the side of the seat and the infinite slide harness adjustment system (no re-rethreading). All the knobs on the Evenflo seat have both fans and detractors—give it a try in the store to see if you find it easy to adjust.

Bottom line: The Triumph Advance is much improved over its previous versions. And the price (half that of Britax's convertible seats that go beyond 40 lbs. for the harness) make this one worthy to consider.
Rating: B+

◆ *Other Evenflo models:* The Evenflo *Tribute I* ($75, rating: C-) is an overhead bar shield seat sold at chain stores like Sears and Baby Depot. We don't recommend bar shields (they aren't as safe as five-point harnesses, in our opinion), so we won't recommend this seat. We did notice that chain stores like Wal-Mart and Babies R Us have a five-point version of the Tribute (Tribute 5) for $60. The Tribute gets poor marks from readers for ease of use; we don't recommend it.

FIRST YEARS TRUE FIT (C630)
Type: Convertible
Weight range: 5 to 35 lbs. rear facing, 20 to 65 lbs. forward facing,
Price: $180-200
Pros: Headrest pops off for easier rear-facing installation. EPP foam, easy-off pad for hand-washing, affordable price.

Cons: Harness can be hard to adjust when rear-facing.

Comments: Here's a great alternative to the Britax Marathon that costs $100 less: the First Years True Fit is an excellent seat that works up to 65 lbs. This seat's most amazing feature is a headrest that pops off. That makes the True Fit easier to install rear-facing in smaller vehicles (you won't need the headrest for newborns riding rear-facing). We also like the automatic harness adjustments (no rethreading), side-impact wings, a seat entirely lined with EPP foam and three crotch positions to adjust for growing babies. Add in the 65 lb. top weight and an affordable $180-$200 list price and we have a winner!

Like the Sunshine Kids Radian seats, the True Fit does not have a base—this enables the seat to be deeper on the inside without increasing its overall dimensions.

Feedback on the True Fit has been very positive: fans love the roomy seat, the "easy off" pad that enables quick cleaning and the overall ease of installation (belt lock-offs are a plus). The downsides? The True Fit doesn't have wide distribution, which can make seeing it in person a challenge. And the harness can be hard to adjust when the seat is in the rear-facing position.

New for 2009, The First Years is coming out with a couple new versions of the True Fit. One (the 650, $230) adds a new recline feature (and indicator) that lets the seat recline whether in rear or forward facing mode. Also new: the True Fit Signature Series (670, $280) which adds an anti-rebound bar—yes, that would make the True Fit the only convertible seat on the market with that feature.

Rating: A

GRACO COMFORTSPORT
Price: $80 to $100.
Type: Convertible, five-point harness. (Wal-Mart has a version with an overhead bar shield, which we don't recommend).
Limits: up to 30 lbs. rear-facing, 20 to 40 lbs. forward-facing.
Pros: Front belt-adjuster, level adjuster, EPS foam.

Cons: Very low harness slots for forward facing. Cheaper versions have skimpy padding; next to impossible to adjust straps in rear-facing mode.

Comments: Despite Graco's success with infant seats, the company hasn't been able to translate this to convertible models. Exhibit #1: The ComfortSport.

On paper, this model looks good: the ComfortSport is a basic convertible that works up to 40 lbs. with EPS foam and a front harness adjuster. At $80 to $100, you'd think it would be a decent buy.

But . . . the seat is flawed. The top slots of the ComfortSport are a measly 14" tall—the lowest slots on the market. That means your child will quickly outgrow this seat, long before the stated limits. And you can only use the bottom two slots for rear-facing (and the top two slots for forward-facing only). That's a strange configuration that truly limits the usage of the seat.

The low weight limits are another major drawback: most seats on the market today work to 35 lbs. rear-facing (the ComfortSport stops at 30) and even Evenflo's entry-level seats work up to 50 lbs. forward-facing (the ComfortSport is 40).

Hence while this seat LOOKS like a bargain, it isn't—your child will outgrow it way too soon. And the ComfortSport is very difficult to install in most vehicles (it lacks belt lock-offs, etc). Bottom line: this seat is a loser.

Rating: D

GRACO COZYCLINE
Price: $130-140
Type: Forward-facing only, five-point harness.
Limits: 20 to 40 lbs. forward-facing.
Pros: EPS foam, five-position easy recline, deep side wings. Easy wash padding.
Cons: Can't use rear facing, so baby must be a year old. Only works to 40 lbs.

Comments: The seat used to be called the Toddler SafeSeat (Step 2)—it was part of Graco's three-step car seat program that flopped. Hence the new name . . . but basically the same seat.

The CozyCline (who thinks up these names?) is a forward-facing seat that is NOT convertible and won't work for rear-facing babies under a year of age.

Graco did a good job with the design features here. Example: you can remove the pad for cleaning WITHOUT removing the harness. The CozyCline also includes items that are standard on more premium seats: EPS foam, deep side wings, plush padding and an easy-install belt path. We also like the seat's easy recline feature, which can be used even AFTER the seat is installed in your vehicle.

Compared to the ComfortSport, this model gets much better marks from readers for ease-of-use, installation and overall quality.

The only bummer: this seat just works to 40 lbs. (we wish Graco could have certified it to 55 or 65 lbs.). At 40 lbs., children will outgrow this seat way too soon . . . and that limits the appeal of the CozyCline.

We recommended this seat in our last book, but since then, many new models have come on the market with higher weight limits. As a result, this seat is past its prime.
Rating: B

GRACO TODDLER SAFESEAT (STEP 2)
See Graco CozyCline

MAXI COSI PRIORI
Seat type: Convertible seat.
Weight range: 5 to 35 lbs. rear-facing, 22 to 40 lbs. forward facing.
Price: $170-200.
Pros: Five harness slots, padded buckle pads, EPP foam, upfront harness adjustment.
Cons: Only works to 40 lbs.
Comments: Maxi Cosi is Cosco/Dorel's European subsidiary. Dorel brought Maxi Cosi to the U.S. as part of their strategy to steal a bit of thunder from Britax's lock on the upper-end car seat market.

It seems to be working: the Maxi Cosi Priori has earned good marks from readers in the short time it has been available stateside. Parents like the comfortable padding, easy LATCH installation and four-position seat recline (nice for younger babies who are still napping). And yes, you can recline the seat while a baby is in it, a nice plus.

But . . . no matter how snazzy this seat looks, remember it only works to 40 lbs. Parents of bigger babies beware: $200 is a chunk of change to spend on a seat with such a low weight limit. You could find yourself with a child who outgrows their seat way too soon.

Bottom line: The Maxi Cosi is a decent alternative to the Britax Roundabout (both work to the same 40 lb. limit) but the Priori is $20 less than the Roundabout.
Rating: A-

ORBIT TODDLER CAR SEAT
Price: $280
Type: Convertible seat.
Limits: 5 to 35 lbs. rear-facing, 20 to 50 lbs. forward facing. 49".
Pros: Docks with Orbit travel system, sunshade, pad removes for easy cleaning.
Cons: Orbit travel system is $900—this $280 "accessory" is extra.
Comments: This unique convertible seat docks into the Orbit base

convertible seats

(see review of the infant car seat earlier in this chapter), but only in the rear-facing mode (so you'll have to rotate it to get it forward facing). The seat also docks with Orbit's stroller frame, which is unique (it includes a detachable UV sunshade just for that purpose). The Orbit features side-impact braces, which are supposed to be used when the seat is in forward-facing mode. We liked the fully removable seat cushion, which doesn't require the harness to be removed.

Feedback on this seat has been limited, given the Orbit system's high price (you first buy the Orbit's $900 infant seat and stroller frame combo before you graduate to this car seat). We'll give this seat the same rating as the travel system—innovative but way overpriced.
Rating: B

RECARO COMO
Seat type: Convertible.
Weight range: Rear facing 5-35 lbs., forward-facing 20-70 lbs.
Price: $250
Pros: Works to 70 lbs., adjustable headrest, EPP foam, side-impact protection wings. Higher harness slots than the Marathon.

Cons: May not fit rear-facing in smaller vehicles. Some kids may find the Como's head pillows too restrictive.

Comments: German car seat maker Recaro hopes to give Britax a run for its money with its new convertible, the Como. And yes, this is the first convertible seat to work to 70 lbs., five more than Britax's convertibles.

Among the Como's unique features: side-impact protection wings made of cushy EPP foam. Similar to the Britax Boulevard, these wings provide both crash protection and head support for napping toddlers. The Como has many seat adjustments and the plush, microfiber fabric is impressive.

The negatives? Well, like the Britax Marathon, this is a big seat—it may not fit rear-facing into smaller vehicles. A few parents told us they found the Como's head pillows to be too restrictive for their older toddlers. And Recaro's thinner distribution (as of this writing, Recaro isn't in as many stores as Britax) means you may have to search for a local store that carries it to see the Como in person.

While this seat and parent feedback has been sparse, we will recommend it, given Recaro's track record for quality seats. With the initial positive reader reports, we think the Como will give Britax much needed competition at the high-end of the car seat market. FYI: While this seat's official retail price is $250, we've seen it discounted to $150, which is a good deal!
Rating: A-

RECARO SIGNO

Seat type: Convertible.

Weight range: Rear facing 5-35 lbs., forward-facing 20-70 lbs.

Price: $290

Pros: Similar to the Como, but adds infinite harness adjustment and additional head support. Side impact protection.

Cons: Pricey.

Comments: The seat is almost exactly the same as the Como, with two major differences: the Signo adds an infinite harness adjustment (like the Boulevard). And the headrest has additional support, plus infinite adjustments. We will give the Signo the same rating as the Como—the initial reader reports are positive and the features (including the 70 lb. limit) are impressive. All in all, we would recommend the Signo. FYI: Like the Como, the Signo is often discounted online ($200 is the lowest price we've seen).

Rating: A-

SAFEGUARD CHILD SEAT

Seat type: Forward-facing harnessed seat.

Weight range: 22 to 65 lbs. with harness.

Price: $300

Pros: Retractable harness, memory foam, special system to ensure tight LATCH fit.

Cons: Price.

Comments: When this seat debuted, its price tag was an eye-popping $400 (as we were going to press, we saw it discounted to $300 or so online).

Made by IMMI (see brand review of SafeGuard earlier in this chapter), the Safeguard Child Seat is impressive: its features include a retractable harness (like those in autos) and a 65-pound weight limit with its five-point harness. Other Safeguard innovations include the "Posi-Latch" system that ensures a snug fit with LATCH. While some features of the SafeGuard are seen on Britax seats (the one-touch height adjuster for the harness is similar to the Boulevard/Decathlon), the overall impression here is quality and design detail. Note the memory foam, aircraft aluminum frame and color-coded knobs.

We were impressed with the SafeGuard's design—the generous 19" maximum harness height means kids will actually be able to use this seat up to 65 lbs.

The Safeguard was unique when it first launched a couple of years ago, but the market has caught up with it. Now there are

convertible seats

CAR
SEATS

quite a few harnessed seats that work to 65 lbs. and beyond . . . and cost less than the SafeGuard.

But parent feedback on this seat is positive. While relatively few of these seats have sold, parents who do have them say the quality and ease of use is excellent.

Minor quibble: no one will accuse the SafeGuard of being the most fashionable seat on the market. Forget cutesy flowers or mod patterns—the SafeGuard has four rather dull color choices. And don't go looking for this seat in big chain stores—at the time of this writing, the SafeGuard was only available in specialty stores as well as online (either direct from SafeGuardSeat.com or on EliteCarSeats.com).

Bottom line: based on the strength of its design alone and the track record of the parent company as a leader in car seat safety, we will give this seat our recommendation.

Rating: A

Safety 1st Avenue

(also known as the Uptown)
Price: $70-80
Type: Convertible
Limits: 5 to 35 lbs. rear-facing, 22 to 40 lbs. forward-facing.
Pros: It's cheap!

Cons: Harness adjuster is almost impossible to access in rear-facing mode.

Comments: This basic convertible seat is similar to the Safety 1st Uptown (a previous model that is still sold online). As a basic convertible, you don't get any fancy features, but a simple convertible that works up to 40 lbs. and costs under $100. The high harness slots and EPP foam are nice, but this seat has one MAJOR negative: the harness adjuster is almost impossible to access, especially when the seat is in rear-facing mode. Between the Avenue and the Cosco Scenera, we'd give the Scenera a nod for this reason alone.

Rating: C

Triple Play Sit ´ n´ Stroll

Price: $220-250
Type: Holy convertible baby product, Batman! It's a car seat! And a stroller!
Limits: 5 to 30 lbs. rear facing, 20 to 40 lbs. forward facing.
Pros: The only car seat that morphs into a stroller.

Cons: Doesn't function well either as a car seat or a stroller. Top harness slot is only 14".

Comments: The Sit 'n' Stroll has won a small but loyal fan base for its innovative car seat/stroller. With one flick of the hand, this convertible car seat morphs into a stroller. Like the Batmobile, a handle pops up from the back and wheels appear from the bottom. Presto! You've got a stroller without having to remove baby from the seat.

We've seen a few parents wheel this thing around, and though it looks somewhat strange, they told us they've been happy with its operation. We have some doubts, however. First, unlike the travel systems reviewed in the next chapter, the Sit 'n' Stroll's use as a stroller is quite limited—it doesn't have a full basket (only a small storage compartment) or a canopy (a "sunshade" is an option). We'd prefer a seat that reclines (it doesn't) and you've got to belt the seat in each time you use it in a car—even if you don't take it along as a stroller. Not only is installation a hassle, but the Sit 'n' Stroll's wide base (17.5") may also not fit some vehicles with short safety belts or contoured seats. Plus, lifting the 14-pound car seat with a full-size child out of a car to put on the ground is quite a workout. Finally, we should note the seat's top harness slot is only 14", much lower than other seats on the market today (that means baby will outgrow it that much quicker). And oddly, even though manufacturer's web site says the car seat can be used from birth to 40 lbs., "we recommend 20-40 lbs." No word on why this is!

So, we're not sure we can wholeheartedly recommend this seat. Yes, we do hear from flight attendants who love their Sit 'n' Stroll—it wheels down those narrow plane aisles. So, it's a mixed bag for the Sit 'n' Stroll. For frequent fliers, the Sit 'n' Stroll is probably heaven-sent. Yet, like many hybrid products, it is not great at being either a car seat or a stroller.
Rating: C+

SUNSHINE KIDS RADIAN 65 / 80 / XT
Price: $190 (65), $250 (80); $280 (XT)
Type: Convertible seat.
Limits: 5 to 33 lbs. rear-facing, up to 65 or 80 lbs. forward facing. Maximum height: 49."
Pros: Folds up! Works to 80 lbs. with five-point harness. Great for airplane travel. EPS foam. Can use a tether rear facing.
Cons: Only works to 49" in height. Heavy weight. Biggest kids may find crotch strap too tight. Not as ideal for kids under one year of age riding rear-facing.
Comments: Sunshine Kids burst onto the car seat market a couple of years ago with their innovative Radian seat. It's unique feature: the Radian is the only car seat on the market that folds up! Yes, we can hear parents of kids in carpools applauding from miles around.

The Radian has another claim to fame: it is one of the few seats that can use a five-point harness up to 65 or 80 lbs. (depending on the model). With all the interest in harnessed seats that work above the traditional 40 lb. limit, Sunshine Kids hit the market at just the right time.

The Radian comes in three versions—the Radian 65 ($190) works up to 65 lbs.; the Radian 80 ($250) works up to (you guessed it) 80 lbs.; the Radian XT ($290) is a new model that works up to 80 lbs. and features side impact protection.

Both the 65 and 80 models are similar: each is lined with EPS foam, but lack the side impact protection wings seen in the XT. This is a trade-off: the lack of head wings or side impact torso protection makes the Radian three inches wider in the shoulder area, again a plus for larger/older toddlers. Yet since the Radian's top height limit is 49", you'll probably have to buy at least a backless booster for the oldest kids to use before they can safely use the auto safety belt.

The Radian accomplishes its folding trick by omitting the base you see on so many convertible seats—the seat actually sits along the back of a vehicle's seat back. One plus to this: the Radian's narrow base allows for a three-across install in the back of a vehicle.

The new Radian XT features side-impact cushions that are height adjustable; this model also features memory foam in the seat.

All in all, we are very impressed with this seat and think it gives Britax a run for its money (the Radian is about $60 less than Britax's 65 lb. limit models). Most of the parent feedback we've received on this model has been quite positive (for the 65 and 80 models; the XT was too new as of press time). The only complaint: the seat is quite heavy (at 20 lbs.)—so while it folds up for carpooling, it does require quite a bit of muscle to haul around. And the youngest babies (under a year, rear-facing) might not find the Radian as comfortable as other seats with side wings and more head support.

One major plus to the Radian: it is approved by the FAA for aircraft use, making it one of the few harnessed seats that can be used for kids over 40 lbs. on a plane. And the Radian can use a tether rear facing, which is rare in this market (Britax is one of the few other seats with this option).

Rating: A

As you can imagine, the child safety seat world changes quickly—read our blog (BabyBargains.com) for the latest news, recalls and more with car seats.

Our Picks: Brand Recommendations

Here are our top picks for infant and convertible seats. Are these seats safer than others? No—all child safety seats sold in the U.S. and Canada must meet minimum safety standards. These seats are our top picks because they combine the best features, usability (including ease of installation) and value. Remember the safest and best seat for your baby is the one that best fits your child and vehicle. Finding the right car seat can be a bit of trial and error; you may find a seat CANNOT be installed safely in your vehicle because of the quirks of the seat or your vehicle's safety belt system. All seats do NOT fit all cars. Hence it is always wise to buy a seat from a store or web site with a good return policy.

FYI: See the chart on pages 418-419 for a comparison of features for both infant and convertible/front-facing car seats.

Best Bets: Infant car seats

Good. Let's be honest: if you're on a super-tight budget, consider not buying an infant car seat at all. A good five-point, convertible car seat (see below for recommendations) will work for both infants and children.

Better. The *Chicco KeyFit 30* is an excellent seat that works to 30 lbs. The KeyFit gets excellent scores from our readers on ease of use—installation is a snap and adjusting the harness is easy. The seat also features EPS foam and a newborn insert. The downsides? The seat is pricey at $170 and doesn't work with as many strollers as our top choice below.

Best. Tie: *Graco SnugRide* and *SnugRide 32*. Both of these seats are excellent, easy to use and install. Each features EPS foam. The key difference: weight limits. The SnugRide works only to 22 lbs., the SnugRide 32 works to (you guessed it) 32. So if you come from a family of six-foot tall folks, the SnugRide 32 is a better bet since you'll use it longer. The trade-off: the SnugRide 32 is heavier and bulkier (and $50 more expensive) than the original SnugRide.

Dark Horses. Two other seats are also worth considering: The *First Years Via* and the *Peg Perego Primo Viaggio 30/30*. The First Years Via ($120) seat's wide and deep carrier, as well as the rock-solid design of the base impressed us. And if fashion is important, the Primo Viaggio is a very good seat that works up to 30 lbs. . . . and has the best selection of luxe fabrics, albeit at a steep price ($250).

car seats

Best Bets: Convertible & Forward-Facing car seats

Good. For a decent, no-frills car seat, we recommend the **Cosco Scenera**. Yes, we realize Cosco's safety track record has been rocky, but this seat is still worth considering for that little-used second car or Grandma's vehicle. The Scenera is a basic, bare-bones convertible that works to 40 lbs., is easy to install and costs $50—no, that's not a typo. With the prices of some car seats pushing $300, it's nice to know you can find a decent seat for just $50. Another good bet for Grandma: the **Evenflo Titan Elite** ($75 to $100), which has a bit more padding than the Scenera.

Better. As its name implies. the **Sunshine Kids Radian 65** works up to 65 lbs. and features EPS foam and a tether can work rear facing. At $190, the Radian 65 isn't cheap . . . but it also has another trick up its sleeve: it is the only car seat that can fold up. That's a plus for carpoolers. FYI: Sunshine Kids also makes a Radian 80 ($250) that works up to 80 lbs. with a five-point harness. And the Radian XT (new for 2009, $280) is much like the Radian 80, but adds side impact cushions.

If you have a compact car, the **First Years True Fit** ($180-200) is an excellent seat that works to 65 lbs. but adds this nifty trick: its headrest pops off to make it easier to install rear-facing in compact cars.

Best. So, what is our top recommendation for convertible car seats? This year, we have a tie between two Britax seats: the **Britax Roundabout** and the **Britax Marathon**. Both seats feature an excellent five-point harness, EPS foam, no-twist traps, easy-to-adjust harness and a "double strap" LATCH system. Best of all, you can tether this seat either rear OR forward facing, for an extra measure of safety. The Roundabout ($200) works up to 40 lbs.; the Marathon ($250) up to 65 lbs.

Since the Marathon is only about $50 more than Roundabout, should you just go for the Marathon? Well, before you buy a Marathon, consider the size of your car. The Marathon is three inches TALLER and 1.5 inches wider than the already big Roundabout—that makes fitting in smaller vehicles a challenge (especially rear-facing). On the other hand, the Marathon is a good bet if you have a big baby (say, above 50% on their growth curves), as it will fit him or her longer with a five-point harness.

If Grandma is buying. What if money isn't an issue when buying a seat? One obvious seat that we'd suggest is the top-of-the-line **Britax Boulevard** ($310-330), which is much like the Marathon, but adds a height-adjuster knob (to better fit the harness to a grow-

Other excellent seats in the "Grandma's buying" category would be the *SafeGuard Child Seat* ($300) and the ***Recaro Signo*** ($290). The Safeguard works to 65 lbs.; the Recaro seats to 70 lbs. Both are excellent, albeit pricey seats.

Booster Seats

So what is a booster? Simply put, this seat boosts a child to correctly sit in an auto safety belt. Yes, some boosters have five-point harnesses (more on this later), but most boosters work with your vehicle's safety belt.

Most parents know they have to put an infant or toddler into a car seat. What some folks don't realize, however, is that child passenger safety doesn't end when baby outgrows that convertible car seat—any child from 40 to 80 lbs. and less than 4'9" (generally, kids age four to eight) should be restrained in a booster seat (or one of the new harnessed seats that work up to 80 lbs.). And in some states, booster seat use is mandated by law. Numerous states have passed laws requiring the use of booster seats. And more states are following their lead.

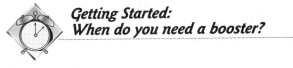

Getting Started:
When do you need a booster?

Your child needs a booster seat when he outgrows his convertible seat. This happens when he exceeds the weight limit or when he is too tall for the harness (his shoulders are taller than the top slots in the seat). For most children, this happens around ages three or four.

In order to sit an a vehicle's safety belt, a child must be mature enough to stay in the seat—since only the belt is holding them in, a toddler can escape the seat easily. If your child is ready for this, you need one of the new hybrid boosters that uses a five-point harness up to 65 or 80 lbs.

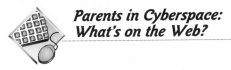

Parents in Cyberspace:
What's on the Web?

We found several booster seat info resources online. Here are a couple to check out:

Continued on page 420

INFANT SEATS

The following is a selection of better known infant car seats and how they compare on features:

MAKER	MODEL	PRICE	WEIGHT/ HEIGHT LIMITS
BABY TREND	FLEX-LOC ADJ. BACK	$90-$100	22 LBS./29" *
BRITAX	CHAPERONE	$200-$230	30 LBS/30"
CHICCO	KEYFIT 30	$160-$180	30 LBS/30"
COMBI	SHUTTLE	$150-$170	22 LBS./29"
EDDIE BAUER	DELUXE/DESIGNER 22	$90	22 LBS./29"
EVENFLO	DISCOVERY	$50-$70	22 LBS./26"
	EMBRACE	$80-$95	22 LBS./29"
FIRST YEARS	VIA/I140	$120	22 LBS./30"
GRACO	SAFESEAT	$130-$140	30 LBS./32"
	SNUGRIDE 32	$150	32 LBS./32"
MAXI COSI	MICO	$150-$180	22 LBS./29"
ORBIT	ORBIT	$900	22 LBS./29"
PEG PEREGO	PRIMO VIAGGIO 30/30	$240-$275	30 LBS./30"

CONVERTIBLE SEATS

The following is a selection of popular convertible car seats and how they compare on features:

MAKER	MODEL	PRICE	WEIGHT LIMITS (IN POUNDS)	
			REAR	FORWARD
BRITAX	BOULEVARD	$310-$330	35 LBS.	65 LBS.
	DECATHLON	$295	35	65
	MARATHON	$250-$280	35	65
	ROUNDABOUT	$180-$200	35	40
COMBI	COCCORO	$200	30	40
COSCO	SCENERA	$40	35	40
EDDIE BAUER	DELUXE 3-IN-1	$160-180	35	100
EVENFLO	SYMPHONY	$200	35	40/100
	TRIUMPH ADVANCE	$120-$170	35	50
FIRST YEARS	TRUE FIT	$180-$200	35	65
RECARO	COMO	$250	35	70
SUNSHINE KIDS	RADIAN 65/80	$190-$280	33	65/80

Infant seat chart:

SIDE IMPACT: Does the seat have side-impact protection?

FOAM TYPE: Does the seat have a EPS or EPP foam (or none at all)? See box on page 373 for a discussion.

*Note: Baby Trend will release a revised Flex-Loc that will work up to 30 lbs. in 2009.

SIDE IMPACT	LEVEL IND.	FOAM TYPE	BASE WIDTH	CARRIER WEIGHT	OUR RATING
◆	◆	EPS	16.50"	9 LBS.	B
◆		EPS	N/A	N/A	NOT YET
◆	◆	EPS	17	9	A
	◆	EPS	17	9.9	C
		NONE	18	8	D+
		EPS	17.50	5.5	D
	◆	EPS	18	N/A	D+
◆		EPS	18.50	8.4	A-
◆	◆	EPS	19	9.75	A
	◆	EPS	19	9.5	A
		EPP	17	8	C
	◆	EPP	15.25	9.8	B
◆	◆	EPS	15.50	11	A-

RATING COMMENT

A-	NEW "CS" VERSION MAKES HARNESS EASIER TO USE.
B+	INCLUDES INFANT BODY PILLOW; AUTO HARNESS ADJUST.
A-	MUST RETHREAD BELTS TO ADJUST HARNESS HEIGHT.
A	EPS FOAM, NO-TWIST STRAPS, TETHER REAR OR FORWARD.
NOT YET	COMPACT CAR SEAT WEIGHTS JUST 11 LBS.
B+	SIMPLE SEAT, GREAT FOR AIR TRAVEL OR GRANDPARENTS.
D	CONVERTS TO BOOSTER SEAT, BUT STRAPS ARE TWISTY.
B+	NEW LATCH SYSTEM MAKES IT EASIER TO INSTALL.
B+	MEMORY HARNESS; CAN ADJUST BELTS WITHOUT RETHREAD.
A	EPP FOAM; HEADREST POPS OFF FOR EASIER INSTALL.
A-	ADJUSTABLE HEADREST, EPP FOAM, SIDE IMPACT WINGS.
A	ONLY SEAT THAT FOLDS UP; CAN USE TETHER REAR-FACING.

LEVEL IND.: Does the seat have a level indicator for easier installation?

CARRIER WEIGHT: This is the weight of the carrier only (not the base).

◆ *SafetyBeltSafeUSA* (carseat.org) has three good reports on booster seats (click on the button, Booster Seats) that explain proper installation and offer other tips. Another great site is CarSeatData.org.

◆ **The National Highway Traffic Safety Administration** (nhtsa.gov) has excellent videos showing proper booster seat installation and use. Click on Child Safety Seats, then on 3Booster Seats. Also cool: the NHTSA now rates and reviews booster seats for ease of use and other factors.

Smart Shopping Tips

Smart Shopper Tip #1
Booster Laws

"My daughter just turned four, and my state doesn't require her to use a carseat anymore. Does she really need a booster?"

A number of states have recently enacted stiffer car seat laws, usually requiring children to use "appropriate restraints" until age six or 60 lbs. (some state laws are now up to age eight or nine and 80 lbs). But other states still only require a car seat until a child turns four (some even just two) years old. So why should you continue to hassle with a car seat or booster after this time?

We like to remind parents that there is the law . . . and then there is the law of physics. Car belts are made for adults, and children (as well as some short adults) just don't fit well, and don't get good protection from those belts. Lap belts used with four- to eight-year old children routinely cause such severe injuries and paralysis that the injuries even have their own name: "lap belt syndrome." Children using lap/shoulder belts often put the shoulder belt behind their back (since it is so darn uncomfortable), giving them no more protection than a lap belt alone. Ejections are another common problem with young children in adult belts, even if they are using both the lap and shoulder belt.

Booster seats (and of course regular car seats) work very simply to eliminate this problem. Boosters properly position the lap part of the belt on a child's hip bone, not their soft internal organs. They elevate the child and include a special adjuster so that the lap shoulder belt fits right on the strong shoulder bones. Booster seats should be used until a child fits the adult belts like an adult. Try out the Five Step Test (later in this section) to see if your child is ready yet.

See our web page for pictures of good and bad fit for a booster (BabyBargains.com, click on Bonus Material).

Smart Shopper Tip #2
Different seats, lots of confusion?

"When I was shopping for a booster seat, I was confused with all the types of seats out there. Why isn't there just one type of booster?"

Good question. We've noticed that buying a booster seat can be a bit more complex than buying another car seat. For example, an infant car seat is, well, an infant car seat. But a booster can come in several versions: high back boosters, backless boosters, combination seat/boosters, and more.

In this chapter, we'll try to simplify things a bit. Any time we refer to a *belt-positioning booster*, we mean a seat that uses the lap/shoulder belt to secure the child. Most other car seats (like convertible seats) use an internal harness to hold the child, while the seat itself is attached to the car with the seat belt or the LATCH system.

What's made this so confusing is that car seat makers have blurred the lines between convertible seats and boosters in recent years by coming out with hybrid models that use a five-point harness up to 65 (or 80) pounds and then convert to a belt-positioning booster. The Britax Frontier and Graco Nautilus are two examples.

Confusing, yes we know. But we want this section to cover all the options for older children who've outgrown their traditional convertible seat . . . so you'll see a variety of options in this section. Let's break down what's out there:

◆ **High back boosters (HBB):** Belt-positioning boosters come in two flavors: high back boosters and backless boosters. High back boosters have often been called "kid's captain's chairs," which they kind of resemble. They are really simple, but provide vital safety features for children who've outgrown a harnessed seats.

These boosters properly position the lap belt on a child's strong hip bones, rather than letting it ride up on the soft internal organs. And they provide correct positioning of the shoulder belt, so the child can comfortably wear it and get critical upper body support. The high back also protects the child's head from whiplash if there are no head restraints in the vehicle, and the high back may also give some side sleeping support. ALL of these boosters require a lap and shoulder belt. FYI: Some high back boosters convert into backless boosters for older kids.

◆ **Backless boosters:** These belt-positioning work the same way as high back boosters—they just don't have a back. Safety-wise, these

can be a bit better than a high back booster, since the child sits right against the vehicle seat. They do the same job positioning the lap belt, and usually include some sort of strap to adjust the shoulder belt. But they don't provide head support if you have low seat backs, and they don't give any side or sleeping support. On the other hand, they are often popular with older kids, since they can be quite inconspicuous.

◆ **Hybrid/Combo seats:** These are probably the most confusing "booster" seats because sometimes they are a booster, and sometimes they aren't. They come with a five-point harness, which can generally be used up to 40 lbs. (some seats now to 65 and even 80 lbs.). Then the harness comes off, and the seat can be used as a belt-positioning booster, usually to 80 or 100 lbs. They get the name "combination" or "combo" for short from the two jobs they do.

A recent report by the Insurance Institute for Highway Safety criticized many older combo seats, saying they poorly fit kids when in booster mode. We factored this report into our ratings.

Newer combo seats (namely the Britax Frontier, Graco Nautilus, among others) now work to 65 or 80 pounds. These combo seats do a better job at fitting older kids, whether in harness or booster mode.

The take-home message hybrid/combo boosters are great for children that have outgrown their convertible seats but aren't mature enough to sit in a belt-positioning booster (the types described earlier). The five-point harness provides that extra measure of safety and security while they are still young (typically, a child has to be three or older to be mature enough to handle the belt-positioners).

◆ **Special Needs Seats:** There are a few seats on the market now that don't really fit into any category. One is the Britax Traveler Plus, which is designed for special needs kids up to 105 lbs. (who can't sit in a regular seat). This seat has a five point harness.

Smart Shopper Tip #3
Avoid Seat Belt Adjusters
"The shoulder belt was bugging my son's neck, so I bought a little adjuster thing. Is that as good as a booster?"

Several companies make inexpensive belt adjusters ($10 or so), which help to properly position the shoulder belt on your child. Sounds good, right? Wrong. Look closely at the pictures on the box. In order to pull the shoulder belt down, and make it more comfort-

Harnessed seats that work beyond 40 lbs.

The following seats can be used with a five-point harness for kids who weigh up to 65 pounds (except as noted):

NAME	HARNESS HEIGHT IN INCHES	HIP WIDTH IN INCHES
Britax		
Advocate	**	**
Boulevard	16.5"	11"
Decathlon	17	11
Frontier	18.25"	13
Marathon	17	11
Regent	20.5	13
First Years (Compass)		
True Fit	17.5	**
Graco		
Nautilus 3-in 1	18	**
Recaro		
Como (to 70 lbs)	19	**
Signo (to 70 lbs)	18.5	**
SafeGuard		
Child Seat	19	10
Go (harness to 60 lbs)	17.5	11
Safety 1st		
Apex 65	17	13.5
Sunshine Kids		
Radian 65	17.5	10.5

*** We were unable to get these dimensions as of press time.*

able for a short passenger, virtually all of these devices also pull the lap part of the belt UP, right back onto the tummy. Marketed to kids 50 lbs. and up, these devices are also packed with statements that confuse even the most safety conscious parents, like "designed to meet FMVSS 213," a reference to a federal safety standard in crash testing. What's wrong with that picture? That federal standard doesn't even apply to items marketed for children 50 lbs. and up! Worse yet, government crash tests show that a three-year-old dummy is less protected when using one of these adjusters compared to using the regular vehicle safety belt. When crash tested with a six-year-old dummy, the seat belt adjusters didn't improve crash protection either. So, bottom line, if your child doesn't fit that adult belt, get a booster.

Smart Shopper Tip #4
Cars with only lap belts

"What if my car has only lap belts in the back seat?"

While lap belts are just fine with infant and convertible seats, they are a no-no when it comes to boosters. If your vehicle doesn't have shoulder belts, check with your vehicle's manufacturer to see if they offer a retrofit kit. If that doesn't work, consider buying a newer vehicle with lap/shoulder belts in the back seat. In the meantime, there are a few seats that can be used with a lap belt for kids over 40 lbs. The Britax Regent, can be used up to 80 lbs., though it requires a tether after 50 lbs. The Britax Marathon, Boulevard and Decathlon seats can be used to 65 lbs.

Smart Shopper Tip #5
LATCH system and boosters

"I have a car with the new LATCH attachments. Do booster seats work with this system?"

We discussed LATCH earlier in this chapter; in short, most booster seats do NOT work with LATCH. There are a couple of exceptions: Clek (reviewed later) makes a couple of models that work with LATCH, as does the new Sunshine Kids Monterey booster.

Smart Shopper Tip #6
Back Harness Adjuster

"I loved our combo seat—until the day I discovered its fatal flaw. When it was cold, my daughter's thick coat required me to loosen the belts on her five-point harness. I discovered this could only be done from the BACK of the seat! What a pain!"

More and more booster seats are adding five-point harnesses so they can be used at younger ages/weights (some seats start as little as 20 lbs.). The problem? The cheapest combo boosters do NOT have up-front belt adjustments. You must adjust the belts from the back of the seat, which is a pain especially in cold weather. A word to the wise: if you get a combo seat, make sure the belt adjustments are UP FRONT and easy to access.

The question of coats/snowsuits and car seats comes up frequently—we should stress that most safety advocates suggest that a child in a safety seat wear a coat that is no thicker than a polar fleece (the Land's End Squall gets good reviews for this job). Big bulky coats are a hazard. Why? In the event of a crash, the coat will compress, creating a gap between the child and the restraint (and possibly ejecting the child from the seat).

Smart Shopper Tip #7
Too Tall for a Convertible

"My daughter is too tall for her convertible car seat but is only 32 lbs. Now what?"

Many children outgrow their convertibles by height before weight. Most convertibles say that they are good to 40" tall, but a better measure is to make sure the child's shoulders are no higher than the top harness slot. If this happens well before a child is 40 lbs., the next step is a combo booster seat. Most have higher slots (17" or so inches, vs. about 15" for the convertibles). The exceptions are combo seats from Cosco. None of their combo booster seats have this feature, so unless you know you've got a very short torso child, skip the Cosco combos.

Smart Shopper Tip #9
Booster Testing—Do they Really Test it to 100 lbs?

"I just bought a booster rated to 100 lbs. What kind of testing is done to make sure that my booster really works for a child that heavy?"

Little notice has been given to the fact that current regulations only require booster seats to be tested with the three-year-old (33 pound) and six year old (47 pound) dummies. In fact, current regulations only apply to seats made for children smaller than 50 lbs. So how can so many seats have an upper limit of 80 or even 100 lbs.?

It all comes down to how the company *thinks* their product will perform. We contacted several companies that offer boosters rated up to 100 lbs. Britax, for example, told us they use "all dummies on the market appropriate for the rating of the restraint", including the 10-year-old, 4'6", 76-pound dummy. We didn't get any response from Cosco. So it appears that some companies are voluntarily using the appropriate weight of dummies to test their products, but we thought you should be aware that this is not required.

Frankly, this appears to be a case of where the market is outpacing safety regulations. More and more states are now requiring that children ride in safety seats (that is, boosters) until six years of age and manufacturers are quickly rolling out new seats to the meet the demand. While that's great, we urge the federal government to catch up with its safety regulations on this matter—if a booster claims to be effective to 80 lbs., we expect the federal government to REQUIRE that seat to be crash tested to 80 lbs.! Having seat makers voluntarily test their seats and assign a weight limit based on what they "think" is the seat's limit sets a dangerous precedent.

Safe & Sound

1 **CHECK YOUR VEHICLE'S OWNERS MANUAL.** We're amazed at the detailed info on installing child safety seats you can find in your vehicle's owners manual, especially for newer vehicles. Car seats also include detailed installation instructions. Unfortunately, some parents don't read these manuals and attempt to "wing it" during installation.

2 **ALWAYS USE THE LAP/SHOULDER BELT WITH THE BOOSTER**—this provides crucial upper body protection in the case of an accident. NEVER use just the lap belt.

3 **DON'T EXPECT TO USE THAT BOOSTER ON AN AIRPLANE.** FAA rules prohibit the use of booster seats on airlines. Why? Booster seats must be used with a shoulder belt to be effective—and airplanes only have lap belts. Our advice: a child under 40 lbs. should ride in a convertible or combo seat on a plane; over 40 lbs., just use the airplane seat belt (no booster). Just make sure to take the booster for the rides to and from the airport. Gate checking (or storing in an overhead bin) will insure that your boosters arrive at your destination with you.

4 **BE CAREFUL OF HAND-ME-DOWN AND SECOND-HAND BARGAINS.** Most old booster seats don't meet current safety standards. Older combo seats usually have the rear harness adjustment, which is a pain to use, as we discussed previously. If you do find a newer used booster, make sure you ask the original owner if it has been in a crash, and then check the seat for recalls (Safety Belt Safe has a great recall list at www.carseat.org). And if your seat has been in a crash, is over six years old or missing its proper labels, stick it in a black garbage bag and throw it away.

5 **ONLY USE CARDBOARD CUPS IN BOOSTER SEAT CUP HOLDERS.** You'll note that some seats now come with cup or juice box holders. These are a great convenience, but most manufacturers only recommend cardboard cups (like to-go cups) or juice boxes be used. Anything harder (plastic, etc.) is more likely to become a dangerous projectile in a crash.

6 **WHEN IS A CHILD BIG ENOUGH TO USE JUST THE AUTO'S SAFETY BELT?** When a child is over 4'9" and can sit with his or her back straight against the back seat cushion (with knees bent over the

---

Booster seat melt-down: safety panel declares 13 seats "poor" in tests

The Insurance Institute of Highway Safety (IIHS) evaluated 41 booster car seats in 2008 to see how well they fit kids—did the boosters correctly position the lap and shoulder belts across a typical child? The short answer: many boosters failed this test. Thirteen of 41 booster seats were deemed poor at protecting kids.

We refer to the IIHS ratings throughout this section. If you'd like to read the entire report, we've put it on our web site at BabyBargains.com/boosters.

---

seat's edge), then he or she can go with just the auto's safety belt. Still have doubts? Try this Five Step Test from Safety Belt Safe, USA:

◆ Does the child sit all the way back against the auto seat?
◆ Does the belt cross the shoulder between neck and arm?
◆ Is the lap belt as low as possible, touching the thighs?
◆ Can the child stay seated like this for the whole trip?
◆ Do the child's knees bend comfortably at the edge of the seat?

If you answered no to any of these questions, your child needs a booster seat, and will probably be more comfortable in one too.

7 **DON'T USE A BOOSTER TOO SOON.** Most safety techs say a child should stay in a harnessed seat as long as possible—four years or at least 40 lbs. is a good rule. Some parents try to switch a too young toddler to a booster . . . but kids that are under four are often not mature enough to correctly sit in a belt-positioning booster.

Booster Car Seats (model by model reviews)

ALPHA

Comments: This Cosco/Dorel brand has its own version of the Safety 1st Apex 65 forward-facing seat (reviewed later in this section). Basically the same seat, just a Babies R Us exclusive fabric pattern.

BRITAX FRONTIER

Booster type: Combo

Weight range: 20-85 lbs. with harness, up to 100 lbs. as a belt-positioning booster. For kids at least two years old, 25 lbs. and 30-53" for the harness, 42" to 60" in height for belt-positioning booster.

Price: $280

Pros: Works to 85 lbs. with five-point harness. A bit wider, deeper than the Graco Nautilus.

Cons: Hard to install, twisty straps, high price.

Comments: Britax's Frontier got off to a rough start in 2008 when no sooner than six months after its release, Britax had to recall the seat for a defective harness.

The Frontier aims for a market similar to the Graco Nautilus (see review later)—it is a harnessed seat that works to a whopping 85 lbs. and then a belt-positioning booster to 100 after that. The Frontier is targeted at kids at least two years old who have outgrown their convertible seats but aren't mature enough to sit in a belt-positioning booster.

While this sounds good on paper, the actual seat falls short when compared to the Nautilus. First, even though the Britax is rated to 85 lbs. and the Nautilus 65, the Nautilus actually has a slightly higher top harness slot. That's important because kids will outgrow the Frontier by height long before they hit 85 lbs.

Safety techs tell us it is much easier to install a Nautilus than the Frontier—and readers concur, complaining about twisty straps that require constant attention. And we can't forget the price issue: Britax prices this seat at a eye-popping $280, while the Graco Nautilus is $135 to $160. Yep, that is about HALF the price.

Bottom line: this seat is a rare flop for Britax. Between the Graco Nautilus and Britax Frontier, we say go for the Nautilus.

Rating: C

Dimensions: 19.5" wide, 22" high, 26.5" deep.

BRITAX REGENT

See review earlier in the chapter (convertible seats).

CHICCO KEYFIT STRADA BOOSTER

Booster type: High back

Weight Range: 33 to 100 lbs.

Price: $130

Comments: It's been "coming soon" for two years, but this year it might actually appear in the wild: the KeyFit Strada is the first belt-positioning booster from Chicco, a brand better known for its strollers and high chairs. We saw a prototype of the seat at a trade show and thought it was well-designed, if a bit overpriced. The KeyFit Strada's unique features include headrest and side wings that adjust up and out and more EPS foam than other seats, Chicco claims. The seat converts to a backless booster for kids up to 100 lbs. and features an adjustable, clip-on cup holder.

The price seems high: $130 is a bit much, when you consider the similar Graco TurboBooster starts at $50. It's hard to image how an adjustable headrest and side wings justifies such a price premium. **Rating: Not yet.**

CLEK OLLI / OZZI

Booster type: Backless booster
Weight Range: 40 to 120 lbs., 57″ tall.
Price: $90 Olli, $60 Ozzi
Pros: Only LATCH backless booster.

Removable, washable seat cover.
Cons: No cup holders. High price.
Comments: Canadian car seat maker Magna's (magnaclek.com) backless booster is unique: it is the only backless booster that uses LATCH for a secure fit to the car. Your child then buckles in with the auto safety belt. We're not quite sure we see the point for the Clek—if your vehicle is in an accident, it is the auto safety belt (not the LATCH connectors) that hold your child in place. So we guess the main advantage of the Clek is that the LATCH connectors hold the seat in place when it is unoccupied. Nice, but is it worth $90 when most other (LATCH-less) backless boosters run $20?

Reader feedback on the Clek Olli has been positive—readers love how easy it is to install and use. The downsides: it is pricey and lacks a cup holder, seen on most other boosters.

FYI: Clek makes a scaled down version of the Olli called the Ozzi: it omits the quick release strap, mesh side storage pocket, carry bag and armrest padding. The Olli comes in several colors and is made of a micro fiber; the Ozzi comes in one color (black) and has less expensive fabric. The Ozzi is $30 cheaper.
Rating: A-

CLEK OOBER

Booster type: High back and backless booster
Weight Range: 33 to 120 lbs., 57″ tall.
Price: $250
Comments: Out by the time you read this, the Clek Oober is a high back booster that has a removable back. As with the Clek Olli/Ozzi, the Oober will

feature LATCH for a secure fit to the car.

The Oober's other main point is that the seat reclines up to 12 degrees and has an adjustable head restraint. AT $250, however, this will be a tough sell for most parents. With the top-selling high back booster (the Graco TurboBooster) selling for $200 less, it is unclear whether these features make it worth five times that amount.

Since this seat wasn't released as of press time, we don't have any parent feedback yet.

Rating: Not yet.
Dimensions. 14″ long, 17.5 wide, 33.5″ high.

COMBI KOBUCK

Backless version is called the Combi Dakota
Booster type: High back and backless booster.
Weight range: 33 to 100 lbs.; 33″ to 57″ in height.
Price: $80-100; backless version is $35-40.
Pros: Side impact protection; can be used as a backless booster.

Cons: Funky cup holder; high price.

Comments: Want side impact protection but turned off by the restrictive wings of other booster seats? Combi's Kobuck aims to fill this niche with a protective headrest, minus the tight-fitting wings. We liked the padding of this seat (even the armrests are padded), but the cheesy cup holder and relatively high price ($20 to $40 more than the Graco TurboBooster) are a turn off. On the plus side, the entire seat is lined with EPS and "egg shock" (comfort) foam. Combi's pitch for the Kobuck includes a claim that its front air vents allow for "healthy ventilation." Well, given parent feedback, we don't think this seat is any cooler than other boosters, but it's hard to measure that claim.

Parent feedback on this seat has been positive. The Kobuck scored as a "good bet" as a high back booster and "best bet" as a backless booster in recent Insurance Institute for Highway Safety ratings.

FYI: Combi sells a backless version of the Kobuck, dubbed the "Dakota" for $35.

Rating: B+
Dimensions. 20″ long, 18″ wide, 27″ high.

COMPASS FOLDING BOOSTER
See First Years Folding Booster

Cosco Ambassador Booster Seat aka High Rise Auto Booster Seat

Booster type: Backless booster
Weight range: 30-100 lbs. Kids must be 52" or less.

Price: $15
Pros: Cheap backless booster. Cup holder.
Cons: None.
Comments: Very simple and affordable backless boosters. Both versions have padded armrests and a fold-down cup holder.
Rating: B
Dimensions: 16"D, 17"W, 9.5"H.

Cosco High Back Booster

(a.k.a. Cosco Complete Voyager)
Booster type: Combo
Weight range: 22-40 lbs. with harness, 30-80 as belt positioning booster. A newer version of this seat goes up to 100 lbs.
Price: Two different versions, $50 to $60.
Pros: Inexpensive, fits great in cars, five-point harness option from 22 to 40 lbs., headrest, armrests, storage bag,.
Cons: Straps twist, Cosco's abysmal safety record. "Not recommended" rating by IIHS.
Comments: Cosco's High Back booster comes in two versions. The Cosco High Back Booster ($50) is a combo booster with a five-point harness from 22 to 40 lbs., then working as a booster from 30 to 80 lbs. But this seat has cut corners at every turn. First and foremost, the top harness slots on this seat are the same as Cosco's convertible, the Touriva, meaning that lots of kids get too tall for this seat before they reach 40 lbs. Second, the tether strap is a total pain to adjust and get tight. An upgraded version of this seat (the Ventura, $60), adds armrests and cup holders.

While this seat does fit well in cars, we don't give it high marks. The too-low harness heights are a deal killer. We also note that parent reviews of Cosco's boosters have been mixed. For every parent we interviewed who liked their Cosco booster, another gave it a thumbs down—some gripes were minor (Cosco's light tan fabric on some of the boosters stains too easily), while other frustrations were more serious (quality complaints, straps that twist and are hard to adjust, etc.). The final blow: the Insurance Institute for Highway Safety gave this seat a "Not Recommend" rating for its poor fit to kids.
Rating: D
Dimensions. Top Harness Slot: 15.3", Back height: 25", Seat width: 17.3".

boosters

COSCO PRONTO

Booster type: High back and backless booster
Weight range: 30-100 lbs. as belt positioning booster, 40-100 lbs. as backless booster.
Price: $35-45.
Pros: Low price, machine washable pad, cup holder.
Cons: None.

Comments: This booster has a roomy seat and adjusts for taller kids. We also like the machine washable pad. And you can't beat the price. This might be a good booster for Grandma's car.

Rating: B

EDDIE BAUER AUTO BOOSTER

a.k.a. Disney enRoute
Weight: 30 to 100 lbs.
Booster type: High back belt-positioning booster
Pros: Affordable.
Cons: Not out as of press time, so no reader feedback yet.
Price: $70 (backless version is $30)
Comments: The Eddie Bauer Auto Booster (also known as the enRoute) features extra padding, double cup holders and converts to a backless booster. Or you can buy just the backless version for $30. It is similar to the Cosco Pronto, but has armrests that pivot and an adjustable headrest plus an extra cup holder.

Rating: B

EDDIE BAUER COMFORT HIGH BACK BOOSTER
See Safety 1st Vantage

EDDIE BAUER ADJUSTABLE HIGH BACK BOOSTER
See Safety 1st Prospect

EDDIE BAUER DELUXE HIGH BACK BOOSTER
See Safety 1st Summit

EVENFLO BIG KID / BIG KID CONFIDENCE

Weight: 30 to 100 lbs.
Booster type: High back booster
Pros: Low price, extras like reading lights, EPS foam.
Cons: Skimpy padding in low-end version. Not recommended" rating by IIHS.

Price: $40-65; a backless version is $20. Big Kid Confidence is $90.
Comments: Evenflo's answer to Graco's TurboBooster, the Big Kid adds a few bells and whistles that Graco doesn't have. Example: two reading lights for "evening activities." Also unique: The Big Kid is adjustable in both height and lap depth (most boosters are just height adjustable). The back removes as kids grow bigger, adding a discreet boost to older kids without having them look "uncool." On the plus side, the Big Kid is less expensive than the Graco Turbo Booster (a $40 version in Target is especially affordable). On the downside, the padding is a bit skimpier than the Graco, making this seat less comfy for longer trips. And the Big Kid has less side impact protection than other seats. As usual, it is the little things about Evenflo that drive you crazy: the reading lights are nice, but lack an auto shut-off feature (and hence, will consume batteries fast if left on).

Evenflo has rolled out a deluxe version of this seat, dubbed the Big Kid Confidence ($90). The Confidence offers "European Styling" (has anyone at Evenflo ever been to Europe?), retractable cup holders and armrests, as well as "visually accented" belt guides to help with correct installation. The backless version of the Big Kid is a mere $20.

This seat earned a "Not Recommended" rating by the Insurance Institute for Highway Safety for its poor fit to kids. As a result, we don't recommend this seat either.
Rating: D

EVENFLO CHASE DLX
Booster type: Combo
Weight: 20-100 lbs.; 20 to 40 lbs. with harness, belt-positioning booster for 30 to 100 lbs.
Price: $60 to $70
Comments: This older model combo seat comes in several versions: the DLX adds fancier padding (the Comfort Touch), armrests and a cup holder. For this, you pay an extra $20 over the LX. These seats are five years old and showing their age. This seat earned a "Not Recommended" rating by the Insurance Institute for Highway Safety for its poor fit to kids. As a result, we don't recommend this seat either.
Rating: D

EVENFLO GENERATIONS
Booster type: Combo
Weight: 20-100 lbs.; 20 to 40 lbs. with harness, belt-positioning booster for 30 to 100 lbs.
Price: $100
Pros: Adjuster knob for belt harness; higher

weight limit than other Evenflo combo seats.

Cons: Pricey. "Not recommended" rating by IIHS.

Comments: This upgraded combo seat from Evenflo is similar to the Chase but features a fancier headrest, better padding and a 100 lb. weight limit. The knob, which adjusts the belts, gets better parent reviews than the harness adjuster on the Traditions. Flip-out cup holder is nice, especially if you have a small back seat. The Generation has a very slight recline feature. This seat earned a "Not Recommended" rating by the Insurance Institute for Highway Safety for its poor fit for kids. As a result, we don't recommend this seat.

Rating: D

FIRST YEARS FOLDING BOOSTER SEAT

Booster type: High back booster

Weight range: 30-100 lbs.

Price: $60-120

Pros: Folds up, nicely padded, flip-up armrests, extra wide seat, good price.

Cons: Not recommended rating by IIHS.

Comments: This seat started life as the Compass Folding booster and is still sold that way on some web sites, even after Compass was acquired by Learning Curve's The First Years a couple of years ago. As you might have guessed from the name, this seat's key selling feature is the ability to fold, unique in the market. That's a boon for carpoolers or anyone who has to shuttle a booster between vehicles. The Folding Booster features excellent padding, side impact protection (EPS foam) and extras like two cup holders, flip-up armrests and six-position height adjustment.

Over the years, The First Years has come out with several different versions of this seat—the Deluxe, Ultra, Premiere, etc. Each is very similar, with the plushness of the fabric being the main difference. The basic model is $60, while some versions soar to $120.

While reader feedback on this seat is very positive and we recommended it in a previous edition, this seat did NOT earn good ratings from the Insurance Institute for Highway Safety (IIHS). In fact, their report said this seat is "Not Recommended" due to poor fit.

Rating: D

GRACO AIR BOOSTER *See Graco TurboBooster*

GRACO CARGO: CHERISHED, ULTRA, AND PLATINUM

Booster type: Combo

Weight range: 20-40 lbs. with harness, 30 to 100 lbs. as high back booster.

Price: $80 to $100

Pros: Good price; starts at 20 lbs., up-front belt adjustment on some models, narrow.

Cons: Skimpy padding, mediocre shoulder belt adjusters.

Comments: The CarGo was Graco's first stab at combo boosters—seats that are harnessed from 20 to 40 lbs. and then convert to a high back booster for kids 30 to 100 lbs. This was innovative ten years ago, but since then the market has passed this seat by—there are many new seats that are harnessed up to 50, 65 and even 80 lbs. Graco's own Nautilus (reviewed below) is a good example and a better bet than the aging CarGo.

The CarGo's biggest selling feature is its narrow width—you can squeeze two or three together in a small back seat. But the CarGo also has its flaws, among them a mediocre shoulder belt adjuster. These clips tend to lock the belt into place, which might introduce dangerous slack in the belt. And they may make it difficult for your toddler to buckle himself into his seat, a major pain as we discussed earlier in this chapter.

The biggest negative to the CarGo: it earned a "Not Recommended" rating by the Insurance Institute for Highway Safety for its poor fit. As a result, we don't recommend this seat.

Ratings: D

Dimensions. Top Harness slot: 17", Back height: 26.5", Outside width: 16".

GRACO NAUTILUS 3-IN-1

Booster type: Combo

Weight range: 20-65 lbs. with harness, 30 to 100 lbs. as high back booster. Backless booster from 40 to 100 lbs.

Price: $135-170

Pros: Works to 65 lbs. with a five-point harness.

Cons: None.

Comments: Graco's Nautilus is a combo booster that works with a five-point harness to 65 lbs. and then converts to high back booster (100 lbs.) and even a backless booster for older kids. The harness is a big plus if you have a toddler who has outgrown his convertible seat, but you wish to keep him in the harness for a while longer (the 65 lb. limit should fit most five year olds).

The Nautilus' other features include over molded armrests (with side storage), three-position recline and decent padding. The seat is lined with EPS foam. Like most Graco seats, Graco makes a few different versions of the Nautilus, which basically boil down to fabric plushness. The basic one is $135; Babies R Us sells a slightly upgraded version that is $170. There is even a "Nautilus Elite" for specialty stores for $220 with a memory foam seat and adjustable head wings.

The Nautilus's biggest competitor is the Britax Frontier, so let's look how they compare. The Britax Frontier is bigger and wider than the Nautilus—and the Britax seat works up to 80 lbs. But, the Britax seat is much more difficult to install and use than the Nautilus, which costs HALF the price of the Frontier.

Overall, we like the Nautilus better—it is our top pick in this category.
Rating: A

GRACO TURBOBOOSTER
(a.k.a. Graco Air Booster)
Booster type: High back and backless booster
Weight range: 30 to 100 lbs. as high back booster (backless, it is 40 to 100 lbs).
Price: $50 to $80. AirBooster: $90. Backless version is $20-25.
Pros: Top choice in booster market—both affordable and well designed.

Cons: No five-point harness; little side impact protection.

Comments: This is our top pick as a great, affordable booster seat. We love the sharp design and open loop belt adjuster, which is a major improvement over Graco's other booster seat (the CarGo). Graco did this one right: you get padded armrests that are height adjustable, EPS foam, hide-away cup holders and more. The seat pad removes for cleaning and there is an easy one-hand adjustment for the headrest. The TurboBooster converts into a backless booster for older kids. As usual, Graco makes the TurboBooster in a bazillion (yes, that is the technical term) colors and fabrics. Hence you'll see a bare-bones version for $50 at Wal-Mart. . . and then "deluxe" models in specialty boutiques for up to $80. What's the difference? Just the fabric pad. More money, fancier pad.

In the past year, Graco debuted a new version of this seat, dubbed the AirBooster. The AirBooster is basically the same shell and features of the TurboBooster, but with a mesh seat like you see in high-end office chairs. With a slightly wider and deeper seat, the AirBooster is $90.

So what are the drawbacks to the Graco TurboBooster? Well, unlike the Graco Nautilus or Britax Frontier, this seat lacks a five-point harness. Hence you must have an older toddler who is mature enough to sit in a safety belt to use the TurboBooster. And other seats have better side impact protection. Finally, the TurboBooster requires quite a bit of assembly with various screws you need to attach.

On the other hand, the TurboBooster is much less expensive the either of those seats. We were also impressed that the TurboBooster scored a "good bet" as a belt-positioning seat and "best bet" as a backless booster by the Insurance Institute of Highway Safety. And reader feedback on the TurboBooster (and AirBooster) has been very positive. Hence, this seat gets our top rating.

Dimensions. Back height: 27", seat width: 16".

Rating: A

JANE INDY PLUS BOOSTER SEAT

This seat is reviewed on our web page BabyBargains.com, click on Bonus Material.

MAXI COSI RODI XR

Booster type: High back booster
Weight Range: 30 to 100 lbs.
Price: $160
Pros: Extra large side wings provide sleep support, adjustable headrest. Seat recline.
Cons: Requires vehicles with rear headrests.
Comments: Dorel brought its European sister brand to the U.S. a couple of years ago, as part of their Quinny stroller launch. The goal was for Dorel to have a premium brand to compete against Britax. The results? If the Rodi is any indication, Dorel needs to rethink its strategy.

The Rodi first debuted as a $100 booster with deep side wings for side impact protection and sleeping support. The Rodi also had a recline feature, yet lacked an adjustable headrest. And at $100, it was hard to justify the extra 50% price premium over seats like the Graco TurboBooster, which basically do the same thing.

The new Rodi XR should be out by the time you read this. It adds an adjustable headrest but is still similar to the old Rodi (seat recline, etc.). At $160, it's overpriced when compared to the similar First Years Folding Booster. Another major negative: like most Dorel boosters, the Rodi requires the rear seat in your vehicle have headrest support—something lacking in many cars.

Rating: C

RECARO START

Booster type: High-back booster
Weight Range: 30 to 80 lbs.
Price: $250
Pros: Very comfortable, many adjustments.
Cons: Shoulder belt lock off makes older children feel confined, adjustments hard to use.

boosters

Comments: When this seat debuted five years ago, it sported a then unheard of price of $350. That seemed like a king's ransom for a booster seat and we wondered if any seat, no matter how good, would be worth that chunk of change.

Well, time rolls on and Recaro has since lowered this seat to $250 at Babies R Us (although Amazon sells it for $275 to $350). And with Britax selling its Frontier booster for $280, suddenly the Start doesn't look so outrageous.

At least for all this money, you do get a darn good seat. According to our child testers, the Recaro Start offers fantastic comfort. It also has more adjustments than most car seats, (height, shoulder width, and seat depth adjustments) and it has one of the highest high backs on the market. The deep side wings provide nice sleeping support and possibly side impact protection. But the adjustments are cumbersome, so this is not a good seat to share between siblings. And it is a lousy choice for carpools at a hefty 26 lbs. The shoulder belt lock off MUST be used on this booster, for all ages, which can feel very confining for older children.

Rating: A-
Dimensions. Back height: 29", Outside width: 16.5"

RECARO VIVO/ VIVO LITE
Booster type: High back booster
Weight Range: 30 to 100 lbs.
Price: $80-90 Vivo Lite, $100 Vivo.
Pros: Side wings provide impact protection and sleep support. Nice fabrics.
Cons: Hard to find in retail stores.
Comments: Recaro's new Vivo high-back boosters are excellent models. The side wings provide side-impact protection and the seat is lined with EPS foam. The Vivo and Vivo Lite are identical, except for the fabric pad: the Vivo has a microfiber pad, while the Vivo Lite has a more breathable fabric with mesh inserts.

Reader feedback on the Vivo has been very positive—parents like the side impact protection and the overall quality of Recaro's seats . . . you can tell the company doesn't cut any corners. Unfortunately, seeing one of these seats in person can take a bit of persistence, as Recaro's retail distribution is thin.

Rating: A

RECARO YOUNG STYLE
This seat is now discontinued; an archive of the review is on our web page at BabyBargains.com (go to Bonus Material).

RECARO YOUNG SPORT

Booster type: Combo
Weight Range: 18 to 80 lbs.; five-point harness to 40 lbs. Up to 59".
Price: $250
Pros: Very comfortable, EPS foam, side impact protection.
Cons: Price. Five point harness only to 40 lbs.?
Comments: This is probably Recaro's best-selling seat—the Young Sport is a combo seat that combines a five-point harness up to 40 lbs. with a belt-positioning booster that works to 80 lbs. Feature-wise, it includes EPS foam, side impact protection and adjustable headrest. The Young Sport also has a removable seat cushion for younger toddlers. As with the Start, kids give high marks to this seat's comfort . . . but, again, the adjustments could be more parent-friendly. Overall, quality (as for all Recaro seats) is high. But the price ($250) is exorbitant, especially compared with the new Graco Nautilus that will feature a five-point harness to 65 lbs. and cost $100 less. FYI: The Recaro Young Sport seat earned a "Good Bet" by the Insurance Institute for Highway Safety.
Rating: A-
Dimensions. Width 18.1", Height 26" to 31.3".

SAFEGUARD GO

Seat type: Combo seat and backless booster.
Weight range: 30 to 100 lbs. To 60 lbs. with five-point harness. 34"-52" height for the five-point harness; 43"-57" for the backless booster.
Price: $150.

Pros: Innovative hybrid seat that works up to 60 lbs. with five-point harness; great for taxis.

Cons: Requires a top tether when used with five-point harness. No cup holder. Pricey. Check LATCH weight limit of your vehicle before ordering.

Comments: Now this seat is impressive—the SafeGuard Go features a five-point harness that can be used to 60 lbs. . . . and then the seat converts to a backless booster to 100 lbs. And it all folds into a travel bag, a boon for carpools or taxis (take note, New Yorkers). This hybrid is probably where the market for boosters is going in the future—a five-point harness for younger toddlers that works beyond 40 lbs. and then a backless booster for older kids up to 100 lbs.

One caveat to the Safeguard Go—it can only be used with its five-point harness in vehicles with LATCH and a top tether. That's

CAR SEATS

not a problem if your car was made after 2003 . . . but if you are driving an older vehicle, it may not be compatible (some car makers added LATCH before 2003, but others did not). SafeGuard has a handy vehicle compatibility function on their web site so you can see if your vehicle would work.

And remember that your vehicle may have low LATCH limits—Honda is just 40 lbs., for example. Most are 48 lbs.; Subaru is 60. If your vehicle has a low limit, you won't be able to use the five-point harness—and hence you just bought yourself a $165 backless booster.

And just to add another layer of confusion: some vehicles have a different (lower) limit for tethers. Saturn has a 48 lb. LATCH limit, but a 40 lb. limit for a tether. In that case, the SafeGuard Go would be a poor choice.

Bottom line: this is a good seat IF your vehicle has high enough LATCH and tether limits to take advantage of its unique design. Reader feedback on this seat has been very positive.

The SafeGuard earned a top rating (Best Bet) from the Insurance Institute for Highway Safety.

Rating: B+

SAFETY 1ST APEX 65
(a.k.a. Safety 1st Apex 65, Alpha Elite Apex)
Type: Combo
Weight range: 20 to 65 lbs. with internal harness; 40 to 100 lbs. as a belt-positioning booster. Kids must be 57" or less.
Price: $110-150

Pros: 65 lb. limit WITH a five-point harness!

Cons: Limiting top harness slot and crotch strap means larger toddlers will outgrow the harness before 65 lbs. Difficult to install. Requires vehicle headrest.

Comments: The Apex was one of the first harnessed booster seats to work to 65 lbs. with a five-point harness. This seat features an adjustable headrest, padded armrests, cup holder and padded insert to fit smaller toddlers.

As a hybrid seat, the Apex morphs into a belt-positioning booster after a toddler has outgrown the harness. And that's the rub with this seat: the top harness slot is only 17.5". Given that harness slot, we'd guess that many toddlers will be too tall for the harness before they reach 65 lbs. And the lack of an adjustable crotch strap (it only has two positions) also limits the Apex's harness use. Another downside to this seat: the arm pads come off too easily, according to reader feedback.

The Apex 65 earned a "Good Bet" rating from the Insurance Institute for Highway Safety for how well it fits children . . . but it is difficult to install. As with all Cosco's boosters, your vehicle must have rear

headrests, which is another negative. While Apex has a slightly wider seat than the Graco Nautilus, it doesn't convert to a backless booster.
Rating: B-

SAFETY 1ST SUMMIT

(a.k.a. the Safety 1st Summit and Eddie Bauer Deluxe High Back Booster)
Booster type: Combo
Weight range: 22-40 lbs. with harness, 40-100 lbs. as belt positioning booster.
Price: $100-$120
Pros: EPP foam.

Cons: Top harness slots no higher than most convertibles, Cosco's abysmal safety record. "Not recommended" by IIHS report.

Comments: The Summit is an old-style booster seat, with a harness that works to 40 lbs. and then to 100 lbs. as a belt-positioning booster. For 2009, Safety 1st is refreshing this model with a new headrest and base with pop-out cup holders.

Sounds perfect, right? Well, not quite. The big disappointment with this seat is that the top harness slots are no higher than an average convertible, about 15." So some kids can use this seat to a full 40 lbs., but many will outgrow it by height before weight. It also comes with the fussy Cosco tether adjuster, and Cosco's dubious safety record.

Another negative: this seat earned a "Not Recommended" rating by the Insurance Institute for Highway Safety for its poor fit as a booster. FYI: There is an Eddie Bauer version of this seat (dubbed the Deluxe High Back Booster) for $120—same seat, just an upgraded fabric pad.

Rating: D
Dimensions. Top Harness Slot: 15", Back height: 27", Seat width: 18".

SAFETY 1ST VANTAGE

(a.k.a. the Safety 1st Surveyor, Eddie Bauer Comfort High Back, Alpha Sport Vantage)
Booster type: Combo
Weight range: 22-40 lbs. with five-point harness, 40 to 100 lbs. belt-positioning booster. 52" height limit. EPP foam.
Price: $80-100.

Comments: A basic combo that is similar to the Cosco High Back Booster, but has a bigger seat area. While the seat now has EPP foam, the Vantage lacks side impact protection and other features you see on other seats in this price category. The shoulder belt guides can adjust to five positions. The Surveyor earned only a "C" in the gov-

ernment's ease of use ratings in the "securing a child" category. All in all, not very impressive. FYI: This seat is sold under the names Vantage, Surveyor, Eddie Bauer Comfort High Back booster and Alpha Vantage.
Rating: C

SAFETY 1ST PROSPECT BOOSTER
(a.k.a. the Eddie Bauer Adjustable High Back Booster)
Booster type: Combo and backless booster.
Weight range: 22 to 40 lbs. with five-point harness, 40 to 100 lbs. as a belt-positioning or backless booster.
Price: $80-100.

Comments: This seat's main advantage is its three uses: first as a combo seat, then as a belt-positioning booster and finally as a backless booster. The Prospect features a wide, well-padded seat and two built-in cup holders. The side wings are lined with EPS. The Prospect is better designed than most Cosco offerings, but we wish the harness worked up to 65 lbs. (like the Apex). One downside: the Prospect earned only a "C" in the government's ease of use rating (NHTSA.gov) when it came to securing a child. FYI: A backless version of the Prospect ($25; 40 to 100 lbs.; pivoting armrests, extra wide seat) is also available.

The Prospect earned a "Not Recommended" rating by the Insurance Institute for Highway Safety.
Rating: D

SUNSHINE KIDS MONTEREY BOOSTER
Booster type: High back
Weight range: 30 to 100 lbs, 60" in height.
Price: $120-140
Pros: Works with LATCH, height adjustable, EPS foam, retractable cup holder, seat recline.
Cons: Short LATCH connectors make it hard to install, difficult to remove.
Comments: A bit taller than the Britax Monarch, the Monterey features a dial-adjustable seat width, EPS foam, a deep seat, retractable cup holders, two recline positions and a cushy foam seat. The Monterey also works with LATCH, among the few boosters on the market with this feature. But . . . the LATCH connectors are very short and hard to attach. Hence moving this seat from car to car would be a chore.

Despite that drawback, most parent feedback on this seat has been very positive. Folks like the roomy seat and easy adjustments.
Rating: A

Our Picks: Booster Seat Recommendations

What's the best booster seat on the market? Before you can answer that question, you must look at your child—his/her weight, height and maturity (ability to stay put in an auto safety belt) are the key factors to consider. In general, we recommend keeping your toddler in a harnessed seat as long as possible . . . whether that is a convertible that works to 65 lbs. or one of the new hybrid boosters that has a five-point harness up to 65 lbs. After that, we suggest a belt-positioning booster.

Here are our top picks for boosters.

◆ *Best Bets: Harness Seats.* Our top pick is the *Graco Nautilus*—this combo seat has a five-point harness that can be used up to 65 lbs. The Nautilus also converts to a belt-positioning booster and even a backless booster to 100 lbs. At $135-170, the Nautilus is half the price of its chief competitor (the Britax Frontier), but is easier to install and use.

◆ *Best Bets: Belt-Positioning Booster.* We have one clear winner here and several other strong runners-ups.

The *Graco TurboBooster* ($50 to $80) is the best belt-positioning booster on the market today. It packs a good number of features into an affordable package: height-adjustable headrest, open belt loop design, armrests, back recline, cup holders and more. Note it comes in two versions: a high-back version and backless (the latter is about $20-$25). And the AirBooster version ($90) of this seat is excellent: its mesh seat wins praise from toddlers for comfort.

Runner up: *Recaro's* excellent boosters, the *Vivo* and *Vivo Lite* feature side impact protection and sleep support, plus EPS foam and Recaro's overall strong reputation for quality. At $80 to $100, these are worth the extra money.

Runner up: The *Sunshine Kids Monterey Booster* works with LATCH and features a dial-adjustable seat width, EPS foam, a deep seat and two position seat recline. The cushy foam seat earns kudos from parents and kids alike. At $120 to $140, it is twice the price of a TurboBooster . . . but worth the investment.

◆ *Best Bets: Backless Booster.* The best backless boosters on the market are the *Graco TurboBooster* backless ($20 to $25) and the *Combi Dakota* ($35 to $40, reviewed under the Combi Kobuck earlier in this chapter). Both are affordable and easy to use boosters for older kids who don't need the high back booster anymore.

CAR
SEATS

Whew! You made it through the car seat chapter. Yes, we know—
it was slightly shorter than the last Harry Potter novel.

Next up: strollers: which brands are best? How can you pick the
best stroller for what you need? We've got it covered, starting on the
next page.

CHAPTER 9

Strollers, Diaper Bags, Carriers and Other Gear To Go

Inside this chapter

W hat are the best strollers? Which brands are the most durable AND affordable? We'll discuss this plus other tips on how to make your baby portable—from front carriers to diaper bags and more. And what do you put in that diaper bag anyway? We've got nine suggestions, plus advice on the best baby carriers.

Getting Started: When Do You Need This Stuff?

While you don't need a stroller, diaper bag or carrier immediately after baby is born, most parents purchase them before baby arrives anyway. And some of the best deals for strollers and other to-go gear are found online, which necessitates leaving time for shipping.

Sources to Find Strollers, Carriers

Like other baby products, the discounters like Target and Wal-Mart tend to specialize in just a handful of models from the mass-market companies like Cosco, Kolcraft, Graco and so on (lately, they've been adding premium brands to their web sites although they aren't available in their stores). The baby superstores like Babies R Us and Buy Buy Baby have a wider selection and (sometimes) better brands. Meanwhile, juvenile specialty stores almost always carry the more exclusive brands.

Yet perhaps the best deals for strollers, carriers and diaper bags are found online—for some reason, this seems to be one area the web covers very well. This is because strollers are relatively easy to ship (compared to other more bulky juvenile items). Of course, more competition often means lower prices, so you'll see many deals online. Another plus: the web may be the only way to find certain premium-brand strollers if you live in less-populous parts of the U.S. and Canada.

Beware of shipping costs when ordering online or from a catalog—many strollers may run 20 or 30 pounds, which can translate into hefty shipping fees. Use an online coupon (see Chapter 7 for coupon sites) to save and look for free shipping specials.

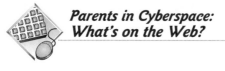

Parents in Cyberspace: What's on the Web?

Online info on strollers, diaper bags and carriers falls into two categories: manufacturer sites and discounters who sell online. Here's a brief overview:

◆ *Discounters.* Stroller deals come and go by the day—track the latest deal news on our message boards. Our stroller message board (BabyBargains.com/strollers) hosts a lively discussion on all things stroller-wise, while the bargain board (BabyBargains.com/coupons) tracks the latest discount codes for major stroller retailers.

◆ *Craigslist.* Stroller deals abound on Craigslist—on the New York City board, we found a Bugaboo Cameleon with extras for $450 (regularly $900), a free Graco stroller in San Francisco and a Chicco Cortina for half price in Dallas. Sure, some deals are dogs . . . but there are also steals. Spend a few moments on Craigslist and you'll quickly see the going rate for used name-brand strollers.

Strollers

Baby stores offer a bewildering array of strollers for parents. Do you want the model that converts from a car seat to a stroller? What about a stroller that would work for a quick trip to the mall? Or do you want a stroller for jogging? Hiking trails? The urban jungle of New York City or beaches near LA?

And what about all the different brand names? Will a basic brand found at a discount store work? Or do you pine after one of the stylish Euro-designed imports? What about strollers with anti-lock brakes and air bags? (Just kidding on that last one).

The $274 million dollar stroller industry is not dominated by one or two players, like you might see in car seats or high chairs. Instead, you'll find a couple *dozen* stroller makers offering just about anything on wheels, ranging from $30 for a bare-bones model to $900 for a Dutch-designed über stroller. A hot recent trend: all-terrain strollers with three wheels, where the front wheel swivels.

We hope this section takes some of the mystery out of the stroller buying process. First, we'll look at the six different types of strollers on the market today. Next, we'll zero in on features and help you decided what's important and what's not. Then, it's brand ratings and our picks as the best recommendations for different lifestyles. Finally, we'll go over several safety tips, money saving hints, and wastes of money.

Whew! Take a deep breath and let's go.

What Are You Buying?

There are six types of strollers you can buy:

◆ **Umbrella Strollers.** The name comes from the appearance of the stroller when it's folded, similar to an umbrella.

WHAT'S COOL: They're lightweight and generally cheap—that is, low in price (about $20 to $40). We should note that a handful of premium stroller makers (Maclaren and Peg Perego) also offer pricey umbrella strollers that sell for $150 to $300. Pictured above is a no-frills Kolcraft umbrella stroller.

WHAT'S NOT: They're cheap—that is, low in quality (well, with the exception of Maclaren and Peg Perego). You typically don't get any fancy features like canopies, storage baskets, reclining seats, and so on. Another problem: most umbrella strollers have hammock-style seats with little head support, so they won't work well for babies under six months of age.

◆ **Carriage Strollers.** A carriage (also called a pram) is like a bed on wheels—the seat lies flat and the leg rest pulls up to form a bassinet-like feature. Clearly, this feature focuses on newborns . . . but these strollers can then be configured for older babies with a seat that sits upright.

WHAT'S COOL: Full recline is great for newborns, which spend most of their time sleeping. Most combo carriage/strollers have lots of high-end features like plush seats, quilted canopies and other accessories to keep the weather out. The best carriage strollers and prams have a dreamy ride, with amazing suspensions and big wheels.

WHAT'S NOT: Hefty weight (not easy to transport or set up) and hefty price tags. Another negative: most Euro-style "prams" have fixed front wheels, which make maneuvering difficult on quick trips. Some carriage/stroller models can top $500, although entry-level carriage strollers start at $200. These strollers once dominated the market but have lost favor as more parents opt for "travel systems" that combine an infant seat and stroller (see below).

◆ *Lightweight Strollers.* These strollers are our top recommendation: they're basically souped-up umbrella strollers with many convenience features.

WHAT'S COOL: Most offer easy set-up and fold-down; some even fold up similar to umbrella strollers. Many models have great features (canopies, storage baskets, high-quality wheels) at amazingly light weights (as little as eight pounds). Graco and Maclaren probably make the most popular lightweight strollers.

WHAT'S NOT: Can be expensive—most high-quality brands run $150 to $300. The smaller wheels on lightweight strollers make maneuvering in the mall or stores easy . . . but those same wheels don't perform well on uneven surfaces or on gravel trails. Skimpy baskets are another trade-off.

◆ *Jogging (or Sport) Strollers.* These strollers feature three big bicycle-tire wheels and lightweight frames—perfect for jogging or walking on rough roads. The front wheel is fixed to maximize glide.

WHAT'S COOL: How many other strollers can do 15 mph on a jogging trail? Some have plush features like padded seats and canopies—and the best fold up quickly for easy storage in the trunk. This category was hip a few years ago, but is now in decline: more popular are the all-terrain strollers (see below).

WHAT'S NOT: They can be darn expensive, topping $300. Jogging strollers are a single-purpose item—thanks to their sheer bulk and a lack of steering (joggers usually have fixed front wheels), you can't use one in a mall or other location. On the plus side, the flood of new models is helping lower prices. New, low-end jogging strollers run $100 to $150. The trade-offs to the new bargain price models: heavier steel frames and a lack of features.

◆ **All-terrain Strollers.** The baby equivalent of sport-utility vehicles, these strollers are pitched to parents who want to go on hikes or other outdoor adventures. All-terrain strollers are similar to joggers with one big difference—the front wheel swivels.

WHAT'S COOL: Big air-filled tires and high clearances work better on gravel trails/roads than standard strollers. These strollers are great for neighborhoods with broken or rough sidewalks. All-terrain strollers have many convenience features (baskets, canopies, etc.) as well as one key advantage over jogging strollers: most all-terrains have swivel front wheels. That makes them easy to maneuver, whether on a trail or at the mall. Pictured here is the Phil & Ted's Sport stroller.

WHAT'S NOT: All-terrain strollers are wider and heavier than other strollers, which make them less useful in a mall or store with tight aisles. And air-filled tires are great for trails . . . but a pain in the neck if you get a flat. If you really want to run with a stroller, all-terrains with a swivel front wheel are not the best choice (a jogger with a fixed front wheel is better). And let's not forget the cost—most all terrains are pricey, some topping $400.

◆ **Travel systems.** It's the current rage among stroller makers—models that combine infant car seats and strollers. Century (now part of Graco) kicked off this craze way back in 1994 with its "4-in-1" model that featured four uses (infant carrier, infant car seat, carriage and toddler stroller). Since then, just about every major stroller maker has jumped into the travel system market. Travel systems have just about killed sales of carriage strollers; now even carriage stroller king Peg Perego has bowed to the travel system trend. Pictured on the previous page is the Graco MetroLite travel system.

WHAT'S COOL: Great convenience—you can take the infant car seat out of the car and then snap it into the stroller frame. Voila! Instant baby carriage, complete with canopy and basket. Later, you can use the stroller as, well, just a stroller.

WHAT'S NOT: The strollers are often junk—especially those by mass market makers Cosco and Evenflo. Quality problems plague this category, as does something we call "feature bloat." Popular travel systems from Graco, for example, are so loaded with features that they tip the scales at nearly 30 pounds! The result: many parents abandon their travel system strollers for lighter weight models after baby outgrows his infant seat. And considering these puppies can cost $150 to $250 (some even more), that's a big investment for such lim-

strollers

ited use. On the up side, better strollers brands such as Maclaren, Perego and Chicco have also jumped into the travel system market, offering alternatives to the heavyweight mass market strollers.

Safe & Sound

Next to defective car seats, the most dangerous juvenile product on the market today is the stroller. That's according to the U.S. Consumer Product Safety Commission, which estimates that over 11,000 injuries a year occur from improper use or defects. The problems? Babies can slide out of the stroller (falling to the ground) and small parts can be a choking hazard. Seat belts have broken in some models, while other babies are injured when a stroller's brakes fail on a slope. Serious mishaps with strollers have involved entanglements and entrapments (where an unrestrained baby slides down and gets caught in a leg opening). Here are some safety tips:

1 **NEVER HANG BAGS FROM THE STROLLER HANDLE**—it's a tipping hazard.

2 **DON'T LEAVE YOUR BABY ASLEEP UNATTENDED IN A STROLLER.** Many injuries happen when infants who are lying down in a stroller roll or creep and then manage to get their head stuck in the stroller's leg openings. Be safe: take a sleeping baby out of a stroller and move them to a crib or bassinet.

3 **THE BRAKES SHOULDN'T BE TRUSTED.** The best stroller models have brakes on two wheels; cheaper ones just have one wheel that brakes. Even with the best brakes, don't leave the stroller unattended on an incline.

4 **FOLLOW THE WEIGHT LIMITS.** Most strollers shouldn't be used by children over 35 pounds.

5 **JOGGING STROLLERS ARE BEST FOR BABIES OVER ONE YEAR OF AGE.** Yes, some stroller makers tout their joggers for babies as young as six weeks (or six months) of age. But after consulting with pediatric experts, we suggest waiting until one year of age to run with baby in a stroller. Why? The neck muscles of infants under a year of age can't take the shocks of jogging or walking on rough paths (or going over curbs). Ask your pediatrician if you need more advice on when it is safe to use a jogger.

 *Smart Shopper Tips*

Smart Shopper Tip #1
Give it a Test Drive
"My friend was thinking of buying a stroller online, sight unseen. Should you really buy a stroller without trying it first?"

It's best to try before you buy. Most stores have at least one stroller set up as a floor model. Give it a whirl, practice folding it up, and check the steering. One smart tip: put some weight in the stroller seat (borrow a friend's toddler or use a backpack full of books that weighs about 15 pounds). The steering and maneuverability will feel different if the stroller is weighted—obviously, that's a more real world test-drive.

Once you've tried it out, shop for price through 'net or mail order sources. Ask retailers if they will meet or beat prices quoted to you online (many quietly do so). What if you live in Kansas and the nearest dealer for a stroller you want is in, say, Texas? Then you may have no choice but to buy sight unseen—but just make sure the web site has a good return policy. Another tip: use message boards like those on our web site (BabyBargains.com) to quiz other parents about stroller models.

If you buy a stroller from a store, we strongly recommend opening the box and making sure everything is in there BEFORE you leave the store!

Smart Shopper Tip #2
What Features Really Matter?
"Let's cut through the clutter here. Do I really need a stroller that has electronic stability assist and anti-lock brakes? What features are really important?"

Walk into any baby store and you'll encounter a blizzard of strollers. Do you want a stroller with a full recline? Boot and retractable canopy? What the heck is a boot, anyway? Here's a look at the features in the stroller market today:

Features for baby:
◆ *Reclining seat.* Since babies less than six months of age sleep most of the time and can't hold their heads up, strollers that have reclining seats are a plus. Yet, the *extent* of a stroller's seat recline varies by model. Some have full reclines, a few recline part of the way (120 degrees) and some don't recline at all. FYI: just because a stroller has a "full recline" does NOT mean it reclines to 180

degrees. It may recline slightly less than that for safety reasons.

◆ *Front (or napper) bar.* As a safety precaution, many strollers have a front bar (also called a napper bar) that keeps baby secure (though you should always use the stroller's safety harness). Better strollers have a bar that's padded and removable. Why removable? Later, when your baby gets to toddler hood, you may need to remove the bar to make it easier for the older child to access the stroller. Some strollers have a kid snack tray, which serves much the same function as a napper bar. FYI: If a stroller has a fully reclining

Guaranteed Frustration: Baby gear warranties can leave you fuming

It's a fact of life: sometimes you buy a product that breaks only days after purchase. So, you pick up the phone and call the manufacturer and ask about their warranty. "Sure, we'll help," says the customer service rep. In no time, you have a replacement product and a happy parent.

Fast forward to real life. Most parents find warranties only guarantee frustration—especially with baby products like strollers and other travel gear. Numerous hassles confront parents who find they have a defective product, from unreturned emails to endless waits on hold to speak with a customer service rep (on a non-toll free line, naturally).

Consider the process of actually registering an item. Filling out a warranty card often requires information that you can only find on the product box or carton. Some parents find this out the hard way . . . after they've hauled all the boxes off to the trash. Even worse: some baby product makers like Peg Perego actually request a copy of the sales receipt for their warranty form. Hello? What about gifts?

Then, let's say something goes wrong. Your new stroller breaks a wheel. That brand new baby monitor goes on the fritz after one week. If it is a gift or you lost the receipt, the store you bought it from may say "tough luck"—call the manufacturer. With many warranties, you have to return the defective item to the manufacturer *at your expense*. And then you wait a few more weeks while they decide to fix or replace the item. Typically you have to pay for return shipping—and that can be expensive for a bulky item like a stroller. And then you must do without the product for weeks while they fix it.

Dealing with the customer service departments at some baby product makers can add insult to injury. It seems like some companies can count their customer service staff with one hand—or one finger, in some cases. The result: long waits on hold. Or it takes days to get responses to emails. The U.S. offices of foreign baby product companies seem to be seat, voluntary safety regulation require the stroller to have an adjustable footrest that can fold up to fully enclose the entire stroller seat—this keeps baby from sliding out.

◆ **Seat padding.** You'll find every possible padding option out there, from bare bones models with a single piece of fabric to strollers with deluxe-quilted padding made from fine fabrics hand woven by monks in Luxembourg. (Okay, just kidding—the monks actually live in Switzerland). For seating, some strollers have cardboard platforms (these can be uncomfortable for long rides) and

---

the worst at customer service staffing, while mass-market companies such as Graco and Evenflo have better customer service.

And customer service can go from good to bad in the blink of an eye. Recalls can cause a huge surge in customer service requests—and many companies fail to adequately staff their customer service departments during such events. Hence even good companies can fall flat on their face during such episodes.

The bottom line: it's no wonder that when something goes wrong, consumers just consider trashing the product and buying a new one. And let's be realistic: paying $30 in shipping to send back a broken $50 stroller doesn't make much sense. Here's our advice:

◆ **Keep your receipts.** It doesn't have to be fancy—a shoebox will do. That way you can prove you bought that defective product. If the item was a gift, keep the product manual and serial number.

◆ **If something goes wrong, call the manufacturer.** We're always surprised by how many consumers don't call the manufacturer FIRST when a problem arises. You might be surprised at how responsive some companies are at fixing an issue.

◆ **If the problem is a safety defect, immediately stop using the product** and file a complaint with the Consumer Product Safety Commission (cpsc.gov). Also contact the company.

◆ **Attack the problem multiple ways.** Don't just call; also send an email and perhaps a written letter. Be reasonable: allow the company one to two business days to reply to a phone call or email.

◆ **Let other parents know about your experiences.** The best way to fix lousy customer service? Shame companies into doing it better. Post your experiences to the message boards on our site (BabyBargains.com) and other parenting sites. Trust us, companies are sensitive to such criticism.

other models have fabric that isn't removable or machine washable (see below for more on this).

◆ *Shock absorbers or suspension systems.* Yes, a few strollers do have wheels equipped with shock absorbers or suspension springs for a smoother ride. This is a nice feature if live in a neighborhood with uneven or rough sidewalks.

◆ *Wheels.* In reality, how smooth a stroller rides is more related to the type of wheels. The general rule: the more the better. Strollers with double wheels on each leg ride smoother than single wheels. Most strollers have plastic wheels. In recent years, some stroller makers have rolled out models with "pneumatic" or inflated wheels. These offer a smoother ride—but they are heavier and can go flat.

◆ *Weather protection.* Yes, you can buy a stroller that's outfitted for battle with a winter in New England, for example. The options include retractable hoods/canopies and "boots" (which protect a child's feet) to block out wind, rain or cold. Fabrics play a role here too—some strollers feature quilted hoods to keep baby warm and others claim they are water repellent. While a boot is an option some may not need, hoods/canopies are rather important, even if just to keep the sun out of baby's eyes. Some strollers only have a canopy (or "sunshade") that partially covers baby, while other models have a full hood that can completely cover the stroller. Look for canopies that have lots of adjustments (to block a setting sun) and have "peak-a-boo" windows that let you see baby even when closed.

What if the stroller you've fallen in love with only has a skimpy canopy? Or lacks a rain cover? Good news: after-market accessories can fill the gap. See the box on the next page for sources.

Features for parents:

◆ *Storage baskets.* Many strollers have deep, under-seat baskets for storage of coats, purses, bags, etc. Yet, the amount of storage can vary sharply from model to model. Inexpensive umbrella strollers may have no basket at all, while other models have tiny baskets. Mass-market strollers (Graco, etc.) typically have the most storage; other stroller makers have been playing catch-up in the basket game. One tip: it's not just the *size* of the storage basket but the *access* to it that counts. Some strollers have big baskets but are practically inaccessible when the seat is reclined. A support bar blocks access to some baskets. Tip: when stroller shopping, recline the seat and see if you can access the basket.

◆ *Removable seat cushion for washing.* Let's be honest: strollers can get icky in a jiffy. Crushed-in cookies, spilt juice and the usual grime can make a stroller a mobile dirt-fest. Some strollers have removable seat cushions that are machine washable—other models let you remove *all* of the fabric for a washing. Watch out for those models with non-removable fabric/seat cushions—while you can clean these strollers in one of those manual car washes (with a high-pressure nozzle), it's definitely a hassle, especially in the winter.

◆ *Lockable wheels.* Some strollers have front wheels that can be locked in a forward position—this enables you to more quickly push the stroller in a straight line (nice for exercising).

◆ *Wheel size.* You'll see just about every conceivable size wheel out there on strollers today. As you might guess, the smaller wheels are good for maneuverability in the mall, but larger wheels handle rough sidewalks (or gravel paths) much better.

◆ *Handle/Steering.* This is an important area to consider—most strollers have a single bar handle, which enables one-handed steering. Other strollers have two handles (example: Maclaren as well as Perego's Pliko line). Two handles require two hands to push, but enable a stroller to fold up compactly, like an umbrella. It's sort of a trade-off—steer-ability versus easier fold. There are other handle issues to consider as well. A handful of strollers feature a "reversible" handle. Why would you want that? By reversing the handle, you can push the stroller while the baby faces you (better for small infants). Later, you can reverse the handle so an older child can look out while being pushed from behind. (Note: models with reversible handles seem increasingly rare in recent years; instead some strollers

strollers

Handy stroller accessories

What if your stroller doesn't have a rain cover? One option is the **Protect a Bub Wind & Rain Cover**, which comes in both single ($23) and double versions ($29; web: protect-a-bubusa. com).

What if you buy a stroller that is great, except for a skimpy canopy? You can fix that with a cool sunshade from Australia called the **Pepeny** (sold on AlbeeBaby. com). The Pepeny screens out the weather, sunlight and UV, comes in several colors and fits most stroller models. Price: $40; This would also be a good idea for California parents to screen out low-angle sun.

have reversible *seats*. We'll note which have this feature later).

Another important factor: consider the handle *height*. Some handles have adjustable heights to better accommodate taller parents. However, just because a stroller touts this feature doesn't mean it adjusts to accommodate a seven-foot tall parent (at most, you get an extra inch or two of height). Finally, a few stroller makers offer "one-touch fold" handles. Hit a button on the stroller and it can be folded up with one motion. Later in this chapter, we'll mention which mention have height adjustable handles as we review stroller brands.

◆ **Compact fold.** We call it the trunk factor—when a stroller is folded, will it fit in your trunk? Some strollers fold compactly and can fit in a narrow trunk. Other strollers are still quite bulky when folded—think about your trunk space before buying. Unfortunately, we are not aware of any web site that lists the size/footprint of strollers when folded. You are on your own to size up models when folded in a store, compared to your trunk (hint: take trunk measurements before you go stroller shopping). Not only should you consider how compactly a stroller folds, but also how it folds in general. The best strollers fold with just one or two quick motions; others require you to hit 17 levers and latches. The latest stroller fold fad: strollers that fold standing UP instead of down. Why is this better? Because strollers that fold down to the ground can get dirty/scratched in a parking lot.

◆ **Durability.** Should you go for a lower-price stroller or a premium brand? Let's be honest: the lower-priced strollers (say, under $100) have nowhere near the durability of the models that cost $200 to $400. Levers that break, reclining seats that stop reclining and other glitches can make you despise a cheap stroller mighty quick. Yet, some parents don't need a stroller that will make it through the next world war. If all you do is a couple of quick trips to the mall every week or so, then a less expensive stroller will probably be fine. However, if you plan to use the stroller for more than one child, live in an urban environment with rough sidewalks, or plan extensive outdoor adventures with baby, then invest in a better stroller. Later in this chapter, we'll go over specific models and give you brand recommendations for certain lifestyles.

◆ **Overall weight.** Yes, it's a dilemma: the more feature-laden the stroller, the more it weighs. And strollers are often priced via the Bikini Principle: the less it weighs, the more it costs. Yet it doesn't take lugging a 30-pound stroller in and out of a car trunk more than a few times to justify the expense of a lighter-weight design. Carefully consider a stroller's weight before purchase. Some parents end up with two strollers—a lightweight/umbrella-type stroller for quick trips (or air travel) and then a more feature-intensive model for extensive outdoor outings.

One factor to consider with weight: steel vs. aluminum frames. Steel is heavier than aluminum, but some parents prefer steel because it gives the stroller a stiffer feel. Along the same lines, sometimes we get complaints from parents who own aluminum strollers because they feel the stroller is too "wobbly"—while it's lightweight, one of aluminum's disadvantages is its flexibility. One tip for dealing with a wobbly stroller: lock the front wheels so you can push the stroller in a straight line. That helps to smooth the ride.

Smart Shopper Tip #3
The Cadillac Escalade or Ford Focus Dilemma

"This is nuts! I see cheap umbrella strollers that sell for $30 on one hand and then fancy designer brands for $900 on the other. Do I really need to spend a fortune on a stroller?"

Whether you drive a Cadillac Escalade or Ford Focus, you'll still get to your destination. And that fact pretty much applies to strollers too—most function well enough to get you and baby from point A to point B, not matter what the price.

So, should you buy the cheapest stroller you can find? Well, no. There *is* a significant difference in quality between a cheap $30 umbrella stroller and a name brand that costs $150, $250 or more. Unless you want the endless headaches of a cheap stroller (wheels that break, parts that fall off), it's important to invest in a stroller that's durable.

The real question is: do you need a fancy stroller loaded with features or will a simple model do? To answer that, you need to consider *how* you will use the stroller. Do you live in the suburbs and just need the stroller once a week for a quick spin at the mall? Or do you live in an big city where a stroller is your primary vehicle, taking all the abuse that a big city can dish out? Climate plays another factor—in the Northeast, strollers have to be winterized to handle the cold and snow. Meanwhile, in Southern California, full canopies are helpful for shading baby's eyes from late afternoon sunshine.

Figuring out how different stroller options fit your lifestyle/climate is the key to stroller happiness. Later in this chapter, we'll recommend several specific strollers for certain lifestyles and climates.

One final note: name-brand strollers with cachet actually have resale value. You can sell that pricey stroller on eBay, at a second-hand store, or via Craigslist and recoup some of your investment. The better the brand name (say, Bugaboo), the more the resale value. Unfortunately, the cheap brands like Graco, Evenflo and Kolcraft are worth little or nothing on the second-hand market—there is a reason for that (beyond snob appeal). Take a quick look at eBay or your local Craigslist stroller section to see what we mean.

Smart Shopper Tip #4
Too tall for their own good

"I love our stroller, but my husband hates it. He's six feet tall and has to stoop over to push it. Even worse, when he walks, he hits the back of the stroller with his feet."

Strollers are made for *women* of average height. What's that? About 5'6". If you (or your spouse) are taller than that, you'll find certain stroller models will be a pain to use.

This is probably one of the biggest complaints we get from parents about strollers. Unfortunately, just a few stroller models have height-adjustable handles that let a six-foot tall person comfortably push a stroller without stooping over or hitting the back of the stroller with his or her feet. One smart shopping tip: if you have a tall spouse, make sure you take him or her stroller shopping with you. Checking out handle heights in person is the only way to avoid this problem.

The best stroller brands for taller parents: Maclaren and Peg Perego (particularly, the Pliko, which has height adjustable handles). The worst? Combi, a Japanese brand that has low-handle heights.

Smart Shopper Tip #5
The Myth of the Magic Bullet Stroller

"I'd like to buy just one stroller—a model that works with an infant car seat and then converts to full-featured pram and then finally a jogger for kids up to age four. And I want it to weigh less than ten pounds. And sell for just under $50. What model do you suggest?"

Boy, that sounds like our email some days! We hear from parents all the time looking for that one model that will do it all. We call it the Myth of the Magic Bullet Stroller—an affordable product that morphs into seven different uses for children from birth to college. Sorry, we haven't found one yet.

The reality: most parents own more than one stroller. A typical set-up: one stroller (or a stroller frame) that holds an infant car seat and then a lightweight stroller that folds compactly for the mall/travel. Of course, we hear from parents who own four, five or six strollers, including specialty models like joggers, tandem units for two kids and more. First-time parents wonder if these folks have lost their minds, investing the equivalent of the gross national product of Aruba on baby transportation. Alas, most parents realize that as their baby grows and their needs change, so must their stroller.

Far be it for us to suggest you buy multiple strollers, but at the same time, it is hard to recommend just one model that works for everyone. That's why the recommendations later in this chapter are organized by lifestyle and use.

Wastes of Money

1 **SILLY ACCESSORIES.** Entrepreneurs have worked overtime to invent all kinds of silly accessories that you "must have" for your stroller. We've seen stroller "snack trays" ($15) for babies who like to eat on the run. Another company made a clip-on bug repellent, which allegedly used sound waves to scare away insects. Yet another money-waster: extra seat cushions or head supports for infants made in your stroller's matching fabric. You can find these same items in solid colors at discount stores for 40% less.

So which stroller accessories are worth the money? One accessory we do recommend is a toy bar (about $10 to $20), which attaches to the stroller. Why is this a good buy? If toys are not attached, your baby will probably punt them out the stroller.

Does your stroller lack a cup holder? Hard to believe, but some pricey strollers actually omit this feature, which you would think would be a no-brainer. We like Kelgar's Stroll'r Hold'r cup holder ($8, call 972-250-3838 or web: kelgar.com).

Valco also makes a Universal Cup Holder for $16 (twice the Kelgar option above) as does Baby Jogger (Liquid Holster, $20). Parents seem to like the Valco, but the Baby Jogger Holster is a disappointment. Apparently it only stays upright (not spilling) some of the time. One parent recommended it only for water bottles, not for cups.

What about stroller handle extensions? If you find yourself kicking the back of the stroller as you walk, you might want to invest in one of these $20 devices. An example: the Stroller Handle Extender from MBS (mbsolutionsinc.com) for $23. It attaches to the stroller handle with Velcro and adds about eight inches.

2 **"NEW" OLD STOCK.** A reader alerted us to this online scam—the problem of "new" old stock. A stroller she ordered from a small web site was described as a "new Chicco stroller." Turns out, the stroller she got was seven years old. Yes, technically it was "new," as in "not previously used" and still in its original box. Unfortunately, since it was sitting in a warehouse for seven years, it had a cracked canopy, torn fabric and other problems. Apparently, there must be warehouses full of "new" old baby products out there for whatever reason. Our advice: request MODEL YEAR info on strollers or other products when that isn't clearly listed online. While previous year models can be a great deal, we wouldn't buy anything over three years old. . . even if a web site says it is "new."

3 **GIVE THE "BOOT" THE BOOT.** Some expensive strollers offer a "boot" or apron that fits over the baby's feet. This padded cover is supposed to keep the baby's feet dry and warm when it rains or snows. Sometimes you have to spend an extra $50 to $100 to get a stroller with this accessory. But do you really need this? We say save the extra cost and use a blanket instead. Or try a product like the Cozy Rosie or Bundle Me (mentioned later in this chapter), which are made of fleece and provide more warmth than a typical stroller boot. Or, if you decide you need a boot, buy a stroller model that includes this feature—several models now include a boot as standard equipment.

Money-Saving Tips

1 **STOP! DON'T BUY A FULL FEATURE STROLLER BEFORE THE BABY ARRIVES.** Here's a classic first-time parent mistake: buying an expensive, giant travel system stroller (a.k.a. the Baby Bus), thinking you need all those whiz-bang features. But the huge bulk and weight of those strollers will have you cursing the thing before your baby hits six months. A better bet: get a basic stroller frame for $60 (more details on these later), strap in an infant seat and voila! You have transport for an infant for up to six months. Trust us, after you've hung out with your baby for a few months, you'll have a much better idea what your stroller needs are. As your baby nears the limits on an infant car seat, THEN you buy a regular stroller.

2 **WHY NOT A BASIC UMBRELLA STROLLER?** If you only plan to use a stroller on infrequent trips to the mall, then a plain umbrella stroller for $40 to $50 will suffice. One caveat: most plain umbrella strollers do NOT recline—you will not be able to use it until your baby is able to hold up his head (around six months).

3 **CONSIDER A CARRIER FOR NEWBORNS.** Yes, a simple baby carrier (sling, front carrier, etc) can be a much more affordable alternative to expensive strollers. The best carriers have padded straps and lumbar support to keep the strain off your back. Sure you will need a stroller at some point as your baby grows . . . but a carrier can be a cost-effective option to take your newborn or young infant to the store or mall.

4 **CHECK FOR SALES.** We're always amazed by the number of sales on strollers. We've seen frequent sales at the Burlington Coat Factory's Baby Depot, with good markdowns on even premium brand strollers. Coupons are also common. Babies R Us offers occasional coupons in newspaper circulars as well as to parents on their mailing list. Another reason strollers go on sale: the manufacturers are constantly coming out with new models and have to clear out the old. Which leads us to the next tip.

5 Look for last year's models. Every year, manufacturers roll out new models. In some cases, they add features; other times, they just change the fabric. What do they do with last year's stock? They discontinue it—and then it's sale time. You'll see these models on sale for as much as 50% off in stores and on the web. And it's not like stroller fabric fashion varies much from year to year— is there really much difference between "navy pin dot" and "navy with a raspberry diamond"? We say go for last year's fabric and save a bundle. See the Email from the Real World on the next page for a mom's story on her last year model deal.

6 Scope out factory seconds. Believe it or not, some stroller manufacturers sell "factory seconds" at good discounts—these "cosmetically imperfect" models might have a few blemishes, but are otherwise fine. An example: one reader told us Peg Perego occasionally has factory sales from their Indiana headquarters. See Peg's contact info later in this chapter to find the latest schedule.

7 Don't fall victim to stroller overkill. Seriously evaluate how you'll use the stroller and don't over buy. If a Toyota Camry will do, why buy a Lexus? You don't really need an all-terrain stroller or full-feature pram for mall trips. Flashy strollers can be status symbols for some parents—try to avoid "stroller envy"!

8 Sell your stroller to recoup your investment. When you're done with the stroller, consign it at a second-hand store or sell it on Craigslist. You'd be surprised how much it can fetch. The best brands for resale are, not surprisingly, the better names we recommend in this chapter.

9 Warehouse club deals. Yes, Sam's and Costco periodically sell strollers, including joggers. At one point before going to press, Costco was selling Schwinn jogging strollers from their web site (Costco.com) at 45% under retail. Of course, these deals come and go—and like anything you see at the warehouse clubs, you have to snap it up quickly or it will be gone.

10 eBay/Craigslist. It's highly addictive and for good reason— these sites are more than just folks trying to unload a junky

E-MAIL FROM THE REAL WORLD
Last year's fashion, 50% off

A reader emailed her tip on how she saved over $100 on a stroller:

"When looking for strollers you can often get last year's version for a big discount. I purchased a previous year Maclaren model from babydealz.com for $190. That compares to the $300 price tag for the current year model from Babies R Us. As far as my research could tell, the models are identical except for the color pattern. A quick web search can turn up a number of sources that are selling last year's strollers; colors are limited (dmartstores.com had the widest selection) but it is a great way to save over $100 for a very nice stroller."

stroller they bought at K-Mart. Increasingly, baby gear retailers are using eBay to discreetly clear out overstock. Better to unload online the stuff that isn't moving than risk the wrath of local customers who bought the model for full price last week. An example: a reader scored a brand new Peg Perego for HALF the stroller's retail price through an eBay auction. Other readers regularly report saving $100 to $200 through eBay. Hint: many strollers sold online are last year's model or fashion. Be sure to confirm what you are buying (is it in an original box? No damage? Which model year?) before bidding.

And don't forget Craigslist either. Yes, this site has both junk and jewels. Be patient and search carefully to find worthwhile stroller buys.

The Name Game: Reviews of Selected Manufacturers

So, how do we rate and review strollers? First, we do hands-on inspections in stores and trade shows. That involves giving the stroller a test spin, checking the fold and more. Next, we listen to you, the reader. The stroller message board on our web site is one of the most popular forums, brimming with over 1000 posts a month. As always, parent feedback is our secret sauce.

One key point to remember: the ratings in this section apply to the ENTIRE line of a company's strollers. No, we don't assign ratings to individual strollers, but we will comment on what we think are a company's best models. Following this section, we will give you several "lifestyle recommendations"—specific models of strollers to fit different parent lifestyles.

The Ratings

A **EXCELLENT**—*our top pick!*
B **GOOD**— *above average quality, prices, and creativity.*
C **FAIR**—*could stand some improvement.*
D **POOR**—*yuck! Could stand some major improvement.*

Aprica *apricausa.com.* Japanese stroller brand Aprica was bought by Graco in 2008. Graco has been mum on its plans for Aprica, but we expect the company to relaunch the brand shortly. See our blog (BabyBargains.com/blog) for the latest updates.

Baby Jogger *Web: babyjogger.com.* Baby Jogger literally invented the jogging stroller category 25 years ago with the first stroller with bicycle tires designed for runners. Since then, the company has been through numerous ups and downs . . . including a bankruptcy back in 2003 that led to new ownership. The company has since refocused on all-terrain strollers with swivel front wheels. Their new models have met with much success, despite the fact the company has drifted away from its "jogger" namesake.

The models. Baby Jogger has three main stroller models: the City Series, Summit and Performance. The City Series has the easiest fold we've seen for such models: one-hand and zip! It's done. That probably explains the strong sales for this series, which is now divided into three models: the Classic, Mini and Elite.

The City Classic (single $350, 21 lbs.; double $450-500, 33 lbs.) features 12" air filled wheels and suspension (on the double only). The City Mini (single $230, 16.8 lbs.; double $400, 26 lbs.) swaps the air-filled tires for 8" plastic tires you see in more traditional strollers—this cuts the weight of the stroller by five pounds. The City Mini has an oversized canopy and fully reclining seat. At the top end, the City Elite (single $350, 24 lbs.; double $570, 33 lbs.) features 12" air-filled wide tread tires and a parent console.

FYI: One major difference between the City models is weight capacity. Both the City Classic and Elite work to 75 lbs. single, 100 double. The City Mini is 50/100 lbs.

If you want to actually jog with a Baby Jogger, the company offers one model for runners: the Performance (single $430, 24 lbs; double $530, 30 lbs.). This stroller has a one-step, quick-release seat recline, floating canopy for extra sun coverage, and a direct-pull brake.

New for 2009, the Summit 360 comes in single ($400, 23lbs.), double ($650, 38 lbs.) and even triple versions ($1000, 43 lbs.). This is Baby Jogger's top of the line model, with 16" rear and 12" front air-filled tires, swivel front wheel that locks, suspension, and the same quick-fold technology you see on the City Series.

strollers

Finally, Baby Jogger has also entered the hybrid jogging stroller/bike trailer segment with the Switchback ($600). It morphs back and forth between being a jogger and bike trailer without any special kit or tools.

Our view. How's the quality? Excellent, report our readers. Parents love the quick-fold and wide selection of accessories. We like how the company has tweaked models to add in features like parent consoles and better folding canopies. Another major plus: Baby Jogger sells a car seat adapter that works with most infant car seats, including Graco and Peg Perego. ***Rating: A***

Baby Planet *630-790-3113, Web: Baby-Planet.com.* Baby Planet is the brainchild of former Kolcraft stroller designers who are aiming to inject a bit of high style into the stroller market. Their first results channel a bit of Maclaren and a touch of Stokke's Xplory.

The models. Baby Planet's most innovative model is the Max, a Stokke Xplory-like tri-wheel stroller that is sold in two versions: Max Traveler and Max Pro. The Max Traveler ($330, 21.2 lbs.) is a tri-

---

Stroller shopping secret: rear wheel width

Weight may be the most important factor to urban parents looking for a new stroller, but we suggest looking at one additional criteria: rear wheel width. Many new strollers have a wide spread between the rear wheels. The problem? Many urban parents have to negotiate tight spaces (grocery store aisles, subways, etc). A stroller with a wide wheel base may not squeeze through small doorways and into tight elevators. Here is a look at the rear wheel widths for some popular urban strollers.

STROLLER	REAR WHEEL WIDTH
Maclaren Techno XT	19.5″
Bugaboo Bee	20.0
Stokke Xplory	22.0
Bugaboo Cameleon	23.0
Peg Perego Skate	23.75
Microlite Toro	24.0
Orbit	24.0
UPPAbaby Vista	25.0
Quinny Buzz	25.5

Our advice: go for the narrowest wheel base you can find—23″ and under is probably best (some doors are a narrow 24″ wide).

---

wheel stroller with a lightweight aluminum frame, adjustable handle, parent tray with two cup holders, front swivel wheel and storage basket. The Max Pro ($400) includes a stroller frame to hold an infant car seat AND the stroller seat.

Baby Planet's other stroller line is a riff on the Maclaren Volo . . . named the Solo Sport ($90). This lightweight model (17.2 lbs.) features a swooping frame coated in a special metallic paint. Features include an oversized basket, adjustable footrest and compact fold. A double version of this stroller is dubbed the Unity Sport ($245, 27.5 lbs) and features a cool, foam-padded "Easy-Steer" handle, which is excellent for taller parents.

To add a bit of eco-cache to its brand, Baby Planet has rolled out an Endangered Species line of strollers—four versions of the Solo Sport that feature animal prints . . . the company will donate $5 per stroller to the Wildlife Conservancy Fund. These strollers sell for $190, which is quite a premium for the animal print since you can find the regular Solo Sport online for half that price.

New for 2009, Baby Planet plans to enhance the Endangered Series line with a deluxe model that adds a telescoping handle and larger wheels for $250. A double model will run $350.

Our view. Baby Planet wins kudos from readers for their Solo Sport—the fabric, padding and canopy are all superior to the similar Maclaren models. Detractors point out the Solo Sport is a few pounds heavier than most Mac models . . . and Maclarens' handle height is better for taller parents. Baby Planet could improve basket access, say most readers. But overall, feedback on the Solo Sport is quite positive. For most suburban mall crawlers, this one is a winner.

Reader feedback for the Unity Sport is a bit more mixed—again, fans like the padding and over design, but more than one parent told us the double is hard to fold up. And, again, the basket is hard to access and the handle height is too low for tall parents.

The Max strollers have been a flop, sales-wise—there is very little reader feedback on these models. One parent told us the fold on the Max is very difficult, requiring you to remove the car seat adapter or toddler seat.

Overall, we will give this brand a B—good, but room to improve.
Rating: B

Baby Trend *(800) 328-7363, (909) 902-5568, Web: babytrend.com.* Baby Trend's biggest selling stroller isn't really a stroller at all—it's a stroller *frame.* Here's an overview of the line:

The models. The Snap N Go is such a simple concept it's amazing someone else didn't think of it years ago—basically it's a stroller frame that lets you snap in most major-brand infant car seats. Presto! Instant travel system at a fraction of the price. The original Snap N

Go was just a frame and wheels and sat low to the ground. Newer model Snap & Go's ($50) now have a big basket and sit higher. And memo to parents of twins: there's even a double version of the Snap N Go that holds two car seats ($90).

Be aware that while most infant car seats snap into the Snap & Go, others merely rest on the top bar. In either case, Baby Trend recommends using the supplied safety belt to make sure the seat is secure.

The Snap N Go has been so successful it has spawned knock-offs from several competitors, namely Kolcraft, Combi and Graco. We will review those options later. All in all, we think the Snap & Go is a winner.

Besides the stroller frame, Baby Trend also offers travel systems, double strollers and joggers.

Baby Trend's travel systems combine their Flex-Loc infant seat (see review in last chapter) with basic low-end strollers. Example: the Trendsport Traveler system for $160-190 (car seat and stroller). That's a low price, but the stroller (18 lbs.) is nothing fancy—steel frame, three-point harness and two-position recline. You do get a decent canopy, one-hand fold and big basket, but the recline is only to 145 degrees (not a full recline). FYI: The company refers to its travel systems by the fabric name (the Zanzibar travel system, for example)—it's the same Trendsport stroller, just a different fabric.

Besides the Trendsport, the company sells a smattering of other stroller models, including a Bugaboo knock off (Euro Buggy, $200) and a lighter weight version of the Trendsport (Trendsport Lite, $40). None of these models are very popular.

Baby Trend is a big player in the jogging stroller market—their flagship model is the Expedition. This steel frame jogger is loaded with features (reclining seat, five-point harness, parent tray with cup holders and ratcheting canopy) and is sold as a travel system ($200) or separately ($120-140).

We should also note that Baby Trend markets their products under the name "Swan" for specialty stores. Basically, these are the same products/models as Baby Trend makes, albeit with a few cosmetic differences (fabric color, etc.).

FYI: Baby Trend still sells the Sit N Stand stroller, an innovative "pushcart" that combines a stroller with a jump seat for an older child. That has prompted a lawsuit from Joovy, a competitor that acquired the patent rights to the Sit N Stand. So you will see versions of this stroller both from Baby Trend (Sit N Stand) and Joovy (Caboose) on the market until a court sorts out the claims.

New for 2009, Baby Trend plans to roll out a redesigned Sit N Stand double that holds two car seats and has a napper bar that rotates away when not in use. It will come in both steel (36 lbs.) and aluminum (30 lbs.) versions that will run $180 to $200. A redesigned

Different versions spark confusion

Here's a common question we get at the home office: readers go into a chain store like Babies R Us and see a major brand stroller they like. Then, they visit a specialty store and see a similar model, but with some cosmetic differences . . . and a higher price tag. What's up with that? Big stroller makers like Graco have to serve two masters—chain stores and specialty retailers. Here's a little trick of the baby biz: stroller makers often take the same basic model of stroller and make various versions for different retailers. Hence, you'll see a Graco stroller with basic fabric in Babies R Us—and then the same model sold with fancier fabric in specialty stores. So is there any real difference besides the fabric color to justify the increase in price? Yes, sometimes the fabrics are upgraded (or there is more padding). But overall, you are basically seeing the same stroller. Our advice: if you can live with the basic version, go for it.

single Sit N Stand will let you attach a car seat in front or back and costs $140.

Our view. As we've noted in other parts of this book, the best word we can use to describe Baby Trend is flakey. The company clearly sells a large number of strollers and car seats . . . yet Baby Trend's marketing and customer service is at best, uh, inconsistent. It announces products that never ship; hot-selling items often go out of stock. And since Baby Trend's distribution is usually limited to chain stores, finding one of their products is hit or miss. Readers complain that Baby Trend's customer service fails to return calls or emails regarding replacement parts.

Based on our reader feedback, parents seem to love some of their products (particularly the Snap N Go) and loathe others (basically, most of their other strollers). Sure, their basic jogging strollers are cheap ($120), but they are designed more for walkers (the heavy steel frames make actually jogging with a Baby Trend quite a chore).

All in all, Baby Trend has been dogged by numerous quality problems when it comes to their regular strollers. Parents say parts break, wheels fall off and worse—"bad engineering" was how one parent put it. Example, on the Baby Trend Shuttle stroller: you can't open the canopy and have a drink in the holder at the same time! Doh! And before you buy a Baby Trend travel system, be sure to read the caveats to their infant car seat in our last chapter. So, it's hard to assign a rating. If we were just looking at the Snap N Go, we'd give them an A. Yet, the other models would barely earn a C. So, we'll compromise. **Rating: B-**

strollers

Bebe Confort *The Bebe Confort Loola is reviewed under Quinny.*

BeBeLove USA *Web: BeBeLoveUSA.com.* These low-end jogging strollers are sold on discount websites for $150 to $180. We weren't that impressed with the stroller design or features. **Rating: Not yet.**

BOB Strollers *Web: bobgear.com.* BOB has won accolades for their innovative joggers—you can tell these were designed by runners for runners. (Trivia note: BOB stands for Beast of Burden trailers—they decided BOB was easier to spell . . . and would avoid a lawsuit from Mick Jagger). BOB's strollers are billed as "sport utility" strollers and that's an apt moniker, as their rugged design (polymer wheels to prevent rust, for example) and plush ride make these strollers best sellers despite their $300+ price tags. The BOB Sport Utility stroller comes in regular ($290, 23 lbs.) and deluxe ($350, 22 lbs.) versions—the latter has aluminum alloy rims.

In recent years, BOB has branched out into strollers with turnable front wheels (the Revolution, $360 single 23 lbs., $530 double). If you don't like the polymer wheels, the Revolution 12" AW stroller ($380 single 22 lbs., $550 double) has aluminum alloy rims.

Yes, BOB has a car seat adapter ($60) that works with the Graco SnugRide and SafeSeat, plus the Peg Primo Viaggio.

BOB hasn't debuted a new stroller model for a while, but the company recently debuted a "Stroller Strides" stroller to coincide with the Stroller Stride fitness program. This model is basically a Revolution with an added handlebar console, exercise manual and tension tubing for resistance exercises. It runs $400.

If you are a serious runner, the BOB Ironman Stroller (single: $350, 21 lbs.; double: $400, 31.4 lbs.) is probably the pick of the litter, with smooth tires, stiffer shocks, suspension wheels and more. Plus the bright yellow color gives it bit of pizzazz lacking in most other joggers.

Parents give BOB excellent marks on quality and durability. Yes, these joggers are expensive, but worth it. Minor quibbles: the handlebars are not height adjustable, frustrating some parents. And the baskets could be a bit bigger and easier to access, especially on the Revolution. Nonetheless, BOB gets our highest rating. **Rating: A**

Britax *Web: britaxusa.com.* Best-known for its well-made car seats, Britax launched a stroller line in 2005 so it could compete in the travel system market.

The Models. Britax offers three stroller options: Preview, Vigour and (new for 2009) Chaperone. Let's take a look at each.

The Preview ($140, 17 lbs.) is Britax's knock-off of the Peg Pliko, down to the two "ergonomic" handles. This stroller, one of the few on the market that works with the Britax Companion infant seat (now discontinued), features a removable hood with window, aluminum frame, five-point harness, four position recline, adjustable leg rest and parent bag with bottle holder (but no cup holder).

The Vigour ($350, 27.5 lbs.) is Britax's take on the Bugaboo—a four-wheel model with 12" rear wheels and smaller front wheels, a la the Cameleon. Compatible with Britax's Companion infant seat, the Vigour features a seat that removes (to fit an infant car seat) or reverses (so you can face your baby), infinite seat recline, removable sun canopy and height adjustable handle. Again, no cup holder.

The new Chaperone (out by the time you read this) is Britax's latest model—it is sold separately ($300) and mates with the new Chaperone infant car seat to form a travel system ($530). The 22 lb. Chaperone features a one-hand fold, extended canopy, height adjustable handles and push down brake.

Our View. Britax has struggled in this category and it's no wonder. For a company that made its name on a slew of *innovative* car seats, Britax initial strollers strangely lacked in both design and features. Let's get real: who comes out with a stroller today WITHOUT a parent cup holder? Spoiler alert: Britax. Yes, the Preview omits this key feature, standard on just about every other stroller on the market.

No wonder that last we looked, Britax's strollers were on clearance at half off—not a good sign for a brand that aims to be a competitor to premium names like Bugaboo.

Britax hopes to hit the reset button once again with the new Chaperone stroller. And the prototype we saw looked encourag-

---

E-MAIL FROM THE REAL WORLD
The Weight Game

"I saw the same stroller listed with two different weights online. How can the same model weigh five pounds less on one site?"

Good question—call it the weight shell game. We've noticed some web sites play fast and loose with the weights of strollers listed on their sites. Why? What parents' value most in a stroller is LIGHT overall weight—and online sellers know this. So, why not cheat and list a stroller's weight . . . minus a few items like a canopy, basket or other amenities? Another explanation: stroller manufacturers often tweak their models from year to year, adding new features. This can add additional ounces, but some web sites "forget" to update the weight. Yes, it is deceptive—but there are ways around the problem. First, this book lists the true weight for most models. If in doubt, check the manufacturer's web site, which almost always lists the correct weight.

ing. But since this wasn't a finished model as of this writing, we will have to reserve judgment.

Hopefully, Britax's new stroller will fare better than the reader feedback on the Preview. Tall parents gripe about the Preview's low handles . . and the fact that you need THREE hands to recline the stroller—two hands to squeeze the release buttons and another hand to actually push the seat down. When you recline the seat, you can't access the basket. While you might expect to see those

Shopping Cart Covers: Advice & Picks

Grocery store carts aren't exactly the cleanest form of transportation—yet once your baby outgrows her infant car seat, you will put likely baby in the little seat up front . . . and quickly realize that keeping the carts clean does-n't seem to be a high priority for most stores. Some stores have added in a wipes dispenser near the carts, but you can't get the gook off the fabric belts—that's just gross.

To the rescue comes the shopping cart cover, basically a fabric seat that provides a clean and safe space for baby while you shop. If you decide one is for you, there are surprisingly quite a few options to choose from in a variety of price ranges. Here's what to look for in a shopping cart cover:

◆ *Washability*. Well, that sounds like a no-brainer, but be sure to check the cover's washing instructions. Machine washable and dryable are key.

◆ *Side coverage*. Cheaper cart covers don't cover the entire cart seat—some leave the sides of the cart exposed.

◆ *Pockets and toy loops.* The best covers have pockets for toys, diapers, wipes, etc. Make sure the pockets have zipper or Velcro closures—and are located on the back of the cover, so they are out of baby's reach. Toy loops are great for attaching toys.

◆ *Flexibility*. Can the cover also work on restaurant high chairs? Will the cover work on those super-sized carts you see at Costco, BJ's or Sam's? Make sure the cover has large enough leg holes to accommodate a growing child.

flaws on a cheap-o $50 stroller sold at Wal-Mart, Britax owes its customers more at this price point. All in all, the durability and overall quality of the Preview is below average.

Readers were a bit more positive about the Vigour—fans like its smooth glide and flat fold. But the skimpy sunshade and heavy weight (it is nearly eight lbs. heavier than the Bugaboo Cameleon) probably explain the Vigour's anemic sales. Last we saw, the Vigour was being sold at about half price ($170 to $210)—that is a much

◆ **Safety**. Make sure the cover has enough padding for smaller infants. Seat belts are a must—the cover should have its own seat belt to secure baby AND securely attach the cover to the cart. Of course, the cover should be easy to install and remove.

Speaking of safety, that's another reason to have a cart cover—falls from shopping carts are the leading cause of head injuries to young children, according to the Consumer Products Safety Commission. Every year, 24,000 kids under age five are taken to the hospital emergency room after falling from shopping carts. A key reason: carts with broken or missing safety belts. Having a shopping cart cover with a secure belt is a smart way to avoid such injuries.

Here are our top picks for shopping cart covers:

◆ **OhSewCuteBoutique.net** Looking for a shopping cart cover that will even work on those oversized warehouse store carts? Oh Sew Cute's $85 cover 100% washable and comes in a plethora of fabrics and colors.

◆ **ChubbySeats.com** is another great choice, with thick batting and customized fabric options. Their $45 cover includes two bungee bands for toys and cups, two pockets an attached tote bag and more.

◆ **The KozyPal** cart cover (kozypalcartcovers.com) is available in 250 different fabrics and wins kudos from our readers for quality. The company has three styles of in-stock covers for $60 to $100 (most are under $70). Or have one made-to-order, with their fabric or yours. Options include diaper pouches, bottle holders and more.

Our readers also recommended the Kangaroodle.com Itzy Ritzy cover ($70), the BuggyBagg ($60), and the Original Clean Shopper ($35). The latter just has quilted cotton fabric, no batting— it is no frills, but does the job. Readers gave much lower marks to the cart covers from Infantino and Nojo, which we would avoid.

strollers

more realistic number than the original $350 price tag.

The take-home message: despite its strength in car seats, Britax has struck out so far in strollers. A lack of quality, design and innovation make Britax strollers not worthy of their namesake brand. If Britax expects to compete against the Maclarens and Bugaboos of the world, they need to try harder. ***Rating: B-***

Bugaboo *800-460-2922. Web: bugaboo.nl.* Bugaboo. It's Dutch for "priced as if from a hotel mini-bar."

The Models. Here's an unlikely recipe for success in the stroller biz. Take a Dutch-designed stroller, attach a $700 price tag and voila! Instant hit, right? Well, chalk this one up to some creative marketing (or at least, lucky timing).

Bugaboo's breakthrough success was the Frog, named as such for its small wheels in front that give it a frog-like look. The Frog is a clever hybrid of an all-terrain and carriage stroller, pitched to parents for its multiple uses. The Frog comprises three parts: an aluminum frame and bassinet that can later be replaced by a stroller seat (included with canopy and basket). It weighs about 20 lbs., which is rather amazing.

Oh, and we forgot the fourth ingredient of the Bugaboo—hype. The Bugaboo folks were in the right place at the right time. How did the Bugaboo become so hot? Sure, it was fashionable, but that doesn't quite explain it. Nope, the answer is Bugaboo had one of the great product placements of all time . . . it was the featured stroller on HBO's *Sex in the City*. The rest is stroller history. In no time, celebs like Gwyneth Paltrow were swishing their Bugaboos across the pages of *People* magazine. The Bugaboo was the first baby stroller to cross paths with the white-hot supernova that is celebrity culture these days.

Cleverly, Bugaboo played on its Dutch design roots . . . even though (shhh! don't tell anyone!) the Bugaboo is made in Taiwan, not Amsterdam.

Figuring a $700 stroller was a bit bourgeois, Bugaboo's sequel to the Frog—the aptly named Cameleon—now costs $900. The Cameleon adds a more springy suspension on the front wheels, plus a slightly larger seat frame and higher chassis. Unlike the Frog, the Cameleon is available in a wide range of color combinations—you can choose from six base colors and nine top colors, mix and match. Also new: a height adjustable handle.

For a while, Bugaboo sold a stripped down version of the Cameleon, dubbed the Gecko. The Gecko omits the front suspension and is lighter (18 lbs. versus 20 lbs. for the Cameleon). It sells for $680. Although it is discontinued, it is still sold in stores as of this writing.

Bugaboo last major stroller launch was in 2007 when the compact Bee ($530, 22 lbs.) debuted. The Bee is pitched to urban dwellers with its narrow width (20", about four inches narrower than other Bugaboos) oversized canopy, reversible seat, and four-position seat recline.

In other news, Bugaboo has brought back the Frog and is selling it at (gasp!) Babies R Us. Sure, BRU just has two colors (black, red), but that is a sure sign that Bugaboo is going mainstream.

FYI: Bugaboo also sells a raft of accessories for its strollers such as cup holders (what? You thought that would be included?). Add in these extras and you could be out $1000 or more. Example: a $45 car seat adapter lets you attach most major brand infant car seats to the frame. That cup holder is $25, parasol $40, foot muff $70 to $130.

Our view. Nothing symbolizes the nation's recent prosperity (some say wretched excess) than the Bugaboo. But where do $900 strollers fit into today's economic reality?

Like all makers of luxury goods, Bugaboo faces uncertain times . . . the company hasn't released a new model in two years, instead they are content to roll out new colors and an occasional "special edition" model (such as the $1500 all-black Marc Jacobs for Bugaboo stroller).

To say it is challenging to rate this stroller is an understatement. On one hand, readers who have bought a Bugaboo almost unanimously praise its quality and ease of use—fans love the smooth steering, cozy bassinet, reversible seat and so on.

The downsides to owning a Bugaboo, besides the price? Assembly is difficult. And unlike other strollers that just pop out of your trunk and set up with one motion, the Bugaboo Cameleon and Frog require a bit of fussing to assemble. Why? To fold a Bugaboo Frog or Cameleon, you must first remove the seat—that's a major pain, especially for folks who live in the suburbs and plan to fold it up frequently to fit in a trunk (and you'll need a big trunk). So, setting up the Bugaboo requires re-attaching the seat to the frame. Sure, this takes 30 seconds or so, which isn't forever—but about 25 seconds longer than most strollers.

Hence a Bugaboo is probably best for urban dwellers or folks who don't plan to break it down and throw it in a trunk frequently. (The Bee is an exception—it is easy to fold and set-up).

But does ANYONE really need a $1000 stroller? (Let's get real—after you add all those cute accessories, we are talking about spending a grand on a baby stroller). We realize this is a rhetorical question . . . and in a country where a pair of Manolo Blahniks are the same price as a Bugaboo stroller, we can see how some folks could do the mental gymnastics to convince themselves this stroller isn't THAT expensive.

On the other hand, we know readers of this book sometimes get a stroller as a gift—and if your relative has the bank roll, why not? So we will give Bugaboo our recommendation . . . if the funds

strollers

are coming out of someone else's wallet. Otherwise, get another of our top-rated strollers and pocket the $700 difference. ***Rating: A—if someone else is paying for it.***

BumbleRide *800-530-3930. Web: bumbleride.com.* BumbleRide's mission is to inject a bit of fashion into a stroller market often marked by models that are dull and duller. Started by a husband and wife team in San Diego, BumbleRide has carved out a small niche in the stroller market.

The Models. The Flyer is a good place to start. This $300 carriage stroller weighs 19 lbs. and features a five-point harness, reversible handle (which is nice), four-position recline, adjustable footrest and mesh basket. Best of all, it is compatible with several major infant car seats. The only negative: it is quite bulky when folded, so you'll need a large trunk to haul it around. In a recent

And now, from Europe . . .

Ah, you've got to love the web. Today you can zip over to European baby product web sites and ogle the latest strollers swishing down the streets of Milan or Paris. Many of these strollers are discussed on our message boards at BabyBargains.com, as parents scheme to find ways to import them to the U.S.

The biggest cross-ocean import in recent years was the Bugaboo, that legendary stroller designed in the Netherlands (but made in Taiwan). So why don't we see more European strollers here? And why are U.S. stores instead filled with cheap Chinese-made models, invariably in navy blue?

Let's take a look at the biggest trends for strollers in Europe . . . and why many of these strollers fail to make a splash here in North America (special thanks to "American Mama," a member of our message boards for sharing these insights after living and traveling extensively in Europe).

◆ ***Pram madness.*** Europeans live a much different lifestyle than your average American—they walk more places, take public transport and don't drive as much. Hence, strollers tend to be heavier since you aren't lifting the thing in and out of a trunk. European strollers feature big wheels, the better to ride over cobblestones and rough sidewalks. Prams are common—these combine a stroller and bassinet. Again, nice when walking from your flat to a café in Rome. Prices for prams run $450 to $700 in Europe—the bassinets alone can cost $170 or more! An odd contradiction: big strollers are popular in Europe, despite the fact that update, BumbleRide made the rear wheels of the Flyer unlock and swivel, which makes pushing easier when the handle is reversed. A detachable cup holder rounds out the features.

New in the past year is the Indie ($400, 20 lbs.), which replaces Bumbleride's most popular model, the Rocket. Much like the model it replaced, the Indie is a tri-wheel stroller with quick release 12" inflated tires, boot, adjustable handle, full recline and deep storage basket. The big difference: the Indie has a much more compact fold, weighs five pounds less . . . and costs about $70 more than the Rocket. Basically, the Indie is a more stylish version of the Mountain Buggy Urban Single or BOB Revolution. FYI: A twin version of the Indie runs $550.

BumbleRide's most expensive model is the Queen B ($430, 31 lbs.), a pram-style stroller with wire basket. Yes, it comes with plush padding, reclining seat, boot and more. Good news: the current

their apartments, elevators and shops are small. And public transport is so crowded.

◆ *My stroller, my country.* Imagine if every state had its own stroller brand—Texas joggers, Utah umbrella strollers, etc. Europe is like that, with many countries boasting their own stroller brands (Emmaljunga in Sweden, Jane in Spain, Bebe Confort in France, and so on). Europeans are often loyal to their own country's stroller maker (thanks to good distribution and marketing), but what sells in Portugal doesn't necessary translate across the border. Or the ocean.

◆ *Cup holder, what cup holder?* Here's one key reason many European strollers fail in the U.S.—no cup holders. Europeans don't understand why mom needs a place to put that Starbucks cup; or why baby would need to have a snack tray. When Europeans want coffee, they go to a café, sit down and drink coffee. The whole concept of toting a beverage is alien. As a result, many European stroller makers fail to include this crucial feature in their models.

◆ *Colors*. Europeans love bright colors—strollers come in bright orange, plaids, two contrasting (clashing?) colors and more. Larger prams let Europeans show off strollers with lots of chrome. Why are dull colors so common here in the U.S.? Hard to say, but we wonder if it has something to do with the chains, which dominate retailing here. There seems to be a mindset among chain store buyers that unless it is dull and blue, it won't sell in South Dakota. Chains must stock one model nationwide, so they play it safe. And stroller makers simply respond to what the chain store buyers say they want.

strollers

Queen B has front swivel wheels, replacing the fixed wheels of previous models.

New for 2009, the Flite ($200, 12 lbs.) is a lightweight stroller with two handles (a la the Peg Pliko), a big canopy and two recline positions. Also new this year: the Indy and Twin get redesigned wheels and larger canopies.

Our view. Reviews for Bumbleride are mixed at best—folks tell us they "like but not love" their Flyers. Fans like the handle that reverses, letting you look at a newborn as you push the stroller and then switch the position for older babies. Other readers laud the Flyer's overall design (decent storage basket, sturdy frame, easy fold, etc). But detractors point out Bumbleride's inconsistent quality (reports of strollers with squeaky wheels, steering that pulls to one side) mar the brand's overall rating. The Flyer's large size when folded is another negative.

The Indie gets somewhat better marks from readers, who often compare it to the BOB Revolution. The Indie is three pounds lighter than the Revolution and fans like its easy fold, adjustable height handle, car seat adapter and more. But critics point out the Indie doesn't have as smooth of a glide as the Revolution and the Indie only has a partial seat recline. Considering both strollers cost about the same, the advantage goes to the BOB Revolution.

The Flite wasn't released as of press time, so no reader feedback yet.

So it is a mixed review for this brand. Customer service, design and fashion are good; but inconsistent quality (especially for the Flyer) drags down Bumbleride's rating a bit. **Rating: B-**

Carter's *These strollers are made by Kolcraft; see their review at the end of this section in "Other Brands."*

Chariot Web: ChariotCarriers.com. Canadian outdoor brand Chariot takes a different approach to the jogger market—Chariot makes bicycle trailers that covert into jogging strollers. If you are an avid bicyclist who also wants to occasionally jog with baby, Chariot offers six models of bike trailers with optional kits that turn the trailers into jogging strollers. Example: the Chariot Cougar 1 ($500), which features plush harness straps, padded seats and adjustable suspension. Add an $80 jogging kit and you've got a stroller. While this is very pricey (some Chariot models run close to $800), we've been impressed with Chariot's quality—no, they aren't cheap . . . but you'll be amazed with the ease of use and adjustments. (Yes, there is even a cross-country ski kit). The downside: these trailers/joggers are too wide to take into most stores, so this isn't a good solution for shopping. Obviously, if you aren't a serious biker or jogger, a Chariot is probably overkill. But if you want a quality bike trailer, this brand should be on the top of your shopping list. **Rating: A**

Chicco *(877) 4-CHICCO or (732) 805-9200. Web: chiccousa.com.* Chicco (pronounced Kee-ko) has a 50-year history as one of Europe's leading juvenile products makers. Along with Peg Perego, Chicco is Europe's biggest producer of strollers and other baby products and toys.

When we first started writing these books, Chicco always played second fiddle to Peg, whose carriage strollers outsold Chicco by a large margin. In recent years, their fortunes have switched: Chicco has seen a string of successes in America, with a popular infant car seat and several lightweight stroller models. Peg, meanwhile, has languished with too high prices and lack of new models.

The models. Chicco's emphasis is on lightweight strollers designed for the mall—the company offers three compact models (Liteway, C5 and C6/Capri) and four full-size options (Cortina, Trevi, S3 and Ct0.1).

New for 2009 in the compact category, the Liteway ($130, 17 lbs.) features two handles, rear wheel suspension, padded five-point harness, cup holder and a full recline. We liked the boot that tucks away when not in use.

The entry level C6 (also known as the Capri; $60, 11 lbs.) features a two-position seat recline, five-point harness and basic canopy . . . a bit like the Maclaren Volo, but almost half the price. The C6 and the Capri are basically the same, but the Capri has an upgraded canopy.

The affordable C5 ($90, 13.7 lbs.) features a multi-position reclining seat, decent size basket and nice canopy. Combine this with a compact, umbrella-style fold and Chicco has a winner. FYI: Chicco plans to discontinue this model sometime in 2009.

The Cortina, Chicco's marquee stroller, is sold separately ($160, 23 lbs.) or as part of a travel system ($300, paired with Chicco's excellent KeyFit infant seat). The Cortina features a more traditional design with height-adjustable handles and decent size basket. We thought it was well designed—we liked the one-hand fold and fully reclining seat.

New in the past year, the Trevi ($130, 19 lbs.) is also designed to work with Chicco's infant car seat and features a full recline, umbrella-style fold, two handles, cup holder and removable child tray.

Also relatively new: Chicco debuted its first tri-wheeled stroller, the S3 ($400, 23 lbs.). This swivel wheel stroller features suspension, foot muff and quick release wheels.

If you are looking for a lightweight double stroller, Chicco offers two options: the Trevi Twin ($170, 23 lbs.) and C5 twin ($190, 29 lbs.). While both are similar, Trevi has fully reclining seats, upgraded canopies and can hold one infant car seat. Chicco told us they are working on a double that will hold two infant car seats, but no word on when that will debut.

Our view. "Cute and cheap" is how our readers sum up Chicco.

Take the 11 lb. Chicco C6 (Capri)—it's half the price of a Maclaren and 40% lighter than the Peg Pliko. That makes it ideal for quick trips to the mall or airplane travel.

Detractors point out that Chicco strollers don't work well for tall folks, who often find the handle heights uncomfortable. And the canopies on many of Chicco's low price strollers don't offer much shade.

But that's the minority view: most readers say they are happy with their Chicco, especially those who mainly use the strollers for quick shopping trips.

So which Chicco strollers get the best marks? Readers give the full-featured Cortina and Trevi very good reviews—fans cheer the easy steering, one-hand fold and padding (critics point out both are a bit bulky).

How about the lightweight strollers? While readers love the design and fashion of most of Chicco's offerings, quality is hit or miss. The C5 scores better than the C6/Capri—but, unfortunately, this model is headed for the discontinued bin. No word on the Liteway, which wasn't out as of press time.

Overall, we think Chicco is a good brand and the prices are a decent value. If you like the look of Maclaren but don't have a Maclaren bank account, Chicco is a good alternative. ***Rating: B+***

Combi *(800) 992-6624, (803) 802-8416; Web: combi-intl.com.* Japanese-owned Combi came to the U.S. in the late 80's and staked out a claim as a leader in lightweight strollers. Their famous Savvy Z was a seven-pound wonder that was often imitated. But Combi has had its ups and downs in recent years; it has shifted strategies more often than Italy changes governments. Here's an overview of their current offerings.

The models. Combi's focus is on lightweight, compact strollers. The company's flagship model, the Cosmo, is a good starting point. The Cosmo ($80-$100, 13 lbs.) features a compact fold, full seat recline for infants, removable napper bar and fits Combi's Shuttle infant car seat. The Cosmo comes in several different versions: DX, EX and a DX special edition, which includes fancier padding and fabric.

Combi's other strollers are variations of the Cosmo. For example, the Flare ($70, 11.7 lbs.) is a touch lighter than the Cosmo, but still has a full recline and compact.

New in the past year, Combi launched the Helio ($150, 13.4 lbs.), which is similar to the Cosmo but a bit wider. It features a taller handle and integrated cup holder.

Combi is discontinuing two of its more expensive strollers in 2009: the Flex ($190) and Torino ($160), but you might see them in the discontinued bin. The Flex featured microfiber fabric and the Torino had a height adjustable handle.

Combi is also cutting back on twin strollers: for 2009, the company will only offer the Twin Sport ($220, 22 lbs.), a side-by-side model that can fit one Combi infant car seat. The Twin Sport features a removable napper bar, machine washable cushions, 165-degree reclining seats and a separate canopy for each seat.

Discontinued but still available as of press time, the Counterpart Tandem is Combi's first front/back stroller in several years. This 25.6 lb. stroller includes a third set of wheels for easy turning, push-button recline and the ability to hold one infant seat. It sells for $230.

Our view. Combi has slimmed down their line in the past year and that's a good thing—in the past, this company's myriad of overlapping offerings made Combi a tough sell. Also gone: many of the super expensive strollers. Again, a good thing, as Combi has decided to concentrate on what it does best: lightweight strollers in the affordable to middle price points.

As for parent feedback, we'd peg Combi's reputation as mixed. Take the simple Combi Flash stroller frame—this $60 product should be a no-brainer. And while most parents praise the Flash's light weight and easy fold, it has one fatal flaw: when you snap in a car seat, the storage basket is inaccessible. Doh! This is the kind of bone-headed design mistake Combi makes.

Other parents gripe about Combi's low handles, which can make their strollers a chore to push for anyone over 5'6". (You'd think the Japanese would have better adapted these model to America after being here for 20 years). And while parents universally like Combi for their lightweight and easy folds, there always seems to be some fatal flaw that pops up . . . a too small basket, difficult seat recline, handle design, etc.

So, we've dropped Combi's rating a bit this year to reflect the disappointing parent feedback. While the company is on the right track in focusing its line on what it does best, more attention to design, quality and ease of use needs to happen. ***Rating B***

Compass *(See the First Years).*

Cosco *(812) 372-0141. Web: djgusa.com.* Dorel (the parent of Cosco), the baby products powerhouse, has struggled in the stroller market for years. Why? The key driver of stroller sales in discount stores are travel systems . . . yet, Dorel/Cosco's main offering for infant car seats (the Designer 22) has failed to win many fans. That has undercut their momentum in this category, forcing the company to come up with several alternatives. Key among these: licensed brand names. Dorel is probably better known for its alter egos: Quinny, Maxi Cosi, Eddie Bauer and Safety 1st.

The models. The biggest news at Cosco in the past year was their launch of Quinny strollers and Maxi Cosi car seats. These are both sister companies to Cosco (part of parent Dorel's global brands). We will review Quinny and Maxi Cosi separately later in this section.

Meanwhile, Cosco is still churning out travel systems and basic strollers, mostly under the Eddie Bauer and Safety 1st nameplates.

A typical offering is the Eddie Bauer Adventurer Travel System ($200). Paired with the Eddie Bauer Comfort (a.k.a. the Designer 22) car seat, you get a stroller that features a one-hand fold and stand feature, big storage basket, parent tray with two cup holders, full reclining seat and upgraded fabric.

We will give Dorel its due—they are trying to innovate in the stroller market. Example: the Safety 1st Acella Sport Travel System. This hybrid jogger features a tri-wheel stroller with turnable front wheel and one-hand standing fold. Price: $150 at Baby Depot. That includes the Designer 22 car seat.

New for 2009, Safety 1st offers the LiteWave Travel System for $150 at K-Mart. Again paired with the Designer 22 infant car seat, the LiteWave stroller stands when folded and features a fully reclining seat and front wheel suspension.

Cosco is a big player in the double stroller market—their Safety 1st Two Ways tandem ($150) has a reversible front seat so kids can face each other. FYI: Cosco sells this same stroller as the All Terrain Tandem under the Eddie Bauer label.

Our view. Cosco has seen improving parent feedback and design features in recent years and our rating reflects this.

That said, Cosco still has a way to go when it comes to quality and durability. We still get emails and message board posts from parents who fall for the cool Eddie Bauer colors . . . and then the regrets start. Complaints about wheels that squeak within the first month, hard-to-adjust harnesses, and other quality woes still dog these strollers. Bottom line: folks are lured in by the Eddie Bauer brand, but then discover too late Cosco has married it to an inferior stroller or car seat.

Since all of Cosco/Eddie Bauer/Safety 1st's travel systems use the same infant car seat (the Designer 22), that seat's poor marks for ease of use drag down the ratings for travel systems.

The take home message: Cosco's basic strollers are probably the best bet . . . but only when on sale or for a steal on Craigslist. A parent who snagged a Safety 1st Acella Alumilite stroller for $60 at Baby Depot complimented the stroller's easy steering and large basket. She felt she got her money's worth and we would agree—set your expectations appropriately and one of these strollers could be a good basic model for the mall or grandma's house. **Rating: C+**

Stroller overload?

Whoa! Finding yourself overwhelmed with all this stroller stuff? Take a break for a minute. We realize making a stroller choice can seem daunting. Here's our advice: first, read our specific recommendations by lifestyle later in this chapter. We boil down all the options to our top picks, whether you live in Suburbia or in downtown Giant Metropolis. Second, realize that you don't have to make all these stroller decisions BEFORE baby is born. Most parents will buy an infant car seat—pair this with an inexpensive stroller frame from Kolcraft (Universal Car Seat Carrier, $55), Combi (Flash EX, $60), Maclaren (Easy Traveler Car Seat Carrier, $70) or Baby Trend (Snap N Go, $50) and you've got an affordable alternative to those pricey travel systems. One of these stroller frames will last you for your baby's first six months . . . or longer. That will give you plenty of time to think about/research your next stroller.

Dreamer Design This brand is reviewed on our web site, BabyBargains.com (click on Bonus Material).

Easy Walker This brand is reviewed on our web site, BabyBargains.com (click on Bonus Material).

Eddie Bauer These strollers and travel systems are made by Cosco. See the above review for more info.

Esprit See Rock Star Baby.

Evenflo (800) 233-5921 or (937) 415-3300. In Canada: (519) 756-0210; Web: evenflo.com. Evenflo's claim to fame, stroller-wise, is their one-hand steering. All of Evenflo's strollers and travel systems have this feature. Here is a breakdown:

The models. Evenflo's flagship stroller is the Aura, which is paired with Evenflo's Embrace infant seat in a travel system. The Aura has probably one of the most amazing parent trays on the market, complete with two cup holders with "automotive cup grippers" and a storage area with "privacy lid." If only Evenflo had put as much effort into the rest of the stroller as they did with the parent tray.

While the Aura has a one-hand fold feature, folding it is not easy or intuitive—and once folded, this thing is big and bulky, clocking in at nearly 30 lbs. and filling up most of just about any vehicle's trunk space. The Aura travel system comes in two flavors: the Select ($160) and the Elite ($180), which offers upgraded fabric and canopy.

Evenflo's other major stroller offering is the Journey. Similar in size and weight to the Aura, it lacks the one-hand fold, cool parent tray (the Journey's parent tray is much simpler) or retracting child tray (to keep it from getting scuffed when folded). The Journey is sold as a stand-alone stroller ($70) and travel system paired with the Evenflo Embrace ($140 to $170).

In the past year, Evenflo debuted a premium travel system, dubbed the EuroTrek ($190-$250, 20 lbs). We're not sure what makes this stroller "Euro," but it does offer a few upgrades not seen on Evenflo's lower-end models such as a height adjustable handle and full coverage canopy. The EuroTrek's aluminum frame makes it significantly lighter than the Aura.

Also new in the past year: a new entry-level model, the XSport Plus ($60, 10 lbs.). This bare bones stroller features a basket, parent console and telescoping handle. A version without the adjustable handle is $35.

Evenflo is a major player in the tandem stroller segment with their Take Me Too. This 29 lb. double stroller has a couple of unique features. First, a side entry step for toddlers lets them get in and out of the back seat better than other models. And they've included an extra large basket. Yes, this unit can hold TWO infant seats (including non-Evenflo seats) and the one-hand fold feature is good. Price: $95.

Our view. Evenflo has slowly improved its quality and durability in recent years. A good example is the newer XSport, which wins rave reviews from parents for ease of use, especially for the Plus version with the height adjustable handles. The only criticism we have for this model is its harness, which is a three point (we think a five-point harness is safer). But overall Evenflo has a big hit with the XSport, which is the first time in years Evenflo has got something right.

Evenflo's travel systems earn lower marks—like Dorel/Cosco, Evenflo's travel systems suffer from a sub-par infant seat that tends to drag down folks' overall impressions. At nearly 30 lbs., Evenflo's full size strollers (especially the Aura) are simply too heavy and bulky for most folks, who fall for that first-time parent trap of buying the SUV stroller only to realize they can't lift it out of their trunk.

So, it's a mixed bag for Evenflo. Thumbs up for the XSport and Take Me Too tandem, which are both affordable AND well designed. We also like Evenflo's customer service department, which earns good marks from our readers for promptly taking care of problems. But we don't recommend Evenflo's travel systems or full-size strollers, which tend to be too heavy and bulky. **Rating: B**

First Years This brand is reviewed on our web site, BabyBargains. com (click on Bonus Material).

GoGo Babyz *Web: GoGoBabyZ.com. This brand is reviewed by on our web page, BabyBargains.com (click on Bonus Material).*

Graco *(800) 345-4109, (610) 286-5951; Web: gracobaby.com.* Graco is a great example of what's right (and wrong) with the stroller biz today. The company (a division of Rubbermaid) is probably the market-leader in strollers, with affordable models that are packed with features like oversized baskets. What drives Graco's success? Well, it is NOT quality or design (Graco's offerings are no better than other mass market strollers). Graco's secret sauce is the runaway success of Graco's SnugRide infant car seat . . . and that feeds travel system sales, the heart of stroller sales at chain stores. You'll find Graco everywhere: discount stores, baby superstores, specialty shops and more.

Graco's primary target market is first-time parents, who want a SUV-like stroller (that is, one packed with tons of features and gizmos). Unlike years past, Graco is now more of a mid-priced brand. Gone are the super-cheap low-end strollers . . . Graco seems to have ceded this market to Cosco.

Graco's line is huge, so let's get to the highlights:

The models. Graco divides their stroller line into four areas: lightweight (Ipo, Mosaic MetroLite), full-size (Quattro, Passage, Vie4, Alano, Glider), travel systems (11 different models) and multi-child strollers (DuoRider, DuoGlider, Quattro Tour Duo, Twin Ipo).

Whew. Deep breath.

In the lightweight category, Graco has three models: the Ipo, Mosaic and MetroLite. The Ipo ($90-$100, 17 lbs.) is Graco's riff on the Peg Perego Pliko—two handles, large basket, one hand fold and tinted sun visor.

The Mosaic ($100, 18 lb.) is an umbrella stroller with two handles, deep basket and partial recline. This stroller has a "three-dimensional" fold—that basically means it folds down to the ground but doesn't scrape or dirty the stroller in the process.

The MetroLite ($130-150 stand alone; $210-260 travel system) is an 18 lb. stroller that features rubber tires for a smooth ride, three-position reclining seat and plush padding. The MetroLite also has a full recline and height adjustable handle.

Graco's best known full-size stroller is the Quattro, a Hummer-like stroller that weighs 26+ lbs. empty. The Quattro comes in two versions: Deluxe and Sport. Both feature a one-hand gravity fold, fully reclining seat, and large parent storage tray that holds two drinks. The difference: the Sport features a more modern, elliptical frame. The Quattro is available as a stand-alone stroller ($140-160 Deluxe; $170 Sport) or part of a travel system ($240-$260).

Graco's other full-size strollers are basically scaled down versions of the Quattro: the LiteRider, Glider, Alano, Vie4 and Passage run

$70 to $100 as stand-alone models or $170 to $210 as travel systems. All feature Graco's voluminous storage basket (which drops down for access when the seat is reclined) and the ability to hold a Graco infant seat.

Finally, double strollers are Graco's last major forte—the DuoRider ($130) is Graco's side-by-side model, while the DuoGlider ($140 to $190, 29 lbs). is a front/back tandem. Graco's claim to fame in the tandem market is their "stadium seating," where the rear seat is elevated. Of course, you get all the standard features: huge storage baskets, removable canopies, etc. Cool feature: The DuoGlider holds two Graco infant car seats.

New in the past year, the Graco Quattro Tour Duo (32 lbs., $220-240) features a curvy frame, fancy cup holders, stadium seating, one-hand "gravity" fold, large basket and a back seat with full recline. The Quattro Tour Duo is about 20% smaller than the DuoGlider.

For 2009, Graco plans to debut a double version of the Ipo that will weigh 32 lbs. and run $190. The Ipo Duo will feature a one-hand fold—this model will eventually replace the DuoGlider as Graco's main side-by-side stroller.

Graco's entry in the stroller frame category, the Snug Rider, is a winner—this $60 frame holds the (what else?) Graco Snug Ride infant car seat with a secure lock-in feature and has a one-hand fold and basket. FYI: The Snug Rider also works with Graco's newer infant seat, the Safe Seat.

Our view. Graco has come a long way and now sits atop the mountain as the top-selling mass market brand for strollers.

We don't fault Graco for focusing on the lucrative first-time parent niche, but we can't help but point out to folks that NO, you do not need a 30 lb. stroller to push around baby. In fact, many parents end up cursing their Graco Hummers as impossible to wrestle in and out of a trunk, among other sins. Stick with the lighter-weight models (Ipo, Mosaic, MetroLite) and you'll be happier here.

And even though Graco's lightweight strollers generally get good marks, we should point out that these strollers stretch the definition of "lightweight"—the Ipo is 17 lbs. . . . that's significantly heavier than the similar Evenflo XSport or UPPAbaby G-lite, both of which are ten lbs. and similar in price. The "lightweight" Mosaic and MetroLite are even heavier (18 lbs.). Heck, a top-of-the-line Maclaren (such as the Techno) still weighs less than that.

If your heart is set on getting a full-size stroller, our pick in this line would be the Quattro Tour Sport—yep, it is way too heavy at 26 lbs. but at least it is loaded with just about every feature you can think of in a stroller. At $170, this model is a decent value.

Much of Graco's good reader feedback stems from their travel systems, which get a halo effect from the strong review of Graco's infant car seats. While we aren't big fans of travel systems, the best Graco option here would probably be the MetroLite travel system, which combines a relatively lightweight (for Graco) stroller at a reasonable price ($210-260).

Of course, despite the generally positive reviews, Graco strollers aren't without their faults. Look at how some Graco strollers fold up . . . when folded, the front tray hits the ground, inevitably damaging or scratching it in a parking lot. Parents also complain about canopies that break or reclining seats that stop reclining. Durability is one of Graco's key weaknesses—these strollers wear out way too quickly (wheels squeak, fabric rips, etc). Forget about a Graco stroller lasting for more than one kid . . . often they don't make it through one year.

Graco strollers are bulky when folded—even the lightweight ones like the MetroLite will eat up the entire trunk of an average sized car. Factor this into your decision if your ride is a small compact.

Bottom line: Graco's strollers are designed for the mall or other light duty shopping trips. Don't expect these strollers to do well in urban environs with cracked sidewalks. Stick with Graco's lightest weight models and set your expectations accordingly. ***Rating: B***

Grand Touring Baby See Rock Star Baby.

Inglesina (877) 486-5112 or (973) 746-5112; web: Inglesina.com. Given the success of fellow Italian stroller makers Peg Perego and Chicco, you'd think Inglesina would be another slam dunk here in the U.S. Yet, the company has struggled for several reasons. First, it lacks an infant car seat—that means Inglesina is frozen out of the big travel system market. Second, prices: Inglesina has raised its prices in recent years, pricing their strollers out of the reach of average buyers. Let's look at the line.

The models. The Zippy is Inglesina's flagship model. Its claim to fame is its amazing one-hand fold—you lift up on a lever on the back of the stroller and poof! Instant folded stroller. This 22.5 lb. model is aimed at urban parents—it has a full recline, adjustable backrest, removable front bumper and storage basket. Best of all: the Zippy has a universal car seat adapter that lets you secure an infant car seat to the stroller (yes, the Graco SnugRide works well with it).

So what's not to love? Well, the Zippy is darn expensive: $400. Yes, you can find previous year models online for about $300, but you've got to question how Inglesina has priced this model. Sure, it is made in Italy, but so are Peg Perego strollers . . . and the similar Pliko P3 is $100 less than the Zippy.

For 2009, the Zippy gets height adjustable handles that rotate so you can steer the stroller with one hand. Also new: the back wheels have suspension and the boot is now included.

Inglesina has two other models: the Trip and Swift. The Trip ($190, 14.5 lbs.) is a lightweight umbrella model with a four-position seat recline, adjustable footrest, cup holder and included rain cover. The Swift (13.5 lbs., $120) is a scaled down version of the Trip, but still has the same seat recline. It omits the cup holder and rain cover and has a less fancy canopy. FYI: the Trip and Swift are made in China.

In previous years, Inglesina also sold a double version of the Swift, but that model is now discontinued.

Our view. Inglesina changed its U.S. distributor in the past year, so 2009 looks like a transition year as the company revamps its strategy. Inglesina hasn't released many new models in recent years; that lack of product is hurting the brand as it falls behind competitors.

Yet the reader feedback on the Zippy, Trip and Swift is positive—parents tell us the brand gets good marks for quality, durability and function. And while the Zippy is probably overpriced, at least the company includes extras like a cup holder and rain cover—many other upper-end stroller makers force you to shell out additional bucks for such accessories. **Rating: A**

InStep is better known by their alter ego, Schwinn—see review on page 508.

i'coo/Traxx See Rock Star Baby.

Jane This brand is reviewed on our web site, BabyBargains.com (click on Bonus Material).

Jeep These strollers are made by Kolcraft, reviewed on page 496.

Joovy (214)761-1809. Web: joovy.com. Joovy was launched in 2002 by a former Baby Trend executive who secured the license to the English pushcart better known as the Baby Trend Sit N Stand. Joovy has re-christened this model the Caboose Stand-on Tandem ($160, 26 lbs.). Compared to the old Sit N Stand, Joovy's Caboose features a higher handle height, foam handle, improved car seat attachment and nicer canopy. The company also brightened up the fashion.

Joovy has made a few improvements to the Caboose—now the seat recline doesn't interfere with the space for the toddler. And the infant car seat attachment sits higher than the previous model. FYI: the Joovy works with 13 infant seats, including the Graco SnugRide and Chicco KeyFit.

In recent years, Joovy has rolled out several spin-offs of the Caboose: the Caboose Ultralight, Big Caboose and (new for 2009) the Ergo Caboose.

The Caboose Ultralight ($260, 21 lbs) is 20% lighter than the original Caboose and features a larger canopy and neoprene parent organizer.

Got three kids? The Big Caboose ($330, 37 lbs.) has two seats plus a toddler jump seat/standing area. This model can also handle two infant car seats—so if you have twins and an older toddler, this would be one of the few models out there to hold all three tykes.

The new Ergo Caboose (28.5 lbs.) is a total redesign—it features air-filed rear tires, ergonomic mesh seat with two-position recline, a longer frame with better access to the storage basket and a slew of accessories (rain cover, fleece canopy, etc). Price: $400.

While the Caboose is Joovy's flagship model, the company has three other models. The Groove ($160-$200, 16 lbs.) is a high-end umbrella with aluminum frame, adjustable footrest, drawstring seat recline, extended canopy and dual cup holders. It also comes in a twin version (Groove 2, $200, 26 lbs.).

Joovy's Zoom ($300) is a jogger with fixed front wheel, no rear axle (so you can run without kicking the back), full canopy and parent tray. Yep it is pricey—but it does include a rain cover. A version of this stroller (Zoom 360, $300) is available with a front swivel wheel.

Finally, the Joovy Kooper is a lightweight umbrella stroller ($200, 15.5 lbs.) with compact fold and quick release wheels.

Our View. Of all the Caboose variations, we recommend the Joovy Caboose Ultralight as tops. Reader feedback on this model is most positive—the lighter weight makes it a worthy upgrade over the regular Caboose.

As for Joovy's other models, feedback is rather sparse, but parents generally like the design touches through out this line (a jogger with parent cup holders—what a concept!) and the bright yet simple fashion is a nice alternative to navy blue. ***Rating: B+***

Kelty (303) 530-7670, web: kelty.com. Kelty is best known for their backpacks, but they jumped into the jogger market back in 2001. Their re-designed jogger won kudos when it was launched in 2005 but it's showing its age. Meanwhile, Kelty has missed out on the swivel wheel stroller boom, belatedly debuting a model in this category only as of last year.

The Speedster is Kelty's key offering. This fixed-wheel jogger features 16" wheels and is $300, while a "deluxe" variation ($335) adds an easier fold, height adjustable handle, hand break and reclining seat. A double version is $390—that's very affordable.

The Speedster Swivel (22 lbs.) is Kelty's belated stab at the all-terrain market: this stroller is similar to the Speedster Deluxe, but has polymer wheels. A single version is $375; double is $475.

How's the quality? Kelty makes an excellent jogging stroller that gets good marks from readers—if you really want to run with a stroller, this is a good choice. The swivel wheel strollers were not out as of press time, so no feedback yet. ***Rating: B+***

Kolcraft *(800) 453-7673. Web: kolcraft.com.* Kolcraft has always been an also-ran in the stroller market—that is, until their recent hot selling Jeep-branded strollers took off. Since Kolcraft exited the car seat business in 2001, the company has no travel systems to offer. That's a blessing in disguise: many Kolcraft models hold other major brands of car seats, giving parents more flexibility.

The models. Kolcraft sells strollers under four brands: Kolcraft, Sesame Beginnings, Jeep and Contours. Kolcraft and Sesame Beginnings are sold as entry-level models at chains stores like Wal-Mart. The real story here is the success of Kolcraft's Jeep line—Kolcraft has an entire line of Jeep strollers, complete with SUV-like knobby wheels, beefed up suspension, and sporty fabrics at affordable prices ($30 to $150). Clever touches like simulated lug nuts on the wheels and a toy steering wheel for baby have made these models quite popular.

The best-selling Jeep is the Liberty Terrain—a three-wheel stroller with turnable front wheel that can be locked in a forward position. This hybrid between jogging and sport strollers features one-hand fold, child snack tray with the aforementioned toy steering wheel and parent tray. At $129 at Wal-Mart, it's no surprise this one has been a hot seller. And surprise: parent reviews have been very positive on this model, albeit with a stray complaint that the handle is too low for very tall parents.

Kolcraft sells several versions of the Liberty—there's a basic model (Sport Urban Terrain, $130) and more deluxe versions (Liberty Limited $170; Liberty Limited Urban Terrain, $165). The more expensive models add extra storage (a bag on the side of the basket), fancier padding and an electronic toy steering wheel.

Kolcraft also makes a raft of other Jeep models, including an umbrella style (Wrangler, 12 lbs., $50) and a more traditional lightweight model, the Cherokee Sport ($60). The Wrangler Twin Sport is a side-by-side model for $120. There's also a jogger, the Jeep Overland Limited with a fixed front wheel for $190.

For 2009, Kolcraft plans to debut an upgraded version of the Wrangler, dubbed the Wrangler Unlimited with a larger canopy for $90.

Besides the Jeep line, Kolcraft also offers strollers under its own brand. Kolcraft's stroller frame (the Universal Car Seat Carrier, $55, 13 lbs.) competes against the Baby Trend Snap & Go, fitting most major brands of car seats and has a large basket and one-hand fold.

Kolcraft's other major stroller label is Contours, which features a bit more style than one would expect from Kolcraft (bright red fabrics, curved tubular frames, etc.). The Contours Option 3 Wheel Stroller ($130, 26 lbs.) has an infant car seat adapter and reversible seat, so you can see baby while pushing, while the Contours Options Tandem ($210, 32 lbs.) is a double stroller with Bugaboo-like front wheels. Speaking of the Bugaboo, Kolcraft also offers the Options 4 Wheel ($140, 25 lbs.), a credible knock-off of the Dutch best seller.

New in the past year, the Contours Options Tandem ($250, 33 lbs.) has seats that can face each other—and the stroller comes with a car seat adapter (a second one is available as an accessory).

For 2009, Kolcraft plans to launch a new tandem dubbed the Traveller ($200, 28 lbs). It will feature a compact fold, height adjustable handle and be car seat compatible.

Our view. Kolcraft has improved its quality in recent years and our rating reflects this. Dollar for dollar, these are the best affordable strollers on the market—the Jeep Liberty is a great example and the pick of the litter. Also winners: Kolcraft's simple umbrella strollers and side-by-side models. Compared to other low-end brands (Graco, Cosco), Kolcraft shines. That said, you can't compare these to high end models . . . Kolcraft still has a way to go to match their durability. But for suburbanites who need a sturdy stroller with lots of storage and decent looks for the mall and occasional outings, Kolcraft's Jeep line fits the bill. **Rating: B+**

Kool Stop *(800)586-3332, 714-738-4973; koolstop.com.* See our web page (BabyBargains.com, click on Bonus Material) for a review.

Maclaren *(877) 504-8809 or (203) 354-4400; Web: maclarenbaby. com.* Maclaren is the brand with British roots that specializes in premium-priced, high-quality umbrella strollers made from lightweight aluminum.

Founded in 1965 by a British test pilot, Maclaren's strollers were a sharp departure from the bulky prams that were the norm back then. By inventing a lightweight stroller that folded up to the size of an umbrella, Maclaren appealed to a generation of mobile parents who wanted to take their strollers on planes, subways, etc.

Maclaren's first efforts to crack the U.S. market were centered on the East Coast, appealing to New Yorkers and Bostonians who needed sturdy yet lightweight strollers that could be hauled up and down subway station stairs. In the last decade, Maclaren has expanded its market by rolling out the brand nationwide to chain stores like Target and Babies R Us.

Most Maclaren strollers run $200 to $300. So, you might be wondering, why buy a Maclaren when you can find a cheap umbrella stroller for under $100 in discounters? Maclaren fans point out these strollers are much more durable, lighter in weight and packed with more urban-friendly features (one-hand folds) than the competition. As a result, Maclaren strollers can last for more than one child and have resale value. Pop onto Craigslist and search for Maclaren versus Evenflo or Graco strollers . . . you'll see what we mean.

The models. Okay, let's take a deep breath. Maclaren offers TEN models, so there is much to cover. There will be a quiz at the end of this review.

FYI: Maclaren quotes weights for its strollers without adding in the canopy or mesh shopping basket. Hence, you'll need to add a couple pounds to each of these weights to compare apples to apples with other brands.

Maclaren's entry-level model, the Volo ($100-130, 8.8 lbs.) is a super light, stripped down stroller. You get a canopy, five-point harness and mesh seat and basket—but that's about it. There are two versions of the Volo: a $100 one with a mesh seat and a $130 version with a seat liner/cushion. The Volo seat does not recline, so this stroller is best for babies six months and up.

A more full-featured model from Maclaren is their Triumph, ($150) which weighs 11.5 lbs. and features a fully enclosed protective hood and one-hand fold. This seat does have a two-position recline (it is designed for babies three months and up).

Next up is the Quest (12.1 lbs.), which adds more padding, a four-position partial seat recline and an extendable footrest. The Quest comes in three versions: the Quest Sport (basic colors, $200), Quest Mod (fancy retro look with circular design fabric, $220) or Kate Spade Quest (a designer fabric print, $300).

The Techno XT ($300, 15 lbs.) is the top of the line Maclaren—it features the most padding, a flip-down sun visor and three-position adjusting handles that can be extended to a height of 42 inches. And yes, Maclaren throws in a cup holder for the Techno, which also has upgraded wheels and reflective trim. The Techno XLR ($350, 16.5 lbs.) is an inch and a half wider than the Techno XT and comes with an infant car seat adapter. You can also use this stroller for a child who weights up to 65 lbs.—ten lbs. more than most other Maclarens.

Maclaren sells two side-by-side strollers, the Twin Triumph ($245, 23.4 lbs.) and the Twin Techno ($380, 26.9 lbs.). The basic difference between these models: the Twin Techno more plush and comes with a boot, head support and upgraded canopy. Parents of twins rave about these strollers, which are among the best made side-by-side models on the market. Maclaren's doubles are good for older child/infant needs as well.

A bit late to the party, Maclaren has debuted their own stroller frame (a la the Snap N Go), dubbed the Easy Traveller ($70, 11 lbs). Mac's stroller frame features a large basket with an easy fold similar the Volo. This model works with most major infant car seats, including Peg Perego and the Graco Snug Ride or Safe Seat.

So, what's new for Maclaren this year? The company is now offering parents a chance to customize their stroller—you can build your own Volo with a frame color, seat fabric, liner and harness color. Price: $250.

But Maclaren's biggest product launch in 2009 is the Grand Tour, the brand's first full-size stroller. The company bills this as a "luxury transport system" and Maclaren has loaded this thing with just about every possible feature: one-hand fold, reversible seat, rain cover, and more. There's even a version (LX) with a clock, thermometer and pedometer.

Unfortunately, all these features add up to one heavy and expensive stroller: the Grand Tour is 27 lbs. and runs $600; the LX weighs in at 31 lbs. and is $900. While we saw a prototype of the Grand Tour, the final production version wasn't on the market as of press time.

Recently, Maclaren rolled out a "Four Seasons" stroller ($430, based on the old Ryder frame) with four different/reversible seat liners to match the changing seasons. You also get a winter foot muff, blanket and carry bag. Maclaren is also offering reversible seat liners for the Twin Triumph.

In the past year or two, Maclaren has been concentrating on beefing up its customizability and accessories rather than rolling out new models. One key accessory: a $20 universal stroller organizer that fits on the back handles—it includes two bottle pockets that can hold drinks, a cell phone pocket and a mesh storage bag. This helps address parent complaints that Maclarens lack adequate storage. They also offer new eco-liners made of corn, bamboo, organic cotton or recycled polyester. Cost: $40 to $75.

One important caveat to this line: all Maclaren strollers lack napper or bumper bars on the front of the seat. Yes, these models all have five-point harnesses to keep baby securely inside the strollers, but the absence of a napper bar will turn off some parents.

Our view. While we still think Maclaren is one of the best quality stroller brands on the market, there are a couple of caveats. First, while this brand stakes its reputation on its British heritage, Maclaren switched all its production to China back in 2001. Maclaren is no more British than Bugaboo is Dutch or Graco is American—all these strollers are made in China (ok, Bugaboo is made in Taiwan, but you get the idea). The point is, don't buy this stroller thinking you are avoiding a made-in-China product.

Another issue: Maclaren's finicky fold. Retailers who sell many

strollers

Macs tell us you must be careful to correctly fold up the stroller (you have to make sure the backrest is completely upright and the canopy is back before folding). You never want to force or jam the stroller, which can bend the frame.

The other perennial Maclaren complaint: skimpy canopies. We wish Maclaren offered an accessory canopy that would really screen out the sun.

Now that we've got the complaints out of the way, we should point out that the majority of reader feedback on Maclaren is very positive. The company has enhanced its customer service reputation by rolling out 35 service centers nationwide in case you need to get your stroller repaired.

The take-home message: these strollers are well made and worth the price premium. ***Rating: A***

Maxi Cosi *maxi-cosi.com* Dorel brought its European subsidiaries Maxi Cosi and Quinny to the U.S. a couple of years ago to bolster the brand's efforts in the upper end of the stroller market.

Maxi Cosi sells both car seats (reviewed in the previous chapter) and strollers here in the U.S.–their two stroller offerings are the Foray and Perle. The Foray ($350, 26.5 lbs.) clearly riffs off that Bugaboo vibe–a modular system that starts with a stroller frame that fits a Maxi Cosi infant car seat and continues with a stroller seat that can face forward or rear. Yes, there's even a cup holder, telescoping handle and weather shield.

Reader feedback on the Foray is mostly positive: fans love the smooth glide, thanks to the wheel design (larger air-filled tires in back, smaller wheels up front). The one-touch push brake is a welcome design improvement over other stroller brakes that can scuff shoes. Of course, the Foray's affordability (less than half the price of a Bugaboo) is a big plus.

But, the Foray is about 30% heavier than a Bugaboo, so there's one trade-off. And the fold is cumbersome and complex, requiring you to remove the seat first. The Foray only works with the Maxi Cosi Mico infant car seat, which we only give a C rating. And the long-term durability of the Foray has been a thorn in the side of some Foray owners, who complain the canopy can tear (among other quality woes) after just a few months of use. If Dorel wants to compete in the luxury stroller segment, it can't cheap out on the quality or fail to answer emails sent to customer service, as some readers allege.

FYI: The Foray is a Babies R Us exclusive as of this writing; and is only available in one fashion (so you better like the black and tan color scheme).

Maxi Cosi's other stroller, the Perle ($180, 17 lbs) also works with the Mico infant car seat as a travel system. The Perle has a two-handle design like the Peg Pliko and features an umbrella fold, partial seat recline, adjustable leg rest and rain cover. Unlike the cumbersome fold for the Foray, the Perle is much simpler and requires just one hand. On the other hand, the Perle's fashion choices are as limited as the Foray: there's just one beige/grey color scheme.

Reader feedback on the Perle isn't as positive as the Foray—quality woes (like fabric that tears after just a few months of use) also dog this stroller. While fans love the easy fold and plush seat, detractors say the kid cup holder is a joke and the weight is several pounds more than a similarly priced Maclaren. The canopy's lack of coverage is another major negative.

So it is a mixed review: the Foray gets better marks than the Perle. But lack of long-term durability hold down this brand's overall rating. *Rating: B-*

Mia Moda   610-373-6888, Web: MiaModainc.com. Former Graco and Maclaren veterans have joined forces to launch Mia Moda. We're not sure where Mia Moda came up with the description of their strollers as "Euro-design"—the company is based in Pennsylvania and imports their strollers from China.

Nonetheless, we will give Mia Moda brownie points for creativity. The clever Cielo Evolution ($150, 18.4 lbs.) has the most amazing fold on the market—basically, the Cielo folds down into the size of a briefcase. (You have to see the video demo on their web site to believe it). While this stroller itself is nothing fancy (basic canopy, five-point harness, cup holder, partial seat recline), the ultra compact fold might be just the ticket for air travelers who fear gate-checking a stroller. (FYI: The Cielo is best for babies over six months of age, as the seat does not fully recline. And there are no sides to this stroller, which makes it more appropriate for toddlers).

We wish the rest of the Mia Moda line was that amazing—the company is launching a slew of mostly me-too models that duplicate what's already on the market. The sleek Energi ($200, 25 lbs.), is a tri-wheel model with full recline, front swivel wheel, child's tray, and height adjustable handle.

Mia Moda's basic umbrella stroller, the Facile ($50, 15.8 lbs) has a four-position seat recline and front wheel suspension—it's a decent buy for the price.

In the past year Mia Moda debuted a knock off of the Baby Trend Sit N Stand: the Compagno ($200, 34.4 lbs). An older toddler can sit or stand in the back, while a younger baby sits in front. The Compagno is also car seat compatible.

New for 2009, Mia Moda plans two new models: the Luce ($80, 14 lbs.), which is an upgraded version of the Facile umbrella stroller,

strollers

adding more padding for the seat, a parent console and a standing fold. Also new: the Veloce ($130, 16 lbs.) a full size model with two handles, an extended canopy, and plush padding.

So, how's the quality? Feedback on Mia Moda is sparse, as the brand is sold in few stores and just a handful of online sites. What little reader feedback we've heard is mixed—the lower price models (Facile) seem to do best; while the three-wheel Energi gets less than glowing marks from readers who say the quality just isn't there for a $200 stroller. **Rating: B-**

Micralite *Web: scichild.com.* UK-import Micralite's most famous stroller is the Toro, which scored as one of *Consumer Reports* top-rated strollers in a recent report. The Toro ($525, 19 lbs.) is a Bugaboo-like modular system with larger air-filled rear wheels. The Toro's most amazing feature is its compact, standing fold—with the seat on (take that Bugaboo!). Infant car seat adapters work with Peg, Graco and Maxi Cosi car seats.

The Toro also has a fully reclining seat, interchangeable seat pads, rain cover, foot muff and an optional carry cot/bassinet ($200 extra).

MicraLite's other model is the FastFold FTS ($300), which is a scaled-down version of the Toro that weighs 15 lbs. The FastFold has an adjustable handle, suspension, and included rain cover and storage pouch. The major negative: there is no seat recline.

Reader feedback on Micralite has been as thin as their distribution—this brand isn't in many stores or sold on many web sites. That may change, as the brand is now distributed by Scandinavian Child (makers of the Svan high chair).

The Toro gets good marks, especially for urban dwellers using public transport and needing a stroller that folds up quick and compact. The smooth ride, fully reclining seat, inflated tires and bright fashion (five solid colors) are the key advantages. Plus, it costs $400 less than a Bugaboo Cameleon.

But . . . detractors point out the seat doesn't reverse to face the parent and the limited canopy doesn't block much sun. Other design flaws: a skimpy basket that is impossible to access and a napper bar that doesn't open or remove. Plus the stroller can be tippy when any weight is put on the back handle—don't hang a diaper bag back there. And you have to adjust the handles with an . . . Allen wrench? For 500 bucks, we'd expect MicraLite to personally visit our home to adjust the handles, much less require a soon-to-be-lost tool. And even when you adjust the handles, the Toro will not work well for tall parents who may find themselves kicking the rear wheels.

The FastFold FTS also is recommended with one caveat: the wide front wheels (24") make it hard to maneuver in tight spaces (unfortunately, the Toro has the same design). Like the Toro, the inadequate canopy and skimpy, hard to access basket come in for the most criticism. FYI: We've seen the FastFold discounted to $200 or so online—that seems like a more reasonable price than the $300 sticker.

So, it is a mixed review for Micralite—the Toro and FastFold's innovative designs are marred by flaws that are disappointing at this price point. **Rating: C**

Mountain Buggy Web: mountainbuggy.com. This little company from New Zealand sells rugged, all-terrain strollers, which have won fans in both urban areas and the 'burbs. These tri-wheel strollers feature lightweight aluminum frames (21-23 lbs. depending on the model), 12″ air-filled wheels with polymer rims (great for use near the beach), full reclining seats, height adjustable handles, one step folds and large two-position sun canopies.

The models. Mountain Buggy's flagship model is the Urban ($530 single, 22 lbs.; $700 double, 30 lbs.), which has a front wheel that can swivel or be fixed. The result is great maneuverability, unlike other joggers with fixed wheels (which limits their appeal for more urban uses). If you don't need the swivel front wheel, Mountain Buggy offers a model with a fixed front wheel—the Terrain ($480).

Got three kids? Mountain Buggy even sells triple versions of the Urban and Terrain that retail for $1200.

In the past year, Mountain Buggy debuted an upgraded version of the Urban: the Urban Elite ($600 single, 23 lbs; $1000 double; 35 lbs). The Urban Elite has an upgraded canvas seat, padded straps, infant insert, diaper bag and bottle holder.

New for 2009, the Swift ($550, 21 lbs.) is a more compact Mountain Buggy, with a smaller frame and 10″ tires. Like the Urban, it features a swivel front wheel but lacks a car seat adapter or carry cot accessory.

Our view. Okay, those prices are high. BUT, Mountain Buggies have a weight limit of 100 lbs., so you can use this stroller for a LONG time. And parents love the slew of optional accessories, including a bug shield and full sun cover . . . AND a clip that lets you attach an infant car seat to their single stroller models.

But the Mountain Buggy's key advantage is its light weight: the Urban Single's 22 lbs. is 10% to 20% lighter than competitors. That makes the Urban easier to push and maneuver.

So, we'll give this brand our top rating despite the stiff prices. Positive parent reviews and added flexibility from all those accessories make these strollers worth the price.

FYI: As we were going to press, we learned that Mountain Buggy has declared bankruptcy and was looking for a buyer. As of now, the company's plant remains open and the strollers are still for sale here in the U.S.—we will post updates on this on our blog. **Rating: A**

Mutsy *(973)243-0234, Web: Mutsy.com.* Dutch-bred Mutsy hoped to follow in the footstep of that other Holland stroller company that made a splash in the U.S. Like Bugaboo, Mutsy offers a series of stroller frames that can fit an infant car seat, stroller frame or bassinet. And like Bugaboo, Mutsy imports its strollers from Asia. So is Mutsy a hit or a flop? Read on.

The models. Mutsy's Urban Rider ($700, 25.4 lbs.) comes complete with bassinet, stroller seat and two sets of wheels—that's right, you can swap out air-filled front tires for smaller, swivel wheels. And the rear wheels swivel, giving the Urban Rider even more maneuverability. Mutsy also sells an upgraded version of the Urban Rider as the Urban Rider Next ($760) with a leather handle, diaper bag and a few other extras.

The 4Rider ($575, 24 lbs.) lacks the Urban Rider's ability to swap front wheels, instead going with 10" single spoke, swivel wheels. The 4Rider includes a car seat adapter, bassinet and stroller seat that is fully adjustable (adjustable leg rest, even seat depth). The 4Rider Light ($545, 19 lbs.) swaps the 4Rider's air-filled tires for rubber versions.

The Spider ($200, 20 lbs.) is a funky tri-wheel model with telescoping handle, partial seat recline and a unique fold (the Spider folds back upon itself).

New in the past year, Mutsy debuted the Slider ($630, 24 lbs.), which features foam wheels (they provide the lighter overall weight), reversible/telescoping handle, bassinet and stroller seat, micro fiber fabric and more. This model is probably Mutsy's closest competitor to the Bugaboo since it also has a reversible seat, infant car seat adapter and bassinet option.

Our view. On paper, Mutsy looked like a slam dunk—multi-function strollers that just oozed cool Euro chic. Unlike other models that tout a faux "European-inspired" patina, Mutsy is the real deal. These strollers are head turners.

Yet, so far, Mutsy has barely been a blip on the sales radar or baby stores. Why the washout? In a word: weight. Mutsy made the mistake of launching strollers that were too heavy for the U.S. market. The Urban Rider is 25% heavier than the Bugaboo Cameleon. Yes, that's works out to four pounds and you might say, big deal. But four pounds in the stroller biz is indeed a big deal—it impacts maneuverability and how easy it is to haul in/out of a trunk or up a set of subway stairs.

Even Mutsy's "light weight" model, the Spider is 20 lbs.—that's much heavier than a comparable Maclaren. Hence it is no surprise that Mutsy's most successful model is the 4Rider Light, which is more in line weight-wise with the Dutch competition.

That doesn't mean Mutsy is a total washout. Fans of the strollers (especially taller parents) love the super-adjustable handles, plush fabrics and ease of use. And readers also tell us they love the head-turning ability of these strollers—you can't go to the park or mall without someone stopping you to ask about the stroller. Quality for Mutsy is high.

The take-home message: these strollers are well designed, but too heavy. Mutsy should have launched its line with lighter-weight models like the newer Slider or the 4Rider Light. By emphasizing the heavy Urban Rider with its awkward swap-able front wheels, the brand has so far failed to gain much traction. **Rating: B**

Orbit Web: orbitbaby.com. Fans of The Office may remember the Orbit fondly, after Dwight Schrute spent an entire episode trying to destroy the pricey travel system to no avail. While that episode may qualify as the best baby product placement in a TV series ever, it showcased the Orbit's quality to withstand the show's extreme road test (you can see the episode on Orbit's web site).

What set off Dwight? It was Orbit's über expensive price tag ("$1200 is more than I spent on my entire bomb shelter!"). Actually, the Orbit runs $900, including the infant car seat reviewed in the past chapter. And no, the Orbit doesn't come with a toddler stroller seat—that's an extra $220.

The verdict? Folks who have the Orbit love it—the unique car seat base makes for simple, rock solid installation, as we noted in the last chapter. The engineering on the Orbit is top notch: parents like the stroller frame's simple one-hand fold and ergonomic handles. And the frame lets you shift the car seat in a 360-degree range of motion.

Downsides? The Orbit car seat only works up to 22 lbs. (compared to other infant seats that work to 30). That means bigger babies will outgrow this travel system before six months—and that's a lot of money to spend for such brief usage. Yes, you can pony up another $220 for a toddler stroller seat—but by now you've spent $1120. And unlike other premium strollers, the stroller seat doesn't reverse to face the parent.

As we noted in the Orbit car seat review, the carrier is heavy (nearly 10 lbs.) and bulky, making it a tight fit in smaller vehicles. Once your baby is near the weight limits of the seat, carrying the Orbit's 30 lb. weight (baby plus car seat) will be a hardy upper-body workout.

Another bummer: there are only two colors to the Orbit—brown and black.

The take-home message: if you are looking for a travel system that is a conversation starter, then Orbit is your brand. Parents love the Jetsons-like look . . . and having a stroller/car seat that no one on the block has. While we understand that appeal, we would be much more excited about the Orbit if it were half the price. That's something we (and Dwight) can agree on. **Rating: B**

strollers

Peg Perego *(260) 482-8191. Web: perego.com.* Peg Perego is the Italian stroller maker that was among the first European brands to land in North America, way back in the 1980's. Actually, the company traces its roots back to 1949 when its founder Giuseppe Perego created a carriage for his infant son.

Unlike most other European brands who long ago abandoned production on the Continent in search of lower labor costs in Asia, Peg Perego still makes all its strollers in Italy. (Ok, there was a brief time when Perego flirted with Chinese imports with one model—the Aria—but that didn't go well and the company returned back to an all-Italian line).

That all-Italian mantra for Peg has been both a blessing and curse. On the upside, the company's fabrics are considered among the most fashionable (although, admittedly, other companies have since closed the fashion gap). Peg's reputation for quality is also excellent. In an era where parents are concerned about Chinese imports and their safety, Peg rarely has a safety recall.

But . . . the made-in-Europe label has its price—in the last few years, Peg's strollers have jumped in price to compensate for a strong Euro. Most Peg strollers run $300, $400 and more . . . that's a tough sell in this economy. And the company has failed to innovate, content to rest on its laurels. The company missed out on the all-terrain three-wheel stroller craze and waited five *years* after the Bugaboo to launch a competitor, which promptly bombed. Peg also lost a bit of its cache after letting its overstock strollers be sold in discounters like Marshall's.

So can Peg get its mojo back? Let's look at their current line up.

The models. Perego has four main stroller offerings: the Pliko P3 Classico, Pliko Switch, Si and Aria. The company also offers two "convertible systems," the Uno and Skate.

The Pliko P3 Classico (18.7 lbs.) is Peg's best-selling stroller. It runs $365, although you can find previous year's Pliko's on sale for less online. The Pliko features a two-handle design, 150 degree reclining seat, adjustable leg rest, adjustable height handle and removable/washable seat cushions. Newer Pliko's have a one-hand fold. For 2009, Peg hasn't changed the Pliko much (just new fashions).

The Pliko Switch ($500, 23 lbs.) is a brand new model with reversible seat that can face forward or rear (hence the Switch name). It features a full recline and most of the same features as the regular Pliko. Yes, you can fold the stroller with the seat on it (unlike Bugaboo).

Also new for 2009, the Si ($280, 12 lbs.) is Peg's stab at a super-lightweight stroller. The Si features height adjustable handles, standing one-hand fold and a seat recline with three positions. The Si holds a Peg car seat, as well as other brands. (In fact, all Peg's strollers work with Peg's infant car seat).

Perego's other major lightweight offering is the Aria ($220, 14.3 lbs.). It features a seat that reclines to 150 degrees (same as the Pliko), decent storage basket, canopy and a five-point restraint. This year's version, the Aria OH ($200) features a one-hand fold (hence the OH suffix), larger canopy that ratchets and adjustable cup holder.

Peg makes two double strollers: the Aria Twin ($340, 17 lbs.), a side by side model and the Duette SW ($880, 32 lbs.), a tandem model. The Aria has a 60/40 configuration that holds a car seat in the larger space.

Peg's "combination" strollers include the Skate and Uno. The Skate was introduced in 2008 with much fanfare—it featured a Bugaboo-like multi-function frame, a height-adjustable handle, four wheel suspension, ball-bearing wheels for a smooth glide, three seat heights and (drum roll) a cup holder. But it also cost an outrageous $900 and weighed 33.7 pounds . . . 68% more than the Bugaboo. The Skate was like a Ford Expedition to the Bugaboo's BMW Z3. As you might guess, the Skate bombed big time.

For 2009, Peg is going back to the drawing board and hopes to fix the Skate with a new lower weight model. The Skate Elite will weigh 27 lbs. and features an $800 price tag, which includes a bassinet, an improved fold and other tweaks. It's hard to say whether these changes will rescue the Skate; we'll have to wait and see as it wasn't out as of press time.

Peg's other combination stroller is the Uno ($400, 23 lbs.), which features a Bugaboo-ish wheel design with smaller wheels up front and larger ones in the back. It features a reversible handle so you can face baby, as well as a boot and height adjustable handle. The only bummer: when you reverse the handle on the Uno, you have the turnable wheels in back (rear-wheel drive), which is rather difficult.

Our view. Despite Peg's reputation for quality, the company has made some bone-headed moves that have damaged its reputation in recent years. Exhibit one: the Aria. For a while, Peg decided to make this model in China . . . and the results were disastrous, with numerous reader complaints about quality and other woes. While Peg has since switched production back to Italy, the damage has been done. There are still hundreds of parent reviews trashing Peg online, with good reason.

Prices for Peg strollers have reached an unreasonable level. The only silver lining: you can often find previous year versions at a steep discount online and in stores.

Despite all this, readers still love the Pliko, even though the basket is hard to reach. And the new Pliko Switch is a home-run—readers love the reversible handle and the fact it folds with the seat on. While the Si wasn't out as of press time, we played with a prototype and thought it could be a winner.

strollers

So it is a mixed review for this Italian brand: the company celebrates its 60th birthday this year. But the company's storied past is no guarantee of future success. ***Rating: B***

Phil & Ted Most Excellent Buggy Company *Web: philandt-eds.com.* It's been the best of times and the worst of times for this brand. On the plus side, Phil & Ted has released a string of hot-selling models, riding a wave of popularity for its all-terrain strollers. At the same time, the company had not one, not two, but THREE safety recalls in the past year—including a serious one involving defective handles that caused strollers to collapse.

On top of it all, Phil & Ted fired its distributor (Regal Lager) and decided to go its own way in 2009. Hence this year will be one of transition for the brand as it sets up its own customer service, sales reps and the like.

Phil & Ted followed their fellow kiwis from Mountain Buggy to the U.S. stroller market in 2000, but it took a while for them to hit their stride. Then Phil & Ted hit a home run with the Sport ($450, 24 lbs.), which used to be known as the e3.

Like Mountain Buggy and Valco, Phil & Ted's flagship stroller is a tri-wheel with a swivel front wheel and air-filled tires. What sets Phil & Ted apart is their second-child seat ($90 extra; for kids six months and up), which can attach to the FRONT or BACK of the stroller (for comparison, Valco's toddler seat only attaches to the front). The rear seat configuration turns off some parents (safety hint: the child in the backseat has to be removed first to prevent tipping). And if you put a larger toddler in the back seat, the access to the stroller's storage basket is limited. But that caveat aside, folks seem to love the Sport. Parents tell us the all-terrain 12" air-filled wheels are perfect for both the mall and hiking trails, plus the wide seat accommodates children for many years.

Phi & Ted also make a side-by-side stroller dubbed the Twin ($600, 36 lbs.) with a 29" width and a maximum capacity of 88 lbs.

In the past year, Phil & Ted rolled out several spin-offs of the Sport. The Classic ($350, 24 lbs.) is a stripped-down model, with only a two-position handle and no bumper bar. The Dash ($550, 23 lbs.) is an upgraded Sport with fancier padding and canopy. Also new: the Vibe ($700, 22 lbs.), a version of the Sport with a Quinny-like aluminum frame. The Vibe's bumper bar has a snack tray and a larger adjustable canopy than the other models.

New for 2009, Phil & Ted plans two new strollers, which are the brand's first attempts at four-wheel models. The unfortunately named Hammerhead ($550) will be much like the Sport, but with two wheels at front that are lockable to push in a straight line. Also new: The Smart, a super lightweight model at 12 lbs. with smaller wheels up front and bigger tires in back. The Smart will feature a compact fold and one-touch brake, but no basket (it will be an optional accessory). No pricing info was available on the Smart as we were going to press.

Our View. Readers give the Sport an enthusiastic thumbs up for its smooth ride and second-seat functionality. The height adjustable handle also wins raves. Sure, folks wish for a bigger canopy and cup holder (there isn't one), but overall the Sport is a winner.

These strollers are designed for the outdoors—the air-filled tires are great for hikes, gravel paths or rough sidewalks.

We are disappointed with all the safety recalls in 2008—with nine years under its belt in the U.S., you'd think the company would have the quality control issues down by now. As a result, we wouldn't recommend buying a first production run Phil & Ted; we'd let a few months go by to make sure all the kinks are worked out.

That said, we still recommend Phil & Ted and specifically the Sport—the overall design and wide range of accessories make this a good choice for parents who want an all-terrain stroller. ***Rating: A-***

Quinny *Web: quinny.com.* Quinny launched in 2007 amid much fanfare as parent Dorel/Cosco tried to steal a bit of the Bugaboo mojo and tap the premium part of the stroller market. Quinny is Dorel's Dutch subsidiary known for its stylish multi-function strollers.

The Buzz 3 (26.4 lbs.) is Quinny's flagship model—this clever tri-wheel stroller has an innovative "automatic unfolding" feature plus a sleek look with a fully reclining seat that can face forward or back toward the parent. Like the Bugaboo, the Buzz is a modular system, albeit sold separately: $580 for a stroller, $160 for a carry cot (Dreami) and $150-180 for a matching Maxi Cosi Mico infant car seat. There is even a two-tone fashion option, like the Bugaboo Cameleon.

New for 2009, the Buzz 4 (27 lbs.) is a four-wheel version of the Buzz with much the same features and a $630 price tag. The Buzz 4 features suspension on all four wheels.

The Zapp ($220, 13 lbs.) is Quinny's ultra-lightweight stroller with compact fold. This model also accommodates a Maxi Cosi car seat. Unlike the Zapp's European counterpart, the U.S. Zapp has a storage basket. A cup holder, however, is an extra $15.

In mid 2009, Quinny plans to debut a new model, the Loola. This stroller was originally a Bebe Confort model (another Dorel Euro subsidiary) but will be released here under the Quinny label. The Loola ($400) will feature a removable, reversible seat, compact fold, and ratcheting canopy.

Our View. Feedback for Quinny has generally been positive. For the Buzz, fans like the automatic unfolding feature, as well as the adjustable canopy and comfy seat. But detractors point out the air-filled tires puncture easily—and Dorel's customer service can be slow and frustrating in providing replacements. The skimpy storage basket also generates complaints, as does the wide 25.5″ spacing of the rear wheels (which makes negotiating narrow spaces difficult). Finally, we should point out the weight of the Buzz is significantly higher than its Bugaboo competition. And the fold (especially on the Buzz 4) can be a challenge, with levers that are hard to push.

The Zapp does better with readers who like its lightweight frame and smooth turning. But the Zapp doesn't recline, so this stroller is better for older babies who are no longer napping.

Much of the original buzz about Quinny has evaporated in recent months—some of this might be the economy, where $600 strollers are sitting on shelves. But some of the blame also rests with Dorel. After a splashy debut, the company hasn't changed the models much, nor addressed the criticisms mentioned above. As a result, Quinny has lost much of its momentum. *Rating: B+*

Rock Star Baby (a.k.a. Esprit, i'coo) *Web: GTBaby.com.* German stroller maker Hauck launched the Rock Star Baby license in 2005, as a partnership with rocker Bon Jovi's drummer Tico Torres. Yes, this brings the number of rock star endorsed strollers to . . . one. Memo to Justin Timberlake: the diaper pail market is wide open.

Rock Star's parent, Grand Touring Baby, markets strollers under four brands: Rock Star, I'coo, Disney and Esprit.

Rock Star Baby's main offering is a Bugaboo knockoff, basically a repurposed stroller with bassinet, originally marketed in Europe as the I'coo Infinity. The Rock Star Baby stroller ($900, 22 lbs.) has a height-adjustable handle, air-filled rear tires, reversible seat and rain cover. You also get a built-in bunting bag. Unlike the Bugaboo, however, a baby can't lie in the bassinet when it is removed from the stroller. FYI: The Rock Star is often referred to by its I'coo model name as well: the Targo.

In the past year, the Rock Star added a bigger canopy, new wheels and a universal car seat adapter that holds 14 different models (including such mainstream brands as Graco, Chicco and Perego).

Rock Star also offers a second stroller, a lightweight umbrella dubbed the Candy ($100-160, 14 lbs.), It features a one-hand fully reclining seat, single hand fold and adjustable leg rest.

Under the I'coo label, the company offers two strollers: the Targo and Pluto. Yes, the Targo is the same as the Rock Star version, just no logo (and presumably, no royalty to Bon Jovi). That makes it less expensive—about $600, depending on the web site and color pattern. Unlike the Rock Star version with its black and skull-and-cross bones fashion, the I'coo Targo comes in more muted, neutral hues.

New for 2009, the I'coo Pluto ($300, 16 lbs.) is a lightweight stroller with two handles, reclining seat, adjustable footrest and large seat. The Pluto also features a one-hand fold and lots of eye candy, courtesy of numerous chrome accents.

Under the Esprit label, the company sells two more umbrella models: the Sun Speed ($130, 13 lbs.) umbrella stroller with two handles and a full recline and the Sun Speed Duo ($200, 25 lbs.), a side-by-side version with full recline.

Finally, we should mention that Grand Touring Baby also makes a Disney version of the I'coo Targo—the same basic stroller but with a Disney-inspired fashion at $900.

How's the quality? Readers tell us they love the Rock Star/I'coo Targo's maneuverability and smooth steering. The few complaints we've noted have been fixed with the new Targo version—the smallish canopy, for example, is now better. Obviously, the I'coo version is a much better deal—we've seen it discounted to about $500 online, compared to the Rock Star's $900 list!

One caveat to the Targo: it is very large when folded and may not fit in the trunk of a compact car.

As for Rock Star's other strollers, the Candy is clearly "inspired" by the Maclaren Quest. But the Candy doesn't steer as well as the Maclaren. On the plus side, the Candy does have a deeper seat recline. Between the two, Maclaren has the quality edge.

We've heard little feedback on the Esprit Sun Speed, although the few comments were positive. One parent who did buy the Esprit Sun Speed Duo told us she loved the low price, light weight and deep seat recline. But there are no cup holders, boot or rain cover.

The Pluto was too new as of press time for any reader feedback.

Bottom line: of all this brand's models, the Targo is a good stroller we would recommend. ***Rating: B+***

Safety 1st *These strollers and travel systems are made by Cosco. See the earlier review for more info.*

Schwinn *Web: instep.net.* Schwinn is made by InStep, which is in turn part of the Dorel/Cosco stroller empire. Basically, Schwinn models are the same as InStep, with upgraded fabric and additional accessories (insulated cooler bag, etc). A single Schwinn is $150-180, while a double is $270. In the past year, Schwinn has redesigned their flagship Safari ($180 single, $250 double) swivel-wheel model with a new oval frame, added headrest, car seat adapter, one-hand fold, adjustable handle and bug screen. A double Safari omits the adjustable handle. These strollers are quite heavy—the single is 30 lbs. and the double is 37 lbs.

If you are looking for a fixed-wheel jogger for running, Schwinn offers the Free Runner, in either steel (ST $150-200) or aluminum (AL $230). Both feature an adjustable handle, suspension and wider tires.

New for 2009, Schwinn will introduce the marker's first TANDEM jogging stroller. The Fit ($350, 38 lbs) will feature a car seat adapter, 16" rear wheels and 12" front wheels that swivel. The Fit's weight capacity will be 50 lbs. per seat.

Bottom line: if you just want a stroller for brisk walks around the neighborhood, we'd stick with the less-expensive InStep versions. A fixed-wheel Instep Run Around jogger is $130 at Target. However, if you want to run (or plan to spend over $200), we'd suggest going with a quality brand (BOB, Dreamer, Baby Jogger). Schwinn/InStep simply doesn't stack up to the competition. ***Rating: C (Schwinn); B (InStep)***

Silver Cross Web: SilverCrossAmerica.com; (858) 587-4745. Silver Cross has been star-crossed in the U.S., after their first distributor collapsed in 2005 amid poor sales. Then the British parent yanked the replacement distributor in 2007, leaving their Canadian sales arm to fill in as of press time.

Silver Cross' specialty is light weight strollers, similar to Maclaren, designed for the mall and quick in-and-out-of-the-car shopping trips.

The models. The Micro V.2 ($125, 12.5 lbs.) is a lightweight cross between the Mac Volo and Peg Pliko—it includes a basket and carry bag. The Pop ($180-200, 15.4 lbs.) is an upgraded Micro, adding a fully reclining seat and upgraded canopy.

New in the past year, the Dazzle ($300, 15.6 lbs.) is a riff on the Maclaren Starck, with a curvy frame, two-position canopy and bright color palette.

Our View. Simply copying a competitor is no business strategy, as Silver Cross has learned the hard way. The company has failed to gain traction here for a simple reason: there's nothing innovative or compelling about Silver Cross' strollers. And the Dazzle is such a blatant copy of the Mac Starck (down to the same price point and solid gray wheels) we're amazed Silver Cross didn't call it the Darck.

Bottom line: Silver Cross has been a bust so far in America, judging from the numerous models we see on clearance online. Given the turmoil in this brand's distribution, we'll pass on recommending it until things settle down. ***Rating: D***

Simmons Sold online on Target.com and Amazon, these strollers are made by Delta, a company better known for its nursery furniture. Simmons sells a couple of Bugaboo knockoffs, including the Pearl ($180) and Onyx ($150). Both are similar but the Pearl features larger rear wheels. Delta mostly sells cheap, low-end umbrella strollers emblazoned with cartoon logos to discount chains, so these strollers are a bit of a departure. Yet we are struck by the amateur design mistakes for the Pearl and Onyx: both lack cup holders, the strollers are hard to fold and open and so on. And given Delta's massive recent safety recalls for furniture, we have serious concerns about the company's commitment to quality and reliability. ***Rating: D***

Stokke *For a dealer near you, call (877) 978-6553. Web: stokkeusa.com.* And now for something totally different: the Stokke Xplory, a stroller so bizarre we have to show you a picture just to explain it. Yeah, it looks like something George Jetson might have pushed Elroy around in, but it's more than a museum piece  about what strollers might look like in the year 2050. We will give Stokke bonus points for creativity (they've tried to push it as the next Bugaboo), but the $1000 Xplory is a bit too funky for its own good. Like the Bugaboo, you get a modular system that includes a frame with rubber tires and a seat that can attach to the frame either forward or rear facing.

The Stokke's key feature is its high-altitude seating. The pitch, according to Stokke, is to keep baby higher off the ground so they are away from exhaust fumes, slobbering Labradors, etc. (the target market is urban parents).

So why haven't you seen the über rich pushing the Stokke Xplory around Greenwich Village? That's because for the most part, the Xplory has been a bust sales-wise. First, most of the Xplory's frame and handle is injection-molded plastic, not something you'd expect from a $1000+ stroller. The "plastic-y" feel turns off many, while the lack of a basket is another major negative. Instead the Xplory has a "shopping bag" that attaches to the frame . . . close, but no cigar.

In the past year, Stokke has rolled out a Complete Xplory for $1200 that includes a bassinet (a la the Bugaboo). Also new: a car seat adapter accessory for the Perego Primo Viaggio or Graco SnugRide, which addresses a key complaint about past versions. So while we still wouldn't recommend the Xplory (its high price alone is a deal killer), we will raise the rating a touch this year to reflect the new car seat adapter. ***Rating: C-***

Stroll Air *(519) 579-4534. Web: stroll-air.com.* Polish-made Stroll Air is another European stroller company hoping to become the next Bugaboo.

The Zoom ($500, 24 lbs.) is Stroll Air's flagship: this modular stroller system comes with three components: aluminum chassis, stroller seat and bassinet. The Zoom includes a wind cover, diaper bag, umbrella, storage basket, mosquito net, boot and rain cover. That's a rather impressive list considering the $500 price. Accessories include a stroller organizer/console ($30, holds bottles and drinks) and infant car seat adapter.

Like the Bugaboo, the Zoom features larger rear wheels and smaller front wheels. Unlike the Bugaboo, you can fold the Zoom with the seat on.

Our View. Parent feedback on Stroll Air is limited, but the few reports we've received are positive. The Zoom was too new as of press time to gauge any parent feedback; however, Stroll Air's previous models generally were good quality with smooth steering.

One bummer: Stroll Air's distribution is so limited (13 stores at last count) that seeing a Zoom in person may require a bit of luck. ***Rating: B***

Strolee *See Combi.*

Swan *See Baby Trend's review earlier in this section.*

Tike Tech *This brand is reviewed on our web page BabyBargains.com, click on Bonus Material.*

Traxx *See i'coo review earlier in this section.*

Teutonia *Web: teutoniausa.com* Teutonia is a 60-year-old German brand of strollers that, like many European stroller makers, churned out large prams and bulky carriage strollers. Owned for several years by Britax, Teutonia tried and failed to crack the U.S. market, thanks to designs that were way to heavy for domestic tastes.

Enter Graco, which bought Teutonia from Britax in 2007 and remade the brand into stylish stroller systems that let you customize various frames, seating options and colors. But unlike Graco's strollers, you won't see Teutonia in chain stores—the brand is only sold in specialty store boutiques.

Graco hopes to steal a bit of Dorel's mojo after their successful Quinny/Maxi Cosi brand launch. Let's take a look at the offerings.

The models. Teutonia lets you pick from three stroller chassis: the t-100 ($425, 19.5 lbs.) is a compact, four-wheel model, while the t-200 ($500, 21 lbs.) is a tri-wheel stroller. The t-300 ($575, 26.5 lbs.) is billed as a full-size stroller with four wheels. Each chassis allows parents to choose between two wheel styles: one is about half a pound lighter than the other (we quoted the above weights with the lighter weight wheel option). Included with the chassis is a car seat adapter that holds all Graco car seats.

Then you pick a stroller seat: the basic stroller seat ($150, 10.7 lbs.)

has a multi-position canopy with one-hand adjust as well as a two position leg support. You can also pair the stroller with the t-tario 32 infant car seat ($225), which is the same as the Graco SnugRide 32, reviewed in the last chapter. Finally, there is also an optional carrycot ($150, 9 lbs.).

Of course, there are a slew of accessories ($75 diaper bag, $80 foot muff, $25 mosquito net, etc.) but oddly, no cup holder. At least Graco/Teutonia offers you a wide choice of fashion options: nine solid colors, three floral prints and another 15 accent colors available on an optional reversible seat insert.

Those of you playing along at home have probably done the math by now: the least expensive frame (t-100) with the stroller seat runs $575. Add that matching car seat and you're up to $800. Add in any accessories and the total could easily top $1000.

Our View. Reader feedback on this line is limited as it only has been in stores for a short period of time before we went to press. But what we've heard so far is quite positive.

The quality is good. Made in Germany and Poland, the Teutonia strollers are easy to steer one-handed, report readers. Folks like the foam-filled tires (no flats), suspension to smooth out bumps and height adjustable handle.

But . . . these strollers are HEAVY. The *lightest* weight configuration of a Teutonia clocks in at 30 lbs. EMPTY. Add baby, a few items in the basket and you've got 40 pounds to push down the street. If you get the full-size t-300 chassis, the total weight would be a stunning 37.2 lbs. empty. We're amazed that Graco put all this time and effort into this line and came out with such a heavy stroller . . . what are they thinking? Can an average parent who isn't bulked up on steroids actually lift this thing in and out of a trunk?

Another negative: the stroller seat doesn't lie flat and when folded, the entire stroller is rather bulky.

So it's a mixed review for this line. While the basic chassis and seat are a decent price at $575, the lack of included accessories make it less of a deal (compared, for example, with the Stroll Air Zoom reviewed earlier). Quality is good, but the heavy weight and bulky fold make this a tough sell whether you live in the city or suburbs. ***Rating: B***

UPPAbaby *(800)760-2060, Web: UppaBaby.com.* Newcomer UPPAbaby was started by Bostonians Bob and Lauren Monahan. Bob worked for First Years and Safety 1st in product development before striking out on his own; Lauren provides the PR and design mojo. Obviously, Bob and Lauren have kids, as you can tell from the well thought-out design of their first strollers.

UPPAbaby has two strollers: the Vista and the G-lite. The Vista ($700, 24 lbs.) is UPPAbaby's take on Bugaboo. Made of an aircraft alloy frame, the VISTA stroller system includes a bassinet and stroller seat, telescoping handle and easy fold. We liked all the included extras, such as a rain shield, mesh sun shade and bug cover. Plus the Vista uses rubber-like foam wheels that give a smooth ride, but don't go flat. Unlike the Bugaboo, you can fold the Vista with the seat attached.

For 2009, the Vista gets a few minor tweaks and upgrades, including an improved canopy with pop-down sunshade and easier to adjust harness. Also new: a $130 rumble seat for a second child that can be used when the Vista is either in infant car seat or stroller seat mode.

UPPAbaby offers car seat adapters for the Graco Chicco and Peg infant seats. While the Vista does include a weather shield, mesh sunshade and bug cover there are few additional accessories available (travel bag, cup holder, all terrain wheels). Fashion is a bit limited, with six solid colors.

UPPAbaby's second offering is the G-Lite ($100, 8.3 lbs.), a super lightweight umbrella stroller with a standing fold and mesh seat (like the Mac Volo) and seat pad. The G-lite doesn't recline, so it is best for babies six months and up.

New for 2009, UPPAbaby will come out with an upgraded version of the G-Lite, dubbed the G-Luxe ($160, 11.25 lbs). It features a standing fold, bigger wheels, and partial seat recline.

Parent feedback on UPPAbaby has been positive. Readers who like the Vista praise its quality, huge basket and high-riding seat and bassinet. The no-flat foam tires also win raves. The negatives include a basket that is a bit hard to reach with the bassinet attached—and the rear wheel base (25") on the Vista is rather wide, making the stroller harder to maneuver in tight aisles or doorways. Another bummer: the seat doesn't have a full recline, which irks some users. But . . . the footrest is adjustable (something the Bugaboo lacks) and the fold is much easier and compact compared to the Bugaboo or I'coo Targo.

Those criticisms aside, folks who have the Vista give it high marks for quality and durability.

The G-lite wins similar kudos, with fans citing its super light weight and included cushions. Readers debate whether the G-lite is really better than a Maclaren—the lack of seat recline in the G-lite is one major negative, but folks with older toddlers say it is fine for them. All in all, we'd give Maclaren a slight edge in overall quality and construction . . . but a typical Mac costs much more than a G-lite. (No feedback yet on the new G-Luxe).

So, we will recommend UPPAbaby—no, the Vista isn't cheap. But at least for the money, you get decent value (example: the sun canopy is included for the Vista; a $40 add-on for Bugaboo Cameleon, which is $200 more than the Vista already!). ***Rating: A***

Valco *(800) 610-7850. Web: valcobaby.com.* Australia-based Valco has made a splash in the all-terrain stroller market with their Tri-Mode (formerly the Runabout), a tri-wheel stroller whose key selling point is its expandability. The basic Tri-Mode comes in both a single ($480, 23 lbs.) and double ($700, 33 lbs.) version and features a five-position, fully reclining seat, large storage basket, aluminum frame, newborn insert and swivel front wheel that can be locked in a fixed position. The Tri-Mode has 12" air-filled tires.

That's nice, but what really has parents jazzed are Valco's add-ons: a bassinet ($180) and toddler seat ($80) that extend the use of this stroller. The bassinet is fine, but the toddler seat is really cool, turning the Valco into a double stroller. Valco's other accessories include a car seat adapter ($40, which holds a Graco or Peg seat) and foot muff ($60).

How does the Valco stack up versus its main competitors in the swivel wheel, all terrain category? Well the Valco is a touch heavier than the Mountain Buggy Urban Single, although Valco has reduced its weight in the past year to be more comparable. And folks seem to like the Valco's toddler seat configuration better than Phil & Ted, although there is a split opinion here. Fashion wise, Valco is a bit dull, with mostly dark/black fabric options.

Valco does have two other models: the lightweight Buggster ($270, 15 lbs.) is like the Tri-Mode on a diet—a bit like the Quinny Buzz in looks. The Buggster comes with a boot, rain shield, bug net and other goodies, which makes the somewhat steep price a bit easier to swallow.

In the past year, Valco debuted the Latitude, a tri-wheel model with smaller (non-air filled) tires, The Latitude comes in both single ($300, 19 lbs.) and double versions ($480, 30 lbs.) and features a telescoping handle, fully reclining seat and a rather amazing fold. Like most Valco's, you get all the accessories included: rain cover, boot, front napper bar, etc. Both Latitudes are car seat compatible (they include straps for a Graco car seat), but the double only fits one car seat.

What's the difference between the Latitude and Buggster? The Latitude is a single-handle stroller while the Buggster has two umbrella-style handles and can hold a bassinet. The Latitude, by contrast, has a bigger basket and standing, umbrella-like fold.

New for 2009, Valco has two models on deck: The Ion ($550, 27 lbs.) is a side-by-side double that features a full recline and flat fold. Also new: the Matrix is a budget version of the Tri-Mode available in two versions: with a bassinet ($500) and without ($375). The Matrix will have EVA (non-air-filled) tires.

Our View. Parent feedback on the Tri-Mode has been positive, with folks lauding Valco's quality, maneuverability and sturdy ride. We've been impressed with how Valco has trimmed the weight on the Tri-Mode, as that was a previous major drawback.

The Buggster also draws kudos for its maneuverability and light weight; but the fold takes practice, the handles don't extend and there isn't a cup holder. Good news: in the past year, Valco tweaked the fold to make it easier.

The Latitude is a newer model with less reader feedback, but what little we've heard so far is positive. The Ion and Matrix were not out as of press time.

Overall, folks like Valco—readers love all the storage and upgraded fashion compared to say, the BOB Revolution. The air-filled tires on the Tri-Mode make it a better bet for folks who want to use it on trails or rough sidewalks. The Buggster and Latitude are more designed for the city and shopping malls.

All in all, Valco is a winner. **Rating: A**

Zooper *This brand is reviewed on our web page at BabyBargains.com, click on Bonus Material.*

◆ **Other brands to consider.** Archived reviews of obscure and previous stroller brands are on our web site. Go to BabyBargains. com and click on Bonus Material.

Our Picks: Brand Recommendations by Lifestyle

Unlike other chapters, we've broken up our stroller recommendations into several "lifestyle" categories. Since many parents end up with two strollers (one that's full-featured and another that's lighter for quick trips), we'll recommend a primary stroller and a secondary option. For more specifics on the models mentioned below, read each manufacturer's review earlier in this chapter. Let's break it down:

Mall Crawler

You live in the suburbs and drive just about everywhere you go. Besides the mall, you take quick strolls around the block, which has paved sidewalks in good condition.

The idea mall crawler stroller has small wheels that enable tight cornering in narrow aisles—it can't be too wide or bulky. As for weight, you'll be hauling this stroller and out of a trunk several times a day . . . so anything over 20 lbs. is asking for trouble.

Trunk space is a concern when considering the fold of a mall stroller—some strollers are more bulky than others. If you have a compact car, take a second to compare the measurements of the folded stroller and your trunk. Good news: most strollers designed for the mall have compact, easy folds that don't require too many steps.

Other nice features for a mall stroller include a decent cup hold-er and good-sized basket. The canopy and accessories like a rain cover are a bit less important, since this stroller is used more indoors than out.

Common first-time parent mistake: buying a giant travel system, with matching infant car seat and stroller. These are common show-er gifts and many folks fall for that coordinated look . . . and think their stroller should be built like a tank to protect a newborn from thermonuclear attack.

But many travel system strollers are behemoths—and that huge weight and bulk make them impossible to use as baby gets older, not to mention wrestling it in and out of trunk.

So, here's our advice: get a stroller FRAME like the **Baby Trend Snap & Go** $50 (pictured) or the **Graco Snug Rider** for $60. The Baby Trend works with most infant car seat brands; the Graco works just with the Graco SnugRide and SafeSeat/SnugRide 32.

FYI: When trying out different stroller frames, take a second and snap your favorite infant car seat into the various stroller frames in the store before purchasing. Some car seats will lock into place; others must be held with straps. Locking is best for safety, of course. Check the instructions, as some stroller frames have bars that have to be adjusted into a certain position to accommodate different brands.

The bottom line: take a stroller frame, pop in a compatible infant seat and poof! Instant travel system . . . without the expense.

When baby outgrows the infant car seat and stroller frame solu-tion, you then go shopping for a real stroller. This is smarter for two obvious reasons: a) you already have a baby and can see what best fits your infant. And b) you're more experienced as a parent, so you'll have an idea where you want to go with a stroller.

"But really, Denise and Alan, which travel system do you like?" No matter how much we editorialize against pre-packaged travel systems, we still get emails from parents who want to go this route. Okay, if you want to ignore the above advice, we'd suggest the **Chicco Cortina** travel system for $300. It combines an excellent infant car seat and 23 lb. full-featured stroller.

Of course, there is another solution for mall crawlers as well: get a stroller that works with your infant car seat. Popular Graco infant car seats work in many strollers, not just Graco's. You may have to buy a separate car seat adapter, but it makes sense to buy a bet-ter quality, lightweight stroller that you can use for years than the bulky travel system stroller that gets trashed after six months.

Second stroller. You've gone the stroller frame route and now your baby is ready to graduate to a real stroller. Again, for the mall, we suggest a compact lightweight model.

At the budget end, consider the **Evenflo XSport Plus:** this ten lb. wonder features height-adjustable handles, parent console and storage basket. For $60, it's hard to beat.

Chicco is another brand we'd recommend for mall crawlers. The **Chicco C6** (also known as the Capri; $60, 11 lbs.; pictured) features a two-position seat recline, five-point harness and basic canopy . . . it is a best bet for the mall.

Finally, we'd recommend a simple Maclaren for the mall: the **Volo** ($100-130, 8.8 lbs.) is bare bones, but features an easy fold and is super-lightweight.

FYI: The Evenflo XSport, Chicco C6 and Mac Volo are best for babies over six months of age, as they don't have fully reclining seats.

Is Grandma paying for your second stroller? The **Baby Jogger City Mini** ($230, 16.8 lbs.) is an excellent tri-wheel stroller with over-sized canopy and fully reclining seat. Baby Jogger's quick fold technology is amazing—you lift a strap in the middle of the stroller and zip! It's folded.

The Maclaren **Techno XLR** ($350, 16.3 lbs.) is another excellent choice if someone else is buying . . . and it includes a car seat adapter so you can skip the stroller frame. The Techno features a fully reclining seat, removable/washable seat and one-hand fold.

If you are planning to do some air travel, we would suggest getting a cheap umbrella stroller from a discount store (Kolcraft has a couple models under $50). Why? You don't want to gate check your pricey mall stroller only to discover it mangled upon arrival. Trust us, it happens.

Urban Jungle

When you live in a city like New York, Boston or Washington D.C., your stroller is more than just baby transportation—it's your primary vehicle. You stroll to the market, on outings to a park or longer trips on weekend getaways.

Weight is crucial for these parents as well. While you are not lugging a stroller in or out of a trunk like a suburbanite, you may find yourself climbing up subway stairs or trudging up to a fourth-floor walk-up apartment. It's a major trade-off here: full-featured strollers that are outfitted for the weather (full boot, rain cover) can weigh more than lightweight models designed for the mall. Basically, you want a rugged stroller that can take all the abuse a big city can dish out—giant potholes, uneven sidewalks, the winter from Hell . . . without the weight of a bulldozer.

In the past, carriage strollers or prams were the primary "urban jungle" stroller, but these have fallen out of favor for their bulk, weight and other disadvantages (prams typically have front wheels that don't turn).

Multi-function strollers are now the rage for urbanites—these combine a chassis with stroller seat for older babies and a bassinet for newborns. Some models include the bassinet, others offer it as an optional accessory.

Our top picks in this category are the UPPAbaby Vista and I'coo Targo. The **UPPAbaby Vista** ($700, 24 lbs., pictured) includes a bassinet and stroller seat, plus many extras (rain shield, mesh sun shade, bug cover, etc). Readers love how functional this stroller is (you can fold it with the stroller seat attached, for example), plus its smooth ride on no-flat foam tires is a must for urban dwellers. New this year: a $130 rumble seat for a second child extends the use of the Vista.

The *I'coo Targo* ($600, 22 lbs.) is very similar to the Vista, but isn't as compact when folded. At $600 the Targo is a good buy. FYI: This stroller is also marketed as the Rock Star Baby with a steep $900 price tag and fancy detailing. Obviously, we'd stick with the I'coo version!

A runner-up for urban dwellers would be the *Valco Tri-Mode*. This tri-wheel stroller ($480, 23 lbs.) has 12" inch air-filled wheels and all the comforts you need for the city: five-position fully reclining seat, decent size storage basket, five-point harness, cushy padding, reflective trim for nighttime visibility and more. The front wheel swivels . . . or can be locked for a little exercise in the park.

But here's the best part: Valco offers a variety of accessories to extend the use of the Tri-Mode. First is a bassinet ($150) that snaps into the aluminum frame. Second, check out the innovative toddler seat ($80) that turns the Tri-Mode into a double stroller. There's also a car seat adapter ($40), foot muff ($50) and full rain cover ($20). All in all, Valco is a great hybrid, combining the plushness of carriage strollers of the past with the flexibility of all-terrain models that can be used both for shopping and the park.

Finally, let's talk about the 800-lb. gorilla in this category: the **Bugaboo Cameleon**. Dutch-designed (but made in Asia), the Bugaboo's claim to fame is its flexibility. Like the multi-function strollers mentioned above, you get an aluminum frame that can hold either a bassinet or stroller seat (both included). It pushes like a dream (and weighs just 20 lbs.) and most parents who have a Bugaboo absolutely adore it . . . but there is a catch.

First, Bugaboo may have been innovative back in 2003 when it

first debuted . . . but it hasn't keep up with the competition, func-
tion-wise. For example, to fold a Bugaboo Cameleon, you first have
to remove the stroller seat. Other multi-function strollers don't
require this maneuver.

And then let's talk about the price: $900. Add in accessories (you
wanted a stroller with a sun canopy?) and you can easily see the
total soar past $1100. So unless you have a rich uncle, we say pass.

There is good news for folks who like the Bugaboo . . . but don't
have the Bugaboo bankroll. A series of knock-offs (both credible
and less so) have debuted in the past few years. See the "Bugaboo
Smackdown" box below for our look at the competitors. As mentioned above, we prefer the UPPAbaby Vista and I'coo Targo as
much better (and less expensive) alternatives.

BUGABOO SMACKDOWN!	The Bugaboo Cameleon ($900, 20 lbs.) is the rein-ing champ of ultra expensive, three component strollers (combining a bassinet, stroller frame and seat). Whether you think it is a cleverly designed

CONTENDER	PRICE	WEIGHT	BUGABOO-ISH?
BRITAX VIGOUR	$350	27.5 LBS.	🥿
KOLCRAFT OPTIONS 4 WHEEL	$140	25 LBS.	🥿
I'COO TARGO	$600	22 LBS.	🥿🥿🥿
MAXI COSI FORAY	$350	26.5	🥿🥿
MUTSY URBAN RIDER	$700	25.4 LBS.	🥿🥿🥿
PEG PEREGO SKATE ELITE	$800	27 LBS.	🥿🥿
QUINNY BUZZ 4	$630	27 LBS.	🥿🥿🥿
STROLL AIR ZOOM	$500	24 LBS.	🥿🥿
TUETONIA T-100	$575	30.2 LBS.	🥿🥿
UPPA BABY VISTA	$700	24 LBS.	🥿🥿🥿

Second stroller. While multi-function strollers are nice, they do have one disadvantage. They're heavy (many are 20+ lbs.) and most don't fold compactly. When you are trying to ascend subway stairs with baby in one arm and a stroller in another, the last thing you need is a bulky stroller.

So we recommend a lightweight second stroller—but unlike a stroller for the mall, this one needs more weather-proofing for the city.

In a word: Maclaren. The entry-level *Maclaren Triumph* ($150; pictured) has all the features you'd need (including a partially reclining seat) yet weighs a mere 11 lbs. For another $50 to $100, you can get a plusher seat and other upgrades with the Maclaren Quest or Techno XT—with the

stroller that embodies urban chic . . . or a sign of wretched yuppie excess, Bugaboo sure has been one thing: a hit. Now competitors are nipping at Bugaboo's wooden shoes. We rate the contenders on a scale of one to three *klompen!* (Google it.)

COMMENTS/VERDICT

While it **lacks design mojo**, reversible seat does remove to fit a Britax infant seat and features infinite recline, removable sun canopy and height adjustable handle. No cup holder. Heavy.

Best value. Holds most infant car seats; reversible seat, child snack tray and yes, even a cup holder. **But weighs 25% more** than Bugaboo.

Best style. Height adjustable handle, reversible seat, rain cover. Baby can't lie in bassinet when removed from stroller.

Reversible seat, weather shield, cup holder. But can't fold with seat on and fold is complex. **Only works with mediocre Maxi Cosi car seat.**

Comes with bassinet and swapable front wheels. **20% cheaper than Bugaboo . . . but 25% heaver.** Euro fashion.

Folds with seat, **includes accessories like car seat adapter,** rain cover and boot. But it is 35% heavier than Bugaboo. Expensive.

Reversible seat; suspension on all four wheels, auto unfold; **carry cot and car seat are extra.** Fold isn't compact. Nice fashion.

Includes bassinet, reversible seat, adj. handle, plush padding, rain cover, diaper bag, umbrella. **Can fold with seat on.**

Customizable; works with Graco car seat. Foam tires, height adjustable handle. But carry cot is $150 extra; **very heavy.**

Pricey, but includes bassinet, height adj. handle, rain shield, mesh sun shade, rubber-like foam wheels. Bonus: extra rumble seat for toddlers.

strollers

caveat of added weight.

Most Maclarens include rain covers and you can buy an accessory foot muffs, parasols and the like.

Another recommendation for a lightweight stroller for urban parents would be the **UPPABaby G-Lite** ($100, 8.3 lbs.). No, that's not a typo: the G-Lite weighs a mere 8.3 pounds yet features a standing fold and mesh seat with included seat pad. FYI: The G-Lite doesn't recline, so this stroller is best for babies over six months of age.

One stroller to watch in this category: Peg Perego will debut the new **Si** ($280, 12 lbs.) this year—it's super lightweight, has a standing fold and seat recline with three positions. If the final production version is actually 12 pounds, it will give Maclaren a run for its money . . . despite the high price tag.

While it's easy to spend less money on other umbrella stroller models, don't be penny-wise and pound-foolish. Less-expensive strollers lack the durability and weatherproofing that living in an East Coast city requires. And since baby spends more time in the stroller than tots in the suburbs, weatherized fabrics and padding are more of a necessity than a luxury.

Green Acres

If you live on a dirt or gravel road or in a neighborhood with no sidewalks, you need a stroller to do double duty. First, it must han-

STROLLER ROUND-UP

Here's our round-up of popular lightweight models by the major stroller manufacturers.

MAKER	MODEL	WEIGHT	PRICE	RECLINE
CHICCO	C6	11 LBS.	$60	PARTIAL
COMBI	COSMO DX	13	$80	FULL
ESPRIT	SUN SPEED	13	$130	FULL
EVENFLO	XSPORT PLUS	10	$60	NONE
GRACO	IPO	17	$90-100	PARTIAL
INGLESINA	SWIFT	13.5	$120	PARTIAL
JEEP/KOLCRAFT	WRANGLER	12	$50	PARTIAL
MACLAREN	VOLO	8.8	$100-130	NONE
PEG PEREGO	SI	12	$280	PARTIAL
QUINNY	ZAPP	13	$220	NONE
UPPA BABY	G-LITE	8.3	$100	NONE
VALCO	BUGGSTER	15	$270	PARTIAL

dle rough surfaces without bouncing baby all over the place. Second, it must be able to "go to town," folding easily to fit into a trunk for a trip to a mall or other store. And what about snow? Most mall strollers simply don't work in snow.

The answer: an all-terrain stroller with air-filled tires.

The best brands for all-terrain strollers are Phil & Ted and BOB. *Phil & Ted's Sport* ($450, 24 lbs., pictured) is a tri-wheel stroller with swivel front wheel and air-filled tires. What's unique about the Sport: a toddler seat accessory ($90) that attaches to the BACK of the seat, giving you added flexibil-

ity if you have multiple kids. That's what makes Phil & Ted special: the flexibility to use the same stroller for newborn, toddler, BOTH toddler and newborn at the same time and two toddlers.

The *BOB Revolution* stroller ($360-380, 22-23 lbs.) comes in two versions—the regular Revolution has polymer wheels (better for the beach or salt air) or the AW model has aluminum wheels (a touch lighter and more stylish). The only bummer about BOB: its handlebar isn't adjustable, so this isn't the best bet for the tallest parents.

A runner-up in the all terrain category is the *Mountain Buggy Urban Single* (22 lbs.) from New Zealand. Nope, it isn't cheap at $530 but it is built to last with quality features like polymer wheels that won't rust (helpful for folks who live near an ocean). FYI: As

strollers

COMMENTS

COMPACT UMBRELLA FOLD, DECENT-SIZE BASKET. AKA THE CAPRI.

AFFORDABLE, COMPACT FOLD, CAN BE PAIRED WITH COMBI INFANT SEAT.

TWO HANDLES, LARGE BASKET, ADJUSTABLE FOOT REST.

HEIGHT ADJUSTABLE HANDLE, PARENT CONSOLE, EASY ACCESSES BASKET.

ONE-HAND FOLD, NO NAPPER BAR; DOESN'T WORK WITH INFANT SEAT.

SKIMPY CANOPY, NO CUP HOLDER, TWO HANDLE DESIGN.

AFFORDABLE, BUT BARE BONES. CARGO BAGS INSTEAD OF BASKET.

MESH SEAT, CARRY STRAP—BUT NO SEAT RECLINE. GOOD QUALITY.

HEIGHT ADJUSTABLE HANDLE, STANDING ONE-HAND FOLD.

COMPACT FOLD, FIT AN INFANT CAR SEAT, BUT NO SEAT RECLINE.

LIGHTEST WEIGHT. STANDING FOLD, MESH SEAT, MACHINE-WASHABLE PAD.

BOOT, RAIN SHIELD, BUG NET, TRI-WHEEL, BASSINET ACCESSORY.

we were going to press, Mountain Buggy's parent declared bankruptcy and is looking for a buyer.

All right, the above strollers are great, but what if you want a simpler all-terrain stroller with a swivel front wheel that costs less than $130? The **Jeep Liberty Terrain** is an excellent choice: it features a one-hand fold, child snack tray with cute toy steering wheel, and parent tray.

What about low-end all-terrain strollers from makers like Baby Trend? We say skip 'em—the quality on these models often disappoints. It probably makes sense to invest in a BOB or Phil & Ted. These models also have resale value.

See the chart below for a comparison of all-terrain models.

Exercise This: Jogging and Sport Strollers

If you want to exercise with a stroller, you have two choices: tri-wheel strollers with fixed front wheels, or a model with a front wheel that swivels.

Fixed-wheel jogging strollers with air-filled tires are best for folks who want to actually jog or run with a stroller—you can push them in a straight line. The disadvantage to these strollers: to turn them, you have to pick up the front wheel and move it. Hence, fixed wheel joggers aren't good for walking or shopping trips.

Strollers with turnable front wheels are NOT recommended for folks who want to run—even if the stroller has the option to lock the front wheel.

That said, strollers with a swivel front wheel are great for folks who just want to walk the neighborhood or trails. So you need to ask yourself, exactly how do you plan to exercise with the stroller?

How young can your baby be and ride in a jogger? First, deter-

ALL-TERRAIN STROLLERS
How top all-terrain strollers compare—each of these

MODEL	WEIGHT	PRICE	BRAND RATING
BABY JOGGER CITY CLASSIC	21 LBS.	$350	A
BOB REVOLUTION	23	$360	A
JEEP LIBERTY TERRAIN	27.25	$130	B+
KELTY SPEEDSTER SWIVEL	22	$375	B+
MOUNTAIN BUGGY URBAN	22	$530	A
PHIL & TED SPORT	24	$450	A-
QUINNY BUZZ 3	26.4	$580	B+
VALCO TRI-MODE	23	$480	A

mine whether the seat reclines (not all models do). If it doesn't, wait until baby is at least six months old and can hold his or her head up. If you want to jog or run with the stroller, it might be best to wait until baby is at least a year old since all the jostling can be dangerous for a younger infant (their neck muscles can't handle the bumps). Ask your pediatrician for advice if you are unsure.

Another decision area: the frame. The cheapest strollers (under $200) have steel frames—they're strong but also heavy (and that could be a drawback for serious runners). The most expensive models ($300 to $400) have aluminum frames, which are the lightest in weight. Once again, if you plan casual walks, a steel frame is fine. Runners should go for aluminum.

Finally, remember the Trunk Rule. Any jogger is a lousy choice if you can't get it easily in your trunk. Check the DEPTH of the jogger when it is folded—compared this to your vehicle's trunk. Many joggers are rather bulky even when folded. Yes, quick release wheels help reduce the bulk, so check for that option.

So, which jogging stroller do we recommend? Let's break that down into two categories: low-end and high-end. Note that all these strollers have fixed front wheels; if you want a stroller with a turnable front wheel (more suited to the mall or light duty outdoor activities), see the Green Acres section on page 516.

Low end (best for power walking). InStep is the best bet here. **InStep's Run Around LTD Jogger** ($130 at Target.com, 29 lbs.) is a good value and features a steel frame, parent console with cup holder and behind seat storage.

High end (serious runners). The top brand for serious runners is BOB. The **BOB Ironman** stroller ($350, pictured) has all the quality fea-

models are tri-wheels with air-filled tires and front wheels that swivel.

COMMENT

EASIEST FOLD ON MARKET. WORKS UP TO 75 LBS. LIGHT WEIGHT.
POLYMER OR ALUMINUM RIMS ($20 EXTRA). CAR SEAT ADAPTER $60 EXTRA.
ONE-HAND FOLD, PARENT AND CHILD TRAY, ADJUSTABLE FOOT REST. HEAVY.
POLYMER WHEELS, HEIGHT ADJUSTABLE HANDLE, EASY FOLD, HAND BRAKE.
MANY ACCESSORIES, SMOOTH GLIDE, FULL RECLINE, LIGHT WEIGHT.
WIDE SEAT, HEIGHT ADJUSTABLE HANDLE. OPTIONAL SECOND CHILD SEAT.
AUTOMATIC UNFOLD, SLEEK LOOK, FULL RECLINE, SEAT CAN REVERSE.
FULLY RECLINING SEAT, LARGE BASKET, TODDLER SEAT ACCESSORY.

tures of a regular BOB, but adds adjustable tracking, stainless steel wheel spokes, new smooth tires and bright yellow fabric. This jogger weighs just 21 lbs.

Another good pick in this category. **the Baby Jogger Performance** ($430, 24 lbs.) with 20″ wheels.

The same advice for brands applies to double joggers—the better brands for single joggers are the same as those for doubles.

Plan to take your jogger out in the cold weather? Instead of bundling up baby, consider a stroller blanket. One of our favorites is **JJ Cole Bundle Me** (web: bundleme.com), which comes in several versions for $25 to $40.

Three mistakes to avoid when buying a jogging stroller

With jogging strollers available everywhere from Target to high-end bike stores, it is easy to get confused by all the options. Keep in mind these traps when shopping for a jogger:

◆ **Rust.** Warning: cheaper jogging strollers are made of steel—rust can turn your jogging stroller into junk in short order. This is especially a problem on the coasts, but can happen anywhere. Hint: the best joggers have ALUMINUM frames. And make sure the wheels rims are alloy, not steel. All-terrain strollers like Mountain Buggy use polymer wheels (in most models) to get around the rust problem.

◆ **Suspended animation.** The latest rage with joggers is cushiony suspensions, which smooth out bumps but can add to the price. But do you really need it? Most jogging strollers give a smooth ride by design, so no added suspension is necessary. And some kids actually LIKE small bumps or jostling—it helps them fall asleep in the stroller.

◆ **Too narrow seats.** Unlike other baby products, a good jogging stroller could last you until your child is five years old—that is, if you pick one with a wide enough seat to accommodate an older child. The problem: some joggers (specifically, Baby Jogger and Kelty) have rather narrow seats. Great for infants, not good for older kids. We noticed this issue after our neighbors stopped using their Baby Jogger when their child hit age three, but our son kept riding in his until five and beyond. Brands with bigger seats include Dreamer Design and BOB. (As always, confirm seat dimensions before committing to a specific stroller; seats can vary from model to model).

Double The Fun: Strollers for two

There are two types of strollers that can transport two tikes: tandem models and side-by-side styles. A tandem stroller has a "front-back" configuration, where the younger child rides in back while the older child gets the view. These strollers are best for parents with a toddler and a new baby.

Side-by-side strollers, on the other hand, are best for parents of twins or babies close in age. In this case, there's never any competition for the view seat. The only downside: some of these strollers are so wide, they can't fit through narrow doorways or store aisles. (Hint: make sure the stroller is not wider than 30″ to insure door compatibility). Another bummer: few have napper bars or fully reclining seats, making them impractical for infants.

So, what to buy—a tandem or side by side? Our reader feedback shows parents are much happier with their side-by-side models than tandems. Why? The tandems can get darn near impossible to push when weighted down with two kids, due to their length-wise design. Yes, side by sides may not be able to fit through some narrow shopping aisles, but they seem to work better overall.

Double strollers can be frustrating—your basic choices are low-price

---

E-Mail from The Real World
Biting the bullet on a pricey twin stroller

Cheapo twin strollers sound like a good deal for parents of twins, but listen to this mother of multiples:

"Twins tend to ride in their strollers more often and longer, and having an unreliable, bulky or inconvenient stroller is a big mistake. As you suggest, it's a false economy to buy an inexpensive Graco or other model, as these most likely will break down before you're done with the stroller. My husband and I couldn't believe that we'd have to spend $400 on a stroller, but after talking to parents of multiples, we understand why it's best to just bite the bullet on this one. We've heard universally positive feedback about the Maclaren side-by-side for its maneuverability, durability and practicality. It fits through most doorways and the higher end model (Twin Techno) also has seats that fully recline for infants. We've heard much less positive things about front-back tandems for twins. These often are less versatile, as only one seat reclines, so you can't use them when both babies are small (or tired). And when the babies get bigger, they're more likely to get into mischief by pulling each others' hair and stuff."

---

duos from Graco or Kolcraft or high-price doubles like those from Maclaren and Baby Jogger. There doesn't seem to be much in between the low-price ($200 range) and the high-end ($400 and up).

Given the choices on the low end for tandems, we like the **Graco Quattro Tour Duo** ($220, 32 lbs.). It features stadium seating, one-hand gravity fold, large basket and a back seat with full recline. It holds one or two Graco infant car seats.

Another top pick for tandem strollers: the **Kolcraft Contours Options Tandem** ($210, 32 lbs.). Cool feature: the seats reverse to face the parents or each other. This model features a few upgrades over the Graco, including adjustable leg rests and each seat can fully recline (only the back seat of the Quattro Tour Duo reclines fully).

Another good bet on the low end: the **Joovy Caboose Stand-on Tandem** ($160, 26 lbs., pictured). It really isn't a tandem, but a pushcart—the younger child sits in front while the older child *stands* in back (there is also a jump seat for the older child to sit on).

What about side-by-side strollers? For parents of twins on a tight budget, we suggest the **Jeep Twin Sport All Weather Umbrella Stroller** (27 lbs., pictured) for $100 on Amazon. It's bare bones (no basket) but will get the job done with reclining seats and a compact fold.

If your budget allows, we recommend the **Maclaren Twin Techno** ($380, 26.9 lbs.) with its fully reclining seats and excellent overall quality. We also recommend the **Baby Jogger City Mini Duo** ($400, 26 lbs, pictured), with its excellent extended canopies and quick fold.

Finally, for outdoor treks with two kids, we'd suggest looking at our top-rated all-terrain stroller brands (Phil & Ted, BOB)—most make swivel wheel doubles that, while pricey, feature great quality and comfort.

Do It By Mail

THE BABY CATALOG OF AMERICA.

To Order Call: (800) PLAYPEN or (203) 931-7760; Fax (203) 933-1147
Web: www.babycatalog.com

This web site won't win any design awards (the main stroller section is just a few paragraphs of advice on buying strollers), but they've added more thumbnail graphics to each category. And the selection is still great. Baby Catalog has it all—over three-dozen models from such brand names as Peg Perego, Maclaren, Chicco and more. Prices are discounted, about 20% to 30% below retail. Once you click to each stroller's page, you'll find detailed pictures and fabric swatches that make shopping easy. The site also includes customer reviews as well as a link to their return policy for that particular item.

Baby Catalog has been in business since 1992, first as a printed catalog and now primarily as a web site (don't waste your time with the printed catalog as it is only produced sporadically and the web site has more up-to-date stuff). The company has a good record when it comes to customer service. The site does offer a baby registry as well.

Of course, this site sells much more than strollers—they also discount Avent bottles, Dutailier gliders, designer bedding and more.

One tip: you can save an additional 10% off the site's prices by purchasing a membership, $25 for a year (or $49.95 for three years). Even cooler: if you're in the military, Baby Catalog offers a free membership. With each membership, you also get three "associate" memberships for friends/relatives to purchase items for you at the same discount. Interestingly, this is a clever way to get a premium brand that is rarely discounted online—for some reason, manufacturers who don't allow sites to discount their products don't seem to mind when Baby Catalog offers their members that 10% discount.

Bike Trailers, Seats & Helmets

Bike Trailers. Yes, lots of companies make bike trailers, but the gold standard is **Burley** (866-248-5634; web: burley.com). Their trailers (sold in bicycle stores) are considered the best in the industry. A good example is the **Burley "d'Lite."** It features a

multi-point safety harness, built-in rear storage, 100 lb. carrying capacity and compact fold (to store in a trunk). Okay, it's expensive at $500 but check around for second-hand bargains. All Burley trailers have a conversion kit that enables you to turn a trailer into a jogging stroller (although we hear mixed reviews on the Burley as a jogging stroller for its wobbly steering). The Burley d'Lite ST includes the jogger conversion kit and additional cargo space for $600.

A close runner-up to Burley in the bike trailer race is Canada's **Chariot** (chariotcarriers.com). "These are the best engineered bike trailers I've ever seen," opined a reader and we agree. Sold at REI, the basic Caddie runs $375, although they sell pricier versions for up to an astounding $925.

Baby Jogger, the jogging stroller company reviewed earlier, has an entry in the bike trailer race as well. As we mentioned earlier, the Switchback is a hybrid jogging stroller/bike trailer. It morphs from one to the other without any special tools or kit. Cost: $600.

What about the "discount" bike trailers you see for $150 to $200? ***InStep*** makes a few of these models: the Quick N Lite ($170), the Rocket ($220), Take 2 ($110), and Quick N EZ ($130). InStep also makes four Schwinn bike trailers, which are upgraded versions of their regular line. Cost: $220 to $320.

What do you give up for the price? In general, lower priced bike trailers have steel frames and are heavier than the Burleys (which are made of aluminum). And the cheaper bike trailers don't fold as easily or compactly as the Burleys, nor do they attach as easily to a bike.

The key feature to look for with any bike trailer is the ease (or lack thereof) of attaching the stroller to a bike. Quick, compact fold is important as well. Look for the total carrying capacity and the quality of the nylon fabric.

So, should you spring for an expensive bike trailer or one of the $150 ones? Like jogging strollers, consider how much you'll use it. For an occasional (once a week?) bike trip, we'd recommend the cheaper models. Plan to do more serious cycling, say two or three times a week? Then go for a Burley or Schwinn. Yes, they are expensive but worth it if you really plan to use the trailer extensively. Hint: this might be a great item to buy second-hand on eBay or Craigslist.

Safety information: you should wait on using a bike trailer until your child is OVER one year of age. Why? Infants under age one don't have neck muscles to withstand the jolts and bumps they'll encounter with bike trailers, which don't have shock absorbers. Remember you might hit a pothole at 15+ mph—that's not something that is safe for an infant to ride out. Be sure your child is able to hold his head up while wearing a helmet as well. Your child should always wear a helmet while riding in a bike trailer—no exceptions. And, no, there is no bike trailer on the market that safely holds an infant car seat, which might cushion the bumps. Most trailers will accommodate children up to about age six. Check the instruction manual for individual trailers.

Bike seats. When shopping for a bike seat, consider how well padded the seat is and what type of safety harness the unit has (the best are five-points with bar shields; less expensive seats just have three-point harnesses). The more expensive models have seats that recline and adjust to make a child more comfortable.

One good model is the ***CoPilot Limo Child Seat***
($110-$140, pictured), which has a florescent orange
safety bar, three-point harness and four-position
reclining seat (sold by LL Bean and REI). A simpler
version of this seat is called the CoPilot Taxi for $90,
which lacks the reclining seat. Another option is the
Topeak BabySitter. It has a spring suspension system to cushion bumps. They also include dual safety latches to lock
the seat to the rack, adjustable foot rests, a quick release padded
safety bar, and four-way safety harness. Cost: $120 to $140.

We've not seen any safety problems with the cheaper bike seats
sold in discount stores; they just tend to lack some of the fancier
features (padding, reclining seats) that make riding more comfortable for a child.

Safety advice: as with a bike trailer, your child should be able to
hold her head up easily while wearing a bike helmet to ride in a
bike seat. We think it's best to use a bike seat for children two or
over. They can accommodate children up to 40 pounds.

Bike helmets. *Consumer Reports* tested kids bike helmets in
2006 with an update in 2007 and recommended options from ***Bell***
(who also makes ***Giro***). CR noted that all toddler models were lacking in ventilation, but the Bell Boomerang ($30) did a very good
job at impact absorption and scored best for ease of use. Although
Bell makes other models of toddler bike helmets, they didn't all
score the same. We would agree with *Consumer Reports*, as their
research matches feedback from parents on Bell. We'd recommend
avoiding the really cheap helmets under $20.

Safety advice: many states are requiring all children to wear bike
helmets when riding in a bike seat or trailer. That makes sense, but
it is sometimes hard to find a helmet to fit such small heads. One
tip: add in thick pads (sold with some bike helmets) to give a better fit. Don't glue pads on top of pads, however—and adding a
thick hat isn't a safety solution either. If your child cannot wear a
bike helmet safely, put off those bike adventures until they are older.
Be sure your child wears the helmet well forward on his head. If a
helmet is pushed back and your child hits the ground face first,
there is no protection for the forehead.

Diaper Bags

We consider ourselves experts at diaper bags—we got five of
them as gifts. While you don't need five, this important piece of
luggage may feel like an extra appendage after your baby's first

bike trailers/seats

STROLLERS AND MORE

year. And diaper bags are for more than just holding diapers—many include compartments for baby bottles, clothes, and changing pads. With that in mind, let's take a look at what separates great diaper bags from the rest of the pack. In addition, we'll give you our list of nine items for a well-stocked diaper bag.

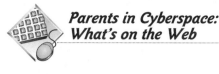

Parents in Cyberspace: What's on the Web

Just because you have a new baby doesn't mean you have to lose all sense of style. And there is good news: an entire cottage industry of custom diaper-bag makers has sprung up to help fill the style gap. One good place to start: our message boards. Go to BabyBargains.com, click on the message boards and then to Places to Go (All Other Gear, Diaper Bags, etc). There you'll find dozens of moms swapping tips on the best and most fashionable diaper bags. Here's a round up of our readers' favorite custom diaper bag makers (most sell direct off their sites, but a few also sell on other sites):

Amy Michelle	amymichellebags.com
California Innovations	californiainnovations.com
Chester Handbags	chesterhandbags.com
Fleurville	fleurville.com
Haiku Diaper Bags	haikubags.com
Holly Aiken	hollyaiken.com
I'm Still Me	imstillme.com
Kate Spade	katespade.com.
Kipling	kipling.com
Oi Oi	oioi.com.au
One Cool Chick	onecoolchick.com
Reese Li	reeseli.com
Skip Hop	skiphop.com
Timbuk2	timbuk2.com
Tumi	tumi.com
Vera Bradley	verabradley.com

No doubt there are dozens more, but that's a great starting point. You can expect prices to be commensurate with style. Kate Spade can cost over $300 a diaper bag. But there are some great looking options for under a $100 too. One caveat: many of these manufacturers are small boutique companies. Often it may be the owner who's taking the order. . . and also sewing the bag! While we admire the entrepreneurship of these companies, many are so small that a minor event can put them off kilter. All it takes is one hurricane or a deluge of orders to turn a reputable company into a customer service nightmare. Check the feedback on these companies on our message boards before ordering.

Smart Shopper Tip #1
Diaper Bag Science

"I was in a store the other day, and they had about one zillion different diaper bags. Some had cute prints and others were plain. Should I buy the cheapest one or invest a little more money?"

The best diaper bags are made of tear-resistant fabric and have all sorts of useful pockets, features and gizmos. Contrast that with low-quality brands that lack many pockets and are made of cheap, thin vinyl—after a couple of uses, they start to split and crack. Yes, high-quality diaper bags will cost more ($50 to $150 versus $30 to $45), but you'll be much happier in the long run. High-end diaper bags (like those made by Kate Spade and other designers) can reach the $300 mark or more. Of course, many of our readers have found deals on these bags, so check out our message boards for shopping tips.

Here's our best piece of advice: buy a diaper bag that doesn't *look* like a diaper bag. Sure those bags with dinosaurs and pastel animal prints look cute now, but what are you going to do with it when your baby gets older? A well-made diaper bag that doesn't look like a diaper bag will make a great piece of carry-on luggage later in life.

Smart Shopper Tip #2
Make your own

"Who needs a fancy diaper bag? I just put all the necessary changing items into my favorite backpack."

That's a good point. Most folks have a favorite bag or backpack that can double as a diaper bag. Besides the obvious (wipes and diapers), put in a large zip-lock bag as a holder for dirty/wet items. Add a couple of receiving blankets (as changing pads) plus the key items listed below, and you have a complete diaper bag.

Another idea: check out the "Diaper Bag Essentials" from Mommy's Helper (web: mommyshelperinc.com). This $20 to $30 kit is basically everything for a diaper bag but the bag—you get an insulated bottle holder, changing pad, dirty duds bag, toiletry kit, etc. That way you can transform your favorite bag or backpack into a diaper bag. We found it online on some web sites for as little as $18.

Top 9 Items for a Well-Stocked Diaper Bag

After much scientific experimentation, we believe we have perfected the exact mix of ingredients for the best-equipped diaper bag. Here's our recipe:

1 **GET TWO DIAPER BAGS**—one that is a full-size, all-option big hummer for longer trips (or overnight stays) and the other that is a mini-bag for a short hop to dinner or the shopping mall. Here's what each should have:

The full-size bag: This needs a waterproof changing pad that folds up, waterproof pouch or pocket for wet clothes, a couple compartments for diapers, blankets/clothes, etc. Super-deluxe brands have bottle compartments with Thinsulate to keep bottles warm or cold. Another plus: outside pockets for books and small toys. A zippered outside pocket is good for change or your wallet. A cell phone pocket is also a plus.

The small bag: This has enough room for a couple diapers, travel wipe package, keys, wallet and/or cell phone. Some models have a bottle pocket and room for one change of clothes. If money is tight, just go for the small bag. To be honest, the full-size bag is often just a security blanket for first-time parents—some think they need to lug around every possible item in case of a diaper catastrophe. But, in the real world, you'll quickly discover schlepping that big full-size bag everywhere isn't practical. While a big bag is nice for overnight or long trips, we'll bet you will be using the small bag much more often.

2 **EXTRA DIAPERS.** Put a dozen in the big bag, two or three in the small one. Why so many? Babies can go through quite a few in a very short time. Of course, when baby gets older (say over a year), you can cut back on the number of diapers you need for a trip. Another wise tip: put whole packages of diapers and wipes in your car(s). We did this after we forgot our diaper bag one too many times and needed an emergency diaper. (The only bummer: here in Colorado, the wipes we keep in the car sometimes freeze in the winter! As they say, you don't know cold . . .)

3 **A TRAVEL-SIZE WIPE PACKAGE.** A good idea: a plastic Tupperware container that holds a small stack of wipes. You can also use a Ziplock bag to hold wipes. Some wipe makers sell travel packs that are allegedly "re-sealable" to retain moisture; we found that they aren't. And they are expensive. For example, a Huggies travel pack of 16 wipes is $6. That works out to 38¢ per wipe compared to 2¢ per wipe if you buy a Huggies refill box of 384 from Kmart.

4 **BLANKET AND CHANGE OF CLOTHES.** Despite the reams of scientists who work on diapers, they still aren't leak-proof—plan for it. A change of clothes is most useful for babies under six months of age, when leaks are more common. After that point, this becomes less necessary.

5 **A HAT OR CAP.** We like the foreign legion-type hats that have flaps to cover your baby's neck and ears (about $10 to $20). Warmer caps are helpful to chase away a chill, since the head is where babies lose the most heat.

6 **BABY TOILETRIES.** Babies can't take much direct exposure to sunlight—sunscreen is a good bet for all infants. Besides sunscreen, other optional accessories include bottles of lotion and diaper rash cream. The best bet: buy these in small travel or trial sizes. Don't forget insect repellent as well. This can be applied to infants two months of age and older.

7 **DON'T FORGET THE TOYS.** We like compact rattles, board books, teethers, etc.

8 **SNACKS.** When baby starts to eat solid foods, having a few snacks in the diaper bag (a bottle of water or milk, crackers, a small box of cereal) is a smart move. But don't bring them in plastic bags. Instead bring reusable plastic containers. Plastic bags are a suffocation hazard and should be kept far away from babies and toddlers.

9 **YOUR OWN PERSONAL STUFF.** Be careful putting your wallet or checkbook into the diaper bag—we advise against it. We left our diaper bag behind one too many times before we learned this lesson. Put your name and phone number in the bag in case it is lost.

Our Picks: Brand Recommendations

We've looked the world over and have come up with two top choices for diaper bags: Lands End and Eddie Bauer (plus a couple of other smaller brands worthy of consideration). They both meet our criteria for a great diaper bag—each offers both full-size and smaller bags, they don't look like diaper bags, each uses high-quality materials and, best of all, they are affordably priced. Let's take a look at each:

Lands End (800) 356-4444 (web: landsend.com) sells not one but five diaper bags: The Do-It-All Diaper Bag ($35), the Diaper Bag Tote ($30-35), the Messenger ($60), the Little Tripper ($25) and the Diaper Clutch for $30. (Side note: Lands End's selections change a lot. It's a bit like nailing Jello to the wall. Visit their web site to check availability. If something is gone, just wait—they usually bring it back eventually.)

The Do-It-All features a wide opening (like a doctor's bag) that lets you see the large main compartment for diapers and wipes. There is also a parent pocket for your stuff, extra long changing pad and exterior bottle pockets. Then there's another zippered compartment for a blanket or change of clothes and an expandable outside pocket for books and small toys. In the past year, Lands End redesigned the bag's strap, making it shorter . . . some users complain it is uncomfortable to carry. Another parent complained that the design of the bag makes it too heavy. Colors (blue and black) are limited.

Despite those drawbacks, the bag does seem to hold a lot of stuff. After all these years of recommending the Do-It-All, it's still a winner with most parents. Readers have hauled this thing on cross-country airline trips, on major treks to the mountains, and more. At $30, it's a good buy considering the extra features and durability.

How about those quick trips to the store? We recommend the Little Tripper ($20) for this purpose. It has a changing pad and two exterior pockets. With just enough room for a few diapers, wipes and other personal items, it's perfect for short outings.

Lands End Diaper Clutch ($30) is another option for short outings—it features a detachable changing pad and a container for wipes. Magnetic closures keep it all self-contained.

This might be a good place to mention the "Overstocks" page on Lands End's web site (landsend.com). This regularly updated section has some fantastic bargains (up to 50% off) on all sorts of Lands End items, including their kids clothing, bedding, diaper bags and more. You can also sign up for their newsletter, which updates you on the site.

Not to be outdone, ***Eddie Bauer*** (800) 426-8020 (web: eddiebauer.com) offers a wide range of diaper bags including a drawstring style ($25), mini bag ($25), the Organizer ($35), and more. Each is made of fabric that's easy to clean and most contain a removable changing pad, bottle pockets, and a detachable wet/dry pouch for damp items. The *Wall Street Journal* called Bauer's offerings "the most manly diaper bag available" and we have to agree.

Carriers

Advocates of baby wearing from pediatricians to your next-door neighbor tout the benefits of closeness with your child. But even if you don't subscribe to attachment parenting, you have to admit carriers are darn convenient. When you have a baby who just won't take a nap and you've got dinner to get on the table, a carrier that gives you two hands free is a godsend.

Just to make it more confusing, though, there are 437 different carrier makes and models on the market, from simple slings to fancy backpacks. And we've noticed over the years that every single one of those models has a fan. Of course, the key is to find the right carrier for you. One idea: we like an instructional DVD on baby wearing called Tummy 2 Tummy (tummy2tummy.com). It covers different types of carriers and how to wear them—a good introduction to the world of carriers. Another tip: we recommend buying a carrier that either has a DVD with instructions or provides an instruction video on their web site.

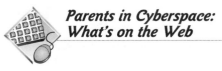

Parents in Cyberspace: What's on the Web

The Baby Wearer
Web Site: thebabywearer.com
What It Is: A resource for parents interested in "baby wearing"
What's Cool: This site is extensive. You'll find articles, reviews, product listings, ads, you name it. The main emphasis seems to be on sling-type carriers, not so much front carriers. There are a couple of great charts that offer detailed comparisons for carriers. In fact, there is so much here, you could spend days on the site. If you're a newbie to baby wearing, be sure to start with the basic articles as well as the glossary of terms. Then you can join chats and message boards or click on product links.
Needs Work: There's a lot of advertising here. And the site is very jumbled. You're probably smart to take their recommendations with a grain of salt and verify reviews with other sites before you buy.

What Are You Buying?

Carriers come in several flavors: slings, hip carriers, front carriers and frame or backpack carriers. Let's take a look at each type:

◆ **Slings.** Slings allow you to hold your baby horizontally or upright. Made of soft fabric with an adjustable strap, slings drape your baby across your body (see picture). The best-known sling is made by NoJo, but many other manufacturers have jumped into the sling market. Whichever brand you choose, devoted sling user Darien Wilson from Austin, Texas has a great tip for new moms: "The trick for avoiding backache when using a sling is to have the bulk of the baby's weight at the parent's waist or above."

Some parents complain that there isn't much between your baby's head and a collision with a wall, furniture, etc. It's true you have to watch where you're going and what you're doing, but sling aficionado's say once you get the hang of it, slings are simple to use.

Weight Limit: 20 pounds. *(Note: weight limits may vary by manufacturer. This is only an approximate weight limit. Please check the directions for each item you purchase.)*

Recommendations: While NoJo was the first, we don't really think they're the best slings out there. Readers complain that they hang too low and hurt their backs. Instead, our readers recommend the **Maya Wrap Sling** ($45-$70; mayawrap.com; pictured) citing its flexibility and comfort. Others praise the **Over the Shoulder Baby Holder** ($45-60; web: otsbh.com).

If you're looking for unusual fabrics so you can be a "stylish" baby wearer, go no further than the **ZoLo** sling (zolowear.com). The silk version (it's machine washable) will set you back a hefty $125 but wow, is it beautiful! And they'll send you fabric swatches if you have trouble deciding from one of their 20+ fabrics (other fabrics start at $80; look for deals on cheaper factory close outs). Another parent recommended the **Moms in Mind** sarong carrier. (momsinmind.com, $42 to $45 with video) saying it had a simpler buckle and enough support to allow for hands-free nursing. **Mamma's Milk** (mammasmilk.com) offers a streamlined sling with "invisibly adjustable pouches." These slings use Aplix (a stronger version of Velcro), to allow for adjustments without using zippers or snaps. Prices range from $30 to $100 depending on fabric.

New Native Baby carriers are yet another option in the sling department (newnativebaby.com, $36 to $160). They tout their streamline design, which allows you to stuff it into a diaper bag for on-the-go convenience, and their organic fabric.

Kangaroo Korner (kangarookorner.com) makes adjustable "pouches" in fleece, cotton, mesh and solarveil. They're the first we've seen to use a UV barrier fabric. And their unpadded pouches can be used in water as well. Cost: $68. We also liked the **Sling Baby** from

Walking Rock Farm (walkingrockfarm.com). The well-padded strap plus soft knit fabrics make this a great option for $58 to $68.

You can't but to love a baby sling called the **Peanut Shell**. And it makes sense that it's a sling. Available in three styles, serendipity, reversible and stretch sateen, the Peanut Shell has a cute little pocket on the front and a variety of cool fabrics from mod to Victorian. The designs sell for $58 to $68 and they sell matching nursing covers for $29.

Looking for a sling that will carry twins? The **Baby K'tan** has a weight limit of up to 42 lbs. Their web site (babyktan.com) describes their sling as a "one-of-a-kind double sling design." It can be used as an infant sling and then adjusted to a hip carrier. The cost: $58 (organic cotton is $68).

Finally, we received a recommendation from a mom for **HotSlings'** (hotslings.com). She loved the fabrics and the light weight of their designs. Fabric options range from organic cotton, designer looks and even "men's looks." Online, HotSlings offers instructions on how to use the product, a nice FAQ and even a sale corner. Prices are affordable and range from $30 to $40. And we agree that the fabric choices are pretty cool.

Where to buy: Kangaroo Korner (kangarookorner.com) is a web site recommended by readers that sells a wide variety of sling brands. The site will even custom design a sling for you. Best of all, they offer tips and advice for sling fans.

◆ *Hip Carriers.* Hip carriers are a minimalist version of the sling. With less fabric to cradle baby, they generally work better for older babies (over six months). Baby is in a more upright position all the time, rather than lying horizontally. And like a sling, the hip carrier fits across your body with baby resting on your hip.

Weight/Age Limit: Manufacturers claim hip carriers can be used up to three years of age. *(Note: weight/age limits may vary by manufacturer. This is only an approximate limit. Please check the directions for each item you purchase.)*

Recommendations: A reader with back problems recommended the **Hip Hammock** ($48; web: swankeltd.com; pictured)—she said this was the most comfortable carrier for her. And the Hip Hammock can be used up to age three.

Cuddle Karrier (cuddlekarrier.com), another hip carrier, claims to do everything but make toast. It converts from a carrier to a shopping cart restraint, high chair restraint, even a car seat carrier. Cost: $48

Walking Rock Farm makes a hip carrier appropriately named **Hip Baby** ($78 to $92). This carrier has a full seat and extra thick shoulder pad. We liked the numerous adjustments—this is one of the few hip carriers you can use hands-free. FYI: Walking Rock Farm also makes a baby sling (Sling Baby, $67).

◆ **Front (Soft) Carriers.** The most famous of all front carriers is the **Baby Bjorn**, that Scandinavian wonder worn by celeb moms among others. Front carriers like the Bjorn are basically a fabric bag worn on your chest. Your baby sort of dangles there either looking in at you (when they're very young) or out at the world (when they gain more head control).

Who Makes Them: Baby Bjorn (babybjorn.com), Ergo (ErgoBabyCarrier. com) Maclaren (maclarenusa.com), Baby Trekker (babytrekker.com), MaxiMom (4coolkids.com), Kelty (kelty.com), Evenflo (Evenflo.com), Infantino (infantino.com) and more.

Weight Limit: 20 to 30 pounds. *(Note: weight limits may vary by manufacturer. This is only an approximate weight limit. Please check the directions for each item you purchase.)*

Recommendations: The Baby Bjorn was our top carrier pick in previous editions of our book, but we now have a new favorite: the Ergo Baby Carrier.

Made by a small Hawaii company, the **Ergo** ($94-$105; pictured; ErgoBabyCarrier.com; 888-416-4888) has won kudos on our boards for its ease of use (you can wear it in front or back) and less strain on the back. While most front carriers put the strain on your shoulders and back, the Ergo comes with a padded hip belt that takes the strain off your upper back. Best of all, you can use it from birth (with a newborn insert, $25-$38) up to an amazing 40 lbs. (toddlers)—most front carriers can only be used for a short time (the Bjorn limit is 22 lbs.).

Given the reader raves on the Ergo, we will give it our top recommendation. One caveat: your baby can't face outward in an Ergo—only towards you. If you prefer a carrier that is more versatile, consider one of the other carriers below. Also: the Ergo is just sold in specialty stores and online (BabyCenter.com and MyFavoriteBabyCarrier.com carry it). So it may be hard to see in person.

Runner up to the Ergo is Eco Baby's **Beco Baby Carrier** ($100-$140, becobabycarrier.com), designed by a mom who is also a rock climber. Yep, it is pricey—but seems to fit shorter parents a bit better than the Ergo. Included in the price is an infant insert for babies as small as 7 lbs. And the best part: when used as a front carrier baby can face in or out (unlike the Ergo), plus eventually it can be used as a soft backpack carrier.

The 800-pound gorilla in the carrier category is the **Baby Bjorn** (babybjorn.com), the Swedish import that comes in five flavors (Original $80, Original Spirit $70, Air $100, Synergy $140 and Active $120). The Original is easy to use and adjust (baby can ride facing forward or rear). Best of all, you can snap off the front of the Bjorn to put a sleeping baby down. The Spirit version is merely a more colorful version of the Original—it comes in new colors like hot pink and lime green. The Active adds lumbar support and wider straps for longer walks and the Air version features a mesh fabric to keep baby cooler in warmer climates. New this year, the Synergy combines the mesh of the Air and the lumbar support of the Active for about $140.

Fans of the Bjorn like the easy adjustments and fashionable fabrics. But detractors point to the high price and limited use (babies outgrow it fast). Back/neck strain is a common complaint of Bjorn users (the Bjorn Active generates fewer complaints on this, thanks to the lumbar support). So while the Bjorn is ok for occasional use, this probably isn't the best choice if you plan to use it daily.

So, what else is out there?

Better known for its strollers, **Maclaren** also has a line of baby carriers (an outgrowth of its acquisition of Theodore Bean in 2004). These front carriers ($80 to $100) work from eight to 12 lbs. with a "pod insert" and up to 25 lbs. otherwise. We liked the one-hand, quick-release buckles and enclosed harness system. For fashionistas, Maclaren offers one version designed by Kate Spade; there's also a leather carrier . . . for $300.

Canadian parents write to us with kudos for the **Baby Trekker** (800-665-3957; web: babytrekker.com). This 100% washable cotton carrier ("green" cotton available too) has straps that wrap around the waist for support. Canadians like the fact a baby can be dressed in a snowsuit and still fit in the Baby Trekker. The carrier ($130 US, $150C) is available in baby stores in Canada or via the company's web site for folks in the U.S.

Lascal (lascal.se), maker of the Buggyboard and Kiddyboard stroller attachments, also makes a front carrier called the **M1**. The M1 is made of bamboo and mesh fabric. The bamboo is anti-bacterial; the mesh keeps baby cool. The front of the M1 is adjustable three ways so parents can use it up to 30 lbs. rather than the usual 22 lbs. for the Baby Bjorn. But you'll pay for the innovative fabric and higher weight limit. The M1 is a pricey $130—almost as much as a top-of-the-line Bjorn.

Looking for a lightweight, easy to pack carrier? **Belle Baby Carriers** (bellebabycarriers.com) forgo all the extra padding to

carriers

make a lighter, cooler carrier that allows baby to face both in and out. Available in four organic fabrics as well as seven other fabrics, the Belle also offers a more ergonomic design for both baby and mom's comfort. Price: $90 to $100.

We've had several readers write to extol the virtues of the **MaxiMom** carrier (4coolkids.com). "It does everything short of making dinner. It can be used as a front carrier facing forward or backward, backpack facing forward or backward, emergency high chair, sling and can be used for a child up to 35 pounds. Here's the great part: MaxiMom is designed to also be used with multiples!" The cost: $65 to $150 depending on how many children you'll be using it for. Look for occasional sales too.

Asian-inspired carriers (called Mei Tai's) that tie instead of snap or buckle have increased in popularity in recent years. Fans love the ability to adjust and configure these carriers—plus they are very comfortable. Among the top Mei Tai-like carriers is the **Kozy Carrier** ($80-85, KozyCarrier.com), which can be can be worn on the front, rear or side. The reader feedback on the Kozy Carrier has been quite positive.

Another, similar tie-on multi-use carrier is the **Ultimate Baby Wrap** from Parents of Invention (parentsofinvention.com). A reader told us she loved how easy it was to use. They have an video on their web site that is simple to follow. Our reader's only caveat: you'll have to make sure it's tied very snugly to make it comfortable to wear. Depending on the fabric, the Ultimate runs from $40 to $120.

What about those low-end carriers like **Snugli, Infantino, Eddie Bauer**? We don't recommend them. Let's be honest here: yes, you can spend $20 on a carrier at a discount store. And that is much less than an Ergo or the other aforementioned carriers. But take a second to read parent reviews of carriers, whether on our site or other baby message boards. Most parents quickly realize a bargain carrier can be a pain to use . . . literally. Cheap-o carriers are more complicated to put on and adjust as well as just being darn painful on the back.

Of all the cheaper carriers, Infantino's models are probably the most well-known. And we will give Infantino kudos for trying to innovate here: their **Comfort Rider Baby Carrier** ($30) has straps with memory foam and breathable mesh panels. Parents complained that the carrier was difficult to put on, requiring help from another adult.

Bottom line: our top pick for a front (soft) carrier would be the Ergo or Beco. If an Asian-inspired (also called Mei-Tai) carrier intrigues you, the Kozy Carrier would be a great choice.

Where to buy: Chain stores only seem to carry the major brands like Bjorn or Snugli; the Internet is your best bet for the more obscure brands. A bargain hint: many carriers are sold second-hand at low prices on boards like TheBabyWearer.com. And be sure to visit our boards (BabyBargains.com) to read the latest on our board dedicated to carriers.

◆ *Frame (or backpack) Carriers.* Need to get some fresh air? Just because you have a baby doesn't mean you can never go hiking again. Backpack manufacturers have responded to parents' wish to find a way to take their small children with them on hikes and long walks. The good news is that most of these frame carriers are made with lightweight aluminum, high quality fabrics and well-positioned straps. Accessories abound with some models including sunshades, diaper packs that Velcro on, and adjustable seating so Junior gets a good view.

Weight Limit: 45 to 50 pounds. *(Note: weight limits may vary by manufacturer. This is only an approximate weight limit. Please check the directions for each item you purchase.)*

Recommendations: **Kelty** (web: kelty.com) and **Sherpani Alpina** (sherpanipacks.com) have come to the rescue of parents with full lines of high-quality backpack carriers.

If you want a frame carrier, Kelty offers seven models, including three Transit Child Carriers ($100 to $150; these are carriers with large back packs attached), and three Frame Child Carriers ($120 to $200). Kelty still offers its combo backpack stroller, the Convertible (basically a Frame pack with wheels) for $200 that weighs just ten lbs.

Sherpani offers frame carriers built specifically to accommodate women's bodies. The Rumba (pictured) is their flagship full feature child carrier. This carrier ($200) has an aluminum frame and suspension system to take the strain off your back. It's also the only backpack carrier that can be adjusted while on your back. It has a five-point safety harness and padded chest plate among other fea-  tures. There is also a "super light" version of the Rumba for $160 (4.5 lbs.). Prices have dropped since our last edition of the book.

What most impressed us with Kelty and Sherpani is their quality—these are real backpack makers who don't skimp on details. Backpack carriers made by juvenile product companies are wimpy by comparison.

If those prices are a bit hard to swallow, check out the **Tough Traveler Kid Carrier** ($176, toughtraveler.com). Adjustable for just the right fit, the Tough Traveler features cushioned pads, tough nylon cloth, and two-shoulder harnesses for baby. A comfortable seat provides head and neck protection for smaller children—you even get a zippered pouch for storage. Tough Traveler has several other models that combine great quality and decent pricing. Check out their web site recommendations regarding the best pack for your height.

So, what's the best backpack among Kelty, Sherpani or Tough Traveler? That's a tough one—each has great features. Readers give the slight edge to the Tough Traveler for its quick and easy adjustments, light weight and great storage. Sherpani, however, is technically amazing, made to fit a woman's body structure better.

Where to buy: A good source for outdoor baby gear is the ***Campmor*** catalog (800) 226-7667 campmor.com). Also try outdoor retailers like REI. FYI: Tough Traveler offers discounts on year's models or factory seconds. Call them at (800) GO-TOUGH for details.

So, how do you decide which carrier is best for you and your baby? The best advice is to borrow different models from your friends and give them a test drive. For most parents, a front carrier is all one really needs, although some parents like slings.

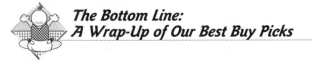

The Bottom Line: A Wrap-Up of Our Best Buy Picks

Wow . . . and you thought car seats were complex!

Here's the take-home message on strollers: match a stroller to your lifestyle. That means thinking about HOW you'll use the stroller—mall? Park? Hikes? Read our lifestyle recommendations to match the right stroller to your needs.

Overall, the best strollers brands are Maclaren, UPPAbaby, Phil & Ted's and BOB. But even brands that get a lukewarm rating can have an occasional winner—witness Graco's twin strollers or Kolcraft/Jeep's affordable all-terrain models.

No matter which stroller you get, it is always smart to go for the lightest weight model you can find. Another key factor: rear wheel width, especially for urban parents. Some new strollers have wide rear wheel widths . . . making negotiating a narrow doorway or tight elevator darn near impossible.

For diaper bags, we like Land's Ends' offerings. Designer diaper bags are nice gifts . . . but go for practical and you'll be happier.

Carriers fall into three categories: slings, hip, front and backpack. One of the best front carriers is the Ergo, an excellent option with one major caveat: baby can only face you, not outward. Another winner is Eco Baby's Beco carrier, which lets baby face both toward you and outward.

Now that we've covered strollers, diaper bags, and carriers, let's take a look at an even bigger expense: child care.

CHAPTER 10

CHILDCARE

Childcare: Options, Costs and More

Inside this chapter

Even stay-at-home parents agree there are days when you need a break. So whether you're a full time executive or a full time diaper changer, childcare will be an issue after your baby arrives. And your choices run from Mom's Day Out services at the local church to full time in-home care and everything in between. In this chapter we'll explain a few of the different options, scare you with the costs of day care and advise you where to look to find the best quality childcare in the best setting for your child.

Childcare

childcare

"It's expensive, hard to find and your need for it is constantly changing. Welcome to the world of child care," said a recent *Wall Street Journal* article—and we agree. There's nothing more difficult than trying to find the best childcare for your baby.

With 65% of moms with children under age five back in the workforce today, wrestling with the choices, costs and availability of childcare is a stark reality. Here's a brief overview of the different types of childcare available, questions to ask when hiring a provider and money saving tips.

What are you buying?

On average, parents pay 10% of their pre-tax income for childcare. And if you live in a high-cost city, expect to shell out nearly 15% of your income for child care. As you'll read below, some par-

CHILDCARE

ents spend $30,000 or more per year. Whatever your budget, there are three basic types of child care:

◆ **Family Daycare.** In this setting, one adult takes care of a small number of children in her home. Sometimes the children are of mixed ages. Parents who like this option prefer the lower ratio of children to providers and the consistent caregiver. About 27% of families place their children in family daycare. Of course, you'll want to make sure the facility is licensed and ask all the questions we outline later. One drawback to family daycare: if there is only one caregiver, you might have to scramble if that person becomes ill. How much does it cost? Family daycare typically runs $6300 to $15,750 per year.

Sources For The Best Child Care Facilities. Which childcare centers have the highest standards? The National Association of Family Childcare (800) 359-3817 (web: www.nafcc.org) offers lists of such facilities to parents in every state.

◆ **Center Care.** Most folks are familiar with this type of daycare—commercial facilities that offer a wide variety of childcare options. And they are by far the most common—66% of parents take their children to child care centers. Convenience is one major factor for center care; you can often find a center that is near your (or your spouse's) place of work. Other parents like the fact that their children are grouped with and exposed to more kids their own age. Centers usually give you a written report each day that details your baby's day (naps, diaper changes, mood). On the downside, turnover can be a problem—some centers lose 40% or more of their employees each year. A lack of consistency can upset your child. Yet center care offers parents the most flexibility: unlike nannies or family care, the day care center doesn't take sick or vacation days. Many centers offer drop-off care, in case you need help in a pinch. The cost: $4000 to $16,000 per year, yet some pricey centers can cost over $30,000. As with family daycare, the cost varies depending on how many days a week your baby needs care.

◆ **Nanny Care.** No, you don't have to be super-rich to afford a nanny. Many "nanny-referral" services have popped up in most major cities, offering to refer you to a pre-screened nanny for $500 to $800 or so. Parents who prefer nannies like the one-on-one attention, plus baby is taken care of in your own home. The cost varies depending on whether you provide the nanny with room and board. Generally, most nannies who don't live-in run $10 to $19 per hour. Hence, the yearly cost would be $10,000 to $25,000. It will cost you more for a live-in nanny: $27,000 to $30,000 a year. And the nanny's salary is just the beginning—you also must pay social security and Medicare taxes, federal unemployment insurance, plus any state-mandated taxes like disability insurance or employment-training taxes. All this may increase the cost of your $20,000 nanny by another $4500 or more per year. And the paperwork hassle for all the tax reporting can be onerous. The other downside to nannies? You're dependent on one person for childcare. If she gets sick, needs time off or quits, you're on your own. Perhaps for these reasons, nanny care is the least popular option with only 7% of families utilizing this option.

Money Saving Tips

1 **ASK YOUR EMPLOYER ABOUT DEPENDENT CARE ACCOUNTS.** Many corporations offer this great benefit to employees. Basically, you can set aside pretax dollars to pay for child-care. The maximum set aside is $5000 (total per couple; single parents can put away $2500). Both parents can contribute to that amount. If you're in the 31% tax bracket, that means you'll save $1550 in taxes by paying for childcare with a dependent care account. Consult with your employer for the latest rules and limits to this option.

2 **SHARE A NANNY.** As we noted in the above example, a nanny can be expensive. But many parents find they can halve that cost by sharing a nanny with another family. While this might require some juggling of schedules to make everyone happy, it can work out beautifully.

3 **GO FOR A CULTURAL EXCHANGE.** The U.S. government authorizes a foreign nanny exchange program, referred to as "au pair." Through this program, you can hire a foreign-born young adult for up to 45 hours a week of childcare. Your kids get exposure to another language and culture, your au pair gets to hang out in the US to learn about our culture and language. What's the catch? See our box on Au Pairs for more information and costs.

4 **TAKE A TAX CREDIT.** The current tax code gives parents a tax credit for childcare expenses. The amount, which varies based on your income, equals about 20% to 35% of childcare costs up to a certain limit. The credit is up to $6000, depending on your income. Another tax break: some states also give credits or deductions for child care expenses. Consult your tax preparer to make sure you're taking the maximum allowable credit/deduction. New in recent years, the federal government expanded the adoption credit up to $12,150 for "qualified" expenses related to adoption.

CHILDCARE

Questions to Ask

Here are questions to ask a daycare provider:

◆ _What are the credentials of the provider(s)?_ Obviously, a college degree in education and/or child development is preferred. Additional post-college training is also a plus.

◆ _What is the turnover?_ High turnover is a concern since consistency of care is one of the keys to successful childcare. Any turnover approaching 40% is cause for concern.

◆ _What is the ratio of children to care providers?_ The recommended national standard is one adult to three babies (age birth to 12 months). After that, the ratios vary depending on a child's age and state regulations. With some day care centers, there is one primary teacher and a couple of assistants (depending on the age of the children and size of class). Compare the ratio to that of other centers to gain an understanding of what's high and low.

◆ _Do you have a license?_ All states (and many municipalities) require childcare providers to be licensed. Yet, that's no guarantee of quality—the standards vary so much from locale to locale that a license may be meaningless. Another point to remember: the standards for family daycare may be lower than those for center care. Educate yourself on the various rules and regulations by spending a few minutes on the phone with your state's child care regulatory body. Check with the state to make sure there are no complaints or violations on record for the provider. Many states are putting this info on the web.

◆ _May I visit you during business hours?_ The only way you can truly evaluate a childcare provider is an on-site visit. Try to time your visit during the late morning, typically the time when the most children are being cared for. Trust your instincts—if the facility seems chaotic, disorganized or poorly run, take the hint. One sign of a good childcare center: facilities that allow unannounced drop-in visits.

◆ _Discuss your care philosophy._ Sit down for a half-hour interview with the care provider and make sure they clearly define their attitudes on breast-feeding, diapers, naps, feeding schedules, discipline and any other issues of importance to you. The center should have established, written procedures to deal with children who have certain allergies or other medical conditions. Let's be honest: child-rearing philosophies will vary from center to center. Make sure you see eye to eye on key issues.

◆ _Do you have liability insurance?_ Don't just take their word on it—have them provide written documentation or the phone number of an insurance provider for you to call to confirm coverage.

◆ _Does the center conduct police background checks on employees?_ It's naive to assume that just because employees have good references, they've never been in trouble with the law.

Au Pair Child Care

Au pairs have become more popular recently for one big reason: the federal government (which regulates au pair programs) changed its rules to allow au pairs, or nannies from other countries, to stay in the U.S. as long as two years. That's up from only one year in the past. So if you find just the right nanny, you won't have to send him or her home in just 12 months and look for another childcare provider.

But how does the au pair idea work? First, only six organizations are allowed by the U.S. government to place au pairs with American families. These agencies must provide the au pair 24 hours of child safety classes and training. Au pairs are also required to have at least 200 hours of infant care experience if they are caring for children under two, be able to speak English proficiently, have a secondary school education (plus six hours of post-secondary education) and pass both reference and background checks. Whew! That's a lot of work you won't have to do as a parent. The age range of au pairs is 18 to 26 years.

If you're interested in hiring an au pair, you contact one of six agencies (see below for a list). There is typically an application fee (about $350) and a program fee. The program fee is $7000 to $8000 and includes all the screening and prep of the au pair, as well as airfare, medical and travel insurance, training materials and support from the agency itself for the period of employment. Families must pay an au pair a weekly stipend and an educational allowance. All these fees work out to about $15,000 per year, comparable to the high end of the family care childcare option (discussed earlier), but less than the cost of a nanny.

So how do you decide if an au pair is for your family? *The Wall Street Journal*, in a 2005 article on au pairs, noted that you should "choose an au pair only if you: can limit her work week to 45 hours a week, 10 hours a day, have a private bedroom available, value cross cultural experiences, can care for the emotions of a teen or young adult, can help and train an inexperienced caregiver, will treat her like a member of the family, (and) don't mind changing caregivers after two years."

Here's a partial list of au pair agencies:

AuPairCare	aupaircare.com
Au Pair in America	aupairinamerica.com
Cultural Care Au Pair (EF au Pair)	culturalcare.com
EurAuPair	euraupair.com
InterExchange	interexchange.org
GoAuPair	goaupair.com

childcare

◆ **Is the center clean, home-like and cheerful?** While it's impossible to expect a childcare facility to be spotless, it is important to check for basic cleanliness. Diaper changing stations shouldn't be overflowing with dirty diapers, play areas shouldn't be strewn with a zillion toys, etc. Another tip: check their diaper changing procedures. The best centers should use rubber gloves when changing diapers and wipe down the diapering area with a disinfectant after each change. Finally, ask how often toys are cleaned. Is there a regular schedule for washing children's hands?

◆ **What type of adjustment period does the center offer?** Phasing in daycare isn't easy—your child may need time to adjust to the new situation. Experienced providers should have plans to ease the transition.

◆ **Show me your security measures.** Every daycare center should be able to show you how they handle drop off and pick up so that no child goes home with the wrong person. Some sophisticated centers even have finger print scanners. At the least, there should be someone blocking the entrance to the main center. And adults should have to sign a child both in and out of the center.

Does your nanny have a past?

Yes, it sounds like the plot of a bad Hollywood thriller—the nanny WITH A PAST! Still, many parents want to feel secure that the person they trust to take care of their child hasn't had any run-ins with the police. In the past, this required laborious background checks with local police or numerous calls to past employers. Today, the web can help. Several web sites now let you screen a nanny's background with a simple point and click. Examples: MyBackgroundCheck.com offers a range of searches for $30 to $60. ChoiceTrust.com has a proprietary criminal records database and court records search for $25 to $100. Wonder if the background checking service you found online is legit? Ask the International Nanny Association (nanny.org), a non-profit group, which keeps tabs on such agencies.

Of course, you can hire someone else to do the checking—most high-quality nanny employment agencies do those background checks, but of course you pay . . . about 10% of the nanny's first year salary as a fee. One note: while criminal background checks are relatively easy, drivers' records are another story. You may need to contact your state motor vehicle's bureau and have the nanny ask for a copy of her own report.

One smart tip: when asking for references from a nanny, get a LANDLINE phone number to call. Why? Some dishonest nannies have faked their references by having friends pose as past employers. That's easier to do with a cell phone versus a landline.

CHAPTER 11 CONCLUSION

What Does it All Mean?

How much money can you save if you follow all the tips and suggestions in this book? Let's take a look at the average cost of having a baby from the introduction and compare it with our Baby Bargains budget.

Your Baby's First Year

ITEM	AVERAGE	BABY BARGAINS BUDGET
Crib, mattress, dresser, rocker	$1500	$1275
Bedding / Decor	$325	$158
Baby Clothes	$600	$311
Disposable Diapers	$860	$300
Maternity/Nursing Clothes	$1130	$540
Nursery items, high chair, toys	$475	$225
Baby Food/Formula	$950	$350
Stroller, Car Seats, Carrier	$600	$490
Miscellaneous	$600	$500
TOTAL	$7040	$4149
TOTAL SAVINGS:		**$2891**

WOW! YOU CAN SAVE NEARLY $2900! We hope the savings makes it worth the price of this book. We'd love to hear from you on how much you saved with our book—feel free to email, write or call us. See the "How to Reach Us" page at the back of this book.

What does it all mean?

At this point, we usually have something pithy to say as we end the book. But, as parents of two boys, we're just too tired. We're going to bed, so feel free to make up your own ending.

And thanks for reading *Baby Bargains*.

APPENDIX A
Canada

$21,400.

Yes, that's the average cost of raising a child to age two in Canada (see chart on the next page). With those costs, Canadian parents need bargains just as much as parents in the U.S.!

Here's an overview of our best bargains sources for Canada.

Recap of Canadian sources

Many of the brands reviewed earlier are based in Canada. For example, crib makers AP, Cara Mia, Morigeau and others are reviewed in Chapter 2. Glider-rockers brands Shermag and Dutailier also are Canadian brands, of course.

In this section, we will focus on Canada's best bargains, baby stores and outlets. But be sure to read earlier sections of this book to find general reviews of Canadian baby product brands.

Layette Items and Diapers

If you're looking for great shoes for your little one, reader Teri Dunsworth recommends Canadian-made **Robeez** (800) 929-2623 or (604) 929-6818; web: robeez.com. "They are the most AWESOME shoes—I highly recommend them," she said in an email. Robeez are made of leather, have soft skid-resistant soles and are machine washable. They start at $26 for a basic pair. "My baby wears nothing else! They have infant and toddler sizes and oh-so-cute patterns." Another reader recommended New Zealand made **Bobux** shoes ($26, bobuxusa.com). These cute leather soft soles "do the trick" by staying on extremely well according to our reader.

A Canadian clothing manufacturer to look for in stores near you is **Baby's Own** by St. Lawrence Textiles (613) 632-8565.

The Mercedes of the cloth diaper category is Canada-made **Mother-Ease** (mother-ease.com), a brand that has a fanatical following among cloth diaper devotees. Suffice it to say, they ain't cheap but the quality is excellent. Mother-Ease sells both fitted diapers and covers; the diapers run $9 to $10 a pop, while the covers are about $9.75. Before you invest up to $400 in one of Mother-Ease's special package deals, consider trying their "introductory offer" for a good deal.

Other parents like **Kushies** (800) 841-5330 (web: kushies. com), another Canadian product. This brand offers several models.

One note: both Kushies and Mother-Ease are sold via mail-order only. Yes, you can sometimes find these diapers at second-hand or thrift stores, but most parents buy them via a catalog or on the 'net. Kushies are trying to branch out into retail stores—check your local baby specialty shop.

My Lil' Miracle (mylilmiracle.com; 877-218-0112 is another Canadian catalog that sells "Indisposables" all-in-one cloth diapers and diaper covers. You can buy from the catalog or from their direct representative. The catalog also has nursing bras, blankets, bibs and more.

Maternity

Toronto-based **Breast is Best** catalog sells a wide variety of nursing tops, blouses and dresses as well as maternity wear. For a free catalog and fabric swatches, call (877) 837-5439 toll free or check out their web site at breastisbest.com.

Carriers

Mountain Equipment Co-operative (MEC; web: mec.ca) is a unique, not-for-profit member owned co-op that sells baby carriers (among other outdoor products). A reader in Ottawa emailed us a rave for their "excellent" backpack carriers that are "renown

---

CANADA COSTS

What does it cost to raise a child in Canada? These figures are from Manitoba, but are a good general guide for most Canadian parents. Costs of raising a child to age two (total cost for two years):

FOOD	$2,399
CLOTHING	2,200
HEATH CARE	292
PERSONAL CARE	116
RECREATION	592
CHILD CARE	11,180
SHELTER	4,621
TOTAL	**$21,400**

Source: "Cost of Raising a Child," Manitoba government report (2004). Adjusted to 2009 dollars, in Canadian currency.

for their excellent quality." At C$109, the MEC Happy Trails back-pack carrier "clearly beats Kelty Kids and other U.S.-made carriers" at a much lower price. MEC has stores in major cities in Canada; call 888-847-0770 for details.

Canadian parents also write to us with kudos for the **Baby Trekker** (800) 665-3957; web: babytrekker.com. This 100% wash-able cotton carrier has straps around the waist for support. Parents like the fact a baby can be dressed in a snowsuit and still fit in the Baby Trekker. The carrier ($130 US, $150 Canada) is available in baby stores in Canada.

Readers also praise the **Tatonka Baby Carrier** ($185 US) from another Canadian manufacturer, Sherpa Mountain (sherpa-mtn.com).

Web Resources

Canadian Parents Online (canadianparents.com) is a great resource, with advice columns, chat/discussion areas and recall info for Canadian parents. We liked their "Ask an Expert" areas, which included advice on childbirth, lactation and even fitness.

The **Childcare Resources and Research Unit** (childcarecana-da.org) has great info and statistics on childcare costs in Canada.

Sears may not have a catalog any more in the U.S., but the Canadian version of **Sears** (sears.ca) has both a web site and print-ed catalog with baby products and clothes. A reader said the cat-alog has a nice selection of products and is a great resource for Canadian parents who might live outside the major metro areas.

Baby gear shopping in Canada

Toronto mom Rhonda Lewis scouted the best baby stores and bar-gain sources in Canada for us (and did a great job, we must say). Here's her report:

Toronto

Macklem's *416-531-7188, macklems.com.* Family run business in Downtown area. Well known for stroller/pram repairs. Friendly and knowledgeable staff. Good selection of strollers, including Zooper Zydeco, Jazz, Boogie ($550), Swing ($249), Waltz ($239), Tango, Rhumba, Maclaren (Triumph $260, Techno $425, Global $475 and other models), Peg (high chairs, double strollers, umbrellas, travel sys-tems), Bertini. They also carry products by Baby Bjorn, Britax and Dutailier to name a few. Good selection of bedding (four, five, and six piece sets from $99) and cribs including: AP, EG, Morigeau Lepine. Parking is available on the street nearby.

Dearborn Baby Express *72 Doncaster Avenue, Thornhill 905-881-3334.* Web: dearbornbaby.com Small store, crammed with merchandise. Wide selection of strollers, car seats, gliders and furniture. Infant car seats range from $159 to $239 and toddler car seats (rear and front facing) range from $189 to $350. Brands include Peg, Graco, Kidco, Evenflo, Inglesina. For furniture, brands include Pali, Morigeau Lepine, Generations and Cara Mia. If you're looking for double strollers they do have a few Peg & Baby Trend. However, it is very hard to maneuver strollers around store as it is so full. Bargains are limited, usually on end of year models. Lots of toys, layette accessories. The parking lot does get very busy, but you can usually find a spot.

Nestings' Kids *418 Eglinton Avenue W, Toronto, 416-322-0511. 2835 W. Fourth Avenue, Vancouver, 604-734-5437. nestingskids.com.* If you want exceptional furnishings, bedding, furniture, look no further than Nestings. They carry Morigeau-Lepine, EP and AG cribs. Their windows are always gorgeous and they carry great, unique items, but at a steep price. Cribs range from $848 to $2695. Lamps can be purchased for up to $395. They have very cute, whimsical lampshade nightlights which are $40 and custom bedding is priced around $1000. Parking is available on the street, or at a lot just to the west of the building.

Baby's Room Warehouse *Hwy 400 & 89, in Cookstown Outlet Mall (705) 458-8050* Specializing in baby bedding, accessories, cribs and furnishings at wholesale prices. Cribs range from $189 to $649. Brands include Little Angel, EG and Cara Mia. They also offer discount packages consisting of a crib, mattress and bedding. There are many kinds of fabric to choose from for bedding ($99-$289), or if you cannot find something you like, simply bring your fabric of choice to them, and they'll create the bedding, typically 5-6 piece sets. Mattresses are $50, $60 or $100. Store is open Monday-Friday 10-9, Saturday and Sunday from 9-6.

Wal-mart. Great place to stock up on accessories and toys Difficult to see car seats and strollers as they are tied down and above eye level for safety reasons. Good place to go if you've done your research elsewhere and are shopping for the lowest prices. Example: Diaper Genie ($35.95 at Wal-mart compared to $49.95 elsewhere, $42.95 at Toys R Us).

Costco often has excellent products at great prices. They have carried highchairs, jogging strollers, gliders and other products. The only problem is that you never know what they will have and once it is out of stock, they typically do not reorder. Check often and ask anyone you

canada

CANADA

know who is going there to check too. Items tend to sell quickly as their prices are superb.

Some **Toys R Us** locations also have **Babies R Us** stores where you can register. Prices relatively competitive, watch for flyers for sales. You receive a free gift package just for registering which is great.

Sears has a wonderful registry program called "Waiting Game" where you can guess the date that your baby will be born. You can change that date twice before you are seven months pregnant. If you guess the correct date, you get gift certificates in the amount of money you and your friends spent on your registry. It is free to join and you also receive a gift package just for taking the time to register.

Toronto Outlets

BABY CITY OUTLET STORE

734 Kipling Avenue, Etobicoke (416) 503-0313; 90 Northline Rd, North York (416) 752-0222; 7 Stafford Dr., Brampton (905) 450-1955; Keel and Wilson, Toronto. (416) 638-8777.

Save up to 45% on baby supplies from cribs, car seats, strollers and playpens to smaller items such as bottles, creams and soothers. A Luna crib is $179. Brands for strollers and car seats include Evenflo, Graco and Eddie Bauer. There are great deals on bulk packages of diapers (generic brand) and baby wipes. Parents of twins can save an extra 10% on purchases. Call store for hours.

ROOTS OUTLET STORE

120 Orfus Rd., (416) 781-8729

Great savings on Roots fashions for babies and the whole family including pajamas, sweats, jeans, hats, jackets. Discounts vary, but items have been seen at 80% off. Call for store hours. Parking is available at the back of the store.

SNUGABYE FACTORY OUTLET

188 Bentworth Ave. (416) 783-0300; snugabye.com

Save up to 50% on Canadian-made, brand-name baby clothing and sleepwear ranging in sizes from newborn to 6X. They have great prices on items like crib sheets ($5.99 to $9.99). Bedding choices change seasonally and they do sell the occasional mobile.

*And more: **Mattel Outlet*** *Mississauga Outlet 905-501-5147. mat-teltoyoutlet.ca* offers a range of discontinued, closeout and excess product stock for toys at value prices, 50% savings on many toy items. Check the web site for monthly specials on toys and baby baskets. In fact, the Cookstown Outlet Mall has many other stores, offering a wide selection of accessories, clothing, footwear, gifts for the whole family. It's worth it to drive up and spend a few hours, you can save hundreds off regular retail prices!

Toronto Maternity Clothing

There are many maternity shops in Toronto which are excellent.

Rhonda Maternity *(416) 921-3116 rhondamaternity.com.* offers a wide range of career wear. Prices are high ($100+ for pants), but quality and service are excellent and they have a wide selection of merchandise including bathing suits in season and evening dresses. Another store that recently opened, ***Kick***, *454 Eglinton Avenue West (416) 488-0255* has the latest trends in maternity wear. Or, try ***Modern Maternity*** *modernmaternity.com.* for casual clothes (Bathing suits $75, long black skirt $105 and tank dresses for fancier outings at $189 plus wrap $49). The brand has a warehouse outlet at 12B Ossington Ave. in Toronto.

Secrets from your Sister *476 Bloor St. W. Telephone: 416-538-1234; secretsfromyoursister.com.* Beautiful lingerie in realistic sizes for all women. Bra fitting experts can fit you in maternity, nursing, sports or everyday bras.

Old Navy has four stores in Canada that sell maternity wear, a few of which are in the Greater Toronto Area (Promenade Mall and Mississauga Square One Mall). They have a great return policy so if you stock up at the beginning of your pregnancy and don't end up needing some items, you can return them at any time with your receipt. Watch for great sales as their merchandise often goes on sale.

If you happen to be near Thunder Bay, there is a store called ***Bambino Paradise Outlet*** where they sell breast pumps, maternity clothes, strollers and bedding (800) 524-6973. bambinoparadise.ca

Thyme Maternity (maternity.ca) is the largest maternity chain in Canada and they have locations in every province. Their fabric choices are at times clingy, but their merchandise turnover is high and they receive new shipments often. The location at Yorkdale Mall probably has the best selection. The prices are a bit high, but often you can find merchandise on sale at the end of season and during promotions. Sweater prices are $30 to $50, pants were on sale at $25 to $60. They also sell bras, underwear, swimwear, pajamas and formal wear.

Bravado Designs *bravadodesigns.com,* a Toronto-based company, has an excellent selection of funky, great quality bras ($37) for both pregnancy and breast-feeding, and underwear ($24). This company encourages women to maintain their style during pregnancy with funky, unique prints.

Toronto Resources & More

Help! We've Got Kids *helpwevegotkids.com* is a unique Children's Reference Directory book for Toronto which was put together over 10 years ago by two young mothers. It is updated yearly. There are many coupons in the back, valued at over $4000.

Cuddle Karrier. *cuddlekarrier.com. 1-877-283-3535* A popular carrier from newborn to toddler. There are eight ways to use it. $63 US.

BabySteps Children's Fund *babystepsgiftshop.com or call 905-707-1030.* Personalized gifts for all. Puzzle stools, coat racks & more. Baby's 1st Year/School Frames for monthly baby/annual school photos. Funky hairbrushes and much more. All proceeds to Hospital for Sick Children. They offer a wonderful selection of great gifts at reasonable prices and the money supports the hospital.

Today's Parent Magazine *todaysparent.com* is available monthly at a price of $18 (savings of 65% off newsstand if you order for one-year). It's an excellent national magazine, offering insight into parenting issues, nutrition, holidays, activities, etc.

Vancouver

Crocodile 2156 West 4th Avenue, Vancouver, 604-730-0232 *crocodilebaby.com.* They carry a wide range of strollers, including the Peg Pliko ($319), Maclaren Techno ($489), Maclaren Triumph ($279), Mountain Buddy Urban Jogger ($499) and the Bugaboo Frog ($1050). They sell cribs (the number one seller is $439), change tables, gliders with ottomans ($529). Peg Perego high chairs are sold from $219-$239. They sell car seats too including Graco, Peg Perego and Britax. You can find toys, videos and other child-friendly items. Parking is available at the back of the store.

Baby's World *6-1300 Woolridge Street, Coquitlam, BC 604-515-0888 itsababysworld.com.* Furniture lines include AP and EG. They have a large selection of strollers including Inglesina and Peg Perego. Sample prices include: Peg Atlantico $449, Peg Pliko $369, Peg Pliko Pramette $519, Snap 'n Go $129, Inglesina Zippy $399 and Inglesina Swift $209. They also have a Chicco Caddy umbrella stroller with tall handles, a rain cover and carrying bag for sale at $129. Peg car seats are $239 and Graco infant car seats are $189. They have Baby Bjorns from $129.

Vancouver Maternity Clothing

Hazel & Company *3190 Cambie St 604-730-8689* They carry a wide selection of their own brands and other well-known brands. Offer casual and dressy clothes (mix & match two-piece set, tops run from $65 to $75 and skirts $59). Jean brands include Rebel, Tummyline, Duet and range from $50 to $95 (low-rise are more expensive). They do carry Bravado undergarments, maternity bras $37 and underwear $15. Open seven days a week. There are two parking spots behind the store, otherwise look for lot parking nearby.

Thyme Maternity *thymematernity.com* has several locations in British Columbia including: Burnaby, Richmond, Victoria, Surrey, Coquitlam, Abbotsford.

Kid Clothing & Consignment

Boomers & Echoes Kid's & Maternity, *1985 Lonsdale Ave. (at 20th) 604-984-6163; web: boomersandechoes.com.* Boomers and Echoes carries: new and consigned quality items; new maternity including Rebel, Ripe, Duet, Bravado & Gem (jeans from $15, tops from $9.95 including tanks, nursing tops); seasonal clothing such as capris, shorts, sweaters is always available. New kids' wear including Robeez, Kushies, Baby Byon, Jelly Beans, Vals Kids & more; consignment including maternity and kids wear (by appointment only); car seats, strollers, furniture. Boomers and Echoes takes great pride in re-merchandising the store with new and consignment and ensures stock reflects current fashions. Large turn-over of inventory but items such as a Chariot Jogger ($375) and Peg Perego Pliko ($149) have been seen there. Plenty of parking in back.

Little Critters Outfitters *5631-176A St., Cloverdale (604) 575-2500* is children's store carrying new and nearly new clothing, toys, furniture and accessories at a fraction of the original price. They offer the style and quality of brand names such as Gap, Oshkosh, Tommy, Gymboree, V-tech, Fisher Price, Little Tikes and Discovery Toys.

canada

Examples of prices include a Gap Fleece Hoody ($15), Girls Cardigan ($18-$20) and toys are for sale at approximately 50% off original prices. They also feature a great selection of new and consigned dance wear. Their Critter Card program gives you 10%-20% back on all your purchases and there is no fee to join.

Trendy Tots: *22344 Dewdney Trunk Rd, Maple Ridge, (604) 467-0330* Name-brand clothing, books, videos, toys and infant care items! Trendy Tots offers a great alternative to consignment. The store buys your items outright. All seasons of clothing from newborn to teen and maternity wear are accepted, as are baby equipment, furniture and toys. Trendy Tots only accepts items in excellent condition. No appointment is necessary.

Online Resources

◆ Don't want to leave the comfort of your home? Visit *canadaretail.ca/Babies.html* for Canadian baby products, priced in Canadian dollars. Tons of links and resources for local and national shopping.

◆ Here are some web sites that offer discounts for parents of multiples: *multiplebirthscanada.org*. Brand offerings include: Huggies, Pampers, Diaper Genie, Similac, Evenflo

◆ For you crafty people out there who are looking to document the first years of their babies lives, check out **Scrapbook Warehouse** *scrapbookwarehouse.com* for the latest in scrapbooks, accessories, cutters, stickers. They carry over 5000 products and have over 100 scrapbooks ranging from $12 to $60. They will teach you how to use the products you buy (i.e. cutters and scissors) so that you will have no problems when you get home. (604) 266-4433. They also offer classes. 8932 Oak St. @ Marine Dr. They are located about 5 minutes from the Vancouver Airport.

◆ *Local Guides to Pregnancy and Parenting Resources*. There are interesting articles/sections on topics including: coupons and freebies, classes for kids, summer camps, pregnancy, breastfeeding, vacation guide, etc. You can also track your pregnancy with a daily journal. Web: parentzone.com

Additional resources for Vancouver and Montreal are on our web site, BabyBargains.com (click on Bonus Material).

APPENDIX B

Sample registry

Here's the coolest thing about registering for baby products at Babies R Us—that neato bar code scanner gun. You're supposed to walk (waddle?) around the store and zap the bar codes of products you want to add to the registry. This is cool for about 15 seconds, until you realize you have to make DECISIONS about WHAT to zap.

What to do? Yes, you could page through this book as you do the registry, but that's a bit of a pain, no? To help speed the process, here's a list of what stuff you need and what to avoid. Consider it *Baby Bargains* in a nutshell:

The order of these recommendations follows the Babies R Us Registry form:

Car Seats/Strollers/Carriers/Accessories

◆ **Full Size Convertible Car Seat.** Basically, we urge waiting on this one—most babies don't need to go into a full-size convertible seat until they outgrow an infant seat (that could be in four to six months or as much as a year). In the meantime, new models are always coming out with better safety features. Hence, don't register for this and wait to buy it later.

If want to ignore this advice, go for the **Britax Roundabout** ($200) or **Marathon** ($250). Two other good choices for less money: the **Cosco Scenera** ($50) or the **Sunshine Kids Radian 65** ($190).

◆ **Infant car seat.** Best bet: the **Graco SnugRide or SnugRide 32** ($80-$160).

◆ **Strollers.** There is no "one size fits all" recommendation in this section. Read the lifestyle recommendations in Chapter 8 to find a stroller that best fits your needs. In general, stay away from the pre-packaged "travel systems"—remember that many of the better stroller brands now can be used with infant seats.

◆ **Baby Carriers.** Ergo Baby Carrier ($94-$105). You really don't need another carrier (like a backpack) unless you plan to do serious outdoor hikes. If that is the case, check Chapter 8 for suggestions.

◆ **Misc.** Yes, your infant car seat should come with an infant head support pillow, so if you buy one of these separately, use it in your stroller. There really isn't a specific brand preference in this category (all basically do the same thing). Any other stroller accessories are purely optional.

Travel Yards/High Chairs/Exercisers/Accessories

◆ **Gates.** The best brand is **KidCo** (which makes the Gateway, Safeway and Elongate). But this is something you can do later—most babies aren't mobile until at least six months of age.

◆ **Travel Yard/Playard.** Graco's **Pack 'N Play** is the best bet. Go for one with a bassinet feature.

◆ **High Chair.** The best high chair is the Fisher Price Healthy Care ($95-$110).

◆ **Walker/Exerciser.** Skip the walker; an excerciser is optional. Good model: ExerSaucer Classic Activity Center. See Chapter 7 for details.

◆ **Swing.** We like Graco's swings ($100 or so) best.

◆ **Hook on high chair.** Graco's Travel Lite table chair is $35—affordable and easy to use.

◆ **Infant jumper.** Too many injuries with this product category; pass on it.

◆ **Bed rail.** Don't need this either.

◆ **Bouncer.** Fisher Price (fisher-price.com) makes the most popular one in the category—their Rainforest bouncer is about $40.

Cribs/Furniture

◆ **Crib.** For cribs, you've got two basic choices: a simple model that is, well, just a crib or a "convertible" model that eventually morphs into a twin or full size bed. In the simple category for best buys, **Graco's** Lauren crib is a basic hardwood crib for just $145. If you fancy a convertible crib, we like the **Baby Cache** Heritage crib (made by Munire) $400 as well as the **Baby's Dream** Serenity ($350).

◆ **Bassinet.** Skip it. See Chapter 2 for details. If you buy a playpen with bassinet feature, you don't need a separate bassinet.

◆ **Dressing/changing table.** Skip it. Just use the top of your dresser as a changing area. (See dresser recommendation below.)

◆ **Glider/rocker and ottoman.** In a word: **Dutailier**. Whatever style/fabric you chose, you can't go wrong with that brand. Hint: this is a great product to buy online at a discount, so you might want to skip registering for one. **Shermag** is another great brand.

◆ **Dresser.** Dressers and other case pieces by **Munire** is our top pick—prices run about $600 for a dresser. Quality is excellent. FYI: Munire sells furniture under the Baby Cache label in Babies R Us. Other good brands for dressers include Westwood and Creations.

◆ **Misc.** Babies R Us recommends registering for all sorts of miscellaneous items like cradles, toy boxes and the like. Obviously, these are clearly optional.

Bedding/Room Décor/Crib Accessories

◆ **Crib set.** Don't—don't register for this waste of money. Instead, just get two or three good crib sheets and a nice cotton blanket or the Halo Sleep Sack. See Chapter 3 for brands.

◆ **Bumper pads, dust ruffle, diaper stacker.** Ditto—a waste.

◆ **Lamp, mobile.** These are optional, of course. We don't have any specific brand preferences.

◆ **Mattress.** We like the foam mattresses from **Colgate** ($100 for the Classica I). Or, for coil, go for **Simmons** Super Maxipedic 160 coil mattress for $115 at Babies R Us. Unfortunately, Babies R Us and other chains don't sell foam mattresses but you can find them online.

◆ **Misc.** Babies R Us has lots of miscellaneous items in this area like rugs, wallpaper border, bassinet skirts and so on. We have ideas for décor on the cheap in Chapter 3.

Infant Toys, Care & Feeding

◆ **Toys:** All of this (crib toys, bath toys, blocks) is truly optional. We have ideas for this in Chapter 6.

◆ **Nursery monitor.** The simple **Graco Ultraclear II** is a good buy at $30. Among the digital offerings, we liked **the Phillips Avent SCD510** for $100—its DECT technology stops interference. A key tip: keep the receipt. Many baby monitors don't work well because of electronic interference in the home

◆ **Humidifier.** The *Holmes/Duracraft* line sold in Target is best. Avoid the "baby" humidifiers sold in baby stores, as they are overpriced.

◆ **Diaper pail.** The *Diaper Genie II or Elite* are best.

◆ **Bathtub.** While not a necessity, a baby bath tub is a nice convenience—try to borrow one or buy it second hand to save. As a best bet, we suggest the *EuroBath by Primo*—it's a $25 bath tub that works well.

◆ **Bottles.** *Avent* and *Dr. Brown's* are the best bet, according to our readers.

◆ **Bottle Warmer.** Also optional—remember, baby doesn't need to have a warm bottle! But if you insist, go for the Avent's *Express Bottle and Baby Food Warmer* ($40). It can heat a bottle in four minutes.

◆ **Sterilizer.** Also optional, *Avent's Microwave Steam Sterilizer* ($30) is a good choice. It holds four bottles of any type and is easy to use—just put in water and nuke for eight minutes.

◆ **Thermometer.** Don't register for a fancy thermometer—the cheap options at the drug store work just as well. *First Years* has a high-speed digital thermometer ($8) that gives a rectal temp in 20 seconds and an underarm in 30 seconds. Ear thermometers are not recommended, as they are not accurate.

◆ **Breast pump.** There isn't a "one size fits all" recommendation here. Read Chapter 5 Maternity/Nursing for details.

◆ **Misc.** In this category, Babies R Us throws in items like bibs, hooded towels, washcloths, pacifiers and so on. See Chapter 4 "Reality Layette" for ideas in this category.

Diapers/Wipes

◆ **Diapers.** For disposables, the best deals are in warehouse clubs like *Sam's* and *Costco*. Generic diapers at *Wal-Mart* and *Target* are also good deals. We have a slew of deals on cloth diapers in Chapter 4.

◆ **Wipes.** Brands like *Pampers* and *Huggies* are the better bets, although some parents love the generic wipes that Costco stocks.

Clothing/Layette

◆ See the "Reality Layette" list (Ch. 4) for suggestions on quantities/brands.

APPENDIX C
Multiples advice

Yes, this year, one in 35 births in the US is to twins. As a parent-to-be of twins and that can mean double the fun when it comes to buying for baby. Here's our round-up of what products are best for parents of multiples:

Cribs

Since twins tend to be smaller than most infants, parents of multiples can use bassinets or cradles for an extended period of time. We discuss this category in depth in Chapter 2, but generally recommend looking at a portable playpen (Graco Pak N Play is one popular choice) with a bassinet feature as an alternative. A nice splurge if your budget allows it: the *Arm's Reach Co-Sleeper*.

Cool idea: a mom of twins emailed us about the *Leachco Crib Divider* for $25 that lets you use one crib for twins. Available on Amazon.

Nursing help

Check out *EZ-2-NURSE's pillow* (800-584-TWIN; we saw it on doubleblessings.com). A mom told us this was the "absolute best" for her twins, adding "I could not successfully nurse my girls together without this pillow. It was wonderful." This pillow comes in both foam and inflatable versions (including a pump). Cost: $40 to $48.

Wal-Mart has a breastfeeding collection with *Lansinoh* products (including their amazing nipple cream). Check the special displays in the store or on their web site at walmart.com.

Yes, nursing one baby can be a challenge, but two? You might need some help. To the rescue comes *Mothering Multiples: Breastfeeding & Caring for Twins and More* by Karen Kerkoff Gromada ($14.95; out of print, but you can find used copies on Amazon). This book was recommend to us by more than one mother of twins for its clear and concise advice.

FYI: Skip buying a glider-rocker if you plan to nurse your twins. The large nursing pillows won't fit! Instead, go for a loveseat.

Car seats

Most multiples are born before their due date. The smallest infants may have to ride in special "car beds" that enable them to lie flat (instead of car seats that require an infant to be at least five or six pounds and ride in a sitting position). The car beds then rotate to become regular infant car seats so older infants can ride in a sitting position.

The **Cosco Dream Ride** ($70-$130, rating: A). Another option: EliteCarSeats.com sells the **Angel Guard AngelRide** infant car bed for $100—it can be used for premature infants up to nine pounds. . The key feature: a wrap-around harness to protect a preemie in an accident. FYI: ALL premature infants should be given a car seat test at the hospital to check for breathing problems—ask your pediatrician for details.

Another idea: check with your hospital to see if you can RENT a car bed until your baby is large enough to fit in a regular infant car seat.

Strollers

Our complete wrap-up of recommendations for double strollers is in Chapter 8 (see Double the Fun in the lifestyle recommendations). In brief, we should mention that the **Graco DuoGlider** accepts two infant seats ($125-$150).

New in the past year, the **Graco Quattro Tour Duo** (32 lbs., $220-240) features a curvy frame, fancy cup holders, stadium seating, one-hand "gravity" fold, large basket and a back seat with full recline. The Quattro Tour Duo is about 20% smaller than the DuoGlider.

Another top pick for tandem strollers: the **Kolcraft Contours Options Tandem** ($210, 32 lbs.). Cool feature: the seats reverse to face the parents or each other. This model features a few upgrades over the Graco, including adjustable leg rests and each seat can fully recline (only the back seat of the Quattro Tour Duo reclines fully).

Those strollers are great since they can handle two infant car seats, but most parents of twins find that side-by-side strollers do better for them than tandem (front/back) models. Why? Tandem strollers typically only have one seat that fully reclines (when parents of twins find they need two reclining seats). And the front/back configuration seems to invite more trouble when the twins get older—the back passenger pulling the front passenger's hair, etc.

Here are our picks for side by side strollers. For parents of twins on a tight budget, we suggest the **Jeep Twin All Weather Twin Sport Umbrella** (27 lbs.) for $100 at Wal-Mart. It's bare bones (no basket) but will get the job done with reclining seats and a compact fold. If you've got a bit more budget, the **Maclaren Twin Techno** ($380, 26.9 lbs.) features fully reclining seats. Finally, for outdoor treks with twins, we like the **Mountain Buggy's** side-by-side double all-terrain strollers—very pricey at $700 but built to last.

In the dark horse category, consider the **Double Decker Stroller** (941-543-1582; doubledeckerstroller.com), a jogging stroller than can accommodate two infant car seats. It runs $275. The same company also sells a "Triple Decker," a model that will hold three babies!

As for other jogging strollers, the side-by-side versions of **Dreamer Design** and **Baby Jogger** are probably best if you really plan to exercise with a sport stroller.

Carrier

A mom of twins emailed us to rave about the *MaxiMom* carrier. She found it easier to use and adjust. The best feature: you adjust it to be a sling and nurse a baby in it. We saw this carrier on 4CoolKids (4coolkids.com) for $85 for twins; a triplet version is $125.

Deals/Freebies

◆ Chain stores like Babies R Us and Baby Depot offer a 10% discount if you buy multiples of identical items like cribs.

◆ Get a *$7 off coupon for the Diaper Genie from Playtex* when you send proof of multiple births to Playtex (800) 222-0453; playtex.com.

◆ *Kimberly Clark Twins Program:* Get a gift of "high-value coupons" for Huggies diapers by submitting birth certificates or published birth announcements. (800) 544-1847).

◆ *The First Years* offers free rattles for parents of multiples when you send in copies of birth certificates. Web: thefirstyears.com.

◆ *The National Mothers of Twins Clubs* (nomotc.org) has fantastic yard/garage sales. Check their web page for a club near you.

Remember that offers can change at any time. Check with the companies first before sending any info.

Don't forget to check out the freebie list on our message board, updated frequently: babybargains.com/freebies. Another good source: Twins Magazine is a bi-monthly, full-color magazine published by The Business Word (twinsmagazine.com).

Miscellaneous

For clothes, make sure you get "preemie" sizes instead of the suggestions in our layette chapter—twins are smaller at birth than singleton babies.

As we discussed earlier in this book, we don't think fetal monitors are a necessary expense for most parents. But, we realize that parents-to-be of multiples are a bit more nervous than others! So, if you plan to get a monitor, *BabyBeat* is one to consider. The company lets you rent the device instead of buying—$20 to $50 per month depending on the model. You can also buy the unit at $450 to $600. For details, see babybeat.com or call 888-758-8822. Unlike cheaper ultrasound monitors that are low-quality, BabyBeat is similar to the Doppler instruments found in doctor's offices. FYI: You must have a prescription from your doctor before purchasing a fetal monitor; be sure to check with your OB before any purchase.

multiples

Contract Name	Toll-Free	Phone	Web Site
General Baby Product Manufacturers			
Baby Trend	(800) 328-7363	(909) 773-0018	babytrend.com
Chicco	(877) 4-CHICCO		chiccousa.com
Cosco	(800) 457-5276	(812) 372-0141	djgusa.com
Evenflo	(800) 233-5921	(937) 415-3229	evenflo.com
First Years	(800) 225-0382	(508) 588-1220	thefirstyears.com
Fisher Price	(800) 828-4000	(716) 687-3000	fisher-price.com
Graco	(800) 345-4109	(610) 286-5951	gracobaby.com
Peg Perego		(260) 482-8191	perego.com
Safety 1st	(800) 962-7233	(781) 364-3100	safety1st.com
Introduction			
Alan & Denise Fields (authors)		(303) 442-8792	babybargains.com
Chapter 2: Nursery Necessities			
JCPenney	(800) 222-6161		jcpenney.com
CPSC	(800) 638-2772		cpsc.gov
Baby Furniture Plus			babyfurnitureplus.com
Baby News			babynewsstores.com
NINFRA			ninfra.com
USA Baby			usababy.com
EcoBaby			ecobaby.com
Hoot Judkins			hootjudkins.com
Crib N Carriage			cribncarriage.com
Baby Furniture Outlet	(800) 613-9280	(519) 649-2590	babyfurnitureoutlet.com
Buy Buy Baby			buybuybaby.com
Babies R Us	(888) BABYRUS		babiesrus.com
Baby Depot	(800) 444-COAT		coat.com
Room & Board			roomandboard.com
Baby Furniture Warehouse			babyfurniturewarehouse.com
Fun Rugs			funrugs.com
Decorate Today			decoratetoday.com
Rugs USA			rugsusa.com
NetKidsWear			netkidswear.com
Baby Bunk			babybunk.com
Kiddie Kastle (outlet)		(502) 499-9667	
Baby Boudoir (outlet)	(800) 272-2293	(508) 998-2166	
Pottery Barn (outlet)		(901) 763-1500	potterybarnkids.com
Baby Catalog America		(800) PLAY-PEN	babycatalog.com
Baby Style			babystyle.com
Pottery Barn Kids			PotteryBarnKids.com
Danny Foundation			dannyfoundation.org
Great Beginnings	(800) 886-9077	(301) 417-9702	childrensfurniture.com
Rocking Chair Outlet			rockingchairoutlet.com
Crib parts			productamerica.com
Amish Furniture Makers			SimplyAmish.com
AmishOak.com			StoneBarnFunishings.com
AmishOakInTexas.com			PureOak.com
AmishEtc.com			

Crib manufacturers

Amby Baby Bed			AmbyBaby.com
Angel Line	(800) 889-8158	(856) 863-8009	angelline.com
AP Industries	(800) 463-0145	(418) 728-2145	apindustries.com
Baby Appleseed			babyappleseed.com
Baby's Dream	(800) TEL-CRIB	(912) 649-4404	babysdream.com
Bassett		(540) 629-6000	bassettfurniture.com
Bellini	(800) 332-BABY	(516) 234-7716	bellini.com
Berg		(908) 354-5252	bergfurniture.com
Bonavita	(888) 266-2848	(732) 346-5150	bonavita-cribs.com
Bratt Déécor	(888) 24-BRATT	(410) 327-4600	brattdecor.com
Cara Mia	(877) 728-0342	(705) 328-0342	caramiafurniture.com
Capretti Home			caprettihome.com
Chanderic	(800) 363-2635	(819) 566-1515	www.shermag.com
Child Craft		(812) 883-3111	childcraftind.com
Corsican Kids	(800) 421-6247	(323) 587-3101	corsican.com
Creations			creationsbaby.com
Generation 2	(800) 736-1140	(334) 792-1144	childdesigns.com
Delta		(718) 385-1000	deltaenterprise.com
Domusindo			domusindo.com
ducduc			ducducnyc.com
Dutailier			Dutailier.com
Eden			edenbaby.com
El Greco			elgrecofurniture.com
Ethan Allen	(888) EAHELP-1		ethanallen.com
LA Baby			lababyco.com
Land of Nod			landofnod.com
Litto			littokids.com
Million Dollar Baby		(323) 728-9988	milliondollarbaby.com
Munire	(973) 574-1040		MunireFurniture.com
Natart		(819) 364-2052	natartfurniture.com
Netto Collection			nettocollection.com
Newport Cottage			newportcottages.com
Nursery Smart			nurserysmart.com
Oeuf			oeufnyc.com
Pali	(877) 725-4772		paliltaly.com
Pottery Barn	(800) 430-7373		potterybarnkids.com
Ragazzi			ragazzi.com
Restore & Restyle			see target.com
Relics		(612) 374-0861	relicsfurniture.com
Romina			rominakidsfurniture.com
Room and Board			roomandboard.com
RT Furniture			rtfurnitureusa.com
Sauder			sauder.com
Simmons		(920) 982-2140	simmonsjp.com.
Simplicity	(800) 448-4308		simplicityforchildren.com
Sorelle	(888) 470-1260	(201) 461-9444	sorellefurniture.com
Stanley	(888) 839-6822		stanleyfurniture.com
Stokke/Sleepi	(877) 978-6553		stokkeusa.com
Stork Craft		(604) 274-5121	storkcraft.com
Westwood Design			westwoodbaby.com
Young America by Stanley			stanleyfurniture.com
Babies Boutique			babiesboutique.com
IKEA		(610) 834-0180	ikea.com
JPMA		(856) 439-0500	jpma.org
Arm's Reach	(800) 954-9353		armsreach.com
Colgate		(404) 681-2121	colgatekids.com
Halo Innovations	(888) 999-4256	(218) 525-5158	halosleep.com
SIDS Alliance			SidsAlliance.org

web/phone directory

Moses Baskets:

| Moses Baskets | | | mosesbaskets.com |
| Badger Baskets | | | badgerbaskets.com |

Sleep Tight Soother	(800) NO-COLIC		colic.com
Burlington Basket Co.	(800) 553-2300	(319) 754-6508	burlingtonbasket.com
Container Store	(800) 733-3532		containerstore.com
Rumble Tuff	(800) 524-9607	(801) 226-2648	rumbletuff.com
Camelot Furniture		(714) 283-4194	
Dutailier	(800) 363-9817	(450) 772-2403	dutailier.com
Rocking Chairs 100%	(800) 4-ROCKER		rocking-chairs.com
Brooks	(800) 427-6657	(423) 626-1111	
Conant Ball	(800) 363-2635	(819) 566-1515	shermag.com
Towne Square	(800) 356-1663		gliderrocker.com
American Health	(800) 327-4382		foryourbaby.com
Lee Rowan	(800) 325-6150		leerowan.com
Hold Everything	(800) 421-2264		holdeverything.com
Closet Factory	(800) 692-5673		closetfactory.com
California Closets	(800) 274-6754		californiaclosets.com
Shades of Light	(800) 262-6612		shades-of-light.com

Mattresses

Moonlight Slumber			moonlightslumber.com
NaturePedic			naturepedic.com
NaturaWorld			naturaworld.com
Container Store			containerstore.com
Best Chair			bestchair.com
Rocky Chairs 100%			rocking-chairs.com
Little Castle			littlecastleinc.com
Plow & Hearth			plowhearth.com

Closet Organizers

Closet Maid			closetmaid.com
Closet Factory			closetfactory.com
Closet Maid	(800) 874-0008		closetmaid.com
Mills Pride	(800) 441-0337		millspride.com
Mommy Bee Happy			mommybeehappy.com
Itzbeen Baby Care Timer			itzbeen.com

Chapter 3: Bedding & Déécor

Baby Supermarket			babysupermarket.com
Overstock			overstock.com
Country Lane			countrylane.com
Basic Comfort	(800) 456-8687		basiccomfort.com
Kiddopotamus	(800) 772-8339		kiddopotamus.com
Clouds & Stars			cloudsandstars.com
Michaels Arts/Crafts	(800) MICHAELS		michaels.com
Stay Put safety sheet			babysheets.com
Baby-Be-Safe			baby-be-safe.com
Wall Nutz			wallnutz.com
Blik Re-Stik stickers			whatisblik.com
WallPops!			Wall-pops.com
Wallies			wallies.com
Creative Images artwork			crimages.com

Outlets

| Garnet Hill | | (802) 362-6198 | |
| The Interior Alternative | | (413) 743-1986 | |

Bedding Manufacturers

Amy Coe		(203) 221-3050	amycoe.com
Baby Guess	(714) 895-2250		crowncraftsinfantproducts.com
Bananafish	(800) 899-8689	(818) 727-1645	bananafishinc.com

Beautiful Baby		(903) 295-2229 bbaby.com
Blueberry Lane		(413) 528-9633 blueberrylanehome.com
Blue Moon Baby		(626) 455-0014 bluebaby.com
Brandee Danielle	(800) 720-5656	(714) 957-1240 brandeedanielle.com
California Kids	(800) 548-5214	(650) 637-9054 calkids.com
Carters	(800) 845-3251	(803) 275-2541 carters.com
Celebrations		(310) 532-2499 baby-celebrations.com
Cotton Tale	(800) 628-2621	(714) 435-9558 cottontaledesigns.com
CoCaLo		(714) 434-7200 cocalo.com
Crown Crafts	(714) 895-9200	crowncraftsinfantproducts.com
Dwell		dwellshop.com
Fleece Baby		fleecebaby.com
Gerber	(800) 4-GERBER	gerber.com
Glenna Jean	(800) 446-6018	(804) 561-0687 glennajean.com
Hoohobbers		(773) 890-1466 hoohobbers.com
KidsLine		(310) 660-0110 kidslineinc.com
Kimberly Grant		(714) 546-4411 kimberlygrant.com
JoJo Designs		amazon.com
Lambs & Ivy	(800) 345-2627	(310) 839-5155 lambsivy.com
Luv Stuff	(800) 825-BABY	(972) 278-BABY luvstuffbedding.com
Martha Stewart		kmart.com
Maddie Boo		maddieboobedding.com
Mr. Bobbles Blankets		MrBobblesBlankets.com
My Baby Sam		mybabysam.com
Nava's Design		(818) 988-9050 navasdesigns.com
Nojo	(800) 854-8760	(310) 763-8100 nojo.com
Nurseryworks		nurseryworks.net
Patchkraft	(800) 866-2229	(973) 340-3300 patchkraft.com
Picci		picci.it
Pine Creek		(503) 266-6275 pinecreekbedding.com
Quiltex	(800) 237-3636	(212) 594-2205 quiltex.com
Red Calliope	(800) 421-0526	(310) 763-8100 redcalliope.com
Sleeping Partners		(212) 254-1515 sleepingpartners.com
Springs		(212) 556-6300 springs.com
Sweet Kyla	(800) 265-2229	sweetkyla.com
Sumersault	(800) 232-3006	(201) 768-7890 sumersault.com
Sweet Pea		(626) 578-0866
Trend Lab Baby		trend-lab.com
Wendy Bellissimo		(818) 348-3682 wendybellissimo.com
Creative Images	(800) 784-5415	(904) 825-6700 crimages.com
Eddie Bauer	(800) 426-8020	eddiebauer.com
The Company Store	(800) 323-8000	companykids.com
Garnet Hill	(800) 622-6216	garnethill.com
Graham Kracker	(800) 489-2820	grahamkracker.com
The Land of Nod	(800) 933-9904	landofnod.com
Lands' End	(800) 345-3696	landsend.com
Pottery Barn Kids	(800) 430-7373	potterybarnkids.com

Chapter 4: Reality Layette

Bella Kids		bellakids.com
One of a Kind Kid		oneofakindkids.com
Preemie.com		preemie.com
SuddenlyMommies		suddenlymommies.com
Kids Surplus		kidssurplus.com
Internet Resale Directory		secondhand.com
Nat'l Assoc. Resale & Thrift		narts.org
Minnetonka Moccasins		(718) 365-7033 minnetonka-by-mail.com
Robeez shoes	(800) 929-2623	(604) 435-9074 robeez.com
Bobux shoes		bobuxusa.com

web/phone directory

Scootees		scootees.com
Once Upon a Child	(614) 791-0000	onceuponachild.com

Outlets

Carter's	(888) 782-9548	(770) 961-8722	
Flapdoodles		(970) 262-9351	
Hanna Andersson		(503) 697-1953	
Hartstrings		(610) 687-6900	
Health-Tex	(800) 772-8336	(914) 428-7551	vfc.com
JcPenney outlet	(800) 222-6161		jcpenney.com
Osh Kosh		(920) 231-8800	oshkoshbgosh.com
Talbot's Kids	(800) 543-7123	(781) 740-8888	talbots.com
Outlet Bound mag	(800) 336-8853		outletbound.com

Clothing Manufacturers

Baby Gap	(800) GAP-STYLE		babygap.com
Baby Lulu			babylulu.com
Carter's	(770) 961-8722		carters.com
Cozy Toes			cozytoes.com
Flap Happy	(800) 234-3527		flaphappy.com
Flapdoodles	(302) 731-9793		flapdoodles.com
Funtasia! Too	(214) 634-7770		funtasiatoo.com
H & M			hm.com
Hanna Andersson			hannaandersson.com
Hartstrings/Kitestrings		(212) 868-0950	hartstrings.com
Hedgehog			hedgehogusa.com
Jake and Me	(970) 352-8802		jakeandme.com
Janie and Jack			janieandjack.com
Little Lubbaloo			littlelubbaloo.com
Little Me	(800) 533-5497		littleme.com
LL Bean			llbean.com
MiniBoden			miniboden.com
MulberriBush (Tumbleweed too)			mulberribush.com
Naartjie			naartjie.com
OshKosh B'Gosh	(800) 692-4674		oshkoshbgosh.com
Patsy Aiken	(919) 872-8789		patsyaiken.com
Pingarama			pingorama.com
Sarah's Prints	(888) 477-4687		sarasprints.com
Sweet Potatoes/Spudz		(800) 634-2584	sweetpotatoesinc.com
Wes & Willy			wesandwilly.com
Zutano			zutano.com
Children's Place			childrensplace.com
Good Lad of Phila.	(215) 739-0200		goodlad.com
Gymboree	(877) 449-6932		gymboree.com
Lands End			landsend.com
Le Top	(800) 333-2257		letop-usa.com
Sprockets (Mervyn's)			mervyns.com
Target (Little Me, Classic Pooh, Halo, Tykes, Circo)			target.com
Wal-Mart (Faded Glory)			walmart.com

Catalogs

Childrens Wear	(800) 242-5437		cwdkids.com
Hanna Andersson	(800) 222-0544		hannaandersson.com
Lands End	(800) 963-4816		landsend.com
LL Kids	(800) 552-5437		llbean.com
Patagonia Kids	(800) 638-6464		patagonia.com
Talbot's Kids	(800) 543-7123		talbots.com
Wooden Soldier	(800) 375-6002	(603) 356-7041	woodensoldier.com
Disney Catalog	(800) 237-5751		disneystore.com
Fitigues	(800) 235-9005		fitigues.com
Campmor	(800) 226-7667		campmor.com
Sierra Trading Post	(800) 713-4534		sierratradingpost.com

Diapers

BioKleen		biokleen.com
All Together Diaper Company		clothdiaper.com
Baby Lane		thebabylane.com
Diapers 4 Less		diapers4less.com
Drug Emporium		drugemporium.com
CVS Pharmacy		cvspharmacy.com
Baby's Heaven		babysheaven.com
Diaper Site		diapersite.com
Costco		costco.com
Weebees		weebees.com
Baby J		babyj.com
BarefootBaby		Barefootbaby.com
Kelly's Closet		kellyscloset.com
Jardine Diapers		jardinediapers.com
Baby Bunz	(800) 676-4559	babybunz.com
Organic Bebe		organicbebe.com
Huggies		huggies.com
Luvs		luvs.com
Diaper Wraps		diaperaps.com
Tushies		tushies.com
Nature Boy & Girl		natureboyandgirl.com

Cloth Diaper Resources

Diaper Changes book	(800) 572-1826	homekeepers.com
Mother-Ease		motherease.com
Kushies	(800) 841-5330	kushies.com
DiaperDance		diaperdance.com
Daisy Diapers		diasydiapers.com
All Together	(801) 566-7579	clothdiaper.com
Bumkins	(800) 338-7581	bumkins.com
Indisposables	(800) 663-1730	
Baby J		babyj.com
Barefoot Baby		barefootbaby.com
		kellyscloset.com
		cottonbabies.com
		aunaturalbaby.com
		babybunz.com
Baby Because		babybecause.com
Seventh Generation		seventhgeneration.com
Sugar Plum Babies		monkeytoediapers.com/sugarplumbaby
Bizzy B Hive		hyenacart.com/bizzybhive
Bijou Baby Gear		bijoubabygear.com
Benjamuffins		benjamuffins.com
AngelDry		angeldrydiapers.com
Bummis		bummis.com
Luxe		Sluxebabydiapers.com
Bizzy B Hive		hyenacart.com/bizzybhive
Proraps		prodiaper.net

All-In –Ones:

Girl Woman Goddess	girlwomangoddess.com
Lullaby Diapers	lullabydiapers.com
Daisy Doodles	daisy-doodles.com
Cuddlebuns	cuddlebunsdiapers.com
DryBees	drybees.com

Pockets:

Happy Heiny's	happyheinys.com
Olive Branch Baby Marathon	olivebranchbaby.com

web/phone directory

Sams Club		samsclub.com
BJ's		bjswholesale.com
Baby Works	(800) 422-2910	babyworks.com
Nurtured Baby	(888) 564-BABY	nurturedbaby.com

Chapter 5: Maternity/Nursing

Expressive		expressiva.com
Motherwear		Motherwear.com
eStyle		estyle.com
2 Chix		2chix.com
Maternity 4 Less		maternity4less.com
Fashion Bug		fashionbug.com
Mom Shop		momshop.com
One Hot Mama		onehotmama.com
Thyme Maternity		thymematernity.com
Birth and Baby		birthandbaby.com
Mommy Gear		mommygear.com
Fit Maternity		fitmaternity.com
Liz Lange Maternity		lizlange.com
Naissance Maternity		naissancematernity.com
Pumpkin Maternity		pumpkinmaternity.com
Twinkle Little Star		twinklelittlestar.com
Baby Becoming		babybecoming.com
Motherhood		maternitymall.com
Plus Maternity		plusmaternity.com
Jake and Me Clothing Company		jakeandme.com
Eva Lillian		evalillian.com
Isabella Oliver		isabellaoliver.com
Prenatal Cradle		prenatalcradle.com
Bella Band		bellaband.com
Bravado Bras		bravadodesigns.com
Playtex Bras		playtex.com
Danish Wool breast pads		danishwool.com
LilyPadz		lilypadz.com
Soothies		soothies.com
Elizabeth Lee		Elizabethlee.com
Majamas		Majamas.com
Wears The Baby		wearsthebaby.com
Yes Breastfeeding		yesbreastfeeding.com
iMaternity		Simaternity.com
Fit Maternity		fitmaternity.com
Due Maternity		duematernity.com
Decent Exposures		decentexposures.com
Birth and Baby		birthandbaby.com
One Hanes Place		onehanesplace.com
Simplicity Patterns		simplicity.com
McCall Patterns		mccall.com
Destination Maternity Superstore		destinationmaternity.com

Chapter 6: Feeding

Breastfeeding

La Leche League	(800) LALECHE		lalecheleague.org
Nursing Mothers' Council	(408) 272-1448		nursingmothers.org
Int'l Lactation Consultants Assoc	(703) 560-7330		iblce.org
Bosom Buddies	(888) 860-0041	(720) 482-0109	bosombuddies.com
Avent	(800) 542-8368		aventamerica.com
Medela	(800) 435-8316		medela.com
White River Concepts		(800) 824-6351	
Ameda Egnell	(800) 323-4060		hollister.com
My Brest Friend	(800) 555-5522		zenoffproducts.com

EZ-2-Nurse	(800) 584-TWIN		everythingmom.com
MedRino			breastpumps-breastfeeding.com
Nursing Mothers Supplies			nursingmotherssupplies.com
Baily Medical			bailymed.com
Affordable Medela Pumps			affordable-medela-pumps.com
Mother's Milk			mothersmilkbreastfeeding.com

Baby Formula

Baby's Only Organic			babyorganic.com
BabyMil	(800) 344-1358		storebrandformulas.com
Mothers Milk Mate	(800) 499-3506		mothersmilkmate.com
Bottle Burper	(800) 699-BURP		

Bottles

Dr Brown's			babyfree.com
Munchkin	(800) 344-2229	(818) 893-5000	munchkininc.com
BreastBottle			breastbottle.com

Baby Food

Beech-Nut	(800) BEECHNUT		beechnut.com
Earth's Best	(800) 442-4221		earthsbest.com
Gerber			gerber.com
Healthy Times			healthytimes.com
Natures Goodness			naturesgoodness.com
Super Baby Food book			superbabyfood.com

High chairs

Boon		(888) 376-4763	booninc.com
Calla Chair			callachair.com
Rochelle			rochellefurniture.com
Stokke			stokkeUSA.com
Svan of Sweden			scandinavianchild.com

Chapter 7: Around the House

Kel-Gar		(972) 250-3838	kelgar.com
EuroBath			primobaby.com
Comfy Kids	(888) 529-4934		comfykids.com
Nature Company			naturecompany.com
Container Store	(800) 733-3532		containerstore.com
Diaper Genie	(800) 843-6430		playtexbaby.com
Toy Portfolio			toyportfolio.com
Buffoodles			marymeyer.com
Infantino	(800) 365-8182		infantino.com
Gymini	(800) 843-6292		tinylove.com
EZ Bather Deluxe	(800) 546-1996		dexproducts.com

Coupon sites

Fat Wallet	fatwallet.com	Clever Moms	clevermoms.com
Mobicam			getmobi.com
Philips Baby Monitors			consumer.Philips.com
BeBe Sounds			unisar.com
Summer Infant Products			summerinfant.com

Chapter 8: Car Seats

NHTSA	(888) DASH2DOT	(202) 366-0123	nhtsa.dot.gov
American Academy of Pediatrics			aap.org
National Safe Kids Campaign			safekids.org
Safety Belt Safe USA			carseat.org
Car Seat Data			carseatdata.org
Fit for a Kid			fitforakid.org
Safety Alerts			safetyalerts.com
ParentsPlace			parentsplace.com
Auto Safety Hotline	(800) 424-9393		
Might Tite	(888) 336-7909		might-tite.com

web/phone directory

Fit for a Kid	(877) FIT4AKID		fit4akid.org
Britax	(888) 4-BRITAX	(704) 409-1700	childseat.com
Compass			compassbaby.com
Orbit			Orbitbaby.com
Recaro			Recaro-nao.com
SafeGuard			safeguardseat.com
Sunshine Kids			sunshinekidsjp.com
Strolex Sit N Stroll			Strolex.com
Kiddopotamus	(800) 772-8339		kiddopotamus.com

Chapter 9: Strollers & To-Go Gear

Traveling Tikes			travelingtikes.com
Lots4Tots			lots4tots.com
PePeny canopies			pepeny.com
Aprica		(310) 639-6387	apricausa.com
Baby Jogger			babyjogger.com
Baby Planet		630-790-3113	Baby-Planet.com
BeBeLove USA			BeBeLoveUSA.com
BOB Strollers			bobgear.com
Britax			britaxusa.com
BumbleRide	800-530-3930		bumbleride.com
Chariot			ChariotCarriers.com
Chicco	(877) 4-CHICCO	(732) 805-9200	chiccousa.com
Compass	888-899-2229		CompassBaby.com
Dreamer Design		509-574-8085	dreamerdesign.net.
GoGo Babyz			GoGoBabyZ.com
Inglesina	(877) 486-5112	(973) 746-5112	Inglesina.com
Joovy		214-761-1809	joovy.com
Kelty		303-530-7670	kelty.com
Kool Stop	800-586-3332	714-738-497	koolstop.com
Maclaren	(877) 504-8809	(203) 354-4400	maclarenbaby.com
Mia Moda		610-373-6888	MiaModainc.com.
MicraLite Strollers	877-844-9575		Euro-Baby.com
Mountain Buggy			mountainbuggy.com
Mutsy		973-243-0234	Mutsy.com
Phil & Ted Most			philandteds.com
Quinny			quinny.com
Silver Cross		858-587-4745	SilverCrossAmerica.com
Stokke	(877) 978-6553		stokkeusa.com
Stroll Air	(519) 579-4534		
Rock Star Baby (Esprit)			GTBaby.com
UPPABaby	800-760-2060		UppaBaby.com
Valco	(800) 610-7850.		valcobaby.com
Cozy Rosie	(877) 744-6367	(914) 244-6367	CozyRosie.com
			SewCuteBoutique.com
			ChubbySeats.com
SnazzySeat			SnazzyBaby.com
			Kangaroodle.com
Burley	(800) 311-5294		burley.com
Schwinn	(800) SCHWINN		schwinn.com
Tanjor			lodrag.com
Rhode Gear			rhodegear.com

Diaper Bags

Amy Michelle		amymichellebags.com
Chester Handbags		chesterhandbags.com
Ella		ella-bags.com
Fleurville		fleurville.com
Haiku Diaper Bags		haikubags.com

Holly Aiken			hollyaiken.com
I'm Still Me			imstillme.com
Kate Spade			katespade.com.
Kecci			kecci.com
Oi Oi			oioi.com.au
One Cool Chick			onecoolchick.com
Reese Li			reeseli.com
Skip Hop			skiphop.com
Timbuk2			timbuk2.com
Tumi			tumi.com
Vera Bradley			verabradley.com

Carriers

Maya Wrap			mayawrap.com
Over the Shoulder Baby Holder			otsbh.net
ZoloWear			zolowear.com
Walking Rock Farm			walkingrockfarm.com
Kangeroo Korner			kangerookorner.com
Cuddle Karrier			cuddlekarrier.com
Hip Hammock			hiphammock.com
Baby Bjorn	(800) 593-5522		babybjorn.com
Baby Trekker	(800) 665-3957		babytrekker.com
Kelty		(303) 530-7670	kelty.com
Tough Traveler	(800) GO-TOUGH	(518) 377-8526	toughtraveller.com
Sherpa Mountain			sherpa-mtn.com
Ergo			ErgoBabyCarrier.com
MaxiMom			4coolkids.com
Water Tot			watertot.com

Chapter 10: Childcare

Nat'l Parenting Ctr	(800) 753-6667	(818) 225-8990	tnpc.com
Au Pair in America	(800) 727-2437 x6188		aupairamerica.com
Cultural Care Au Pair (AKA EF au Pair)			culturalcare.com
EurAuPair			euraupair.com
InterExchange			interexchange.org
GoAuPair			goaupair.com

Nat'l Assoc Family Child Care (800) 359-3817			nafcc.org
Nat'l Assoc Educ Young Child. (800) 424-2460			naeyc.org
My Background Check			mybackgroundcheck.com
Choice Trust	choicetrust.com	US Search	ussearch.com
International Nanny Association			nanny.org
National Association of Family Childcare			nafcc.org

Appendix A: Canada

Transport Canada		(613) 990-2309	tc.gc.ca
Canadian Auto. Assoc			caa.ca
British Columbia AAA		(604) 268-5000	bcaa.bc.ca
Canadian Parents Online (877) 325-8888			canadianparents.com
Maternal Instinct	(877) MATERNAL		maternal-instinct.com
Mountain Equip Coop			mac.ca
Child Resources			childcarecanada.org

Appendix C:Twins

Twins Magazine	(800) 328-3211	(303) 290-8500	twinsmagazine.com
Baby Beat	(888) 758-8822		babybeat.com
Kimberly Clark Twins (800) 544-1847			
Double Decker Stroller		(941) 543-1582	doubledecker.com
Maxi Mom Carrier			twinsstuff.com

web/phone directory

index

index

How to Reach the Authors

Have a question about

Baby Bargains?

Want to make a suggestion?

Discovered a great bargain
you'd like to share?

Contact the Authors, Denise & Alan Fields
in one of five flavorful ways:

1. By email:
authors@BabyBargains.com

2. By phone:
(303) 442-8792

3. On our web page:
BabyBargains.com

If this address isn't active, try one of our other URL's:
DeniseAndAlan.com or www.WindsorPeak.com.
Or call our office at 1-800-888-0385
if you're having problems accessing the page.

What's on our web page?

◆ *Parent product reviews.*

◆ *The latest updates and safety recalls on our BLOG.*

◆ *Bonus material—more reviews and reports.*

◆ *MESSAGE BOARDS with in-depth reader feedback.*

◆ *The latest coupons and freebies.*

◆ *CORRECTIONS and clarifications.*

◆ *Look for our Kindle ebook, iPhone apps and more!*

If this book doesn't save you at least

off your baby expenses, we'll give you a complete refund on the cost of this book!

NO QUESTIONS ASKED!

Just send the book and your mailing address to

Windsor Peak Press • 436 Pine Street, Suite T Boulder, CO, 80302.

If you have any questions, please call
(303) 442-8792.

Look at all those other baby books in the bookstore—no other author or publisher is willing to put their money where their mouth is! We are so confident that *Baby Bargains* will save you money that we guarantee it in writing!